BEOWULF AND THE CRITICS

by J. R. R. Tolkien

MEDIEVAL AND RENAISSANCE
TEXTS AND STUDIES

VOLUME 248

BEOWULF AND THE CRITICS

by J. R. R. Tolkien

Edited by

MICHAEL D. C. DROUT

Arizona Center for Medieval and Renaissance Studies

Tempe, Arizona

2002

Library of Congress Cataloging-in-Publication Data

Tolkien, J. R. R. (John Ronald Reuel), 1892–1973.
    Beowulf and the critics / by J. R. R. Tolkien ; edited by Michael D. C. Drout.
      p. cm. — (Medieval & Renaissance texts & studies ; v. 248)
    Includes bibliographical references (p.) and index.
    ISBN 0-86698-290-6 (acid-free paper)
    1. Beowulf. 2. Tolkien, J. R. R. (John Ronald Reuel), 1892–1973 — Knowl-
edge — Literature. 3. Epic poetry, English (Old) — History and criticism —
Theory, etc. 4. Scandinavia — In literature. 5. Monsters in literature. 6. Dragons in literature. 7. Heroes in literature. I. Drout, Michael D. C., 1968–
II. Title. III. Medieval & Renaissance Texts & Studies (Series) ; v. 248.
PR1585.T6 2002
829'.3—dc21   2002074612

This book is made to last.
It is set in Baskerton,
smythe-sewn and printed on acid-free paper
to library specifications.

Printed in the United States of America

TABLE OF CONTENTS

ACKNOWLEDGMENTS

This project has been possible only due to the kindness of many individuals and institutions. I would like to thank the Tolkien Estate for its generosity in allowing me first to use material from *Beowulf and the Critics* in my 1997 Loyola University Chicago Ph.D. dissertation and then to develop this current edition of the text. I am exceedingly grateful for the trust placed in me by the Estate, and I hope I have lived up to its expectations and to the example of Professor Tolkien, whose fiction has brought me many years of joy and whose scholarship has been a long-time inspiration.

This project began when my mother-in-law, Elizabeth Canton, sent my wife and me to England in 1996, thus enabling me to examine the drafts of *"Beowulf: The Monsters and the Critics"* and find *Beowulf and the Critics* lurking in a box in the Tolkien collection at the Bodleian Library at Oxford. I would like to thank her and Mrs. Helen Kennedy Vyse for their kindness and encouragement.

Part of the work for the project was included in my dissertation, the writing of which was supported by the Arthur J. Schmitt Foundation. That dissertation was directed by Allen J. Frantzen, for whose friendship, counsel, encouragement, and teaching I am thankful. My working with Allen was a direct result of the good advice of John Miles Foley at the University of Missouri-Columbia. I am grateful for that advice, and for his teaching me Old English, as I am grateful to Peggy Knapp of Carnegie Mellon, who first taught me medieval literature and encouraged my interest in the subject.

The rest of the project has been completed while I have been Assistant Professor of English at Wheaton College, Norton, MA. I would like to thank Wheaton's Committee on Faculty Scholarship for financial support that enabled me to return to Oxford and collate my transcriptions of the microfilm against the manuscript. I would especially like to thank my colleagues in the Department of English at Wheaton, Deyonne Bryant, Claire Buck, Beverly Lyon Clark, Sam Coale, Katherine Conway, Susan Dearing, Paula Krebs, Richard Pearce, Sheila Shaw, Pamela Stafford, Sue Standing, Josh Stenger, and Kathleen Vogt, for teaching me so much, supporting me with friendship and advice, and most of all for providing an invigorating intellectual environment in which to work.

That environment is also due in large measure to the tireless work of Marilyn Todesco, who has been a friend, supporter, and confidante throughout the project. Her student assistants Suzanne Lima and Libby Bixby were also exceptionally helpful. To Beth Affanato, who did so much to help organize the early stages of the project, I owe a special debt of gratitude.

My students at Wheaton have also been a catalyst for the project. Many of the ideas I have developed about Tolkien's work were formulated in the context of the Spring 1999 and Fall 2000 Senior Seminars on the Sources and Uses of Fantasy Literature. I would like to thank those entire classes, and in particular Teresa Mac-Namara, Candace Castro, and Laura Comoletti, who with their insight and sharp questions did much to refine my arguments. Laura Comoletti also deserves special thanks for proofreading large portions of the manuscript. John Walsh has been a source of interesting and provocative questions about Tolkien's work, as have Rachel Kapelle, Hilary Wynne, and Kate Malone.

At the Bodleian Library the staff of the Modern Papers Reading Room were of immense help, particularly Judith Priestman and Colin Harris, and I would like to thank them for their kindness and patience. The Newberry Library in Chicago much aided my research, as did Brown's Hay Library and Harvard's Houghton Library. Wheaton's Madeline Clark Wallace Library's Interlibrary Loan staff performed miracles, and to them I am especially grateful, as I am to the library's research staff, particularly Marcia Grimes and Judy Aaron, who helped so much with the explanatory notes.

The International Society of Anglo-Saxonists kindly allowed me to present a paper on *Beowulf and the Critics* at the 1997 meeting in Palermo, and I would like to thank Patrizia Lendinara and the Università di Palermo for hosting the conference, the executive committee for inviting me, Wheaton College for providing a research travel grant, and the membership of the International Society of Anglo-Saxonists for asking good questions and being enthusiastic about the project, both at ISAS '97 in Palermo and ISAS '99 at Notre Dame University.

Gale Owen-Crocker of the University of Manchester found for me the page from the minutes of the Manchester Medieval Society that documents Tolkien's presentation of a version of "The Monsters and the Critics" at Manchester in 1936. Other eminent Anglo-Saxonists, George Hardin Brown of Stanford University, Michelle Brown of the British Library, Katherine O'Brien-O'Keefe of Notre Dame, and Allen J. Frantzen of Loyola University Chicago supported me with letters of recommendation to the Tolkien Estate, and for this they have my thanks, as does Donald Scragg of the University of Manchester for his good advice, support and friendship. The "virtual" scholarly communities on the electronic networks ANSAX-NET and OLDNORSE-NET were a valuable source of ideas and help. Douglas A. Anderson also provided a number of helpful suggestions. Two anonymous readers for Medieval and Renaissance Texts and Studies saved me from a number of errors, and changes made at their recommendation greatly improved the edition. It has been a pleasure to work with Robert Bjork, Roy Rukkila, and Karen Lemiski of MRTS, and Dr. Leslie S. B. MacCoull's meticulous and inspired editing has been invaluable.

At Wheaton, Joel Relihan of Classics has been an enormous help in going over my translations of Latin (it goes without saying that the remaining infelicities are my own). I thank him and my other colleagues for their encouragement and their willingness to listen to my ideas in the faculty dining room and on the basketball court.

A preliminary version of my Introduction to *Beowulf and the Critics* was presented in May 1996 at the Thirty-First International Medieval Congress at Western Michigan University, Kalamazoo, MI. I would like to thank Michael Matto for organizing the session and James Earl and Pauline Head for sharing their papers and their ideas with me. In this session I had the good fortune of having my paper responded to by the late Edward B. Irving, who gently corrected some rather foolish errors and overstatements and had the immense kindness to take the entire paper seriously. Anglo-Saxon studies will miss Ted's insightful criticism and his generosity to other scholars.

Alyson Cox, Stephen Harris, Christina Heckman, Sylwia Ejmont, Kathryn Powell, and Susan Rosser have provided both specific advice and more general warmth and support. Mary Dockray-Miller has been my advisor and friend, and I thank her and Michael, Cordelia, and Bryn for their generosity. My *staþolfæst* friend Christiane Noll has for fourteen years been a constant supporter, and she always knew, even when I didn't, that I could finish the project.

Finally, my beloved wife, Raquel M. D'Oyen, deserves to have her name on the cover of this book as much as I do. It is not possible to express how grateful I am for the innumerable times that she has carried both her and my shares of the daily load so that I could complete this project. She and Rhys Miranda, the *ides ælfsciene*, have turned struggles into joys.

PREFACE

"Two different kinds of people are going to read this book," said my student Laura Comoletti when I told her about the project: "people who read it because it says 'J. R. R. Tolkien' on the cover, and people who read it because it says 'Beowulf' on the cover. And whatever you do to make the one group happy is going to irritate the other."

She is probably right. There is no one form of a book that will please both audiences equally. As Tolkien noted himself in a 1956 letter, different readers want different materials:

> Musicians want tunes, and musical notation, archaeologists want ceramics and metallurgy. Botanists want a more accurate description of the *mallorn* ... and historians want more details about the social and political structure of Gondor; general enquirers want information about the Wainriders, the Harad, Dwarvish origins, the Dead Men, the Beornings, and the missing two wizards (out of five). It will be a big volume, even if I attend only to those things revealed to my limited understanding! (*Letters*, 248–49)

But while this is not a big enough volume, even though I have tried to attend only to those things revealed to my limited understanding, I have taken some measures to accommodate both potential audiences (and of course provide for that most valued audience of all: those who read the book because it says *both* "J. R. R. Tolkien" *and* "Beowulf" on the cover). First, I have presented the main text of the argument in both its versions (I follow Christopher Tolkien in labeling them "A" and "B"): there was simply too much variation between the two and between each and the published text of "*Beowulf:* The Monsters and the Critics" to redact some kind of "best text" from the multiplicity of readings. Also, it is my contention — shared by many — that "*Beowulf:* The Monsters and the Critics" is an important monument of literary history. Both texts of *Beowulf and the Critics*, then, are essential for scholarship because they illustrate the development of Tolkien's ideas. The full two texts of *Beowulf and the Critics*, taken together and compared, allow readers a glimpse into the workings of a great mind engaged in a struggle with a complex problem.

After the decision (not a difficult one) to present both versions of the main text had been made, there was still the problem of editing and the preservation of information. To put it simply, I wanted to lose nothing. The manuscript of *Beowulf and the Critics* is not written on acid-free paper. It is faded and difficult to read in a great many places. The microfilm version is even more difficult to read. Each year that goes by will cause more information to be lost. While the question of what words lie beneath the crossed-out and replaced sections of the manuscript is not today a burning issue, we do not and cannot know what the scholars of the future will desire. Had the scribe of the *Beowulf* manuscript known that today scholars would expend vast energies trying to decipher the words he scraped out and wrote over on the palimpsest page, he might have done things differently. In the future someone may wish to write a dissertation on Tolkien's revisions. I wanted to allow for that possibility even if the manuscript becomes unreadable (despite the Bodleian's excellent conservation efforts).

But such a truly diplomatic text would be almost impossible to read and would tax the patience of even the most ardent philologists and Tolkien fans. Thus I have "cleaned up" the manuscript to make it easily readable. All editorial emendations, both Tolkien's and mine, are documented in the Textual Notes, where I have attempted to give as clear a description and as accurate a picture of the actual manuscript pages as can be presented short of a photographic facsimile. The notes have been created with the idea of avoiding complicated sigla, apparatus, and abbreviation, so while they may be ugly to look upon, they do provide the key information in such a fashion, I believe, that a novice reader can immediately see what is actually on the manuscript page.

Next arises the issue of the many quotations from ancient languages that Tolkien uses throughout his text. While I did not want to alter the manuscript and present my words as Tolkien's, I was also aware that many sympathetic and interested readers are not equally fluent in Old English, Middle English, Old Saxon, Old High German, Latin, and Old Norse. I could have relegated translations to the notes, but then readers would have to continually flip back and forth in the book just to follow the main text. I have therefore taken the liberty of providing such translations as I can for the quotations from ancient languages. In the case of Old Saxon, Old Norse, Old High German, and Virgilian Latin I have relied upon the work of other, more qualified, scholars to provide translations of the material. Old English translations are my own, and are intentionally literal and plodding rather than impressionistic. I have also translated some of the Latin texts that are otherwise untranslated. To distinguish Tolkien's translations from my own I have used smaller type to indicate the translations that I have provided. I have followed an analogous procedure to indicate where I have inserted quotations from outside the text at places where Tolkien indicated he wanted them to be inserted (for instance: where he writes the title of his poem on the dragon hoard, I have inserted the complete text of the poem).

Beowulf and the Critics is a beautifully crafted piece of rhetoric. It is as insightful and readable a critical commentary as one is likely to find in medieval studies (or literary criticism in general). But it is in the end a series of lectures combined together into what eventually became a technical paper delivered before an audience of high scholarly achievement. To expect readers not familiar with the problems and issues of *Beowulf* study in the 1930s to follow every nuance of the argument would be foolish. Thus as I have provided, to the best of my ability, Explanatory Notes. These notes attempt to document all of Tolkien's sources (a daunting task, given how widely ranging they are) and explain how his references and comments fit into his argument and the larger issues of *Beowulf* criticism. If my notes are too detailed for the professional philologist, I apologize, but I hope that by being so explicit (perhaps even pedantic) I have managed to provide all the information that the interested student needs to set *Beowulf and the Critics* in the intellectual context in which its author created it. Let me then, at the close of this Preface, address the two (possibly) separate audiences for the book.

To the pure Tolkien enthusiasts:
The single best way to understand and appreciate Tolkien's fiction is to become literate in medieval literature. Optimally, one would learn Anglo-Saxon and Old Norse and Latin and read the many works that T. A. Shippey and others have shown to be the sources of Tolkien's world. But, sadly, not everyone has time to learn the old languages. For those enthusiasts of Tolkien's work who cannot come to Wheaton and enroll in my Anglo-Saxon class (or a class taught by a better teacher somewhere else) I suggest reading medieval literature in translation. Seamus Heaney's deservedly famous recent translation of *Beowulf* could be one good starting point, as could the equally excellent new translation of the poem by Roy Liuzza, or the CD of Benjamin Bagby's recitation (accompanying himself on the harp) of the poem. After reading *Beowulf*, I suggest working through a good anthology, such as Oxford University Press' *Medieval English Literature*. You might also read thoroughly T. A. Shippey's *The Road to Middle-earth*, which is far and away the best book of Tolkien criticism yet written. Shippey identifies many of the sources and inspirations for Tolkien's fiction, and these sources are in themselves worth reading. In any event, you could do nothing that would please Tolkien more, I believe, than, inspired by *The Hobbit* or the *Lord of the Rings*, read *Beowulf* and see what it was in the poem that inspired Tolkien for so many years.

To my colleagues, the Anglo-Saxonists:
I hope this book raises as many questions as it answers. I hope it provides ample fodder for challenges to our thinking about *Beowulf* and the discipline that we love. I hope some of you will find it to be a useful resource, a critical foil, a source of inspiration for books and articles and, most importantly, lectures and classroom discussion.

Anglo-Saxon studies are, I firmly believe, entering into a period no less exciting than were the decades in which Tolkien opened up *Beowulf* for real literary analysis. But if Old English is to survive as an academic discipline beyond the rarefied heights of the big, rich universities, we need the enthusiasm and excitement of those who are drawn to the medieval through Tolkien's work. I recognize how irritating it can be to have in a class a person who believes he or she is an expert on things medieval but whose only background is the reading of a few books of fantasy literature and the perusal of a few sites on the Internet. But very soon a three-part *The Lord of the Rings* film will be released (over which, sadly, the Tolkien Estate has no control). There will be, surely, a renewed interest in Tolkien's work — though repeated reports of its loss of popularity have been greatly exaggerated. We should work to channel the enthusiasm of Tolkien fandom into the scholarly study of Old English.

What have Hobbits to do with Danes and Geats? The two are now, for better or for worse (and I think much for the better), completely intertwined in the cultural imagination. We can lament the joining or praise it, but we must deal with it. If we make a narrow house we will surely end up sitting in it by ourselves. Slowly with the rolling years the obvious becomes evident: *The Hobbit* and *The Lord of the Rings* are important and influential works of twentieth-century literature. And yet the literary criticism of High Modernism (post-modernism is really just the most recent form of this criticism) that is and has been the dominant intellectual literary discourse for fifty years is completely incapable of dealing with Tolkien's work. As Anglo-Saxonists, as trained philologists, as readers who know there were and are other kinds of literature with different conventions, intentions, and effects, we have the means to understand and explain these texts.

Finally, I would encourage all readers to simply enjoy Tolkien's words. They have been a source of wonder and inspiration to me for the years I have worked with them. I hope you will share some of the same feeling of discovery I felt, and that you will learn as much as I have.

Michael D. C. Drout
October 2001
Dedham and Norton, MA

DESCRIPTION OF THE
MANUSCRIPT

The manuscript of *Beowulf and the Critics* is Oxford, Bodleian Library, Tolkien A26/1–4. It is held in the Modern Papers collection of the Department of Western Manuscripts and is catalogued with the rest of the Tolkien collection in the paper catalogue in the Modern Papers Reading Room.

Upon the donation of the manuscript to the Bodleian in 1985 Christopher Tolkien described it thus:

> This file contains two versions (an earlier, 'A', and a later, expanded, 'B') of a very substantial work of much interest entitled *Beowulf and the Critics*.
>
> From it was directly derived the much shorter "The Monsters and the Critics," the famous lecture delivered to the British Academy in 1936. This original work is entirely unknown.
>
> I do not know whether *Beowulf and the Critics* was composed with the British Academy lecture already in mind, or whether when the occasion arose to give such a lecture my father decided to draw on and reduce *Beowulf and the Critics* already in existence for another purpose. There are suggestions that *Beowulf and the Critics* was intended for oral delivery, but I do not know whether it was so delivered (as a series of Oxford lectures).
>
> At the end of 'A' are notes associated with the work, passages relevant to the argument, and a further version (see note on file A 29, item A) of *Beowulf* lines 210ff translated into modern English alliterative verse.

Physical Description

According to Dr. Judith Priestman of the Modern Papers collection, the manuscript was bound by the Bodleian and had most likely been a collection of loose papers at the time of its donation in 1985. Tolkien A26 is bound into four slim, blue-covered volumes (1–4), each of which is approximately 50 pages long.

The manuscript leaves are unlined paper 8.5 inches high by 6.5 inches wide. Tolkien generally wrote on the recto of each leaf, leaving the verso blank (although there are some exceptions). In a number of places (17, 57, 67, 149, 158, 167, 170) the writing on the verso is upside down, suggesting that Tolkien jotted notes on the blank pages and then flipped and inverted them once he had incorporated the notes into the main text. The jottings and notes on folios 71–91 are on miscellaneous pieces of paper, including at least one (87) which seems to have come from an examination book, since it is ruled with black lines and "Do not write in this margin" is printed in the upper left margin.

The writing is in pen, both black and blue, and in pencil. Red pencil is used for re-numbering in a few places towards the end of the manuscript. The handwriting is unmistakably Tolkien's.

Organization of the manuscript

Tolkien A 26 / 1: folios 1–52.
Tolkien A 26 / 2: folios 53–100.
Tolkien A 26 / 3: folios 101–148.
Tolkien A 26 / 4: folios 149–198.

Folios 1–71:   A-Text of *Beowulf and the Critics*
Folios 72–91:   Assorted notes and jottings (some illegible), most of which are incorporated in some form into *Beowulf and the Critics*. I have provided below in Appendix I a transcript of what I have been able to make out from the notes.

Folio 86 includes a page of Tolkien's partial translation of *Beowulf* into alliterative verse (the rest of the translation is to be found in manuscript Oxford, Bodleian Library, Tolkien A 29/1).
Folios 91–198: B-Text *of Beowulf and the Critics*
Folio 95 verso is a page of paradigms and exercises in Gothic. Folio 178 is misbound upside-down.

Numbering

The first 71 leaves are numbered only with the Bodleian's penciled folio numbers. From 92–146, the B-Text of *Beowulf and the Critics*, the folios are also numbered in pencil from 1–56, and each of these numbers is circled. Folios 146 through 196 are numbered continuously from 60–109, and each of these numbers is circled. The numbers, from 1–56 and 60–109, are Tolkien's original foliation for the manuscript. The lacuna in numbering is explained by three missing folios, originally 57–59, on which is written a copy of Tolkien's poem "Iúmonna Gold Galdre Bewunden," which Tolkien at some point removed from the manuscript in order to use it for publication in the *Oxford Magazine* of 4 March 1937. Christopher Tolkien has found these missing folios, which are indeed numbered 57–59 and notes that the text is nearly identical to that of the published 1937 version of the poem.[1]

---

[1] Personal communication, 21 August 2001.

In addition to these two sets of numbers, folios 116–121 are also numbered 28–43 (in sequence), but each of these numerals is crossed out. Folios 125–135 are also numbered 25–35, with these numbers crossed out. On folio 136 the number 44 is both circled and crossed out. Folios 138–141 are additionally numbered 45–48 (in sequence) with these numbers crossed out.

At the end of the manuscript several folios have additional numbering in red pencil:

Bodleian's numbering	red pencil	
154	~~25~~	
182	~~2~~	
184	3	4
185	~~4~~	5
186	~~5~~	6
191	~~7~~	8
192	~~8~~	9
193	~~5~~	10 (circled)
196	14 (circled)	
197	~~14~~	15
198	~~15~~	16

The red-pencil numbers appear be related to Tolkien's re-organizing the end of the essay for its eventual publication as "*Beowulf*: The Monsters and the Critics."

Date

The British Academy lecture "*Beowulf*: The Monsters and the Critics," was delivered on 25 November 1936, setting this as the latest possible date for the composition of *Beowulf and the Critics*.

The earliest possible date is harder to determine. The reference to "students trained in this scholarly Oxford school" on folio 18 allows us to place the composition of the text (at least from folio 18 on) as dating from after 1926, when Tolkien moved from Leeds to Oxford and began teaching there.

The inclusion of C. S. Lewis's poem "The Northern Dragon" (not given a title in the manuscript) sets an earliest possible date of composition for folios 38 and 39 of January 1927, when Tolkien and Lewis first became friends. But according to Humphrey Carpenter, Lewis wrote all of *The Pilgrim's Regress: An Allegorical Apology for Christianity* in one two-week period in August 1932 (*The Inklings*, 47), and in fact there was no separate publication of the poem. The inclusion of "The Northern Dragon" pushes the earliest composition of this portion of the manuscript to August 1932 (unless Lewis had composed the poem previously). The text of the dragon poem in the manuscript is identical to that of the published text of Lewis's book, and while this correspondence does not prove that Tolkien copied it from a printed version of *The Pilgrim's Regress*, it does at least strongly suggest that *Beowulf and the Critics* was written after the publication of Lewis's book in 1933.

There are other factors that also point to a date after the latter part of 1932 for the composition of most of the manuscript. Christopher Tolkien writes (of *The Hobbit*) that "it seems that the greater part of the story was in written form by the winter of 1932, when it was read by C. S. Lewis" (*The Hobbit* [1987], 7). It seems probable that Tolkien's work as a creator of an original tale had sensitized him to the difficulties of maintaining consistency. On folio 186 (page 140) he writes:

> I have not discussed minor discrepancies. They are at any rate no proof of a composite authorship in this final stage. It is extraordinarily difficult, even in a newly invented tale of any length, to avoid minor discrepancies; more so still in re-handling old and oft-told tales. Critics would seem seldom themselves to have experienced the difficulties of narration. The points they fix on in the study, with a copy that can be turned back and forth for reference, are usually such as may easily escape an author, and still more easily an audience.

In his Foreword to the fiftieth anniversary edition of *The Hobbit*, Christopher Tolkien shows Tolkien struggling with problems of consistency, stating that Michael Tolkien (Christopher's older brother) remembered that Christopher, then between four and five years old:

> was greatly concerned with petty consistency as the story unfolded, and that on one occasion [he] interrupted: "Last time you said Bilbo's front door was blue, and you said Thorin had a golden tassel on his hood, but you've just said that Bilbo's front door was green, and the tassel on Thorin's hood was silver"; at which [his] father muttered "Damn the boy," and then "strode across the room" to his desk to make a note. (*The Hobbit* [1987], 7)

While such a coincidence cannot prove that Tolkien had composed almost all of *Beowulf and the Critics* (there are only twelve additional folios after 186) after the winter of 1932, it does suggest composition of at least the end of the manuscript after this time, which does not contradict a date of composition after August 1933.

Additional evidence for a date after 1933 can be found in the text itself. On folio 138 (page 106) of *Beowulf and the Critics* Tolkien remarks of a quotation from W. P. Ker's *The Dark Ages*: "There is much that is excellent here. It becomes still more remarkable if one reflects that it was written at least thirty years ago and has not seriously been surpassed." *The Dark Ages* was published in 1904. If Tolkien was writing folio 138 thirty years after Ker, he should be writing no earlier than 1934. Of course Tolkien may be factoring into his dating a publication delay (i.e., Ker may have written the words in 1903 but not published them until 1904), but that seems unlikely. Thus we can perhaps date the composition of from folio 138 to the end to some time in 1934. On folio 33 (page 52) Tolkien wrote of the same quotation from Ker: "There is much that is excellent here. Still more so when it was written," not giving a specific date. It is possible that Tolkien wrote the first draft before 1934 and the second after 1934, but it is equally possible that the round number of thirty years only occurred to Tolkien in the later stages of the composition of the manuscript. In any event, the comment about Ker would strongly suggest that *Beowulf and the Critics* was being composed in 1934, 1935, or 1936.

The inclusion, on folio 133, of the marginal jotting "Oct 23" leads me to believe that the latest possible date should be pushed to before 1936. It is hard to imagine Tolkien not only composing the additional sixty-five pages of *Beowulf and the Critics* in one month but also revising the work, preparing a typescript, and substantially cutting it to fit the time constraints of the British Academy lecture. In addition, the note on folio 158 verso, "Part reached last time," at least suggests a two-phase process of composition. If the "Oct 23" does indicate that Tolkien was working on that portion of the text at that date (of course this is impossible to prove; the date written in the manuscript may be unrelated) it seems to me reasonable to view the composition of the manuscript up through 133 as occurring before 23 October 1935. Thus it seems possible to place the composition of much of *Beowulf and the Critics* between August 1933 and 23 October 1935. Unless there is additional information in Tolkien's diaries or in other archival materials that I have not examined, the manuscript cannot be dated with any greater accuracy.

INTRODUCTION

Seeds, Soil, and Northern Sky

For it is said that, though the fruit of the Tree comes seldom to ripe-
ness, yet the life within may then lie sleeping through many long years,
and none can foretell the time in which it will awake.

— J. R. R. Tolkien, *The Return of the King*

"Beowulf: The Monsters and the Critics" in Literary History

It is fair to say — and no slur on the profession — that scholars of Anglo-
Saxon agree on very, very little beyond that "it is worth studying!" The date of
Beowulf, the provenance of the *Exeter Book*, the trustworthiness of the *Anglo-Saxon
Chronicle*, the usefulness of the penitentials, the prevalence of dialect forms, the
existence of secular scribes, the most effective translation for the refrain of *Deor*,
the actual subject of *Wulf and Eadwacer* . . . all are just a very few examples of the
thousands of vexed and debated questions in the study of Old English language,
literature and culture. It is almost frightening, then, to find something upon which
all Anglo-Saxonists agree. But in fact we do concur, and have for more than a half
century, that J. R. R. Tolkien's "*Beowulf*: The Monsters and the Critics" is the single most important critical essay ever written about *Beowulf*, that most revered and
studied of all Anglo-Saxon literary monuments.[1]

Delivered as a British Academy lecture and published in 1936, "*Beowulf*: The
Monsters and the Critics" is a watershed, an origin, a turning point. While it does
not mark the moment that *Beowulf* was first studied as literature (W. P. Ker and R.
W. Chambers, among others, had in fact already much advanced that study), it
does begin the study of the poem and its workings as legitimate in their own right,
as something worth studying to see how it worked rather than simply comparing
it (unfavorably) with other literature.

Critics may complain about the essay, but they still feel required to include it
in their anthologies. R. D. Fulk, for instance, writes that:

---

[1] In fact, "*Beowulf*: The Monsters and the Critics" casts its imposing shadow even beyond Anglo-Saxon
studies and into the field of children's literature. In researching another project I discovered that at least
two-thirds of the scholars writing about Ursula Le Guin's *Earthsea* books quote not only Tolkien's "On Fairy
Stories" (which is perhaps to be expected), but also "*Beowulf*: The Monsters and the Critics."

Any editor worth his salt, and with an adequate understanding of the changing critical winds in the profession, would no doubt remark at this point that Tolkien's lecture on the monsters and the critics has become the object of mindless veneration, is over-anthologized, hopelessly retrograde, and much too long, and so can safely be set aside now to make way for more important matters. But since my wit is short (as you may well understand), against all reason Tolkien is included here. No one denies the historical importance of this lecture as the first sustained effort at viewing the poem on its own terms, according to aesthetic guidelines discoverable in the work itself, thus opening the way to the formalist principles that played such a vital role in the subsequent development of *Beowulf* scholarship. But Tolkien's study is not just a pilgrim's stop on the road to holier shrines: his explanation of the poem's larger structure, though frequently disputed, has never been bettered, and the methodology inherent in his practice of basing claims about the macrostructural level on patterns everyone discerns in the microstructure remains a model for emulation. His view of the poet as an artist of an antiquarian bent remains enormously influential (and a major obstacle to dating the poem); and although the issue of the appropriateness of the monsters is not as pressing as it was in 1936, it is not superfluous in the context of some subsequent criticism. . . . (*Interpretations of Beowulf*, xi–xii)

In 1968 Donald K. Fry felt compelled to remind readers that "*Beowulf* criticism did not begin in 1936," when Tolkien first read his British Academy lecture (*The Beowulf Poet*, ix). Fry's comment is not facetious, and a glance through *Beowulf* criticism shows that he hardly exaggerated. C. L. Wrenn called Tolkien's essay "exceptionally important: probably the most widely influential critical appreciation of the poem" (*A Study of Old English Literature*, 606). George Clark recognizes it as "a turning point in the history of *Beowulf* in the modern age" (*Beowulf*, 7–8), and John Niles sees it as marking the admission of *Beowulf* "fully into the ranks of English literature" (*Beowulf: The Poem and its Tradition*, 4). Gillian Overing (*Language, Sign and Gender in Beowulf*, 33–35), James Earl (*Thinking About Beowulf*, 74), Clare Lees ("Men and *Beowulf*," 130), Kevin Kiernan (*Beowulf and the Beowulf Manuscript*, 251), and Edward Irving (*Rereading Beowulf*, 30) concur. E. G. Stanley writes that Tolkien's essay should be seen "not as the end of the first age of *Beowulf* scholarship, but the beginning of a new age" (*In the Foreground: Beowulf*, 37–38).

Undoubtedly Tolkien's immense popular success has also served to increase his stature within medieval studies. While there are still some voices within Old English criticism that call Tolkien's fiction a distraction from serious study, a sufficient number of generations of scholars and students have been introduced to Old

English through the names and language in *The Hobbit* and *The Lord of the Rings*[2] to develop a widespread, pro-Tolkien bias, and student predilections for Tolkienian fantasy are often used by teachers to generate enthusiasm for Old English language and literature. Tolkien, unlike many other significant scholars of Anglo-Saxon, has shaped the field from both the top down and the bottom up, influencing popular as well as elite perceptions of Anglo-Saxon.

Thus while no one would claim "*Beowulf*: The Monsters and the Critics" as *the* origin of *Beowulf* studies, it is *a* recognized point of origin for modern *Beowulf* study. Criticism requires origins; not every discussion of *Beowulf* can begin with Thorkelin or Wanley, nor must every conversation about literature begin with the *Epic of Gilgamesh*. But at the same time (as the critical discussion of "*Beowulf*: The Monsters and the Critics" shows) dealing with an origin is exceptionally tricky: the tools of criticism were not designed for such an undertaking. Origins are a center that the criticism, in the words of Allen J. Frantzen, "cannot do without, and yet a center with which it can do nothing" (*Desire for Origins*, 109). Or to appropriate one of Tolkien's most famous metaphors, attempting to investigate "*Beowulf*: The Monsters and the Critics" is like trying to excavate the foundations of a tower without toppling it over. Such attempts, it seems to me, have ended either in full-scale attacks on Tolkien's view of the poem (such as George Clark presents) or, more generally, in an invocation of "*Beowulf*: The Monsters and the Critics" that seeks the touchstone of the origin but then proceeds elsewhere.

Beowulf and the Critics is not "*Beowulf*: The Monsters and the Critics." It is thus free of the taboo of the origin while at the same time preserving and in fact more fully illustrating Tolkien's complex, nuanced, and difficult argument — upon which so much has been built. For the two texts of *Beowulf and the Critics* illustrate the evolution of Tolkien's thought on the poem (or, more likely, an evolution in the presentation of Tolkien's thought on the poem, which for his posthumous readers is effectively the same thing), and they also present the argument of "*Beowulf*: The Monsters and the Critics" in a simplified form more easily apprehended and examined than the published essay, the rhetorical virtuosity of which can at times impede direct analysis even as it compels assent. I am surely not the only scholar who has found himself, after reading "*Beowulf*: The Monsters and the Critics," agreeing completely with Tolkien but at the same time not being completely sure of all the particulars with which I am in agreement. *Beowulf and the Critics* makes the points of agreement that much more clear and outlines the specific areas of dispute. It also provides the detailed background evidence of quotation and analysis that in the published essay is either compressed and relegated to the appendices or altogether eliminated due to constraints of space.

---

[2] Among them this editor, who took his first course in Old English in 1991 when he recognized that an Old English quotation used in John Miles Foley's University of Missouri-Columbia course catalogue description, "wes thu hal" had appeared in the speech of the Rohirrim (*The Two Towers*, 122).

History and Influence

Beowulf and the Critics (its original title was *Beowulf with Critics*) may have been delivered as a series of Oxford lectures. It was certainly begun with that intention, for Tolkien on folio 17–18 writes: "I have lectured before and shall again on this aspect of 'Beowulf' separately. And in any case I leave here the poem itself in the hands of students trained in this scholarly Oxford school with *confidence*" (page 42). This remark is excised from the revised B-Text (though Tolkien's use of "ars longa, vita brevis" remains), suggesting that Tolkien was no longer considering the text as a series of lectures. Another mention of Oxford, in the B-Text, is more ambiguous: "But even in Oxford, where we have a school of English studies knowledgeable intelligent and even diligent and scholarly, strange ignorances and prejudices lurk still in the fens and dark places" (page 91). The deictic marker "this" is here absent, and the comment could easily be appropriate for a non-Oxonian audience that would have known where Tolkien was professor. Other comments about Oxford relating to the relative lack of respect given to philological studies (page 99), and the how little Oxford changes in regard to a failure to purchase the Cotton collection (pages 42 and 98), could be read as indicating an internal rather than external audience, but cannot prove definitive.

But whether or not *Beowulf and the Critics* was presented as a series of lectures at Oxford, sometime between 1933 and 1936 Tolkien undertook the major revision and condensation of the text that led to the British Academy lecture, which he presented on 25 November, 1936.[3] Tolkien also took *Beowulf and the Critics* on the road, presenting the lecture to the medieval society at Manchester University (he arrived late for the talk because his train was delayed by fog), presumably having been invited by his old friend E.V. Gordon.[4] Tolkien also sent a draft of the manuscript to R. W. Chambers around this time, for in a letter dated 2 February 1937 Chambers writes:

> Dear Tolkien,
> You must not delete a single word or line from your lecture. I have read it through twice over with the greatest enjoyment.
> Also the appendices must be printed. . . .
> Get it printed straight away, and don't omit anything.[5]

---

[3] Douglas A. Anderson informs me that Tolkien began a regular series of lectures entitled "The Historical and Legendary Tradition in *Beowulf* and other Old English Poems" in the Michaelmas term of 1933.

[4] Professor Gale Owen-Crocker informed me of the general knowledge at Manchester that Tolkien had presented a version of "*Beowulf*: the Monsters and the Critics," and she and Professor Alexander Rumble were kind enough to unearth the medieval society minute book that records in the hand of E.V. Gordon the visit on 9 December 1936 (the date of the minutes is 21 January 1937).

[5] The letter from Chambers may be found in Oxford, Bodleian Library, MS Tolkien 4, fol. 58.

Before June of the same year Tolkien must have arranged to print the entire lecture, for in a letter dated 2 June, Chambers writes: "So glad to know that you are printing without any cuts, appendices and all. It all hangs together, and any cuts would be disastrous."[6]

"*Beowulf*: The Monsters and the Critics" had finally appeared in print by the end of 1937; Chambers writes to Tolkien on 14 December that he has "just finished a review of your splendid Beowulf lecture."[7] But Tolkien was not finished with *Beowulf and the Critics*. Selections from the work appear in "On Translating *Beowulf*," an essay that is included as "Prefatory Remarks on Prose Translation of *Beowulf*" to John R. Clark-Hall's *Beowulf and the Finnesburg Fragment, A Translation into Modern English Verse*, in the 1940 revised edition by C. L. Wrenn. The section of alliterative translation that Tolkien includes in "On Translating *Beowulf*" can be found on folio 86 of *Beowulf and the Critics*, although Tolkien modified and improved the translation between the manuscript page and the published version ("On Translating *Beowulf*," 63). Tolkien also adapts analysis from *Beowulf and the Critics* for "On Translating *Beowulf*." In the former he writes of Old English prose: "For long reasonably competent translations of Old English prose, such as that of Ælfric, had been possible, but verse remained a practically unintelligible riddle" (page 43). In the latter: "So the early scholars of the seventeenth and eighteenth centuries thought: to them, even when they understood Ælfred or Ælfric well enough, 'Saxon poetry' often seemed a tissue of riddles and hard words woven deliberately by lovers of enigma" ("On Translating *Beowulf*," 52). Other parallels — such as Tolkien's discussion of the mythological "geography" of the *Beowulf*-poet — between *Beowulf and the Critics* and "On Translating *Beowulf*" are more difficult to prove, since they also appear in the published version of "*Beowulf*: The Monsters and the Critics."

Material from *Beowulf and the Critics* also appears in the long note on W. H. Auden's review of *The Return of the King* which Tolkien most likely wrote (though he never sent it) in 1956. Some similarity of phrasing can be found in the long discussion of *Beowulf*, though here also it is difficult to differentiate between material that may have come from *Beowulf and the Critics* and that from "*Beowulf*: The Monsters and the Critics." And of course similarities may be due to Tolkien's having, after so many years of giving lectures, practically memorized phrases originally composed in the early thirties. Nevertheless, the use of the uncommon word "naif" in both "in that political world Grendel looks silly, though he certainly is not silly, however naif may be the poet's imagination and description of him" (*Letters*, 242) and "Are we to refuse 'King Lear' either because it is founded on a silly folk-tale

---

[6] Oxford, Bodleian Library, MS Tolkien 4, fols. 61–62. Douglas A. Anderson points out that "*Beowulf*: The Monsters and the Critics" was published as a pamphlet on 1 July 1937; the lecture then appeared in *Proceedings of the British Academy* 22(1937): 245–95, which was published on 30 December 1937.

[7] Oxford, Bodleian Library, MS Tolkien 4, fols. 63–64.

(the old naif details of which still peep through as they do in *Beowulf*) or because it is not 'Macbeth'?" (page 55) are at least suggestive. And in any event, the ideas that Tolkien first articulated in *Beowulf and the Critics* — about the human value of a story about monsters, about the *Beowulf*-poet's technical virtuosity and the capabilities of Old English verse, and about the essential value of "Northern courage" in the poem — obviously continued to influence Tolkien's thought and writing throughout his fictional and critical work.

Sources

In writing *Beowulf and the Critics*, Tolkien used a multitude of sources, from which he drew quotations, allusions, turns of phrase and general guidance. There are four authors in particular upon whom he relied: R. W. Chambers, Archibald Strong, John Earle, and W. P. Ker. Tolkien viewed Chambers as the greatest of contemporary *Beowulf* critics and drew constantly upon his essay "*Beowulf* and the Heroic Age" and his book *Beowulf: An Introduction to the Study of the Poem with a Discussion of the Stories of Offa and Finn.* Tolkien also found the title of *Beowulf and the Critics* in Chambers's edition of *Widsith*, the fourth chapter of which is entitled "*Widsith* and the Critics."

Strong was for Tolkien more of a foil than a support, but he was an effective and challenging foil (unlike J. J. Jusserand, whose multifaceted errors and obvious pomposity Tolkien enjoyed lampooning). Strong's approach to *Beowulf* summed up for Tolkien much that was wrong with *Beowulf* criticism even in the hands of sympathetic and interested readers. John Earle supplied the background: much of Tolkien's summary of the history of *Beowulf* criticism comes directly from Earle's introduction to *The Deeds of Beowulf*, and this survey provides Tolkien with jumping-off points from which he developed his own analysis of the historiography of the poem.

But W. P. Ker's presence looms larger than any other in *Beowulf and the Critics*, though Tolkien cites Chambers and Strong far more frequently. Tolkien seemed to feel keenly the influence of Ker. Even in the corrected typescript of "*Beowulf*: The Monsters and the Critics," Tolkien was modifying and re-wording his remarks about Ker: "The chief points with which I feel dissatisfied I will now approach by way of W. P. Ker" (here Tolkien colored in Ker's initials, giving them almost an appearance of manuscript illumination). Tolkien then wrote "I revere his name" but then crossed it out and replaced it with "whose name and memory I honor." A few lines down, after some criticism of Ker's conclusions, Tolkien adds "In any case, I do not lightly criticize the dead before whom I should humbly bow," though he then crossed out this sentence.[8]

It is clear that Tolkien much admired the work of Ker, whose *The Dark Ages* is a true monument of learning. It was Tolkien's respect and admiration for Ker,

---

[8] Oxford, Bodleian Library, MS Tolkien 1, fol. 27.

I believe, that made several passages of *The Dark Ages* so galling to him. For Ker finds much fault with *Beowulf*, arguing that the poem is misshapen and "cheap." So in *Beowulf and the Critics*, many turns of phrase (which I have tried to identify in the Explanatory Notes) come from Ker. And even where Tolkien is quoting other sources, the original reference for him is frequently Ker. The quotations from the *Fóstbræðra Saga*, for instance, are found verbatim in Ker. More significantly, the famous "allegory of the tower" has its source ultimately in a lecture by Matthew Arnold, but the relevant portion of that lecture is quoted by Ker in *The Dark Ages*.

Tolkien's other sources are nothing less than the length and breadth of early Northern literature. I am convinced that he was quoting from memory much Old Norse (at one point he correctly quotes, but misattributes to *Völsunga Saga* a quotation from *Hálfs Saga*, an error which he later corrects). The most important source from the primary texts is of course *Beowulf*, but the Old Norse poem *Völuspá*, the Prophecy of the Seeress, is also referred to many times. Other Anglo-Saxon poems, particularly the "Wanderer" and the "Seafarer," are also significant for the argument. Of the works cited from later periods of literature, the most important as a source is H. Rider Haggard's *Eric Brighteyes*, not so much because of its influence in *Beowulf and the Critics*, which is slight, but because Tolkien's reference to it in this work helps identify a link between Haggard and Tolkien's fictional writings: there are great similarities of style and material between Haggard and Tolkien, though Tolkien eschews the bizarre misogyny that is so much a part of Haggard. References to *King Lear* and *Macbeth* confirm T. A. Shippey's contention that these two Shakespearean plays (despite Tolkien's much-quoted comment that he "cordially disliked" Shakespeare) were particularly important to Tolkien not only as argumentative foils — the purpose for which he uses *Lear* in particular in *Beowulf and the Critics* — but also as direct sources for his fiction (see *Author of the Century*, 192–95).

Beowulf and the Critics and Tolkien's Thought: A Reading

All the elements of Tolkien's British Academy lecture are present in the first draft of *Beowulf and the Critics*,[9] but the argument proceeds more slowly and methodically. It is the severe compression of the complex logical structure of *Beowulf and the Critics* that enables the rhetorical style of "Monsters": the impression of vast depth behind the essay is not an illusion. Compression was Tolkien's most significant task in modifying "Critics" for oral delivery and publication, but he also changed the content and style of the piece as he progressed. Many references to individual critics, for example, are made less pointed. In both the A and B texts of "Critics," Tolkien says that Oswald Cockayne's disparaging remarks about Joseph Bosworth "may have been unfair" (pages 31 and 79). In "Monsters" he is kinder,

---

[9] I will hereafter refer to the published British Academy lecture as "Monsters" and the book from which Tolkien drew the lecture as "Critics."

calling the remarks "doubtless unfair" (5). Tolkien greatly reduces his many scath-
ing comments on the deficiencies of Strong's treatment of *Beowulf* in *A Short History
of English Literature*. He also reduces to the single sentence "it is the confused product of a committee of muddle-headed and probably beer-bemused Anglo-Saxons
(this is a Gallic voice)" an eight-page, savage — and wickedly funny — attack on
Jean J. Jusserand's commentary on *Beowulf*, which Tolkien shows to be linguistically inaccurate, illogical, and, most enraging to the Gallophobic Tolkien (Carpenter, *J. R. R. Tolkien: A Biography*, 67), condescending (pages 48–53).

For the purposes of this study, however, the most telling changes Tolkien
made to "Critics" as he modified it into "Monsters" can be found in the famous
allegory of the tower. This is the most frequently cited passage of "Monsters," and
is, as critics have recognized, essential for understanding Tolkien's thoughts about
Beowulf. The published version runs as follows:

> A man inherited a field in which was an accumulation of old stone, part
> of an older hall. Of the old stone some had already been used in build-
> ing the house in which he actually lived, not far from the old house of
> his fathers. Of the rest he took some and built a tower. But his friends
> coming perceived at once (without troubling to climb the steps) that
> these stones had formerly belonged to a more ancient building. So they
> pushed the tower over, with no little labour, in order to look for hidden
> carvings and inscriptions, or to discover whence the man's distant fore-
> fathers had obtained their building material. Some suspecting a deposit
> of coal under the soil began to dig for it, and forgot even the stones.
> They all said: 'This tower is most interesting.' But they also said (after
> pushing it over): 'What a muddle it is in!' And even the man's own de-
> scendants, who might have been expected to consider what he had been
> about, were heard to murmur: 'He is such an odd fellow! Imagine his
> using these old stones just to build a nonsensical tower! Why did he not
> restore the old house? He had no sense of proportion.' But from the
> top of that tower the man had been able to look out upon the sea.
> ("Monsters," 7–8)

Thomas Shippey's is the clearest exegesis of this passage. The man is of
course the *Beowulf* poet, Shippey writes. The friends are scholars of *Beowulf*. The
tower is the poem itself. From the remaining elements of the allegory:

> one can deduce that Tolkien thought that there had been older poems than
> *Beowulf*, pagan ones, in the time of the Christian past already abandoned;
> they are the 'older hall'. However debris from them remained available,
> poetic formulas and indeed stray pagan concepts like *Sigelware*; that is the
> 'accumulation of old stone'. Some indeed of this was used for Biblical poems

like *Exodus* . . . that is 'the house' in which the man 'actually lived'. (*Road to Middle-earth*, 36–37)

Shippey goes on: "the gist of all this is that no one, friends or descendants or maybe even contemporaries, had understood *Beowulf but Tolkien*." This understanding depended on Tolkien's "being a descendant, on living in the same country and beneath the same sky, on speaking the same language, on being 'native to that tongue and land' " (*Road to Middle-earth*, 37, Shippey's emphasis). Shippey perhaps overstates the case here. I am certain that Tolkien would have replied that if he was the first to understand *Beowulf* it was because he had both inherited an immense amount of philological learning from the previous generations of scholars and had also read the poem with an open mind and heart, trying to understand what it was attempting to do in and of itself rather than merely comparing it (unfavorably) to other works.

But in support of Shippey's idea we have a letter from Tolkien to his son Christopher, in which Tolkien remarks that after reading Sir Frank Stenton's *Anglo-Saxon England*, "I'd give a bit for a time-machine." But he would not use it to fill in specifically historical gaps because "it is the things of racial and linguistic significance that attract me and stick in my memory." Tolkien hopes that his son will be able to read *Anglo-Saxon England* and so "delve into this intriguing story of our particular people. And indeed of us in particular. For barring the Tolkien (which must long ago have become a pretty thin strand) you are a Mercian or Hwiccian (of Wychwood) on both sides" (*Letters*, 108). Tolkien thus identifies himself with a particular ethnic stock firmly rooted in the Anglo-Saxon period and in the West Midlands. In a letter to W. H. Auden, Tolkien wrote that he was "a West-midlander by blood (and took to early west-midland Middle English as a known tongue as soon as I set eyes on it)" (*Letters*, 213).

This ethnic identity added to Tolkien's philological training provided self-justification for what Shippey calls Tolkien's "rather curious beliefs" expressed indirectly in "Monsters." Tolkien was convinced, Shippey argues, "that he knew exactly when and under what circumstances the poem was written" (*Road to Middle-earth*, 36). Despite this rhetorical stance, which I believe Shippey characterizes accurately, Tolkien treats date and provenance in one sentence in "Monsters," accepting the attribution of the poem "to the 'age of Bede' " ("Monsters," 25). Tolkien is less coy, however, in the two drafts of "Critics." After reviewing and agreeing with arguments made by Chambers (Tolkien does not quote them but merely writes "Cha. Introd. II. p 391–392" in the center of the page), he writes: "we are face to face with a poem by an Englishman c. 725–750!" (page 48). The poet's ethnos is significant to Tolkien. The poem is English, not Scandinavian or primitive Germanic (Teutonic); or as Tolkien puts it earlier in "Critics," "so Norse is Norse and English English" (page 36).

This strain of thought is evident in "Monsters," particularly in the final lines of the essay: *Beowulf* "is in fact written in a language that after many centuries has still essential kinship with our own. It was made in this land, and moves in our northern world beneath our northern sky, and for those who are native to that tongue and land, it must ever call with a profound appeal — until the dragon comes" ("Monsters," 36). Most telling in this lyrical passage is Tolkien's use of pronouns and determiners, the genitive plural "our" and the deictic marker "this." "Our" indicates possession; "this" indicates proximity. *Beowulf* becomes a possession of a people of a certain background ("native") that is both linguistic ("to that tongue") and mystically tied to the soil. The first proposition is eminently rational; the second is more a matter of feeling than of logic, but the idea informs all of Tolkien's scholarly work. A concern with land, custom, and ethnos is most clearly visible in Tolkien's first draft of the allegory of the tower. Here he writes:

> I would present you with the following allegory, and would have it borne in mind. A man found a mass of old stone in an unused patch, and made of it a rock-garden; but his friends coming perceived that the stones had once been part of a more ancient building, and they turned them upside down to look for hidden inscriptions; some suspected a deposit of coal under the soil and proceeded to dig for it. They all said "this garden is most interesting," but they said also "what a jumble and confusion it is in!" — and even the gardener's best friend, who might have been expected to understand what he had been about, was heard to say: "he's such a tiresome fellow — fancy using these beautiful stones just to set off commonplace flowers that are found in every garden. He has *no* sense of proportion, poor man." And, of course, the less friendly, when they were told the gardener was an Anglosaxon and often attended to beer, understood at once: a love of freedom may go with beer and blue eyes, but that yellow hair unfortunately grows always on a muddled head. (page 32)

Obviously the tower's genesis as a rock garden is the most striking element of the passage. A rock garden used to "set off commonplace flowers" immediately brings to mind the stereotyped and often caricatured (but containing some kernel of truth) image of the Englishman devoted to flowers and plants. This is an image that Tolkien did not necessarily disavow — he thought the language of the *Ancrene Wisse* to retain "the air of a gentleman, if a *country* gentleman" ("*Ancrene Wisse* and *Hali Meiðhad*," 106, my emphasis). In *The Fellowship of the Ring*, Frodo, deep in the Mines of Moria, thinks of his home in the Shire: "he wished with all his heart that he was back there . . . mowing the lawn, or pottering among the flowers" (332). All three of these images suggest a class identification by Tolkien. Hobbits are decidedly rural middle-class, and Frodo, before his quest, could easily be described as a "country gentleman." After all, the very upper classes do not concern themselves with making rock gardens (that being the job of servants). Nor can the low-est classes go in for ornamental horticulture. Rather, the rock garden is a sign of the middle classes of the countryside, the classes to which Tolkien at heart belonged.[10]

In fact rock gardens were invented in England,[11] and by invoking the rock garden in which the ancient stones set off commonplace (but nevertheless beauti-ful) flowers, Tolkien is saying much about *Beowulf* that is elsewhere in the essay supported by argument but which is lost in the published version of the allegory of the tower — although of course that allegory is more rhetorically powerful than the allegory of the rock garden. For if we read the rock garden as Shippey reads the tower, the stories of the monsters in *Beowulf*, although they are in ruinous con-dition, the vestiges of folk-tale commonplaces, perhaps, are nevertheless trans-formed by the poet in some particularly English fashion. Ancient ruin combined with common nature and beauty create something better than either the original scattered stones or the flowers themselves. In fact the allegory of the rock garden more clearly marks the class identification that Tolkien wished to make. The most treasured monument of ancient English verse, though it depicts the deeds of kings and heroes, of Danes and Swedes, is in the end transformed into its most valuable form through the creativity and genius of a representative of the English middle classes (a poet, after all must work for his bread), living close to both nature and history, and willing to combine them both.

As interesting as the class identification in the allegory is the explicit racial categorization of the *Beowulf* poet in the final lines. As an "Anglosaxon," he is possessed of "yellow" hair, blue eyes, and a fondness for beer. This last detail is clearly part of Tolkien's gut-level reaction to what he calls the "drink-complex" — Jusserand's tendency to read any reference to drink in *Beowulf* as indicating wide-spread inebriation among the Anglo-Saxons ("Critics," pages 50–51). But even if these final lines of the allegory are a reaction to Gallic condescension, the identi-fication of the *Beowulf* poet with stereotyped phenotypic racial features might be cause for concern (particularly in the mid-1930s) if we did not possess the follow-ing letter written by Tolkien to his son Michael in 1941:

> I have spent most of my life, since I was your age, studying Germanic
> matters (in the general sense that includes England and Scandinavia).
> There is a great deal more force (and truth) than ignorant people

---

[10] Carpenter notes that while Tolkien spent most of his youth in the urban settings of Birmingham and Leeds, and in the suburbs of Oxford, his familial and psychological roots had been put down in Sarehole, in the Warwickshire countryside outside of Birmingham (Carpenter, *Biography*, 124–25).

[11] Rock gardens were invented in England in the late Victorian period but only perfected in the early part of the twentieth century: the most important early book on rock gardening, Reginald Farrer's *The English Rock Garden*, was published in 1919 and led to the immense popularity of such gardens in the 1920s and 30s, when Tolkien was developing the ideas for and then writing *Beowulf and the Critics*.

imagine in the "Germanic" ideal. I was much attracted by it as an
undergraduate (when Hitler was, I suppose, dabbling in paint, and had
not heard of it), in reaction against the "Classics" . . . But no one ever
calls on me to "broadcast," or do a postscript! Yet I suppose I know better than most what is the truth about this "Nordic" nonsense. Anyway
I have in this War a burning private grudge — which would probably
make me a better soldier at 49 than I was at 22: against that ruddy little
ignoramus Adolf Hitler . . . Ruining, perverting, misapplying, and
making for ever accursed, that noble northern spirit, a supreme contribution to Europe, which I have ever loved, and tried to present in its
true light. Nowhere, incidentally, was it nobler than in England, nor
more early sanctified and Christianized. . . . (*Letters*, 54–55)

In 1938, Tolkien had written a razor-tongued reply to the German firm
Rütten und Loening Verlag, who, upon negotiating the publication of a German
translation of *The Hobbit*, dared to ask Tolkien if he was "arisch" [Aryan]. Tolkien
replied with insulting philological precision that since he was not aware that any of
his "ancestors spoke Hindustani, Persian, Gypsy, or any related dialects," he could
not to claim to be Aryan. He adds, "but if I am to understand that you are enquiring whether I am of *Jewish* origin, I can only reply that I regret that I appear to
have *no* ancestors of that gifted people." He then continues with an explanation of
his German name (Tolkien's ancestors had immigrated to England in the eighteenth century), and closes with the following:

I have been accustomed . . . to regard my German name with pride, and
continued to do so throughout the period of the late regrettable war
. . . I cannot, however, forbear to comment that if impertinent and
irrelevant inquiries of this sort are to become the rule in matters of
literature, then the time is not far distant when a German name will no
longer be a source of pride. (*Letters*, 37–38)

In a letter to his own publishers about the same issue Tolkien calls the
German race laws "lunatic" and notes "I do not regard the (probable) absence of
all Jewish blood as necessarily honourable . . . and should regret giving any colour
to the notion that I subscribed to the wholly pernicious and unscientific race-
doctrine" (*Letters*, 37). Tolkien's understanding of the English "race" was not generally influenced by the " 'Nordic' nonsense" promulgated by the Nazi party.[12]

---

[12] In fact Tolkien's ideas about race are almost shockingly "progressive" (particularly for a man who
claimed that he was by no means a "democrat"). In his valedictory address to Oxford delivered in 1959 (!)
he notes that he was born in a place "under the Southern Cross, but I have a hatred of *apartheid* in my
bones" ("Valedictory Address," 238).

And if Tolkien did not accept the notion of a single, superior, "Nordic" race (and it is clear from his letters than he did not), how could he construct an "English" race characterized by blond hair, blue eyes, and a fondness for beer?

First, I think Tolkien was exaggerating the caricature of the Anglo-Saxons that he found in Jusserand and linking that insulting characterization to his strong personal animus against all things French (Carpenter, *Biography*, 67, 235–36). This animus in scholarly matters dates back at least as far as 1923, when Tolkien wrote sarcastically in a review, "these remarks are tempered by regret that they do not reflect more plainly the cordiality with which we should wish to greet any mark of attention shown by French philology to English matters" ("Philology: General Works" [1923], 36–37). As part of his long attack on Jusserand, Tolkien brutally criticizes an "underlying assumption" that all English from the sixteenth century on is a more or less homogenous "modern" English, and the best is " 'polite' — and the Frencher the politer" (page 49). Clearly Jusserand's assumption that Anglo-Saxon England was "primitive" (the characterization is Tolkien's on the same folio) continued to sting Tolkien although Jusserand had died (in 1932) before "Critics" was written. Thus the external view of the *Beowulf* poet in the allegory is the cartoon of the "Anglo-Saxon" (a term which is still a common descriptive term for English and Americans in contemporary chauvanist French political discourse, where it is un-historically set in opposition to "European") that Tolkien believed Jusserand and other critics saw. The man described as yellow-haired and blue-eyed is, after all, not meant to be truly muddle-headed — only those who fail to understand his purpose perceive him thus. More importantly, I do not think Tolkien's view of the English "race" was truly genetic. As a linguistic scholar he knew that this English "race" was a complex mixture, each of whose components was likewise mixed and blended through centuries of migrations and conquests. Nevertheless, Tolkien did believe that there was something essentially "English" about *Beowulf* and about the allegorical man with the rock garden.

The only way to reconcile these two apparently opposing viewpoints is to take seriously and literally those final lines of "Monsters" and the related sentiments in "*Ancrene Wisse* and *Hali Meiðhad*": *Beowulf* was "made in this *land*, and moves in our northern world beneath our northern sky, and for those who are native to that tongue and *land*, it must ever call with a profound appeal" ("Monsters," 36, my emphasis). The language of the Katherine Group texts "is also in close touch with a good living speech — a *soil* somewhere in England" ("*Ancrene Wisse* and *Hali Meiðhad*," 106, my emphasis). A long discussion of *The Lord of the Rings* and *The Silmarillion* sent to the publisher Milton Waldman (probably in late 1951) shows that these sentiments persisted throughout Tolkien's lifetime:

> Do not laugh! But once upon a time (my crest has long since fallen) I had a mind to make a body of more or less connected legend, ranging from the large and cosmogonic, to the level of the romantic fairy-story

— the larger founded on the lesser in contact with the *earth*, the lesser
drawing splendour from vast backcloths — which I would dedicate
simply to: to England; to my country. It should possess the tone and
quality that I desired, somewhat cool and clear, *be redolent of our "air"*
(the clime and soil of the North West, meaning Britain and the hither parts of
Europe: not Italy or the Aegean, still less the East), . . . it should be "high,"
purged of the gross, and fit for the adult mind of a land long now
steeped in poetry. I would draw some of the great tales in fullness, and
leave many only placed in the scheme, and sketched. The cycles should
be linked to a majestic whole, and yet leave scope for other minds and
hands, wielding paint and music and drama. Absurd. (*Letters*, 144–45,
my emphasis)

In each case English identity is based upon contact with the earth itself, with
the physical land of the British Isles. Englishness derives from persistent presence
in England, not from solely genetic connections, and not from purely cultural
antecedents, either. Being native to the English tongue is not enough; one must
also be native to the land. In other words, an English racial identity is made
through participation in two related traditions: physical occupation of England
(preferably in close contact with the soil and growing things of the countryside)
and participation in the English speech community. The traditions could both be
entered — the Tolkiens eventually become completely English after their arrival
from Germany — but such an enlistment was slow and, most importantly, required
participation in both traditions. English speakers in America, for example, were
not part of the first; the Irish, whose tongue Tolkien found not only difficult but
unpleasant, were not part of the second. Or, as Tolkien put it in a letter to his son
Christopher, "I love England (not Great Britain and certainly not the British
Commonwealth (grr!))" (*Letters*, 65).

Understanding Tolkien's semi-mystical connection between English identity
and the land itself sheds light on Tolkien's fiction and his personal beliefs. Discussing the beauty of the Golden Wood, Lothlórien,[13] in *The Fellowship of the Ring*,
Sam Gamgee says "Whether they've made the land, or the land's made them [the
Elves], it's hard to say" (376). In *The Two Towers*, the true horror of the land of
Mordor, "the lasting monument to the dark labour of its slaves that would endure
when all their purposes were made void," is the desecration of the earth itself and
the creation of "a land defiled, diseased beyond all healing" (239).

---

[13] Even *The Lord of the Rings'* harshest critics have praise for Tolkien's invention of this magical woodland
of the Elves. Edmund Wilson, in one of the more vitriolic and, as Shippey shows, self-contradictory (*Road
to Middle Earth*, 1–3, 19–20, 218–19) reviews written of *The Lord of the Rings* has kind words for Lothlórien
(and also for the Ents) ("Oo, Those Awful Orcs!" 59).

Tolkien's ambivalent feelings towards the United States can be seen as arising from Americans' usage of the same tongue as England on another continent. In unpublished notes dating, according to a small penciled note in the upper margin, from 1937 or before, Tolkien writes that he has no use for "Big Business (on the transatlantic model)" (A28 B, fol. 160v). In a letter to Christopher Tolkien dated 9 December 1943, he writes that he finds "this Americo-cosmopolitanism very terrifying," and wonders if American victory in World War II, while certainly preferable to Nazi domination, "is going to be so much better for the world as a whole and in the long run" (*Letters*, 65).

On the other hand, Tolkien was apparently fascinated by "tales of Kentucky folk ... family names like Barefoot and Boffin and Baggins and good country names like that" (Guy Davenport, "Hobbits in Kentucky," *New York Times*, 23 February 1979: A 27). Shippey is likely correct in interpreting this interest as related to a belief by Tolkien that "in Kentucky and its neighbors ... there had for a time been a place where English people and English traditions could flourish by themselves free of the chronic imperialism of Latin, Celtic and French." But Tolkien would not have agreed with Shippey's invocation of the idea that "Once upon a time all Americans were English: *caelum non animum mutant qui trans mare currunt*" ["the sky, not the spirit, changes for him who crosses the sea" (Horace, *Epistles* 1.11.27)] (*Road to Middle-earth*, 223). First of all, to pursue briefly an overly-literal reading of the Latin phrase, being "beneath our northern sky" was almost as important to Tolkien as being connected to the land; secondly, Americans were not directly connected to England's soil, but participated in the English tradition only in terms of language. A good start, perhaps, but not enough.

Tolkien believed that in some way English soil and northern sky had forged an important and valuable identity for the people of his country. This identity had been encapsulated in the speech, stories, and traditions of Old English, and had been mostly shattered by the Norman Conquest and the subsequent imposition of French upon the common speech of England. Tolkien's work on the language of the Katherine Group showed that the Old English roots ran deep, and had persisted in spite of the onslaught of French. But even if an Old English culture had valiantly held on in the West Midlands, it had, long before Tolkien's time, succumbed. In unpublished lecture notes Tolkien suggests that Laȝamon's *Brut* illustrates a "breach" that had occurred in English cultural continuity:

> The breach was precisely in kinship, dynasties and politics, largely in language, but not in religion. It is as if far off rumours of Celtic lore, the Roman invasions and conquest, the Roman imperial troubles and the abandonment of Britain, the invasions and conquests of the English and the Saxons, their resistance under Æthelwulfing kings to the Norse invaders, had all become jumbled in a vast haze of battle, in which the

only constant is the land, Britain, without even an imaginative poetic sense of chronology or sequence.[14]

The land itself is the "only constant," and has the ability, abetted by the power of philological study, to help heal the breach in culture and continuity. Tolkien's work on such words as "eaueres" and "sigelwara," whereby he recaptured scraps of the mythology of the Anglo-Saxon culture that had, however changed, persisted in some way into the twelfth century, suggests that at least some of the old Northern culture could be recaptured. But only so much of the lost culture could be re-animated directly by philology. Much of what was important to Tolkien, like the connection between earth and identity, is mythical, and he would not have found it appropriate for the pages of *Medium Ævum* or *Essays and Studies*. He therefore tried to build a tower of the accumulation of old stone; that tower was the mythology of Middle-earth: *The Silmarillion, The Hobbit,* and *The Lord of the Rings*.

But at the time of the writing of *Beowulf and the Critics* the essential continuities of land and blood were under an ever-increasing threat that Tolkien clearly recognized. In the same pre-1937 lecture notes for *Beowulf* quoted above he writes: "but we — if we read our northern poetry to any profit of soul — are not dismayed. The Giants come out of the East, and destroy us, as they did the gods of Asgard. But they shall perish with us. And it is not the Giants that arise again, when the waters pass off from the foundered Earth."[15] These references to the end of *Völuspá* where we learn of the end of the gods and a new rebirth (which is focused on a new, bright and shining hall interestingly enough called Gimlé) suggest that Tolkien was trying to find in *Beowulf* and other northern poetry an antidote to despair and fear: the courage of Beowulf when faced with his death is conflated with the courage that would soon be required of the English in the face of the "monsters" of World War II.

The genesis of the allegory of the tower in the allegory of the rock garden shows the linkage between Tolkien's ideas about identity and tradition and his own fiction (which he called "sub-creation"). Tolkien saw himself as a builder,[16] using the old ruins to create something new that would allow readers (and himself as author) to achieve a transcendent purpose, to view the sea otherwise out of sight.[17]

---

[14] This comment is found in Oxford, Bodleian Library, MS Tolkien A28, a collection of commentary on *Beowulf* that was used for lectures at Oxford, both pre- and post-war. The quoted passage is found on folio 171.

[15] Oxford, Bodleian Library, MS Tolkien A28, fol. 160v.

[16] Edward B. Irving suggested this metaphor in his response to my paper at the 1996 International Congress on Medieval Studies in Kalamazoo, MI.

[17] It is interesting to note that some of the "builder" figures in Tolkien's mythology — Aulë, Fëanor, and Celebrimbor, as well as Sauron, who was a Maia of Aulë — create objects that can lead to a kind of transcendent sight, but these objects (the Palantíri, the Silmarils, the Rings of Power) are subject to misuse, and their creators can be rebellious and disobedient towards higher powers (of course the 'disobedience' of Aulë, a Vala, is rather different than that of the lower-ranking builders).

The tower from which the *Beowulf* poet and Tolkien achieve this gaze is built up of old stone that has already been used in building the ancestral home of the builder. That is, it is composed of inherited material, and this inherited material is valued primarily because it is old:

"Slowly with the rolling years, the obvious (so often the last revelation of analytic study) has been discovered: that [in *Beowulf*] we have to deal with a poem by an Englishman using afresh ancient and largely traditional material" ("Monsters," 9).[18] At first glance this sentence appears to suggest a Miltonic value for tradition: it is validated by being used "afresh." Such an interpretation fits well with reading Tolkien as a proto-New Critic (a fallacy I shall discuss later), and is certainly defensible when applied in light of *The Lord of the Rings*. But I think Tolkien really wants to suggest something simpler; that, just as is the case in *Beowulf*, the material is valuable because it is "eald" ("old"). In the first version of the allegory of the rock garden, which is one hundred thirty-two words long, the word "old" occurs once, as does "more ancient" (page 32). In the B-Text version, which is one hundred sixty-seven words long, there are two occurrences of "old" and one of "more ancient" (page 81). But in the two hundred and twenty-two words of the published version of the allegory of the tower there are five occurrences of "old," and one each of "older," "more ancient," and "distant forefathers." Clearly the age of *Beowulf* and the antiquity of the materials of which it is constructed create much of the poem's value for Tolkien, and just as clearly this valuation for "old" was emphasized as Tolkien rethought and revised his work. I think this value is analogous to the value of inherited objects in *Beowulf*: an object (or, for Tolkien, a tale, story, or word) is made particularly precious by its participation in a lineage, by its connection with a tradition.[19]

In the same lecture notes mentioned above, Tolkien suggests that a reverence for tales and objects possessed of a lineage was part of the English temperament: "The English of the earlier days had a marked 'historical mood' and interest not only in tales of the Past as tales of wonder, but in history as such: the history of their own country and people in particular. They had a wealth of traditions in their own tongue . . ."[20] These English are given their identity from their language and their lineage; they were "freemen who knew the names of their fathers and their fathers' fathers, who spoke undebased English in the manner of them, and knew and appreciated the literary (as we must call it) English of their long inherited tradition."[21]

---

[18] Note also that "slowly with the rolling years" is an uncited reference to Ker's *The Dark Ages* (252–53).

[19] For the sense of "eald" meaning "time-honored" or "especially valuable" see *Beowulf* lines 472, 795, 1488, 1688, 2763 and 2774.

[20] Oxford, Bodleian Library, MS Tolkien A28, fol. 170.

[21] Oxford, Bodleian Library, MS Tolkien A28, fol. 174.

Yet the language had changed and the lineage had been broken. Direct inheritance by blood was no longer possible.[22] Englishmen had forgotten the names of their forefathers, or these names had changed beyond recognition. So Tolkien created the inheritance anew in his mythology that he had originally wished to dedicate "to England; to my country." More importantly, he worked to weave together the loose strands of Anglo-Saxon culture into a comprehensible inheritance just as he illustrates the *Beowulf* poet weaving together Christian and heathen, mythological and religious, into one effective poem. As he writes in *Beowulf and the Critics*:

> Christianity infused into the northern world (if we consider England), or the infusion of the North into the southern world (if we consider Europe more generally) make what we call the *mediæval*. That process begins at once — some of the most fundamental changes of that alchemy are almost immediate, indeed instantaneous. In a Christian country (including one thoroughly reacquired by Christendom as was England) it is not a random mixture, to be judged by the vagaries of wandering and ill-instructed vikings who had no foothold in Christendom; it is a conversion. (page 119)

A conversion re-organizes the minds and the culture of those who convert. It creates something new and (Tolkien clearly believed) better out of the pre-conversion material. And what was special about the English conversion was that everything old did not have to be destroyed or cast away:

> It was the English temper — in its strong Englishry connected with its nobility and its dynasties and many small courts, assisted, it may be by the humaner and less severe Celtic tradition of learning — that preserved so much tradition of the past to interweave with southern learning. The ancestors were not banned (as some would have wished) but we could hardly expect the gods to be given yet the twilight reverence of antiquarian record. (page 63)

Thus in other lecture notes (which, according to dates on some associated envelopes, seem to have been written or at least re-copied in 1962), Tolkien suggests that the *Beowulf* poet should be called "Heorrenda rather than X."[23] Heorrenda is the "scop" ("poet" or "minstrel") who replaces the aging "scop" Deor in

---

[22] If for no other reason than the changes in Anglo-Saxon blood lineages brought about by the introduction of French bloodlines as a result of the Conquest.

[23] Oxford, Bodleian Library, MS Tolkien A28 C, fol. 6v; "rather than X" is written interlinearly in pencil and marked for insertion with a caret.

the poem of that name.[24] Here we see the elements of the synthesizing practice that led directly to the Rohirrim in *The Lord of the Rings*.[25] In the manner of the *Beowulf* poet, who links up the legends surrounding Heorot with the story of the Geats, Tolkien is forging a synthetic mythical "history" to explain certain perceived truths about the ancestry of his people.

The Rohirrim speak Old English, lament their dead in alliterative verse, and, with the exception of their extensive use of horses, are for all intents and purposes Anglo-Saxons (see Shippey, *Road to Middle-earth*, 93–98). In creating them Tolkien took an enormous number of disputed ideas about the Anglo-Saxons and synthesized them into a seamless whole. In *The Two Towers* he describes this idealized view of the Anglo-Saxons thus: "They are proud and wilful, but they are true-hearted, generous in thought and deed; bold but not cruel; wise but unlearned, writing no books but singing many songs . . ." (33). In *Beowulf and the Critics* Tolkien sees the *Beowulf*-poet performing a similar alchemy:

> *Beowulf* is not a 'primitive' poem; it is a late one, at the end of an epoch, using the materials, then plentiful, of a day already changing and passing, which has now for ever vanished, swallowed in oblivion, and using them for a new purpose with a wider sweep of imagination, if with a less bitter and concentrated force of mood. *Beowulf* was already antiquarian in a good sense. (page 145)

Tolkien thought that some kind of warrior society lay behind the later culture documented by monastic scriptoria. In other words, the characterization of the Riders of Rohan as (it seems) pre-Christian Anglo-Saxons, perhaps the companions of Hengest and Horsa, works to fill in the gaps of Anglo-Saxon history.[26] Likewise by bringing Heorrenda into the world of *Beowulf* and *Beowulf* into the world of *Deor*, Tolkien weaves a tapestry of Anglo-Saxon culture that, while not controverted by the fragmentary evidence, cannot be substantiated either. In other

---

[24] In *The Book of Lost Tales, Part Two*, much-purchased by the public but, it seems to me (after having read much exceptionally confused criticism of Tolkien's fiction) very little read by putative critics, Christopher Tolkien lays out his father's development of an English mythology, a mythology that includes the equivalence of the elvish city of Kortirion with Warwick and the use of Heorrenda and Deor as the names of poets (*Book of Lost Tales, Part Two*, 278–334 at 322–26).

[25] Geoffrey Russom suggested this link between Tolkien's use of Heorrenda and the creation of the Rohirrim (Personal Communication).

[26] As Christopher Tolkien notes in *Unfinished Tales*, the names of the leaders of the Rohirrim (which in *The Lord of the Rings* are all Anglo-Saxon words for "king") before their migration into the known lands of Middle Earth are Gothic (*Unfinished Tales*, 311). Tolkien, it seems to me, is here suggesting that the Anglo-Saxons, before their migrations, were related to the Goths (see also Shippey, *The Road to Middle-earth*, 12). The parallel between the founding of the Shire by two brothers, Marcho and Blanco, and the legend of the Anglo-Saxon migration led by Hengist and Horsa has also been noted by many critics (see Shippey, *Author of the Century*, 59–60).

words, Tolkien's synthesis is very much an "invention" of the Middle Ages as discussed by Norman Cantor (*Inventing the Middle Ages*, 31–47).[27]

This invention is Tolkien's tower. But what was the sea he was able to view from its top? In her perceptive reading of "Monsters," Clare Lees argues that seeing from the top of the tower allows "the poem, the poet and the critic to transcend time, conquering it as does the hero, Beowulf, at the moment of his death" ("Men and *Beowulf*," 134). This transcendent gaze (and the very idea of such a view) is enmeshed in "masculinist" ideology; that is, it is inextricably linked with the gender role, politics, and ideology of the poet and critic. I agree with Lees that Tolkien's reading of *Beowulf* (and the poem itself) promote an exceptionally "masculinist" viewpoint, but I believe she is incorrect in several particulars of her argument. "Tolkien's New Critical Reader" is Lees's title for the section of her essay "Men and *Beowulf*" that deals with "Monsters," and in this section she argues that Tolkien is a New Critic ("Men and *Beowulf*," 130–31). This assertion is exceptionally problematic, and illustrative of a tendency widespread in post-structuralist criticism to make "New Criticism" the "other" of any favored contemporary critical approach. As I have discussed above, the two versions of "Critics" show that the ideas behind "Monsters" were present as early as 1927 (although the text was likely written between 1933 and 1936). Although, as Gerald Graff shows, the elements of the New Criticism began to be developed in America as early as the late 1920s and early 1930s (*Professing Literature*, 144–47), it would be most anomalous for Tolkien, a man educated in the specific Oxford tradition of philological inquiry and hardly an Americanophile, to adopt so early the work of an originally American school of thought that was just beginning to coalesce at the time "Critics" was being drafted. In addition, C. S. Lewis (presumably with Tolkien's blessing; the two were exceptionally close at this time) as early as 1939 vigorously attacked both F. R. Leavis and I. A. Richards as being part of a "tradition of educated infidelity" overly influenced by the "personal heresy," and arguing that Leavis's positions were based only on subjective judgment and were therefore unsound (Carpenter, *The Inklings*, 64).[28]

Tolkien does criticize former historical scholars for producing very little

---

[27] Cantor recognizes that Tolkien and his close friend C. S. Lewis saw a continuity between their own culture and that of the Middle Ages, but the rest of his discussion of Tolkien is riddled with factual errors (the two most egregious examples: Tolkien had four children, not three — though perhaps Cantor is suggesting that Tolkien wrote his stories only for his first three sons, although such a view is not substantiated in the biographical information; "Mordor," the evil Land of Shadow, is misspelled as "Modor" — a rather amusing Freudian slip in Old English, since the final verse of the *Lord of the Rings* poem would then be: "One Ring to bring them all and in the darkness bind them / In the land of Mother, where the shadows lie"). More damaging to his argument, Cantor completely misses the subtleties of Tolkien's scholarly work and his fiction, and reads *The Lord of the Rings* as an allegorical interpretation of the Middle Ages. Thus the ridiculous suggestion that the trilogy "communicates the experience of endemic war and the fear of armed bands that was a frequent condition of the period from 400 to the middle of the eleventh century . . ." (*Inventing the Middle Ages*, 231). Of course the protagonists and sympathetic heroes of the epic are themselves an "armed band," and we read little of the terror *they* inspire.

[28] "Zeitgeist" arguments — in this case the idea that New Critical ideas leapt *ab ovo* from the brows of scholars between the years of, say, 1925 and 1955 — are unhistorical and unconvincing.

criticism that is composed of "actual judgments of *Beowulf*, as a thing itself, as a poem, as a work of art, having structure and motive" ("Monsters," 2). In "Monsters" he writes that *"Beowulfiana"* is weak in "criticism that is directed to the understanding of a poem as a poem" (5). Both appear to be New Critical sentiments, and both were enthusiastically supported by the great historical critic R. W. Chambers in letters to Tolkien. In a letter dated 14 December 1937 Chambers writes:

> You will, I hope, long outlive me, and I do trust that you will go on impressing on Oxford that to give too serious attention to the 'literature' of Beowulf, Shakespeare, or any classic imposes an obligation which is not consistent with a free and untrammelled (or is it untrammeled) study of the thing itself. I feel this at the moment very much about *Piers Plowman*.[29]

But New Critical sentiments do not a New Critic make, and if an exhortation to discount the "literature" of a poem is New Critical, then nearly every scholarly practice can be so considered. It is only in the context of previous historical criticism that Tolkien's statements (and Chambers's response to them) can be understood. Tolkien was reacting specifically to the tendency, exemplified in his view by Strong, to interpret *Beowulf* as primarily a historical document ("Monsters," 6).[30] Looking at the poem as a poem is a reaction to severely historical criticism of Strong's kind, in which *Beowulf* is viewed as a window onto ancient Anglo-Saxon life and nothing more. This view of the poem was for Tolkien both frustratingly circular and emotionally empty. It is not, however, the (only somewhat accurately) stereotyped practice of New Critics' viewing the poem in a cultural, political, and social vacuum. Tolkien's essay, with its focus on etymology and philology (particularly in the little-read appendices), religious interpretation, and historical speculation (particularly in "Critics") does not in fact fit into any particular school.

Lees supports her assertion that "Monsters" is "an early and important example of New Criticism in Anglo-Saxon studies" ("Men and *Beowulf*," 131) with a reference to Frantzen's *Desire for Origins*. But Frantzen does not in fact state that Tolkien was a New Critic, only that "Monsters" claimed that "historical analysis had swamped the poetic merits of the texts, and set about to reassert the balance between history and criticism" (*Desire for Origins*, 113). Tolkien did indeed open the door to New Critical readings of the poem, a door, as George Clark notes, that postwar critics were happy to walk to through (*Beowulf*, 9). But there is an important distinction between unlocking the door and taking a seat in the parlor.

---

[29] Oxford, Bodleian Library, MS Tolkien 4, fol. 61.

[30] George Clark argues a similar point in the analysis of "Monsters" in his *Beowulf* (Boston: Twayne, 1990, 8–11).

Lees's assumption that Tolkien was a New Critic causes her to assimilate Tolkien's essay to a standard trope of post-modern criticism that is fast becoming a critical cliché: the misidentification as universal of something that is in fact particular. In the case of "Monsters," it is the false perception that something gendered male necessarily can stand in for all humans of both genders. But, as my argument above shows, Tolkien did not regard *Beowulf* as universal. Not everyone could climb the tower, which had been built for Englishmen who shared a tongue, a soil, and a life beneath a northern sky. Likewise I do not believe that Tolkien creates a reader who is the "liberal humanist construct of the universal male, 'we'" (Lees, "Men and *Beowulf*," 133). Lees is undoubtedly correct in arguing that the "universal" reader constructed by "Monsters" is in fact male, but I think Tolkien intended this to be the case.[31] Lees notes that in the allegory of the tower, "critic and author come perilously close to being the same" ("Men and *Beowulf*," 132), a point analogous to Shippey's contention that Tolkien believed that he shared motive and technique with the *Beowulf* poet (*Road to Middle-earth*, 37). This identification across the centuries relies on the recognition (or, if you prefer, the illusion)[32] of fundamental continuities between one time and another. These continuities, as constructed by the poem and its reader Tolkien, are those of masculine, same-sex, non-biological reproduction of identities.

Such reproduction carries as a concomitant and inescapable attribute the ultimate "tragedy" of its own failure. Lees notes that "the maintenance of patrilineal genealogy is no easy thing." "Patrilineal genealogy cannot guarantee the continuity of kingly life," she adds, "but it is the only institution available" ("Men and *Beowulf*," 141–42). In fact, patrilineal genealogy, inheritance by blood, will always fail if construed in narrow terms. There is, however, another institution available, namely the reproduction of identities through culture, inheritance by deeds. But that sort of inheritance is doomed to dissolution without at least some component of blood to stabilize and restrain masculine competition for supremacy.

Tolkien located civilization in the masculine institutions of the *Beowulf* poet (in particular the bright hall), outside of which the chaos-monsters ruled. The primary theme of *Beowulf*, Tolkien wrote, is "that man, each man and all men and all their works shall die." *Beowulf* is not subject to reproach for fighting with the dragon because he would have died anyway, albeit from a different sling or arrow of fortune. In *Beowulf and the Critics* Tolkien quotes both the "Seafarer" and Hrothgar's words to Beowulf:

---

[31] Tolkien had particularly fierce ideas about the benefits of excluding women from the Inklings' literary activities, and in a 1941 letter to his son Michael suggested that in general women, while "sympathetic" and "understanding," did not have the ability to pursue study (or possibly literary art) without the guiding hand of a male teacher (*Letters*, 49–50). But on the practical — as opposed to the ideological — side he did zealously promote the careers of a number of his female Oxford students.

[32] Though I must admit that I do not understand why such an illusion, if illusion it is, would be perilous.

ic gelýfe nó
þæt him eorðwelan   ece stondað
simle þreora sum   þinga gehwylce
ær his tíd-dæge   to tweon weorþeð
ádl oþþe yldo   oþþe ecghete
fægum from weardum   feorh oðþringeð.

[I believe not that the joys of earth will abide everlasting. Ever and in all cases will one of three things trouble his heart before the appointed day: sickness, or age, or the foeman's sword from the doomed men hastening hence will his life ravish.]

eft sóna bið
þæt þec ádl oððe ecg   eafoþes getwæfeð,
oððe fýres feng,   oððe flódes wylm,
oððe gripe méces,   oððe gáres fliht,
oððe atol yldo;   oððe éagena bearhtm
forsiteð ɟ forsworceð.   Semninga bið
þæt ðec, dryhtguma,   déað oferswýðeð.

[Soon hereafter it will come to pass that sickness or sword shall rob thee of strength, or grasping fire, or heaving flood, or biting blade, or flying spear, or dreadful age; or the flash of eyes shall foul and darken. Swiftly will it come that thee, O knight, shall death conquer.] (page 132)[33]

This fatalism is a logical and inevitable consequence of historical knowledge: "as the poet looks back into the past, surveying the history of kings and warriors in the old traditions, he sees that all glory (or as we might say 'culture' or 'civilization') ends in night" ("Monsters," 23).

In an important 1993 article, John Niles suggests a reorientation of scholarly attention to *Beowulf* from the question "What does [the poem] mean?" to "What work did the poem do?" (Niles, "Locating *Beowulf* in Literary History," 79). Gillian Overing proposes that critics ask the question "who wants what in *Beowulf* and who gets it?" (*Language Sign, and Gender in Beowulf*, 69). I would apply both sets of questions to *Beowulf and the Critics* and its offspring, "Monsters." First, the work of *Beowulf and the Critics* is the work of the recovery and reproduction of historical identities. The institutions it reproduces are not the warrior *comitatus* or the Anglo-Saxon hall-retinue of kings, but rather the scholarly, religious, and emotional

---

[33] The translations are Tolkien's. Square brackets are given in the manuscript. Sources are *The Seafarer*, lines 66b–71, and *Beowulf*, lines 1762b–68. In line 69a of *The Seafarer*, Tolkien emends the manuscript reading of "tid aga" to "tid-dæge."

matrix in which Tolkien's identity was constituted. As Shippey notes, in 1921 the British Board of Education had printed a report condemning philology because this "German-made" science had helped lead to the outbreak of the first world war by leading to "German arrogance" (*Road to Middle-earth*, 7). Tolkien felt such sentiments painfully, as is shown not only by the letters quoted above but also by remarks printed in the 1924 issue of *The Year's Work in English Studies*:

> 'philology' itself, conceived as a purely German invention, is in some quarters treated as though it were one of the things that the late war was fought to end ... a thing whose absence does credit to an Englishman, especially when engaged in work where some philological training and competence are an essential piece of apparatus. ("Philology: General Works" [1924], 36–37)

In Tolkien's reaction to political events beyond his control we see self-reproducing effects of the desire for continuity. Having through study and training constructed himself as *Beowulf*'s ideal reader, Tolkien is concerned that the specific cultural influences that shaped his life will no longer be in existence to shape others. The old traditions may have reproduced in him, but they may lose their ability to reproduce by-means-of him. While he had provided fertile earth for the seeds of Anglo-Saxon culture, his ability to be a gardener was called into question by an outside threat to the land.[34] Rightly or wrongly, Tolkien saw as gendered masculine the courage and determination needed to fight a losing battle without surrender. The characters in *The Lord of the Rings* who fight an analogous fight are (with only two exceptions, one, Éowyn of Rohan, admittedly not minor) male. As Overing notes, an inevitable consequence of such masculine ideology is the difficulty women have in speaking within the symbolic economy of both *Beowulf* and its critical tradition (*Language, Sign, and Gender in Beowulf*, xxiii).

What Beowulf and Tolkien both want is to reproduce their identities. Beowulf does not, dying as he does without a son. Tolkien did have sons, but during the war — when he composed much of the second half of *The Lord of the Rings* as a serial sent to his son Christopher stationed in South Africa with the R.A.F. — he feared for their lives and futures. Even after the war, Tolkien had reason to fear for the loss of continuity, since he saw the countryside and the life of England being transformed by technology and economics. Lees argues that the masculine

---

[34] Tolkien himself used the seed/gardener metaphor in an unsent response to W. H. Auden's review of *The Return of the King* in the New York Times Book Review: "A great part of the 'changes' in a man are no doubt unfoldings of the patterns hidden in the seed; though these are of course modified by the situation (geographical or climatic) into which it is thrown, and may be damaged by terrestrial accidents. But this comparison leaves out inevitably an important point. A man is not a seed, developing in a defined pattern, well or ill according to its situation or its defects as an example of its species; a man is both a seed and to some degree also a gardener, for good or ill" (*Letters*, 240).

symbolic economy of *Beowulf* leads inevitably to blood and death. That she means this as a criticism shows just how far her assumptions (which I believe are rather representative of contemporary criticism) are from Tolkien's. The ethos of heroism in *Beowulf* leads logically to the inevitability of the hero's death: "the only good hero, after all, is a dead one" (Lees, "Men and *Beowulf*," 145). Overing also notes that "death seems to be a pervasive value in *Beowulf*" (*Language, Sign, and Gender in Beowulf*, xxiii). Tolkien, I believe, would agree with this point, but he would not have found it a cause for blame. And this is where Tolkien's point of view does become universalist — not in terms of his critical reader, but in terms of his understanding of human nature and the place of human beings in the world.

For Lees and many other contemporary critics of Anglo-Saxon — James Earl immediately comes to mind (*Thinking About Beowulf*, 76) — conditioned as they are by their historical situation and political beliefs, any violence is cause for blame. Therefore the essential tragedy of masculinist culture is that it inevitably leads to violence. As Lees puts it, "the ethos of the heroic world demands it" ("Men and *Beowulf*," 143). For masculinist culture then, in the words of Berger and Leicester, social structure *is* doom ("Social Structure as Doom," 77). But Tolkien did not believe in such points of ideology. For him the violence required by masculinist culture was an unavoidable reaction to human existence in a fallen world.[35] That is, Tolkien's religious convictions as a devout Roman Catholic, and as a man who had personally sacrificed and suffered for his religious convictions, set up the framework by which he interpreted human existence. It is no accident that the entire *Silmarillion*, Tolkien's first fictional work and the set of legends that underlies all the rest, is at heart a reworking of the story of the Fall of Man (Shippey, *Road to Middle-earth*, 179).[36] The sufficient tragedy of *Beowulf* and the entire "northern" legendary world was for Tolkien not that the poem participated in a social structure that inevitably leads to violence and death, but that the social structures inherent in the literature are responses to a human fate that inevitably ends in violence and death. There is what Thomas Sowell calls "a conflict of visions" between Tolkien and his most perceptive critics (*Conflict of Visions*, 33). This gap cannot be bridged without determining which vision is "true," and any critic who believes that he or she can definitively make such a determination on anything but purely personal biases is deluded.

For the purposes of this argument, then, I will accept Tolkien's assumptions that the tragedy of *Beowulf* reflects something of the inherent truth and sorrow of the world rather than the arbitrary constructions of human cultures. The tragedy

---

[35] Tolkien is influenced by E. V. Gordon's ideas given in the latter's *Introduction to Old Norse* (see particularly xxviii–xxxv).

[36] Tolkien's theological and moral speculations on the Fall of Man and his adaptation of this material in his fictional creations was not published until 1993, in the section of *Morgoth's Ring* entitled "Athrabeth Finrod Ah Andreth" (303–66).

of *Beowulf*, then, the tragedy to be faced with "Northern courage," is not that the hero dies. In *The Silmarillion*, Tolkien calls the death of men "the gift of Ilúvatar [the Creator] to Men." The Númenóreans fall because they cannot accept this gift, which they call the Doom of Men, and attempt to wrest eternal life from the Valar and the Elves (*Silmarillion*, 187, 265).[37] All humans must die, and Tolkien was too devout to interpret this fate as an evil. But Beowulf's overarching tragedy, the one that he does not necessarily share with all other human beings, is that he fails to reproduce. The traditions of behavior and the inheritances of identity which he possesses are not passed on. At some point the chain is broken. This tragedy, Tolkien points out in *Beowulf and the Critics*, is how it should be for the purposes of the poem:

> That the actual bearer of enmity, the dragon, dies also is important chiefly to Beowulf himself. He was a great man. Not many even in dying can achieve the death of a single dragon or the temporary salvation of their kindred. Within the limits of human life and its ineluctable end, Beowulf neither lived nor died in vain — so brave men might say. Though there is no hint (indeed there are many hints to the contrary) that it was a war to end war, a dragon fight to end dragons or the foes of men. It is the end of Beowulf, and with him dies the hope of his people. (pages 142–43)

Tolkien wished for the revival of what he saw as the best parts of the culture of "the great time of the Anglo-Saxon Christian spring" ("Critics," page 88) — the strength of faith, the willingness to confront the dark, the fortitude in the face of death — though even as early as the writing of *Beowulf and the Critics* he believed that such renewal was unlikely. But even as the clouds gathered over Europe in the 1930s there was still the hope in the face of destruction and dissolution, and thus remained the duty to preserve what could be preserved, to treasure the memory of the long-dead ancestors (and in so preserving that memory, mitigating if not reversing the defeats of death). The Christian spring of the Anglo-Saxon eighth century had ended in fire and Viking swords in the ninth century only to be rebuilt by Æthelwold, Oswald, Dunstan, and Edgar in the tenth century, when the *Beowulf* manuscript was copied. The Norman Conquest destroyed much of English culture and language, and yet, as Tolkien showed in his work on the Katherine Group texts, there remained traces "in the West of a centre where English was at once more alive, and more traditional and organized as a written form, than anywhere else" ("*Ancrene Wisse* and *Hali Meiðhad*," 116). Through philology Tolkien had been able to reconstruct a lost history of the West Midlands, a history in which

---

[37] See also "Athrabeth Finrod Ah Andreth" (*Morgoth's Ring*, 330–34).

Old English has persisted not as a subaltern gutter tongue but as a language of learning and refinement even in the face of conquest by a foreign enemy:

> It is not a language long relegated to the 'uplands' struggling once more for expression in an apologetic emulation of its betters or out of compassion for the lewd, but rather one that has never fallen back into 'lewdness,' and has contrived in troubled times to maintain the air of a gentleman, if a country gentleman. It has traditions and some acquaintance with books and the pen, but it is also in close touch with a good living speech-soil somewhere in England. ("*Ancrene Wisse* and *Hali Meiðhad*," 106)

In some ways the defeat and elimination of heathen mythology by the Conversion was a greater defeat even than the Norman Conquest, for in Tolkien's Christian view the defeat of the pagan gods was the success of truth over falsehood: the old gods deserved to lose, and the loss of paganism was a gain for the souls of those who otherwise would not know the light of the Christian God. But yet there was sadness from the loss of the lost stories, the stirring tales of "man upon earth and his war with the inhuman world" (page 75), which Tolkien (again, as a Christian) saw were in substance if not ostensible content, in *fruyt* rather than *chaff*, consistent with a Christian world-view.

Beowulf and the Critics, then, is one step in a lifelong intellectual project of recovering (as Tolkien believed the *Beowulf*-poet had) the old, lost stories and harmonizing them with the new Christian truth. While the *Beowulf* poet and Tolkien looked back with sadness and a knowledge of ultimate ends, there were reasons for hope, if not for the Geats, then for the hearers and readers of Beowulf's poem, if not for Tolkien's beloved English countryside, then perhaps for other men in another day. For only one seed, carefully preserved, was necessary. It needed only to find the proper gardener, as *Beowulf*, coming to Tolkien across the centuries, had found a critic who could bring the poem to new life.

Tolkien was surely familiar with the anonymous "Life" of Ceolfrith, the Abbot of Monkwearmouth and Jarrow in the late seventh and early eighth centuries. According to the "Life," at some time in the 680s a pestilence struck the monastery, and

> all who could read or preach, or say the antiphons and responses, were carried off, except the abbot himself and one little boy, who had been brought up and taught by him, and who now at this day, being in priest's orders in the same monastery, duly commends the abbot's praiseworthy acts both by his writings and his discourse to all desiring to know them. He — the abbot that is — being very sorrowful by reason of the aforesaid pestilence, ordered that the former use should be

suspended, and that they should conduct all the psalm singing without antiphons, except at vespers and matins. When this had been put into practice for the space of a week, with many tears and laments on his part, he could not bear it any longer, and resolved to restore again the course of the psalmody with the antiphons according to custom; and, all exerting themselves, he fulfilled what he had resolved, with no small labor, by himself and the boy whom I mentioned, until he could either himself train, or gather from elsewhere, sufficient associates in the divine work. (Whitelock, *English Historical Documents*, 2nd ed., 1: 762)

The monastic community had been reduced to the very edge of extinction, but by 716 the abbeys of Monkwearmouth and Jarrow housed six hundred monks, and the little boy who had been Ceolfrith's only surviving companion had grown up (scholars believe) to become the Venerable Bede, the greatest English scholar of the Middle Ages (Shirley-Price, introduction to Bede, *Ecclesiastical History*, 20). Through the transmission of identities through discipline and teaching, monastic life was restored, and the abbeys of Monkwearmouth and Jarrow waxed great in power and influence for many years. It had taken only two men, a father figure and his monastic "son," to restore a nearly extinct community. Likewise what Tolkien called the "the patient work of philologists for 150 years" had revived the language of men dead long before the Norman Conquest.[38] *Beowulf and the Critics* worked to allow that long-dead language to speak to us across the centuries and rekindle in the readers of *Beowulf* what Tolkien believed to be an essential truth about the poem and the world:

We get in fact a poem from a pregnant moment — by a man who knew enough of the old heroic tales (preserved to him undoubtedly in traditional forms that descended often from actual pre-christian authors) to perceive their common tragedy of inevitable ruin, and to feel this perhaps more poignantly because he was himself a little removed from the direct pressure of its despair. He could view from without but still feel immediately and from within the old dogma — the huge pessimism as to the event, combined with the obstinate faith in the value of the doomed effort. (pages 129–30)

"Obstinate faith in the value of the doomed effort" is Tolkien's legacy to us as readers, scholars, Anglo-Saxonists — as human beings. By demonstrating (or even, if you will, creating) this effect of *Beowulf*, *Beowulf and the Critics* resurrects the life and power of a poem that

---

[38] Oxford, Bodleian Library, MS Tolkien A28B, fol. 269.

is now itself to us ancient; and yet its maker was telling of things already old and weighted with regret, and he expended his art in making keen that touch upon the heart which sorrows have that are both poignant and remote. So that if the funeral of Beowulf moved once like the echo of an ancient dirge, it is to us as a memory brought over the hills, an echo of an echo. There is not much poetry in the world that has this effect; and though *Beowulf* may not be among the very greatest poems of our western world and its tradition, it has nonetheless its own individual character and peculiar solemnity which no comparisons can take away, its own ancient cadences of verse, and its own thought. To recapture such echoes is the final fruit of scholarship in an old tongue (and it is the most honourable object — rather than the analysis of an historical document), fruit that is good for all to eat if they may, but which can be gathered only in this way. For such reasons ultimately do we study 'Anglo-Saxon' (pages 145–46).

'BEOWULF' & THE CRITICS (A)

The Reverend Oswald Cockayne wrote (in 1864) of the Rev. Joseph Bosworth, D.D, F.R.S., Rawlinsonian Professor of Anglo-Saxon: "I have long entertained [the conviction] that Dr. Bosworth is not a man so diligent in his special walk as duly to read the books . . . which have been printed in our old English, or so-called Anglo-saxon tongue. He may do very well for a Professor . . ." The remarks were inspired by annoyance with Bosworth's dictionary, and may have been unfair, but certainly the period was one of a certain decline in Anglo-Saxon study in England, one in which it was not so much dependent on foreign work as behind it and largely in-competent to appreciate it. However that may be, a modern professor, even if he is not troubled by books printed in Anglo-Saxon, through limiting himself to one, Beowulf, is faced by the serious problem of books about them. I am not a man so diligent in my special walk as duly to read all the books that have been printed about, round, or touching on Beowulf. But I have, in compensation, given a good deal of attention to Beowulf itself; and it has repaid me. The intensive student has some reward denied to the travelling giant of mighty range. At least he escapes sophistication; and that is important. The critic who knows too much is only too likely to go wrong in estimating a poem from a period when literature was not wide in range, or in possession of a diversified store of themes and ideas, and took such as it had all the more vividly and earnestly for that.

In speaking of 'Beowulf and the critics' therefore, I do not attempt an elab-orate study of Beowulf criticism: I am not trying to trace in full its history. The eye is fixed primarily on the poem itself, and such criticism as I notice is principally that which is still current, potent, and influential, and even interesting; and insofar as I allude to its history at all it is to point to what I think is the explanation of certain critical commonplaces which I attack. Beowulf criticism now has a history of its own, and therein is to be found the seeds of the malady from which it suffers still. And all this is but a background against [2] which to place my own view. I pass over, therefore, not only all that is detailed and technical, that slow hammering of scholars great and small, whose results we inherit, and which has gradually made what was still a hundred years ago mainly unintelligible — the real effective beginning of modern scholarship was made by Kemble[1] — a thing about which it

---

1)   First edition 1833, 2nd edition 1835; and especially "A translation of the Anglo-Saxon poem of Beowulf, with a copious Glossary, Preface and Philological notes," 1837.

is possible to have general ideas, but also the mass of disquisition and theory, which has in the main been directed to the <u>origin</u> of the story of <u>Beowulf</u>, or of the allusions in <u>Beowulf</u>, rather than the understanding or valuation of <u>Beowulf</u> as it is, and was made. Indeed antiquarian analysis of the content of <u>Beowulf</u>, and research into this, has usually been considered identical with 'criticism,' or so inextricably confused with it that the confusion has (in my opinion) never been yet dissolved. What I am concerned with, therefore, is that relatively small department of <u>Beowulf</u> bibliography: the actual judgements on <u>Beowulf</u> as a thing itself, as a poem, as a work of art, showing structure and motive.

So overshadowed, as I have said, has this critical function been by the other, that even the greatest critics (such as W. P. Ker or R. W. Chambers) are, I think, still clouded or troubled by this shade. Even, for instance, in the inimitable foreword — the best thing written on the subject — 'Beowulf and the Heroic Age in England' (xxvi pages and all too short) contributed by Chambers, the greatest of living Anglo-Saxon scholars, to Sir Archibald Strong's translation, I see this shadow still. But to this I shall return. For the moment my point is this, and it is my main point, and the one on which I hope to convince you: nearly all censure, and a great deal of the praise, of <u>Beowulf</u>, has been due either to believing it to be something that it is not (e.g. primitive, or rude, or Teutonic) or to disappointment because it was not itself like something else the critic would have preferred [3] (e.g. an ancient heroic lay of slaughter and divided allegiances). And this, even where the intention has been 'pure' criticism (as in the case of Ker or of Chambers), and the acumen and originality displayed has been great, is due to a mental background due to 'research' — to too much 'research' of the kind that is not so much criticism of the poem as mining in it.

I would present you with the following allegory, and would have it borne in mind. A man found a mass of old stone in a unused patch, and made of it a rock garden; but his friends coming perceived that the stones had once been part of a more ancient building, and they turned them upsidedown to look for hidden inscriptions; some suspected a deposit of coal under the soil and proceeded to dig for it. They all said "this garden is most interesting," but they said also "what a jumble and confusion it is in!" — and even the gardener's best friend, who might have been expected to understand what he had been about, was heard to say: "he's such a tiresome fellow — fancy using those beautiful stones just to set off commonplace flowers that are found in every garden: he has <u>no</u> sense of proportion, poor man."

And of course, the less friendly, when they were told the gardener was an Anglo-Saxon and often attended to beer, understood at once: a love of freedom may go with beer and blue eyes, but that yellow hair unfortunately grows always on a muddled head.

That allegory is perfectly just. I will quote from some critics — only very few and generally the most recent, for I am attacking the picture of 'Beowulf' as it is becoming fixed and perpetuated — and you shall see. In the meanwhile let us skip swiftly over the heads of the mass of the critics. Their conflicting Babel mounts up to us, and very little can we make of it. It sounds something like this: 'the poem is due to the imitation of Virgil and inspired by emulation of Latin literature introduced by Christianity — it is a half-baked native epic the development of which was killed by the same influence; it is feeble and incompetent as a narrative — the rules of narrative are cleverly observed [4] in the manner of the learned epic; it is Christian poetry antiquarianly aping a half-forgotten paganism — it is pagan poetry edited by a monk; it is a silly folk-tale — it is a poem of an aristocratic and courtly tradition; it is a hotch-potch; it is 'small beer'; it is a sociological document; it is a mythical allegory; it is rude and rough — it is a masterpiece of metrical art; it was sung or bellowed — it was composed in the study and never even recited; the author had no clear plan or idea at all — it is a clever allegory of a contemporary political situation; it is thin and cheap — it is solemn and weighty; it is the accidental product of blind accretion and senseless elaboration.

The odd thing is that amidst all this Babel we catch one constant refrain: it is steadily said to be 'worth studying'. It is true that this is often qualified thus: 'it is the most worthy of study amongst Anglo-Saxon remains' (this being said in sometimes in tones that suggest that Andaman-islanders could be substituted for Anglo-Saxons); but nowhere is at least this qualified commendation missing. Why? The answer is important.

I will read you a passage from one of the more recent compendia of English literary history — the sort of thing that scholars do not read, though (when they are hard-up in cash or ideas) they occasionally write them: they are, however, very important. Students without formed ideas read them; and if one wonders whence the strange nonsense comes which examinations produce, in spite of ex cathedra vociferations, the answer is from statements in these books transformed in minds that contain little else. These books are the index of what the 'widely-read and cultured' man makes of the 'special literature' mole-like scholars fling up in their chosen field. They are the quintessence of 'research'; they are what of it, finally selected, gets home to the public and makes the background of current ideas. In fact we ought to [5] be more aware of them — most of them ought to be on an <u>index expurgatorius</u> or publicly burnt. Now the passage I will read serves a double purpose. First of all it gives in a few lines 'the plot' of <u>Beowulf</u>, and it is necessary to have this stated in its barest terms for my purpose. Secondly it states explicitly the reasons why, amid all the dispraise, we have an agreement that <u>Beowulf</u> ought to be studied — why, indeed, it burdens 'English' syllabuses up and down the land. And the compendium is a competent one, that of the late Sir Archibald Strong,[2] who had read <u>Beowulf</u> with attention, indeed he cared for it sufficiently to

---

2)   <u>A Short History of English Literature</u>, Milford, 1921.

translate it into verse,[3] and in the Introduction to his translation said many things nearer to the point than any critic other than Chambers. But this was four years later than the compendium. This latter crushes the crowded scene of English literature from 700–1900 into 368 closely printed pages — how much longer will this ridiculous jig-saw work continue to be thought worth while! — of which <u>Beowulf</u> (one of the greatest single things in that tongue) gets less than two.

It would take far too long, however, to criticize all the remarks even in this brief entry; and I pass now over the first and longest paragraph (mostly tentative and not dogmatic and therefore innocuous, more or less, even in error), [6] though, before I leave Sir Archibald I shall draw attention to two sentences. But I want first to exhibit some of his later remarks, which throw a light on the earlier ones. He thus summarizes the 'plot': "The main story deals with the adventures of Beowulf in his contest with ogres and dragons" — there is bias in these plurals. "We are told how the hall of Hrothgar, King of the Danes, is devastated for the space of twelve years by a demon called Grendel. Beowulf, nephew of Hygelac, king of the Geats, a tribe of South Sweden, crosses the sea to help Hrothgar, and in a fight in his hall mortally wounds Grendel. Grendel's mother, seeking vengeance for the death of her son, renews the attacks. Beowulf tracks her to her lair, a cave at the bottom of a deep mere, and slays her. Loaded with gifts he returns to his native land, where he ultimately succeeds to the throne. In his old age a fire-breathing dragon lays waste the land. Beowulf attacks and kills it, but is himself wounded to death in the fray. The poem ends with an account of his burial amid the mourning of his whole people. This short summary does scant justice to the poem."

Exactly Sir Archibald — then why give it? It can only be for the benefit of people who have never read <u>Beowulf</u>, and it will not benefit them any more than the plot of the 'Iliad.' A story cannot be judged from its summarized plot, but only from the way this is told, and from the ideas and feelings which are stirred in the author — whether ever consciously formulated by him or not — in the telling, and which breathe a life and purpose into it. To judge of <u>Beowulf</u>, to try indeed to form any conception of it from stuff of this sort is to attempt an estimate of a great man from his skeleton. But I have quoted it because it is accurate (which cannot be said of other summaries which are still before a cozened public[4] and because this mental subtraction from a story of all that gives it life [7] must precede the forming of such judgements as the following. The critic immediately goes on: "in outline

---

3)   <u>Beowulf, translated into modern English rhyming verse</u>, Constable, 1925: on the whole the best modern English translation of <u>Beowulf</u> that I know, though it is rather a transformation, since in spite of the reasons urged by the translator, I remain of opinion that he selected the metré (that of Morris' <u>Sigurd</u>) which is the most foreign in mood and style to the original of almost all the available metrés.

4)   For example from a baser variety of the genre to which Sir Archibald's book belongs, I would refer to <u>A History of English Literature</u> (in 111 pages!) by Dr. Compton Rickett, a potting of his longer work (which is as erroneous . . .

the story is <u>trivial</u> enough, a <u>typical folktale</u>; but it is interspersed with many subsidiary legends, historical and mythical, and with allusions to legends, which open up for us the life of Teutonic heathendom and lift the story far above a <u>mere recital of the deeds of a giant killer</u>. Beowulf is the picture of a whole civilization, of the Germania which Tacitus describes" — this is, of course, nonsense; but the cat is just about to leap from the bag. "The <u>main interest</u> which the poem has for <u>us</u> is thus <u>not a purely literary interest</u>. <u>Beowulf</u> is an important <u>historical document</u>, recreating for us a whole society, telling us, in most authentic fashion, of life as it was lived in far-off heathen days." There is more to follow, but I cannot deal with all the errors (as they seem to me) of still current criticism of <u>Beowulf</u>, I must omit all except one sentence (a hackneyed one): "The Christian allusions show up rather incongruously against the pervading paganism." This taken with what I have just cited, and with two sentences from the opening paragraph originally passed by, — (i) "<u>Beowulf</u> is the only poem of any length . . . which has come down to us, of the early heroic poetry of the Teutons," and (ii) "Though biblical allusions abound, and the heathen deities have, for the most part, vanished before the editing — if we may call it editing — of the Christian reviser, the background is not Christian but heathen" — contains, explicitly, the views which I principally intend to attack. Though they are closely interconnected one can discern some distinct points. 'The story is trivial a typical folk-tale' is the main objective of my attack, but we shall meet this again and in more unexpected quarters, so for the moment I reserve my fire. At this point I should like attention concentrated on Sir Archibald's frank statement of the reasons for studying <u>Beowulf</u>. He should be thanked for it. It throws light on much that was to me dark before I read it. It had never occurred to me to approach this or any other poem in such a spirit — but once one knows the spirit exists, one sees in this spirit an admirable explanation of the errors in <u>Beowulf</u>-criticism; it is their natural source.

[8] We need not pause to quarrel over 'authentic fashion' — in my opinion it is probably a delusion[*] — but we will ponder "the main interest is for us not purely literary. <u>Beowulf</u> is an important historical document." I protest that there is here either a confusion of thought or a falsehood. Either it is held that the literary merits of <u>Beowulf</u> are so small that its <u>historical</u> interest (which no one doubts — though it is accidental, and due to our poverty of other records of a more suitable type) is the only one which can to-day attract a rational person of culture (or in search of it) — <u>which is false</u>, or else the two different attitudes which one can have towards a document which is at once old (and preserved from an important but ill-represented period) as well as a work of art, have been confused. They can be studied as poetry, or they can be quarried for information. The

---

[*]   i.e. we have insufficient knowledge to judge by, but the probabilities are that it is as authentic and as unauthentic as an historical novel concerning the days of Queen Anne written by a competent person of today who had read much of the literature and something of the history of that period.

operations are distinct, and no excuse for confusing them is provided by the facts that they are often prosecuted in conjunction even by the same persons, or that the 'research' process may, and sometimes does, assist and illuminate the other. For this is accidental. The quarrying would be perfectly legitimate if it did not assist 'criticism' at all (so long as it was not mistaken for criticism). Yet if a thing does in fact possess any literary merit at all, the appreciation of that merit is the right and natural and indeed the prime function of its study. The works of Homer contain some of the greatest of the recorded verse of the world, and the Homeric language is probably the greatest instrument of poetry of which we have knowledge. Yet the Iliad and the Odyssey are great quarries for information, and there are doubtless perfectly worthy persons to whom their main interest is not purely literary, to whom they are important historical documents. But I have never heard any of them prescribe their attitude as inevitable for 'us' — the lordly 'us' that means all reasonable living men. Though the literary merit of Homer be much greater than that of Beowulf (in nearly all respects), the principle is the same.

[9] This then is the shadow that hangs still over Beowulf — it is primarily an historical document, a source of information about things we otherwise should not know. It will be valuable I think to see what an effect this has still, and how subtly this attitude pervades and twists the judgement even of those who do not consciously and frankly avow it like Sir Archibald.

It is a cause of what is false in the sentences I have already quoted. But for it the critic would never have written "Beowulf is the only poem of any length ... which has come down to us, of the early heroic poetry of the Teutons." The historian would like some of this early heroic poetry, but he has not got it, and so he sees it where it is not, and does not in consequence see what is there.

There is something in the background of Northern Europe — an ancient community of temper and spirit and ideals, to some extent of custom, law, and social arrangements, which corresponds roughly to the known and definite community of language which we express by the terms Teutonic, or now more generally Germanic, and by the hypothesis of an actual linguistic unity in the far past. But the linguistic hypothesis — a necessary and inevitable one, though all the problems connected with it are far from settled — is not instantly convertible into terms of race or ethics. Too many other factors, some known, some unknown, intervene in the course of the spread of the Germanic languages to areas where they were certainly not indigenous (such as Britain or Southern Germany). It is no longer good criticism to speak of things written in Norse or English or German or Gothic as just "Teutonic." Or rather it is just as good and just as bad as lumping all the products of Spain, Portugal, Italy and France as Romance or Latin. There is, or may be, a truth in it, but it is not always the most important truth — especially in dealing with individual works of literature: namely that Spanish is Spanish, Italian Italian, and French French.

[10] So Norse is Norse and English English. Though there is indeed some-

thing which may be called a common Germanic (or Teutonic) spirit, and is appreciable (with admiration or distaste) by all, even if it is not easily caught in a few words. It is true too that <u>Beowulf</u> is illuminated by a knowledge of early Germanic languages and literary remains, and of history in the North. Yet the differences are at least as important as the resemblances, and <u>Beowulf</u> is primarily, for its critic, an <u>English</u> poem <u>of a special period</u>, and not a Teutonic one. For that it is several hundreds of years too late. There is extant <u>no</u> "Teutonic" literature, still less any early Teutonic heroic poems; and for these lost things "Beowulf" is neither a satisfactory substitute, nor to be judged as if it were.

Were all mediæval English literature swept away, but for a few scraps, and the allusions and stories in the plays of Shakespeare — even perhaps what survives of the mediæval temper in those plays, it would still be untrue to say that the works of Shakespeare were "the largest body of medieval poetry that has come down to us." It might be an unfortunate fact that we could only guess at "medieval literature" by investigating Shakespeare and comparing him with other material of similar period outside England, and so seeking to detect what in him was derived from the period behind him in matter or in spirit. This would be a legitimate procedure — to use Shakespeare in the course of research prompted by a special curiosity about the past. But it would <u>not</u> be the chief function of Shakespearean criticism; for real Shakespeare criticism Shakespeare was a dramatist, an English dramatist, and an English dramatist of a special English period. Also Shakespeare was an individual and himself.

[11] We will then emend our inaccurate and hasty critic: — "'<u>Beowulf</u>' is then the only poem of any length which had come down to us of the early heroic poetry of the <u>English</u>."[†] Or, if you don't mind sacrificing snap for exactitude: "It is the longest and most elaborate surviving poem which may be held to be in the main in a direct line of descent from ancient Germanic or Northern heroic verse, now lost; it is the principal surviving example of the early heroic poetry of this vernacular tradition as it developed under peculiar circumstances <u>in England</u>; and it comes probably from the end of that development."

Also it is by an author, and is a thing in itself.

For a moment we will turn to this last point, usually unnoticed. While the individualism and the proprietary rights of authorship were less and different we may assume in ancient days, we still cannot dismiss the author and thrust him back into the tribal genius. The ancient legends mention no less the particular fame of the maker of verse such as <u>Heorrenda</u> than the maker of jewel or sword such as <u>Wéland</u>. The fame and names of individual Icelandic poets have been better preserved even than their works. "Beowulf" it is true has been preserved and not the

---

†   Even 'early' is here misleading. It means early one presumes relatively to the whole later course of English to the present. Of the actual <u>heroic poetry</u> of the English "Beowulf" is, of course, to be viewed as a very <u>late</u> example.

name of its author; but we have no right to assume that he was ordinary and negligible or that his authorship was of no concern to him; or that the personal factor can be safely forgotten. This "Teutonic" criticism suggests, however, that 'Teutons' had a universal kind of poetry and no individual poets. Since Teutons were thoroughly Teutons, so Teutonic poetry was all Teutonic. But what of the makers? Great differences can be detected even among the lays of the Elder Edda. What of Anglo-Saxon poets? What of the maker of "Beowulf" in particular?

[12] He seems to be lost in a crowd of 'ancestral voices prophesying war.' But he must be distinguished, and his voice heard as his own. If one really comes to think of it, he would have disliked many of these Teutons heartily, and would have failed to recognized his identity with them as readily as our critics do. His grand-children were at grips with such Teutons par excellence, the viking invaders, and regarded them as the very devil. What ever their tongue they would have written them down rather in the kin of Grendel than of Hrothgar (for even Grendel may probably well have spoken Danish). And there is the rub. "Beowulf" may be a poem about Danes, but it is an English poem about them, or rather the poem of a particular Englishman using in a particular way English tradition about them.

The life and spirit of the poem "Beowulf" is then not Teutonic, still less a specimen of Teutonic heathendom. It has its roots in a past which was shared by at least some of the historical speakers of Teutonic tongues (it has much that is perceptibly common to the spirit of the men say of Norway or Iceland) and with that past it has definite tangible links in manners, things, and code (kinship and loyalty for example). But all these are transmuted: they belong to a special time, with a special temper, and also to a special man.

The special man, in a period whose original wealth is now represented only by a selection so haphazard and so very scanty, we can perhaps not define — no more than to recognize the general unity and harmony of the whole he has produced. But we must not forget him even if this means no more than a caution in ascribing everything in "Beowulf" to Anglo-Saxons in general (let alone Teutons), and a remembrance that a factor exists, the personal one, for which we have not allowed (even if we cannot help this omission).

[13] The special period can be made more clear. We do know much, if much too little, of early Anglo-Saxon history. And it is the duty of the critic to attempt the setting of "Beowulf" correctly against that background. 'Correctly' I say because Anglo-Saxon history is not one thing, uniform in mind and texture from Aidan to Stigand any more than Icelandic is all one and the same from the Landnám in the 9th century to the cruel feuds of the great houses and the submission to the Norwegian crown in the 13th century, or Rome from Romulus to Constantine.

This is the reverse of the historical document bias of which I have spoken — valuing "Beowulf" primarily or solely as an historical document, even a document for a period of history to which it did not belong. It is true that if once we can make even an approximate and probable guess as to the period when "Beowulf" as we have it was composed,* then this great poem becomes a chief document of the times and an illumination of those days, of prime importance to the <u>historian as such</u> (though usually neglected). But the "Beowulf" critic, <u>as such</u>, must go first to the evidence for the period outside his poem. The process must not for him become a vicious circle in which the poem is used to depict a period, and that picture is then used to explain the poem. There is not much danger of this, or at least no need for it. The poem fits well into the period (8th century) to which it can be assigned on dry and logical and unsubjective grounds, and is so illuminated by that placing that it cannot any longer be doubted that so set it is seen against its <u>natural background</u>. The murmurs of the primeval Teutonic forest, and the sounding of the Scandinavian seas, may still be heard there and move the imagination of the listener, but they are memories already in that day of a far past caught and coloured in the shells and amber of tradition, and refashioned by the jeweler of a later day — the great day of the Anglo-Saxon spring.

[14] If that is so, small wonder that the discerning critic will boggle at that other sentence of Strong's that I have quoted above — his remark that in '<u>Beowulf</u>' '<u>biblical allusions abound, and the heathen deities have, for the most part, vanished before the editing, — if we may call it editing — of the Christian reviser, the background is not Christian but heathen</u>." The inaccuracies are the least important part of the error here: '<u>Biblical allusions</u>' do not '<u>abound</u>' in "Beowulf", and heathen deities have not <u>for the most part</u> <u>vanished</u> but vanished altogether. The biblical allusions are rare and of one special and peculiar kind — references to Cain, and to the giants, the origin of monsters. This and <u>not</u> their relative frequency is the important point, and will later be considered. No heathen deity is ever named. Nor does a heathen deity enter even into proper names, save in the one curious case of <u>Ingwine</u>, twice used as a name of the Danes; a fossil which may indicate the character of the stones used in the building, but says nothing of the use to which the architect has put them. <u>Wyrd</u> is mentioned, but this is quite another matter: <u>wyrd</u> was not and is not a god, but the master of gods and men, a theory that was absorbed insensibly by an omnipotent god, or rather was indeed from the beginning an apprehension of Him. The only important thing about this 'heathenism' in fact, if we are considering the <u>author</u>, is that he consciously and explicitly regarded his story as taking place in <u>heathen times</u> and also in <u>past times</u>, but either could not or would not name any of the ancient divinities.

Well Sir Archibald says "<u>background</u>" doesn't he? Certainly but look at the contrast made, the creation (half heartedly it is true) of an editor who is not the poet. Background! Of course the background is heathen and not Christian. The background of all humanity is heathen; the background of Christianity is heathen.

---

*   This can be done. I do not (at any rate at the moment) enter into the arguments or allude to the evidence, linguistic or of other kind. The 8th. century is now, probably universally agreed to fit all the various lines of enquiry.

If you really mean "background" and not immediate setting — not spirit and temper, indeed of the actual original author — it is not worth saying. To do Sir Archibald justice he plainly did mean not "background" but original author. That is
worth discussing; and becomes, so expressed, a natural part of the story of the
"Beowulf" period we have spoken of just previously. Its discussion can be delayed,
therefore; and we need for the moment say no more than that Sir Archibald himself after profounder study speaks in his own introduction to his translation not of
the "heathen background" but of the "Christian colouring" which the author has
"given to his story".

[15] And so we pass slowly towards sanity, and from pseudo-historical phan-
tasy to genuine criticism. In Chambers' Foreword to this same translation (which
should be read by all whatever else, save the poem itself, is unread) only the shadow of the old historical document bias is left, and the final solution of the Christian-heathen debate is trembling on the verge of expression, only just not explicit.

The shadow is there in the tone, which suggests that if "Beowulf" analysed is
not quite so good as it is in general impression (in style and dignity) at least it gives
a picture of the times and perhaps the mood of a great moment in our history.
Chambers' method is nonetheless right. In a few brilliant strokes and a few quotations the period to which "Beowulf" belongs is delineated, and against that
period "Beowulf" is set.

One thing only remains unresolved — and here the shadow of the old bias is
most dark. Still the folk-tale motive stands like a spectre of old research gone
wrong. On page xxvi, when everything seems going right, we hear once again that
"the main story of Beowulf is a wild folk-tale." Quite true of course, as it is of King
Lear except that silly would in the latter case be a better adjective. But more — we
are told that the same sort of stuff is found in Homer, yet it is kept in its proper
place. "The folk-tale is a good servant but a bad master: it has been allowed in
'Beowulf' to usurp the place of honour, and to drive into episodes and digressions
the things which should be the main stuff of a well-conducted epic."

But why class 'Beowulf' as an "epic" however conducted; and who has legislated for what should be the main stuff of any poem. Only, I fear, the antiquarian
historian, who prefers semi-historical legend to folk-tale (whatever that may be)
which he calls "wild."

And so we have come full circle, and the cloud hangs over us still!

[16] I started with a chance-selected but not unrepresentative criticism from
a recent compendium. But criticism of that criticism has already almost let several
cats out of the bag, cats whose release were better kept until nearer the end. We
will push them back a moment. I have been led to digress from the path I perhaps
ought to have followed: I have hurried on too far and left out the beginning, and
must loop backward. I should have begun with the antiquated, the beginnings of
"Beowulf" criticism and progressed to the "modern," and surveyed the minor and
the ridiculous as well as the greater and more wise. But since I have already

glimpsed the most important critics (such as Chambers) and the most important problems I shall not now survey the whole course of "Beowulf" criticism maximal and minimal. I never really wished to, and I do not really think it very necessary or desirable. One may assent to Earle's quotation from Dowden "The happiest moment in a critic's hours of study is, when seemingly by some divination, but really as the result of patient observation and thought, he lights upon the central motive of a great work" — but one need not (as Earle himself admitted) still bother about Earle's particular divination, which ascribed the work to Hygeberht, Archbishop of Richfield (787 – 803?) and made the whole poem into a kind of early political Utopia.

I shall present a casual selection dictated largely by chance and memory and this will (unless I turn aside for some deserved merriment, at the expense of the fools who have trespassed in the confidence of their ignorance on paths too difficult for their dainty feet) chiefly illustrate what we have already seen are the principal points of critical debate.

(1) Poetic merit —— historical document

(2) Christian or heathen.

(3) a medley, an accretion; or a constructed whole.

(4) and finally we shall reach at the end as at the beginning the old ogre in his lair — the typical (or the 'wild') folk-tale usurping even in the courtly Anglo-Saxon 8th century the throne of the heroes. If we can deal this old ogre a knock, or show him to be phantom, then indeed 'Beowulf' the poem will be <u>gefælsod</u>.

[17] The exaltation of the 'historical document' value, as greater than, or a substitute for poetic merit is due to two distinct things. Primarily and principally it is due to the fact that many critics have failed from lack of training, superciliousness, sheer ignorance or mere insensitiveness to poetry (especially in unfamiliar mould) to grasp — to hear or to feel — the poetic merit of *Beowulf* in detail or general. Many have been frankly unqualified for their self-appointed pulpits. Others have been but indifferently equipped.

Thus the introduction to Mr. Shane Leslie's anthology of (I believe he said) Catholic poets speaks of "Beowulf" "as small beer." I hope in depending on memory (for I do not possess the worthless book) I am not wrong in ascribing these introductory words to Mr. Chesterton. This ascription alone causes me to mention them. On such a matter Mr. Shane Leslie is of course already honoured more than he deserves by the mere mention of his name: his book includes what by its title seems intended for the "Dream of the Rood" in translation, but in content is more wholly unlike that poem than the versions of plough-candidates in a provincial university. But Mr. Chesterton is difficult. Still one may guess he could not construe a line of the original and had depended on translation (if on anything but imagination). He might as well judge of English beer by visiting an American speak-easy.

Old English verse — less perhaps in essence than because it is now strange and unfamiliar in metré and manner and methods of diction — does not unlock the treasures of its <u>word hord</u> readily, and least to the hasty and conceited. This department, the texture of Old Verse (of which "Beowulf" is a part but yet an individual, and much the best individual), though it is a department of 'general criticism,' I shall not here in detail explore. I have lectured before and shall again on this aspect of 'Beowulf' separately. And in any case I leave here the poem itself in the [18] hands of students trained in this scholarly Oxford school with <u>confidence</u>. <u>Ars longa vita brevis</u> (art is long; life is short) — <u>The lyf so schort, the craft so long to lerne so hard the assay so scharp the conqueryng</u> as Chaucer says; long study has its rewards, yet the poetic merits of Beowulf verse are not inaccessible entirely even to the first assay, if the will is there and the scholar humble.

But as we has seen, this "historical bias" lingers still even unto those whose knowledge and feeling for Old English is eminent. This is due of course, to the fact that "Beowulf" actually is full of things that <u>are</u> of historical and antiquarian interest; and no real critic of its poetry has ever been not also to some extent an amateur as well of history and antiquity. And so far have the days when it was written receded from us that this historical interest — this ancestral voice out of the distance — has an inscrutable appeal. Nonetheless it remains true that this is only an accident, and not an essential.

But the very origin of "Beowulf" studies also helps to explain this bias. It first awakened real interest and attracted close attention as an historical document.

The one surviving manuscript of the poem is contained in a composite Mss. together with other pieces (such as the <u>Epistola Alexandri</u> and the <u>Wonders of the East</u>) that occurred before and after it. For this reason — whatever its first possessors after the scattering of Ms remains of the 16th century, such as Laurence Nowell, may have made or thought of it — our first notice of it is that of the great Humphrey Wanley He describes it thus on p. 218 of his <u>Catalogus</u> of Mss. [*] [19] in Vol. II (1705) of Hickes <u>Thesaurus</u>.

"In hoc libro qui Poeseos Anglosaxonicae <u>egregium est exemplum</u> descripta videntur bella quae Beowulfus quidam Danus ex regio Scyldingorum stirpe ortus gessit contra Sueciae regulos."

(In this book, which is an excellent example of Anglo-Saxon poetry, it seems that there are wars described which a certain Beowulf, a Dane sprung from the royal race of the Scyldings, waged against the princes of Sweden.)

This is of course largely untrue — it comes of looking only hastily at the beginning and the end, very excusable in this monumental and admirable catalogue. But so far no great damage is done. It is <u>poetry</u> you notice (and quite rightly <u>egregium exemplum</u>, a criticism that has constantly been repeated even amidst mispraise and has never been reversed), though it deals with "history," and with

---

[*]   Who tried so hard in vain to get the Cotton Collection, amongst which is Beowulf, for Oxford. Oxford changes little.

Danes and Swedes. Wanley's words in fact suggest that if he had had more time for scrutiny he would have said more that was pertinent and as far ahead of the scholarship of his own time (and of a century to come) as he usually was. For in general the language of Old English verse was as yet in his time almost entirely unknown. For long reasonably competent translations of Old English prose, such as that of Ælfric, had been possible, but verse remained a practically unintelligible riddle.

So far little harm has been done. But though we do not yet see the "historical document" bias, we see already the germ of it. The subject of the poem was the wars of Sweden and Denmark.

It is not surprising therefore that the story goes next to Denmark, to <u>Grim Johnson Thorkelin</u> — who eventually published the *editio princeps* in 1815. Thorkelin thought the work was a translation, of the age of Alfred, from a <u>Danish</u> original written by contemporaries with the events described. This "translation from Scandinavian" was one of the earliest red herrings, and long confused the scent. Thorkelin's first interest dates from 1786 when he visited England and had his transcripts made.

[20] By 1807 his edition was practically ready for press, but it was destroyed by the gentle descendants of the barbarous Anglo-Saxons when they bombarded and stormed the old city of Copenhagen. Thorkelin's house was burned and his property mostly destroyed although his two transcripts were saved. It took him eight years to do the work again — a gallant effort for an old man. And from Thorkelin we pass to Pastor <u>Grundtvig</u> — one of the greatest single names in the history of Beowulf -criticism [*] — another Dane, under the patronage of the same Privycounselor Bülow, the Mæcenas of his time, who had encouraged and munificently aided Thorkelin. This is the first stage of <u>Beowulf</u> criticism — and though criticism rapidly [21] shifted as knowledge grew, we must note that this stage was due to the view of "Beowulf" as a <u>document for early Scandinavian history</u>, [*] sufficiently

---

[*]   I have not here time to say much about him. With practically no material for study he tackled the elucidation of Old English verse language brilliantly, and made such advances that his own <u>Anglo-Saxon verse</u> in commendation of <u>Bülow</u>, though it will not now pass muster except where it is mere quotation is nonetheless recognizably "like" in metré and idiom. His "emendations" of Thorkelin's faulty text were often found actually to be in the Mss (which he had not seen when he made them) — a thing which seemed almost like sorcery to those unable yet to swallow the notion that other languages than Latin, Greek and Hebrew had any shape or rules. This ensured him nonetheless a hospitable welcome in England and Oxford; and served to reawaken a belief that there might be something in this Anglo-Saxon stuff after all. A large part of Oxford remains, however, as secure in its ignorance of the field and the achievements of Anglo-Saxon scholarship as it was when it shook its head in half incredulous wonder over N. F. S. Grundtvig, Præst. Among examples of Grundtvig's sagacity one may mention that it was he who first made out many of the proper names in the text, first discerning Sigemund the Volsung for instance; and it was he who first identified <u>Hygelac</u> with the <u>Chochilaicus</u> in Gregory of Tours, a discovery of cardinal importance. It was Grundtvig who published the first translation of <u>Beowulf</u> into any modern language: <u>Bjowulfs Drape. Et Gothisk Helte-Digt fra forrige Aar-Tusinde af Angel-Saxisk paa Danske Riim</u> ved. Nic. Fred. Sev Grundtvig, Præst. Kjöbenhavn, 1820.

[*]   So it is to Prof. B. Nerman in <u>Det Svenska Rikets Uppkomst</u> "Beowulf" is still a prime document — rightly. I am not complaining, only indicating the atmosphere in which "Beowulf" criticism was born.

indicated by the title of Thorkelin's edition: <u>De Danorum Rebus Gestis Secul. III & IV. Poema Danicum Dialecto Anglosaxonica</u>. (History of the Danes of the 3rd and 4th Centuries, a Poem about Danes in the Anglo-Saxon Dialect)

Thorkelin was not the first to mention "Beowulf" after Wanley. This distinction, such as it is, goes to <u>Sharon Turner</u> in 1807 in his <u>History of the Anglo-Saxons</u>. But though he gave some extracts with such "translation" as he could manage, he was not only too incompetent in the verse language to 'qualify him' even for this moderate part, but probably too little able to imagine that any Anglo-Saxon might be too difficult for him without further study to appreciate the magnitude of his offence. He only replaced the pardonable errors of Wanley by nonsense. He pronounces <u>Beowulf</u> — "the most interesting relic of Anglo-Saxon poetry which time has suffered us to receive. The subject is the expedition of Beowulf to wreak the fæhðe or deadly feud on Hrothgar, for a homicide which he had committed. It abounds with speeches, which Beowulf and Hrothgar and their partisans make to each other, with much occasional description and sentiment."

As Earle says, proper names excepted, this has no more to do with Beowulf than with the Iliad or the Chanson de Roland. But we need not be too harsh upon Turner — his nonsense is no worse in proportion to available knowledge than other stuff supposing itself criticism that we meet much later. Sharon Turner is then negligible, and in so far as he ever learned more sense, a disciple of the more humble and patient Thorkelin. In his History of 1823 there is a considerable change, and the poem is a "poetical Romance" or "metrical Romance"* which celebrates the heroic deeds [22] of a Beowulf who fell in <u>Jutland</u> in the year 340 A. D. This is a borrowing from the Danes from Thorkelin, from Suhm the Danish Historian, and by him got from <u>Saxo Grammaticus</u>, by identifying Beowulf with <u>Bous</u> son of Odin, whom Saxo relates to have fallen in battle with <u>Hotherus</u> about that date. With this identification or <u>confusion</u> of Geats and Jutes was foreshadowed a long controversy which has complicated the detail of Beowulf criticism — and which we can safely neglect, as it concerns primarily the elucidation for their own sake of the traditions enshrined in Beowulf and not the criticism of the poem as a whole.

It is to Conybeare perhaps in "Illustrations of Anglo-Saxon Poetry" (1826) that we may give the credit of finally dismissing the uncritical belief that 'Beowulf' was derived from a hand contemporary with the events described. This was, of course, due to total misunderstanding of the frequent expressions such as <u>mine gefræge</u> (it was learned by me) and <u>we gefrignon</u> (we have learned) and so on. The appeal is rather to <u>tradition</u> and the time envisaged by the poet already the distant past, as Conybeare pointed out. But this was his only real contribution; though we may note that he rejects Thorkelin's <u>Bous</u> and Jutland, and remains an agnostic

---

* These titles are challenges to Ritson, and others, who denied the existence of poetical Romance before the Norman Conquest

about ultimate origins (<u>Illustrations</u>. p 33); and says of the writer (or perhaps the translator or modernizer of the Dano-Saxon period to whom he is inclined to ascribe Beowulf as we have it) that "<u>it is evident that he was a Christian</u>." His translations, although often absurd and never even reasonably close, are at least recognizably related to the original.

Little later however with the work of J. M. Kemble (of Trinity College Cambridge) accurate scholarship began — also comparative philology of a scientific kind was introduced, and proved here its worth: by it the meanings of innumerable words have been recaptured, and if we can now to a great extent appreciate the diction and verbal effects of Old English verse it is due in the main to philology. [23] This in turn was due to Germany where Kemble had studied, and in general to Germany after Kemble the ball passed — in some ways much for the good of the game, but not in all.

Kemble's first limited edition in 1833 — <u>The Anglo-Saxon Poems of Beowulf, The Traveller's Song</u>[+] <u>and the Battle of Finnesburh, edited together with a glossary of the more difficult words and an Historical Preface</u>. London. Pickering. was sold out in a few months and soon replaced by the corrected second edition (1835). But though the text represents a great advance on Thorkelin, and the discussion of archaic and difficult words was something quite new, it is Kemble's work of 1837 that marks a definite crossing to a new era. This is <u>A Translation of the Anglo-Saxon Poem of Beowulf</u> with a copious Glossary, Preface and <u>Philological Notes</u>. London. Pickering. 1837. The glossary was copious and in its day invaluable — it was indeed the foundation of Grein's <u>Sprachschatz</u>, the possession of which puts the merest beginner of today in a position which 100 years ago could only be gained by years of work on largely unprinted manuscripts. But in this preface we begin that swing from a blind belief in the historicity of the hero and all other characters in the poem to the "mythological" explanation of everything which is now as wearisome as it was once fascinating. And already research begins to bury the poem, and the poet. What the author made of and meant by his use of his material is lost in speculation as to what is the nature and ultimate origin of that material in itself. So deep has the dust grown since that it is difficult now to see the poem beneath it, except by the clean sweep of a broom.

It is to Germany or scholars there trained and writing in German, as I have said, that in the main the history of research into <u>Beowulf</u> now passes. I say research advisedly, for it produced rather the materials of criticism (and as plentifully lumber that was of no use) [24] than criticism, constructive criticism itself. One does not necessarily advance in acquaintance with a man, or understanding of his thought, either by studying his ancestors, or by dissecting his person. But dissection was for long the order of the day: dissection not only into heathen original and Christian interpolation, but into the component lays which had somehow

---

+   sc. <u>Widsith</u>

— it never became clear quite how, fortuitously or arbitrarily — became conjoined into an "epic." The notions were grafted upon Beowulf-criticism in Germany, and came from current classical scholarship; for Beowulf if welcomed there was welcomed by scholars with ingrained beliefs about the accidental growth of epics, founded upon the authority of Wolf and Lachmann, and their sentence upon it was foregone.

As Earle says[‡] "That great works in early literature forsooth were not made by art and device, but that they grew spontaneously and blindly, this was that imagination in the air which attended the first entertainment of Beowulf in the Fatherland."[*] It is small wonder that little illuminating general criticism was produced in such an atmosphere, or in later work still tainted with such an origin. Though the contributions of many illustrious German scholars cannot be despised — we depend heavily upon their patient and ingenious work — we can understand why it is that Chambers notes[‡] almost with surprise that it is on such a piece as Widsith that older scholars are at their best — Kemble, Leo, Lappenberg, Ettmüller and later Möller, Ten Brink, Müllenhoff. Precisely on such a poem — which has little poetry and only that of a glittering catalogue when patience has rubbed the rust of oblivion and obscurity off the names therein — is 'research' at its best; and the dissection and the dissector and mythomaniac most innocuous.

Small wonder then that in his appendix to the second edition (1932) of his Introduction on recent work down to 1930, Chambers begins with Klæber's edition Beowulf (1922 2nd 1928) and calls it rightly the most important since Kemble's in 1833. Since it is written in English, but in America, and yet by a German, it may be taken as symbolic [25] of changes in the world, and in the lesser world of Beowulf studies in the intervening century. And it contains in its introduction studies of structure tone, ideas, style and language in which we have some synthesis as well as research, and some sanity as well as learning.

Decision, a view, a conviction are as Chambers says essential and now imperative; yet with few exceptions Beowulf study has wandered in a maze of theories for 90 years and more. This wandering and development until we come to Lawrence, Klaeber and Chambers I make no attempt to sketch. I will quote you Chambers' own summary of the principal points in his neglected synthetic and constructive side — since 1890 (it was hardly in evidence before) and pass on.

So it is time to try and reach a decision with regard to the controversial problems of Beowulf.

For although, about 1890, a number of efforts were made to get a comprehensive view of these problems, little was done in the following thirty years by way of a general survey. In 1883 Rönning had published his study, Beovulfs-Kvadet — a study which, in a remarkable way, anticipates the results to which scholars, after nearly half

---

‡   "Deeds xxix"
*   All Earle's Introduction is valuable, except his own private gambol at the end.
‡   Preface to Widsith.

a century, are now returning. Then, in 1888–9, had appeared the three monographs of ten Brink, Sarrazin and (posthumously) Müllenhoff. These had been followed by the "Introduction" which Earle prefixed to his translation of *Beowulf* in 1892.

The theories expressed in these five books differed fundamentally, and no prospect of agreement seemed to be in sight. Röning's work, in many ways the best balanced of all five, was handicapped partly by its appearance in Danish, and partly by the fact that the views which it put forward were at the moment unpopular.

During the thirty years following (1892–1921) there had been comparatively few and brief attempts at synthesis (honourable mention must be made of Brandl's fine sketch in *Pauls Grundriss*). Yet during all this time there had appeared a constant stream of publications on the subject of *Beowulf* or on allied subjects. And the study had been revolutionized in many ways, of which at least five need special mention.

W.P. Ker in his *Epic and Romance* (1896) had done a good deal to shatter the belief that (in the words he was fond of quoting) "all epic poetry is written by A, B, and an Interpolator."

Ker's work had more influence after its importance had been emphasized by Andreas Heusler in his *Lied und Epos* (1905). Heusler followed this up by a number of invaluable contributions to the study of Germanic heroic legend.

Olrik published in 1903 and 1910 his studies of early Danish history as reflected in Denmark's ancient heroic poetry.

In 1910 Friedrich Panzer brought a vast knowledge of folk-tale to bear upon *Beowulf*, thus reinforcing the view that Beowulf's adventures with Grendel and Grendel's mother belonged rather to folk-lore than to mythology.

In a number of ways Knut Stjerna placed his large archæological experience at the service of *Beowulf* students, and this led to further studies by other Swedish historians and archæologists, notably Birger Nerman and Sune Lindqvist.Contemporary with these definite contributions, there had been that slow shifting of standpoint which comes with the years. The view as to the amalgamation of epics from earlier lays, which had seemed axiomatic to Lachmann and his pupil Müllenhoff, and the mythological and allegorical assumptions which Müllenhoff had inherited from Kemble, had ceased to be generally believed.

It has therefore become necessary to hew a way through the jungle. Now, whilst the monographs of 1883–92 leave one with a bewildered wondering where truth is to be found amid all this difference, I find an agreement between the views of Klæber, Lawrence and myself which is almost embarrassing. A hostile critic might liken our voices to the docile harmonious utterance of a stage crowd: "where they do agree on the stage, their unanimity is wonderful."

And indeed it must be granted to such a potential critic that we are not absolutely independent of each other. What Klaeber published in 1922 he had written in 1918, and therefore without any knowledge of my book, which was not then out; but I, on my part, had learnt a good deal from various monographs which he had printed; whilst (as I said in my preface) my debt to Lawrence, who read the proofs of my book and discussed all its details with me, is a heavy one. Still none of us would, I hope, accept any view on trust from the other. We have all tried to use independent judgment, and on some subjects, of which *Finnsburg* is the most important, we differ. But these differences are episodic, hardly affecting the main argument.

In brief this summary means that mythological fantasy is dead; the dissector has vanished with the ghost of his own interpolation and we are face to face with a poem by an Englishman circa. 725–750!

But knowledge percolates slowly, and the dead dogmas of buried scientists often in mythopoeic perversion are the science of popular belief and the journalist today. So we can still hear of Grendel as symbolic of the sea, and Beowulf of the sun and of the redacting Christian monks in popular compendia still on the shelves of responsible book-shops. But we pass over such "small beer." There is still some fun to be got out of the major critics, the monuments of learning, indeed the very reverend masters who remain our masters, and from whom we get all that we know.

[26] We can turn now to the polymaths — in whom great reading was (or is) combined with literary ability, so that their works are received with authority and read — sometimes with pleasure — so that they have a considerable influence.

Of these Chambers is the most technical, though his wit and wisdom are ever ready to burst out unexpectedly. Of all the critics of "Beowulf" he is the most sympathetic and the most penetrating, and the least condescending. Old English verse, as I have said, unlocks its treasury to the devoted stay-at-home rather than the ever-ranging traveler however piercing-eyed. Though 'stay-at-home' is only relatively true, of course, of this learned critic. His criticism offers little opportunity to the critic of criticism, since he has done more than any one other person to set criticism right and heal it of its madness. If one may say so humbly, W. P. Ker on the other hand, suffered from the weakness of his greatness — though he never lacked depth and insight in spite of his enormous literary and linguistic range, he could not achieve both depth and width equally. I cannot help feeling that stories or plots may sometimes have seemed triter to him the much-read than they were to some less-read old or medieval authors and their audiences, and that he did not always realize this.

But first I will take a representative of quite a different class and temper. While men like Ker — and this is perhaps a token of the peculiar intermediary cultural and mental (and linguistic) situation of the English-speaker in Europe, a situation already preparing in the days when "Beowulf" was written — seem no less at home or understanding in Latin or in Norse in French or in German, in Italian or in Russian, there is a Gallic kind (whether so in blood or by adoption) which is far more limited, even it would sometimes seem blind altogether in one eye. Jusserand is perhaps not much read now — one hopes not, but one never knows whither the thirst for second-hand opinions upon literary works will take people. To the least worthy, by some perverse instinct, it often [27] seems to be, and even to tomes the perusing of which is more irksome and more dull than reading the originals. This critic is so easy a target to shoot at that it might seem unfair — like potting a one-eyed rabbit on the blind side. If I begin on him it is primarily because in The Literary History of the English People are contained splendid examples of a critical method as popular as it is worthless; and secondarily because it offers an example, though an exaggerated one, of the weakness and insensitivity of the Latin or Latinized in dealing with the un-Latin elements in English, or with (shall we say) the Teutonic.

This weakness is not solely (though it is often) due to ignorance, nor the insensitiveness always (though it is sometimes) due to ill will. If any reason for them is to be sought, beyond that curious incompatibility of temper and intelligence which is one of the problems of Europe, it is to be sought, I fear, in an easy sense of patronage, a consciousness of superior worth, which is as pleasant as it is fatal to possess.

For first of all we see here clearly the idea which is still prevalent — indeed of Chaucer, not to mention other things more dark and ancient — that early English verse, and especially Old English, is <u>primitive</u>, and has the savage and rustic vices of incoherence and boorishness (normally) — <u>the village pub</u>; but occasionally an artless charm (<u>the village maiden</u>). The former is an axiom, the latter a charitable afterthought — the "wood-notes wild" idea. But Jusserand says actually "the charm of a wild flower." Such notions always go with, and are founded upon mere linguistic ignorance.

The underlying assumption, whether consciously acknowledged or not, is that English from (say) the sixteenth century on is one homogeneous thing, modern English, and "polite" — and the Frencher the politer; and that all that is not familiar to "modern English" ears is almost barbarous, at best quaint. That one can, or should at least [28] attempt, if the period is worth considering at all, to study its language and idiom until one recaptures something of the full meaning and the connotation of what is said, and has some idea of what was normal and what unusual <u>at the time when the thing was written</u>, does not seem usually to occur to such minds. Ignorance is bliss, and their private reading is strewn with howlers which they are unaware of. The language of a past period is a foreign language, and the acquiring of literary understanding of another tongue, whether of another country or another day, requires a humble apprenticeship. Occasionally we catch such people in the act. Jusserand, for instance — just after delivering himself of "the charm of a wildflower" (said of Ælfric, forsooth!!)[*] — jots down as a sample of delicious quaintness a sentence from the Old English translation of Boethius, treating of the legend of Eurydice and Orpheus. It is cast before you without context, and your indulgent smile is awaited, as you listen to the lisping of the village maiden. 'The dog of hell he should have three heads.'   !!

First of all this is a misquotation and a mistranslation. The original is a pretty competent straightforward bit of prose with no quaintness at all, no wildflower charm whatever, but something of the air of a schoolmaster; and it says of the dog of hell <u>þæs nama wæs Cerverus, se sceolde habban þrio heafdu.</u> That means in modern English precisely: "whose name was Cerberus, and who has been reported to have three heads." A common idiom. A most unrustic attitude (the comment is

---

[*] Ælfric though he actually deserves admiration, can be attacked, of course. You may have so little liking for his matter, that the virtues of his manner are obscured. But neither friend nor foe could see in the writing of this learned, painstaking, polished, meticulous ecclesiastic scholar the "charm of a wildflower" unless he knew no Anglo-Saxon (and one suspects no wildflowers).

not in the original) of doubt towards legend. [29] The man who thought se was the same as he or that "should" was quaint enough for quotation — in a work giving only brief attention to Beowulf, — would be considered inept, if he trespassed with such little knowledge, into any other language. But we have to suffer the opinions of the condescendingly ignorant; and it is still believed by many that Old English (or Middle English) should yield its meaning readily to the moderns; and if it does not, so much the worse for the stuff itself.

And thus with this magnificent equipment we pass to Beowulf — with a bias, as I say, which notices, when the village maiden does not briefly appear like a wood-anemone, only the hoarse and incoherent clamour of the pub. For example, the speech of Beowulf to Unferth (ll. 530–606), we are told, may be summed up thus: "liar, drunkard, coward, murderer!" So may many brilliant speeches in the houses of Parliament to-day, and possibly more in the house of deputies. Many indeed are less civilized than Beowulf's. But that is scarcely the point. Were the summary true, it would tell us still nothing of the manner or the artistic purpose of that speech in the poem. Here we have once more the "historic document" fallacy, and the drink-complex combined. Anything that any character says or does in a poem is any 'Anglo-Saxon' so behaving. The speech itself, of course, is actually well done, and rises slowly from an ironic beginning to crushing accusation — though the actual words liar, drunkard, coward, or murderer are not anywhere used. It serves at once the purpose of depicting Beowulf and his character as a high spirited proud young man, and of bringing in part of his early history before us, at the same time relating it and interlinking it cunningly with the tremendous background against which we now see him: the great court of Heorot, the am- biguous figure of Hroðulf and the sinister figure of the evil counsellor.

[30] The method here adopted of criticizing such matter, would reduce all poetry to vulgarity — and its use can proceed only from malice, or from an igno- rance and insensibility to an ancient mode which is almost as criminal.* But we will pass now to major points — observing nonetheless, that throughout Beowulf is taken as if it were a photograph of 'The Anglo-Saxon Period,' whatever that may have been, not a poem creating a special story with a special purpose. "To their excessive enthusiasm" we are told "succeed periods of complete depression, their

---

* It should scarcely be necessary to point out to this audience that the germ of the whole misconception is druncen in beore druncen l. 531. So certain is it that all Anglo-Saxons were "drunken" that it has not been observed that our modern used of drunk(en) = helplessly inebriated is a litotes, and that in Old Eng- lish druncen means still normally as here "having drunk." That a man has spoken rashly owing to wine or beer at a feast is a thing that can be observed even in Latin countries. In Old English and Old Norse poetry, however, words of this kind imply more — not bestial orgy, but the mirth, freedom, and sense of security where friends were gathered in hall about their patron. What would these drink-maniacs make of the tragic words concerning Guðrún in Atlakviða, where of the great Lady of the Burgundians, Queen of the Goths, it is said as she greets her brothers riding to their fate in Attila's hall bjori vas [hon] litt drukkin. This means, of course, that none of the joy of the alien hall in which she was queen was hers (cp. the similar symbolism at the beginning Drukku dróttmegir . . . vin í valöllu). But our discerning critic would doubtless imagine that the poet was recording the fact that on this great occasion the queen was only partially inebriated!

orgies are followed by despair." Whose? The Anglo-Saxons! [31] You could hardly guess that the critic is speaking of a poem, to which contrasts and changes of fortune are a necessary narrative method; still less that "Anglo-Saxons" are nowhere in that poem referred to at all!

And actually, in Anglo-Saxon, as we have it, not as it might have been, no orgies are recorded, unless it be of alien pirate chieftains, or of Assyrians and suchlike highly cultured people of the ancient world. "They sacrifice their life in battle without a frown," the critic proceeds. Dear old nonsense, recently dealt with by Professor E. V. Gordon in his *Introduction to Old Norse*. "And yet when the hour for the fight comes they are harassed by the thought of death." What heroes! What convulsions they must have endured to suffer harassment and yet not frown! Unless it can be, perhaps, that the critic has himself got mixed, drunk with words rather than beer, and fallen somewhat short of that Gallic lucidity he so much admires.

"The strange poem of <u>Beowulf</u>" he wanders on, "<u>the most important monument of Anglo-Saxon literature</u>" (the poor poet lifts his nose out of his beer-horn and humbly acknowledges the gentleman's condescension) "... like Old Celtic tales ... is a medley of pagan legends, which do not concern Beowulf (the hero) in particular, and of historical facts. ... New discrepancy is introduced in trying to adapt the old tale to the faith of his (the author's) day. No need to expatiate on the <u>incoherence of a poem formed of such elements</u>." (the poor poet here hastily hides his blushes in the beer-horn again). "Its heroes are at once pagan and Christian, <u>they believe in Christ and Wéland</u>" — deathly and completely flabbergasted silence throughout the hall, while a horrible suspicion crosses the poet's mind that the magnificent gentleman is an idiot. "They fight against the monsters of Scandinavian mythology, and see in them the descendants of Cain; historical facts such as the battle of the sixth century (mentioned by Gregory of Tours) are mixed up with fantastic deeds beneath the waves" At this point the gentleman is seized by Grendel and put in a bag, and for once one's sympathies are with Grendel.

[32] Old Celtic tales! If there is one kind of thing in the range of human knowledge which is least like <u>Beowulf</u> it is old Celtic tales, but we will let that pass, though the difference is fundamental, and its perception essential to an understanding of England and Europe. <u>Christ and Wéland</u> of course robs any critic capable of such confusion of any authority to speak at all — on any subject! They believe in the Trinity and Merlin, in God and Sir Orfeo; while professing Catholics they imagine good violins were made by Stradivarius; while serious Calvinists they tell tales of Robin Hood — the joke allows of infinite expansion, but its original perpetrator never smiled: he offers us his gem as "criticism." Even the famous Anglo-Saxons must look to their laurels as champions of muddle and incoherence. Poor fellow — groping under the shadow of 'research.' Somewhere he has read that <u>Beowulf</u> is composed of many diverse elements. Therefore it is a <u>medley</u>. Q. E. D. What brilliance! We have only to apply the method to all living poems to see how thoroughly satisfying it is. No need to expatiate on the incoherence to be

perceived in Europe wherever you like to turn — compound of many elements, made of commixture of Palestine, Greece, Rome, and other things. You imagined that you perceived a culture, which has been held worthy of honour; and you find a 'medley'.

And Cain. Here was a chance for a real critic. The making of the monsters the children of Cain, is used as a stone to throw at a fool. The thrower is the fool. It is one of the central points for a critic to seize upon, to ponder, and if he can, explain, [33] why Cain and Abel alone of the names of Scripture appear. But before we deal with that there is some more elementary work to be done. We will turn again to W. P. Ker — a name of great reverence, a critic who could read and move as in his home in many tongues, ancient medieval and modern, as illuminating as a critic of prose and verse as he was biting as a critic of critics. This makes it all the more unfortunate that on literature in the old Germanic tongues he has among things of astonishing worth said several that are ill considered. And his influence has been strong — for instance on Chambers who often repeats his words and quotes them.

I shall read you a passage from the Dark Ages pp. 252–3.

> A reasonable view of the merit of Beowulf is not impossible, though rash enthusiasm may have made too much of it, while a correct and sober taste may have too contemptuously refused to attend to Grendel or the Firedrake. The fault of Beowulf is that there is nothing much in the story. The hero is occupied killing monsters, like Hercules or Theseus. But there are other things in the lives of Hercules and Theseus besides the killing of the Hydra or of Procrustes. Beowulf has nothing else to do, when he has killed Grendel and Grendel's mother in Denmark: he goes home to his own Gautland, until at last the rolling years bring the Firedrake and his last adventure. It is too simple. Yet the three chief episodes are well wrought and well diversified; they are not repetitions, exactly; there is a change of temper between the wrestling with Grendel in the night at Heorot and the descent under the water to encounter Grendel's mother; while the sentiment of the Dragon is different again. But the great beauty, the real value, of Beowulf is in its dignity of style. In construction it is curiously weak, in a sense preposterous; for while the main story is simplicity itself, the merest commonplace of heroic legend, all about it, in the historic allusions, there are revelations of a whole world of tragedy, plots different in import from that of Beowulf, more like the tragic themes of Iceland. Yet with this radical defect, a disproportion that puts the irrelevances in the centre and the serious things on the outer edges, the poem of Beowulf is unmistakably heroic and weighty. The thing itself is cheap; the moral and the spirit of it can only be matched among the noblest authors.

There is much that is excellent here — still more so when it was written. The great dragon it is true, if not quite turned down, is turned into a firedrake vaguely suggestive of some contraption, a Brock-effect for the amazement of the simple. But the sentence chiefly to note is: "Yet with this radical defect, a disproportion that puts the irrelevances in the centre and the serious things on the outer edges, the poem Beowulf is unmistakably heroic and weighty."

This — the two points the radical defect and yet at the same time the dignity, loftiness in converse, the well-wrought finish — has become, apparently, a commonplace of criticism, a paradox whose oddity has been forgotten in the process of swallowing it whole. We may compare Chambers, Widsith p. 79 where he is studying the story of Ingeld son of Froda and his feud with the great Scylding house, which is in "Beowulf" introduced merely as an allusion.

"Nothing" he says, "could better show the disproportion of 'Beowulf' which" — and here he goes into quotation marks — "puts the irrelevances in the center and the serious things on the outer edges" than this passing allusion to the story of [34] Ingeld. For it is in this conflict between plighted troth and the duty of revenge that we have a situation, which the old heroic poets loved, and would not have sold for a wilderness of dragons." Alas the poor rock-gardener — he gave them flowers and they wanted only stones!

And there is a flick of malice here too — the sharper for coming from Chambers, the Beowulf-poets' best friend; we might have expected it of Jusserand, who speaks of "one of these ever-recurring treasures." A "wilderness of dragons"! This is à la The Book of St. Albans — then why not say "a pride of lions, a draught of butlers, a kindle of young cats, and a raffle of knaves" as that book does? They would have been as much in point. One dragon is not a host. And dragons, real dragons, essential to the plot, interwoven with its machinery and its ideas, are actually rare. In all Northern literature there are but three that really count: the Encircler of the World of Men (Miðgarðsormr), the doom of the gods in what is left of Norse mythology; the dragon of the Völsungs; and Beowulf's bane. The last two are both in Beowulf (one in the main story and the other spoken of) it is true; but this is not a wilderness. Indeed their presence is sufficient proof that the poet chose a dragon of well-founded purpose, even as he carefully compared Beowulf to the prince of the heroes of the North, the dragon-slaying Wælsing.

He knew the uses of dragons as I hope some do still; he liked them — as a poet and an artist; and he had his reasons, which were not those of wild romance.

Chambers later repeats this same criticism, and even in the Foreword to Strong's Translation we meet it still — though it is now toned down, and is no longer in Ker's actual words. But still, as we have seen, the folk-tale "has been allowed in Beowulf [35] to usurp the place of honour, and to drive into episodes and digressions the things which should be the main stuff of a well-conducted epic."

Very well then Beowulf is not a 'well-conducted epic.' Perhaps it is something else altogether. At any rate there is something odd about all this. Higher praise than we find in Ker and Chambers could hardly be given to the "civilization" in tone of Beowulf. Yet it is all wasted on an unprofitable theme, we are to understand, as if Milton had conducted a Children's Bed-time Hour and told the story of Jack and the Beanstalk in blank verse. A man may depict lower things than he knows — for example Beowulf as a proud young man; but not higher. This high tone and sense of propriety is real evidence of the presence of a man with a mind. It is, I should have said, antecedently improbable that such a person should have

spent 3000 lines on matter that is not worth serious attention — that is thin and
'cheap' as Ker says. A theory that will at least allow that what he did was of design
or choice, and the choice rational is plainly in itself a deal more probable.

Why have the great critics thought otherwise? There are a variety of reasons.
The virtues of myth — or folktale, if you like to be patronising, or misleading for
folk-tales contain a good deal of what actually is thin and cheap with little imaginative value besides much that is far more powerful — the virtues of myth are at
once vaster and more vague (less able to be penned on paper by mere reasoning)
than those of heroic legend on a strictly human plane. It is perfectly possible to be
moved by myth and misunderstand the sensation yourself— to deny the attraction
or to ascribe it wholly to something also present, tone, style, or what not. The sophisticated scholarly intelligence may refuse to admit that it has been moved by
ogres or dragons, since it believes such things have in our day long been relegated
to the nursery. O impoverished day! Also, it is an odd [36] fact that myth is best
treated by an author who feels, rather than makes consciously explicit what his tale
portends; who even presents it as a fact in time, and bolsters it about with history
(as our poet has done): we desire our myths to be incarnate. Myth at its best <u>never</u>
points a moral — and so, if you are looking for a moral pointed as the hero-worshippers do — (how they seize on Byrhtwold's words in <u>Maldon</u>!) — you are puzzled or disappointed.

And behind this lies the shadow of nineteenth-century 'research', modeled
partly after, and directed according to the purposes of analytic science. The 'heroic,' as Chambers calls it, is the <u>more</u> valuable — an axiom, there is no argument
about it. Why? In a measure, I fear, this is due to the fact that it is <u>older</u>. Research
suggests that in the development of Old English poetry the 'heroic' lay precedes
such stuff as <u>Beowulf</u>; and by the preservation of <u>Beowulf</u> and the loss of practically all save allusions to the "heroic" lays the antiquarian has been cheated. Deliberately provocative this. "No!" The hero worshippers cry in chorus. "The heroic-
stories are in themselves more valuable." 'There is no disputing about tastes' it is
said — foolishly; for we must dispute about them. Yet here indeed there has hardly been any dispute; the proposition has appeared self-evident.

Were it really self-evident we could still make two points. First that Chambers
fights on poor ground when electing to give battle on Ingeld's behalf. This story of
Ingeld the twice faithless and easily led (and the not too intelligent) has to me —
and I suspect its undoubted popularity among the English was due to much the
same course — its chief interest not in itself but its being part of a great whole, part
of a tradition concerning moving <u>historical</u> events, the arising of Denmark and the
wars in the islands. And in any case even granting the superlative merit of the
"heroic" in general, we have yet given no reason for refusing to consider stuff of
other kind, for valuing <u>Beowulf</u> as it is.

Are we to have no tragedy of fact but dealing death in a narrow place against
overwhelming odds, no tragedy of the mind but divided allegiances or conflicting

duties? Are we to refuse "King Lear" either because it is founded on a silly folk-tale (the old naif details of which still peep through as they do in Beowulf) or because it is not "Macbeth"? Need we even debate which is more valuable?

[37] There is of course, a value in heroic tales of divided allegiance and unacknowledged defeat. But it is not the only mode of imagination. Almost an element of cant creeps in, as if such things had a mysterious, almost magical virtue. The musical critic Ernest Newman I remember once commented on a similar superstition that there was something inexplicable by analysis, inimitable, about old traditional 'airs' — remarking that any competent modern musician with any melodic invention could turn them out by the score to defeat the powers of discrimination of their most enthusiastic admirers. He may or may not have been right. But I feel it is true at any rate of these 'heroic-tales.' Rider Haggard's Eric Brighteyes is as good (if rather longer) and as heroic as most of such things. There are many good heroes (and rather similar), but there are few good dragons (and each different). Beowulf's dragon, if you wish to criticize still, is not to be criticized for being a dragon, but rather for not being dragon enough, plain pure dragon. * Already nonetheless he approaches "draconitas" rather than 'draco' — a personification of malice, greed, destruction (the evil side of heroic life), and of the indiscriminating cruelty of fortune that distinguishes not good or bad (the evil aspect of all life). But actually for Beowulf the poem this is as it should be. In the poem the balance is nice, but it is preserved. The vast symbolism is near the surface of the exterior narrative but it does not quite burst through. Something larger than a standard hero, faced with a foe greater than any human enemy of house or realm is before us, and yet incarnate in time, walking as it were in heroic history, and treading the named lands of the legendary North. And this we are told is the radical defect of Beowulf — that its poet coming in a time rich in legends and histories of heroic men, has used them afresh: he has not given us just one more, but given us something different and also unique.

[38] "No, no" they say impatiently — "It won't do. He has given us a dragon." But a dragon is not an idle or a silly tale. Whatever dire origins it has in prehistoric fact, the dragon is as we have it one of the most moving creations of the imagination, richer in meaning than his barrow is in golden treasure. Even today you may find men not ignorant of legend and of literature, who have heard about the hero, and indeed seen him, and who yet though they would scarcely dream of writing an heroic tale, have been caught by the fascination of the 'worm.'

I will quote you — though this may seem an unpardonable digression in the manner of the poor Beowulf-poet — two modern poems on the dragon. The two together for all their defects (especially the first I shall quote) seem to me more

---

*   Although there are some vivid touches (2293ff) in which the dragon is real enough with an animalic life and thought of his own.

important for <u>Beowulf</u>-criticism, for which they were not written, than very much
that has been written with that purpose.

(i)

Iúmonna Gold Galdre Bewunden.

When the moon was new and the sun young
of silver and gold the gods sung;
in the green grass they silver spilled,
the white waters they with gold filled.
Ere the pit was dug or Hell yawned,
ere dwarf was bred or dragon spawned,
there were elves of old, and strong spells
under green hills in hollow dells
they sang as they wrought many fair things,
the bright crowns of the elf-kings.
But their doom fell, and their song waned,
by iron hewn and by steel chained.
Greed that sang not, nor with mouth smiled,
in dark holes their wealth piled,
graven silver and carven gold:
over Elvenhome the shadow rolled.

There was an old dwarf in a dark cave,
silver and gold his fingers clave
with hammer and tongs and anvil-stone
he worked his hands to the hard bone,
and coins he made and strings of rings,
and thought to buy the power of kings.
But his eyes grew dim and his ears dull,
and the skin yellow on his old skull;
through his bony claw with a pale sheen
the stony jewels slipped unseen.

No feet he heard, though the earth quaked,
when the young dragon his thirst slaked,
and the stream smoked at his dark door,
and flames hissed on the dank floor.
He died alone in the red fire,
and his bones were ash in the hot mire.

[58]

There was an old dragon under grey stone;
his red eyes blinked as he lay alone.
His joy was dead and his youth spent,
he was knobbed and wrinkled and his limbs bent
with the long years to his gold chained;
in his heart's furnace the fires waned.

To his belly's slime gems stuck thick,
silver and gold he would snuff and lick —
he knew the place of the least ring
beneath the shadow of his black wing.
Of thieves he thought on his hard bed,
and he dreamed that on their flesh he fed,
their bones crushed and their blood drank:
his ears drooped and his breath sank.
Mail-rings rang. He heard them not.
A voice echoed in his deep grot:
a young warrior with a bright sword
called him forth to defend his hoard.
His teeth were knives, and of horn his hide,
but iron tore him, and his flame died.

There was an old king on a high throne:
his white beard lay on knees of bone;
his mouth savoured neither meat nor drink,
nor his ears song; he could only think
of his huge chest with carven lid
where pale gems and gold lay hid,
in secret treasury in the dark ground
whose strong doors were iron-bound.
      The swords of his thanes were dull with rust,
his glory fallen, his rule unjust,
his halls hollow, and his bowers cold,
but king he was of elvish gold.
He heard not the horns in the mountain pass,
he smelt not the blood on the trodden grass,
but his halls were burned, his kingdom lost;
in a cold pit his bones were tossed.

Here we see that the old enemy is within man as well as without
Lewis's poem: —

Once the worm-laid egg broke in the wood
I came forth shining into the trembling wood.
The sun was on my scales, dew upon the grasses,
The cool, sweet grasses, and the budding leaves.
I wooed my speckled mate. We played at druery
And sucked warm milk dropping from the goats' teats.

Now I keep watch on the gold in my rock cave
In a country of stones: old, deplorable dragon,
Watching my hoard. In winter night the gold
Freezes through toughest scales my cold belly.
The jagged crowns and twisted cruel rings,
Knobbly and icy are old dragon's bed.

[39] Often I wish I had not eaten my wife,
Though worm grows not to dragon till he eat worm.
She could have helped me, watch and watch about,
Guarding the hoard. Gold would have been the safer
I could uncoil my weariness at times and take
A little sleep, sometimes when she was watching.

Last night under the moon-set a fox barked,
Woke me. Then I knew I had been sleeping,
Often an owl flying over the country of stones
Startles me, and I think I must have slept.
Only a moment. That very moment a man
Might have come out of the cities, stealing, to get my gold.

They make plots in the towns to steal my gold.
They whisper of me in a low voice, laying plans,
Merciless men. Have they not ale upon the benches,
Warm wife in bed, singing, and sleep the whole night?
But I leave not the cave, but once in winter
To drink of the rock-pool: in summer twice.

They feel no pity for the old lugubrious dragon.
O Lord that made the dragon, grant me thy peace!
But ask not that I should give up the gold,
Nor move, nor die; Others would get the gold.
Kill, rather, Lord, the men and the other dragons
That I may sleep, go when I will to drink.

[40] So much (at the moment) for the foe: If we return to the hero we find a curious thing. We have not denied his value by accepting Beowulf. Let us have our old heroes — men caught in a net of fate, or torn between duties equally sacred, and dying with back to the wall against human enemies. Yet without Beowulf— to me at any rate — the Germanic hero, of the sort that Chambers insists on having and says that the 'old poets' would not have sold for a 'wilderness of dragons,' is an animal in a trap, fierce, sad, brave, and bloody, but not very intelligible (nor always very intelligent), as moving as a baited badger. Or rather, perhaps fairer, I fancy Beowulf plays a larger part than is recognized in assisting in the understanding of him; and if these very critics had not had Beowulf to read they would have less loved the other heroes.

The heroic lay may have dealt in its own way, more vigorous and brief perhaps, if more harsh and noisy (has not Chambers himself made a motorbike the symbol of the lay, and a Rolls Royce of the epic) with the action of a hero, pitted against a particular set of circumstances, which more or less conform to the simple recipe for an heroic situation. In it we could have seen the exaltation of the will undefeated, which receives excellent doctrinal expression, as all know, in the mouth of Byrhtwold in the Battle of Maldon:

> Hige sceal þe heardra, heorte þe cenre,
> mod sceal þe mara þe ure mægen lytlað.[*]

An expression which we are not to take as struck off by Byrhtwold himself in the heat of battle, or even by the poet of Maldon, but a solemn repetition of a received and honoured gnome; a terse exposition of a dominant idea.

[41] But though, with sympathy and patience, we might gather from stray words, from a line here or a tone there, the background of imagination which gives to this indomitability, this paradox of defeat inevitable and yet unacknowledged, its real significance, it is in Beowulf that a poet has devoted a whole poem to the theme, has drawn the struggle in vaster proportions on a larger stage, so that we may see man at war with the infest world and his inevitable overthrow in time. I don't mean necessarily to say that the poet, if questioned, would have replied in the Old English equivalents of such terms. Had the matter been so explicit to him his poem would probably have been the worse. Nonetheless we at any rate against his great scene — hung with tapestries woven of ancient tales of ruin (each in itself a little world) — may see the hæleþ walk. And we perceive at the end that he who wrote hæleþ under heofenum may have 'meant' — in dictionary terms — 'heroes under the heavens' or 'mighty men on earth', but he and his audience were thinking of the eormengrund, the great earth, ringed with gársecg, the shoreless ocean unknown beneath the sky's inaccessible roof, wherein as in a little circle of light defended by mortal hands, men with courage as their stay, went forward to that battle with the dark and its offspring, which ends for all, even the great champions in defeat. That even this geography (once held as material fact) might now by the supercilious be classed as 'mere folk-tale,' affects its value little or nothing. It transcends astronomy. Beowulf is not a hero of an heroic lay — not quite. He has no enmeshed loyalties or hapless love. He is a man, and that for him and many is a sufficient tragedy.

[42] It is then not an irritating accident that the tone of Beowulf is so high and its theme so low. It is the theme in its deadly seriousness that makes us feel so deeply. For all the machinery of "dignity" is present elsewhere. Cynewulf or the author of St. Guthlac had a great feel for dignified verse, and there you will find lofty converse, weighty words, high-wrought finish: all in fact precisely that which they say is the real beauty of Beowulf. Yet there is no one at all who doubts that Beowulf is more beautiful, that a line (even when it is the same line) is more beautiful in Beowulf than in the other Old English poems. Where then lies the special virtue of Beowulf if the common element is withdrawn? It is the theme. So

---

[*]   The spirit shall be more resolute, the heart more bold, the courage greater as our strength grows less.

deadly and so ineluctable is the theme that those who play only in the little circle of light with the toys of wit and refinement, looking not to the battlements, either hear not the theme at all, or recoiling shut their ears to it. Death comes to the feast, and they say He gibbers.

It has been said that there is mirth and music and gentle talk in <u>Beowulf</u>, but the 'light is but a foil to the dark'. It may seem a meaningless distinction, but this should really be the other way about. The dark is foil to the light — or rather the light is encircled by the dark, but not because the Old English poet did not value the light, passionately. If we like to forget the encircling foe and its ultimate victory in the temporal order, he did not forget it. He was on a besieged island and knew it; but he loved the island all the more.

It is at this point that the question of Cain becomes most important. Though I have long laboured the point myself, I have only observed. Chambers has grasped it (in one aspect) and put it in words that I shall not attempt to better — indeed the only criticism that I have to make on them is that they are destructive of traditional strictures on "Beowulf" to which he still elsewhere to some extent adheres. They should lead direct to an appreciation of Beowulf and its theme as a whole. In any case they cut right to the heart of the Christian-heathen controversy, and dispel the last illusion of a muddleheaded Anglo-Saxon who did not distinguish clearly between paganism and Christianity.

Yet Professor Chadwick has shown us how a study of *Beowulf* can be made to throw new light upon the study of Homer. For in both we have a picture of society in its Heroic Age. The society of *Beowulf* is in many respects cruder and less developed, just as the hall of Hrothgar is a less elaborate thing than the hall of Odysseus. But there is a fundamental likeness in the life depicted.

Now in Anglo-Saxon England this Heroic Age was brought into contact with Christianity, and with all the civilization of the Mediterranean which came to England with Christianity. It is just this which makes the Seventh Century in England so exciting an epoch. Christian gentleness, working upon the passions of the Heroic Age, produces at once a type which is the rough outline of what later becomes the mediæval ideal of the knight, or the modern ideal of the gentleman.

In the Heroic Age, elementary passions are still very near the surface. This causes the tension in the twenty-fourth *Iliad*. In spite of the command of Zeus, in spite of the laws of hospitality, there is always the possibility that the wrath of Achilles may overmaster him, and that he may slay Priam within his hut. And the history of Europe during the incursion of the Germanic barbarians tells of many a deed as grisly as that to which Achilles feared that he might, despite himself, be driven.

In the epoch of *Beowulf*, a Heroic Age more wild and primitive that that of Greece is brought into touch with Christendom, with the Sermon on the Mount, with Catholic theology and ideas of Heaven and Hell. We see the difference if we compare the wilder things — the folk-tale element — in *Beowulf* with the wilder things in Homer. Take for example the tale of Odysseus and the Cyclops, the No-Man trick. Odysseus is struggling with a monstrous and wicked foe, but he is not exactly thought of as struggling with the powers of darkness. Polyphemus, by devouring his guests, acts in a way which is hateful to Zeus and the other gods: yet the Cyclops is himself god-begotten and under divine protection, and the fact that Odysseus has maimed him is a wrong which Poseidon is slow to forgive.

But the gigantic foes whom Beowulf has to meet are identified with the foes of God. Grendel and the dragon are constantly referred to in a language which is meant to recall the powers of darkness with which Christian men felt themselves to be encompassed. They are 'inmates of Hell,' 'adversaries of God,' 'offspring of Cain,' 'enemies of mankind.' Consequently, the matter of the main story of *Beowulf*, monstrous as it is, is not so far removed from common mediæval experience as it seems to us to be from our own. It was believed that Alcuin as a boy had been beset by devils because he neglected divine service in order to read Virgil. Grendel hardly differs from the fiends of the pit who were always in ambush to waylay a righteous man. And so Beowulf, for all that he moves in the world of the primitive Heroic Age of the Germans, nevertheless is almost a Christian knight. If Spenser had known *Beowulf*, he would have found a hero much nearer his Red Cross Knight than Achilles or Odysseus. The long sermon on humility which Hrothgar preaches to Beowulf after his victory, is as appropriate as the penance in the House of Holiness which the Red Cross Knight has to undergo (and, the scoffer will here interject, hardly less painful).

Beowulf, then, has yet a third claim on our attention. Here we find the character of the Christian hero, the mediæval knight, emerging from the turmoil of the Germanic Heroic Age. Not but what many of Beowulf's virtues can be traced back to that Heroic Age. For example, Beowulf's loyalty, when he refuses to take the throne at the expense of his young cousin Heardred, is a part of the Teutonic code of honour, though a part not often put into practice. But the emphasis placed upon gentleness, humility, and judgment to come is a thing in which we can trace the influence of the new faith. In his dying speeches, Beowulf rejoices that he has sought no cunning hatreds, nor sworn oaths unrighteously: 'For all this may I have joy, though sick with deadly wounds, that the Ruler of men may not charge me with the slaughter of kinsfolk.' And he thanks the Lord of all, the King of glory, that he has been able to win such treasure for his people. And so the poem ends:

> So did the people of the Geatas, his hearth companions, bewail the fall
> of their lord: they said he was a mighty king, the mildest and gentlest of
> men, most kind to his people, and the most desirous of praise.

It is with reason that Professor Earle quoted the words of Sir Ector de Maris over Lancelot dead as being 'like an expansion of the closing lines of the *Beowulf*':

> And now I dare say, said Sir Ector, thou, Sir Launcelot, there thou liest,
> that thou were never matched of earthly knight's hand; and thou were
> the courteoust knight that ever bare shield; and thou were the truest
> friend to thy lover that ever bestrad horse: and thou were the truest
> lover of a sinful man that ever loved woman: and thou were the kindest
> man that ever struck with sword: and thou were the goodliest person
> that ever came among press of knights: and thou were the meekest man
> and the gentlest that ever ate in hall among ladies: and thou were the
> sternest knight to thy mortal foe that ever put spear in the rest.

[43] In other words Christianity — which had provided even outside its proper realms most of the dynasties and aristocracies of Europe by this time — infused into the Northern would make what we call the <u>medieval</u>, and that process begins <u>at once</u> — some of the most fundamental changes of that alchemy are almost immediate. You do not have to wait until all the tales and lays and the native

traditions of the older world have been forgotten — for the minds that still retain them are changed and the memories themselves are seen in different perspective. It is a lesser error to think of Beowulf as an early medieval poem than as an old Germanic one. It is better than either as an Old English one. It has a kinship with St. Guthlac, Ælfric, even with medieval homilies on hell equally balanced with a lay like Voluspá, Hávamal or Sigurd's lay.

But there is yet one point remarkable. It came from a learned age, and yet (though the accidents of survival tend constantly to make us forget this) from a two-sided one. Not all the learning was book-Latin nor all the love of the learned for what was written in the new letters. There was never any sign of a new pseudo-Latin people being fabricated — within Christendom there was the Angolcynn, with its own language, its own laws, its own history, and its own poetry. And these were not beneath the study of the early scholars such as Aldhelm (whom Theodore considered best of the vernacular poets — though his vernacular verse is lost), and were loved no less by Alfred the revivalist than the Latin learning which he strove to reestablish. It is thus that we have available to a poet such as the man who wrote "Beowulf" not only education in the newer sense which some have thought discernible in Beowulf itself [44] — a poem that supposes the knowledge of classical Latin epic they say — but also a body of northern historical and legendary tradition for the "educated" and christianized mind to ponder.[†] That this tradition was kept alive itself by an 'education' is seen plainly enough from the connected and analyzable character that its fragments still possess — even in "Beowulf" a poem that only draws upon it at will for the purposes of a later day: as a modern poet may still (or once used to) draw upon his history and his classics and expect to be understood. The "Beowulf" poet in fact was quite learned enough in this vernacular department to have an historical even antiquarian perspective. He is not a bad Christian because he describes heroic sea-burial, or the blazing pyre, and piled tumulus! He casts his time back into the long ago — because the long ago has for him a poetic appeal and also justly because so set the struggle of man stands out all the more naked — but he knew much about the old days: not least (because indeed it is of the marrow of his theme) that the days were heathen. This is specifically recognized even of Hrothgar and his Danes. The discrepancy is dealt with later in the famous passage from 175–178: <u>Hwílum hie geheton æt hærgtrafum wigweorþunga, wordum bædon þæt him gastbona geoce gefremede wið þeodþreaum</u> (At times they offered — at the heathen temple — sacrifice to heathen idols, bade with words that the spirit-slayer might give them help against the nation's calamity). Avoidance of all glaring anachronism in this respect (such as is found heedlessly in <u>Judith</u>) in the absence of all

---

[†]   Virgil, Statius and Lucan are given among the books studied in the school of York, by Alcuin in his poem on the Church of York. Alcuin from circa 725 must have been nearly contemporary with the Beowulf poet.

specifically <u>Christian</u> references* is natural, deliberate, and essential. One can only stand amazed at the willful stupidity that has turned this into a charge of a half-baked Christianity. Of course we at this distance of time [45] had we old traditions still surviving (such as we have for Scandinavia) to work upon might be more specific. We should not hesitate to trot out references to <u>Woden</u> and Þunor — so far have they faded that we can feel only a distant antiquarian interest in these figures (once so dominant, so mighty and so strong).

That we could hardly expect in the 7th or the 8th centuries. The last heathen kingdom Sussex had only been converted in 681–6. In protesting against a view that a man sufficiently cultured to write a long poem did not clearly know the difference between Christian and pagan, we rather emphasize than obscure the potency still of paganism — as a belief. Saxons (or the Frisians and the continental Saxons which were later and the Swedes later-still) had been fanatically heathen — the sort of pale lassitude without resistance which we get in Bede's story of Coifi and his sparrow is not a picture that can be applied universally to Germanic heathendom or to all parts of England. It is precisely therefore that part of the old traditions that are suppressed. We get no heathen gods, only the Lord, the Almighty, often Metod the Apportioner — in which the conception of him falls back almost into that of <u>wyrd</u> "fate," the dim and unintelligible and all-powerful, which is the first glimmering, and which remains in all times a natural colloquial method of reference to the scheme of the Universe as extended into our individual wills. This is indeed to be expected — it has indeed been pointed out that in Ireland of the seventh century profane classical literature with its inherent mythology was widely cultivated even in monasteries — in marked contrast to the Latin lands while the pagan religion of the Empire was still a serious thing, and indeed in marked contrast to the attitude of churchmen in Gaul much later, where a suspicious attitude long survived active paganism. But a foreign paganism has little danger for a Christian.

[46] It was the English temper — in its strong Englishry connected with its nobility and its dynasties and many small courts, assisted, it may be by the humaner and less severe Celtic tradition of learning — that preserved so much tradition of the past to interweave with southern learning. The ancestors were not banned (as some would have wished) but we could hardly expect the gods to be given yet the twilight reverence of antiquarian record.*

There are not wanting 'Gallic' voices. St. Paulinus of Nola (born at Bordeaux)

---

*   It should be noted that Abel 108 Cain 107 (1261) only occur where the poet is speaking. He is giving you his view of the origin and nature of such monsters; not a view contemporary with his hero.

*   The special conditions that obtained in Iceland — and the very special nature of the fragments of Norse mythology — must not be allowed to confuse this judgement. The Odin and Þór of Snorri in the early 13th century are in any case nearly as remote from Woden or Þunor (or any ancient tradition concerning Danish heathendom the English may have possessed) as Jupiter and Apollo or mythology in Ovid is from Greek <u>religion</u> in the days of the long-haired Achaeans.

— 5th century — cried that 'Hearts vowed to Christ have no welcome for the goddesses of song; they are barred to Apollo." Sulpicius Severus in the preface to his life of St. Martin asks "what good will it do posterity to study the philosophy of Socrates or to read the battles of Hector." Apocryphal[**] — but nonetheless to be noted for such an attitude was possible — is the famous story concerning the Frank St. Wulfram of Sens (died 695). Radbod (successor of Aldgisl who had harboured the English St. Wilfrid) was a fierce enemy of Christian and Frank and the last defender both of Frisian heathenism and Frisian independence. The story relates that once he approached the baptismal font but stopped on the way [47] to ask Wulfram whether, if he were baptized, he might hope to meet in heaven his Frisian ancestors. 'Do not deceive thyself' was Wulfram's reply, 'it is certain that they have received the just sentence of damnation.' Radbod therefore withdrew from the font, and said that he preferred to join his own people, wherever they might be, rather than sit down in the Kingdom of Heaven with a handful of beggars. He remained heathen to his death in 719.

It was perhaps not altogether in the result regrettable that the Gallic or rather now Frankish church fell into confusion, demoralization and decay and that the re-energizing of it and the reclamation by missions of Frisia and large areas of Germany was due in principal measure to the English (of the age of 'Beowulf' the muddleheaded!), to whom may be ascribed indeed the foundation of the medieval church in Europe.

Yet even of the best known figure in that process <u>Alcuin</u> (born about 735 and therefore almost certainly alive at the same time as the poet of Beowulf) we have received a saying that sounds similar. In a letter to Speratus Bishop of Lindisfarne of A.D. 797 we read: Verba Dei legantur in sacerdotali convivio; ibi decet lectorem audiri, non citharistam, sermones patrum, non carmina gentilium. Quid Hinieldus cum Christo? Angusta est domus; utrosque tenere non poterit (Let the words of God be read at the refectory of the priests; there it is fitting that the lector be heard, not the lyre-player, the sermons of the fathers, not the songs of the heathens. What has Ingeld to do with Christ? Narrow is the house; it cannot hold both of them) — the King of Heaven must not be mentioned with pagan kings who are now lamenting in Hell. This reference to Ingeld is <u>not</u> in the received text of the letter (see Chambers note <u>Widsith</u> p. 78). In any case it is rather evidence that in England even those trained and professed in religion as monks could preserve ancient tradition. It might [48] certainly be regarded then, as still, <u>indecens</u> that the harpist should usurp the <u>lector</u> in the refectory, but it was not necessarily improper that the same minds should contain the old histories and the new faith. The house is wide and has many rooms. To such a view, to such a time and temper 'Beowulf belongs.

[**]   The missions to Frisia were English begun by Wilfrid in 679 and after 10 years interval by Wictberct in 689 soon after Radbod's succession. Wulfram died 695, and there is no evidence (outside the late <u>vita Sancti Wulframni</u>) that he even visited Frisia. Radbod died 719.

The old Gods disappeared — partly because they were strong and still connected with <u>religion</u> not solely with a world-mythology, partly because, as I shall suggest, their going was nonetheless not disastrous to the theme — and the heroic figures, the men of old, <u>hæleþ under heofenum</u> (heroes under the heavens) remained and not only were not ousted by Moses or the warriors of the Israelites, or by St. Matthew and St. Andrew, but transmuted and recoloured the conception of these figures of Christian tradition.

A point especially to note in Chambers' remarks is this: "<u>the Cyclops is himself god-begotten, and under divine protection, and the fact that Odysseus has maimed him is a wrong Poseidon is slow to forgive.</u>" But of Grendel it is said <u>godes yrre bær</u> (he bore the anger of God). God is on the side of him who wrestles with him. "<u>But the gigantic foes whom Beowulf has to meet are identified with the foes of God</u>".

This is suggestive — one may pause indeed to wonder whether we do not miss an essential stage here, if we pass on too quickly to Christianity. There is probably a truth in a generalization which contrasts the <u>inhumanness</u> of the Greek deities with the <u>humanness</u> of the Northern — remember that we may well paint in what is left us of later mythologies that do not exactly fit; [49] alive though we may be to the danger of accepting late Norse mythological traditions as any parallel or illustration of the lost English ones — though the similar temper of the two peoples and their "heroism" can hardly be founded on a radically discrepant mythological philosophy.

The fair Gods of Greece are yet in alliance with the horrors — even akin to them — at the least not partners of lesser men in war against them. Their race is rather like that far off vision of men in Wells' <u>Time Machine</u> divided into two, the fair who live in the sun, and the dark cannibals beneath the earth, beautiful and hideous yet of one origin. Man may worship or propitiate the one or the other, but he is not ally of either. Maybe this makes them better gods, more fair, more lofty more mighty or more dark. They are timeless and know not death — and such beliefs hold promise of a higher or profounder thought, so that Greece could make philosophy, but the Germanic north claimed especially the 'hero', the artist in conduct.

For in Norse at any rate the gods are enmeshed within time, they are doomed to the agony of death — even if a rebirth glimmers faintly far ahead; their battle is with the monsters, and with the dark. They fight along with men and gather heroes from the same war. They are men writ large on a vaster scale of time. Already before euhemerism saved them by embalming them, and they dwindled in belief to the mighty ancestors of the northern kings, that had been raised by ancestor worship to false lords. [50] They are in their very beings but the shadows of great men and warriors cast upon the walls of the world. (Hel: Gods can go there and not come out — Baldr). Loki is among them it is true, an evil and a lying and a clever spirit — of whom many monsters come. But this is true of humanity in whom both Grendel and the dragon in their hatred, cruelty, malice and greed find part. But the Gods of Asgard do not recognize kinship with the Wolf of Fenrir anymore than men with Grendel.

Thus though the passages in Beowulf concerning the giants and their war with God (1689–1693 and 113–114) are certainly related directly (as are the names of Cain and Abel) to Scripture; as is especially Genesis chapter II, they cannot nonetheless be dissociated from the giants of northern mythology, the ever encircling foes of Asgard — just as the undoubted reference to Cain connects him with eoten and ylfe, the álfar and jötnar of Norse mythology.

It is precisely therefore at this point that Christian Scripture and pagan tradition fused — and the point is the right one. Need we any longer wonder that Cain and Abel alone of Scriptural names appear.

The monsters were the foes of the Gods, and the monsters would win; and in the heroic siege and the last defeat alike men and Gods were in the same host. And though the old Gods departed men remained, the heroes who had in fact in reversal of mythology begotten the gods fought on, or wove from splendid forms the fantastic banners of human courage, until defeat. [51] For the monsters remained — indeed they do remain; and a Christian was no less hemmed in by the world that is not man than the pagan. Yet the war had changed. For now there is one Lord and Dryhten, Líffreá, and the monsters are His foe. Even as the contest on the fields of time thus takes on its greatest aspect — and is still one doomed to defeat: the vision is dissolving and the visible world is changing into an incarnation spiritual and an allegory is near.

But this is not yet complete in "Beowulf." "Beowulf" is not a stupid medley of Christian and pagan but a re-treatment of a theme which had already been hammered out; that man not only as an individual, but as a whole, and all his works shall die: a theme acceptable by a Christian as it still is — within the temporal order. Yet it would not be so treated, but for the nearness of paganism. The shadow of its despair, if only in a mood, is still there. As the poet looks back into the past, he sees that all that man as man can accomplish ends in night. He is still thinking primarily of man and men in the world and their glory (or as we should put it meaning nothing very different, in essence their culture and civilization, their art and science).

In spite of the terminology applied to Grendel he is not yet "medieval" — we have not yet devils as hideous as this þyrs (monster),[+] this ogre and his dam, and as fleshly, who are yet "evil spirits" whose proper purpose is to destroy the soul, to tempt the spirit.

[52] Grendel although a feond on helle (enemy in hell) is primarily a feond mancynnes (enemy of mankind), he and his kin are in this world eaters of the very flesh of men, they are in the physical world and of it — because they are indeed it

---

+   This very word in Middle English survives only precariously as a synonym of the Devil

itself. We are dealing still with the tragedy of man in time. The solution of that tragedy is not treated — it does not arise out of this material.[†]

We are in fact just in time to get a poem from a man who knew enough of the old heroic tales, as his contemporaries did (vide <u>Wanderer</u> and <u>Seafarer</u>), to perceive their common tragedy of inevitable ruin, and to feel it perhaps more poignantly because he was a little removed from the direct pressure of its despair; who yet could view it with a width and depth only possible in a period which has in Christianity a justification of what had hitherto been a dogma not so much of faith as of instinct — a huge pessimism as to the event, combined with an obstinate belief in the value of the doomed effort, though in what plane such value was realized the Germanic North never found (and probably unaided never would have found) a coherent or explicit theory. He was still dealing with this old universal theme.

The wise myths — the counterparts of which in pagan England are lost — such as we find in fragmentary state in Old Norse (largely preserved only in ruinous condition in a time of faulty memories during the disappearance of paganism or even long after it when such things had become only conventional properties like Jove and Mars): a warrior's heaven and a shadowy hell.

[53] Of pagan English eschatology we know nothing — except our guess that the similar heroic temper cannot have had a fundamentally different background of mythology, however different the details, from the Scandinavian. What little we know of the latter is, however, difficult enough to estimate as a picture of Scandinavian imaginative beliefs — paganism is rarely a unified system, it is variable locally and in time; and its fragments in the North reach record in tattered form from times of confused or faulty memories, the periods of decay, or periods long after such things had become only conventional trappings of poetry and the amusements of antiquarians like Snorri — almost as far from real paganism as an 18th century Jove or Mars. We glimpse there a heaven and a hell — the one rather the reward of courage the other the punishment of feebleness; but among much that is crude or unshapen, or confused with other ideas ill assimilated[*] (possibly of extraneous, or Christian origin), the most dominant motive is that of courage, apprehended mystically as valuable in the war of Gods and men against their common enemy in Chaos and Darkness.

But of definite mythological treatments of this idea we naturally have nothing left in English. Its spirit survives as a flavour, a temper, a mood. Far more definite, indeed clearly explicit, is the idea of <u>lof</u> (praise) — the noble pagan's desire for the <u>merited praise</u> of the noble, which is not confined to northern pagans. For if this

---

† Yet the "mediæval" is fully developed already in Old English in this respect. The devils that tempt and torment St. Guthlac have nothing to distinguish them from the mediæval assailants of saints. The Sigelhearwan in Ælfric are perfectly mediæval bogeys.

* Partly due to a lack of development (primitiveness), partly due to accidents of tradition, but that actual <u>debasement</u> took place in the viking period — a crueler colder and more barbarous one exalting slaughter and rapine, and encouraging at once unbelief and fantasy — is a possibility to bear in mind.

"limited immortality" or prolonged life can exist as a strong motive together with detailed pagan beliefs and practices, it can long outlive them. It is in fact the natural residuum when the pagan gods decay whether unbelief comes from within or from without.

The dominance of this motive in Beowulf we may interpret then both as a sign that a pagan time was not far away from the poet, and its mood was well grasped imaginatively by him, and also that [54] the end of English paganism was marked (at least among the noble and the courtly classes for whom and by whom such traditions were preserved) by a twilight period similar to that which we see historically in Scandinavia. The gods faded and man was left to carry on his war alone; his trust was in his own power and will and his reward the praise of his own peers now and afterward. So was it explicitly said of men of might in the last days of Norwegian heathendom that their fate was simply ek trúi á mátt ok megin (I believe in my own might and main). Certainly we see them often godlausir (godless) or at best patronising towards to their eclectically formed deities — giving them a belief often of not much greater than that which modern men will accord to omens, or talismans in motorcars.

Earle long ago pointed out the prominence of lof in Beowulf. At the beginning of the poem at the end of the first 'strophe' of the exordium occurs as a leitmotif: lofdædum sceal in mægþa gehwam man geþeon (By praiseworthy deeds a man shall prosper anywhere). The last word in the poem is lofgeornost (most eager for praise), the climax of the praise of its hero — to make an Anglo-Saxon pun this is lastworda betst (best last-word). For Beowulf had lived according to his own philosophy explicitly avowed in 1386ff Ure æghwylc sceal ende gebidan worolde lifes. Wyrce se ðe mote domes ær deaþe; þæt bið drihtguman unlifgendum æfter selest (Each one of us must must live in expectation of the end of this worldly life. Let him who can earn good fame before death; that is the best thing, afterwards, for the unliving man). The poet himself as commentator recurs again to this in 1534 swa sceal man don þonne he æt guðe gegan þenceð longsumne lof; na ymb his lif cearað (So must a man do, when he hopes to win long-lasting glory at battle; he will not be too concerned about his own life). Lof is ultimately 'value' or 'valuation'; dom is assessment, judgement, and so 'esteem.' Their differentiation is not in such passages important[*] — yet it has an importance, since the two words were not commensurable in significance, and when Christianity came the one flowed rather into the idea of heaven and the heavenly choirs, the other into the conception of the judgement seat of God, the particular and the general judgements of the dead.

[55] The subtle change which comes about in this way can be observed curiously in the Seafarer. To appreciate this it is necessary to compare Seafarer 66

---

[*]   C.f. the end of Widsith referring to the minstrel's part in achieving for the noble and their deeds the prolonged life of fame — He says of his noble patron: lof se gewyrceð, hafað under heofonum heahfæstne dom (He earns praise who has under heaven enduring fame).

ic gelyfe no carefully with Hroðgar's sermon or gidd — noting especially the close resemblances between Beowulf 1735 ff and especially 1761–8 (which I believe original and not "revised") and Seafarer 66–71. After teaching that man will die, the Seafarer-poet says: "Therefore this is for all noble men the best "last word" (i.e. memorial in tale and song) and praise of the living that commemorate him in words, that ere he is obliged to depart, he merit and achieve on earth by heroic deeds against the maker of enemies (feonda) opposing the Devil (deofle) so that the children of men may praise him afterwards and his "lof" thereafter may live with the angels for ever and ever, the splendour of eternal life, rejoicing (dream) among the hosts (dugeþum)."

This is a passage which certainly seems to have been revised. In any case it is a modification of heathen lof in two directions. (1) by saying that this lof on earth should be for deeds of Christian value, heroic deeds against the spiritual foes. (2) by enlarging lof to include the future life.

But we do not get anything like this in "Beowulf." Lof remains pagan lof — the esteem of one's peers, perhaps prolonged vaguely awa to ealdre (always for life) in song. There is in Beowulf hell* There is nowhere any mention of heaven*

[56] I mean to 'heaven' as a place of reward, eternal bliss in the presence of God.* An exception might be made in case of 186 ff. Wel bið þæm þe mot æfter deaðdæge Drihten secean, 7 to Fæder fæþmum freoðo wilnian (It shall be well for him who on his death day is able to seek the Lord, and to seek safety in the embrace of the Father). If this and the passage in which it occurs is genuine and not a later addition (as I believe — I will return to this point) then it marks the point still more clearly; for it must be taken as an exclamation of the Christian author, who clearly understood about 'heaven.' But the characters in his story did not. They refer to hell** — "helle gemundon" — they know about hell and this is a fact. Beowulf prophesies it for Unferð 588; but even the noble monotheist Hroðgar (as he is painted quite apart from the question of the bulk of his sermon 1724–1760) refers to no heavenly bliss. The reward which he foretells to Beowulf (955) is that his dom shall live awa to ealdre (always for life), a fortune also in Norse bestowed on Sigurd (that his name æ mun uppi [while men still live]). As we have seen this is capable of Christianization, but in Beowulf is it not Christianized — on purpose — when the characters are speaking in the proper persons, or their thoughts reported. Thus the author tells

---

* heofon in the singular or plural, and synonyms such as rodor, are of course frequent, but refer either to the particular landscape, or to the sky under which men dwell in general. These words are of course used with names of God — Lord of the Heavens and so on — but are parallels rather to God's general governance of nature (e.g. 1609 ff), and His realm which includes land and sea, even if heofon is His especial seat and the sun His candle.

** A native word — and also a native idea the symbolism of which is seen coloring references first in Christian literature. C.f. the celebrated reference to the death of Holofernes which so remarkably recalls certain features of Völuspá. Judith 115 wyrmum bewunden (wound round with snakes), 119 of ðam wyrmsele (from the snake-hall) — Völuspá 38 sá er undinn salr orma hryggjum (its [the hall's] walls are clad with coiling snakes).

us that Beowulf's soul <u>gewat .. secean soðfæstra dom</u> (departed to seek the judgment of those fast in truth) — that is not to hell but was reckoned among the just; and here we may see a transmutation of significance: <u>soðfæstra dom</u> by itself could have meant "the esteem of the just and good," the <u>dom</u> which Beowulf [57] himself as a young man had declared to be the prime motive of good conduct, but here it means either "the judgement (of God) upon the just" or else "the glory that belongs (in eternity) to the just." Yet <u>Beowulf</u> himself though troubled by dark doubts at first (2729), and later declaring his conscience clear, thinks at the end only of his barrow and memorial among men, and of his childlessness, and of Wiglaf the sole survivor of his kin to whom he bequeaths his helm and gear. His funeral is quite unchristian, and his memorial is the virtue of his kingship and the hopeless sorrow of his people.

This question of the Christian and heathen in <u>Beowulf</u> is then usually misconceived. Though there are special problems such as Hroðgar's <u>gidd</u> (sermon) (especially 1724–1760) and particularly lines 175–188, we have no right to speak in general either of confusion (in one poet's mind or of a whole period's thought!) or of patch-work revision — without first considering whether more sense can be made of the poem starting with the hypothesis that the poet tried to do something definite, perhaps something difficult, perhaps not with complete success, but at least something with reason and thought in it.

I should say that the strongest argument that the actual situation in the poem is not the product either of stupidity or of accident (or later patchery) is to be found in the fact that we find in the poem <u>differentiation</u>. That is in the matter of religious sentiment and philosophy we can distinguish plainly for instance (a) the poet as narrator and commentator (b) Beowulf (c) [58] Hroðgar. This would not be achieved either by a man who did not know what he thought himself (and could in consequence hardly conceive of other people's minds), or by mere accidental tinkering by "monks" or others concerned only to graft on at random familiar Christian matter. The sort of thing that is achieved by the latter process is illustrated by the <u>drihten wereda</u> (lord of hosts) for <u>drihten Wedera</u> (lord of the Weders) in 2186. Though this is clearly ultimately due to some gentleman more familiar with the biblical "Lord of Hosts" than with Hreðel Lord of Wederas (to whom the words clearly refer) no one has ventured to ascribe his 'confusion' to the poet.

That this differentiation does occur I leave to your study. The simplest method is to extract from the poem all references to religion, fate or mythology, and observe their circumstances, paying special attention to those things <u>which are said in speech or reported</u> as actually said or thought by characters. The poet as narrator and commentator obviously stands apart. But the two characters who do most of the speaking, <u>Hroðgar</u> and <u>Beowulf,</u> are quite distinct.

Hroðgar is for some reason constantly regarded as wise and pious, a noble monotheist who refers all things to the favour of God* and never omits explicit thanks for mercies. Beowulf refers to God only on following occasions (1) He says that Dryhten (Lord) will decide the issue of his combat with Grendel, and follows immediately with gæð a wyrd swa hio scel (fate goes always as it must) (441 ff). (2) In 570 ff in describing his escape from the sea he calls the sun leoht eastan .. beorht beacen Godes, (light from the east, the bright beacon of God) but ascribes his conquest of the nicors to luck, saying [59] hwæþere me gesælde (so it was given to me) 574 (words which are precisely repeated of Sigemund later, to whom Beowulf is compared, 890). Grendel's success he ascribes simply to Danish feebleness 591.

(3) It is said by the poet that Beowulf on the eve of his combat (669) trusted in Metodes hyldo (the favor of the Measurer), but this was manifested in his possession of modgan mægnes — georne truwode modgan mægnes, Metodes hyldo (his own mighty strength, the protection of the Measurer). It would be quite wrong to put an "and" in here.

(4) Beowulf says that witig God .. halig Dryhten (wise God ... holy Lord) (685ff) can decide the combat as He wishes.

(5) 967: Beowulf says that Metod (the Measurer) did not will that he should kill Grendel outright.

(6) 977: Beowulf says that Grendel shall abide miclan domes (the great judgment) and what scir metod (the glorious Measurer) shall doom for him.

(7) 1272–3 The poet says that Beowulf gemunde mægenes strenge, gimfæste gife, ðe him God sealde ond him to Anwaldan are gelyfde frofre ond fultum. (remembered the strength of might, the wonderful gift, which God gave to him, and he entrusted himself to the One-Ruler, to his relief and support). Though we still see the preeminent trust in personal might — even of God's gift. This was not said by Beowulf. We note in his comforting of Hroðgar he says domes ær deaþe (fame before death) is the best thing for a dead man; and in his speech before he plunges into the accursed waters he makes no reference to God. His last 'will' is that Hroðgar should secure his dom by sending his "gifts" to Hygelac.

(8) Beowulf (1658–1665) acknowledges God's protection nymðe mec God scylde (if God had not shielded me); and says that by his favour (me geuðe ylda Waldend)(it was granted to me by the Ruler) he saw the giant sword which enabled him to win the battle under the water. He adds oftost wisode winigea leasum (often he has guided the friendless).

[60] (9) In his recapitulation of events to Hygelac (2000–2151) he makes no reference to God at all. Næs ic fæge þa gyt (I was not yet then fated) (2141) is his explanation of his escape from the water.

---

* halig god (holy God) 381; god (god) 478, 930, 1397; Alwealda (All-Ruler) 928, 955, 1314; wuldres hyrde (guardian of the world) 931; Dryhtnes miht (power of the Lord) 939; Eald metod (the ancient Measurer) 945; mightig Drihten (mighty Lord) 1398; mihtig God (mighty God) 1716; Metod (the Measurer) 979; ecean Dryhtne (Eternal Lord) 1779; wigtig Drihten (wise Lord) 1841. — I omit the gidd (sermon) 1724–1760.

(10) (2329 f) Beowulf in his old age — now <u>frod</u> (wise) cyning — is said by the poet to wonder if he had offended God (who was consequently punishing him with the dragon) : <u>wende se wisa þæt he Wealdende ofter ealde riht ecean Dryhtne bitre gebulge</u> (the wise one wondered if he had bitterly enraged the Ruler, the eternal Lord). Perhaps the <u>least</u> Christian thing said of him — unwitting trespass bringing penalty as if "sin."

(11) 2469. Beowulf says of the heartbroken death of Hreðel: <u>gumdream of-geaf, Godes leoht geceas</u> (gave up the joy of men and chose the light of God). But this is a mere phrase (from Christian poetry?). The story itself is a pagan and hopeless one, and its telling by Beowulf a mere device — long before end it has ceased to have any "dialogue" character, and the expression is therefore rather that of the poet as narrator.

(12) 2526f. Beowulf definitely equates <u>wyrd</u> (fate) and <u>metod</u> (the Measurer) : ac unc sceal weorðan æt wealle, <u>swa unc wyrd geteoð Metod manna gehwæs</u> (so we two will fare as our fate determines, the Measurer of man). Compare his words again 2814f ealle <u>wyrd</u> forsweop mine magas to <u>metodsceafte</u> (fate swept away all my kinsmen to their destiny). And contrast the words of the poet 1056 <u>nefne him witig God wyrd forstode 7 þæs mannes mod</u> (except that wise God and the courage of that man staved off fate) where God and <u>wyrd</u> — become merely death or ill fate — are opposed. It is in <u>Metod</u> originally measure or measurer — ordainer or ordinance — destiny[*] we see a coalescence point of the pre-Christian with the Christian in both ideas and words.

[61] (13) Beowulf in his penultimate speech (2729ff) — reflects on his career: he regrets he has no son. He has ruled for 50 years, and no king has dared to assail him. He has held his own with justice, he worked no treachery. <u>ne swor fela aþa on unriht</u> (nor swore many false oaths). He says <u>Waldendfira</u> (the Ruler of men) cannot impute to him <u>morðorbealo maga</u> (the murder of kin). The list of crimes (avoided) is similar to those which in Völuspá doom men to wade in the heavy streams (þunga stramma) of Hell: there are <u>menn meinsvara, ok morðvarga</u>, ok þanns <u>annass glepr eyrarúnu.</u> namely perjurers, murderers, and adulterers.

His death is however comforted by no thought of heaven, but by the gold he has won on earth.

(14) In his last speech Beowulf says thanks to <u>Frean Wuldorcyninge . . . ecum Dryhtne</u> (Lord, King of the world, eternal Lord) for all that his eyes now see of treasure, and because in dying he has won treasure for his people. But his last thoughts are

---

*   Compare Old Norse mjötuðr, dispenser (of fate), ruler — also doom, fate, death. Old Saxon metod is singly "ambiguous" and like Old English. Gabriel in the <u>Heliand</u> says of John the Baptist that he will not touch wine — <u>so habed</u> im <u>uurd giscapu metod gemarcod endi maht godes</u> (this is the way the works of fate made him, time formed him, and the power of God as well) (128); again it is said of Anna the widow when her husband died that sie thiu mikila maht metodes tedelda uured uurdigiscapu (that the mighty power of the Measurer separated them, the cruel workings of fate) (511). In both "fate" is nearer than God. In Old Saxon metod uurd <u>giscapu</u> and <u>metodigesceaft</u> equals fate as Old English meotodsceaft.

for his barrow, and his kindred — ealle wyrd forsweop mine magas to metodsceafte (fate swept all my kinsmen to judgment).

Beowulf refers sparingly to God — except as the arbiter or decider of critical
events (Metod) in which He approaches nearest to the old Fate — so 441ff, 685ff,
967. Thus we have in Beowulf's language close assimilation of two, even (to our
minds) paradoxical conjunctions — as where gæð a wyrd swa hio scel (fate goes always as it must) immediately follows his assertion (441) that Dryhten (Lord) holds the
balance in his combat; or where wyrd (fate) and metod (Measurer) are definitely
equated (2526f — with which compare 2814f. where wyrd is more active and metodsceaft equals doom, death). It is Beowulf who says Wyrd oft nereð unfægne eorl
þonne his ellen deah (fate often saves an un-fated earl if his valor endures) (immediately
after calling the Sun beacen Godes (beacon of God), which contrasts (Wyrd taking
place of God) with the poet's comment on the man who escapes the dragon 2291f
Swa mæg unfæge eaðe gedigan wean 7 wræcsið se ðe Wealdendes hyldo gehealdeþ
(so may an unfated one easily endure woe and the exile-journey, he who holds the favor of the
Ruler).

[62] Beowulf twice explicitly thanks God or acknowledges His help: (1) 1658–
1661 he acknowledges God's protection and the favour of ylda Waldend (the Ruler
of men) — oftost wisode winigea leasum ([who has] often guided the friendless) — in his
combat under water. (2) in his last speech of all he thanks Frean Wuldorcyning
. . . ecum Drhytne (the Ruler, the king of the world) for all the treasure his eyes can see
and for helping him to win it for his people. But his last thoughts are for his memorial on earth, and his family, and successor. Usually he makes no such reference. He ascribes his conquest of the nicors (570ff) to luck — 'hwæþere me
gesælde' (so it happened to me) (cf Sigemund episode 890). In his account to Hygelac
his only explanation of preservation from the water-den is Næs ic fæge þa gyt (I was
not yet fated) 2141: he never in this speech refers to God.

Other references are the merely formal beorht beacen Godes (bright beacon of
God) (571) and Godes leoht geceas (chose God's light) 2469 — both have 'escaped'
from Christian poetry,[*] the first an innocent example, the second a piece of unsuitable diction, which however is under no possible suspicion of later addition or
revision. More remarkable, but having some similarity to Beowulf's other references to God as Doomsman, is his declaration (977) that Grendel shall abide
miclan domes (the great judgment) and the decision of scir metod (the glorious

---

[*]   It would be truer to regard the language of Beowulf as Christian diction partly "paganized" for a
specific reason than to regard it as pagan poetry clumsily revised. Throughout the poem it seems to me
clear that the language of poetry — as known to the poet, as it was before our Beowulf poem ever took the
shape we see — was already Christianized, and familiar with Christian and Hebraic terms (Old and New
Testament). We have therefore in Old English not only "heroic" language misused for unsuitable items
themes, but also Christian language misused or rather casually used. Godes leoht geceas (chose God's light)
is an example (all is not perfect in Beowulf) — (a) the tale actually told is pagan and despairing (b) the poet
forgets long before this phrase that technically Beowulf is telling it — it ceases to be a monologue in
character.

measurer). There remains 2729ff: where Beowulf examines his conscience and says that Waldend fira (the Ruler of men) cannot accuse him of morðorbealo maga (the murder of kin) — his death is, however, actually comforted by the sight of the gold he has won. (With the crimes Beowulf says he has avoided compare the crimes that are punished in hell in Völuspá 36).

[63] This is a very different picture to that of Hroðgar. Even where reference to Beowulf's thought is made by the poet we note that his real trust was in his own might — that this is a "favour of God" is rather a comment of the poet, and reminds us of comments in Christianized saga.* Thus 669 georne truwode modgan mægnes Metodes hyldo (eagerly trusted in the mighty power, the favor of God) [N.B. no "and" should be inserted; the favour of Metod is the possession of strength]; and 1272-3 gemunde mægenes strenge gimfæste gife ðe him God sealde ond him to Anwaldan are gelyfde frofre ond fultum. (he remembered the strength of might, the wonderful gift which God gave to him and he entrusted himself to the One-Ruler, to his relief and support). Finally the poet tells us that when the dragon's ruinous attack was reported wende se wisa þæt he Waldende ofer ealde riht ecean Dryhtne bitre gebulge (the wise one wondered if he had bitterly enraged the Ruler, the eternal Lord, due to an offense against ancient law).

We have thus actually in "Beowulf" an historical poem or an attempt at one (though literal historical fidelity was not ever attempted). It is in the main a poem by a Christian writing of old times: looking back on the heroism and gloom and seeing in it something permanent, and something symbolical. The man who wrote Beowulf so far from being a muddleheaded semi-pagan — an historical improbability in any part or period of England to which our poem can be ascribed — brought first to his task a knowledge of Christian poetry, and especially that of the Cædmonian tradition (among which ranks especially the Genesis of which we have a damaged and late copy). He also was deeply [64] learned in native English (northern) traditions. It is not unnatural then in the circumstances that in delineation of the great king of Heorot we see strongly the influence of the Old Testament — and in the folces hyrde (the herdsman of the people), Hroðgar, have something of the devout shepherd patriarchs, servants of the one God. It is a Christian English conception of the noble pre-Christian who can lapse nonetheless (as could the Israelites) in times of stress into "idolatry." It is of Old Testament lapses and idolatries rather than of events in England (such as northern reversions in the 7th century)

* E.g. Fostbræðra where it is said describing a grim character ekki var hjarta hans sem fóarn í fugli, ekki var þat blóð ult, svá af þat skylfi at hræðslu, heldr var þat hert af enum hæsta höfuðsmið í öllum hvatleik (For his heart was not like the crop of a bird, nor was it so full of blood that it shook with fear. It had been hardened in the Almighty Maker's forge to dare anything). Fostbræðra – Chapter 2 (page 8 Reyky) again Chapter. 17 (Reyky page 73) Almáttigr er sá sem svá snart hjarta ok óhrætt lét í brjóst orgeiri: ok ekki var hans hugþryði af mönnum ger né honum í brjóst borin, heldr af enum hæsta höfuðsmið (It was the Almighty who touched Thorgeir's heart and put such fearlessness into his breast, and thus his courage was neither inborn nor of humankind but came from the creator on high).

that he is thinking in l. 175ff,[*] and which colour his manner of allusion to knowledge of the Danes as heathens and probably of <u>Heorot</u> (Hleiðr) as a place of
originally heathen religious import which he derived from native tradition. On the
other hand this same traditional history and poetry — not to mention its living
survival in the code of conduct of the nobles of England — enable him to draw
differently and far more near to the northern "hero" the [65] character of Beowulf
— who used his great gift "mægen" to earn <u>dom</u> and <u>lof</u>. "Beowulf" is not an actual
picture of historic Denmark and Sweden circa 500 A.D. But it is with certain
defects, of course, at a general view, a self-consistent picture, an imaginative construction. The whole must have succeeded admirably in creating in the minds of
the poet's contemporaries the illusion of surveying a past, pagan but not ignoble
and fraught still with deep significance — indeed a past that had itself depth and
reached back into the mists. This last is an effect of and a justification of the use of
episodes and allusions to old tales — which are all notably darker more pagan and
despairing than the foreground.

The old fashioned criticism of "putting the best things on the fringes" entirely misses this — fails indeed to see part of the reason for the special appeal of
these old things in "Beowulf." The poet has made the appeal of antiquity so deeply
appealing.

To us perhaps, in a way he could hardly have hoped for, this appeal is
strengthened, since the poet himself and his work have slipped back far into time
and we hear this only now, we learn of sorrows that were ancient already in ancient days.

[66] The poem has then both a theme (or interwoven themes) and a structure
— discernible if not faultless.

The pagan theme <u>man upon earth</u> and his war with the inhuman world,
doomed to perpetual defeat in particular, and to <u>final defeat in general</u> — in
which his chief stay and reward is <u>dom</u> (self-approval and the approval of all good
men) — is presented not only by a contrast in the foreground between successful
youth and old age defeated, which is made sharp and definite, but also symbolized
by the nature of his adversaries. But this is somewhat changed by Christian
thought. The defeat in time, in spite of favours and answers to prayer, <u>death in-
evitable</u>, is still emphasized, remains in fact the really dominant idea. But there is

---

[*]   From 175–179 <u>hæþenra hyht</u> (hope of the heathens) we can confidently accept as original. The status
of the remainder to 188 is really suspect on wholly different grounds — style, rhythm, tone. I find it very
difficult to believe that 180–188 was by same hand as rest of the poem <u>on these grounds</u>. If they are accepted then the reference can only be to <u>certain of the Danes</u>. But it is really preposterous that an author
who has carefully (and for good reason) depicted <u>Heorot</u> and symbolized its <u>'dream'</u> (joy) — its <u>culture</u>
which enraged Grendel — by a minstrel's song of Creation by se Ælmihtiga (the Almighty) should say 180
<u>Metod hie ne cuþon</u> (they did not know the Measurer) etc. of Danish counsellors. It is the very marked character
given to Hroðgar which has made it possible to sense and expand the <u>gid</u> (sermon) without doing any
serious damage. The reviser's hand was in that case not so much at fault. I do not here enter into reasons
for suspecting lines 1724–1760 to be an addition considerably subsequent to the original composition.

a shift: the monsters are the foes of God. The battle is not in vain ultimately and though all human glory, success, victory, wealth, power, majesty, wisdom will fall defeated physically by the inhuman, man's destiny is not thus ended or completed. In the war with the world his battle is that of the Spirit. Grendel, too, as we have seen becomes more "devilish" and less merely elemental — more like the inner enemy, the evil possibilities of debased human nature, just as in defining him and his broods as <u>Godes andsaca</u> (the enemy of God) he has become in fact offspring of Cain; that is ultimately of Adam. The Dragon remains more elemental, more pure malice whelming good and evil alike, at once the destroyer of Beowulf individually, and also the kin of the great serpent devourer of the world at last.

[67] The structure of the poem is plain enough — if we take only the main points, the strategy, and neglect the many points of minor and occasional tactics (in which much is worthy of high praise). But we must dismiss, of course, the idea that "Beowulf" is a <u>narrative</u> poem — that it tells a tale sequentially or meant to. What tale? The life of Beowulf? Certainly if that is how it is taken criticism will be vociferous. It "lacks steady advance" — so Klaeber heads a critical section. But it does not mean to advance steadily or unsteadily. It is based on a contrast of ends with beginnings. It is in simplified form a description of two "moments" in a life. It is divided therefore into two contrasting portions, different in matter manner and length: <u>A</u> from 1–2199 including the Exordium of 52 lines. <u>B</u> 2200–3182. The proportion cannot be caviled at — it is for the purpose and the production of the effect right.

This simple structure is in each portion much diversified and adorned. In the conduct of the presentation of Beowulf's youth on the one hand, and the conduct of his full manhood, kingship, and old age on the other criticism can find much to question, especially if it is captious, malicious, or stupidly unsympathetic. But to my mind there is actually one point in each portion which can be seriously raised. In the first portion I would instance the report of Beowulf to Hygelac — to which I will return. In the second half it must be admitted that though the interweaving by speech and allusion of past events has often in itself virtues, and is in any case imposed on the poet by his more or less static contrast-structure with its two opposed pictures, it is not wholly successful. [68] The surface is too broken; reminiscence is too long in proportion and not always sufficiently suitable in the character and atmosphere of the things told and recalled to the general theme of Beowulf's fall. Yet without <u>all</u> that we have got the magnificent final movement, 3137 – end, <u>a very great piece of poetry</u> where it stands and with the rest behind it would not be so full of content.

The other weakness, the one in the first "half," is more interesting. The recapitulation, granted, is necessary, is done very well; without serious discrepancy it retells rapidly the events and retouches them, and serves to demonstrate vividly the portrait of a young man, singled out by destiny for great things as he steps suddenly out into his full powers. Yet this is not quite enough justification for it. I suspect that if not justification at least explanation can be found in different directions.

The old tale was not first told by our author. The sluggish bear's son with his hug who wakes up and becomes famous is a very old folk tale, the legendary association of the Danish and Heorot with a marauding monster, and of the arrival from abroad of a "champion" of the "bear-anger" was not invented by our poet. There are clear traces of it in Scandinavian tradition. The "plot" is not his, though he has poured feeling into it quite different from its simple crude essentials. And that plot is not perfect as the vehicle of the ideas aroused in the poet in making his poem. For the contrast, the rise and fall, it would have been better if we had no journeying. If the single nation and land of the Geatas had been concerned we should have felt the stage not narrower, but symbolically more wide. More easily should we have felt in one people and their hero, the human whole and their heroes.

[69] I always feel this in reading 'Beowulf', and I always feel that this defect is to some extent rectified by the bringing of the tale of Grendel to Geatland — as Beowulf stands and tells his story to Hygelac he sets his feet firm again in the land of his people, and is no longer in any danger of being a wrecca, a wandering adventurer, an errant slayer of bogies that do not concern him. There is in fact a double division of the poem. The fundamental one at 2200 between age and youth. A secondary (but deep) one at 1888. In a sense at 1888 we have "summary of previous events now read on" — the essentials of the previous part are taken up and compacted so that all the tragedy of "Beowulf" is contained in essentials in the section 1888–end — though missing much of incidental illustration and the secondary contrast of age and youth in the persons of Hroðgar and Beowulf — The one really silly thing to do with "Beowulf" therefore is to read only 1–1888 and not the rest. I do not defend the English syllabus on this score.

An interesting point may be mentioned here. There is a special connexion between Beowulf and Andreas — Andreas being usually considered the imitation since the passages of close similarity in the two poems are found in natural surroundings and applications in Beowulf rather than in the Christian 'romance.' But whether that be so or not — the connexion is undoubted and serves to suggest that "Beowulf" itself has some relation to the great missionary epoch of the 8th century. Just so did many young Englishmen untried, while those at home hoped and feared, set out to win their spurs in foreign lands, in Frisia and Saxony. They went to the courts of kings and wrestled with godes andsacan (the enemies of God), and some were destroyed like Beowulf's companion. Sometimes the enemy [70] in new form returned to the attack in the moment of apparent triumph. Granted that "Beowulf" was written in the 8th century — which seems secure enough on independent grounds — then one can imagine why especially the "plot" attracted a poet of this temper. The "allegory" could hardly have escaped contemporaries, although the poet has actually done nothing to underline it. But we can see both how the tale came to be chosen, and why imitated closely in a definitely missionary romance like Andreas, even perhaps a subsidiary reason for the half surprised almost ironic question of Hygelac (ac ðu Hroðgare widcuðne wean wihte gebettest)(But did you, for Hrothgar, remedy at all his widely known affliction?), the joy in the return, and eagerness for a full account, the emphasis on the friendly relations now established between nations once hostile: All this is nonetheless purely subsidiary — and hardly affects the real feeling and movement of the poet's mind.

But whichever portion we read or criticize do not let us imagine that this poem is primarily an exciting narrative or a romantic tale. In the second portion for instance . . .

[71] In final conclusion.

Since there is a little time and one ought as a kind of appendix to General Criticism point out that it should fall in his department to assess the art and technique in detail of the poet — was he good as Old English poets go, was he good in a general literary view.

It is one of the misfortunes of English which possesses at the beginnings of its career a language and a verse technique such as Old English. For this language and verse is a true one — we have just enough preserved to reveal that. And (since this is but another way of saying the same thing) this requires considerable study for literary appreciation. Old English is not ?strong? — the language is nonetheless full of those tones and echoes that come from long literary cultivation. It is slow laborious, compact and often taken ???? but full of feeling. ??? ??? what the ???? same time is large and ??????.

'BEOWULF' & THE CRITICS (B)

<u>'Beowulf' and the Critics.</u>

The Rev. Oswald Cockayne wrote (in 1864) of the Rev. Joseph Bosworth, D. D., F. R. S., Rawlinsonian Professor of Anglo-Saxon: 'I have long entertained [the conviction] that Dr. Bosworth is not a man so diligent in his special walk as duly to read the books . . . which have been printed in our old English, or so-called Anglo-saxon tongue. He may do very well for a Professor . . .' These words were inspired by annoyance with Bosworth's dictionary, and may have been unfair; but the period was certainly one in which the study of Anglo-Saxon had perhaps declined in England, and where this study was not so much dependent on foreign (German) work as behind it and largely incompetent to appreciate it. However that may be, a modern professor, even if he is not troubled by books printed <u>in</u> Anglo-Saxon, and limits himself to one, to <u>Beowulf</u>, is still faced by the serious problem of books <u>about</u> Anglo-Saxon. I am not a man so diligent in my special walk as duly to read all the books that have been printed on about, around, or touching on <u>Beowulf</u>. But oddly enough I have read <u>Beowulf</u> itself, with some attention and with some understanding of its language — though this does not appear to have been the universal practice of the critics. Yet this concentration on the poem itself has certain compensations denied to a wider learning. The dwarf on the spot sometimes sees deeper than the travelling giant ranging over many countries. At least the intensive and stay-at-home student is less likely to become bored and sophisticated. The critic who knows too much is likely to go wrong in estimating a poem written in a [93] period when literature was less wide in range, and possessed a less diversified stock of ideas and themes, but perhaps for that reason felt more deeply and pondered more profoundly such as it had.

In speaking of '<u>Beowulf</u> and the critics', therefore, I do not attempt a study, hardly even a sketch, of the history and present state of <u>Beowulf</u> criticism. My eye is fixed primarily on the poem itself, and such criticism as I notice is principally that which is still current and influential, whether for bad or good. Its history I refer to chiefly in order to point to what I think is the explanation of certain critical commonplaces, or falsehoods, that I attack. The criticism and study of <u>Beowulf</u> has now, of course, a considerable history. It began over two hundred years ago, and for a hundred years a 'litteratur' has been accumulating till it has become a veritable library. But my chief concern with the past, is the discovery there of the seeds of the malady from which the criticism still suffers, ideas which are still afloat although supposed to have been long exploded.

I pass, therefore, in the first place over the matters of detail, the slow hammering and digging of scholars, great and small, whose accumulated results we inherit — their work has gradually made what was still one hundred years ago largely unintelligible in detail a poem which it is now possible to read with understanding and pleasure. I also pass by, with a few glances, the mass of disquisition and theory which has in the main been directed to determining the origin of the story of Beowulf, or of the allusions in Beowulf, rather than to the understanding or valuation of Beowulf as it is, or as its author made it. I am chiefly concerned with that relatively small department of Beowulf bibliography, judgements passed on Beowulf as a thing in itself, as a work of art, as a poem having (or not having) structure and motive.

It is of course true that the labour in other departments has among much rubbish now discarded or discardable, produced results essential to any general estimate. It was indeed long before any such estimate could be made with any hope of success. In the early stages [94] of the study much elementary work had to be done, the text had to be deciphered, the language learned, the darkness of the allusions as far as possible illuminated, and later actually in time (though not least in importance) the metre comprehended. But the fact that Beowulf belonged to a past, the tradition of which was almost completely lost (unlike the case of the classical tongues), so that a long apprenticeship of 'research' was necessary, has had a considerable effect on the general criticism that finally emerged. History, Mythology, Folk-lore, Archaeology, and Philology were the Fairy-godmothers at the Christening: few thought of inviting Poetry. Poetry has indeed been so over shadowed by others, especially History and Antiquarian Curiosity, that even now, when general criticism is and has long been possible, the best criticism (such as that of W. P. Ker or R. W. Chambers) is, as it seems to me, still clouded by that shade. Even, for instance, in the admirable foreword — probably the best thing written on the subject — Beowulf and the Heroic Age in England, sixteen pages and all too short, contributed by Chambers to Sir Archibald Strong's translation, that shadow is still to be seen. But to that I shall return later. For the moment my point is this — nearly all censure, and much also of the praise, of Beowulf has been due either to believing that it was something it was not (e.g. primitive, or rude, or Teutonic) or to disappointment because it was itself and not something the scholar would have preferred (e.g. an ancient lay of heroic slaughter and divided allegiance, or a Germanic dictionary of antiquities, or a Nordic Summa Theologica). And this even where the intention has been literary criticism, as in the case of Ker, or of Chambers (when that is his object) is ultimately [95] due to a mental background produced by 'research' — to a preponderance of that 'research' that is not so much criticism of a poem as quarrying in it.

I present you with the following allegory, which I should like to have borne in mind. "A man found a mass of old stone: it was part of the old wall of his small house and garden which had recently been considerably altered and enlarged. Of this stone he made a rock-garden. But his friends coming at once perceived that the stones had formerly been part of a more ancient building; and they turned the stones upside down to look for hidden carvings and inscriptions; some suspected a deposit of coal under the soil and began to dig for it. They all said "This garden is <u>most</u> interesting!" but they also said "What a jumble and confusion it is in!" And even the gardener's best friend, who might have been expected to understand, or at least to enquire, what he had been about, was heard to say: "He's such a tiresome fellow — imagine his using these beautiful old stones just to set off commonplace flowers that are found in every back-garden: he has no sense of proportion, poor man!" I might add that, of course, the less friendly when they were told that the gardener was an Anglo-Saxon and often alluded to beer, understood at once. A love of freedom may go with beer and blue eyes, but that yellow hair unfortunately grows always on a muddled head.

That allegory is quite just — as you will see even when we come to consider the more recent or more intelligent of the critics, and the notion of <u>Beowulf</u> [96] which is becoming more or less fixed and accepted. To reach these we have to skip swiftly over the heads of the mass of critics. As we do so their conflicting babel mounts up to us, and very little sense can we make of it. It sounds something like this: '<u>Beowulf</u> is an imitation of Virgil inspired by the emulation of Latin literature introduced by Christianity — it is a half-baked native epic the development of which was killed by classical learning; it is feeble and incompetent as a narrative — the rules of narration are cleverly observed in the manner of the learned epic; it is Christian poetry treating half-forgotten paganism in an antiquarian spirit — it is pagan poetry edited by a monk; it is a silly folk-tale; it is a poem of an aristocratic and courtly tradition; it is a hotch-potch; it is 'small beer'; it is a sociological document; it is a mythical allegory; it is rude and rough — it is a masterpiece of metrical art; it was sung or bellowed — it was composed in the study and never even recited; the author had no clear plan or idea at all — it is a clever allegory of contemporary politics; it is thin and cheap — it is solemn and weighty; it is the accidental product of stupid accretion and senseless elaboration'. The odd thing is that amidst all this babel we catch one constant murmur: <u>Beowulf</u> is steadily pronounced to be 'worth studying'. It is true that this is often qualified — 'it is the most worthy of study amongst Anglo-Saxon remains' (said somewhere in a tone that suggests that Andaman Islanders might be substituted for Anglo-Saxons); but nowhere do we miss at least this [97] qualified commendation. Why is this so? The answer is important.

I will now read you a passage from one of the more recent compendia of English literary history — the sort of thing that scholars, young or old, do not read though they occasionally write them (when they are hard up for cash or ideas).

These compendia are nonetheless important, owing to the pressure of the examination-system which they serve and by which they are served. It would appear that so-called students read them; and if one wonders whence the strange nonsense comes that appears in examinations (or in the press), the answer is from the statements in such books transformed in minds that contain little else. These books are the index of what the 'widely read' or 'cultured' make of the special literature mole-like scholars pile up in their chosen fields; they are the quintessence of 'research'; they are that part of it which finally selected gets home to the public. They are the milk of bottle-fed infants (and later boneless men). In fact we ought to be more aware of them — most of them should be on an index expurgatorius and publicly burnt.

Now the passage I will read serves a double purpose. First, it gives in a few lines the 'plot' of Beowulf, and it is necessary to have that stated in barest terms for my purpose. Secondly, it states explicitly the reason why, amid all dispraise, we have an agreement that Beowulf should be studied — why, indeed, it burdens English syllabuses up and down the land. Also, let me say, the compendium is a fairly competent one — that of [98] the late Sir Archibald Strong,[1] who had read Beowulf with attention; indeed he cared for it sufficiently to translate it into verse[2] and in the introduction to his translation said many things worthy of attention, and was nearer to the point than any critic other than Chambers. But this was four years later than the compendium. This latter crushes the crowded scene of English literature from 700–1900 into 368 closely printed pages — one wonders how much longer this painful and ridiculous jig-saw work will be considered worth while! — of which Beowulf, probably justly (though it is one of the more important single pieces produced in all those 1200 years) gets less than two. It would take far too long, all the same, to criticize all the assertions and assumptions in this brief entry. I pass over therefore the first and longest paragraph — more or less innocuous even in error — pausing only to note that it opens thus: Beowulf is the only poem of any length — it runs to 3182 lines — which has come down to us, of the early heroic poetry of the Teutons. And it ends: Though biblical allusions abound, and the heathen deities have, for the most part, vanished before the editing — if we may call it editing — of the Christian reviser, the background is not Christian but heathen. Bear these in mind. We will now pass on and consider the summary and the comment on it. Strong pots the 'plot' as follows:

[99] "The main story deals with the adventures of Beowulf in his contest with ogres and dragons" — there is bias in this plural! "We are told how the hall of

---

1)   A Short History of English Literature. O. U. P. (Milford) 1921.
2)   Beowulf, translated into modern English Rhyming verse. Constable 1925 on the whole the best English translation of Beowulf that I know, though it is a transformation rather than a close representation of the original, since, in spite of the reasons urged by the translator, I remain of opinion that he selected from all those available the one metre most foreign in mood and style to the original (the metre used by Morris in Sigurd) and not in itself a good metre.

Hrothgar, King of the Danes, is devastated for the space of twelve years by a demon called Grendel. Beowulf, nephew of Hygelac, King of the Geats, a tribe of
South Sweden, crosses the sea to help Hrothgar, and in fighting in his hall mortally
wounds Grendel. Grendel's mother, seeking vengeance for the death of her son,
renews the attacks. Beowulf tracks her to her lair, a cave at the bottom of a deep
mere, and slays her. Loaded with gifts he returns to his native land, where he ultimately succeeds to the throne. In his old age a fire-breathing dragon lays waste the
land. Beowulf attacks and kills it, but is himself wounded to death in the fray. The
poem ends with an account of his burial amid the mourning of his whole people.
This short summary" says the critic "does scant justice to the poem." Exactly —
and why then give it? It can only be for the benefit (or delusion) of people who
have never read the poem, and it will not help them any more than the plot of the
Iliad. No story can be judged from its summarized plot — but only from the way
it is told, and from the ideas and feelings which its telling stirs in the author, so
that (whether he ever consciously formulates them or not) he infuses a life and
meaning into his tale. To judge of Beowulf, to try indeed to form any conception
of it at all, from stuff of this sort, is to attempt an estimate of a great man from his
skeleton. But I have quoted this 'summary' because it is accurate — more than can
be said of other summaries which are still before a cozened public;[1] and because
this mental [100] subtraction from a story of all that gives it life leads naturally to
such judgements as the following — a common-place of Beowulf criticism. Strong
immediately proceeds thus: "In outline the story is trivial enough, a typical folk-
tale; but it is interspersed with many subsidiary legends, historical and mythical,
and with allusions to legends, which open up for us the life of Teutonic heathendom, and lift the story far above a mere recital of the deeds of a giant-killer. Beowulf is a picture of a whole civilization, of the Germania which Tacitus describes"
— this is, of course, nonsense, but the real cat is about to leap from the bag —
"The main interest which the poem has for us is thus not a purely literary interest.
Beowulf is an important historical document, recreating for us a whole society,
telling us, in most authentic fashion, of life as it was lived in far off heathen days."

There is more, but as I cannot deal with all the errors (as they seem to me) of
still current criticism of Beowulf, I must omit all except one further sentence (a
hackneyed one): The Christian allusions show up rather incongruously against the
pervading paganism.

In this summary and the comments on it, taken with the two sentences I have
quoted from the opening paragraph, you have, succinct and explicit, the views on
Beowulf which I intend principally to attack. Though they are closely inter-
connected, there are some distinct points in all this for consideration. The story is

---

1) For example there is a more meagre and baser variety of the genre to which Strong's book belongs: A
History of English Literature (in 111 pages) in the 'Peoples Books,' a potting by Dr. Compton Rickett of his
own larger work. This is so entirely inaccurate as to show that the author had not even perused an English
version of the poem he presumed to talk about.

trivial, a typical folktale — not so much as a statement of fact, but in its critical implications, is the main objective of my attack, but we shall meet this again [101] in more unlikely places and for the moment I reserve my fire. Let us turn to this explicit statement of the reasons why 'we' should study Beowulf. It would not have occurred to me to approach this poem, or any other, primarily as an 'historical document' — unless, either (a) I was not concerned with poetry at all, but merely seeking for information wherever it could be found, or (b) it seemed clear that the so-called poem contained actually no poetry. But there are, of course, these two attitudes which one can have towards a document which is at once old and a poem. It can be studied as poetry, or quarried for facts, references and allusions. The two operations are quite distinct, and should not be confused, even though they are often performed in conjunction and by the same student, even though the 're-search' process may sometimes assist and illuminate the other.[2] The quarrying would, of course, be perfectly legitimate, even if it did not assist criticism in general at all — so long, that is, as it is not mistaken for criticism. The works of Homer contain some of the greatest of recorded poetry, and Homeric language is perhaps the most admirable instrument of poetry that we know of. Yet the Iliad and the Odyssey are vast quarries for information; and there are doubtless worthy persons to whom the main interest of these works is 'not purely literary', to whom they are primarily 'important historical documents.' [102] But I have never heard any of them prescribe their attitude as inevitable for 'us' — the lordly 'us' that means all reasonable living men. Though the literary merit of Homer is much greater (in most all respects) than that of Beowulf, the principle is the same. If a poem has any poetry in it, the understanding and estimation of this is naturally the prime object of reading and study, as long as we are concerned with literature. To class a 'poem,' a thing to say the least in metre, as mainly of historical interest in a literary survey should be tantamount to saying that it is a very poor poem, whenever it was written. But such a judgement on Beowulf is doubly false. So far from being a poem so bad that only its accidental historical interest can still recommend it, Beowulf is in fact so interesting as poetry, in places poetry so powerful, that any historical value it may possess must always be of secondary importance. While in truth its historical value is dubious and debatable, and needs in any case much inde-

---

2)   Criticism and interpretation may assist 'research' as much — at least in keeping it within bounds and ensuring it some measure of practical sanity. Sometimes it alone can give the decision when the technical experts reach a deadlock. Thus the old and rather dreary debate, which shows signs of breaking out like measles again, whether the Géatas of Beowulf are the Gautar of Sweden or Jutes has much technical evidence in favour of either side, but though to my mind the probability on linguistic and historical grounds lies with the Gautar, the real decision lies with the interpreter rather than the philologist or historian; for the Jutish case is really founded on the notion that Beowulf being in Old English must be a "national epic" and must relate the glories of Jutes not Swedes. But this is a primitive and quite erroneous conception and with its dismissal the Jutish-case with all its special pleading fails. It should never have been brought forward. If Beowulf is a national epic it is an epic of a peculiar kind which includes both Gautr and Jutes.

pendent exterior evidence for its appreciation; its poetic merit is patent and indisputable, and needs only an approximate mastery of the idiom in which it is written for immediate, if not full, appreciation.

But the air has been clouded for Strong, as for critics worse and better, by the dust of the mining researchers; his ear confused by the very rumour of their subterranean dynamite. Really he felt deeply the appeal of Beowulf as poetry (as we can see in his translation) and it was the poetry that cast its glamour over the supposed 'historical' content, and made it seem so worthy of study. He thought he was attracted by fragments of historical information, but he was really in large measure moved by the poetical treatment. The illusion of historical truth and perspective in Beowulf, that has made it seem so attractive a quarry, is largely a product of art — an art that has used indeed a sense of history, but for the purposes of poetry, with a poetical not an historical object. [103] The lovers of poetry can safely study the art, but the seekers after historical fact must beware at every step, or fall into fallacies after Sir Archibald Strong, lest the glamour of Poesis overcome them.

But this confusion of purpose, which directs scholars when reading Beowulf to consider it primarily as an historical document, as a source of information about things we otherwise should not know, twists the judgement even of those who do not explicitly approve of it, as Strong does. It is the cause of most of what is false in the sentence I have quoted from Strong. But for this false historical bias the critic would never have written: "Beowulf is the only poem of any length . . . which has come down to us, of the early heroic poetry of the Teutons." The historian would like to have some of this early poetry of the Teutons (as documents doubtless not poems), but he has not got any; and therefore he is determined to find a substitute; he sees it where it is not, and does not in consequence see what is there. Alas, there is no "early heroic poetry of the Teutons" of any kind or any size in existence. It is a matter for legitimate doubt whether there ever was any such poetry or indeed any such Teutons. There is indeed something in the background of Northern Europe, something as potent as it is elusive — an ancient community of temper and spirit, to some extent of custom, law, and social arrangements, which roughly corresponds to the known and definite community of language which we express by the term 'Teutonic,' or now more generally 'Germanic,' and by the hypothesis of an actual linguistic unity more or less complete, in the remote past. But that linguistic hypothesis — a well-founded one — is not instantly convertible into terms of race, or ethics, or of poetry. Too many other factors, some known, some unknown, intervene in the course of the spread of Germanic (Teutonic) languages to regions [104] where they were certainly not indigenous (such as Britain, Russia or Southern Germany). It is no longer good criticism of any kind to speak of things written in Norse or English or German or Gothic as just 'Teutonic.' Or rather, it is just as good and just as bad as lumping all the products of Portugal, Spain, France and Italy together as Romance or Latin. There is, or may be, some sort of truth in either, but it is seldom the more important truth, especially when it comes to individual works of literature: namely that these works are Spanish, or Italian, or French, or English or Icelandic.

There is, of course, something which may be called a common Germanic (or Teutonic) spirit, and it is appreciable (with liking or distaste) by all, even if it is not easily caught in a few words. Beowulf has much of it, and Beowulf is illuminated by a knowledge of other early Germanic languages and remains. Yet the differences are at least as important as the resemblances — between say Old Norse and Old English verse; and Beowulf is primarily an English poem of a special period, and not a Teutonic one. For that it is several hundred of years too late. For those lost and unguessable 'Teutonic' things Beowulf is neither a satisfactory substitute, nor to be judged as if it were. Were all mediaeval English literature swept away but for a few scraps and the allusions and stories in the plays of Shakespeare, even perhaps what survives of mediaeval ideas and temper in those plays, it would still be untrue to say that the works of Shakespeare were "the largest body of mediaeval poetry that has come down to us." It might be an unfortunate fact that we could only guess at "mediaeval literature" by investigating Shakespeare and comparing him with other material of similar period outside England, and so seeking to detect what in him was derived from the periods behind him, in matter or in spirit. This would be a legitimate procedure, to use Shakespeare thus in the course of research prompted by [105] curiosity about the past. But it would not be the chief function or the main interest of Shakespearean criticism. For essential criticism Shakespeare was a dramatist, an English dramatist of a special English period. Also he was probably an individual!

We will emend then our hasty and inaccurate critic, thus: — "Beowulf is the only poem of any length which has survived from the early heroic poetry of the English." But here 'early' is still misleading. It means, one presumes, early relatively to the whole later millennial course of English. Of the actual heroic poetry of the English, so far as we can judge, Beowulf is probably a very late example. So, if you do not mind sacrificing snap to exactitude, let us say: "It is the longest and most elaborated surviving poem which may be held to be in the main line of descent from ancient Germanic or Northern heroic verse; it is the principal surviving example of the early poetry of this vernacular tradition as it developed under peculiar circumstances in England, and it came probably from the end of that development." Also it was by an author, and is an individual work. This last point is important, and though our own ignorance may be unable to make much of it, that is a defect in criticism to be deplored rather than concealed. While the individualism and the proprietary rights of authorship may be assumed to have been less and different in ancient days, we still cannot dismiss the author and thrust him back into the tribal genius. The ancient legends mention the particular fame of the maker of verse such as Heorrenda no less than the maker of sword or jewel such as Wéland. The fame and names of the individual Icelandic poets have been better preserved even [106] than their works. Beowulf it is true has been preserved, but not the name of its author. Still we have no right to assume that he was unknown or negligible, or that his authorship was of no concern to him or to others, and that the personal factors can be safely overlooked. The "Teutonic" kind of criticism suggests that 'Teutons' had a universal kind of poetry and no individual poets. Since Teutons were all thoroughly Teutons, Teutonic poetry was all Teutonic. But what of the makers? Great differences can be observed even among the Norse lays of the so-called Elder Edda. What of Anglo-Saxon poets, and of the maker of Beowulf in particular? He seems to be lost in a crowd of 'ancestral voices prophesying war'. But we should at least wish to distinguish him, and to hear his voice as his own. One may reflect that he would have disliked many of these 'Teutons' heartily, and would have been much slower than the critic to recognize his kinship (and indeed identity) with them. His grandchildren were at grips with such Teutons par excellence, the viking invaders, and regarded them as the very devil. Whatever their tongue, they would have written them down rather in the kin of Grendel than of Hrothgar (for even Grendel may have spoken Danish). And there is the rub. Beowulf may be a poem about Danes (and others), but it is an English poem about them, or rather the poem of a particular Englishman using in a particular way certain English traditions about them.[1]

[107] The life, the times and the spirit, then of the poem Beowulf is not Teutonic, still less a specimen of Teutonic heathendom. This poetry has its roots in a past which was shared by some at least of the speakers of other "Teutonic" tongues in later days — it has much that is perceptibly similar to the spirit of the men of Norway and Iceland, for instance. And with that past it has definite tangible links in manners, and code (views of kinship and loyalty, for example) and artifacts, and last but not least in metre. But all these are transcended: they belong to a special time with a special temper as viewed by an individual man.

The individual man, in a period whose original wealth is now represented by a selection so haphazard and so meagre, we can scarcely define — no more than to recognize the general unity and harmony of the whole he has produced. But we must not forget him entirely, even if this means no more than using caution in ascribing everything in Beowulf to 'Anglo-Saxons' in general (let alone Teutons).

The special period can be made more clear. We know much, if still too little, of early Anglo-Saxon history. And it is essential to criticism that we should attempt to set Beowulf correctly against such historical background as we can reconstruct. I say "correctly" because Anglo-Saxon history is not one thing, uniform in mind and mood from Aidan to Stígand any more than Icelandic history from the Land-nám to the cruel feuds of the great houses and the submission to the Norwegian crown in the 13th century; any more one might add than Rome from Tarquin to

---

1)   This is the most rational view. I pass over in any case as fantastic the now obsolete idea that Beowulf is a translation of Scandinavian originals, or an imitation of them. More recent hypotheses concerning Frisian intermediaries seem hardly less fantastic, but do not radically affect what is here said.

Augustus or Augustus to Diocletian. This setting is the <u>reverse</u> of the using of <u>Beowulf</u> itself as a prime historical document, even as a document for a period of history to which it does not belong. It is true, of course, that if once we can with any certainty fit <u>Beowulf</u> [108] as we have it into the period in which it was composed, then it is not only illuminated by history, but illuminates that history in return. It becomes a considerable document for the times of great importance to the historian (and usually neglected by him). But the critic of <u>Beowulf</u> as such, must seek first the evidence for the dating of his poem, and secondly the evidence concerning that period <u>outside</u> his poem. The process must not for him become a vicious circle in which the poem is used to depict a period, and that picture is then used to explain the poem. The poem fits so well into the period, the <u>eighth century</u> to which it must almost certainly be assigned on dry, logical unsubjective grounds,[1] that it can hardly any longer be doubted that so set it is seen against its natural background. The murmurs of the primeval Teutonic forest, and the thunder of the Scandinavian seas, may still be heard there, and move the imagination of listeners, but they are memories, already in the poet's day memories of a far past, caught and coloured in the shells and amber of tradition, and refashioned by a jeweler of a later time — the great time of the Anglo-Saxon Christian spring.

But if such a time in history is the time of <u>Beowulf</u>, what are we to make of such statements as the one I quoted above? — in <u>Beowulf</u> "Though biblical allusions abound, and the heathen deities have, for the most part, vanished before the editing — if we may call it editing — of the Christian reviser, the background is not Christian but heathen."

There are serious inaccuracies here which show the bias of the writer and help us to perceive what he really means by the somewhat vague and ambiguous language. He really means <u>Beowulf</u> was written by a heathen (or at best a half-baked Christian) and that such signs of Christianity as are to be perceived are not integral, but due to the confused mind of the original author or [109] perhaps of some later writer who recast the antique poem.†

But <u>biblical allusions</u> do not 'abound' in <u>Beowulf</u> ; while on the other hand <u>heathen deities</u> have not 'for the most part vanished,' but vanished altogether. There is not indeed the slightest evidence that they ever appeared in the poem at all. The <u>biblical allusions</u> are rarer, and are of one special and peculiar kind: references to Cain, to the giants, and the origin of monsters. This <u>not</u> their relative frequency is the important point, as we shall see later. No <u>heathen deity</u> is ever named. Nor does a heathen deity appear even as an element in proper names, save for the obscure name of <u>Ing</u>, occurring in Ingeld and in <u>Ingwine</u> (an 'epic'

---

1)   linguistic, metrical, and so on.

†   It would be only fair here to remark that better criticism is actually moving in the direction I intend. Namely (1) towards regarding the Christianity as produced by an editor (2) by later making that editor an effective adaptor who was trying to Christianize pagan tradition. But as you will see, this seems to me, though a saner view, probably a perversion of the truth

name of the Danes): the first was doubtless the historical name of a real person and no longer analyzed any more than <u>Edward</u> is today; the latter is a fossil (interesting to the antiquarian) which may indicate the character of the stones used in the building, but says nothing of the purposes or knowledge of the architect. <u>Wyrd</u> is, of course, mentioned, but that is quite another matter: <u>wyrd</u> was not and is not a 'god,' but the master of gods and men, the total history past present and destined within which they are; a theory or conception that was absorbed insensibly by an omnipotent God, or rather was indeed from the beginning an apprehension of Him, and survived and survives as a natural aspect of the world's working. The only important thing about this 'heathenism' in fact, if we are considering the poem as we have it, and as some writer left it (even if he did not write it all for the first time), is that the story is consciously and explicitly regarded as taking place in <u>heathen times</u>, and also in <u>past times</u>, and yet the names of ancient divinities are, it would seem of set purpose (since we know their names were <u>not</u> forgotten), <u>never mentioned</u>.

[110] Well, but you may object: "The critic only said the <u>background</u> was heathen." Certainly he did. But observe the contrast made and the creation (half-hearted it is true) of an editor or scriver who is not the poet and it would appear not in sympathy with the poet. <u>Background</u> — of course the 'background' is heathen and not Christian. The background of all humanity is heathen; the background of Christianity is heathen. If you really mean 'background', and not "immediate setting', not spirit or temper indeed of the actual original and effective author, it is not worth saying. But to do this critic and the criticism of which he is a mere representative specimen, justice — it is not 'background' that is meant, but original and effective author or authors. That is worth saying or at least considering. But whether we can really envisage our 'author' as a heathen, and our actual poem as a 'redaction' is a fundamental question — to which I will return later. For the moment I need say no more than that Sir Archibald Strong, chosen to represent a common and still current kind of criticism, himself makes after profounder study an almost complete somersault: in his own introduction to his translation he speaks not of the '<u>heathen background</u>' nor of the '<u>Christian editor</u>,' but of the <u>Christian colouring</u> which the <u>author</u> has given to <u>his</u> story. But Strong was essentially more intelligent and perceptive than the criticism he had at first imbibed. When we pass from his compendium to his translation and introduction we are moving towards sanity, from 'research' to understanding, from hypothetical Teutons to Englishmen, from bogus history to real poetry.

[111] In Chambers' Foreword to this same translation — this Foreword should be read by all, whatever else, save the poem itself, is unread — only the shadow of the historical document fallacy is left, and the solution of the Christian-heathen debate is trembling on the verge of explicit expression.

The shadow is there, however, still — we gather that if <u>Beowulf</u> scrutinized is not quite so good as it is in general and more distant impression (of style and dignity), at least it gives a picture of the times, and perhaps the mood of a great moment in our history. But nonetheless it is real history not a theoretic Teutonic age. And Chambers' method is right. With a few strokes and a few quotations the period to which 'Beowulf' belongs is delineated, at least in certain features, and against that period Beowulf is set. One thing only remains a riddle unresolved — and here the shadow of old error is most dark. Still the 'folk-tale' motive stands like the spectre of old research gone wrong, dead yet unquiet in its grave. On page xxvi, when everything seems to be going right, we hear yet once again "that the main story of 'Beowulf' is a wild folk-tale." Quite true, of course. It is true of King Lear, unless in that case one would prefer to substitute silly for wild. But more — we are told that the same sort of stuff is found in Homer, yet there it is kept in its proper place. "The folk-tale is a good servant," Chambers says and does not realize the great importance of the admission (made though it is to save the face of Homer to throw stones at whom would be impious), for he continues "but a bad master: it has been allowed in 'Beowulf' to usurp the place of honour, and to drive into episodes and digressions the things which should be the main stuff of a well-conducted epic." But why class Beowulf as an 'epic' however conducted? And who has legislated for what 'should' be the main stuff of any poem? The answer is: the antiquarian historian, who prefers semi-historical legend to 'folk-tale' (whatever that may be), which he calls 'wild.'

[112] And now, after what I fear you will consider an unduly long preparation, too much bayonet-practice in prodding a man of straw, the real battle-field is set. I started with a deliberately selected, a fairly representative, piece of compressed criticism from a recent compendium, and in the preliminary commentary we have already glimpsed some of the really important points of debate. It may be felt that I have digressed from the proper path, and have hurried on too far and left out the beginning. I should have begun with the antiquated, the beginnings of Beowulf-criticism and progressed to the modern, surveying the minor and ridiculous as well as the greater and the more wise. But as I said at the beginning I do not really wish to do this, and do not think it either necessary or desirable. One may assent to Earle's quotation from Dowden: 'The happiest moment in a critic's hours of study is, when seemingly by some divination, but really the result of patient observation and thought, he lights upon the central motive of a great work'; but one need not (as Earle himself admitted) give serious attention to Earle's particular divination, which caused him to ascribe Beowulf to Hygeberht, bishop, and temporary archbishop, of Lichfield (787–?803), and to view the whole poem as a kind of early political Utopia. The jetsam of criticism, whatever patient observation and thought and whichever ingenuity may have produced it, need not necessarily now be collected and piously scrutinized.

Though I am obliged now to leap backwards for a moment, and work forward again to the more important and recent critics, such as Chambers whom we have already met, I select from the past only casually, and though I may turn aside for a moment for a little deserved merriment at the expense of fools who have rushed in with clumsy and blundering feet, I do so chiefly to illustrate and bring out what we now [113] perceive to be the chief points requiring consideration: (1) the poetic or literary merit of Beowulf, especially as compared with its value as an 'historical document'; (2) the Christianity or the paganism of the poem, and what is meant in either case; (3) the incoherence, and shapelessness of the poem, or possibly its structure and form; and (4) finally the old ogre in his lair — the 'typical' or the 'wild' folk-tale, that like Grendel in Heorot, is said wið rihte, against all propriety, to have usurped, even in the courtly eighth century of England, the throne of the heroes. There are a good many bogeys here. If we can slay them, then indeed criticism of Beowulf will be gefælsod (cleansed).

The assumption that the value of Beowulf as an 'historical document' is greater than its poetic merit, or that it is some compensation for the absence of any, is due to various causes. For one thing, the antiquarian interest of any piece of connected writing in a vernacular, were it no older than the mere manuscript date of Beowulf (c. 1000 A.D.), is obvious and cannot be denied. Few European vernaculars have anything so old to boast, good or bad. The appreciation of this requires no effort. But the assessor of poetry requires both the knowledge of the language and some sensibility, some ability to escape from the prejudices of his own time and tongue. Many who have criticized have possessed none of these. They have been in fact quite unqualified for their self-appointed pulpits. Thus to take a recent example — so recent that there can be no excuse for the extremity of its impudence —, the introduction to an anthology compiled by Mr. Shane Leslie speaks of Beowulf as 'small beer.' I hope in depending on memory — for I do not possess the worthless book — I am not wrong is ascribing these introductory words to Mr. Chesterton. This ascription alone causes me to mention them. Mr. Leslie hardly merits notice of any kind — his anthology at any rate includes what by the title one perceives is intended for a version of the Vercelli Vision of the Cross (Dream of the Rood), though its content is remoter from the original than the translation of plough-candidates in a minor university (it is in fact so bad that it would seem to be by Mr. Leslie himself). Mr. Chesterton, however, is different, and deserves at any rate on some topics, some attention. Yet one may guess that he could not construe a line of the poem he slightingly refers to, but has depended, if on anything other than imagination [114] and Bellocian prejudice, on Shane-Leslian translation. He might as well judge of English beer from hooch in a speakeasy. It is casual 'criticism' of this Chestertonian kind, of course, that is really the 'small beer' or the sour wine. In a book on Beowulf addressed to the knowledgeable and intelligent it would not be necessary to allude to it. But even in Oxford, where we have a school of English studies knowledgeable, intelligent and even diligent and scholarly, strange ignorances and prejudices lurk still in the fens and dark places. There is a kind of criticism, and an attitude which is a bogey — it may be as unworthy of mention in serious lectures as Grendel has been held to be in an epic poem, yet it still comes out and stalks even in high places — feond on helle (enemy in hell). It catches the slow and stupid, of course, but also sometimes the innocent. I will venture to its lair.

While men like W. P. Ker — and this is perhaps a token of the intermediary position of the English-speaker in Europe, balanced linguistically and culturally between what we may casually define as the Latin and Germanic (a situation already preparing when Beowulf was written) — seem to be at home, or at least not to fail of some measure of sympathy and understanding, in Latin, French, Italian, Spanish and in English (old or modern), Norse or German, there is a Gallic kind, whether by blood or adoption, which is far more limited, often it would seem blind in one eye, or lame in one leg. Of these there are several examples (more important in such affairs than Mr. Chesterton). Jusserand is an extreme example — but not an unfair one to choose. His work used to be much recommended, though it is perhaps not much read now. I hope not. But one never knows whither the thirst for second-hand opinions upon literary works will take people. Often it would seem by some perverse instinct they are led to the least worthy, and even to tomes the perusing of which is more irksome and laborious than the reading of the originals.

[115] At any rate Jusserand's Literary History of the English People is on the shelves of the English library — neither stolen nor locked up, I regret to note. I turn to briefly to this great work — though this critic is so easy a target that to shoot seems almost unfair, it is like potting a one-eyed rabbit on the blind side — because it contains characteristic specimens of a critical method, as popular still as it is worthless. It offers us an example, exaggerated perhaps but the more unmistakable, of the feebleness and obtuseness of the Latin (or especially the Gallic) when he attempts to deal with non-Latin ingredients of English (and especially therefore Old English). The feebleness is often due to carelessness and ignorance, the obtuseness is sometimes due to prejudice or ill will — though one has to reckon also with that curious incompatibility of temper and mind which is one of the factors of Europe (making the Frenchman a problem to his neighbors, and his neighbors to the Frenchman). There is a deal of history behind this, and the men of today cannot be held entirely to blame. Yet there is usually present also an easy sense of patronage, a lofty consciousness of superior worth, which it is as pleasant as it is fatal to possess. There is in any case no insularity quite so insular as that of the Île de France.

[116] First of all we see here clearly the idea which is still prevalent — indeed of Chaucer, not to mention other things more dark and ancient — that early English verse, and especially Old English, is primitive, and has the savage or rustic vices of incoherence and boorishness (normally) — the village pub; but (occasionally) an artless charm — the village maiden. The former is an axiom, the latter a charitable afterthought — the 'woodnotes wild' idea. Jusserand says actually 'the

charm of a wildflower'! Such notions go with and are usually founded upon mere linguistic ignorance. The underlying assumption, whether consciously acknowledged or not, is that English from (say) the sixteenth century onwards is one, homogeneous, thing, modern English and polite (and the Frencher the politer); and that all that is not familiar to 'modern English' ears is at worst barbarous, at best quaint. That one should at least attempt, if the period is worth considering at all even as a stage in an ascent, to study its language and idiom, until something at least of the meaning and implications of what is said can be understood, indeed until one has some idea of what was normal and what unusual <u>at the time when a thing was written</u>, does not seem to occur to such minds. If it occurs the notion does not commend itself. And actually therefore this sort of criticism commends itself specially to the idle or the stupid. Ignorance is bliss, and their private reading (upon which sweeping judgements are founded) is strewn with howlers which they are unaware of. Occasionally we catch such people in the act. Jusserand, for instance [117] delivers himself first of the precious reference to 'the charm of a wildflower.' This, by the way, he says of Ælfric! Ælfric actually deserves praise, though he is open to criticism. But neither friend nor foe could see in the writing of this learned, painstaking, polished, and meticulous ecclesiastic scholar the 'charm of a wildflower,' unless he knew very little Anglo-Saxon and (one suspects) no wildflowers. However we soon see whence this delusion of charm is derived. Jusserand jots down as a sample of delicious quaintness a sentence from the Old English translation of Boethius, treating the legend of Orpheus and Eurydice. This is cast before you without context, and your indulgent smile is awaited as you listen to the lisping of the village infant. '<u>The dog of hell he should have three heads</u>' !

First of all, this is a misquotation and a mistranslation. The original Old English is a competent, straightforward, bit of prose, with no quaintness at all, no wildflower charm whatever, but something of the air of a schoolmaster. Actually, it says of the dog of hell <u>þæs nama wæs Cerverus, se sceolde habban þrio heafdu</u>. That is precisely in modern English: 'whose name was Cerberus, and who has been reported to have three heads.' The <u>sceolde</u> idiom is common. The attitude is the quite unrustic one of incredulity — the comment is Anglo-Saxon and not in the original. The man who thought that <u>se</u> was the same as he, or that 'should' was quaint enough for special quotation — in a work giving only brief attention to <u>Beowulf</u> — would be considered inept, if he trespassed with such little knowledge into any modern language. But archaic English has still constantly to suffer the condescending opinions of the ignorant, and it is still believed by many that English (Old or Middle) [118] should yield its meaning readily to the casual moderns; and if it does not, so much the worse for the stuff itself.

Well, with this admirable equipment, we pass to <u>Beowulf</u> — prepared, as I have said, to notice, when the village maiden does not briefly appear like a wood-anemone, only the hoarse and incoherent clamour of the pub. For example, the speech of Beowulf to Unferth (ll. 530–606), we are told, may be summed up thus:

'liar, drunkard, coward, murderer!' So may many brilliant speeches in the houses of Parliament today, and judging by report still more in the similar institutions in Paris. Some indeed seem less civilized utterances than Beowulf's. But this is not really the point. Were the summary true, it would still tell us nothing of the manner, or of the artistic purpose of that speech in that poem. Instead we have once more the 'historical-document' fallacy, now confused in addition with an alcohol-complex. Anything that any character says or does in a poem written in Anglo-Saxon is just a picture of 'Anglo-Saxon behaviour'. The speech itself is, of course, actually well done, and rises slowly from an ironic beginning to crushing accusation, and the actual words 'liar, drunkard, coward or murderer' are, of course not employed at all. It serves at once the purpose of depicting Beowulf and his character as a proud, highspirited, young man, and of bringing part of his earlier history before us, at the same time relating it and interlinking it cunningly with the large and ominous background against which we now see him: the great court of Heorot, the ambiguous figure of Hroðulf, and the sinister figure of the evil counselor Unferth. The Jusserandian method of [119] criticizing such a passage would reduce all poetry to vulgarity; and its employment can proceed only from malice, or from an ignorance and an insensibility to an ancient mode, which is in one presuming to criticize almost as criminal. It is hardly necessary to point out that the whole prejudiced misconception is founded upon beer — it starts from beore druncen, in line 531. So certain is it that all 'Anglo-Saxons' were drunk, that it has not been observed that our modern use of 'drunk' and 'drunken', meaning 'helplessly inebriated' is a litotes, and that in Old English, druncen means here and normally 'having drunk'. That a man has spoken rashly owing to wine or beer at a feast is a thing that can be observed even in Latin countries. In Old English and Old Norse poetry, however, with their constant recourse to concrete symbols, words of this kind imply more than mere drinking — not bestial or stupid fuddlement, but the mirth, freedom, and sense of community and security where friends were gathered in hall about their patron. What would these beer-bemused critics make of the tragic words concerning Guðrún in the 'Lay of Attila', where of the great Lady of the Burgundians, Queen of the Goths, it is said, as she greets her brothers riding to their doom in Attila's hall, bjóri vas [hón] lítt drukkin (little beer had she drunk). This means, of course, that none of the joy of the alien folk and hall in which she was perforce queen was hers. But our discerning critics would doubtless imagine that the poet was recording the fact that on this anxious occasion the queen was only partially inebriated!

But we will pass now to more important points in this 'criticism'. Yet we shall still observe that, throughout, Beowulf is taken as if it were a photograph of the 'Anglo-Saxon period' (whatever that may have been), not a poem creating a special story with a special purpose. "To their excessive enthusiasm" we are told "succeed periods of complete depression, their orgies are followed by despair." The word their, I may say, refers [120] to the "Anglo-Saxons." You would hardly guess that the critic is speaking of a poem, to which contrasts, and changes of fortune, are a necessary narrative method; still less that "Anglo-Saxons" are nowhere in that poem referred to at all. The poet speaks of Danes. On such principles it is plain that the 'swaggering upspring' and heavy headed revel that the Prince of Denmark thought 'a custom more honoured in the breach than the observance' should be ascribed to the "Elizabethans." As it might with more justice — but not on such evidence. Actually in 'Anglo-Saxon' as we have it, and not as it might have been, 'orgies' are nowhere praised and very seldom recorded — unless it be of alien pirate chieftans, or of Assyrians and such highly cultured people of the ancient world. But the critic has not finished his sketch of his apocryphal 'Anglo-Saxons.' He proceeds: "They sacrifice their life in battle without a frown, and yet when the hour for fight comes they are harassed by the thought of death'. This is nonsense, and an almost exact reversal of the spirit we actually see portrayed.[1] But we can hardly withhold admiration from these strange heroes, and sympathy for the convulsions they must have known in suffering harassment without allowing themselves to frown. Though we can hardly avoid also the suspicion that the critic has himself got mixed, and, drunk with words rather than beer, has fallen somewhat short of the Gallic lucidity he admires." The strange poem of 'Beowulf' " he wanders on, "the most important monument of Anglo-Saxon literature" (the humble poet lifts his nose out of the beer-horn and acknowledges gratefully the gentleman's condescension) " . . . like Old Celtic tales — it is a medley of pagan legends, which [121] do not concern Beowulf (the hero) in particular, and of historical facts . . . New discrepancy is introduced in trying to adapt the old tale to the faith of his (the author's) day. No need to expatiate on the incoherence of a poem formed of such elements." (the poet here hastily hides his blushes in the beer-horn again). "Its heroes are at once pagans and Christian, they believe in Christ and Weland." At this there falls a dead and flabbergasted silence throughout the hall, while a horrible suspicion crosses the poet's mind that the magnificent gentleman is after all a wandering idiot. "They fight against the monsters of Scandinavian mythology, and see in them the descendants of Cain; historical facts such as the battle of the sixth century (mentioned by Gregory of Tours) are mixed up with fantastic deeds beneath the waves." At this point the gentleman is seized from behind by Grendel and put in a bag, and for once one's sympathies are with the troll.

Old Celtic Tales! If there is anything in the range of European literature of all ages which is least like Beowulf it is old Celtic Tales — but we will let that pass, though the difference is fundamental and its perception essential. The conjunction of Christ and Wéland, however robs any 'critic' capable of such confusion of the authority to speak at all. They believe in the Trinity and Merlin; while professing

---

1)   E.V. Gordon has dealt recently with this piece of traditional nonsense concerning the Germanic warrior in literature in his Introduction to Old Norse. In point of origin it is derived rather from classical accounts of ancient Celts and Gauls than from attention to Old English or Old Norse literature.

Catholics they imagine good violins were made by Stradivarius; though serious
Calvinists they ascribe their furniture to Chippendale — the joke allows of indefinite expansion; but its original perpetrator does not smile, he offers his gem as
serious criticism! Even the legendary Anglo-Saxons must look to their laurels as
champions of muddle and incoherence. Yet one cannot help feeling sorry for Jusserand, impostor though he is, groping under the shadow of 'research.' Somewhere he had read that Beowulf is compound of many diverse elements. Therefore
it is a 'medley' Q.E.D. Roma locuta, causa finita! (Rome has spoken, the matter is settled!).

[122] As for Cain — here is a chance for a genuine critic. The making of the
monsters the offspring of Cain is used as a stone to throw at a fool. The thrower is
the fool. For this is one of the central points for a critic to seize upon — in order to
comprehend not sneer — and any satisfactory interpretation of the poem has to
explain why Cain and Abel alone of the names of Scripture appear in Beowulf. I
shall return to this point later. But there is some elementary work to do first.

The digression on bad criticism, with Jusserand as an example, has at any
rate I hope sufficiently emphasized the point that neither supercilious contempt
nor slipshod scholarship are good critical weapons. Old English verse does not
unlock the treasure of its word-hord readily, not at least at the first casual knock of
the vain or hasty, though this is less of its own nature than through the mere lapse
of time that has rendered it now unfamiliar in vocabulary, modes of diction, manner and metre. There is no reason why it should be expected to do so. But though
it might be considered a department of 'general criticism', I do not deal here with
the diction and texture of Old English verse, and of Beowulf in particular. There
is in any case substantial agreement concerning it among those competent to
judge. The writing in detail, the tactics, as opposed to the criticized strategy, and
the metrical accomplishment of Beowulf is good — one's estimate improves steadily with acquaintance. The poem itself indeed can in this respect be safely left in the
hands of readers. Ars longa (art is long) indeed — the lyf so schort, the craft so long
to lerne, so hard th' assay, so scharp the conquering, as Chaucer says. Long study
has, of course, its special rewards, yet the virtue of the language, style, and metre
of Beowulf is not inaccessible even to the first 'hard assay,' if the scholar have wit
and will.

But though some may have lacked, not a few critics of Beowulf have possessed an eminent scholarship in Old English. And the 'historical document' bias
is still found even among these. It is not solely due then to inability to 'read' Old
English with understanding; and we [123] need to consider the causes of this attitude (in different degrees) even among the better equipped for the reading of a
poem as poetry. It is due in some part to the fact that Beowulf does actually contain much that is of historical or antiquarian interest, an interest that time and accident has now increased so that it is much greater than the importance or function that the reference or allusion originally possessed in the economy of the poem.
Real critics of Beowulf as poetry have always also been in varying degrees lovers of

history and antiquity as well. Moreover — though this anticipates a point that should arise later, and to which we must return — the poet himself had a special share of this love: his poem probably had historical and antiquarian interest when it was composed, certainly when the surviving manuscript was written out. And so far have the days, when either the original or the copy was made, receded now from us, that this 'history' it enshrines, comes like an ancestral voice from far away, and has a specially strong appeal for those that feel such things.

Nonetheless a far more potent cause, I fear, is the belief that the intelligent people of today cannot be expected even in verse to take high pleasure in the actual 'main story' of Beowulf — in the 'wild folk-tale' — so that they are thrown back upon the descriptions and on the legendary allusions, and these are in the main (not entirely) of a more historical kind. This article of the critic's creed seems to me quite false, though I have never seen anyone so bold as to attack or question it in print. It has, however, become established chiefly because Beowulf-study has painfully progressed through nineteenth-century 'research' towards poetic under-standing. Thus the 'story' of Beowulf has tended to be considered as just one further collector's specimen of a wide-spread group, family, or type of folk-tale, as if on a par with any other [124] variant jotted down from an old wife's lips, or un-earthed in an old chap-book. So considered it remains, of course, just a 'typical folk-tale'. Yet it is not — for it is a 'folk-tale' used by a considerable poet for the plot of a great poem, and that is quite a different thing. As different as the Lear of Shakespeare from the same tale recounted in the chronicle of Layamon — indeed the difference is greater, for already in Layamon we have a tale told with art, not a mere example of 'story-motives'.

It is thus, as I said earlier, that the germ of the malady from which Beowulf criticism — or critical estimates — still suffers is to be found in the past history of the subject. A glance at the rise and progress of Beowulf studies will help us to understand how we have got to our own present position, and may help us to go on further. For Beowulf started with the historians, and then on to the folk-lorists, philologists, archaeologists, and yet more historians; and in all its modern wan-derings has seldom met the poets. Its meeting with William Morris was not under the happiest auspices; but in any case Morris was not a learned or scholarly poet. He was too fond of employing a living crib or interpreter. In his dealings with Beo-wulf he was perhaps not so fortunate in his crib as in his (still somewhat casual) dealing with Icelandic through Magnússon. But Morris had a wild and willful way even with his cribs, and these cannot take the blame of his transgressions. The 'Morris and Wyatt' translation of Beowulf remains an oddity — quite outside the main line of development.

If we glance back briefly to the beginnings we perceive that Beowulf in mod-ern times began its career, first attracting the curiosity and attention of scholars, as an historical document. The sole manuscript in which it is preserved is a composite one, and it there appears [125] together with other pieces (such as the Epistola

Alexandri and the Wonders of the East) that occurred before it and after it. For this reason, whatever its first possessors after the scattering of manuscript remains in the sixteenth century, such as Lawrence Nowell, may have made or thought of it, our first notice of it comes from the great Humphrey Wanley.[1] On page 218 of his Catalogus of manuscripts in volume II of Hickes Thesaurus (1705) he describes it thus: "In hoc libro qui Poeseos Anglosaxonicae egregium est exemplum descripta videntur bella quae Beowulfus quidam Danus ex regio Scyldingorum stirpe artes gessit contra Sueciae regulos." (In this book, which is an excellent example of Anglo-Saxon poetry, it seems that there are wars described which a certain Beowulf, a Dane sprung from the royal race of the Scyldings, waged against the princes of Sweden.)

This is of course largely untrue — it comes of looking only hastily at the beginning and the end, though this is excusable in the making of his monumental catalogue. But so far no great damage is done. It is poetry you notice, and quite rightly egregium exemplum (an excellent example) (a criticism that has been constantly repeated even amidst mispraise, and has never been reversed); though it deals with history and with Danes and Swedes. Wanley's words in fact suggest that, if he had had more time for scrutiny, he would have said more that was pertinent, and as far ahead of the scholarship of his own time (or of a century to follow) as he usually was. For in general the language of Old English verse was as yet in his day almost entirely unknown. For long reasonably competent translation of Old English prose, such as that of Ælfric, had been possible, but verse remained an almost unintelligible riddle. However, we see here if not the 'historical document' bias, already its germ. The subject of the poem was the early wars of Sweden and Denmark.

[126] It is not surprising, therefore, that the story — after a long silence — goes next to Denmark, to Grim Johnson Thorkelin, who eventually published the 'editio princeps' (first edition) in 1815. Thorkelin thought Beowulf was a translation, made in the age of Alfred, from a Danish original written by a contemporary or contemporaries of the events described. This 'translation from Scandinavian' was one of the earliest red herrings and long confused the scent. Thorkelin's first interest in the poem dates from 1786, when he visited England, and had two transcripts made. By 1807 his edition was practically ready for press, but it was destroyed by the gentle descendants of the barbarous Anglo-Saxons, when they bombarded the old city of Copenhagen. Thorkelin's house was burned and his property mostly destroyed, though the two transcripts were saved. It took him eight years to do the work again — a gallant effort for an old man.

From Thorkelin we pass to Pastor Grundtvig — one of the greatest single names in the history of Beowulf study — another Dane, under the patronage of the same Privy-counsellor Bülow, the Mæcenas of his time, who had encouraged

---

1)   Who tried so hard in vain to get for Oxford the Cottonian Collection in which is Beowulf, for Oxford. Oxford changes little — at any rate in its contempt and ignorance of the national linguistic and literary antiquities.

and munificently aided Thorkelin. I have not here time to say much about him. With practically no materials for study he tackled the elucidation of the Old English verse language brilliantly, and made such advances that his own 'Anglo-Saxon Verse' written in dedicatory commendation of his patron <u>Bülow</u>, though it will not now pass muster at all, except where it is mere quotation, is nonetheless recognizably 'like' in metre and idiom.

> Froedoric siteþ   On fæder-stole
>
> Gumena baldor   Þæt is god cyning.
>
> Swylcum gifeþe biþ   Þæt he Grendles cynn
>
> Denum to dreame   Dæda getwæfe
>
> A þone sinc-gyfan   Ymbe-scinon
>
> Witena betstan   wis-fæste eorlas
>
> Monige swylce   on Middan-gearde
>
> Swylce Bilof is   Byrne æþelinga

(Frederik sits on the father-seat, the master of men. That is a good king. It is given to him that he should deprive the race of Grendel of their deeds, to the delight of the Danes. Wise earls, the best of councilors, always shone around the treasure-giver, many such on middle-earth, as is Bülow, protector of princes.)

His emendations of Thorkelin's faulty text were often found actually to be in the manuscript, which he had not seen when he made them — a thing which seemed almost like sorcery to those unable yet to swallow the notion that other languages than Latin and Greek and Hebrew had any shape or rules. This ensured him [127] nonetheless a hospitable welcome in England and Oxford, and served to awaken the notion that there might be something in this Anglo-Saxon stuff after all. Most of Oxford remains, however, as secure still in its ignorance of the field and the achievements of Northern scholarship as when it shook its head in half incredulous wonder over N. F. S. Grundtvig, Præst. Among examples of Grundtvig's sagacity one may mention that it was he who first made out many of the proper names in the text, first discerning <u>Sigemund Wælsing</u> for instance; and it was he who first identified <u>Hygelac</u> with <u>Chochtilaicus</u> in Gregory of Tours, a discovery of cardinal importance. It was Grundtvig also who published the first translation of <u>Beowulf</u> into any modern language (Thorkelin's 'translation' parallel to his text was in Latin): <u>Bjowulfs Drape. Et Gothisk Helte-Digt af Angel-Saxisk paa Dansk Riim ved Nic. Fred. Seve. Grundtvig, Præst. Kjöbenhavn, 1820.</u>

So ended the first stage — criticism rapidly shifted as knowledge, especially of the language, grew, but we may note that the first stage was one in which <u>Beowulf</u> was valued mainly as a <u>document for early Scandinavian history,</u>[1] as is sufficiently indicated by Thorkelin's title: <u>De Danorum Rebus Gestis Secul. III & IV</u>

---

1)   So it is, and so it still may be treated. Thus to Professor B. Nerman in <u>Det Svenska Rikets Uppkomst</u>, <u>Beowulf</u> is still a prime document. But Nerman is not posing as a critic of <u>Beowulf</u> in a history of literature.

Poema Danicum Dialecto Anglosaxonica. (A Danish Poem in the Anglo-Saxon Dialect about the History of the Danes of the 3rd and 4th Centuries) In this atmosphere Beowulf study was born.

[128] Thorkelin, or at any rate his edition of 1815, was not the first to mention Beowulf after Wanley. This distinction, such as it is, goes to Sharon Turner in 1807, in his History of the Anglo-Saxons. But though he gave some extracts with such "translation" as he could manage, he was not only too incompetent in the verse language to qualify him even for this moderate part, but probably too little able to imagine that any Anglo-Saxon might be too difficult for him (without further study) to appreciate the magnitude of his offence. He only replaced the pardonable errors of Wanley by nonsense. He pronounced Beowulf : "the most interesting relic of Anglo-Saxon poetry which time has suffered us to receive. The subject is the expedition of Beowulf to wreak the fæhðe or deadly feud on Hrothgar for a homicide which he had committed. It abounds with speeches, which Beowulf and Hrothgar and their partisans make to each other, with much occasional description and sentiment." As Earle says, proper names excepted, this has no more to do with Beowulf than with the Iliad or the Chanson de Roland. But we need not be too severe upon Turner: his nonsense is less bad in proportion to easily available knowledge than other pronouncements that can be met much later, even today. Sharon Turner is all the same negligible, and in so far as he ever learned more sense, a disciple of the humbler and more patient Thorkelin. In his History of 1823 there is a considerable change, and Beowulf has become a 'poetical Romance' or a 'metrical Romance'[1] which celebrates the heroic deeds of Beowulf who fell in Jutland in the year 340 A.D. This is a borrowing from the Danes — from Thorkelin, from the [129] Danish historian Suhm, who derived it from Saxo Grammaticus, by identifying Beowulf with the Bous son of Odin, whom Saxo relates to have fallen in battle with Hotherus about that date. With this theory we are introduced not only to the histories of Saxo, which still remain an essential quarry for Beowulf commentators, but also we have foreshadowed the approach of myth which was soon to compete with history for the 'main interest' of Beowulfiana. Foreshadowed also in this identification (or mere confusion) of Geats and Jutes is that long controversy, which has complicated the detail of Beowulf-criticism, concerning the identity of the Géatas. This we can safely neglect, both because a decision depends rather on our primary view of the nature of Beowulf than the reverse, and because the elucidation of the problem concerns the study of the traditions enshrined in Beowulf for their own sake rather than for the sake of their poetic employment.†

---

1)   These titles are challenges to Ritson and others, who denied the existence of poetical Romance before the Norman Conquest.

†   The Jutish hypothesis has still vigorous supporters such as Professor Elis Wadstein. Ultimately to my mind the Jutish theory, in any case the weaker, breaks down since its foundation (the only thing that would give it any probability) is the view that Beowulf is a national epic glorifying the English or some part of their supposed ancestry.

It is to Conybeare perhaps in Illustrations of Anglo-Saxon Poetry (1826) that we may give the credit of finally dismissing the uncritical belief that Beowulf was derived from a hand contemporary with the events described. This delusion was primarily due to a mis-understanding of the frequent expression mine gefræge, we gefrugnon, (I have heard tell, we have heard tell) and so on. But these appeal rather to tradition and view the times treated of as already in the far past, as Conybeare pointed out. But this was his only real contribution. Yet we may note that he re-jects Thorkelin's Bous and Jutland, remains an agnostic about ultimate origins (Il-lustrations, page 33), and says of the writer (or perhaps the translator or modern-izer of the 'Dano-Saxon' period to whom he is inclined to ascribe the poem as we have it) that "it is evident that he was a Christian." Conybeare's translations, though often absurd [130] and seldom even approximately accurate, are at least recognizably related to the original.

Accurate scholarship began soon after, with the work of J. M. Kemble of (Trinity College, Cambridge). Now comparative philology of a scientific kind was introduced as a critical weapon, and immediately proved its worth. By it the mean-ings of very many words have been recaptured, and if we can now to a very large extent appreciate the diction and the verbal effects of Old English verse, it is due in the main to philology. The philology Kemble derived from Germany, where he had studied; and in general after Kemble to Germany the ball passed — in some ways much for the good of the game. Kemble's first limited edition — the effective beginning of Anglo-Saxon scholarship — came out in 1833: The Anglo-Saxon Poems of Beowulf, the Traveller's Song,[1] and the Battle of Finnesburh edited together with a glossary of the more difficult words and an Historical Preface. Lon-don. Pickering. It was sold out in a few months (!) and soon replaced by the cor-rected second edition (1835). But though the text shows a great advance on Thor-kelin, and the discussion of archaic and difficult words was something quite new, it is Kemble's work of 1837 that marks the definite crossing to a new era. This was A Translation of the Anglo-Saxon Poem of Beowulf with a copious Glossary, Pref-ace and Philological Notes. London. Pickering. The glossary was copious as it claimed to be, and in its day invaluable. It was indeed the foundation of Grein's Sprachschatz and so of the modern 'Grein-Köhler', the possession of which puts the merest beginner of today (provided of course that he knows a little Latin and German) in a position which one hundred years ago could only be gained by years of work among manuscripts still largely unedited.

[131] But already in the Preface we begin that swing from a blind belief in the historicity of the hero and all other characters in the poem, save perhaps Grendel and the Dragon, to the "mythological" or "allegorical" explanation of everything which is now as wearisome as it was once irresistibly fascinating. And already 're-search' begins to bury the poetry and the poet. What the author made of, and

---

1)   i.e. Widsith.

meant by his use of his material, is lost in speculation as to what is the nature and ultimate origin of that material in itself. So deep has the dust grown since that it is difficult now to see the poem beneath it.

It is to Germany, or to scholars there trained and writing in German, that, as I have said, the history of 'research' into Beowulf now passes. I say 'research' advisedly, for there was produced the materials for criticism (among much lumber of little use for any purpose) rather than criticism, constructive criticism, itself. One does not necessarily advance the knowledge of a man, or understanding of his mind, either by studying his ancestors, or by dissecting his person. Of these the less useful process is dissection. But dissection was for long the order of the day: dissection not only into heathen original and Christian interpolation, but even into the component lays which had somehow — it never became clear just how, fortuitously or arbitrarily — became conjoined into an 'epic.' These notions were grafted upon the criticism of Beowulf in Germany, and were derived from current classical scholarship.[2] For Beowulf, if welcomed there, was welcomed by scholars with firm beliefs in the accidental growth of epics, founded upon the authority of Wolf and Lachmann, and their sentence upon it was inevitable. As Earle says: "That great works in early literature forsooth were not made by art and device, but that they grew spontaneously and blindly, this was that imagination in the air which attended the first entertainment of Beowulf in the Fatherland." It is small wonder that little illuminating [132] general criticism was produced in such an air, or in later work still tainted with it. Though the contribution of the many illustrious German scholars cannot be overlooked, nor ever despised — we depend heavily in nearly every department upon their ingenious and patient labour — it can be understood why it is that Chambers notes (with something, it would seem, of unnecessary surprise) that it is on such a piece as Widsith that the older scholars were at their best: Kemble, Leo, Lappenberg, Ettmüller, and later Möller, Ten Brink, Müllenhof. It is precisely in dealing with such a piece — which has little poetry, and only that of a glittering catalogue when patience has rubbed the rust of oblivion and obscurity off the names therein — that 'research' is at its best, while the dissector and nature-myth-monger is most innocuous.

It is no great wonder either that in the appendix to the second edition (1932) of his Introduction, dealing with recent work down to 1930, Chambers begins with Klaeber's edition of Beowulf (1922, 1928[2]), and rightly calls it the most important since Kemble's nearly a century ago, in 1833. Since it is written in English, but in America, and yet by a German, it may be taken as symbolic of the changes in the world, and in the lesser world of Beowulf studies, in that intervening century. It is on bad paper, in ugly type, and a depressing binding, but amidst a vast amount of critical and illustrative matter of all sorts (often compressed to a distasteful form)

---

2)   It was not formerly usual for students to study the ancient northern tongues without being first trained in the yet older and more reverend tongues of the South.

it does also contain in its introduction studies of structure, tone, ideas, style and language, in which we have some synthesis as well as research, and some sanity as well as learning. That Klaeber in spite of an almost unique mastery of and familiarity with Old English verse idiom, and great tact in detail, is not a man of great originality nor of great penetration and poetic insight, cannot be helped. He has at least something of these things, and he regards them as important. Decision, a view, a conviction are now imperatively desired as Chambers rightly says: but oddly, since he is himself a master of indecision and takes characteristically as the motto of his [133] voluminous Introduction the words of Uncle Remus, when faced with the problem of the comparison of the history of the flood in his animal story and in Scripture : Dey mout er ben two deloojes : en den agin dey moutent (there might have been two deluges, and then again there might not). The wanderings of Israel in the desert would have been a fitter symbol of the history of Beowulf study. It wandered, with much retracing of steps, in a maze of theory for ninety years or more. I do not attempt to sketch the course of that peregrination. Synthesis and general literary interpretation and judgement was the most neglected, and it is not until we approach the year 1890 that attempts in this direction assume importance.

As a representative of the sort of effort then made at last to take a comprehensive view, amid the tulgey wood of conjecture and the burbling of the jabberwocks, we may take the Introduction which Earle wrote for his translation, The Deeds of Beowulf, in 1892. It is still very well worth reading, apart from his own private theory at the end, the political allegory to which I have already alluded, which only added one more tum-tum tree to the forest. There was also other work, of equal or greater importance on the continent, in Danish and in German. Almost the only considerable attempt at synthesis after that down to the period of the War, indeed until recently, was the sketch by Brandl in Pauls Grundriss. But of course all the time there was a constant stream of writings and monographs on, or touching on, Beowulf appearing, and contributing to the slow revolutionizing of the study. Among the most important I should class the metrical work of that renowned scholar Sievers, appearing first in the 'eighties' and issuing in his Altgermanische Metrik 1893. Since then the metre of Old English — after grammar and dictionary the first essential (and not the last luxury) of the study of poetry — has become a thing which [134] not only can be employed as a weapon of textual criticism, but can be appreciated as an instrument of art. Debate, of course, still rages. Odium prosodicum excels odium theologicum in bitterness, and is apt to seize on less intelligent minds, and has curiously a special attraction for those with small experience of poetry itself, and none of its composition. But the debate concerns rather musical, or prosodic, or phonetic theory, and metrical origins rather than the writing of verse. The essential 'metre' is established. We know what it was — the metric properly so-called, the measure, the pattern selection from the rough material of language. It is significant, nonetheless, of the prevailingly unpoetic attitude of criticism that to the metrical side of Beowulf, to its author's accomplishment in this essential of his art, reference is seldom made in general estimates. To the fundamental connexion between the nature of Old English verse and the structure of the poem itself, there is no reference whatsoever.

Turning once more to the general literary study of early poetry one of the principal things of the period to mention is W. P. Ker's Epic and Romance (1896); and one of the principal services of this work was, as has been said, to assist in shattering "the belief that (in the words he was fond of quoting) 'all epic poetry is written by A, B, and an Interpolator.' " The study of legends and their interconnexion, and of the history enshrined in legends, especially in Denmark, is in this period especially associated with the great [135] name of Olrik. The 'folk-lorists' are also busy, and especially in Panzer's Studien zum germanischen Sagengeschichte (1910) a vast knowledge of "folk-tale' is brought to bear on Beowulf. The distinction that became drawn between 'mythology' or 'myth' and 'folk-tale' has some value, and truth is contained in the view that has resulted from such research that "Beowulf's adventures with Grendel and Grendel's mother belonged rather to folk-lore than to mythology." The death-blow was dealt to the mythical-allegorical interpretation of the central Beowulf-story. At least it could not longer be believed that this story was actively mythopoetic, or even apprehended as a myth of nature, the sun, the seasons and the sea, when the poem was written, if indeed it ever had any such significance. Yet the exchange was hardly one of poetic profit. The primitive mythopoeia which is abandoned had at least something large and significant. A wide-spread motive of folk-tale — mere folk-tale, trivial folk-tale, as the language of somewhat cloyed research tends to call it — begins to seem hardly strong meat enough for a noble hall. But a really hard and sharp distinction cannot be drawn between mythology and folklore, and the 'mere folktale' exists rather as an abstraction of the student of origins than as a thing ever anywhere actually and individually met, certainly not set out in sonorous verse. At the same time modern archaeology began to be important for Beowulf study also — especially in the many essays of Knut Stjerna, and in further studies by Swedish historians and archaeologists (such as Professor Birger Nerman).

There was thus a slow shifting of view, as the result of the passing years, and of the general increase of knowledge in the archaeology, antiquities, and philology of the northern world. "The views as to the amalgamation of epics from earlier lays, which had seemed axiomative to Lachmann and his pupil Müllenhoff, and the mytho-allegorical and allegorical assumptions which Müllenhoff had inherited from Kemble, had ceased to be believed." Slowly but inevitably the obvious becomes discovered, that we have to deal with a poem by an Englishman using afresh ancient and traditional material, and it becomes plain that at any rate in addition to enquiring whence this matter came from, we must now consider what the poet did with it. If we ask that, there is still something lacking even in the major critics, the acknowledged pundits, the monuments of learning, indeed the very reverend masters from whom we humbly derive what little we know. Even, for instance, in the Lawrence-Klaeber-Chambers combine, [136] which Chambers himself, in his Introduction (2nd ed. pp. 392 ff) sets forth, perhaps a shade too solemnly, as an almost undivided trinity. The general agreement of this reigning triarchy — it does not reign in any part of its realm undisputed, though it reigns, I think, on the whole de jure — is that Beowulf is at least as much the work of one man and mind, in all its parts, as, say, an undisputed major play of Shakespeare, though it may have suffered accidents of tradition (even occasional alterations here and there) — as may an Elizabethan play. Its 'religion' belongs to that man and is not a product of mere editing. Its themes — especially the legendary allusions — though largely concerned with Scandinavian tradition and history, are English traditions, or traditions thoroughly Anglicized prior to being used by the poet, concerning these things, and are either as old as their importation into this island as are the idiom and the metric, or are at the least of very early importation. And the poem, essentially as we have it, though the language has been modernized and the dialect partly altered, was composed in the age of Bede — in the 'Anglian,' not the 'Saxon' parts of England.

All this is very satisfactory. But when we approach the final solemnity of Beowulf it is not possible to feel the same satisfaction. The major points I will approach now, by way of W. P Ker the revered master of Chambers. He would deserve reverence, of course, even if he had not ellor gehworfen on Frena wære (was turned elsewhere, to the Lord), on the high mountain in Switzerland. He was [137] a scholar who could read and move intelligently in many tongues, ancient and mediaeval and modern, often as illuminating himself as a critic of prose and verse as he was biting as a critic of critics. But this makes it the more unfortunate that on literature in the old Germanic tongues, among things of eminent worth, he has said several that were ill-considered. If one may say so humbly, he suffered perhaps from the weakness of his greatness. Though he seldom failed in sympathy and insight, in spite of the width of his literary and linguistic range, he could not achieve both depth and width equally, at least at all points. I cannot help feeling that stories and plots sometimes seemed triter to him, the much-read, than they were to some less-read of the old and mediaeval authors and their audiences. His influence has been potent, especially on his disciple Chambers, who often repeats and quotes his words.

I will quote you a well-known passage from his Dark Ages (pp. 252–3): 'A reasonable view of the merit of Beowulf is not impossible, though rash enthusiasm may have made too much of it, while a correct and sober taste may have too con-[138] temptuously refused to attend to Grendel or the firedrake. The fault of Beowulf is that there is nothing much in the story. The hero is occupied in killing monsters, like Hercules or Theseus. But there are other things in the lives of Hercules and Theseus besides the killing of the Hydra or Procrustes. Beowulf has nothing else to do, when he has killed Grendel and Grendel's mother in Denmark: he goes home to his own Gautland, until at last the rolling years bring the Firedrake and his last adventure. It is too simple. Yet the three chief episodes are well wrought and well diversified; they are not repetitions exactly; there is a change of temper between the wrestling with Grendel in the night at Heorot and the descent under water to encounter Grendel's mother; while the sentiment of the Dragon is different again. But the great beauty, the real value, of Beowulf is in its dignity of style. In construction it is curiously weak, in a sense preposterous; for while the main story is simplicity itself, the merely commonplace of heroic legend, all about it in the historic allusions there are revelations of a whole world of tragedy, plots different in import from that of Beowulf, more like the tragic themes of Iceland. Yet with this radical defect, a disproportion that puts the irrelevances in the centre and the serious things on the outer edges, the poem of Beowulf is unmistakably heroic and weighty. The thing itself is cheap; the moral and the spirit of it can only be matched among the noblest authors."

There is much that is excellent there. It becomes still more remarkable if one reflects that it was written at least thirty years ago and has not seriously been surpassed. Yet it curiously fails to penetrate the heart of the matter, and is content to state a paradox which should have strained belief as much then as it does now. Its chief virtue (not the one for which it is usually esteemed) is that it does accord at least [139] some attention to the monsters, in defiance of 'correct and sober taste.' The great Dragon is not quite turned down, though he is turned into a Firedrake, a little suggestive of some contraption or Brock-effect, for the astonishment of the simple. But the sentence chiefly to note is the concluding one of my quotation. "The thing itself is cheap; the moral and the spirit of it can only be matched among the noblest authors."

This — the contrast made between the radical defect and at the same time the dignity, loftiness in converse, well-wrought finish — has become a commonplace of the better criticism, a paradox the strangeness of which has been forgotten in the process of swallowing it on authority. We may compare Chambers in Widsith (p. 79), where he is studying the story of Ingeld son of Froda and his feud with the great Scylding house of Denmark, which is in Beowulf introduced merely as an allusion. "Nothing" he says "could better show the disproportion of Beowulf" — and here he goes into quotation marks — "which 'puts the mere irrelevances in the centre and the serious things on the outer edges' than this passing allusion to the story of Ingeld. For it is in this conflict between plighted troth and the duty of revenge that we have a situation, which the old heroic poets loved, and would not have sold for a wilderness of dragons." Alas! the poor gardener — he gave them flowers and they wanted only stones! And there is a flick of malice here, the sharper for coming from Chambers, the Beowulf-poet's best friend; we might have expected it of Jusserand, who speaks contemptuously of 'one of these ever-recurring treasures.' A wilderness of dragons! This is borrowed from the Book of St. Albans. Let the poet retort upon his critics from the same Book a 'pride of lions, a kindle of young cats, a raffle of knaves, and a gaggle of geese.' It would be more pointed and more just to the critics. As for the poem, one dragon does not [140] make a summer nor a host. And dragons, real dragons, essential to the plot, part both of the machinery and the ideas of a poem or tale, are actually rare. In all Northern literature there are only two that really count. If we omit from consideration the vast and vague figure of the Encircler of the World (Miðgarðsormr), the doom of the Gods, we have but the dragon of the Volsungs (Fáfnir), and Beowulf's bane.

It is true that both these are in Beowulf, one in the main story and the other spoken of by a minstrel praising Beowulf himself. But even this is not a "wilderness of dragons." Indeed the allusion to the more renowned and ancient worm killed by the Wælsing, is sufficient indication that the poet of Beowulf selected a dragon of well-founded purpose (or saw its significance in the plot as it had come down to him), even as he was careful to compare his hero, Beowulf, to the prince of the heroes of the North, the dragon-slaying Wælsing. He valued dragons, as rare as they were dire, as some do still. He liked them — as a poet not a zoologist; and he had his reasons.

But Chambers later repeats this same criticism; and even in the Foreword to Strong's translation we meet it still, though it is now toned down, and is no longer in Ker's actual words. There still, as we have seen, we are told that the folk-tale "has been allowed in Beowulf to usurp the place of honour, and to drive into episodes and digressions the things which should be the main stuff of a well-conducted epic."

Very well then: Beowulf is not a 'well-conducted epic.' It may, after all, be something altogether different. At any rate there is something irritatingly odd about all this. Higher praise than we find in Ker and Chambers could hardly be given to the detail, the tone, the style, the total effect of Beowulf. Yet this has [141] all been wasted, we are to understand, on an unprofitable theme, as if Milton had conducted a children's Bed-time Hour and told the story of Jack-and-the Beanstalk in excellent blank verse. Even if Milton had done this, we should probably look twice and pause to consider what in the process of his poetic effort he had made of it, what alchemy he worked upon his trivial tale.

A man may depict things lower than the highest he can conceive of; but not things higher. This high tone, this sense of propriety and dignity in converse alone, is evidence of the presence of a mind lofty and thoughtful. It is, one would have said, à priori improbable that such a person should have written 3000 lines (wrought to a high finish, we are told) on matter that is really not worth serious attention, that remains 'thin and cheap' when he has finished with it; or that he should in the selection of his material, in the choice of what to put forward, what to keep subordinate "upon the outer edges," have shown a puerile simplicity much below that of the characters he himself draws in his own poem. A theory that will at least allow us to believe that what he did was of design, and that for that design there is a defense that is still of some force, is plainly in itself a good deal more probable.

Why then have the great critics thought otherwise? There is a variety of reasons. The value of myth or folk-tale — the latter is the more patronizing term, and the more misleading, for 'folk-tales' contain a certain amount of what actually is thin and cheap, with little potential virtue, besides much that is far more powerful, and which cannot be sharply separated from 'myth' being derived from it, or capable in poetic hands of turning into it — the virtues of 'myth' are at once vaster and more vague, less able to be penned on paper by plain reasoning than those of heroic legend on what would be called a strictly human scale. It is quite possible to be moved by 'myth' [142] and yet misunderstand the sensation — to deny it, or ascribe it wholly to something that is also present, style, tone, or what not. The sophisticated mind, or 'correct and sober taste,' may refuse to admit that there can be anything in ogres or dragons, since it believes that such things have in our day long been relegated to the nursery (whence they are now being cast forth onto the rubbish heap). O Impoverished day! But it is not the first time that valuable things have been cast upon the rubbish heap at the bidding of fashion — to be painfully sought for again later. 'Myth' also labours under this disadvantage — it is at its best when it is treated by an author who feels, rather than makes explicit (even to himself), what his theme portends; who even presents it as a fact in time and bolsters it about with history (as our poet has done). A myth must be incarnate in human form, and better also in place and time. Myth too points no 'moral', and so, if you are looking for a moral and like it pointed, as the hero-worshippers do — how they seize on Byrhtwold's words in Maldon! — you are puzzled or disappointed. It follows that the defender of the mythical is also handicapped — unless he is careful he will kill what he is studying by vivisection, and the myth will turn into a formal even mechanical allegory.

We have also, of course, in the criticism of the 'virtue' of old tales and stories to face what might almost be called a Shakespeare-complex, certainly a drama complex. We must have tragedy, and tragic conflict, and that of an especial kind, a kind and form that drama could treat with success. If other modes of imagination, or of presentation, are not wholly ruled out, at least the taste for them is blunted or confused. They are appreciated or comprehended, or they are judged by criteria that do not apply. [143] And on top of all lies still the shadow of 'research.' The story of Beowulf is told to you, you have only to read the poem to get it, such as it is. Research is here quite unnecessary — except of course in an enquiry into origins or parallels, and such 'research' does not lead you into the higher regions of literature. But the allusions in Beowulf are half-tellings, or hints, or mere names, and these require a great deal of 'research.' So much that there is not much time left for the poem in general; so much that you come eventually to value the "outer edges" chiefly — especially since there you find the kind of tragic stories, of inner and external conflict, that your prejudices of taste prefer. Moreover the tragic heroic 'lays,' research suggests, were actually in point of time and development older — what more needed to convince the antiquarian of their superior worth? He becomes seriously annoyed with the tantalizing allusiveness of Beowulf, and feels cheated. Though he might reflect that it is time rather than Beowulf that has cheated him. Had time been less chary, we should have had plenty of this heroic stuff to feed him with, maybe nearly the whole catalogue of Widsith and more besides, and he could have left Beowulf alone for rarer and more discerning palates.

'Nonsense!' the hero-worshippers cry in chorus. 'The heroic stories are in themselves essentially more valuable!' There is no disputing about tastes, it is said, foolishly; for we must or should dispute about them. Yet on this point there has indeed been hardly any dispute. The proposition seems to have been passed as self-evident. I would challenge it. I should like to know why.

[144] I do not question the virtue of heroic or 'tragic' stories, but their exclusive claims. There are others; and I do not see why we need even debate which is in general, or as a kind, more valuable. Some 'fairy stories' are very poor even in their own line; some are very great in any line. Some heroic-tragic stories are potent, some are dismal failures. In any case Chambers is not, I think, very happy in his particular choice. He gives battle on dubious ground. In so far as we can now grasp its detail and atmosphere the tale of Ingeld the twice faithless, the easily persuaded (and perhaps not too intelligent) is chiefly interesting as an episode in a longer theme, as part of a tradition, that had acquired legendary and dramatically personalized form, concerning moving events in history, the arising of Denmark and the wars in the isles of the North. In itself it is not a supremely potent story (qua 'plot,' there may have been a treatment that made it so).

Let us get rid, then, of the cant, as it has almost become, on this subject. There is no indefinable magical virtue about heroic-tragic stories as such, and apart from the particular merits of each individually (especially as handled by individual authors). The recipe for such stories is after all as "simple" and as "typical" as that of "folk-tales." Even simpler. It is arguable that they are even simpler to manage. There are in any case many good heroes (and rather similar), but there are few good dragons (and each different). Beowulf's dragon, if you wish really to criticize, is not to be criticized for being a dragon, but rather for not being dragon enough, plain pure fairy-story dragon. Although there are in the poem some vivid touches (2285, 2293 ff) of the right kind, in which the dragon is real worm, with a bestial life and thought of its own,[†] the conception nonetheless approaches draconitas [145] rather than draco — a personification of malice, greed, destruction (the evil side of heroic life), and of the undiscriminating cruelty of fortune that distinguishes not good or bad (the evil aspect of all life). But for Beowulf, the poem, this is as it should be. In this poem the balance is nice, but it is preserved. The vast

---

† Þa se wyrm onwoc, wroht wæs geniwad, stonc þa æfter stane . . . hat 7 hreohmod hlæw oft ymbe hreaf, ealne utan weard (then the dragon awoke, the strife was renewed, a stench arose from the stone . . . Hot and fury-minded, he searched all around the outside of the barrow).

symbolism is near the surface of the exterior narrative, but it does not quite burst through and become allegory. Something more significant than a standard hero, a man faced with a foe greater than any human enemy of house or realm, is before us, and yet incarnate in time, walking in heroic history, and treading the named lands of the North. And this we are told is the "radical defect" of <u>Beowulf</u>, that its poet coming in a time rich in the legends and histories of heroic men, has used them afresh in an original fashion, he has given us not just one more, but some-thing different, something unique, a measure and an interpretation of them all.

Let us now consider the <u>foe</u> — the dragon. I doubt very much whether an-cient taste was quite what Chambers would have us believe. These ancient min-strels, or "old heroic poets": as far as we know anything about them, we know this. There was among them a strange unanimity — the prince of the heroes of the North, supremely memorable, whose fame æ <u>man uppi</u> (while men still live), was the Wælsing or Völsungr — Sigemund (Old English), Sigurðr, Siegfried. And his most memorable deed, from which in Norse he derived his title <u>Fáfnisbani</u>, was the kill-ing of a dragon, of <u>the</u> dragon, the prince of legendary worms. Although there is plainly a considerable difference between the ancient form of the story alluded to in <u>Beowulf</u>, already it had for the author these two salient features — the Dragon, the killing of which is mentioned as his greatest deed, and the supreme glory of the dragon-slayer: <u>he was wreccena wide mærost ofer werþeode</u> (he was the most widely known of warriors-in-exile throughout the nations of men).

And of course, a dragon is not an idle or silly tale. Whatever dire origins He has in prehistoric facts or fears, the dragon as we have him in legend, is one of the [146] more potent creations of men's imagination; richer in significance than his barrow is in gold. Even today you may find men not ignorant of legend and litera-ture, who have heard about the hero, and indeed seen him, and who yet, though they would scarcely think of writing an heroic tale, have been caught by the fas-cination of the worm.

Though this may seem an unpardonable digression, in the manner of the author of <u>Beowulf</u>, — I will quote you two modern poems on the dragon. The two together, whatever their defects as poems, or dragon-poems, are in some respects, I think, more important for <u>Beowulf</u>-criticism (for which they were not written) than much that has been written with that purpose.

[147]

Eft ongan eldo gebunden gioguðe cwíðan He wintrum fród worn gemunde
(Afterwards it happened that the man bound with age lamented for his youth.
He, wise in winters, remembered much.)

(i)

Iúmonna Gold Galdre Bewunden.

When the moon was new and the sun young
of silver and gold the gods sung;

in the green grass they silver spilled,
the white waters they with gold filled.
Ere the pit was dug or Hell yawned,
ere dwarf was bred or dragon spawned,
there were elves of old, and strong spells
under green hills in hollow dells
they sang as they wrought many fair things,
the bright crowns of the elf-kings.
But their doom fell, and their song waned,
by iron hewn and by steel chained.
Greed that sang not, nor with mouth smiled,
in dark holes their wealth piled,
graven silver and carven gold:
over Elvenhome the shadow rolled.

There was an old dwarf in a dark cave,
silver and gold his fingers clave
with hammer and tongs and anvil-stone
he worked his hands to the hard bone,
and coins he made and strings of rings,
and thought to buy the power of kings.
But his eyes grew dim and his ears dull,
and the skin yellow on his old skull;
through his bony claw with a pale sheen
the stony jewels slipped unseen.
No feet he heard, though the earth quaked,
when the young dragon his thirst slaked,
and the stream smoked at his dark door,
and flames hissed on the dank floor.
He died alone in the red fire,
and his bones were ash in the hot mire.

There was an old dragon under grey stone;
his red eyes blinked as he lay alone.
His joy was dead and his youth spent,
he was knobbed and wrinkled and his limbs bent
with the long years to his gold chained;
in his heart's furnace the fires waned.
To his belly's slime gems stuck thick,
silver and gold he would snuff and lick —
he knew the place of the least ring
beneath the shadow of his black wing.

Of thieves he thought on his hard bed,
and he dreamed that on their flesh he fed,
their bones crushed and their blood drank:
his ears drooped and his breath sank.
Mail-rings rang. He heard them not.
A voice echoed in his deep grot:
a young warrior with a bright sword
called him forth to defend his hoard.
His teeth were knives, and of horn his hide,
but iron tore him, and his flame died.

There was an old king on a high throne:
his white beard lay on knees of bone;
his mouth savoured neither meat nor drink,
nor his ears song; he could only think
of his huge chest with carven lid
where pale gems and gold lay hid,
in secret treasury in the dark ground
whose strong doors were iron-bound.
        The swords of his thanes were dull with rust,
his glory fallen, his rule unjust,
his halls hollow, and his bowers cold,
but king he was of elvish gold.
He heard not the horns in the mountain pass,
he smelt not the blood on the trodden grass,
but his halls were burned, his kingdom lost;
in a cold pit his bones were tossed.

There is an old hoard in a dark rock
forgotten behind doors none can unlock;
that grim gate no man can pass.
on the mound grows the green grass;
there sheep feed and the larks soar,
and the wind blows from the sea-shore.
While gods wait and the elves sleep,
its old secret shall the earth keep.

(ii)

Atol inwit gæst
(terrible unwanted guest)

Once the worm-laid egg broke in the wood,
I came forth shining into the trembling wood,
The sun was on my scales, dew upon the grasses,
the cool, sweet grasses, and the budding leaves.
I wooed my speckled mate. We played at druery
And sucked warm milk dropping from the goats' teats.

Now I keep watch on the gold in my rock cave
In a country of stones: old deplorable dragon,
watching my hoard. In winter night the gold
Freezes through toughest scales my cold belly.
The jagged crowns and twisted cruel rings,
Knobbly and icy are old dragon's bed.

Often I wish I had not eaten my wife,
Though worm grows not to dragon, till he eat worm.
She could have helped me, watch and watch about,
Guarding the hoard. Gold would have been the safer.
I could uncoil my weariness at times and take
A little sleep, sometimes when she was watching.

Last night under the moon-set a fox barked,
Woke me. Then I knew I had been sleeping,
Often an owl flying over the country of stones
Startles me, and I think I must have slept
Only a moment. That very moment a man
Might have come out of the cities, stealing, to get my gold.

They make plots in the towns to steal my gold.
They whisper of me in a low voice, laying plans,
Merciless men. Have they not ale upon the benches,
Warm wife in bed, singing, and sleep the whole night?
But I leave not the cave, but once in winter
To drink of the rock-pool: in summer twice.

[148] They feel no pity for the old lugubrious dragon.
O Lord that made the dragon, grant me peace!

> But ask not that I should give up the gold,
> Nor move, nor die; Others would get the gold.
> Kill rather, Lord, the men and the other dragons
> That I may sleep, go when I will to drink!

[149] These have at any rate 'a sense of proportion' lacked by Beowulf. They have not even any 'outer edges' at all. They are just wild folk-tale and nothing else. And worse still one of the ever-recurring treasures recurs again. But they are not by beer-fuddled Anglo-Saxons. They have, in fact, no excuse.

So much, at the moment, for the foe. If we return to the hero, we find a curious thing: we have not denied his value by accepting Beowulf, Grendel, dragon and all. Let us have our old heroes — men caught in a net of fate, or torn between duties equally sacred, dying with back to the wall against human enemies. Yet without Beowulf, to me at any rate, the Germanic hero, of the sort Chambers insists on having and declares that the 'old poets' would not have sold for a wilderness of dragons, is often an animal in a trap, fierce, sad, brave, and bloody, but not wholly intelligible (not always very intelligent), as moving as a baited badger. Or rather, I fancy Beowulf plays a larger part than is recognized in assisting in the understanding of him; and if these very critics had not had Beowulf to read, they would have less esteemed the other heroes — unless of course they are merely counting the heads of slain in the spirit of the game-hunter.

The heroic lay may have dealt in its own way, more brief and vigorous perhaps, though perhaps also at times more harsh and noisy — Chambers himself has made a motor-bicycle the symbol of the lay, and a Rolls-Royce of the epic — with the action of a hero, pitted against a set of circumstances, which conform more or less to the simple recipe for an heroic situation. [150] In it we could have seen the exaltation of the will undefeated, which receives doctrinal expression in the mouth of Byrhtwold at the battle of Maldon:

> Hige sceal þe heardra, heorte þe cenre,
> mod sceal þe mara þe ure mægen lytlað.

(The spirit shall be more inflexible, the heart more bold, the courage greater, as our strength grows less.)

This expression we are probably not to take as struck off by Byrhtwold himself in the heat of battle (though he may well have said precisely these words), nor invented by the poet of Maldon, but as a solemn repetition of a received and honoured, and indeed honourable gnomē, a terse repetition of a dominant idea.

But, though with sympathy and patience we might gather from stray words, from a line here or a tone there, the background of imagination which gives to this indomitability, this paradox of defeat inevitable yet unacknowledged, its real significance — it is in Beowulf that a poet has devoted a whole poem to the theme, has drawn the struggle in vaster proportions on a larger stage, so that we may see man at war with the infest world, and his inevitable overthrow in Time. The particular and accidental is on the 'outer edges,' the essential is in the very centre, or rather the spirit which informs the whole.

Of course I do not mean to say that the poet, if questioned, would have replied in the Anglo-Saxon equivalents of such terms. Had the matter been so explicit to him, his poem would certainly have been the worse. Nonetheless we at any rate against his great scene, hung with tapestries woven of ancient tales of ruin (each in itself a little world), may see the hæleþ walk. And at the end we perceive that he who wrote hæleþ under heofenum may have meant, in dictionary terms, 'heroes under the heavens,' or 'mighty men on earth,' but he and his audience were thinking of the eormengrund, the vast earth, ringed with gársecg, the shoreless ocean, beneath the sky's inaccessible roof, whereon as in a little circle of light, defended by mortal hands, men with courage as their stay went forward to that battle with the dark and its offspring, which ends for all, even the great champions, in defeat.

[151] That even this 'geography,' once held as a material fact, might now by the supercilious be classed as a mere folk-tale, affects its value little or nothing. It transcends astronomy. Indeed astronomy has done nothing to make the island more secure, or the outer seas less formidable. Beowulf is not the hero of an 'heroic lay' — not quite. He has no enmeshed loyalties or hapless love. He is a man, and that for him and many is sufficient tragedy.

It is not an irritating accident that the tone of Beowulf is so high, and its theme so low. It is the theme in its deadly seriousness, that makes us feel so keenly the dignity of tone. So deadly and ineluctable is the theme that those who in the little circle of light play only with the toys of wit and refinement, looking not to the battlements, either hear it not at all, or recoiling, shut their ears to it. Death comes to the feast, and they say He gibbers.

For it has been too little observed that all the machinery of 'dignity' is to be found elsewhere. Cynewulf or the author of Guthlac had a great command of dignified verse. In them you will find well-wrought finish, weighty words, lofty converse, all precisely of that which we are told is "the real beauty of Beowulf." Yet it cannot be disputed that Beowulf is more beautiful; that each line there is more significant, than a line (even when, as occasionally happens, it is the same line) in the other long Old English poems. Where then resides the special virtue of Beowulf, if the common element which of course to some extent belongs to the language itself, to a greater extent to a literary tradition — if this is deducted? It must be in the theme, and the spirit this has infused into the whole. [152] It has been said that there is mirth and music and gentle talk in Beowulf, but 'the light is but a foil to the dark.' This should perhaps have been reversed. The dark is a foil to the light. The dark is the background, and the light is encircled by it. But not of course because mirth and music were 'vain' and the light too fleeting for esteem. They were valued passionately. But if we now like to forget the encircling foe and its ultimate victory on the temporal plane, for each individually and for mankind as a whole, despising Beowulf and preferring politics and economics, the poet did not forget. He was on a besieged island and he knew it. It was the foundation of his love of the island.

It is at this point that the question of Cain becomes most important. It has long been used as a stick to beat an ass. They (says Jusserand, meaning the Anglo-Saxons who he seems to think wrote Beowulf in committee over a surfeit of beer) fight against the monsters of Scandinavian mythology and see in them the descendants of Cain. But here is the critical point for criticism (as distinct from contempt) to seize. I have often laboured this point before. But — though I am not a man, as I say, so diligent as to read all the books on <u>Beowulf</u> — Chambers is as far as I am aware, the only one who has grasped the point (and recorded this in print), in one aspect at least. <u>He has put it in words I shall not attempt to better — indeed my chief criticism of them is that they are destructive of the traditional strictures upon Beowulf to which he still appears to some extent to adhere. They should lead direct to a more penetrating apprehension of Beowulf and its theme as a whole; but do not seem quite to have done this.</u> In any case they cut to the heart of the christian-heathen controversy, and dismiss the illusion of a muddleheaded Anglo-Saxon who could not clearly distinguish between paganism and Christianity.

To quote Sir Arthur Quiller-Couch:

> I ask you but to note the difference of note, of accent, of mere music. And I have quoted to you but a passage of the habitual Homer. To assure ourselves that he can rise even from this habitual height to express the extreme of majesty and of human anguish in poetry which betrays no false note, no strain upon the store of emotion man may own with self-respect and exhibit without derogation of dignity, turn to the last book of the *Iliad*, and read of Priam raising to his lips the hand that has murdered his son. I say confidently that no one unable to distinguish this, as poetry, from the very best of *Beowulf* is fit to engage upon business as a literary critic.

[153] The context is a comparison between <u>Beowulf</u> and Homer (containing the words about the folk-tale being 'a good servant but a bad master' that I quoted above). The comparison goes naturally very much against <u>Beowulf</u>. But as Chambers says:

> "A champion of <u>Beowulf</u> might reply that it is doing that poem a great honour to pit it (even in comparison to its disadvantage) against the greatest thing in all secular literature — the twenty-fourth <u>Iliad</u>: perhaps the greatest thing even when read in translation: and what in the original? in language compared with which . . . 'Virgil's seems elaborate, Dante's crabbed and Shakespeare's barbarous.' "

Yet Professor Chadwick has shown us how a study of <u>Beowulf</u> can be made to throw new light upon the study of Homer. For in both we have a picture of society in its Heroic Age. The society of <u>Beowulf</u> is in many respects cruder and less developed, just as the hall of Hrothgar is a less elaborate thing than the hall of Odysseus. But there is a fundamental likeness in the life depicted.

Now in Anglo-Saxon England this Heroic Age was brought into contact with Christianity, and with all the civilization of the Mediterranean which came to England with Christianity. It is just this which makes the Seventh Century so exciting an epoch. Christian gentleness, working upon the passions of the Heroic Age, produces at once a type which is the rough outline of what later becomes the mediæval ideal of the knight or the modern ideal of the gentleman.

In the Heroic Age, elementary passions are still very near the surface. This causes the tension in the twenty-fourth <u>Iliad</u>. In spite of the command of Zeus, in spite of the laws of hospitality, there is always the possibility that the wrath of Achilles may overmaster him and that he may slay Priam within his hut. And the history of Europe during the incursions of the Germanic barbarians tells of many a deed as grisly as that to which Achilles feared he might, despite himself, be driven.

[154] In the epoch of Beowulf as (he says) a Heroic Age more wild and primitive than that of Greece is brought into touch with Christendom, with the Sermon on the Mount, with Catholic theology and ideas of Heaven and Hell. We see the difference if we compare the wilder things — the folk-tale element — in <u>Beowulf</u> with the wilder things in Homer. Take for example the tale of Odysseus and the Cyclops — the No-Man trick. Odysseus is struggling with a monstrous and wicked foe, but he is not exactly thought of as struggling with the powers of darkness. Polyphemus, by devouring his guests, acts in a way which is hateful to Zeus and the other gods yet the Cyclops is himself god-begotten and under divine protection, and the fact that Odysseus has maimed him is a wrong which Poseidon is slow to forgive.

monstrum horrendum, informe, ingens (a horrible monster, unformed, bizarre).

But the gigantic foes whom Beowulf has to meet are identified with the foes of God. Grendel and the dragon are constantly referred to in language which is meant to recall the powers of darkness with which Christian men felt themselves to be encompassed. They are the 'inmates of hell,' 'adversaries of God,' 'offspring of Cain,' 'enemies of mankind.' Consequently the matter of the main story of <u>Beowulf</u>, monstrous as it is, is not so far removed from common mediæval experience as it seems to us to be from our own. . . . . Grendel hardly differs" — this is going too far, but I shall return to this point — "from the fiends of the pit who were always in ambush to waylay a righteous man. And so Beowulf, for all that he moves in the world of the primitive Heroic Age of the Germans, nevertheless is almost a Christian Knight. If Spenser had known

Beowulf, he would have found a hero much nearer to his Red Cross
Knight than Achilles or Odysseus . . . ."

. . . . Here we find the character of the Christian hero, the mediæval Knight, emerging from the turmoil of the Germanic Heroic Age.
Not but what many of Beowulf's virtues can be traced back to that Heroic Age. For example, Beowulf's loyalty, when he refuses to take the
throne at the expense of his young cousin Heardred, is a part of the
Teutonic code of honour, though a part often not put into practice. But
the emphasis placed upon gentleness, humility, and judgement to come
is a thing in which we can trace the [155] influence of the new faith. In
his dying speeches, Beowulf rejoices that he has sought no cunning
hatred, nor sworn oaths unrighteously: 'For all this may I have joy,
though sick with deadly wounds, that the Ruler of men may not charge
me with the slaughter of kinsfolk.' And he thanks the Lord of all, the
King of Glory, that he has been able win such treasure for his people.
And so the poem ends:

> So did the people of the Geatas, his hearth-companions,
> bewail the fall of their lord: they said that he was a mighty
> king, the mildest and gentlest of men, most kind to his people,
> and the most desirous of praise.

It was with reason that Professor Earle quoted the words of Sir
Ector de Maris over Lancelot dead as being 'like an expansion of these
closing lines of the Beowulf':

> And now I dare say, said Sir Ector, thou, Sir Launcelot,
> there thou liest, that thou were never matched of earthly
> knight's hand; and thou were the courteoust knight that
> ever bore shield; and thou were the truest friend to thy lover
> that ever bestrad horse; and thou were the truest lover of a
> sinful man that ever loved woman; and thou were the kind-
> est man that ever struck with sword; and thou were the
> goodliest person that ever came among press of knights; and
> thou were the meekest man and gentlest that ever ate in hall
> among ladies; and thou were the sternest knight to thy mor-
> tal foe that ever put spear in the rest.

And the stories told by Bede are enough to prove that the
combination in Beowulf of valour with mildness and gentleness is no
mere idealization. Seventh-Century England did produce men of that
type . . ."

[156] Several distinct points have here combined. Beowulf as an historical document of the seventh and eighth centuries; the absolute literary ability of its author; the relative potentiality for poetry of Old English, as compared with Greek; the mood of the times and the author, and the background, the essential cast of the imaginative apprehension of the world. The last is the one which directly concerns us. The history of the early Christian period in England is for us only a means to the understanding of this. We have to consider the product of a fusion, not a half-hearted lukewarm affair, but one filled with thought and emotion. One of the most potent elements in this is the Northern courage — the theory, one might call it, of courage, that is the great contribution of early Northern literature. This is not a military judgement — we are not here asserting that, if the Trojans had employed a Northern king and his warriors, they would have driven Agamemnon and Achilles and all the Achaeans into the sea more decisively than the Greek hexameter routs the alliterative line (though this is highly probable). But rather — since with due reserve we may here turn to the tradition of pagan imagination in Icelandic — with the central position this creed of resistance holds in the North. Ker has said: 'What is distinctively Northern in the myth of the Twilight of the Gods is the strength of its theory of life. It is this intensity of courage that distinguishes the Northern mythology ... from all others. The last word of the Northmen before their entry into the larger world of Southern culture, their last independent guess at the secret of the Universe, is given in the Twilight of the Gods. As far as it goes, and as a working theory, it is absolutely impregnable. It is the assertion of the individual freedom against [157] all the terrors and temptations of the world. It is absolute resistance, perfect because without hope. The Northern gods have an exultant extravagance in their warfare which makes them more like Titans than Olympians; only they are on the right side, though it is not the side that wins. The winning side is Chaos and Unreason; but the gods, who are defeated, think that defeat no refutation. The latest mythology of the North is an allegory of the Teutonic self-will, carried to its noblest terms . . .".

This is a summing up of the specifically Norwegian-Icelandic traditions; but it is plain that apart from the particular form of the myths (what the heathen English mythology was we do not know) that the same temper was possessed by the ancient English — it survived among the feudal lieges and retainers of the great nobles and houses into the tenth century.

Christianity infused into the northern world (if we consider England), or the infusion of the North into the southern world (if we consider Europe more generally) make what we call the mediæval. That process begins at once — some of the most fundamental changes of that alchemy are almost immediate, indeed instantaneous. In a Christian country (including one thoroughly reacquired by Christendom as was England) it is not a random mixture, to be judged by the vagaries of wandering and ill-instructed vikings who had no foothold in Christendom; it is a conversion. It is as difficult to separate out the thread of old and new as it is in the case of an individual. The new is a spirit, the old is the material. You do not have to wait until all the tales and lays and the native traditions of the older world have been forgotten; for the minds which still retain [158] them are changed, and the memories themselves are viewed in a different perspective. It would thus be a lesser error to think of Beowulf as an early medieval poem than a 'primitive Teutonic' one — though it is actually something different from either, and in some respects better than either: an Old English poem. It has a kinship with Cynewulf, St. Guthlac, Ælfric, even with mediæval homilies, no less than with the lays of the gods and heroes of the North preserved in Icelandic.

Take Ælfric, for instance; he is classed by Ker as belonging "to the Latin world, the common educational tradition." Yet his homilies are written in Anglo-Saxon, in a prose "which is English in rhythm and founded on the model of Teutonic verse," though it is also greatly under the influence of Latin ornamented prose. And even the bogies of Ælfric, the Sigelhearwan, with fiery eyes, that are regarded as devils, and yet equated with Ethiopians, have a purely native name and derive in one line from native northern 'folk-tale,' and are distant relatives of Grendel.

The earlier age was not less learned than the days of Eadgar and Æthelred II, but more learned and certainly not less two-sided. The accidents of survival, which have left so little of the native tradition, should not obscure this fact. Not all the learning was in 'Book-Latin,' nor all the love of the learned for what was written in the new letters. There was never any tendency for a new pseudo-Latin people to be fabricated — within Christendom there was the Angolcyn, converted, yet nonetheless of the North, with its own language, its own laws, its own history, and its own poetry. And these were not beneath the study of the early scholars, such as Aldhelm, whom Ælfred considered the best of the vernacular poets (though his vernacular verse is lost); and they were still loved no less by Ælfred the revivalist than the Latin learning and education which [159] he strove to re-establish. It is the blending of the Northern pagan and Christian. It is thus we have available to a poet who sets out to write a poem such as Beowulf — write it on a scale and with a structure of epic proportions quite unlike any mere minstrel's lay — both education in the newer sense of the word, and also a body of northern historical and legendary tradition for the educated and christianized mind to ponder. Virgil, Statius, and Lucan are cited among the books studied in the school of York by Alcuin in his poem on the church of York — Alcuin was born about A.D. 735, and must have been nearly contemporary, possibly actually contemporary, with the author of Beowulf. It has been held that the influence, if no more than the exciting of emulation, of the classical Latin epic, is perceptible in Beowulf, and a necessary part of the explanation of the development of the long poem in England in the eighth century. However that may be, it is plain that the native tradition was itself kept alive by 'education.' This is clear both from the volume that it once possessed, and its connected character. Both these are evidenced even in Beowulf, a poem that merely draws upon the traditions at will for its own purposes, in the manner in which a modern poet might draw upon history or the classics and expect his references and allusions to be understood. The poet of Beowulf was in fact quite learned enough in this vernacular department to have an historical, even an antiquarian, perspective. He is not a half-Christian because he describes heroic seaburial, or the blazing pyre! He casts his time back into the long-ago, because the long-ago has for him a poetical attraction, and also because, so set, the struggle he depicts stands out all the more naked. He knew much about those days, and though his knowledge may [160] have been rich, rather than accurate with the accuracy of modern archaeology (such as that is), one thing he knew clearly — it was the marrow of his theme — was that the days were heathen. This is specifically recorded even of Hroðgar and his Danes in the famous passage 175 ff: Hwílum hie gehéton æt hærgtrafum wígweorþunga (At times they offered — at the heathen temple — sacrifice to heathen idols) (of which more later). Avoidance of all obvious anachronisms in this respect (such as are found heedlessly in Judith, for instance), and the absence of definite Christian terms and names, is natural, essential, and plainly deliberate.* One can only be amazed that this silence has been construed as evidence of a half-baked Christianity. Of course we, at our distance of time, had we ancient English traditions like those of Scandinavia, to work upon, should in writing a poem about the pagan past no doubt attempt historical colour, and should not hesitate to trot out references to Woden and Þunor. But to expect the same of the Beowulf-poet is to misunderstand the situation. The English showed a liberalism and good sense in preserving the pagan ancestors but the gods were, or had been, gods — and false gods. They have faded now, so that we can feel only a distant antiquarian interest in their figures, once so dominant, and so strong. But that was not so in the seventh or eighth centuries. The last heathen kingdom, Sussex, had only been converted in 681-6. In protesting against the view that a man sufficiently cultured to write a long poem did not [161] clearly know the difference between Christian and pagan, we emphasize rather than minimize the potency still of paganism — as a belief or group of beliefs. Saxons in England, as the Saxons on the continent and Frisians still were later (and the Swedes later still) had been fanatically heathen. The pale lassitude, as it were, without resisting power, which we get in Bede's story of Coifi and the sparrow, even if it is itself historical, is not a picture that can be applied universally to Germanic heathendom, or to all parts of England. If the Incarnation and the Trinity, therefore, on the one hand are not referred to, on the other hand the gods of the old world are also suppressed, or referred to generally by the poet himself, speaking as a Christian, as the devil (gást-bona). Their names were not forgotten. In the Gnomic Verses of the Exeter Book

---

* It should be noted that Abel 108, Cain 108 (1261), only occur where the poet is speaking in his own person, and giving you his own view of the origin of the monsters, of human or half-human form — it is not intended to be a theory known to or propounded by Hroðgar! Hroðgar in fact denies any knowledge of Grendel's ancestry (1355).

we are told that <u>Wóden worhte wéos, wuldor Alwalda, rume roderas: þæt is ríce
God</u>. (Woden wrought idols, the All-Ruler the world, the wide heavens; that is the kingdom of
God.) But in <u>Beowulf</u> we get no heathen gods, only the Lord, the Almighty, often
<u>Metod</u> (Order or Ordainer) in which the conception of him falls back almost into
that of <u>wyrd</u>, the all-powerful and unintelligible, which remained and remains today a natural mode of reference to the scheme of the world as contrasted with the
individual will. This cannot be defended as archeologically strictly accurate for the
times depicted; we know nothing of ancient English accounts of their Gods; but of
neither <u>Þunor</u>, nor <u>Woden</u>, can they have formed anything but the merest glimmer of an Almighty God, at most. But the old English poet was not attempting ar-
chaeological accuracy in this point — and he had other models for his conception
of the noble pre-Christian: the Old Testament. The taboo its only to be expected.
It has been observed that in Ireland of the seventh century profane classical literature, with its inherent [162] mythology was widely cultivated even in monasteries,
in marked contrast to the Latin lands, where the pagan religion was still in being,
or later (as in Gaul) when a tradition of warfare had survived it. A foreign paganism has little danger.

It was part of the English temper — its strong Englishry, connected especially
with its dynasties, and noble houses, and many small courts — strengthened, it
may be, by the more inquisitive and less severe Celtic traditions of learning, that it
should preserve much of the vernacular tradition of the pagan past to interweave
with southern learning. The ancestors were not banned (as some would have
wished), but the gods could not yet be given the twilight reverence of antiquarian
fancy.*

There were not wanting (even in England) "Gallic" voices. Abroad they are
stronger and more frequent. St. Paulinus of Nola (born at Bordeaux), in the fifth
century, had cried that "Hearts [163] vowed to Christ have no welcome for the
goddesses of song; they are barred to Apollo." Sulpicius Severus in the preface to
his life of St. Martin asks: "What good will it do posterity to study the philosophy
of Socrates or to read the battles of Hector?" Such utterances reflect the unease of
the Christian teacher amid the classical learning that by historical accident had
become associated with the Church. But the same severity is also occasionally

---

*   The special conditions in Iceland, and the very special nature of the fragments of Norse mythology,
must not be allowed to confuse the judgement of this matter. The Óðinn and Þórr of Snorri in the early
13th century, are nearly as remote from Wóden and Þunor or Ing as divine beings, and the persons of cult
and temple-worship, as Jupiter and Apollo in Ovid are from Greek <u>religion</u> in the days of the long-haired
Achaeans. As the names of the 'classical' gods eventually survived for all Christian children who learned
letters to read aloud because of the value set upon the ancient literature as literature, so it was in Iceland.
The northern gods or stories about them (very little understood — we can glimpse dark and terrible things
often in the tales, that were probably not perceived at all by the Icelanders who handed them on) were <u>nec-
essary</u> to courtly and <u>cultured</u> verse. But in the North there was a slow fading. In England there was a
definite and rapid (but at the same time astonishingly effective and deep-going) conversion taking place at
a much more primitive, more religious and less literary, stage.

found in dealing with the barbaric. Apocryphal, but nonetheless to be[†] noted as dramatizing an attitude that was possible, is the well known story concerning the Frank St. Wulfram of Sens. King Radbod of Frisia, the successor of Aldgísl who had harboured the English St. Wilfrid, was a fierce enemy of Christians and Franks, and the last defender both of Frisian heathendom and Frisian independence. The story tells that once he approached the baptismal font, but stopped on the way to ask Wulfram whether, if he were baptized, he might hope to meet in heaven his Frisian ancestors. 'Do not deceive thyself' was the reply; 'it is certain that they have received the just sentence of damnation.' Radbod therefore withdrew from the font, and said that he preferred to join his own people wherever they might be, rather than sit down in the Kingdom of Heaven with a handful of beggars. He remained heathen to his death in 719. One may be permitted to reflect that he was evidently imperfectly instructed and no fit candidate for baptism, while the missionary left much to be desired. But the story is chiefly of interest in showing a possible attitude to the ancestors — the heathen heroes; and on the other hand the <u>aristocratic</u> nature of pagan tradition

[164] It was perhaps not altogether in the result regrettable that the Gallic, or rather now Frankish, Church fell into confusion demoralization and decay, and that the re-energizing of it, and the reclamation by missions of Frisia and large areas of Germany, was due in chief measure to the English — of the age of <u>Beowulf</u> and its muddleheaded poet! — to whom may thus be ascribed the foundation of the mediæval church and Europe.

Yet even of the best known figure in that process, Alcuin, we have recorded a saying that sounds similar. In a letter to Speratus,[*] bishop of Lindisfarne, of A.D. 797 we read: Verba Dei legantur in sacerdotali convivio; ibi decet lectorem audiri, non citharistam, sermones patrum, non carmina gentilium. Quid Hinieldus cum Christo? Angusta est domus; utrosque tenere non poterit (Let the words of God be read at the refectory of the priests; there it is fitting that the lector be heard, not the lyre-player, the sermons of the fathers, not the songs of the heathens. What has Ingeld to do with Christ? Narrow is the house; it cannot hold both of them) — the King of Heaven must not be mentioned with pagan kings who are lamenting in hell.

But this is also evidence that in England even those trained and professed in religion could, whatever high authority felt, find room for both, and could preserve ancient heroic tradition. It might certainly be regarded by most then (as still) <u>indecens</u> (inappropriate) that the harpist should usurp the place of the lector in the

---

†   The missions to Frisia were English not Frankish — partly because of the interference of politics, and the intense hatred of Frisians, in their struggle for independence, of the Frankish realm. The missions were begun by Wilfrid in 679 and again by Wihtberht in 689, soon after Radbod's succession. Wulfram died in 695, and there is no evidence, outside the late <u>Vita Sancti Wulframni</u>, that he ever visited Frisia. Radbod died in 719.

*   The reference to Ingeld is not, however, in the received text of the letter (see Chambers nota to <u>Widsith</u> p. 78) and may possibly therefore not derive actually from Alcuin, though the name <u>Hinieldus</u> seems to show that it is of English origin.

refectory; but it was not necessarily improper that the same minds should contain
the old histories and the faith. This was evidently a prevalent feeling. "The house
is wide and has many rooms." To such a time and temper <u>Beowulf</u> belongs.

     The old gods disappeared. Partly because they were strong and still con-
nected in memory not only with such fairy-story matter as we find in <u>Gylfaginning</u>
but with religion; partly because [165] nonetheless their going was not disastrous
to the theme. But the heroic figures, the men of old, <u>hæleþ under heofenum</u> (heroes under the heavens) remained; and not only were they not wholly ousted by Moses
or the Israelite warriors, or by St. Matthew and St. Andrew, but coloured the whole
conception of these figures of Scripture as Christian tradition and mythology.

     A point especially to note in Chambers' words is this: <u>the Cyclops is himself</u>
<u>god-begotten, and under divine protection, and the fact that Odysseus has maimed</u>
<u>him is a wrong Poseidon is slow to forgive</u>." But of Grendel it is said <u>Godes yrre</u>
<u>bær</u> (he bore God's anger). God is on the side of him who wrestles with Grendel,
though He may accord victory to either side, and — viewed as <u>wyrd</u> (fate) — may
allow the ogre in certain cases to triumph.

               'per sidera testor,
          per superos atque hoc caeli spirabile lumen,
          tollite me, Teucri; quascumque abducite terras:
          hoc sat erit. scio me Danais e classibus unum
          et bello Iliacos fateor petiisse penatis.
          pro quo, si sceleris tanta est iniuria nostri,
          spargite me in fluctus vastoque immergite ponto;
          si pereo, hominum manibus periisse iuvabit.'
          dixerat et genua amplexus genibusque volutans
          haerebat. qui sit fari, quo sanguine cretus,
          hortamur, quae deinde agitet fortuna fateri.
          ipse pater dextram Anchises haud multa moratus
          dat iuveni atque animum praesenti pignore firmat.
          ille haec deposita tandem formidine fatur:
               'Sum patria ex Ithaca, comes infelicis Ulixi,
          nomine Achaemenides, Troiam genitore Adamasto
          paupere, mansissetque utinam fortuna! profectus.
          hic me, dum trepidi crudelia limina linquunt,
          immemores socii vasto Cyclopis in antro
          deseruere. domus sanie dapibusque cruentis,
          intus opaca, ingens. ipse arduus, altaque pulsat
          sidera; di talem terris averite pestem!
          nec visu facilis nec dictu adfabilis ulli;
          visceribus miserorum et sanguine vescitur atro.
          vidi egomet duo de numero cum corpora nostro
          prensa manu magna medio resupinus in antro
          frangeret ad saxum, sanieque aspersa natarent
          limina; vidi atro cum membra fluentia tabo
          manderet et tepidi tremerent sub dentibus artus:
          haud impune quidem, nec talia passus Ulixes

oblitusve sui est Ithacus discrimine tanto.
nam simul expletus dapibus vinoque sepultus
cervicem inflexam posuit, iacuitque per antrum
immensus saniem eructans et frusta cruento
per somnum commixta mero, nos magna precati
numina sortitique vices una undique circum
fundimur, et telo lumen terebramus acuto
ingens quod torva solum sub fronte latebat,
Argolici clipei aut Phoebeae lampadis instar,
et tandem laeti sociorum ulciscimur umbras.
sed fugite, o miseri, fugite atque ab litore funem
rumpite . . .
nam qualis quantusque cavo Polyphemus in antro
lanigeras claudit pecudes atque ubera pressat,
centum alii curva haec habitant ad litora vulgo
infandi Cyclopes et altis montibus errant.
tertia iam Lunae se cornua lumine complent
cum vitam in silvis inter deserta ferarum
lustra domosque traho, vastosque ab rupe Cyclopas
prospicio sonitumque pedum vocemque tremesco.
victum infelicem, bacas lapidosaque corna,
dant rami, et vulsis pascunt radicibus herbae.
omnia conlustrans hanc primum ad litora classem
conspexi venientem. huic me, quaecumque fuisset,
addixi: satis est gentem effugisse nefandam.
vos animam hanc potius quocumque absumite leto.'
Vix ea fatus erat summo cum monte videmus
ipsum inter pecudes vasta se mole moventem
pastorem Polyphemum et litora nota petentem,
monstrum horrendum, informe, ingens, cui lumen ademptum.
trunca manum pinus regit et vestigia firmat;
lanigerae comitantur oves; ea sola voluptas;
solamenque mali . . .
postquam altos tetiget fluctus et ad aequora venit,
luminis effossi fluidum lavit inde cruorem
dentibus infrendens gemitu, graditurque per aequor
iam medium, necdum fluctus latera ardua tinxit.

['In heaven's name,' he said,
'By all the powers, I beg you —
Oh, by the light and air we breathe! Take me
With you, Trojans! Anywhere at all
Will be good enough for me. I am, I know it,
One of the Danaans, one from the fleet;
I won't deny I fought to take Troy's gods.
For that, if so much harm came of our devilry,
Cut me to bits, scatter me on the water,
Drop me in the sea. If I must die,
Death at the hands of men will be a favor!'

With this he took our knees and groveled, kneeling,
Clinging there. We told him to speak out,
Say who he was, born of what blood, what fortune
Put him in such a panic; and my father
After a moment gave the man his hand
To calm him by that touch and sign of mercy.
In the end he put aside his fear and said:

'I am an Ithacan, of Ulysses' company —
That man beset by trouble. Achaemenidës
I'm called. My father, Adamastus, lived
In poverty, so I shipped out for Troy.
Would god our life of poverty had lasted!
My shipmates left me here, they all forgot me,
Scrambling to get away from the cave mouth
And frightfulness in the cavern of the Cyclops.
That is a blood-soaked hall of brutal feasts,
All gloom inside, and huge. The giant rears
His head against the stars. Oh heaven, spare earth
A scourge like this — unbearable to see,
Unreachable by anything you say.
The innards and the dark blood of poor fellows
Are what he feeds on; I myself looked on
When he scooped up two crewmen in his hand
Mid-cave, and as he lay back smashed them down
Against the rockface, making the whole floor
Swim with spattered blood; I saw him crunch
Those dead men running blood and excrement,
The warm flesh still a-quiver in his teeth.
Not that he did not suffer for the act!
Not that Ulysses put up with that outrage
Or lost his self-possession in the pinch.
Gorged with feasting and dead-drunk with wine,
The giant put down his lolling head, lay down
Enormous on the cave floor. In his sleep
He dribbled bile and bits of flesh, mixed up
With blood and wine. We prayed to the great gods,
Drew lots for duties, and surrounded him.
Then with a pointed beam bored his great eye,
His single eye, under his shaggy brow,
Big as a Greek shield or the lamp o' Phoebus.
So we got back at him — some cause for pride,
Avenging our friends' shades.
            As for yourselves,
Put out to sea, put out to sea, poor fellows;
Break your hawsers! Tall and dangerous
As Polyphemus, penning and milking sheep
In his rock cave, there are a hundred more
Unspeakably huge Cyclops everywhere
At large along these bays and mountain-sides.

And now three times the long-horned moon has filled
With a new glow since I've dragged out my days
In woods, among the wild things' lonely dens,
And from a peak spied on the Cyclops there,
My heart a-tremble at their great footfalls,
Their shouts. Thin fare I've had, such as the boughs
Would yield me: berries, cornel fruit, all stones,
With roots and grasses. As I looked out seaward
These were the first ships that I saw put in.
Whatever ships they might turn out to be,
I handed myself over. Boon enough
Just to escape these unholy savages.
Better you take this life, by any form
Of death you choose.'
     He had no sooner spoken
Than we all saw, high on the mountainside,
The shepherd Polyphemus' giant mass
In motion with his flocks, advancing shoreward.
Vast, mind-sickening, lumpish, heaven's light
Blacked out for him, he held a pine tree staff
To feel his way with, and the woolly sheep
Were all his company and the ease
Of comfort that he had.
On reaching the seashore and the deep water
He washed the fluid from his gouged eye-pit
And gnashed his teeth and groaned, then waded out
To the middle depth where still the swell came short
Of dampening his haunches.]

This is suggestive; and at this point in particular we may regret that we do
not know more about pre-Christian English beliefs. At any rate we may pause to
wonder whether something on the heathen side did not assist in the formation of
this attitude. It is possible to guess, with due caution, that there was a fundamental
difference between Northern and Greek gods. Though we may remember the
many points in which it does not work, there is probably truth in a generalization
that contrasts the "inhumanness" of the Greek deities, and the "humanness" of the
Northern. The late Norse mythological survivals are not English, and are only at
best a possible illustration — yet the similar temper of the two peoples and their
'heroism' can hardly have been founded upon a mythological philosophy divergent on this fundamental point.

[166] Of the fair gods of Greece we also hear rumour of wars with giants and
great powers not Olympian. Yet this distinction is not clearly conceived. The gods
are not in any case an ever-present danger: the war is rather in a chaotic past.
Though the seed of the gods may be heroes, it is also other creatures hostile to
men and monstrous. The monsters may be akin to the gods, and the gods are not
partners of lesser men in their war against them. The gods neither need men's
help, nor are concerned in their struggles. Men may worship or propitiate one or

the other, gods or monsters, but he is not an ally of either. The interest of the gods
is in this or that man as part of their whims or private schemes, not as part of a
great strategy that includes the whole of mankind, if only as the infantry of battle.
The wages of heaven are deeds. This perhaps makes the gods more godlike —
more lofty, more dread, more inscrutable. They are timeless and do not know or
fear death. Such beliefs may hold promise of a profounder thought, so that the
Greeks could make philosophy, but the Germanic North created specially the <u>hero</u>.
Though the word we use in English is Greek (instead of the ancient <u>hæleþ</u> or the
German cognate <u>Held</u>), the notion we have of it is rather Germanic than Greek.

In Norse at any rate the gods are enmeshed within time; they are doomed to
the agony of death — though (probably by a late addition) a rebirth glimmers
faintly far ahead for some of them. Their battle is with the monsters and with the
darkness. They fight along with men and gather heroes for the final battle. Already
before euhemerism saved them by embalming them, and they dwindled in learned
antiquarian fancy to the mighty ancestors of [167] northern kings, they are in their
very being but the enlarged shadows of great men and warriors cast upon the walls
of the world. When Baldr is slain and goes to Hel, he cannot escape thence any
more than mortal man. Loki is among the gods, it is true, an evil and a lying and
clever spirit, of whom many monsters come. But this is true of men, in whom both
Grendel and the Dragon in their hatred, cruelty, malice and greed find part. But
the gods of Ásgarðr do not recognize kinship with Fenris wolf anymore than men
with the Dragon.

Thus though the passages in <u>Beowulf</u> concerning the giants and their war
with God (1689–93 and 113–114) are certainly related directly, as are the names of
Cain and Abel, to Scripture, especially <u>Genesis</u> vi, they cannot at the same time be
dissociated from the giants of northern myth, the ever-watchful foes of Ásgarðr.
The undoubted mention of Cain connects him with <u>eotenas</u> (giants) and <u>ylfe</u> (elves),
the <u>jötnar</u> (giants) and <u>álfar</u> (elves) of Norse mythology. It is not surprising therefore
that at this precise point Christian Scripture and pagan tradition fused. We need
no longer wonder that Cain and Abel alone of Scriptural names appear in a poem
<u>dealing deliberately with the noble heathen before Christ and his war with the
world.</u>

The monsters had been the foes of the gods, who were the captains of men,
and the monsters would win in time; and in heroic siege and last defeat alike men
and gods were in the same host. And, though the old gods departed, men remained. The heroes, who had, in reality and in reversal of myth, begotten the
gods, devising their grim shapes as the emblems of their own courage, fought on
until defeat. For the monsters also remained. They remain still. A Christian was
still hemmed in by the hostile world.

[168] Yet the war had changed. There was now one Lord and Captain (Dryhten), and the monsters were <u>His</u> foe as of the old feuds. But even as the contests on
the fields of Time thus takes on its largest aspect, the vision is dissolving. The

tragedy of the great temporal defeat is poignant, but no longer of final importance. It is indeed no defeat: the end of the world is but part of the design of its own Maker, an Arbiter above and beyond the visible and mortal world. There is a possibility of eternal defeat and eternal victory; the real battle is of the soul and of the soul's enemies. So the old monsters became symbols of the devil — or the devils blended into the monsters and took visible shape in the hideous bodies of the þyrsas (monsters) and sigelhearwan (fiery monsters) of heathen imagination.

But this shift is not complete in <u>Beowulf</u>. At any rate its author is still primarily concerned with <u>man on earth</u>. <u>Beowulf</u> is not a stupid medley of Christian and pagan, but a re-treatment of a theme that had already been hammered out: that man, individually and as a race, and all his works shall die. A theme acceptable within the temporal order to a Christian. Yet this theme would not be so treated in this poem but for the <u>nearness</u> of paganism. The shadow of its despair, if only as a mood, as an intense emotion of regret, is still there. The work of defeated valour in the world is still felt deeply. As the poet looks back into the past surveying the history of kings and warriors in the old traditions he sees that all that man as man can accomplish ends in night; and he is still thinking primarily of men in the-world and their glory (or as we should put it, meaning in the end nothing very different, their culture and civilization). In spite of the terminology [169] applied to Grendel (as a déofol (devil)) he is not yet mediæval. He is not a materialized evil spirit — he cannot disappear, or enter houses save by the door. Later we have devils as hideous as this þyrs (monster),[+] as fleshly-seeming, as capable even of doing bodily hurt, who are yet 'evil spirits,' whose proper purpose is to injure the soul, to tempt to evil. But Grendel though called <u>feond on helle</u> (enemy in hell) is primarily <u>feond mancynnes</u> (enemy of mankind); he and his kin are in this world, eaters of the flesh of men, they are in the physical world and of it — they are indeed in a sense <u>it</u> itself.[*]

We are dealing still in <u>Beowulf</u> with the tragedy of man in time. The solution of that tragedy is not explicitly treated — it does not arise out of the material. We get in fact a poem from a pregnant moment — by a man who knew enough of the old heroic tales (preserved to him undoubtedly in traditional forms that descended often from actual pre-christian authors) to perceive their common tragedy of inevitable ruin, and to feel this perhaps more poignantly because he was himself a little removed from the direct pressure of its despair. He could [170] view from without but still feel immediately and from within the old dogma — the huge pessimism as

---

+   This very word — an extremely ancient northern word — survives in Middle English only precariously as a synonym of '<u>devil</u>.

*   The 'mediaeval' is fully developed already in later Old English. There is nothing but the older language and the metre to distinguish Cynewulf's <u>Juliana</u> from the thirteenth century homily <u>Juliene</u> of MS. Bodley 34 (which is probably lineally connected with Cynewulf). The devils that tempt and physically torment <u>St. Guthlac</u> cannot be distinguished (save perhaps by the odd fact that they speak Welsh) from the mediæval assailants of Saints.

to the event, combined with the obstinate faith in the value of the doomed effort. He was still dealing with the old universal theme, and not yet writing an allegorical homily in verse. Beowulf's <u>byrne</u> (corselet) was made by Wéland, and the iron shield he bore against the dragon was made by his own smiths: it was not the breastplate of righteousness, nor the shield of faith for the quenching of all the fiery darts of the wicked.

Virgil: multa putans sortemque animo miseratus iniquam (pondering on so much, and stood in pity for the souls' inequitable fates).

Of pagan English eschatology, as I say, we know nothing definite — apart from the guess that the closely similar heroic temper cannot have had a fundamentally different background of mythology from the Scandinavian, however different the details may have been. What we know of Scandinavian paganism is not easy to estimate as a representation of genuine heathen tradition. Paganism is not usually unified and coherent; it is variable locally and in time, and the fragments in the North achieve written record in a tattered form at a time of confused or faulty memories, and in some cases in a period when such traditions had become no more than the conventional trappings of a special poetry, or the amusement of antiquarians such as Snorri Sturlson — nearly as far from real paganism as Jove and Mars in our eighteenth century. In the Norse traditions we glimpse a future life — the reward of courage, and a hell that is the punishment of feebleness, as much as of wickedness. Among much that is crude or unshapen, or confused with other ideas not wholly assimilated* (possibly in some cases echoes of Christianity), the dominant motive is that of courage, apprehended mythically as valuable [171] in the war of gods and men against their common enemy in Chaos and Darkness. But of definite mythological treatments of this idea we have nothing left in English. Its spirit only survives. Far more definite, indeed clearly explicit, is the idea of <u>lof</u> or dóm — the noble pagan's desire for the <u>merited praise</u> of the noble, a desire which is not, of course, peculiar to northern pagans. For if this limited immortality of praise naturally exists as a strong motive together with detailed heathen practices and beliefs, it can also long outlive them. It is in fact the natural residuum when the pagan gods fade, whether unbelief comes from within or from without.

The prominence of the motive of <u>lof</u> in <u>Beowulf</u> we may interpret, then, both as a sign that a pagan time was not far away from the poet (and its mood was well grasped imaginatively by him), and also as a probable indication that the end of English paganism, (at least among the noble classes for whom and by whom such traditions were preserved) was marked by a twilight period similar to that which

---

* Partly due to lack of development (primitiveness), partly due to accidents of tradition. But that actual <u>debasement</u> had taken place in the North in the viking period is a possibility to bear in mind. Between the old Germanic North and Christianity intervened an age crueller, colder and more barbarous, one exalting slaughter and rapine, and encouraging both unbelief and fantasy.

we observe in Scandinavia later. The gods faded and man was left to carry on his war alone. <u>His trust was in his own power and will</u> and <u>his reward the praise of his own peers during life and after death</u>. So was it explicitly said of men of might in the last days of Icelandic heathendom that their creed was simply <u>ek trúi á mátt ok megin</u> (I believe in my own might and main). We see them often <u>goðlausir</u> (godless), as almost patronising towards their eclectically favoured deities, to whom they accorded, in return for services rendered, a belief not much greater that a modern pagan will give to omens, or talismans on his motor-car.

[172] Earle long ago pointed out the prominence of <u>lof</u> in Beowulf. At the beginning of the poem, at the end of the first "strophe" of the exordium there occurs as a <u>leitmotif</u>: <u>lofdædum sceal in mægþa gehwam man geþeon</u> (By praiseworthy deeds a man shall prosper anywhere). The last word of the poem is <u>lofgeornost</u> (most eager for praise), the summit of the praise of the dead hero. To make an Anglo-Saxon pun, this is <u>lást worda betst</u> (the best last-word). For Beowulf had lived according to his own philosophy, which he explicitly avowed (1386ff): <u>úre æghwylc sceal ende gebídan worolde lífes. Wyrce se ðe móte dómes ær déaþe: þæt bið dryhtguman æfter sélest</u> (Each one of us must live in expectation of the end of this worldly life. Let him who can earn good fame before death; that is the best thing, afterwards). The poet himself as commentator recurs again to this in 1534: <u>swá sceal man don, þonne he æt guðe gegan þenceð longsumne lof: na ymb his líf cearað</u> (So must a man do, when he hopes to win long-lasting glory at battle; he will not be too concerned about his own life).

<u>Lof</u> is ultimately (and etymologically) 'value' or 'valuation' — praise as we say (itself derived from <u>pretium</u>). <u>Dóm</u> is assessment, judgement, and so esteem. Their differentiation is not in such passages important.* But it <u>has</u> an importance, since the two words were not identical nor entirely commensurable in meaning. When Christianity came the one (<u>lof</u>) flowed rather into the ideas of heaven and of the heavenly choirs, the other (<u>dóm</u>) rather into the idea of the judgement-seat of God, the particular and general judgements of the dead. The change that is worked in this way can be observed curiously in the <u>Seafarer</u>. To appreciate this one should compare closely the passages in the <u>Seafarer</u> from lines 66 to 80 with Hroðgar's <u>giedd</u> or sermon in <u>Beowulf</u>, [173] from 1735 onwards. There is a specially close resemblance between <u>Seafarer</u> 66–71, and Hroðgar's words, 1761–8 (a part of his speech that I believe is certainly original whatever revision or expansion the <u>giedd</u> in general may have suffered).

The Seafarer says:

               ic gelýfe nó
þæt him eorðwelan   ece stondað
simle þreora sum   þinga gehwylce

---

* C.f. the end of <u>Widsith</u> which refers to the minstrel's part in achieving for the noble and their deeds the prolonged life of fame. It is said of the noble patron: <u>lof se gewyrceð, hafað under heofonum heahfæstne dom</u> (he earns praise who has under heaven enduring fame).

ær his tíd-dæge⁺   to tweon weorþeð
ádl oþþe yldo   oþþe ecghete
fægum from weardum   feorh oðþringeð.

[I believe not that the joys of earth will abide everlasting. Ever and in all cases will one of three things trouble his heart before the appointed day: sickness, or age, or the foeman's sword from the doomed man hastening hence will his life ravish.]

Hroðgar says to Beowulf [2]:

eft sóna bið
þæt þec ádl oððe ecg   eafoþes getwæfeð,
oððe fýres feng,   oððe flódes wylm,
oððe gripe méces,   oððe gáres fliht,
oððe atol yldo;   oððe éagena bearhtm
forsiteð 7 forsworceð.   Semninga bið
þæt ðec, dryhtguma,   déað oferswýðeð.

[Soon hereafter it will come to pass that sickness or sword shall rob thee of strength, or grasping fire, or heaving flood, or biting blade, or flying spear, or dreadful age; or the flash of eyes shall foul and darken. Swiftly will it come that thee, O knight, shall death conquer].

[174] The Seafarer, after thus proclaiming that all men shall die, goes on: "Therefore this is for all noble men the best 'lást-word' (i.e. memorial in tale or song) and praise of the living that commemorate him in words after his death, that ere he must go hence, he merit and achieve on earth by heroic deeds against the malice of enemies (feonda which is ambiguous) opposing the devil (deofle) that the children of men praise him afterwards, and his 'lof' may live with the angels for ever and ever, the glory of eternal life, rejoicing (dréam) among the hosts (mid dugeþum)."

This is a passage which, for its syntax alone, would certainly appear to have been revised. In any case it is a modification of heathen lof in two directions: first in making the deeds that are to be the basis of glory resistance to spiritual foes — the sense of the ambiguous feonda (of enemies) is in the surviving poem made clear to be deofle togeanes (against the devil); secondly in enlarging the lof to include the angels and the future life. Lofsong; loftsong (praise-song) are in Middle English

---

+   Manuscript: tidaga
2)   Somewhat expanding the þreora sum (one of three) are lines found elsewhere either in great elaboration as in the Fates of Men or in briefer allusion to the well recognized theme as in Wanderer 80ff.

specially used of the heavenly choirs. But we do not get anything like this in Beo-wulf. There lof remains pagan lof, the praise of one's peers, perhaps vaguely pro-longed among their descendants awa to ealdre (always for life). In Beowulf there is hell. But there is not explicit reference to heaven. Not to heaven, that is, as a place or state of reward, of eternal bliss in the presence of God.*

[175] An exception might be made in the case of lines 186 ff: wel bið þæm þe mot æfter deaðdæge Drihten secean, 7 to Fæder fæþmum freoðo wilnian (Well will it be for one who is permitted to seek the Lord and to seek after peace in the bosom of the Father). If this and the passage in which it occurs is genuine (descends, that is, from the poet who wrote Beowulf as a whole) and is not a later addition, as I believe, then the point is lost.* For the passage is definitely an exclamation of the Christian auth-or, who understood about heaven, and expressly denies any such knowledge to the Danes. Nowhere do the characters in the poem understand heaven or have hope of it. They refer to hell.* Beowulf prophesies it for Unferð (588). Even the noble monotheist Hroðgar (so he is painted, quite apart from the question of the bulk of his sermon from 1724–1760) refers to no heavenly bliss. The reward which he fore-tells to Beowulf is that his dom shall live awa to ealdre (always for life), a fortune also in heathen Norse bestowed on Sigurðr (that his name live æ mun uppi) (always among men). This is, as we have seen, capable of being Christianized, but in Beowulf it is not Christianized, probably deliberately, when the characters are speaking in their proper [176] persons, or their actual thoughts are reported. Thus the author tells us that Beowulf's soul gewat . . . secean soðfæstra dom (departed . . . to seek the truth-fast judgment). This we may take as implying that it did not go to (Christian) hell, but was reckoned among the just. (What the precise theology concerning the subject of the just heathen was is now perhaps not important, but we may take this as a comment. Beowulf was too distant to allow little of punishment being rec-koned.) There is probably a Christian transmutation of significance, soðfæstra dóm could by itself have meant merely 'esteem of the just and true-judging,' that dóm

---

*   heofon in the singular and plural and its synonyms such as rodor are, of course, frequent but refer either to the particular landscape, or the sky under which men in general dwell. Such words are of course also used with the names of God — who is 'lord of the heavens,' and so on — but these expressions are rather parallels to others describing His general governance of nature (e.g. 1609 ff), and His realm which includes land, sea, and sky, even if heofon is already regarded as his especial seat and the sun as his candle. We may have simply lack of differentiation between symbol and state. But in the pagan North the sky was not a symbol of the opposite of Hell — which had originally been the place of all departed (so Baldr).

*   Decision is not possible. But suspicion must not, of course, be allowed to rest on the lines solely be-cause of what they say. My view is based on the feeling that in metre and style they introduce a 'voice' quite different to that of Beowulf as a whole, while they interrupt both the rhythm and the thought of the narrative.

*   A native word, free from definite physical location, for an originally native pagan conception, symbol-ism of which is seen colouring the references to hell in Christian literature. A celebrated example is the reference in Judith to the death of Holofernes, which recalls remarkably certain features of Hel in Völuspá. Cf. Judith 115 wyrmum bewunden (wound round with snakes), 119 of ðam wyrmsele (from the snake-hall) — with Völuspá 38 sá er undinn salr orma hryggjum (its [the hall's] walls are clad with coiling snakes) (which would translated into Old English be se is wunden sele wyrma hrycgum).

which Beowulf himself, as a young man, had declared to be the prime motive of noble conduct, both here combined with <u>gewat secean</u> (departed to seek) it seems to mean either the 'judgement of God upon the 'just' or 'the glory that belongs in eternity to the just.' Yet Beowulf himself expressing his own opinion, though troubled by dark doubts at first, and later declaring his conscience clear, thinks at the end only of his barrow and memorial among men, of his childlessness, and of <u>Wigláf</u>, the sole survivor of his kindred to whom he bequeaths his helm and gear. His funeral is quite unchristian, and his memorial is the recognized virtue of his kingship and the hopeless sorrow of his people.

This question of the Christian and heathen thought in <u>Beowulf</u> has often been misconceived. So far from being a man so simple or so confused that he muddled up Christianity and Germanic paganism, the author probably drew on or attempted to draw distinctions (more than one distinction), and to represent moods and attitudes of characters conceived of dramatically and in the past. Though there are special problems, concerning the tradition of the poem and its possible occasional later retouching (such as 168–9, the <u>giedd</u> (sermon) 1724–1760, and especially lines 175–188), we cannot speak in general either of confusion (in one poet's mind, or in the mind of a whole period), or of patch-work revision producing confusion. More sense can be made of the [177] poem, if we start rather with the hypothesis (not in itself actually at all unlikely) that the poet tried to do something definite, and difficult, which had some reason and thought behind it, though the execution may not have been entirely successful.

The strongest argument that the actual situation in the poem is not in general the product either of stupidity or of accident, is to my mind to be found in the fact that we can observe <u>differentiation</u>. We can, that is, in the matter of philosophy and religious sentiment, distinguish plainly for instance: (<u>a</u>) the poet as narrator and commentator; (<u>b</u>) Beowulf; (<u>c</u>) Hroðgar. Such differentiation would not be achieved either by a man who was himself confused in mind, or by haphazard later tinkering, by monks or others concerned only to graft on at random familiar Christian matter. The kind of thing that 'accident' achieves is illustrated by <u>drihten wereda</u> 'lord of Hosts,' a familiar Christian expression, which is plainly an alteration, probably casual, of <u>drihten Wedera</u> 'Lord of the Geats' in line 2186. This alteration is plainly due to some man (the actual scribe of the line or some predecessor) more familiar with <u>Dominus Deus Sabaoth</u> than with <u>Hreðel</u> and the <u>Weder-Geatish</u> house. But no one has ventured to ascribe this confusion at any rate to the poet.

That the differentiation does occur would take long to show by quotation of chapter and verse. But it can I think be observed if we extract from the poem all references to religion, fate, or mythology, and remember the circumstances in which each appears, paying especial attention to those things which are <u>said in speeches</u> or <u>reported as being said or thought</u> by characters in the poem. The poet as narrator and commentator obviously stands apart. But the two characters who do most of the actual speaking, Hroðgar [178] and Beowulf, are quite distinct.

Hroðgar is consistently portrayed as a wise and pious and noble monotheist, who refers all things to the favour of God, and never omits explicit thanks for mercies.* Beowulf refers sparingly to God, except as the arbiter of critical events, principally as <u>Metod</u>, in which the idea of God approaches nearest to the old Fate. Of course the expressions implying a belief in 'fate' — whatever degree of belief remains — at no time disappear. There is no reason, theological or linguistic, why they should. Certain words such as metod — ordinance or ordainer — naturally took over that part of the action of the God as the ruler of all the apparent chances of the world which remain inscrutable, and is for all practical daily purposes dealt with as fate or else luck. The Christian poets continue to use wyrd which did not become a word equatable with God — Thus Cynewulf - Elene: Huru wyrd gescreaf (indeed, fate declared).

We have in Beowulf's language little differentiation of God and Fate. For instance he says <u>gæð á wyrd swa hio scel</u> (fate goes always as it must) and immediately continues that <u>dryhten</u> (Lord) holds the balance in his combat (441); or again he definitely equates <u>wyrd</u> (fate) and <u>metod</u> (the Measurer) (2526f).* It is Beowulf who says <u>Wyrd oft nereð unfægne eorl, þonne his ellen deah</u> (fate often saves an un-doomed earl, when his valor endures) (immediately after calling the sun <u>beacen Godes</u> (beacon of God)), which contrasts strongly with the poet's own comment on the man who escaped the dragon (2291): <u>swa mæg unfæge eaðe gedígan wean 7 wræcsíð, se ðe Wealdendes hyldo gehealdeþ</u> (So may an unfated one easily endure woe and the exile-path, he who holds the favor of the Ruler). Beowulf only twice explicitly thanks God or acknowledges His help: (a) in ll. 1658–61 where he acknowledges God's protection and the favour of <u>ylda Waldend</u> (the Ruler of men) (. . . <u>oftost wísode winigea léasum</u> . . .(often he has helped the friendless)) in his combat under the water; (b) in his last speech of all, where he thanks <u>Frean Wuldorcyninge</u> . . . <u>ecum</u> [179] <u>Dryhtne</u> (the Lord of World-Kings, the Eternal Lord) for all the treasure his eyes see, and for helping him to win it for his people. (But as I have said his last thoughts are for his memorial on earth, his family and successor.) Usually he makes no such references. He ascribes his conquest of the nicors (570 ff.) to luck — <u>hwæþere me gesælde</u> (whatever was given to me) (cf. the similar words used of Sigemund 890). When he plunges into the mere he offers no prayer, and his only request is that Hygelac should be

---

*   He refers to <u>halig god</u> (holy God) 381; <u>god</u> (god) 478, 930, 1397; <u>Alwealda</u> (All-Ruler) 928, 955, 1314; <u>wuldres hyrde</u> (guardian of the world) 931; <u>Dryhtnes miht</u> (power of the Lord) 939; <u>Eald metod</u> (the ancient Measurer) 945; <u>mightigan Drihten</u> (mighty Lord) 1398; <u>mihtig God</u> (mighty God) 1716; Metod (the Measurer) 979; <u>ecean Dryhtne</u> (Eternal Lord) 1779; <u>wigtig Drihten</u> (wise Lord) 1841 (the <u>giedd</u> 1724–60 is omitted).

*   Compare 2814f where <u>wyrd</u> is more active while <u>metodsceaft</u> equals doom, death. Cf. Old Norse <u>mjötutr</u> which has the senses 'dispenser, ruler' — and also 'doom, fate, death' to the side of the inscrutable (and even hostile) Fate applied to worldly works. Gabriel in <u>Héliand</u> says of John the Baptist that he will not touch wine <u>so habed im uurd (equals wyrd) giscapu metod gemarcod endi maht godes</u> (this is the way the works of fate made him, time formed him, and the power of God as well) (128); or it is said of Anna the widow when her husband died that sie thiu mikila maht metodes tedelda uured uurdigiscapu (that the mighty power of the Measurer separated them, the cruel workings of fate) (511). In Old Saxon <u>metod(o)giscapu</u> and <u>metodigisceft</u> equals Fate as Old English <u>metodsceaft</u>.

told of his bravery. In his account given to Hygelac his only explanation of his preservation in the water-den is næs ic fæge þa gyt (I was not yet then fated) (2141). He does not allude to God throughout this report. Other references he makes are casual and formal such as beorht béacen Godes (bright beacon of God) of the sun (571). An exceptional case is Godes leoht geceas (chose God's light) 2469 describing the death of Hréðel Beowulf's grandfather. This would appear to refer to heaven. But both these expressions have escaped, as it were, from Christian poetry. The first béacen Godes (beacon of God) is even for a heathen passable. The second is, if we press the fact that Beowulf himself is formally the speaker, a piece of unsuitable diction — though it cannot be dismissed as a later addition or revision. A didactic Christian reviser would hardly have added this detail in the description of the pagan king Hréðel's death. The whole story is a heathen and hopeless one turning on blood-feud, and the motive that when a son kills his brother by accident the father's sorrow is intensified because no vengeance can be exacted. The explanation is not to be sought in Christian revision, but in the fact that before Beowulf was written Christian poetry was already well-developed, and was well known to the author. The diction of Beowulf is in fact 're-paganized,' with a special purpose by its author, rather than Christianized later without clear purpose by revisers. Throughout the poem the language becomes intelligible, if we assume that the diction of poetry — as known to the Beowulf-poet, and before ever his poem took the shape in which he has given it to us — was already Christianized (there is probably nearly one hundred years between Cædmon and Beowulf), and familiar with Christian and Old Testament themes. We have in Old English, therefore, not only the old heroic language occasionally misused in application to Christian legend (as in Andreas or Elene), but in Beowulf Christian language occasionally (actually very seldom) placed in the mouth of [180] of a heathen character. We observe in godes leoht geceas (chose God's light) an instance of this. All is not perfect in Beowulf. In the very long speech of Beowulf from 2425–2525 the poet has hardly attempted to keep up the pretense of oratio recta throughout. Just before the end he reminds us and himself that Beowulf is supposed to be speaking with a renewed Beowulf maðelode (Beowulf spoke) (2510). From 2446–2489 it is hardly a monologue in character at all.

There remain in considering the utterances of Beowulf himself his declaration that Grendel shall abide miclan domes (the great judgment) and the judgement of scír metod (the glorious Measurer) — which resembles Beowulf's other references to God as doomsman; and finally his last examination of conscience where he says that Waldend fira (the Ruler of men) cannot accuse him of morðorbealo mágu (the murder of kinsmen). The crimes which he claims to have avoided, treachery, false oaths, and murder, are closely paralleled in the heathen Völuspá, where the grim hall Náströnduá contains especially menn meinsvara ok morðvarga (perjurers and murderers).

When we have made allowance for Godes leoht geceás (chose God's light) and even for some modification of character in age (when Beowulf becomes much more like Hroðgar before him), it is plain that the characters and sentiments of the two kings are quite different. Even where Beowulf's thoughts are revealed by the poet, we can observe that his real trust was in his own might. That the possession of this might was a 'favour of God' is actually a comment of the poet's and is similar to the comments of later Christians upon the heathen heroes of Norse saga. Thus 669: georne truwode modgan mægnes, metodes hyldo (Indeed the leader of the Geats eagerly trusted in his own mighty strength, the protection of the Measurer). No and is possible metrically in the original, none should appear in translation: the [181] favour of God was the possession of mægen (strength). Again 1272–3: gemunde mægenes strenge, gimfæste gife ðe him God sealde, and him to Anwaldan áre gelýfde frófre and fultum (he remembered the strength of might, the wonderful gift, which God gave to him, and he entrusted himself to the One-Ruler, to his relief and support). * Finally the poet tells us that when the dragon's ruinous assault was reported Beowulf was filled with doubt and dismay and wénde se wísa þæt he Wealdende ofer ealde riht écean Dryhtne bitre gebulge (The wise one wondered if he had bitterly enraged the Ruler, the eternal Lord, due to an offense against ancient law). It has been said (Klaeber note to 2330) that ofer ealde riht, 'contrary to ancient law' is here given a Christian interpretation; but this would not seem to be so. This is a heathen or unchristian fear — of an inscrutable power that can be offended inadvertently.

We have in Beowulf then an historical poem about the pagan past, or an attempt at one — literal historical fidelity accompanied with research was of course not attempted. It is a poem by a learned Christian writing of old times, and looking back on the heroism and gloom, and feeling in them something permanent, and something symbolical. The man who wrote this, so far from being a bewildered semi-pagan (historically improbable for a man of this sort in the period to which Beowulf belongs) brought first to his task a knowledge and admiration of Christian poetry, especially that of the Cædmon tradition, and among this especially Genesis.* He [182] makes his minstrel sing of the Creation of the earth and the lights of heaven in Heorot. So excellent is this choice as the theme of the harp that maddened Grendel lurking joyless in the dark without that we do not care whether it is anachronistic or not. Actually the poet may have known what we can

---

*   Compare, for instance, the Christian commentary in Fóstbræðra saga where it is said in describing a grim pagan character: ekki var hjarta hans sem fóarn í fugli, ekki var þat blóð ult, svá af þat skylfi at hræð-slu, heldr var þat hert af enum hæsta höfuðsmið í öllum hvatleik (For his heart was not like the crop of a bird, nor was it so full of blood that it shook with fear. It had been hardened in the Almighty Maker's forge to dare anything) (Ch. 2. Reykjavík edn. p. 8); or again Almáttigr er sá sem svá snart hjarta ok óhrætt lét í brjóst orgeiri: ok ekki var hans hugþryði af mönnum ger né honum í brjóst borin, heldr af enum hæsta höfuðsmið (It was the Almighty who touched Thorgeir's heart and put such fearlessness into his breast, and thus his courage was neither inborn nor of humankind but came from the creator on high).

*   The Genesis which we have is a late and damaged copy of a poem that certainly belongs to this same tradition ultimately, and goes back to the same period as Beowulf. The actual priority in composition of Genesis A compared with Beowulf is generally recognized.

still now guess, that such creation-themes were also ancient in the heathen North. The Völuspá describes Chaos and creation of sun and moon, and extremely similar language appears in the Old High German fragment (Wessobrunner Gebet). The song of the minstrel in the first Æneid is also in part a song of origins.[†] Secondly to his task the poet brought a considerable learning in vernacular traditions (for only by training and learning could such things be acquired, they were no more born naturally into seventh- or eighth-century Englishmen than ready-made knowledge of modern poetry or history is inherited at birth by British School boys). It is thus not unnatural that a poet who sets out to tell of old pre-Christian days, but intends to emphasize their nobility, and the desire of the good of all ages for truth, should in his delineation of the great king of Heorot turn largely to the Old Testament.[♦] In the folces hyrde (herdsman of the folk) of the Danes we have much of the devout shepherd patriarchs, servants of one God. We have in fact a Christian English conception of the noble pre-Christian, who nonetheless lapse, as could the Israelites, in times of stress or temptation into idolatry. It is probably of Old Testament lapses rather than of any events in England (of which he is not speaking), that the poet is thinking in line 175ff,[*] and these colour his manner [183] of allusion to knowledge which he probably derived from native traditions concerning the Danes and the special religious significance of Heorot and its site in the heathen North and the point of fusion between old lays and new. On the other hand, the traditional history and poetry in English, not to mention the living survival of the heroic code and temper among the nobles of ancient England, enabled him [184] to draw differently, and far closer to the actual northern pre-

---

[†]   "Cithara crinitus Iopas / personat aurata, docuit quem maximus Atlas / hic canit errantem lunam solisque labores, / unde hominum genus et pecudes, unde imber et ignes" (And Lord Iopas / With flowing hair, whom giant Atlas taught, / Made the room to echo to his golden lyre. / He sang the straying moon and toiling sun / The origin of mankind and the beasts) (Virgil I, 740 ff)

[♦]   "Saturni gentem haud vinclo nec legibus aequam, sponte sua, veterisque dei se more tenentem" (we who come of Saturn's race, that we are just — / Not by constraint or laws, but by our choice/And habit of our ancient god) (Virgil VII 202 ff).

[*]   From 175 to helle gemundon in modsefan (remembered hell in their hearts) (which is strikingly true) 180 we can confidently accept as original. The status of the rest of the passage metod hie ne cuþon (they did not know the Measurer) to freoðo wilnian (to seek after peace) 188 is partly suspect on grounds of style and rhythm. If the whole passage is original then the poet must have mentally distinguished between Hroðgar (who certainly knew of God) and a certain section of more pagan Danes. But it would remain a blemish on the poem. For it is undeniably as inept for an author who has (with startling poetic propriety and effect) depicted Heorot by a minstrel's song of how se Ælmihtiga (the Almighty) wrought the world, to say that the Danes heofena Helm herian ne cuþon (they did not know to praise the Protector of heaven). But this is the only really serious poetic discrepancy in the whole poem. When we consider both the special temptation to enlargement here, and the ease with which it could be achieved without gross dislocation, and note at the same time that there is some dislocation, and that 180–188 is unlike the rest of the poem in style and verse or rhythm, it becomes a more than probable certainty that we have here an instance of later interference with the poet's plan and purpose. Similarly it is the very marked character already by the poet given to Hroðgar which has made possible the probable revision and expansion of the giedd without serious damage — though, well done as the passage is in itself, the poem would be better with the excision of 1724 wundor is to secgan (it is a wonder to tell) to 1760 éce rædas (eternal wisdom), which are on independent grounds (that I do not here go into) under very strong suspicion as a later addition.

Christian 'hero,' the character of Beowulf, especially as a young knight — who used his great gift of mægen (strength) to earn dóm and lof among men and posterity.

The 'discrepancies' are no greater than those to be found in Virgil's Æneid. Beowulf is not an actual picture of historic Denmark or Gautland or Sweden circa A.D. 500. But it is (with of course certain defects here and there of minor detail) at a general view a self-consistent picture, an imaginative construction. The whole must have succeeded admirably in creating in the minds of the poet's contemporaries the illusion of surveying a past, pagan but not ignoble and fraught still with a deep significance, a past that itself had depth and reached back into the mists of countless human sorrows. This impression of depth is an effect and a justification of the use of episodes and allusions to old tales — which are all notably darker, more pagan, and despairing than the foreground. The same sort of change is probably due to the similar effect of antiquity in the Æneid — especially felt as soon as Æneas reaches Italy, and the Saturni gentem .... Sponte sua veterisque dei se more tenentem. (Know that our Latins /Come of Saturn's race, that we are just — /Not by constraint or laws, but by our choice/ And habit of our ancient god). Ic þa leode wat ge wið feond ge wið freond fæste geworhte, æghwæs untæle ealde wisan (I know that nation, fast in purpose against enemy and with friend, in every respect blameless, as known from of old). Alas for the lost lore, the annals and the old poets Virgil knew, and only used in the making of a new thing. The criticism of Ker that the important matters are put on the 'outer edges' misses this essential point of artistry, indeed it fails to see one of the very reasons why the old things have in Beowulf such a special appeal. It is the poet himself who has made antiquity so appealing. Yet there is no doubt of his allegiance. He is viewing pagan heroism with sympathy, not regretting its supersession. His poem has more value in consequence and is a greater contribution to mediæval thought than the hard and intolerant view that consigned all the ancestors to the devil. For preservation of this noble monument [185] of a great moment in our history from the dragon of reckless destruction we may be thankful.

The general structure of the poem is not really difficult to perceive, if we look only to the main points, the strategy, and neglect the many points of minor and occasional tactics (in which much is deserving of high praise). We must dismiss, of course, from mind the notion that Beowulf is a "narrative poem", that it tells or intends to tell a tale sequentially. The poem "lacks steady advance" — so Klaeber heads a critical section in his edition. Yet the poem does not mean, was not meant, to advance steadily or unsteadily. It is based on a balance, and a contrast of ends with beginnings. In its simplest form it is a contrasted description of two moments in a great life; an elaboration of the extremely ancient and intensely moving contrast between youth and age, first achievement and final death. It is divided in consequence into two opposed portions, different in matter, manner, and length: A from 1–2199 (including an exordium of 52 lines); B from 2200 to 3182 (the end). This proportion cannot be caviled at; it is, for the purpose and the production of the required effect, right.

This simple and <u>static</u> structure is in each portion much diversified and adorned. In the conduct of the presentation [186] of Beowulf's youth on the one hand, and of his kingship and old age on the other, criticism can find much to question, especially if it is captious or malicious, but also much to praise if it is attentive. But to my mind there is only one point in each portion that merits serious attention. In the first portion I should select the report of Beowulf to Hygelac — to which I shall return. In the second it must be admitted that, though the interweaving of past and dramatically present events by means of speeches and allusions has in place great virtues, and is in any case imposed upon the poet by his static contrast-structure, it is not wholly successful. The surface is too broken; reminiscence is too long in proportion and the nature and atmosphere of the things told is not always sufficiently suitable to the general theme of Beowulf's fall. Yet without <u>all</u> that we have of the glimpses of Beowulf's life, and the tragedies of the Geatish house in their long struggle, the magnificent final movement of the poem (3137–end), a piece of great poetry where it stands and with the rest behind it, would not be so full of content.

The other weakness, the recapitulation, is more serious and more interesting. This recapitulation, granted its necessity, is done very well. Without serious discrepancy* it [187] retells rapidly the events in Heorot, and retouches the account, and serves to illustrate (since he himself describes his own deeds) yet more vividly the portrait of the young man, singled out by destiny for great achievements, as he steps suddenly out in his full powers. Yet this is perhaps not quite sufficient to justify the repetition. I imagine that, if not complete justification, at least explanation is to be sought in different directions.

For one thing, the old tale was not first told or invented by our author. The sluggish bear's son, with his dreadful hug, who suddenly wakes up and surprises his family and becomes famous is a very old folk-tale. Even the legendary association of the Danish court with a marauding monster, and with the arrival from abroad of a champion of bear-origin, was not invented by our poet. There are clear traces of it in Scandinavian tradition. The plot is not his, though he has poured a feeling and significance into it quite different from its simple and crude essentials. And that plot is not perfect as the vehicle of the theme or themes that come to hidden life in the poet's mind as he makes his poem of the old material.* For the contrast — the rise and fall — it would probably have been better, if we had no journeying. If the single nation and land of the <u>Geatas</u> had been the scene, we should

---

* I have not discussed minor discrepancies. They are at any rate no proof of a composite authorship in this final stage. It is extraordinarily difficult, even in a newly invented tale of any length, to avoid minor discrepancies; more so still in re-handling old and oft-told tales. Critics would seem seldom themselves to have experienced the difficulties of narration. The points they fix on in the study, with a copy that can be turned back and forth for reference, are usually such as may easily escape an author, and still more easily an audience. Let us think, say, of Malory, were all his sources lost beyond recall.

* As is true enough of Shakespeare's use of old material. <u>King Lear</u> is a specially clear example.

have felt the stage not narrower, but symbolically wider. More easily should we have felt in one people and their hero, all mankind and its heroes.

[188] I always feel this in reading Beowulf, but I always feel that this defect is rectified by the bringing of the tale of Grendel to Gautland. As Beowulf stands in Hygelac's hall and tells his story, he sets his feet firm again on the land of his own people, and is no longer in danger of becoming a mere wrecca, a wandering adventurer, an errant slayer of bogies that do not concern him. There is thus a double division in the poem. There is the fundamental one at 2200 between age and youth. There is a secondary one, but an important one, at 1887–8. In a sense at 1888 we have "summary of previous chapters: now read on!" The essentials of the previous part are taken up and compacted so that all the 'tragedy of Beowulf' is contained in the section 1888–the end; though without the first half we should miss much incidental illustration, and (most important) the subordinate contrast between age and youth in the persons of Hroðgar and Beowulf, which is one of its chief purposes (the first half ends with the pregnant words oþ þæt hine yldo benam mægenes wynnum, se þe oft manegum scód) (That was an incomparable king, without any flaws, until old age, which has destroyed many, took from him the joys of strength). The one really absurd thing to do with Beowulf, therefore, is to read only 1–1888 and not the rest. This procedure is in consequence directed or encouraged by several 'English syllabuses'!

For full understanding of this point we may also consider a further matter — interesting if subsidiary. There is a special connexion between Beowulf and Andreas, both in the language and phraseology and in the 'plots.' Andreas [189] is usually considered the imitation, that is a poem written by a man who knew Beowulf more or less as we have it, since the similar passages and expressions in the poem are found in Beowulf in their more natural surroundings and applications rather than in the romance of the apostle. But what ever be the truth of the matter, the connexion is undoubted, and serves to suggest that Beowulf itself has some relation to the great missionary epoch of the eighth century. Just so did many a young Englishman of that day, untried, while those at home hoped and feared, set out to win their spurs déorum dædum déofle tógéanes (with brave deeds against the devil) in foreign lands, in Frisia or Saxony. They went to the courts of kings and wrestled with Godes andsacan (the enemies of God), and some were destroyed like Beowulf's companion. Sometimes the enemy in new form returned to the attack in the moment of apparent triumph. If we suppose Beowulf to have been written in the eighth century — and this seems secure enough on grounds quite independent of its theme — then one can perceive why the tale had a special attraction. Contemporaries could not fail to have felt something allegorical, something of a topical significance in it, although the poet has done nothing to emphasize this. But in the great activity and deep enthusiasm and interest of the English of the time [190] in missions we can see a subsidiary reason for the choosing of the story, and a plain reason for close imitation of the poem in a definitely missionary romance such as <u>Andreas</u>. We get thus a sidelight, as it were, on the surprised and almost ironic question of Hygelac: <u>ac ðu Hróðgáre wídcúðne wéan wihte gebéttest?</u> (But did you, for Hrothgar, remedy at all his widely known affliction?) on the <u>joy in the traveller's return</u>, the <u>eagerness for a full account</u>, and the emphasis laid on the friendly relations now established between kindred nations that had been estranged. But, of course, <u>Beowulf</u> will not work out into a full 'allegory' of missionary enterprise, and it was certainly not written as one. The real movement of the poet's mind lay far deeper.

In any case, whichever section of the poem we read or criticize, we must not allow ourselves to view the poem as in intention primarily an exciting narrative or a romantic tale. The very nature of Old English metre is often misjudged. In it there is no single rhythmic pattern progressing from the beginning of the line to the end; the lines do not go according to a tune. They depend on a balance and an opposition between two halves of roughly equivalent phonetic length and weight and emotional content, which are more often rhythmically contrasted rather than similar. They are more like masonry than music. In this there is undoubtedly a parallel to the total structure of <u>Beowulf</u>. Beowulf is in fact the most successful Old English poem because there the elements are all most nearly in harmony, language, metre theme and structure. Judgement of the verse has often gone astray through listening to it as if it were in modern accentual lines. Judgement of the theme goes astray through considering [191] it as the narrative handling of a plot. Language and verse, of course, differ from stone or wood or paint in that they occupy time and can only be heard or taken in in a time-sequence, so that in any poem that deals with characters or events (unlike <u>Wanderer</u> or <u>Seafarer</u>) some narrative element must be present. We have nonetheless, in <u>Beowulf</u> a method and structure that, within the limits of the verse kind, approaches rather to sculpture or painting. It is a composition not a tale.

This is clear in the second half. Though in the struggle with Grendel one can as reader dismiss the practical certainty of literary experience that the hero will not in fact perish in his encounter, and allow oneself to share the hopes and fears of the Danes and Geats upon the shore, in the second part the author has not the slightest wish that the outcome of the struggle should remain open, even according to literary convention. By now you are supposed to have grasped the poem's plan. Disaster is foretold. Defeat is the theme. Triumph over the foes of man's precarious fortress is over, and we approach the inevitable victory of the finally untameable. We have the end of 'glory', which fades to the praise of 'those that come after': and at the end we feel that too dwindling to the voices of the ghosts of ghosts as the ages lengthen.

[192] That the actual bearer of enmity, the dragon, dies also is important chiefly to Beowulf himself. He was a great man. Not many even in dying can achieve the death of a single dragon or the temporary salvation of their kindred. Within the limits of human life and its ineluctable end, Beowulf neither lived nor

died in vain — so brave men might say. Though there is no hint (indeed there are many hints to the contrary) that it was a war to end war, a dragon fight to end dragons or the foes of men. It is the end of Beowulf, and with him dies the hope of his people.

'In structure' it is said of Beowulf 'it is curiously weak, in a sense preposterous,' while allowing great merits of detail. In structure it actually is curiously strong, in a sense inevitable, though there may be defects in detail. The proportion (3:2) observed between rise and fall is natural, and right. It is artistically just to apportion these amounts to each. And the general method of the poet, in spite of all that may have been said, is defensible, indeed I think admirable.

There may have previously existed stirring verse dealing in a straightforward manner and even in natural narrative sequence with the fall of Hygelac, with Beowulf's deeds, or again with the fluctuations of the feud between the houses of Hréðel the Geat and Ongenþeow the Swede, or with the tragedy of the Heathobards, or the treason that destroyed the glory of the Scyldings. Indeed we must admit this to be practically certain: it was the very existence of such connected legends (making [193] a largely connected and known whole, though not of course, dealt with in the chronicle fashion in long historical poems) that permitted the peculiar use of them in Beowulf. You cannot criticize or comprehend the poem, if you argue as though its original audience was in like case to ourselves and possessed Beowulf in splendid isolation. For Beowulf was not designed to tell the tale of Hygelac's fall, or for that matter the whole biography of Beowulf, still less the history of the downfall of the Geatish kingdom — but it used knowledge of these things for a different purpose.

The poet might reply thus if he could be got to understand the modern critics: "The history of the Danes, and Frisians, and Geats has often been treated before, and well-handled — you have surely heard the poems? In any case the gentle and learned had, in my day. I chose a tale that touched on these things, and dealt with it in rather a new fashion, somewhat elaborately, allowing Beowulf's temper and youthful style to be caught (portrait of a brave eorl in early manhood), while I sketched in with allusions to well-known things the background of his achievements, the traditional heroic history of the northern world. Beowulf, I understand, you do you not think 'historical.' At any rate, I made him walk in poetic history. The things which now interest you most (poetry in itself does not seem to be one of them), and about which you clamour for more details, because you have hardly any other sources of information, are on the "outer edges" in my poem, because in my poem they belong there.

[194] I put Beowulf in the centre, because my poem is about him. Do not blame me, but time and your ancestors who have reduced the ancient poetry of England to such a few fragments. I was well enough esteemed in my time, but Beowulf was not my only poem, nor was I the chief Anglo-Saxon poet ancient or modern. There were many good poems that were then well-known, though I never saw

a copy of them or heard of them being written down. Still chance has preserved my <u>Beowulf</u> for you — why not listen to it, as I made it. It has been fairly well preserved on the whole.

You do not think much of trolls and dragons? Then our tastes differ, and living a thousand years later does not prove without further argument that your taste is superior. You are too sophisticated, and many of you have read too much too carelessly. I do not think most of you have seen the point of it all, or caught the significance of the dragon. Yes, I know, I have heard it said by more than one <u>úþwita</u> (scholar) of yours that it is monsters in both halves that is so disgusting. One they could have stomached more easily. But that is <u>nonsense</u>. I can see the point of asking for <u>no</u> monsters — only in that case do not bother with my poem, for it is not that sort of poem. There is something to be said for <u>none</u>. Also something for the situation in <u>Beowulf</u>. But nothing at all for mere reduction in numbers. It would really have been preposterous, if I had recounted Beowulf's rise to fame in commonplace wars in Sweden or Frisia, and had then ended him with a dragon. Or if I had told of his cleansing of Heorot and brought him [195] to death and defeat in a Swedish invasion! If the dragon is the right end for Beowulf — and I will not argue that any more — then Grendel is the right sort of beginning. They are creatures of similar orders, symbols (not allegories, my good sir) of a similar kind, and of like significance. Triumph over one is balanced by defeat by the other. And the Grendel-feat comes at the right moment: not in the earliest youth (though the <u>nicors</u> that I alluded to show from the beginning that Beowulf is not just an ordinary <u>hæleþ</u> on a strictly historical scale), and not during the later humdrum of recognized ability and carrying out of early promise, but in the first moment, which does come in the lives of remarkable men, when men look up with surprise and see that a 'hero' has unawares leaped forth in power. The placing of the dragon is inevitable: a man can but die upon his death-day."

I will for all represent my view in this way.

Let us to conclude consider this once more on our own account. If Alfred had perished in old age in actual battle with the Danes, and by the sacrifice of his life in some desperate assault had achieved a victory that saved his stricken people for the moment, and had been buried among lamentation and the boding of final ruin not far off — then a poet might have arisen who told first of Ashdown, when Alfred, not yet king, left his brother and charged up the hill to the bitter fight about the thorn-tree, achieving great victory, and who then passed to his last campaign and his dying battle, while he introduced allusively (or omitted) all the rest of Alfred's [196] long life and achievements and the traditions of his royal house. To any one but an historian in search of facts and relative chronology this would have been a fine thing, an heroic elegiacal poem <u>in the ancient English manner</u> — already perhaps a little enlarged owing to the greater and more impersonal import, transcending the mere fortunes of the house of Wessex, of the struggle in which Alfred was engaged. It would be much better poetry than a verse narrative chronicle, however spirited, or steadily advancing of his birth, deeds, battles and death in due order and proportion. This mere arrangement would give it already a greater significance than any straight account of one man's deeds: the contrast of youth and achievement with sacrifice, defeat and death. But even so it would still not be so large as the rise and fall of poor 'folk-tale' Beowulf with his 'incredible and childish' monsters. You would have to turn your Danes into dragons for that. It is just because the main foes in Beowulf are inhuman, that the story has something more large and permanent than this imaginary epic of a great king. It glimpses the cosmic and moves with the thought of all men, and the fate of human life and effort; it escapes from the petty wars of princes, and overleaps the dates of historical periods, however important. At the beginning, and during its process, and most of all at the end, we look down as if from a visionary height upon the house of men in the valley of the world. A light starts — lixte se léoma ofer landa fela (light from it shone out over many lands) — and there is the far sound of music, but the outer darkness and its hostile offspring lie ever in wait for [197] the torches to fail and the voices to cease. Grendel is maddened by the sound of the harp.

One may ask what from the purely human point of view could be, however simple or obvious, yet more moving and profound than such a theme? What symbol better than the dragon, mightiest of elemental creatures, filled with fire, he that covets gold wrought to shape by human art, and gathering it lies upon it, hoarding it but not using it, keeping it in the dark. That the dragon-spirit is found among men — that the enemy is not only outside the gates — does not alter this, though it complicates it. Even so in Grendel we see, as well as one of troll-kind, in original conception the offspring of the earth made of the very stone of the world, also a parody of man misformed by hate (earmsceapen on weras wæstmum) (a wretched creature in the shape of a man), who bears hell with him, feond on helle (enemy in hell) even as he walks in Denmark, being rejected by God. The poet has made him spring ultimately from Adam. But neither the dragon nor Grendel have become abstract, or allegorical. We have myth in history, and history turned myth.

And one final point — which those will feel who today preserve still the ancient human piety toward the past. Beowulf is not a 'primitive' poem; it is a late one, at the end of an epoch, using the materials, then [198] plentiful, of a day already changing and passing, which has now for ever vanished, swallowed in oblivion, and using them for a new purpose with a wider sweep of imagination, if with a less bitter and concentrated force of mood. Beowulf was already antiquarian in a good sense. And it now produces a singular effect. For it is now itself to us ancient; and yet its maker was telling of things already old and weighted with regret, and he expended his art in making keen that touch upon the heart which sorrows have that are both poignant and remote. So that if the funeral of Beowulf moved once like the echo of an ancient dirge, it is to us as a memory brought over the hills, an echo of an echo. There is not much poetry in the world that has this effect; and though Beowulf may not be among the very greatest poems of our western world and its tradition, it has nonetheless its own individual character and peculiar solemnity which no comparisons can take away, its own ancient cadences of verse, and its own thought. To recapture such echoes is the final fruit of scholarship in an old tongue (and it is the most honourable object — rather than the analysis of an historical document) fruit that is good for all to eat if they may, but which can be gathered only in this way. For such reasons ultimately do we study 'Anglo-Saxon.'

EXPLANATORY NOTES

In these notes I have attempted to explain, as best I can, the background and source material as well as the general thrust of Tolkien's arguments. I apologize if the notes seem pedantic, or if I explain what are (to some) obvious or simple terms and ideas, and I particularly apologize for explaining Tolkien's various jokes. But it is my hope that those who get any given joke will not need to use the notes and will thus be spared my dissection (and hence destruction) of the humor. The aim of the notes is to provide an easy reference for both interested readers of Tolkien's fiction and professional scholars of Old English. At times these two audiences will have different needs. I have tried to accommodate them.

While considerations of space make it probably impossible for every single potential reference to be captured in the notes, I do hope that the present construction of this section will allow for the book to be useful as well as interesting to its readers, both casual and specialized.

Tolkien relied upon a prodigious number of sources for *Beowulf and the Critics*. I have tried to the best of my ability to cite the particular editions of works that he used, but in some cases I have not been able to determine a specific edition or even (in the case of many works in Old Norse poetry and prose, much of which I am convinced Tolkien was able to quote from memory) the editor of the work used. In those cases I have tried to cite a "standard edition" or, failing that, the most readily available. In no case have I cited a work that I have not personally examined.

It is my hope that students of *Beowulf*, particularly beginning students (and most particularly my own students), will find these notes helpful. They can be used as a sort of concise *Encyclopedia Anglo-Saxonica*, at least for the history of *Beowulf* criticism up until the 1930s. They also show the process by which a great scholar creates an important work, and the glimpse they give into the mind of J. R. R. Tolkien has been for me, and will be, I hope, for readers, valuable indeed.

'A' Text

Folio 1

1. The Reverend Oswald Cockayne

Thomas Oswald Cockayne (1807–1873) was a major nineteenth-century scholar of Anglo-Saxon. The first chapter in his book *The Shrine: A Collection of Occasional*

Papers on Dry Subjects, entitled "Dr. Bosworth and his Saxon Dictionary," is a plea for Oxford to remove its name from Bosworth's dictionary so that the responsibility for what Cockayne saw to be the many errors in grammar in the first edition of the dictionary would rest solely with Bosworth. Cockayne's hostility to the dictionary is clearly related to Bosworth's reliance on the new field of Germanic philology: ". . . it is not comparative philology (filology) nor Bopp nor Pott nor an army of German fanatics, that we want in a Saxon dictionary."

Cockayne's references are to Franz Bopp and August Friedrich Pott, both nineteenth-century German philologists.

2. **The Rev. Joseph Bosworth, D.D., F.R.S., Rawlinsonian Professor of Anglo-Saxon**
Joseph Bosworth (1789–1876), Doctor of Divinity, Fellow of the Royal Society. Bosworth, who is best known for his *Anglo-Saxon Dictionary*, held the Rawlinson Professorship, an endowed chair at Oxford that was later, after he donated £10,000 to Oxford, renamed the Rawlinson Bosworth Professorship of Anglo-Saxon. The chair was founded in 1750, when Richard Rawlinson gave rents of £87. 16s. 8d. for the support "forever" of an Anglo-Saxon professor; it is the most prestigious academic position in the field of Anglo-Saxon studies. John Earle was also Rawlinsonian Professor of Anglo-Saxon. The Rawlinson Bosworth Professorship was awarded to Tolkien in 1925.

3. **"I have long entertained [the conviction] that Dr. Bosworth is not a man so diligent in his special walk as duly to read the books . . . which have been printed in our old English, or so-called Anglosaxon tongue. He may do very well for a Professor."**
The complete quotation is:

> Up to this point I have tried to lend to others the conviction I have long entertained, that Dr. Bosworth is not a man so diligent in his special walk, as duly to read the books, especially the Gospels, which have been printed in our old English or Anglosaxon tongue. He may do very well for a professor, but before the University of Oxford shares with him the title page of a dictionary I will try to make my voice, feeble as I know it to be, heard on the other side.

Thomas Oswald Cockayne, *The Shrine: A Collection of Occasional Papers on Dry Subjects* (London: Williams and Norgate, 1864), 1: 4.

4. **Bosworth's dictionary**
This work remains, and will remain until the Toronto *Dictionary of Old English* project is completed, the standard lexicon of Old English.

Joseph Bosworth, *An Anglo-Saxon Dictionary, Based on the Manuscript Collections of the late Joseph Bosworth . . . Edited and Enlarged by T. Northcote Toller* (Oxford: Clarendon Press, 1898).

Folio 2

5. **the real effective beginning of modern scholarship was made by Kemble**
John Mitchell Kemble (1807–1857) was a scholar of Anglo-Saxon who studied at Trinity College, Cambridge, and then at Göttingen, where he was a pupil of Jakob Grimm. Kemble applied the techniques of the newly developed Germanic philology to Old English texts. Tolkien is referring to his translation of *Beowulf* into Modern English.

John Mitchell Kemble, *A Translation of the Anglo-Saxon Poem of 'Beowulf' with a Copious Glossary Preface and Philological Notes* (London: William Pickering, 1837).

6. **W. P. Ker**
William Paton Ker (1855–1923), fellow of All Souls College, Oxford, 1879–1923. A literary scholar whose erudition in many languages and literatures was matched by his influence both within academe and in the more popular versions of literary study, Ker published some of the first criticism to take *Beowulf* seriously as a poem rather than simply as a historical document. His *Epic and Romance* and *The Dark Ages* attempted to provide a complete picture of the range of medieval European literature. Ker set *Beowulf* in a context of "Northern" poetry, comparing and contrasting the poem to Icelandic, Old High German, and other "epic" poems. He claims that the merits of *Beowulf* have perhaps been overstated, and that *Genesis* and *Judith* are in fact better poems than *Beowulf*, as is *The Battle of Maldon* (*Dark Ages*, 251–63). Ker was the teacher of R. W. Chambers (about whom see below note 8). Chambers wrote Ker's entry in the *Dictionary of National Biography 1922–1930* (London: Oxford University Press, 1937), 467–69, and included a treatment of him in *Man's Unconquerable Mind: Studies of English Writers from Bede to A. E. Housman and W. P. Ker* (London: Jonathan Cape, 1939), 386–406. See also B. I. Evans, *W. P. Ker as a Critic of Literature* (Glasgow: Jackson, 1955).

W. P. Ker, *The Dark Ages* (London: Blackwood and Sons, 1904), 26.
W. P. Ker, *Epic and Romance: Essays on Medieval Literature* (London: Macmillan and Co., 1897; repr. New York: Dover, 1958).

7. **'Beowulf and the Heroic Age in England' (xxvi pages and all too short) contributed by Chambers, the greatest of living Anglo-Saxon scholars, to Sir Archibald Strong's translation**
R. W. Chambers, "Beowulf and the Heroic Age," in *Beowulf Translated into Modern English Rhyming Verse*, ed. Archibald Strong (London: Constable, 1925), vii–xxxii.

Beowulf Translated into Modern English Rhyming Verse, ed. Archibald Strong (London: Constable, 1925).

8. **R. W. Chambers**

Raymond Wilson Chambers (1874–1942) was one of the great Anglo-Saxonists of the early twentieth century. Chambers's monumental work on *Beowulf* remains essential for those who wish to study the poem seriously. Chambers was Professor of English language and literature at University College, London. In 1925 he was the senior and most respected Anglo-Saxonist in England. He was offered, but turned down, the Rawlinson Bosworth Professorship of Anglo-Saxon, and his deferral allowed Tolkien to be awarded the post. Chambers gave the first W. P. Ker lecture in Glasgow.

9. **Sir Archibald Thomas Strong (1876–1930)**

A professor at the University of Melbourne, Strong wrote *A Short History of English Literature* and *Beowulf Translated into Modern English Rhyming Verse*. The commentaries on *Beowulf* in both books are important foils for Tolkien's arguments in *Beowulf and the Critics*.

Folio 3

10. **'research'**

This passage reflects Tolkien's dislike of the newer practice of postgraduate degree programs at Oxford. See Carpenter, *The Inklings*, 228–29, and cf. idem, *J. R. R. Tolkien: A Biography*, 134, 237; see also R. Currie, "The Arts and Social Studies, 1914–1939," in *History of the University of Oxford* 8: *The Twentieth Century*, ed. B. Harrison (Oxford: Clarendon, Press, 1994), 109–38, here 124–27, and cf. 217–18.

11. **A man found a mass of old stone in a unused patch, and made of it a rock garden; but his friends coming perceived that the stones had once been part of a more ancient building, and they turned them upsidedown to look for hidden inscriptions;**

This passage, the genesis of Tolkien's famous allegory of the tower, seems to refer to a passage from Matthew Arnold quoted by Ker. Compare:

> The very first thing that strikes one in reading the *Mabinogion* is how evidently the mediæval story-teller is pillaging an antiquity of which he does not fully possess the secret; he is like a peasant building his hut on the site of Halicarnassus or Ephesus; he builds, but what he builds is full of materials of which he knows not the history, or knows by a glimmering tradition merely — stones 'not of this building,' but of an older architecture, greater, cunninger, more majestical.

The phrase "not of this building" is from Hebrews 9:11 in the Authorised (King James) Version of the Bible; the Douai-Rheims Version that Tolkien as a Roman Catholic would have used has "not of this creation."

Ker, *Dark Ages*, 59.

Matthew Arnold, "On the Study of Celtic Literature," in *Lectures and Essays in Criticism*, ed. R. H. Super (Ann Arbor: University of Michigan Press, 1962), 322.

12. it is a half-baked native epic the development of which was killed by the same influence
The source for this comment seems to be:

We have thus in *Beowulf* a half-finished epos, as if benumbed in the midst of its growth. The introduction of Christianity was doubtless one of the causes that destroyed the productive power of epic poetry. The vital continuity of the mythical tradition was interrupted; new material and new ideas came gradually to the foreground in the nation's mind. The elements which, though developed simultaneously with the epos, as we have seen, bore the germs of the decay of the epic style, were greatly increasing; vis., the inclination to reflection, to elegiac tenderness. Besides this, the founding of a literature raised a barrier between the learned and the unlearned. But even had Christianity and literature not been introduced, *Beowulf* would hardly have become an English *Iliad*. Such poems arise only among nations that victoriously maintain ideals of higher culture against inimical forces.

Bernhard ten Brink, *History of English Literature*, trans. Horace M. Kennedy (London: George Bell and Sons, 1895), 1: 28.

Folio 4
13. Andaman-islanders
The Andaman Islands are a group of remote and numerous small islands in the Bay of Bengal. The islanders have, over the years, been portrayed as barbaric cannibals; for example, an Andaman Islander is a villain in Sir Arthur Conan Doyle's *The Sign of Four*. Tolkien is here using the stereotype of the undeveloped islanders (whose culture was often referred to as "Stone Age") in contrast to the comparatively more developed technology of the Anglo-Saxons, and is implying that many critics fail to recognized that the Anglo-Saxons, even in the earlier stages of their history, had produced a written literature and a culture superior to that of a supposedly "Stone Age" tribe.

Arthur Conan Doyle, *The Sign of Four* (London: Spencer Blackett, 1890).

Folio 5

14. **<u>index expurgatorius</u>**

Literally "a list of things that should be expunged." Tolkien is here referring in passing to the practice of banning and burning certain books thought to contain heretical ideas. The destruction of an unknowable number of precious Anglo-Saxon books and manuscripts during such purges (particularly in the sixteenth century), and the sadness that Tolkien undoubtedly felt at the enormous and unrecoverable loss of literature, makes the jest all the more telling: that Tolkien would even joke about putting some books on an "index expurgatorius" suggests how awful he believes them to be. The actual Roman Catholic *Index Librorum Prohibitorum* was abolished only in the 1960s.

15. **Strong, *Short History of English Literature.***

For Strong, see note 9 above.

16. **Strong, *Beowulf Translated.***

For Strong, see note 9 above.

17. **Morris' <u>Sigurd The Volsung</u>**

There was a dwelling of Kings ere the world was waxed old;
Dukes were the door-wards there, & the roofs were thatched with gold;
Earls were the wrights that wrought it, and silver nailed its doors;
Earls' wives were the weaving-women, queens' daughters strewed its floors,
And the masters of the its song-craft were the mightiest men that cast
The sails of the storm of battle adown the bickering blast.
There dwelt men merry-hearted, and in hope exceeding great
Met the good days and the evil as they went the way of fate:
There the Gods were unforgotten, yea whiles they walked with men,
Though e'en in that world's beginning rose a murmur now and again
Of the midward time and the fading and the last of the latter days,
And the entering of the terror, and the death of the People's Praise.

Thus was the dwelling of Volsung, the King of the Midworld's Mark,
As a rose in the winter season, a candle in the dark . . ."

William Morris, *The Story of Sigurd the Volsung and the Fall of the Nibelungs*, in *The Collected Works of William Morris: With Introductions by his Daughter May Morris* (London: Longmans Green and Company, 1811), 12: 1.
Strong, *Beowulf Translated*. For Strong, see note 9 above.

Folio 6

18. **The main story deals with the adventures of Beowulf in his contest with ogres and dragons . . . This short summary does scant justice to the poem.**

Strong, *Short History of English Literature*, 2. For Strong, see note 9 above.

19. **A History of English Literature (in 111 pages!) by Dr. Compton-Rickett, a potting of his longer work (which is as erroneous …**
Arthur Compton-Rickett, *A History of English Literature* (London: People's Books, 1912).

Folio 7

20. **the Germania which Tacitus describes**
The Roman historian Tacitus' descriptions of the customs of the barbarian German tribes is our source for much of what we think we know of the life of the ancestors of the Anglo-Saxons before they migrated to Britain in the fifth century and, eventually, converted to Christianity. But Tacitus can not be relied upon uncritically: he was using his description of the "Germans" in part to criticize what he saw as the softness and corruption of the Roman empire around 100 A.D.

Tacitus, *The Agricola and The Germania*, trans. H. Mattingly (New York: Penguin, 1971).

21. **in outline the story is trivial enough … telling us, in most authentic fashion, of life as it was lived in far-off heathen days.**
The Christian allusions show up rather incongruously against the pervading paganism.
***Beowulf* is the only poem of any length … which has come down to us, of the early heroic poetry of the Teutons,**
Though biblical allusions abound … the background is not Christian but heathen
All quotations are verbatim from: Strong, *Short History of English Literature*, 2–3. For Strong, see note 9 above.

Folio 8

22. **the days of Queen Anne**
Queen Anne ruled from 1702 to 1714.

Note that W. P. Ker also uses Queen Anne as a touchstone:

Most of the intellectual things on which [the educational work and general culture of the Dark Ages] set most store are derived, on the one hand, from ancient Greece, and on the other are found surviving as respectable commonplaces, scarcely damaged, in the Augustan Ages of Louis XIV and Queen Anne.

Ker, *Dark Ages*, 26. For Ker, see above, note 6.

Folio 11

23. **Even 'early' is here misleading. It means early one presumes relatively to the whole later course of English to the present. Of the actual <u>heroic poetry</u> of the English "Beowulf" is, of course, to be viewed as a very <u>late</u> example.**

    Here Tolkien is arguing that Anglo-Saxon "heroic" poetry would have been composed and popular during the migration period (during the fifth and sixth centuries) or even earlier, when the ancestors of the Anglo-Saxons still lived on the European continent. If these ancestors did indeed possess heroic poetry (which might have included some form of the *Beowulf* story), then indeed *Beowulf*, which Tolkien believed to have been written in the eighth century, would be at the later end of the period of the composition of heroic poetry.

24. **The particular fame of the maker of verse such as <u>Heorrenda</u> than the maker of jewel or sword such as <u>Wéland</u>.**

    Heorrenda and Weland are both mentioned in the poem *Deor*, which is found in the *Exeter Book* miscellany of Anglo-Saxon poetry: Heorrenda is a scop, a court poet, who has replaced Deor, another scop and the narrator of the poem, as the favorite minstrel of the lord of the Heodeningas.

    > Þæt ic bi me sylfum   secgan wille,
    > þæt ic hwile wæs   Heodeninga scop,
    > dryhtne dyre.   Me was Deor noma.
    > Ahte ic fela wintra   folgað tilne,
    > holdne hlaford,   oþþæt Heorrenda nu,
    > leoðcræftig monn   londryht geþah,
    > þæt me eorla hleo   ær gesealde.

    > [I wish to say this about myself, that I for some time was the scop of the Heodeningas, dear to the lord. Deor was my name. For many winters I had good office and a loyal lord, until now Heorrenda, a poet-crafty man, has received the land-rights that to me the protector of men had previously given.]

    Weland is the archetypal Germanic smith, cognate with the Roman Vulcan. Beowulf says that his corselet, an heirloom of his grandfather Hrethel, is "Welandes geweorc" (the work of Weland). Close to Oxford, and probably well known to Tolkien, is a prehistoric barrow called "Wayland's Smithy." Local legend has it that if one left a horse and a silver penny overnight at the barrow, Wayland would shoe the horse and take the penny as payment. For a possible link between Wayland's Smithy and Tolkien's work see Shippey, *Road to Middle-earth*, 23 and *Author of the Century*, 92.

    Deor, lines 35–41

    G. P. Krapp and E. van K. Dobbie, *The Exeter Book*, The Anglo-Saxon Poetic Records 3 (New York: Columbia University Press, 1936), 178–79.

Beowulf, line 455

Friedrich Klaeber, ed., *Beowulf and the Fight at Finnsburg*, 3rd ed. (Boston: D. C. Heath, 1950), 17–18.

Thomas A. Shippey, *The Road to Middle-earth* (Boston: Houghton Mifflin Company, 1983), 23.

Thomas A. Shippey, *J. R. R. Tolkien: Author of the Century* (Boston: Houghton Mifflin, 2001), 92.

25. **The fame and names of individual Icelandic poets have been better preserved even than their works.**

The name of Úlfr inn Óargi, who lived in the eighth century, has been preserved, but none of his poems. Likewise we know that Stúf the Blind in the eleventh century knew many poems by heart, but we have none of his compositions (that we know of) extant.

E. V. Gordon, *An Introduction to Old Norse* (Oxford: Clarendon Press, 1927), xlii, lviii.

26. **Great differences can be detected even among the lays of the <u>Elder Edda</u>.**

The *Elder Edda* are a group of poems written in Old Icelandic that were assembled by an unknown collector at the end of the twelfth century. Some of the poems themselves may be as old as the ninth century; most probably date from between 900 and 1050; and a few may even date from the early twelfth century. The *Elder Edda* (or Poetic Edda) preserve the oldest poetic treatment of Norse mythological material.

For an edition and translation see:

Lee M. Hollander, ed., *The Poetic Edda* (Austin, TX: University of Texas Press, 1962).

Folio 12

27. **a crowd of 'ancestral voices prophesying war.'**

This is a quotation from Samuel Taylor Coleridge's "Kubla Khan":

> But Oh! that deep romantic chasm which slanted
> Down the green hill athwart a cedarn cover!
> A savage place! as holy and enchanted
> As e'er beneath a waning moon was haunted
> By woman wailing for her demon-lover!
> And from this chasm, with ceaseless turmoil seething,
> As if this earth in fast thick pants were breathing,
> A mighty fountain momently was forced:
> Amid whose swift half-intermitted burst
> Huge fragments vaulted like rebounding hail,
> Or chaffy grain beneath the thresher's flail:

> And 'mid these dancing rocks at once and ever
> It flung up momently the sacred river.
> Five miles meandering with a mazy motion
> Through wood and dale the sacred river ran,
> Then reached the caverns measureless to man
> And sank in tumult to a lifeless ocean:
> And 'mid this tumult Kubla heard from far
> Ancestral voices prophesying war!

Samuel Taylor Coleridge, "Kubla Khan," in *The Poems of Samuel Taylor Coleridge*, ed. Ernest Hartley Coleridge (London: Humphrey Milford for Oxford University Press, 1927), 297–98.

28. **His grandchildren were at grips with such Teutons par excellence, the viking invaders, and regarded them as the very devil.**
If *Beowulf* was written in 750, as Tolkien believed, then the grandchildren of the poet would have been adults in the early part of the ninth century, when Vikings (who were Northern Germanic tribes, i.e., "Teutons" in the old nomenclature) were sacking and destroying, and eventually invading and occupying, much of the eastern part of England.

29. **What ever their tongue they would have written them down rather in the kin of Grendel than of Hrothgar (for even Grendel may probably well have spoken Danish). And there is the rub. "Beowulf" may be a poem about Danes, but it is an English poem about them.**
Tolkien is here pointing out the obvious: that even if *Beowulf* is about Danes and Geats, the poem is in fact written in English and thus in some essential way more closely connected to English history and culture than it is to the history and culture of Denmark or Sweden. His use of the reference to *Hamlet*, "there is the rub" (literally, there is the obstacle), emphasizes that this other most famous work of English literature is nominally about Danes but is in fact considered a wholly English work of art, involved in English themes and a part of English, not Danish, culture. Tolkien wants his readers to recognize the parallel and accept *Beowulf*, regardless of the "nationality" of its characters, as being as much a part of English cultural history as is Shakespeare.

> To sleep, perchance to dream. Ay, there's the rub,
> For in that sleep of death what dreams may come,
> When we have shuffled off this mortal coil,
> Must give us pause.

Hamlet, Act 3, Scene 1, lines 66–69
William Shakespeare, *Hamlet*, ed. David Bevington, in *The Complete Works of William Shakespeare*, Vol. 3 (New York: Bantam Books, 1988).

Folio 13

30. **. . . from Aidan to Stigand any more than Icelandic is all one and the same from the Landnám in the 9th century to the cruel feuds of the great houses and the submission to the Norwegian crown in the 13th century, or Rome from Romulus to Constantine.**

St. Aidan was a seventh-century monk from the island of Iona who, under the auspices of King Oswald of Northumbria, began the conversion of the north of England in 635. He established the monastery on the island of Lindisfarne. Stigand was the chaplain to King Cnut and later bishop of Winchester and (uncanonically) archbishop of Canterbury in 1052. "From Aidan to Stigand," therefore, covers the entire Christian period of Anglo-Saxon history with all the cultural, social, and political changes that occurred in those five centuries.

The Landnám ("Land-naming") in Iceland is the period, beginning around 874, when Norwegian settlers first migrated to Iceland. The "cruel feuds of the great houses" is a reference to a period of political chaos in Iceland caused by a small number of extremely powerful families struggling for political dominance. This struggle in the thirteenth century finally ended when Iceland submitted to the Norwegian crown in the years 1262–1264. From Landnám to the submission to the Norwegian crown, therefore, covers the entire early independent history of Iceland, with all the changes in cultural, social, and political life that took place in those four centuries.

Romulus is the legendary king who supposedly founded Rome in 735 B.C. Constantine is the Roman emperor who with the edict of Milan in 313 A.D. gave civil rights to Christian throughout the empire. Thus the period from Romulus to Constantine comprises the entire pre-Christian history of Rome.

Tolkien's point here is that no one would say that Roman history is monolithic throughout such a long period. Likewise no one should believe that Icelandic or Anglo-Saxon history is monolithic and "one thing" across the changes of the centuries.

31. **The 8th. century is now, probably universally agreed to fit all the various lines of enquiry.**

Such agreement is no longer the case in *Beowulf* study. In fact, the date of the poem is the single most discussed (some Anglo-Saxonists would say it has been discussed far too much) topic in *Beowulf* criticism. Credible and respected critics have put forth strong arguments that date the poem anywhere from the seventh to the early eleventh century. General agreement does not seem to be likely in the near future. The only date we can be absolutely certain of is the date of the manuscript in which *Beowulf* is found: it was written, experts agree, between 975 and 1025.

Folio 14

32. . . . . 'Beowulf' 'biblical allusions abound, . . . the background is not Christian
but heathen.'

Strong, *Short History of English Literature*, 2. For Strong, see note 9 above.

33. **references to Cain**

Lines 107 and 1261 of *Beowulf* are presumed by scholars to be references to
Cain, the son of Adam who slays his brother Abel in Genesis 4:1–16. Line 107
contains the word "Caines" but it is altered by a scribe from "Cames." We can
nevertheless presume that the reference is to Cain because the poet then tells us
that Cain received the punishment of God because he slew Abel. In line 1261
the word "camp" is emended by scholars to "Cain." In medieval tradition a race
of giants and monsters had arisen from the cursed lineage of Cain; they are
destroyed by the flood. This is the story Hrothgar "reads" on the sword hilt that
Beowulf brings back from the cave of Grendel's mother.

34. **one curious case of <u>Ingwine</u>, twice used as a name of the Danes;**

The literal translation of "Ingwine" would be "friends or followers of Ing." The
word is used to describe the Danes in *Beowulf* lines 1044 and 1319. Ing is apparently the name of a heathen deity, but Tolkien clearly believed that "Ingwine" was merely a compound that had lost any specifically religious meaning;
just as the majority of Modern English speakers use "Tuesday" without any
knowledge of the pagan god Tiu.

35. **a fossil which may indicate the character of the stones used in the building,
but says nothing of the use to which the architect has put them.**

This seems to be a reference to a passage from Matthew Arnold quoted by Ker.
See above note 11.

36. **<u>Wyrd</u> is mentioned, but this is quite another matter: <u>wyrd</u>**

The question of the exact meaning of "wyrd" is one of the great arguments in
Anglo-Saxon studies. The term is usually translated as "fate," but, as Tolkien's
remarks indicate, it can convey a complex range of meanings, many of which
are ambiguous, particularly in regard to the ways in which "wyrd" relates to the
Christian idea of providence, or God's plan for the world.

37. **Sir Archibald himself after profounder study speaks in his own introduction
to his translation not of the "heathen background" but of the "Christian
colouring" which the author has "given to his story".**

Strong, *Beowulf Translated*, xxxv–xxxvi. For Strong, see above, note 9.

Folio 15

38. **In Chambers' <u>Foreword</u> to this same translation (which should be read by all whatever else, save the poem itself, is unread)**
R. W. Chambers, "Beowulf and the Heroic Age," vii–xxxii. For Chambers, see above, note 8.

39. **On page xxvi, when everything seems going right, we hear once again that "the main story of <u>Beowulf</u> is a wild folk-tale."**
Chambers, "Beowulf and the Heroic Age," xxvi. For Chambers, see above, note 8.

40. <u>**King Lear**</u>
The story of King Lear is first told in detail by the early medieval historian Geoffrey of Monmouth in his *Historia Regum Britanniae* (*History of the Kings of Britain*). Geoffrey's work dates from approximately 1136, but scholars agree that the tale almost certainly has much older folk-tale roots probably related to the sources of the fairy tale of Cinderella.

While Tolkien, in a 1963 letter to W. H. Auden, had claimed to have "disliked cordially" the works of Shakespeare (*Letters*, 213) as T. A. Shippey has shown, several Shakespearean plays, particularly *Macbeth, King Lear, The Tempest* and *A Midsummer Night's Dream*, were influences upon and sources for *The Lord of the Rings* (*The Road to Middle-earth*, 133–48 and see also Shippey, *Author of the Century*, 289). If critics had any doubts about Shippey's conclusions, the mention of *Lear* several times, and in a positive context (obviously Tolkien is suggesting that the "folk-tale" aspect of Lear is "silly" but that Shakespeare has worked an important transformation upon his material), should support the idea that Tolkien respected the play.

And in fact it is possible to identify *Lear* even more closely with Tolkien's work (particularly in Book Five of *The Lord of the Rings*, the first half of *The Return of the King*) than has previously been noted. For instance, in Act I, Scene I, line 122, Lear says "come not between the dragon and his wrath," to which may be compared "Come not between the Nazgûl and his prey!" said by the Lord of the Nazgûl to Éowyn (*Return of the King*, 116). In Act I, Scene 1, line 170, Lear calls Kent "recreant." Denethor similarly cries to his servants: "Come, if you are not all recreant" (*Return of the King*, 130). The scene in which Lear asks Kent what services he can perform (Act I, Scene 4, line 31) could be a source for the scene where Denethor asks Pippin what services the hobbit can perform as esquire (*Return of the King*, 79–80). The Fool mentions seven stars in Act I, Scene 5, line 35 of *Lear*; in Act IV, Scene 7, lines 82–83 the words of the Doctor, "Be comforted, good madam. The great rage / You see, is killed in him" are similar to those of Aragorn in the Houses of Healing, "The worst is now over. Stay and be comforted" (*Return of the King*, 141). In Act V, Scene 3, line 266–268, Lear commands his men to "Lend me a looking glass; / If that her breath will mist or stain the stone, / Why, then she lives." Imrahil, seeing Éowyn seemingly dead, "held the bright-burnished vambrace that was upon his arm before her cold lips, and behold! A little mist was laid on it hardly to be seen." The madness of Denethor, in any event, is quite similar to the madness of Lear, and Éomer's blood-fury — "Death, death, death! Death take us all!" after he finds Éowyn seemingly dead (*Return of the King*, 119) has echoes of Lear's "No, no, no life? / Why should a dog, a horse, a rat, have life? / And thou no breath at all? Thou'lt come no more,/ Never, never, never, never, never!" when he knows that Cordelia is dead in Act V, Scene III, lines 311–314

William Shakespeare, *King Lear*, ed. David Bevington, in *The Complete Works of William Shakespeare*, Vol. 5 (New York: Bantam Books, 1988).

41. **The folk-tale is a good servant but a bad master: it has been allowed in 'Beowulf' to usurp the place of honour, and to drive into episodes and digressions the things which should be the main stuff of a well-conducted epic.**
Chambers, "Beowulf and the Heroic Age," xxvi. For Chambers see above, note 8.

And compare:

"Yet with this radical defect, a disproportion that puts the irrelevances in the centre and the serious things on the outer edges . . ."

Ker, *Dark Ages*, 253.

Folio 16
42. **John Earle**
John Earle (1824–1903) was Rawlinsonian Professor of Anglo-Saxon at Oxford. His translation of *Beowulf* into prose and his summary of the critical history of the poem were attempts to bring *Beowulf* to the attention of a larger and more general audience than the scholarly and antiquarian community. Earle's *The Deeds of Beowulf* is a particularly important source for *Beowulf and the Critics*.

John Earle, *The Deeds of Beowulf: An English Epic of the Eighth Century Done into Modern Prose* (Oxford: Clarendon Press, 1892).

43. **One may assent to Earle's quotation from Dowden 'The happiest moment in a critic's hours of study is, when seemingly by some divination, but really as the result of patient observation and thought, he lights upon the central motive of a great work'**
Earle, *The Deeds of Beowulf*, xcix.

Earle is quoting from:

Edward Dowden, "The Interpretation of Literature," in *Transcripts and Studies*, 2nd ed. (London: Kegan Paul, Trench, Trübner & Co, 1896), 237–68, here 264–65.

44. **Earle's particular divination, which ascribed the work to Hygeberht, Arch-bishop of Lichfield (787–803?) and made the whole poem into a kind of early political Utopia.**
Earle believed that *Beowulf* had been composed for the court of Offa, the king of Mercia, by Hygeberht, Archbishop of Lichfield. He interpreted Scyld as an allegory of Offa and Beowulf as an allegory of Ecgferth, the son of Offa, and he thought that the theme of *Beowulf* was: "mutual dependence is the law of human society":

> The general sense of the poem is this. There is work for the age of Blood and Iron, but such an age must yield to a better. Force is not the supreme and final arbiter of human destiny; above and beyond Might is enthroned the diviner genius of Right. In this idea we recognize the essential thought of Civilization, the clue to emergence out of barbarism. And even further back, as if in barbarism itself, we see a germ of culture and the gentler form of life. The honoured position of woman, which here rests upon an-cestral custom, is full of promise for the development of the nobler instincts of Society.

Earle, *The Deeds of Beowulf*, lxxxvii–lxxxviii, xc–xcviii.

45. **'Beowulf' the poem will be <u>gefælsod</u>.**
The word means literally "cleansed" or "purged." In line 430 Beowulf asks Hrothgar for permission "Heorot fælsian" ("to cleanse Heorot") from the scourge of Grendel. In line 825 Beowulf is said to have "gefælsod" ("cleansed") the hall by tearing off Grendel's arm. In line 1176 Queen Wealhtheow says that now, due to Beowulf's deeds, "Heorot is gefælsod" ("Heorot is cleansed"). Finally, in line 2352 the poet reminds us that long before the attack of the drag-on on the Geatish kingdom Beowulf had "sele gefælsode" ("cleansed the hall") of Hrothgar.

Tolkien's reference is meant to liken bad criticism in the study of *Beowulf* to the infestation of Heorot by monsters. This line is, I believe, the germ of the brilliant double meaning of the eventual title of the essay "*Beowulf*: The Mon-sters and the Critics," which can be read as simply indicating the interaction of the monsters in the poem with the critics who have discussed them or, if one takes another view, differentiating between the true critics (such as Chambers and Ker) and other critical "monsters" who have misread the poem.

Folio 17

46. **Mr. Shane Leslie**

Shane Leslie (1885–1971) was a poet, novelist (*Doomsland, The Oppidan*, and *The Cantab*), biographer, and memoirist.

47. **Mr. Shane Leslie's anthology of (I believe he said) Catholic poets speaks of "Beowulf" "as small beer." I hope in depending on memory (for I do not possess the worthless book) I am not wrong in ascribing these introductory words to Mr. Chesterton.**

The entire quotation is:

"Beowulf is small beer compared to the rich honey ale of Cuchulain Saga."

Tolkien is incorrect in ascribing the remark to Chesterton. It is Leslie's own, found in Leslie's 1924 introduction and persisting in the 1954 reprint.

Shane Leslie, ed., *An Anthology of Catholic Poets* (London: Burns Oates, 1924; repr. 1952), 2–3.

48. **Mr. Chesterton**

Gilbert Keith Chesterton (1874–1936), English novelist and poet, was one of the most famous literary critics of the early twentieth century. Tolkien clearly would be more troubled about the insulting "small beer" remark coming from Chesterton than he would if he had owned the "worthless book" and been able to check and note that in fact the remark comes from Leslie.

Tolkien appears to want to distance his own position from what was popularly thought to be Chestertonian "beer and Catholicisim." Compare C. S. Lewis's evenings of "beer and *Beowulf*." Tolkien did not want to be thought of as a "Chesterbellocian" Roman Catholic (Carpenter, *The Inklings*, 19, 26). And see below, note 336.

49. **his book includes what by its title seems intended for the "Dream of the Rood" in translation**

Anonymous (eighth century)
The Dream of the Rood

The Holy Cross speaks:

I am remembering in the long ago:
How at the forest-edge they hewed me low,
And stem-cut thence strong foes took me to stare
Upon and bade me outcast men to bear
And hillward bore me shoulder high and then
Foes fixed me there. I saw the Lord of men
In his might hastening to me to ascend,

Yet dared not break asunder nor me bend
Nor disobey for god's commandment's sake
Though Earth I saw in all her bosom quake.
I stood, who might have thrown the foes to sod.
Then gathered Him, the Warrior young called God
Almighty; resolute and strong; unbowed
Of courage went He up in sight of crowd
Upon the lofty Cross mankind to fend.
I trembled in His arms but dared not bend
Or earthward fall: but firmly had to stand.
On me, the Cross, the mighty King was spanned
The Heaven's Lord, yet dared I not to quail.
You see the Wounds, dark piercing of the Nail
And open gashes. To none dared bring I bane.
They scorned us both and I was made astain
With Blood forth from His Side that flowed,
When He like Man His Ghost sent on its road.
And many were the bitter pangs I bore
Upon that hill. The Lord of Hosts I saw
Unkindly set upon and darkness shroud
The Ruler's corpse with covering of cloud.
In face of shadowy night day's splendour leapt
All wan beneath the welkin. All creation wept.

In Leslie, ed., *An Anthology of Catholic Poets*, 21–22.

50. Dream of the Rood

Found in the *Vercelli Book*, one of the great Anglo-Saxon poetic codices (manu-script books), *The Dream of the Rood* (or *The Vision of the Cross*) is widely regarded as one of the finest of all Old English poems, blending Christianity with the ethos of the Germanic warrior culture. Christ is portrayed not as sacrificial victim but as an active young warrior who "mounts" the cross of his own volition.

The Dream of the Rood, in G. P. Krapp and E. van K. Dobbie, *The Vercelli Book*, The Anglo-Saxon Poetic Records 2 (New York: Columbia University Press, 1936), 61–65.

51. plough-candidates in a provincial university

According to the OED, "being ploughed" is university slang for failing an examination, first recorded in 1853. There is no entry for "plough-candidates," but the meaning is obvious. I have not been able to determine whether this par-ticular term was current in the 1930s or if Tolkien was being deliberately archaic.

52. **Old English verse does not unlock the treasures of its <u>word hord</u> readily**
"Word hord" ("hoard of words") is a poetic phrase that means something like "the collection of all possible words held in a person's mind." It is used in *Beowulf*, line 259, when the poet tells us that Beowulf "wordhord onleac" ("unlocked his word-hoard") and in so doing spoke to the Danish coast-guard.

Folio 18

53. **students trained in this scholarly Oxford school with <u>confidence</u>.**
This line clearly indicates that *Beowulf and the Critics* was, at this point in its composition, intended as a series of Oxford lectures (as Christopher Tolkien noted in his description of the manuscript upon its donation to the Bodleian Library).

54. **<u>Ars longa vita brevis</u> —**
Latin for "art is long, life is brief" — it takes much time to learn any art well, but our lives are finite and all too short for this work. The Latin commonplace is the source of Chaucer's opening for the *Parliament of Fowls* (see below, note 55).

55. **<u>the lyf so schort, the craft so long to lerne, so hard th' assay, so scharp the conquering</u>, as Chaucer says.**
    The lyf so short, the craft so long to lerne,
    Th'assay so hard, so sharp the conquerynge

Geoffrey Chaucer, *The Parliament of Fowls*, lines 1–2, in Larry D. Benson, et al., eds., *The Riverside Chaucer*, 3rd ed. (Boston: Houghton Mifflin, 1987), 385.

56. **in a composite Mss.**
The manuscript in which *Beowulf* is found is London, British Library, Cotton Vitellius A. xv (the manuscript name means that it was part of Sir Robert Bruce Cotton's collection of manuscripts in the seventeenth century, and that it was stored on a shelf under the bust of the Roman emperor Vitellius; it was the fifteenth manuscript on the first shelf). The *Beowulf* manuscript is sometimes called the "Nowell Codex" because the name of "Laurence Nouell" and the date 1563 is written at the top of the first page. Nowell was one of the earliest (he died in 1576) sixteenth-century students of Anglo-Saxon; see below, note 59.
    Cotton Vitellius A. xv is a composite made up of two unrelated manuscripts that were arbitrarily bound together in the seventeenth century. The half of the manuscript that contains *Beowulf*, however, was put together in the Anglo-Saxon period. It contains the texts of a prose homily on St. Christopher, the *Epistola Alexandri* (The letter of Alexander to Aristotle), *The Wonders of the East*, *Beowulf*, and *Judith*. Some critics have argued that the manuscript is a collection of materials relating to monsters: St. Christopher is a giant, various monstrous and wondrous beings are discussed in the *Letter* and the *Wonders*, and there are,

obviously, three monsters in *Beowulf*. The argument requires a bit of special pleading, however, when *Judith* is brought into the picture. Holofernes intends to do horrible things to Judith, and he is a drunkard, a lecher, and a violent man, but to interpret him as a monster *per se* is perhaps stretching the point. In fact we cannot be sure how the medieval scribes chose their material for Cotton Vitellius A. xv. But for the most convincing argument for the idea that the manuscript is a collection of texts about monsters, see:

Andy Orchard, *Pride and Prodigies: Studies in the Monsters of the Beowulf-Manuscript* (Cambridge: D. S. Brewer, 1995).

And also:

Michael Lapidge, "*Beowulf*, Aldhelm, the *Liber Monstrorum* and Wessex," in idem, *Anglo-Latin Literature (600–899)* (London: Hambledon Press, 1996), 271–311, 507.

57. (such as the <u>Epistola Alexandri</u> and the <u>Wonders of the East</u>) that occurred before it and after it.
Both of these texts are found in the same manuscript as *Beowulf*, British Library, Cotton Vitellius A. xv.

The *Epistola Alexandri* ("Letter of Aristotle") is a "letter" from Alexander the Great to his tutor, Aristotle. The *Wonders of the East* is a medieval text describing the various monsters and strange creatures purported to live in the East.

Editions of both texts can be found in:
Orchard, *Pride and Prodigies*, 173–253.

58. the scattering of MS remains of the 16th century
When Henry VIII dissolved the English monasteries in 1536, Thomas Cromwell, "the hammer of the monasteries," supervised the burning and destruction of much of England's early medieval cultural heritage, including an untold number of Anglo-Saxon manuscripts. A very few were saved in the sixteenth century by antiquarians like Laurence Nowell.

59. Laurence Nowell
Laurence Nowell (died 1576) was one of the earliest students of Anglo-Saxon in the sixteenth century. Somehow he came into possession of the *Beowulf* manuscript after the dissolution of the monasteries and the wholesale destruction of Anglo-Saxon literary remains in the sixteenth century. Also see above, note 58.

60. Humphrey Wanley
Humphrey Wanley (1672–1726) was an antiquarian scholar who first catalogued the vast majority of the Anglo-Saxon manuscripts still in existence.

61. Cotton Collection

The collection of books and manuscripts assembled in the early seventeenth century by Sir Robert Bruce Cotton of Denton, Huntingdonshire. Cotton devised the idea of an order of baronets who could purchase their titles from King James for one thousand pounds. He became a baronet himself in 1611 after being knighted. He angered King Charles I because he disapproved of the lack of a parliament, and as a result he was barred from his own library. Cotton died in 1631. The library was sold to the government of England in 1700 by Sir John Cotton, Robert Bruce Cotton's great-grandson. It was housed in Ashburnham House, where, in 1731, a fire completely destroyed 114 volumes and badly damaged another 98 (of the original 958). *Beowulf* was damaged, but escaped with only minor burns along the edges.

See:

John Earle, *Anglo-Saxon Literature* (London: Society for Promoting Christian Knowledge, 1884), 32.

Folio 19

62. in Vol. II (1705) of Hickes Thesaurus. "In hoc libro qui Poeseos Anglosaxonicae egregium est exemplum descripta videntur bella quae Beowulfus quidam Danus ex regio Scyldingorum stirpe ortus gessit contra Sueciae regulos."

[In this book, which is an excellent example of Anglo-Saxon poetry, it seems that there are wars described which a certain Beowulf, a Dane sprung from the royal race of the Scyldings, waged against the princes of Sweden.]

Humphrey Wanley, *Librorum Veterum Septentrionalium, qui in Angliae Bibliothecis extant, nec non multorum Veterum Codicum Septentrionalium alibi extantium Catalogus Historico-Criticus cum totius Thesauri Linguarum Septentrionalium sex Indicibus*, ed. George Hickes (Oxford, 1705), vol. 2.

George Hickes, ed., *De Antiquæ Litteraturæ Septentrionalis Utilitate, sive De Linguarum Veterum Septentrionalium Usu Dissertatio Epistolaris ad Bartholomæum Showere, Equitem Auratum, Non ita pridem Jurisconsultum apud Anglos, & Causarum Patronum Celeberrimum* (Oxford: E Theatro Sheldoniano, 1703).

63. Old English prose, such as that of Ælfric

Ælfric, who was abbot of Cerne Abbas in Dorset and later the first abbot of Eynsham in Oxfordshire, lived at the end of the tenth and the beginning of the eleventh century. He was a pupil of the great bishop Æthelwold of Winchester, who was responsible for beginning the Benedictine Reform of the monasteries in England. Ælfric is known for his grasp of Latin and his particularly clear and readable Old English prose. His most famous works are a series of homilies, a paraphrase of the first seven books of the Bible into Old English, and a book of the Lives of the Saints.

64. **Grim Johnson Thorkelin**
Grímur Jónsson Thorkelin (1752–1829), a Danish scholar, was the first to produce an edition of *Beowulf*. He viewed the poem as an important source for early Danish history (and see below, note 67).

65. **editio princeps in 1815.**
The first edition of *Beowulf*, published by Grímur Jónsson Thorkelin.

Grímur Jónsson Thorkelin, *De Danorum rebus gestis secul. III et IV. Poëma Danicum dialecto Anglo-Saxonica* (Copenhagen: Typis Th. E. Rangel, 1815).

66. **of the age of Alfred**
King Alfred ruled the West Saxon kingdom from 871 to 899. He was able to preserve Wessex against Viking incursions and eventually rebuild and then again defend the kingdom. Alfred strove to restore the Latin learning of the eighth century's "golden age" of English monasticism, learning which, according to Alfred's introduction to his translation of Gregory the *Great's Pastoral Care*, had been lost to England as part of the aftermath of the Viking incursions of the ninth century. Alfred translated a number of important works into English from Latin, and he imported books and learned monks from the continent.

67. **Thorkelin's first interest dates from 1786 when he visited England and had two transcripts made.**
The transcripts, known as *Thorkelin A* and *Thorkelin B* (A was made by an unnamed scribe who did not read Anglo-Saxon, and B was made by Thorkelin himself), are exceptionally important sources for *Beowulf* study. In the transcripts are preserved many manuscript readings that have since either been lost due to the gradual deterioration of the burnt edge of the manuscript or covered over by the paper frame put in place to protect those edges. But there are also a fair number of errors or divergent readings in both transcripts, and scholars have debated fiercely as to which readings should be believed for any given passage. See J. Gerritsen, "What Use are the Thorkelin Transcripts of *Beowulf*?" *Anglo-Saxon England* 28 (1999): 23–42.

Folio 20

68. **By 1807 his edition was practically ready for press, but it was destroyed by the gentle descendants of the barbarous Anglo-Saxons when they bombarded and stormed the old city of Copenhagen.**
During the Napoleonic Wars, England bombarded Copenhagen to force the Danes to surrender their navy (England feared that the continental powers would use the Danish navy for the invasion of England). The bombardment and capitulation occurred in 1807.

69. **It took him eight years to do the work again — a gallant effort for an old man.**

Thorkelin describes the work thus:

> O! luctuosos dies illos (qvorum acerba recordatio veteres animi curas, infandosqve dolores renovat) qvi me lauto orbarunt lare, et tota supellectile literaria, qvam per triginta et amplius annos impiger collegeram. Periit isto excidio Scyldingidos mea versio cum toto apparatu suo: et periisset æternum una animus eam iterandi, nisi Heros illustrissimus JOHANNES BULOWIUS, dynasta Sanderumgaardi, exhortatus fuisset me, consiliis et ære suo adjutam, opus iterum incoare, ut publicam videret lucem.

> Verum rei gravitas a tam difficili negotio me diu deterruit. At vicit amor patriæ et auctoritas Mæcenatis optimi, cujus magnificam ac singularem in doctis hominibus fovendis, juvandis, et ad præclara studia erigendis indolem sancte colo. Qva re factus audacior novam interpretationem, infelici augurio olim exactam, melioribus avibus de novo susceptam molitus sum, et tandem consummavi.

> [O! Those woeful days (the bitter memory of which brings back my old troubles and ineffable sorrows) that robbed me of my sumptuous home and all my scholarly tools, which I had assiduously gathered for thirty years or more. My rendering of the Scylding epic, together with its entire scholarly apparatus, perished utterly; my resolve to start again would have perished eternally along with it had not that most noble hero, Johan Bülow, Lord of Sanderumgaard, encouraged me with advice and money, to resume the work so that it would see the light of day. Nevertheless the immensity of the task deterred me for a long time. Love of country, however, prevailed, as did the council of my Maecenas, whose magnificent and singular nature in cherishing, aiding, and guiding scholars, I reverently honor. Thus encouraged, I worked anew at the translation, completed under unlucky circumstances, then begun again under better auspices. At last, I am finished.]

Thorkelin, *De Danorum rebus gestis*, xvi. For Thorkelin, see above notes 64, 65, 67.

Translation by Robert E. Bjork, "Grímur Jónsson Thorkelin's Preface to the First Edition of *Beowulf*, 1815," *Scandinavian Studies* 68 (1996): 291–323.

70. **Pastor <u>Grundtvig</u>**

Nikolai Frederik Severin Grundtvig (1783–1872) was a Danish theologian, poet, and scholar. He translated *Heimskringla* and Saxo Grammaticus as well as *Beowulf*. Grundtvig brought to Denmark ideas that led to the creation of the Folk High Schools. He became titular bishop of Zealand in 1862. See *Heritage and*

Prophecy: Grundtvig and the English-Speaking World, ed. A. M. Allchin, et al. (Aarhus: Aarhus University Press, 1993).

71. **Privy-counselor Bülow, the Mæcenas of his time**
Johan Bülow (1751–1828), Knight of the Order of the Elephant, Grand Cross of the Order of the Dannebrog, was a Danish diplomat and advisor to the court. He supported both Thorkelin and Grundtvig, as well as many other poets and scholars, including Rasmus Rask. See Johannes C. H. R. Steenstrup, *Historieskrivningen i Danmark i det 19de Aarhundrede (1801–1863)* (Copenhagen: B. Lunos Bogtrykkeri, 1898).
Gaius Cilnius Mæcenas (died 8 B.C.) was a Roman statesman and advisor to Augustus. He was a patron of literature, and his name has become synonymous with the support of letters.

72. **his own Anglo-Saxon verse in commendation of Bülow**
See below, note 380.
As Tolkien notes, Grundtvig's verse often violates the rules of Anglo-Saxon metrics and grammar.

73. **proper names in the text, first discerning Sigemund the Volsing for instance; and it was he who first identified Hygelac with the Chochilaicus in Gregory of Tours**
Grundtvig connected the Sigemund whose story is told in lines 874b–902a of *Beowulf* with the hero Sigmund of the *Völsunga Saga*. He also noted that the name Chochilaicus mentioned in the *History* of Gregory of Tours can be shown, using basic philological procedures, to be equivalent to the name of Hygelac in *Beowulf*. See below, note 131.

74. **Bjowulfs Drape. Et Gothisk Helte-Digt fra forrige Aar-Tusinde af Angel-Saxisk paa Danske Riim ved. Nic. Fred. Sev Grundtvig, Præst. Kjöbenhavn, 1820.**
Nikolai Frederik Severin Grundtvig, *Bjowulfs Drape. Et Gothisk Helte-Digt fra forrige Aar-Tusinde af Angel-Saxisk paa Danske Riim* (Copenhagen: Trykt hos A. Seidelin, 1820).

75. **under the patronage of the same Privy-counselor Bülow, the Mæcenas of his time, who had encouraged and munificently aided Thorkelin.**
John Bülow aided both Thorkelin (see above, notes 64, 67, 69) and Grundtvig (see above, note 70). The "Mæcenas" reference Tolkien takes from Earle:

"But when Privy-Councilor Bülow, the Mæcenas of that time, saw Grundtvig's work . . ."

Earle, *The Deeds of Beowulf*, xii.

Earle takes the Mæcenas reference from Thorkelin's dedication (and from the section of Thorkelin's introduction quoted above, note 68):

Illustrissimo Heroi
Domino Johanni de Bülow
Dynastæ Sanderumgaardi,
Eqviti magnæ crucis Danebrogicæ,
commendatori Stellæ Polaris,
S.R.M. Intimo Conferentiæ Consiliario,
ETC. ETC. ETC.
Grimus Johnson Thorkelin
S.

Cui, potius, qvam Tibi, Mæcenas optime! opus hoc inscriberem, prædem meæ perpetuæ in Te venerationis et testem gratæ mentis? Etenim Tu, et præsidium meum, mearumqve columen rerum multis fuisti annis, et Tuis auspiciis Tuaqve munificentia fecisti, ut in dulcissimam patriam nostram monumentum, qvod suum ante plus qvam mille annos fuit, postliminio rediret.

Qvoties igitur, dum in præterita redeo, et animo præsentia lustro, non possunt non Tua in me beneficia ante oculos versari: qvæ si publice non profiterer, foedæ oblivionis notam nulla posset dies delere.

Ego sane hanc mei in Te studii et amoris omnibus probandi occasionem nolui amittere. Cæterum Te, etiam atqve etiam rogo, velis Scyldingorum promeritas virtute laudes, qvas alioqvin nox æterna premeret, eadem facilitate admittere, qvâ me olim in Tuam clientelam suscepisti.

Faxit Deus ter opt. max., ut vitæ longam inoffenso pede teras orbitam, tardaqve sit illa dies, qvæ Te in publica commoda natum reposcet ad debita virtutis Tuæ præmia. Havniæ die I Mensis Maii Anno MCDDDXV.

[Grim Johnson Thorkelin sends greetings to that most illustrious hero Lord John Bülow of the house of Sanderumgaard, knight of the Grand Cross of Denmark, Commander of the North Star, personal advisor to the audience of his royal Majesty etc., etc., etc.

O great Mæcenas, to whom should I dedicate this work if not to you? It is the reward of my constant veneration of you and a witness to my grateful mind. For you have been for many years my protection and the support of all my efforts; under your auspices and by your generosity you have brought it about that into this most sweet country of ours a monument which had belonged to it for more than a thousand years has returned from exile. Therefore, as often as I return in mind to times past, and consider in mind the present times, your kindnesses to me cannot help but appear before my eyes; no day could possibly erase the mark of my foul forgetfulness if I were not to confess them in public.

To be sure, I had no desire to let pass this occasion for demonstrating to all people my affection and my love for you. Furthermore, I ask again and again that it be your desire to take to yourself the praises of the Scyldings, earned by their virtue, which otherwise eternal night would conceal, with the same ease with which you once took me into the company of your friends. And may God, thrice greatest and best, bring it about that you walk with unoffending foot a long path of life, and that that day may come slowly which will summon to the rewards that your virtue deserves you who have been born for the public good. Copenhagen, 1 May 1815.]

Thorkelin, *De Danorum rebus gestis*, 1–3.

Sharon Turner, in his 1823 edition, also mentions the "Mæcenas" trope:

"Ten years after the first edition of this part of the Anglo-Saxon history, Dr. G. J. Thorkelin, in the year 1815, printed this work at Copenhagen, which he addressed to the Lord John de Bulow, as his Mæcenas optime! by whose private munificence, he says, he had been enabled to bring into his country a monument of literature which was above a thousand years old."

Sharon Turner, *The History of the Anglo-Saxons: Comprising the History of England from the Earliest Period to the Norman Conquest*, 3 vols., 4th ed. (London: Longman, Hurst, Rees, Orme and Brown, 1823), 2: 280–81.

76. **Sharon Turner**
Sharon Turner (1768–1847) wrote the earliest popular history of the Anglo-Saxons, a work which he revised many times. Turner could read Old English prose well enough but, as Tolkien notes, he had great difficulty with the poetic language used in *Beowulf*.

Turner, *History of the Anglo-Saxons*.

Folio 21

77. **Thorkelin's edition: <u>De Danorum Rebus Gestis Secul. III & IV. Poema Danicum Dialecto Anglosaxonica.</u>**
Thorkelin, *De Danorum rebus gestis*. And see above notes 64, 67, and 69.

78. **Thorkelin was not the first to mention "Beowulf" after Wanley. This distinction, such as it is, goes to <u>Sharon Turner</u> in 1807 in his <u>History of the Anglo-Saxons</u>.**

Tolkien takes this from Earle, *The Deeds of Beowulf*, xvi, but both Earle and Tolkien are incorrect. Turner first mentions *Beowulf* in the 1799–1805 first edition of his *History of the Anglo-Saxons*:

> "The most interesting remains of the Anglo-Saxon poetry which time has suffered to reach us, are contained in the Anglo-Saxon poem in the Cotton library, Vitellius, A 15. Wanley mentions it as a poem in which "seem to be described the wars which one Beowulf, a Dane of the royal race of the Scyldingi waged against the reguli of Sweden" But this account of the contents of the MS. is incorrect. It is a composition more curious and important. It is a narration of the attempt of Beowulf to wreck the fæhthe or deadly feud on Hrothgar, for a homicide which he had committed. It may be called an Anglo-Saxon epic poem. It abounds with speeches which Beowulf and Hrothgar and their partisans make to each other, with much occasional description and sentiment."

Turner, *History of the Anglo-Saxons* (London, 1799–1805), 4: 398–99.

However, the 1807 edition provides the revised quotation used by both Tolkien and Earle:

> The origin of the metrical romance has been lately an interesting subject of literary research and as it has not been yet completely elucidated, it seems proper to enquire whether any light can be thrown upon it from the ancient Saxon poetry.
>
> It was asserted by Mr. Ritson, in conformity with the prevailing opinion of antiquaries, that the Anglo-Saxons had no poetical romance in their native tongue. But he grounds this opinion on the fact, that no romance had been at that time discovered in Saxon but a prose translation from the Latin of the legend of Apollonius of Tyre. The Anglo-Saxon poem on Beowulf, first described in the former edition of this history, proves that this opinion was erroneous. This poem is certainly a metrical romance in the Anglo-Saxon language. It is the most interesting relic of the Anglo-Saxon poetry which time has suffered us to receive. It is in the Cotton Library, Vitellius, A. 15. The subject is the expedition of Beowulf, to wreak the fæhthe, or deadly feud, on Hrothgar for a homicide which he has committed. It abounds with speeches which Beowulf and Hrothgar, and their partisans, make to each other, with much occasional description and sentiment.

Turner, *History of the Anglo-Saxons*, 2nd ed. (London: Longman, Hurst, Rees and Orme, 1807), 2: 294.

79. **Prof. B. Nerman in Det Svenska Rikets Uppkomst**

Birger Nerman (1888–1971) was a Swedish archeologist and historian whose work has been used to investigate the potential relationship of the Geatas in *Beo-wulf* to the tribe of the Gautar in Sweden.

Birger Nerman, *Det Svenska Rikets Uppkomst* (Stockholm: Generalstabens Lito-grafiska Anstalt, 1925).

80. . . . the most interesting relic of Anglo-Saxon poetry which time has suffered us to receive. The subject is the expedition of Beowulf to wreak the fæhðe or deadly feud on Hrothgar, for a homicide which he had committed. It abounds with speeches, which Beowulf and Hrothgar and their partisans make to each other, with much occasional description and sentiment.
Turner, *History of the Anglo-Saxons*, 2nd ed., 2: 294.

81. As Earle says, proper names excepted, this has no more to do with *Beowulf* than with the *Iliad* or the *Chanson de Roland*.
Earle, *The Deeds of Beowulf*, xvi. For Earle see above, note 42.

82. Chanson de Roland
The Song of Roland, the great French epic of Roland, one of the retainers of Charlemagne.

83. Sharon Turner
See above, note 76.

84. In his History of 1823 there is a considerable change, and the poem is a "po-etical Romance" or "metrical Romance" which celebrates the heroic deeds of a Beowulf who fell in Jutland in the year 340 A. D.
The complete quotation from Turner is:

This work is a poem on the actions of its hero Beowulf. If it describes those deeds only which he actually performed, it would claim the title of an his-torical poem; but if, as few can doubt, the Anglo-Saxon poet has amused himself with pourtraying [sic] the warrior, and incidents of his fancy, then it is a specimen of an Anglo-Saxon poetical romance, true in costume and manners, but with an invented story.

Turner, *The History of the Anglo-Saxons*, 3 vols, 4th ed. (London: Longman, Hurst, Rees, Orme and Brown, 1823), 2: 280–81.

85. These titles are challenges to Ritson, and others, who denied the existence of poetical Romance before the Norman Conquest
Earle notes that Turner's mention of *Beowulf* was ". . . little more than a trium-phant assertion of its importance, as establishing, against Ritson and other lit-

erary antagonists, the existence of poetical Romance before the Norman period."

Earle, *The Deeds of Beowulf*, xvi.

Joseph Ritson had claimed that:

> The first metrical romance, properly and strictly so call'd, this is known to
> have existed, and may possibly be still extant, in the dark recess of some
> national or monkish library, is the famous *chanson de Roland*, which was
> sung by a minstrel, or jugler, named Taillefer, riding on horseback, at the
> head of the Norman army, when marching, under duke William, to the
> battle of Hastings.

Joseph Ritson, *Ancient English Metrical Romances* (London: W. Bulmer and Company, 1802), 1: xxxiv–xxxv.

Turner addresses Ritson thus:

> It was asserted by Mr. Ritson, in conformity with the prevailing opinion of
> antiquaries, that the Anglo-Saxons had no poetical romance in their native
> tongue . . . the Anglo-Saxon poem of Beowulf, which was particularly rec-
> ommended to the notice of the public in the first edition of this history in
> 1805, proves that this opinion was erroneous.

Turner, *History of the Anglo-Saxons*, 4th ed., 2: 280–81.

86. **Ritson**

Joseph Ritson (1752–1803) was an English antiquarian who specialized in the
study of literature. Ritson exposed John Pinkerton's forgeries in *Select Scottish
Ballads* as well as the Shakespeare forgeries of Samuel Ireland.

Folio 22

87. **This is a borrowing from the Danes from Thorkelin, from Suhm the Danish
Historian, and by him got from <u>Saxo Grammaticus</u>, by identifying Beowulf
with <u>Bous</u> son of Odin, whom Saxo relates to have fallen in battle with <u>Hoth-
erus</u> about that date.**

Here Tolkien paraphrases and condenses Earle's summary of Turner's methodology:

> Turner took his ideas about *Beowulf* from Thorkelin, "Thorkelin from Suhm the
> Danish historian, and Suhm from Saxo Grammaticus."

Earle, *The Deeds of Beowulf*, xvii.

In his 1823 edition, Turner writes:

> Beowulf's "author, in several places, speaks as if he had been a contem-
> porary of the events he describes; but this may be considered as a poetical

license, especially if it be historically true that Beowulf fell in Jutland in the year 340"

Turner gives the following footnote:

"Dr. Thorkelin mentions this on the authority of Suhn [sic], in his *Geschichte der Danen*. I can neither deny nor confirm the chronology."

Turner, *The History of the Anglo-Saxons*, 4th ed., 2: 281–82.

Thorkelin's citation of Suhm may be found in a footnote on page ix:

Quod autem ad Scyldingidem nostram attinet, eam vere Danicam esse, nemo non ibit inficias, qvi observaverit auctorem rerum a Regibus HROD-GARO, Beowulfo et Higelaco gestarum oculatum fuisse testem, et in Beowulfi exseqviis encomiasten adfuisse cecidit autem Beowulfus in Jutia anno æræ nostræ CCCXL.

[Let no one doubt that the epic of the Scyldings is Danish who notes that the author of the deeds of the Kings Hrodgard, Beowulf, and Higelac was an eye-witness, and was present as a singer-of-praises at the funeral of Beowulf (Beowulf fell in Jutland in the year 340 of our era).]

Thorkelin, *De Danorum rebus gestis*, ix.

Dieser Fürst wurde von seinen Jarl Gunnar in der Nacht überfallen und verbrannt. Hother heilt es für Pflicht, seinen Tod zu rächen, bekam auch Gunnarn gefangen, lieb ihn zur gerechten Strafe ebenfalls lebendig auf einem Jofurs Söhn, Herlit und Gerit, in das väterliche Reich ein. Diesen Krieg hatte er bald zu Ende gebracht, aber kurz darauf stand ihm ein härterer bevor, denn Boe, Odins Sohn, griff ihn mit einem mächtigen Heere an. Diebmal ward Hother bedenklich, und gab auf dem Thing, oder der Volksversammlung, zu erkennen, dab er in diesem Krieg seinen Tod voraussehe, und dab ihm auch die Wahrsager solchen geweissagt hälten; er bitte daher die Volksversammlung, dafs man nunmehr seinen Sohn Rerek an seine Stelle zum König ernennen möchte; dann wollte er mit Freuden sterben. Dieses Begehren ward ihm auch verwilligt. In der darauf folgenden Schlacht verlor er wirklich sein Leben, Boe ward ebenfalls so hart verwundet, dab er auf seinem Schilde musste in Zelt getragen werden, wobei das Fussvolk mit einander abwechselte.

Peter Friedrich Suhm, *Geschichte der Dänen*, trans. Friedrich Dav. Gräter (Leipzig: Heinrich Gräff, 1803), 231–32.

This is a German translation of Suhm's Danish text:
Peter Friedrich Suhm, *Historie af Danmark far de oeldeste Lider* (København: Ernst med Brøðrene Berlings Strifter, 1782), 1: 158–59.

The relevant section in Saxo Grammaticus is:

> Post haec, vocatis in contionem maioribus, bello, quo Boum excipere debeat, periturum se refert idque non dubiis coniecturae modis, sed veris vatum praedictionibus expertum. Orat proinde, filium suum Roricum regno praeficiant, ne ius hoc ad externas ignotasque familias improborum censura transfunderet, plus voluptatis se ex filii successione quam amaritudinis ex propinqua morte percepturum testatus. Quo ocius impetrato, pugna cum Boo congressus occiditur. Nec iucunda Boo victoria exstitit; quippe tam graviter affectus acie excessit, ut scuto exceptus atque a peditibus vicissim subeuntibus domum relatus postridie vulnerum dolore consumeretur. Cuius corpus magnifico funeris apparatu Rutenus tumulavit exercitus, nomine eius insignem exstruens collem, ne tanti iuvenis monumenta a posterorum memoria citius dilaberentur.

J. Olrik and H. Ræder, eds., *Saxonis Gesta Danorum* (Hauniæ: Apud Librarios Levin og Munksgaard, 1931), 1: 73.

> Later, after he had called his chieftains to a meeting, Høther announced that he was bound to take on Bo and would perish in the fight, a fact he had discovered not by doubtful surmises but from the trustworthy prophecies of seers. He therefore begged them to make his son Rørik ruler of the kingdom and not let the votes of wicked men transfer this privilege to unknown foreign houses; he would experience more delight in the assurance of his son's succession than bitterness at his own approaching death. When they had readily acceded to his request he met Bo in battle and was slain. But Bo had little joy in this victory; he was so badly stricken himself that he withdrew from the skirmish, was carried back home on his shield in turns by his foot-soldiers, and expired the next day from the agony of his wounds. At a splendidly prepared funeral the Rutenian army buried his body in a magnificent barrow erected to his name, so that the record of this noble young man should not fade soon from the memory of later generations.

Hilda Ellis Davidson, ed., *Saxo Grammaticus' History of the Danes*, trans. Peter Fisher (Haverhill, Suffolk: D. S. Brewer, 1979), 79.

88. **Saxo Grammaticus**

Saxo Grammaticus ("Saxo the Scholar") was a Danish historian born in Zealand. He lived from approximately 1150 to 1220 and compiled the *Gesta Danorum* ("History of the Danes") in Latin. The *Gesta Danorum* is the earliest source for much of the history and legend of Northern Europe.

89. **Conybeare**

John Josias Conybeare (1779–1824) was an antiquarian and literary scholar who understood *Beowulf* and its language more clearly than any previous researcher. His work was edited and published by his brother, William Daniel Conybeare (1787–1857) who took over his brother's work after the former's untimely death.

90. **Conybeare perhaps in "Illustrations of Anglo-Saxon Poetry" (1826)**
John Josias Conybeare (ed. William Daniel Conybeare), *Illustrations of Anglo-Saxon Poetry* (London: Harding and Lepard, 1826).

91. **mine gefræge and we gefrignon**
"Mine gefræge" means "I have heard tell." The phrase is used in *Beowulf* in lines 776, 837, 1955, 2685, and 2837. "We gefrignon" means "we have heard tell." These phrases are formulaic, or at the very least are the poet calling attention to his speaking. They are not, Tolkien and other scholars note, an attempt to claim that the poet actually witnessed the events he is narrating.

92. **He rejects Thorkelin's Bous and Jutland, and remains an agnostic about ultimate origins (Illustrations. p 33); and says of the writer (or perhaps the translator or modernizer of the Dano-Saxon period to whom he is inclined to ascribe Beowulf as we have it) that "it is evident that he was a Christian."**
Conybeare rejects the speculations of Thorkelin thus:

> "It is with some diffidence, and not till after an extensive examination, that the present editor ventures to doubt, with a single exception, the whole of these conjectures."

He says, of the author of *Beowulf*:

> "Whatever his age it is evident that he was a Christian, a circumstance which has perhaps rendered his work less frequent in allusions to the customs and superstitions of his pagan ancestors, and consequently somewhat less interesting to the poetical antiquary than if it had been the production of a mind acquainted only with the wild and picturesque mythology which forms so peculiar and attractive a feature of the earlier productions of the Scandinavian muse."

Conybeare, *Illustrations of Anglo-Saxon Poetry*, 33–34. For Conybeare see above, note 89.

93. **J. M. Kemble (of Trinity College Cambridge)**
See above, note 5.

Folio 23
94. **Kemble's first limited edition in 1833 — The Anglo-Saxon Poems of Beowulf, The Travellers Song and the Battle of Finnesburh, edited together with**

a glossary of the more difficult words and an Historical Preface. London. Pickering. was sold out in a few months and soon replaced by the corrected second edition (1835).

John Mitchell Kemble, *The Anglo-Saxon Poems of Beowulf, The Traveller's song, and the Battle of Finnesburh* (London: William Pickering, 1833; 2nd ed. 1835).

Tolkien must have copied his citation from the later edition, whose title includes "edited together with a glossary of the more difficult words and an Historical Preface," words which are not found in the title of the 1833 edition.

95. sc. Widsith

The standard edition of the poem "Widsith" is:
"Widsith" in Krapp and Dobbie, *The Exeter Book*, 149–53.

96. Kemble's work of 1837 that marks a definite crossing to a new era. This is A Translation of the Anglo-Saxon Poem of Beowulf with a copious Glossary, Preface and Philological Notes. London. Pickering. 1837

Kemble, *A Translation of the Anglo-Saxon Poem 'Beowulf'*. For Kemble, see above, note 5.

97. Grein's Sprachschatz,

Christian Wilhelm Michael Grein (1825–1877) was one of the German pioneers of Anglo-Saxon studies. His *Sprachschatz* ("Vocabulary") of Anglo-Saxon is the first true Old English dictionary. Grein also published the first relatively complete corpus of Anglo-Saxon poetry, the *Bibliothek der angelsächsischen Poesie* ("Library of Anglo-Saxon Poems").

Christian W. M. Grein, *Sprachschatz der angelsächsischen Dichter* (Cassel: G. H. Wigand, 1861–1864).

Folio 24

98. Wolf and Lachmann

Tolkien and John Earle both spell Wolf's name "Wolff," with two f's. But they are clearly talking about Friedrich August Wolf (1759–1824), the German classical scholar who argued that the works of Homer were composed of various ballads that had been joined together into longer works by later editors.

Friedrich August Wolf, *Prolegomena ad Homerum, sive de operum Homericorum prisca et genuina forma variisque mutationibus et probabili ratione emendandi*, vol. 1 (Halis Saxonum: Libraria Orphanotrophei, 1795), ed. Anthony Grafton, et. al. (Princeton: Princeton University Press, 1985).

Karl Konrad Friedrich Wilhelm Lachmann (1793–1851) was a professor at Königsberg and Berlin. He was one of the founders of modern textual criticism, and argued that the *Iliad* was composed of separate lays enlarged and joined together (see Sebastiano Timpanaro, *La genesi del metodo di Lachmann* [Padua: Liviana, 1985]). Lachmann's influence on *Beowulf* criticism is found in the work of his pupil, Karl Müllenhoff (1818–1884).

Karl Müllenhoff, "Die innere Geschichte des Beovulfs," *Zeitschrift für deutsches Altertum und deutsche Literatur* 14 (1869): 193–244.

Reprinted and revised in:
Karl Müllenhoff, *Beovulf: Untersuchungen über das angelsächsische Epos und die älteste Geschichte der germanischen Seevölker* (Berlin: Weidmann, 1889).

99. **As Earle says "That great works in early literature forsooth were not made by art and device, but that they grew spontaneously and blindly, this was that imagination in the air which attended the first entertainment of Beowulf in the Fatherland."**
The complete quotation from Earle is:

> Long ingrained notions about the fortuitous growth of Epics, grounded upon the authority of Wolff [sic] and Lachmann, had prepared in the German learned mind a welcome for the Beowulf, and at the same time a foregone sentence upon the nature of its composition. That great works of literature forsooth were not made by art and device, but that they grew spontaneously and blindly, this was the imagination in the air which attended the first entertainment of Beowulf in the Fatherland.

Earle, *The Deeds of Beowulf*, xxix. For Earle, see above, note 42.

100. **All Earle's Introduction is valuable, except his own private gambol at the end.**
See above, note 44.

101. **Chambers notes almost with surprise that it is on such a piece as Widsith that older scholars are at their best**
Raymond W. Chambers, *Widsith: A Study in Old English Heroic Legend* (Cambridge: Cambridge University Press, 1912), 135–36. See also above, note 8.

102. **Kemble, Leo, Lappenberg, Ettmüller and later Möller, Ten Brink, Müllenhoff.**
For Kemble, see above, note 5.

Heinrich Leo (1799–1878) was a professor at Halle who wrote on *Widsith* and *Beowulf*.

Johann Martin Lappenberg (1794–1865) was a German historian who wrote on *Widsith* and (perhaps) defended *Beowulf* against the charge of being inferior to Old Norse; see T. A. Shippey and Andreas Haarder, *Beowulf: The Critical Heritage* (London: Routledge, 1998), 50, 259–60.

Ernst Moritz Ludwig Ettmüller (1802–1877) was a German scholar who became professor of literature at Zürich. He published an edition of *Beowulf* in 1840.

Martin Thomas Hermann Möller (1850–1923) was a Danish scholar (professor at Copenhagen), who was raised in the North Frisian Islands and considered himself German. He published, among other things, an edition of *Widsith* in 1883.

Bernard Ægidius Konrad ten Brink (1841–1892) was a Dutch philologist who became professor of literature at Marburg and later at Strasbourg. He published *Geschichte der englischen Literatur* (*A History of English Literature*) in 1874 and *Beowulf-Untersuchungen* (*Beowulf: Researches*) in 1888. Note that one of ten Brink's given names, Ægidius, is the same as that of Farmer Giles of Ham. Perhaps ten Brink was the inspiration for Tolkien, though the character and the scholar seem to have little in common.

Karl Müllenhoff (1818–1884) was a pupil of Karl Lachmann and brought to bear upon *Beowulf* his teacher's methods of textual criticism and mytho-allegorical analysis. Müllenhoff became embroiled in a exceptionally nasty dispute with Christian Grein who criticized his and his teacher's methods of analysis.

T. A. Shippey's and Andreas Haarder's magisterial compilation *Beowulf: The Critical Heritage* was not available to me until research for *Beowulf and the Critics* was complete, but I have checked my work against their text and updated the note on Möller based on their commentary. Shippey and Haarder's book supercedes all previous studies and is essential to anyone interested in the critical history of *Beowulf*.

Shippey, T. A. and Andreas Haarder, eds., *Beowulf: The Critical Heritage* (London: Routledge, 1998).

J. R. R. Tolkien, *Farmer Giles of Ham* (London: Allen and Unwin, 1949; repr. 1975).

103. **which has little poetry and only that of a glittering catalogue**
"Glittering catalogue" seems to be inspired by "glimmering tradition" in the passage from Matthew Arnold quoted by W. P. Ker; see above, note 11. Its ultimate source is probably the "Catalogue of the Ships" in the *Iliad* 2. 494–759.

104. **in his appendix to the second edition (1932) of his <u>Introduction</u> on recent work down to 1930, Chambers begins with <u>Klæber's</u> edition Beowulf (1922 2nd 1928) and calls it rightly the most important since Kemble's in 1833.**
Friedrich Klaeber (1863–1954) was the author of the what has been the "standard" edition of *Beowulf* for well over fifty years. He was born and trained in Germany, but spent most of his most productive and influential years as a professor at the University of Minnesota. There is some confusion in a few sources over Klaeber's given name, which is printed as "Frederick" in a number of library catalogues.

Friedrich Klaeber, ed., *Beowulf and the Fight at Finnsburg: Edited with Introduction, Bibliography, Notes, Glossary, and Appendices with Supplement* (Boston: D. C. Heath and Company, 1922; 2nd ed. 1928).

Chambers, *Beowulf: An Introduction to the Study of the Poem*, 391. For Chambers see above, note 8.

Kemble, *The Anglo-Saxon Poems of Beowulf, The Travellers Song, and the Battle of Finnesburh*. For Kemble see above, note 5.

Folio 25

105. This wandering and development until we come to <u>Lawrence</u>, <u>Klaeber</u> and <u>Chambers</u> I make no attempt to sketch.

William Witherle Lawrence (1876–1958) was professor of English at Columbia University. He published extensively on *Beowulf*, taking a literary rather than purely historical approach to the poem.

William Witherle Lawrence, *Beowulf and Epic Tradition* (Cambridge, MA: Harvard University Press, 1928).

For Klaeber see above note, 104. For Chambers see above, note 8.

106. So it is time . . . hardly affecting the main argument

Chambers, *Beowulf: An Introduction to the Study of the Poem*, 391–92. For Chambers see above, note 8.

107. So we can still hear of Grendel as symbolic of the sea, and Beowulf of the sun and of the redacting Christian monks in popular compendia still on the shelves of responsible book-shops.

For Grendel as symbolic of the sea:

Karl Müllenhoff, "Sceáf und seine Nachkommen," *Zeitschrift für deutsches Altertum und deutsche Literatur* 7 (1849): 410–19.

Karl Müllenhoff, "Der Mythus von Beóvulf," *Zeitschrift für deutsches Altertum und deutsche Literatur* 7 (1849): 419–41.

For the mythico-allegorical interpretations of the poem summarized in English, see:

Chambers, *Beowulf: An Introduction to the Study of the Poem*, 45–47.

Lawrence, *Beowulf and Epic Tradition*, 147–48.

For the case for redacting Christian monks, see:

ten Brink, *History of English Literature*, 1: 26–29.

108. But we pass over such 'small beer.'

See above, notes 46 and 47.

Folio 26

109. **Jusserand is perhaps not much read now**

Jean (Adrien Antoine) Jules Jusserand (1855–1932) was a French writer and diplomat who served in the French embassy in London and was ambassador to the United States from 1902 to 1925. He wrote and published in both French and English.

Folio 27

110. **The Literary History of the English People**

J. J. Jusserand, *A Literary History of the English People from the Origins to the Renaissance*, vol. 1 (London: G. P. Putnam's Sons, 1895).

111. **the "wood-notes wild" idea.**

The quote is a reference to John Milton's poem "L'Allegro" (Italian for "the cheerful man"). Tolkien clearly did not approve of the idea that Shakespeare's literary work was the production of some sort of natural and uncultivated genius.

> Then to the well-trod stage anon,
> If Jonson's learned sock be on,
> Or sweetest Shakespeare, Fancy's child,
> Warble his native wood-notes wild.
> And ever, against eating cares,
> Lap me in soft Lydian airs,
> Married to immortal verse,
> Such as the meeting soul may pierce,
> In notes with many a winding bout
> Of linked sweetness long drawn out
> With wanton heed and giddy cunning,
> The melting voice through mazes running,
> Untwisting all the chains that tie
> The hidden soul of harmony;
> That Orpheus' self may heave his head
> From golden slumber on a bed
> Of heaped Elysian flowers, and hear
> Such strains as would have won the ear
> Of Pluto to have quite set free
> His half-regained Eurydice.
> These delights if thou canst give,
> Mirth, with thee I mean to live.

John Milton, "L'Allegro," in Roy Flanagan, ed., *The Riverside Milton* (Boston: Houghton Mifflin, 1998), 66–71, here 70–71.

112. **But Jusserand says actually 'the charm of a wild flower.'**
Jusserand writes of King Alfred's Boethius translation:

> "each episode is moralised; the affected elegance of the model disappears, and give place to an almost childlike yet captivating sincerity. The story of the misfortunes of Orpheus, written by Boethius in a very pretentious style, has in Alfred's translation a charm of its own, the charm of the wild flower."

Jusserand, *Literary History of the English People*, 85.

Folio 28

113. **Jusserand, for instance — just after delivering himself of "the charm of a wildflower" (said of Ælfric, forsooth!!**
For the quotation from Jusserand, see above, note 112.

Tolkien here is incorrect. The insulting comment by Jusserand is directed at King Alfred's translation of Boethius. Ælfric, as far as we know, never translated Boethius or the story of Orpheus.

114. **Ælfric**
See above, note 63.

115. **'The dog of hell he should have three heads.'**
"He goes down to the nether region, at the sweetness of his harping, Cerberus "began to wag his tail." Cerberus was "the dog of hell; he should have three heads." "A very horrible gatekeeper," Charon by name, "had also three heads," according to the calculation of Alfred, whose mythology is not very safe."

Jusserand, *Literary History of the English People*, 86.

116. **the Old English translation of Boethius**
Anicius Manlius Severinus Boethius (c. 480–524) was a Roman philosopher and chief minister to the Gothic king Theodoric, who occupied Rome. Boethius was accused of treason and put to death in 524, but while in prison he wrote *De Consolatione Philosophiae* (*The Consolation of Philosophy*), the most influential work of Christian philosophy for the following millennium (though Boethius does not specifically mention Christianity in the text).

Some time between 878 and 892 King Alfred undertook to translate the *Consolation* from Latin into Old English, and he modified and augmented the text, making his translation more specifically Christian than the original.

117. **Eurydice and Orpheus.**
The Greek myth of Orpheus and Eurydice (the basis for the Middle English *Sir*

Orpheo, which Tolkien edited and translated) tells of the great minstrel Orpheus who rescues Eurydice, his beloved, from Hades. His music so charms the denizens of hell that Hades agrees to set Eurydice free, provided that Orpheus does not look back to see if she is following him. But Orpheus looks back just before they have escaped from the underworld, and Eurydice is forced to return to Hades.

118. dog of hell . . . Cerberus
In Greek mythology Cerberus is a three-headed dog who guards the gates of the underworld.

Folio 29
119. the speech of Beowulf to Unferth (ll. 530–606), we are told, may be summed up thus: "liar, drunkard, coward, murderer!"
Beowulf crushes all he touches; in his fights he upsets monsters, in his talks he tumbles his interlocutors headlong. His retorts have nothing winged about them; he does not use the feathered arrow, but the iron hammer. Hunferth taunts him with not having had the best in a swimming match. Beowulf replies by a strong speech, which can be summed up in a few words: liar, drunkard, coward, murderer! It seems an echo from the banqueting hall of the Scandinavian gods; in the same manner Loki and the goddesses played with words. For the assembled warriors of Hrothgar's court Beowulf goes in nowise beyond bounds; they are not indignant, they would rather laugh. So did the gods.

Jusserand, *Literary History of the English People*, 55.

Hwæt! þu worn fela,   wine min Unferð,
beore druncen   ymb Brecan spræce,
sægdest from his siðe.   Soð ic talige,
þæt ic merestrengo   maran ahte,
earfeþo on yþum,   ðonne ænig oþer man.
Wit þæt gecwædon   cnihtwesende
ond gebeotedon   (wæron begen þa git
on geogoðfeore)   þæt wit on garsecg ut
aldrum neðdon,   ond þæt geæfndon swa.
Hæfdon swurd nacod,   þa wit on sund reon,
heard on handa;   wit unc wið hronfixas
werian þohton.   No he wiht fram me
flodyþum feor   fleotan meahte,
hraþor on holme;   no ic fram him wolde.
Ða wit ætsomne   on sæ wæron
fif nihta fyrst,   oþ þæt unc flod todraf,

wado weallende,   wedera cealdost,
nipende niht,   ond norþanwind
heaðogrim ondhwearf;   hreo wæron yþa.
Wæs merefixa   mod onhrered;
þær me wið laðum   licsyrce min,
heard, hondlocen,   helpe gefremede,
beadohrægl broden   on breostum læg
golde gegyrwed.   Me to grunde teah
fah feondscaða,   fæste hæfde
grim on grape;   hwæþre me gyfeþe wearð
þæt ic aglæcan   orde geræhte,
hildebille;   heaþoræs fornam
mihtig meredeor   þurh mine hand.
Swa mec gelome   laðgeteonan
þreatedon þearle.   Ic him þenode
deoran sweorde,   swa hit gedefe wæs.
Næs hie ðære fylle   gefean hæfdon,
manfordædlan,   þæt hie me þegon,
symbel ymbsæton   sægrunde neah;
ac on mergenne   mecum wunde
be yðlafe   uppe lægon,
sweordum aswefede,   þæt syðþan na
ymb brontne ford   brimliðende
lade ne letton.   Leoht eastan com,
beorht beacen godes;   brimu swaþredon,
þæt ic sænæssas   geseon mihte,
windige weallas.   Wyrd oft nereð
unfægne eorl,   þonne his ellen deah.
Hwæþere me gesælde   þæt ic mid sweorde ofsloh
niceras nigene.   No ic on niht gefrægn
under heofones hwealf   heardran feohtan,
ne on egstreamum   earmran mannon;
hwæþere ic fara feng   feore gedigde,
siþes werig.   Ða mec sæ oþbær,
flod æfter faroðe   on Finna land,
wadu weallendu.   No ic wiht fram þe
swylcra searoniða   secgan hyrde,
billa brogan.   Breca næfre git
æt heaðolace,   ne gehwæþer incer,
swa deorlice   dæd gefremede
fagum sweordum   (no ic þæs fela gylpe),
þeah ðu þinum broðrum   to banan wurde,

heafodmægum;   þæs þu in helle scealt
werhðo dreogan,   þeah þin wit duge.
Secge ic þe to soðe,   sunu Ecglafes,
þæt næfre Grendel swa fela   gryra gefremede,
atol æglæca,   ealdre þinum,
hynðo on Heorote,   gif þin hige wære,
sefa swa searogrim,   swa þu self talast.
Ac he hafað onfunden   þæt he þa fæhðe ne þearf,
atole ecgþræce   eower leode
swiðe onsittan,   Sige-Scyldinga;
nymeð nydbade,   nænegum arað
leode Deniga,   ac he lust wigeð,
swefeð ond snedeþ,   secce ne weneþ
to Gar-Denum.   Ac ic him Geata sceal
eafoð ond ellen   ungeara nu,
guþe gebeodan.   Gæþ eft se þe mot
to medo modig,   siþþan morgenleoht
ofer ylda bearn   oþres dogores,
sunne sweglwered   suþan scineð.

[Listen, Unferth my friend. For one who has drunk some beer you speak much about Breca and tell about his journey. Truth I tell, that I possess greater sea-strength for hard struggles in the waves than any other man. We two said — we were both then in youth — that we would venture our lives out on the sea, and we did so. We had a naked sword hard in our hands as we swam into the sound — we intended to protect ourselves against the whales. He was not able to fare a bit away from me into the flood waves, for I was quicker in the water, nor did I wish to flee. Then we were together in the sea for five nights' time, until the flood separated us, the sea surged, the coldest of weather and the night growing dark and the north wind, battle grim, turned against us.

The ocean waves were rough, and the enmity of the ocean fishes was stirred up. Then my corselet, hard and made of hand-locked rings, helped me against the enemies. The woven war-garment adorned with gold lay on my breast. A hateful enemy dragged me to the bottom of the sea; it had me fast in its grip. But it was granted to me that I was able to hit the monster with the point of my sword, the battle blade. The battle-rush completely carried off the mighty ocean beast by my hand.

The hateful despoilers frequently harassed me severely. I served them with my precious sword, as it was fitting. The wicked destroyers did not have joy at that feast, of partaking of me as they gathered around their planned banquet at the sea-bottom. But in the morning, wounded by swords, they became the leavings of the waves, lay upon the shore, put to sleep by swords, so that afterwards they would not hinder the journey of seafarers across the deep crossing.

Light came from the east, the bright beacon of God. The seas became still, that I might see the headlands, the windy walls. Fate often protects an eorl who is not fated to die, when his valor is strong. So to me it befell that I with my sword slew nine nicors. Never have I heard of a harder fight beneath the vault of heaven, nor of a man more forlorn in the sea streams. Nevertheless I escaped, weary of the journey, from the grasp of the hostile ones. Then the sea bore me off, the flood and the current, the surging waters, to the land of the Finns.

I have never heard anything of such skillfully waged battles, the terror of swords, said about you. Breca never yet, not either of you, accomplished with blood-stained swords a deed so brave in battle. I do not boast too much about this. And you became a killer to your brothers, your near kin. For that you must endure punishment in hell even though your will be strong.

I say then in truth, son of Ecglaf, that Grendel, the terrible monster, would never have performed so many horrors against your lord, humiliations in Heorot, if your heart and will were as fierce in battle as you believe. But he has discovered that he does not need to fear revenge, the terrible sword-storm of the Victory-Scyldings, very much. He continues taking his toll, nor does he spare the people of the Danes, but he desires battle, kills and tears them. He does not expect fighting from the Spear-Danes.

But I will soon now offer him the might and valor of the Geats. He who is permitted will go to the mighty mead-hall after the morning light, the sun clothed with radiance, shines from the south over the sons of men.]

Beowulf, lines 530–606
Klaeber, ed., *Beowulf and the Fight at Finnsburg*, 20–23.

120. **So may many brilliant speeches in the houses of Parliament to-day, and possibly more in the house of deputies.**
Here Tolkien is suggesting that many speeches in the British Parliament, and perhaps more in the French (the Chamber of Deputies) can be reduced to invective or *ad hominem* attacks. That the lowest common denominator of aggressive political speech can be expressed thus, he suggests, does not take into account rhetoric, eloquence or other aspects of the sorts of verbal sparring illustrated by Beowulf's and Unferth's confrontation.

121. **the great court of Heorot, the ambiguous figure of Hroðulf and the sinister figure of the evil counselor.**

Whatever its historical roots, the hall of Heorot appears to symbolize (as does the legendary court of Camelot in the later Middle Ages in such works as *Sir Gawain and the Green Knight*) the greatest and most important court of its time.

Hrothulf is Hrothgar's nephew, the son of Hrothgar's brother Halga. His figure is "ambiguous" because he is older than Hrothgar's sons, Hrethric and Hrothmund. As Chambers says, "very small acquaintance with the history of royal houses in these lawless Teutonic times is enough to show us that trouble is likely to be in store" (*Beowulf: An Introduction to the Study of the Poem*, 15). In addition, some of the phrases used to describe Hrothulf and his relationship with Hrothgar may be translated to indicate a coming conflict (see *Beowulf*, lines 1188–1191). Finally, a close reading of Saxo Grammaticus suggests that in at least one story Hrethric son of Hrothgar is slain by Hrothulf (Chambers, *Beowulf: An Introduction to the Study of the Poem*, 26–27).

The "sinister figure of the evil counselor" is Unferth, who has slain his own kin, has been unable to defend Heorot from the depredations of Grendel, and who greets Beowulf with hostile words of challenge (see Chambers, *An Introduction to the Study of the Poem*, 27–29).

Folio 30

122. **"To their excessive enthusiasm" we are told "succeed periods of complete depression, their orgies are followed by despair."**

> The same unchanging genius manifests itself in the national epic, in the shorter songs, and even in the prose chronicles of the Anglo-Saxons. To their excessive enthusiasms succeed periods of complete depression; their orgies are followed by despair. They sacrifice their life in battle without a frown, and yet, when the hour for thought has come, they are harassed by the idea of death. Their national religion foresaw the end of the world and of all things, and of the gods even.

Jusserand, *Literary History of the English People*, 56.

123. **It should scarcely be necessary to point out to this audience that the germ of the whole misconception is <u>druncen</u> in <u>beore druncen</u> l. 531.**

> Beowulf maþelode,   bearn Ecgþeowes:
> 'Hwæt, þu worn fela,   wine min Unferð,
> beore druncen   ymb Brecan spræce,
> sægdest from his siðe.'

> [Listen, Unferth my friend. For one who has drunk some beer you speak much about Breca and tell about his journey.]

Beowulf, lines 529–532a
Klaeber, ed., *Beowulf and the Fight at Finnsburg*, 20–21. And see above, note 119.

124. A "litotes" is a deliberate understatement, often used in poetry. "He'd had a few sips of beer" to describe someone helplessly inebriated would be an obvious litotes. Tolkien points out that the root of Modern English "drunken" is similar, meaning simply "having had a drink." A use of litotes in *Beowulf* can be found in lines 562–563a, where Beowulf, having killed the sea-beasts who had tried to eat him, says "the wicked destroyers did not have joy at that feast."

125. **Guðrún in *Atlakviða*, where of the great Lady of the Burgundians, Queen of the Goths, it is said as she greets her brothers riding to their fate in Attila's hall bjori vas [hon] litt drukkin. This means, of course, that none of the joy of the alien hall in which she was queen was hers**
Atlakviða, "The Lay of Atli" (Atli is very loosely based on the historical figure of Attila the Hun) is one of the poems of the Elder or Poetic Edda (see above, note 25). *Atlakviða* tells the story of the fall of the Niflung house. Guðrun, Queen of the Goths and the daughter of Gjúki, avenged the death of her brothers by killing Atli's sons, then Atli himself. She then burned his hall and all of his court. When the poet comments that she has drunk little beer in the hall of her husband, he is commenting (as Tolkien notes) that she has not truly entered into the bond of synthetic kinship with Atli and his kin.

Systir fann þeira
snemst at [þeir] í sal kómu
bræðer hennar báðir,
bjori vas [hon] litt drukkin.

Finnur Jónsson, *Atlakviða* (Copenhagen, 1912), 102.

Their sister first saw them   as the seats they neared,
both her dear brothers —   little beer had she drunk.

Hollander, ed., *The Poetic Edda*, 285–86.

126. **(cp. the similar symbolism at the beginning <u>drukku dróttmegir vín í valhöllu</u>).**
Atli sendi
ar til Gunnars
kunnan segg at riða,
Knéfröðr vas sá heitinn;
at görðum kom [hann] Gjuka
ok at Gunnars höllu,
bekkjum aringreypum
ok at bjóri svósum.
Drukku þar dróttmegir

en dyljendr þögðu,
vin í valöllu

Jónnson, *Atlakviða*, 99.

Of yore sent Atli   on errand to Gunnara
cunning king's man —   Knéfroeth was he hight;
to Gjúki's court came he,   and to Gunnar's beer hall,
to the benches hearth-girding,   to the beer of welcome.
The doughty ones drank,   their dark thoughts hiding,

Hollander, ed., *The Poetic Edda*, 285–86.

Folio 31

127. **no orgies are recorded, unless it be of alien pirate chieftains, or of Assyrians and such-like highly cultured people of the ancient world.**
In *Judith* the evil Holofernes, leader of the Assyrians, attempts to hold what can
be interpreted as an orgy: he and his men drink themselves into a state of total
inebriation and, so incapacitated, the chieftain orders that Judith, the captive
maiden of the Bethulians, be brought to his tent to satisfy his lustful desires.

Judith, lines 15–72
Elliott Van Kirk Dobbie, ed., *Beowulf and Judith*, The Anglo-Saxon Poetic Records 4 (New York: Columbia University Press, 1953), 99–101.

128. **"They sacrifice their life in battle without a frown," the critic proceeds.
. . . "And yet when the hour for the fight comes they are harassed by the
thought of death."**
Jusserand, *Literary History of the English People*, 56.

129. **Dear old nonsense, recently dealt with by Professor E.V. Gordon in his
Introduction to Old Norse.**
The greatness of Icelandic literature lies primarily in its understanding of
heroic character and the heroic view of life. This means much more than
the representation of courage; the hero of this literature was not merely a
courageous man, he was a man who understood the purpose of his courage. He had a very definite conception of the evil of life, and he had courage to face it and overcome it; he had a creed of no compromise with
anything that gave him shame or made him a lesser man. The heroic
problem of life lay primarily in the struggle for freedom of will, against the
pains of the body, and the fear of death, against fate itself. The hero was in
truth a champion of the free will of man against fate, which had power
only over material things. He knew that he could not save his body from
destruction, but he could preserve an undefeated spirit, if his will were

strong enough. To yield would gain nothing, since 'old age gives no quarter, even if spears do,' and yielding made him a lesser man; so the hero resisted to the end, and won satisfaction from fate, in being master of his life while he had it. The courage of the hero rose higher, and his spiritual energy was more concentrated as the opposing forces were stronger. He might win the struggle, or he might know that it was hopeless; but it was almost better to die resisting than to live basely (xxix–xxx).

The chief evil in life which men had to face in those violent days was death by the sword. That is why Norse authors usually have feuds or battles as the setting of heroic story. Their motives for doing so are often misunderstood, for many critics have attributed to them a delight in battle and killing for its own sake; but on the contrary, they saw in it the greatest evil, the one that required the most heroic power to turn into good. The authors' delight was only in the man who had this power (xxx).

Heroic character had its lighter side too, seen in the courageous humour of the saga heroes, as when Hjalti stood up among the heathen and told them in verse, 'I do not wish to blaspheme the gods, but I think Freyja is a bitch.' The hero was not made gloomy by facing the evil of life so sternly; he had the cheerfulness of the man who feels that he is a master of life (xxxi).

E. V. Gordon, *An Introduction to Old Norse* (Oxford: Clarendon Press, 1927), xxviii–xxxv.

130. **"The strange poem of <u>Beowulf</u>" he wanders on, "<u>the most important monu-</u> <u>ment of Anglo-Saxon literature</u> . . . like Old Celtic tales . . . is a medley of pagan legends, which do not concern Beowulf (the hero) in particular, and of historical facts. . . . New discrepancy is introduced in trying to adapt the old tale to the faith of his (the author's) day. No need to expatiate on the <u>inco-</u> <u>herence of a poem formed of such elements.</u> Its heroes are at once pagan and Christian, <u>they believe in Christ and Weland.</u> They fight against the monsters of Scandinavian mythology, and see in them the descendants of Cain; historical facts such as the battle of the sixth century (mentioned by Gregory of Tours) are mixed up with fantastic deeds beneath the waves."**

The strange poem of "Beowulf," the most important monument of Anglo-Saxon literature, was discovered at the end of the last century, in a manuscript written about the year 1000, and it is now preserved in the British Museum. Few works have been more discussed; it has been the cause of literary wars, in which the learned men of England, Denmark, Sweden, Germany, France, and America have taken part; and the peace is not yet signed.

This poem, like the old Celtic tales, is a medley of pagan legends, which did not originally concern Beowulf in particular, and of historical facts; the various parts, after a separate literary life, having been put together, perhaps in the eighth century, perhaps later, by an Anglo-Saxon Christian, who added discrepancies in trying to adapt the old tale to the faith of his day. No need to expatiate on the incoherence of a poem formed of such elements. Its heroes are at once pagan and Christian; they believe in Christ and in Weland; they fight against the monsters of Scandinavian mythology, and see in them the descendants of Cain; historical facts, such as a battle of the sixth century, mentioned by Gregory of Tours, where the victory remained to the Frankish ancestor, are mixed up with tales of fantastic duels below the waves.

Jusserand, *Literary History of the English People*, 48–49

131. the battle of the sixth century (mentioned by Gregory of Tours)
Historia Francorum (*History of the Franks*), Book III, Chapter 3.

His ita gestis, Dani cum rege suo nomine Chlochilaico evectu navali per mare Gallias appetunt. Egressique ad terras, pagum unum de regno Theudorici devastant atque captivant, oneratisque navibus tam de captivis quam de reliquis spoliis, reverti ad patriam cupiunt; sed rex eorum in litus resedebat, donec navis alto mare conpraehenderent, ipse deinceps secuturus. Quod cum Theudorico nuntiatum fuisset, quod scilicet regio eius fuerit ab extraneis devastata, Theudobertum, filium suum, in illis partibus cum valido exercitu ac magno armorum apparatu direxit. Qui, interfecto rege, hostibus navali proelio superatis oppraemit omnemque rapinam terrae restituit.

Gregory of Tours, *Historia Francorum*. Monumenta Germaniae Historica, Scriptores Rerum Merovingicarum 1 (Hanover: Impensis Bibliopolii Hahniani, 1884), 110–11.

After these events the Danes and their king Chlochilaichus crossed the seas with their fleet and came to Gaul. They landed, devastated one region of Theuderic's kingdom, and took the people prisoners, after which they loaded their vessels with captives and other spoils, and were ready to return to their own country. Their king remained on shore until the ships took the high sea, intending himself to follow later. News was brought to Theuderic that his land had been ravaged by foreigners, whereupon he sent his son Theudebert into those parts with a strong force and great armament. The Danish king was killed and the enemy severely defeated in a sea battle; all the booty was brought on shore again.

Gregory of Tours, *The History of the Franks*, trans. O. M. Dalton (Oxford: Clarendon Press, 1927), 2: 87.

132. **At this point the gentleman is seized by Grendel and put in a bag, and for once one's sympathies are with Grendel.**
When Beowulf returns to Gautland and tells the story of his fight against Grendel to Hygelac, he reveals that Grendel carried with him a great bag, literally a "glof" ("glove") made of a dragon's skin, into which the monster hoped to stuff his victims.

Beowulf, lines 2085b–2091a
Klaeber, ed., *Beowulf and the Fight at Finnsburg*, 78.

Folio 32
133. **They believe in the Trinity and Merlin, in God and Sir Orfeo; while professing Catholics they imagine good violins were made by Stradivarius; while serious Calvinists they tell tales of Robin Hood**
Tolkien's point here is that the mention of both Weland and Christ by Anglo-Saxon poets proves no confusion, heterodoxy, or blend of pagan and Christian religion, since Weland is not a god who is worshipped but rather (in the case of *Beowulf*) the supposed master-craftsman of a great heirloom. Weland was no more worshipped by Christian Anglo-Saxons than Merlin is by Catholics who read tales of King Arthur as fiction, not religion.

Folio 33
134. **why Cain and Abel alone of the names of Scripture appear.**
See above, note 33.

135. **I shall read you a passage from the <u>Dark Ages</u> pp. 252–3.**
Ker, *Dark Ages*, 252–53.

136. **But there are other things in the lives of Hercules and Theseus besides the killing of the Hydra or of Procrustes.**
The Hydra is a multi-headed monster killed early in the adventures of Hercules. Procrustes is a giant possessed of a bed upon which he forces travelers to lie. Those who are too short for it, he stretches to fit; he hacks the limbs from those who are too long. Theseus kills him. But both Hercules and Theseus also accomplish feats that have political and social dimensions beyond the mere destruction of marauding monsters.

137. **some contraption, a Brock-effect for the amazement of the simple.**
The *Oxford English Dictionary* gives the term as "Brock's Benefit," but the sense is the same: a spectacular display of fireworks and thus by extension a "special effect" used to dazzle a crowd. C. T. Brock provided fireworks for a display held annually at the Crystal Palace from 1920 to 1957. The *OED* quotations illus-

trating "Brock's Benefit" are all dated between 1920 and 1957, suggesting that
the term came into and went out of use rather quickly.

138. **We may compare Chambers, <u>Widsith</u> p. 79 where he is studying the story
of <u>Ingeld</u> son of <u>Froda</u> and his feud with the great Scylding house, which is in
"Beowulf" introduced merely as an allusion.**

As far as this story can be reconstructed from hints in *Beowulf*, *Widsith* and Saxo
Grammaticus, it runs thus: Froda, king of the Heathobards, slays Healfdane,
Hrothgar's father. The Danish Scyldings then try to avenge Healfdane and in
so doing slay Froda. Froda's son Ingeld makes peace with Hrothgar by marry-
ing Hrothgar's daughter, Freawaru. But, as Beowulf suggests in his report to
Hygelac, the peace does not last long. A Heathobard warrior who has survived
the death of Froda encourages a younger warrior to renew the fight against the
Danes. It seems that the Heathobard attack is repelled by the combined might
of Hrothgar and Hrothulf, but Heorot is burned. Ingeld is seen by Chambers
and others as a tragic figure because he is caught between his duty to revenge
his father and his oath, sealed by his marriage to Freawaru, of peace with the
Danes.

See:

Klaeber, ed., *Beowulf and the Fight at Finnsburg*, xxxvi.

Chambers, *Beowulf: An Introduction to the Study of the Poem*, 22–23. For Chambers,
see above, note 8.

139. **"Nothing" he says, "could better show the disproportion of 'Beowulf'
which" — and here he goes into quotation marks — "puts the irrelevances in
the center and the serious things on the outer edges" than this passing allusion to the story of Ingeld. For it is in this conflict between plighted troth and
the duty of revenge that we have a situation, which the old heroic poets loved,
and would not have sold for a wilderness of dragons."**

Chambers, *Widsith*, 33–34.

Tolkien continues to press this allusion, which is to Shakespeare's *Merchant
of Venice*, Act III, Scene 1, line 128: "I would not have given it for a wilderness
of monkeys." See below, note 141.

Folio 34

140. **Jusserand, who speaks of "one of these ever-recurring treasures."**

"According to a legend partly reproduced in [Beowulf], the Danes had no
chief. They beheld one day a small ship on the sea, and in it a child, and
with him one of those ever-recurring treasures."

Jusserand, *Literary History of the English People*, 50.

141. **This is à la Book of St. Albans — then why not say "a pride of lions, a draught of butlers, a kindle of young cats, and a raffle of knaves" as that book does?**
All of these phrases are found in the *Book of St. Albans*, but they are widely separated from each other. As can be seen from the revisions made between versions of *Beowulf and the Critics* and *Beowulf: The Monsters and the Critics*, Tolkien chose his phrases carefully from the list (see Textual Notes, page 303).

Rachel Hands, ed., *English Hawking and Hunting in* The Boke of St. Albans: *A Facsimile Edition of sigs. a2–f8 of the* Boke of St. Albans *(1486)* (London: Oxford University Press, 1975), 83–85. For a discussion of Tolkien's uses of the *Book of St. Albans* terms, see Shippey, *Road to Middle-earth*, 21.

142. **the Encircler of the World of Men (Miðgarðsormr), the doom of the gods in what is left of Norse mythology;**
The Midgard Serpent (Miðgarðsormr) is the offspring of the Norse "god" Loki and a giantess. It has been cast into the sea and encircles the world, biting its own tail. At the time of the doom of the gods it will rise up and be battled by Thor. Both thunder-god and monster will perish.

143. **the dragon of the Völsungs**
In the *Völsunga Saga*, the hero Sigurd slays Fafnir, a terrible dragon who is in fact a person transformed into serpent-shape. Fafnir had killed his father Hreidmar to seize the gold that Andvari the dwarf had paid as a weregild for slaying Otr, son of Hreidmar and the brother of Regin and Fafnir. It is Regin, who hopes to betray the hero and recover the hoard, who goads Sigurd into attacking Fafnir. A version of this story is told in *Beowulf*, lines 874–902.

Beowulf, lines 874–902
Klaeber, ed., *Beowulf and the Fight at Finnsburg*, 33–34.

144. **the prince of the heroes of the North, the dragon-slaying Wælsing**
Tolkien here refers to Sigurd, the hero of the *Völsunga Saga*, who slew the dragon Fafnir as his greatest deed (a version of the story is told in *Beowulf*, lines 874–902). In *Beowulf* lines 875–877, his name is given as "Sigemund" "Wælsinges gewinn" ("kin of Wæls"). "Kin of Wæls" can be translated as "Völsung."

Beowulf, lines 874–902
Klaeber, ed., *Beowulf and the Fight at Finnsburg*, 33–34.

145. **even in the Foreword to Strong's Translation we meet it still — though it is now toned down, and is not longer in Ker's actual words. But still, as we have seen, the folk-tale "has been allowed in Beowulf to usurp the place of honour, and to drive into episodes and digressions the things which should be the main stuff of a well-conducted epic."**

The folk-tale is a good servant but a bad master: it has been allowed in *Beowulf* to usurp the place of honour, and to drive into episodes and digressions the things which should have been the main stuff of a well-conducted epic.

Chambers, "Beowulf and the Heroic Age," xxvi. For Chambers see above, note 8. For Strong, see above, note 9.

Folio 35

146. **Milton**

The reference is to John Milton (1608–1674), the great English poet and author of *Paradise Lost*. Tolkien is suggesting that such a poet as Milton could, by the power of his poetic gifts, transform even a simple story into great art. Simply because we do not know who the *Beowulf* poet was, the argument would go, we cannot be certain that he did not have the same ability as Milton to take something "base" and raise it to the level of great poetry.

147. **'cheap' as Ker says.**

"The thing itself is cheap; the moral and the spirit of it can only be matched among the noblest authors."

Ker, *Dark Ages*, 253. For Ker, see above, note 6.

Folio 36

148. **we desire our myths to be incarnate.**

See Carpenter, *J. R. R. Tolkien: A Biography*, 90–92; Carpenter, *The Inklings*, 42–45.

149. **(how they seize on Byrhtwold's words in <u>Maldon</u>!)**

Hige sceal þe heardra,   heorte þe cenre,
mod sceal þe mara   þe ure mægen lytlað

Tolkien translated these lines as:

(The spirit shall be more inflexible, the heart more bold, the courage greater, as our strength grows less.)

Byrhtwold, an English warrior, says these words at the end of the *Battle of Maldon*, after it is clear to all participants that the Vikings will win and the English will be slaughtered. Byrhtwold states that he would rather be killed and lie dead next to his lord (who has already been killed) than survive the battle.

The Battle of Maldon, lines 312–313
Elliott Van Kirk Dobbie, ed., *The Anglo-Saxon Minor Poems*, The Anglo-Saxon Poetic Records 6 (New York: Columbia University Press, 1942), 15.

150. **The 'heroic,' as Chambers calls it, is the <u>more</u> valuable**
Chambers, "Beowulf and the Heroic Age," vii–xxxii; see particularly xxix. For Chambers, see above, note 8.

151. **'There is no disputing about tastes' it is said — foolishly; for we must dispute about them.**
Tolkien is here translating a Latin commonplace: "de gustibus non est disputandum" ("there is no disputing about tastes"), a phase often used to attempt to avoid undesired arguments about subjective matters. Tolkien says that the phrase is used foolishly because a very important part of literary study is analysis of — and disputing about — literary "tastes."

152. **This story of Ingeld the twice faithless and easily led (and the not too intelligent)**
For the story of Ingeld, see above, note 137.

Ingeld is "twice faithless" for first betraying his duty to revenge his father and then turning around and betraying the peace he had made as part of his first betrayal (in "*Beowulf:* The Monsters and the Critics," Tolkien calls Ingeld "thrice faithless," presumably because he betrays his duty to his father, to his wife, and to his oath of peace). He is "easily led" because the mere goading of one aged warrior (if Beowulf's tale that is put into the future subjunctive mood is to be-lieved) caused him to break his word and his peace. The "not too intelligent" description may be unfair, given that Ingeld did not choose his situation, but nevertheless Ingeld seems less heroic and more foolish than Chambers paints him. See above, note 138.

Klaeber, ed., *Beowulf and the Fight at Finnsburg*, xxxvi.

153. **a tradition concerning moving <u>historical</u> events, the arising of Denmark and the wars in the islands**
Tolkien is here referring both to the development of Scandinavian sea-power in the fifth century and the Germanic colonization of Britain in the same period. Tolkien discusses this presumed historical background in *Finn and Hengest*.

J. R. R. Tolkien, *Finn and Hengest: The Fragment and the Episode*, ed. Alan Bliss (Boston: Houghton Mifflin, 1983), 12–16.

154. **Are we to have no tragedy of fact but dealing death in a narrow place against overwhelming odds,**
Compare:

No kind of adventure is so common or better told in the earlier heroic manner than the defense of a narrow place against odds.

W. P. Ker, *Epic and Romance*, 5.

155. Are we to refuse "King Lear" either because it is founded on a silly folk-tale (the old naif details of which still peep through as they do in <u>Beowulf</u>)
For *King Lear* see above, note 40.

The folk-tale whose details "peep through" in Beowulf is the "Bear's Son" tale. As summarized by Chambers, who takes it from *Der Starke Hans* in Grimm's Fairy Tales:

> Hans is brought up in a robber's den: but . . . this is a mere toning down of the original story, which makes a bear's den the nursery of the strong youth. Hans overcomes in an empty castle the foe (a manikin of magic power) who has already worsted his comrades Fir-twister and Stone-splitter. He pursues this foe to his hole, is let down by his companions in a basket by a rope, slays his foe with his club and rescues a princess. He sends up the princess in the basket; but when his own turn comes to be pulled up his associates intentionally drop the basket when halfway up. But Hans, suspecting treason, has only sent up his club. He escapes by magic help, takes vengeance on the traitors, and weds the princess.

Chambers, *Beowulf: An Introduction to the Study of the Poem*, 365–81.

Folio 37

156. The musical critic Ernest Newman I remember once commented
Ernest Newman (1868–1959) was the highly respected music critic of the *Manchester Guardian*, *Birmingham Post*, and *London Times*. He is most well known for his four-volume biography of Wagner. I have been unable to find in Newman's extensive writings the exact source of the sentence Tolkien paraphrases.

157. Rider Haggard's <u>Eric Brighteyes</u>
Henry Rider Haggard (1856–1925) was a Victorian writer of popular adventure stories, including *King Solomon's Mines* and *She*; see Tom Pocock, *Rider Haggard and the Lost Empire* (London: Weidenfeld and Nicolson, 1993), here 78–79; and compare Robert Fraser, *Victorian Quest Romance* (Plymouth, England: Northcote, 1998), 28–46. *Eric Brighteyes* is an agglomeration of characters, episodes and themes from various Norse sagas compiled into one tale of a great and powerful young Icelander, his love for a beautiful woman, and the destruction wrought upon him by another woman who desires to possess him and is herself gifted with evil magical powers. There are many similarities in style between *Eric Brighteyes* and Tolkien's fiction. One Sigfriður Skaldaspillir wrote a sequel, *Eric Brighteyes 2: A Witch's Welcome* (New York: Kensington, 1979).

H. Rider Haggard, *Eric Brighteyes* (London: Longmans Green and Co., 1891).

158. **Although there are some vivid touches (2293ff)**

> Hordweard sohte
> georne æfter grunde,   wolde guman findan,
> þone þe him on sweofote   sare geteode,
> hat ond hreohmod   hlæw oft ymbehwearf
> ealne utanweardne,   ne ðær ænig mon
> on þære westenne;   hwæðre wiges gefeh,
> beaduwe weorces,   hwilum on beorh æthwearf,
> sincfæt sohte.   He þæt sona onfand
> ðæt hæfde gumena sum   goldes gefandod,
> heahgestreona.   Hordweard onbad
> earfoðlice   oð ðæt æfen cwom;
> wæs ða gebolgen   beorges hyrde,
> wolde se laða   lige forgyldan
> drincfæt dyre.   Þa wæs dæg sceacen
> wyrme on willan;   no on wealle læng,
> bidan wolde,   ac mid bæle for,
> fyre gefysed.

[Eagerly the hoard-guardian sought, going over the ground. He wished to find the man who had trespassed against him while he was sleeping. Hot and fury-minded, he searched all around the outside of the barrow. There was not a single man there in all that wasteland, but he desired war, the work of battle. After a while he returned to the barrow to seek the treasure-cup. He soon found that a certain man had tampered with the gold, the wonderful treasures. The hoard-guardian bided his time impatiently until evening came. Then he, the guardian of the barrow, was enraged. The hateful one intended to repay the dear drinking cup with flame. Then the day was departed as the dragon wished. He did not intend to abide long inside the walls, but went forth with fire, impelled by the blaze.]

Beowulf, lines 2293b–2309a
Klaeber, ed., *Beowulf and the Fight at Finnsburg*, 86–87.

159. **Already nonetheless he approaches "<u>draconitas</u>" rather than '<u>draco</u>' —**
"Draconitas" can be translated as "dragon-ness" or "the qualities of a dragon." In adjective form it could just as easily be used to describe a person or a monster. "Draco" on the other hand, is a noun and is the beast, the dragon, itself.

Folio 38

160. **<u>Iúmonna Gold Galdre Bewunden</u>. (omit last stanza). Here we see that the old enemy is within man as well as without.**
'Iúmonna Gold Galdre Bewunden' (the title comes from line 3052 of *Beowulf*

and means "the gold of ancient men, wound with spells"), was first published in the Leeds literary magazine *Gryphon*, n.s. 4 no. 4 (January 1923): 130. There is a revision of the poem in the 4 March 1937 issue of *The Oxford Magazine*.

There is a small textual puzzle in the manuscript of *Beowulf and the Critics* at this point, but with the help of Christopher Tolkien I have been able to resolve it.

The MS of Beowulf and the Critics contains two pairs of dragon poems. In the 'A' text (on page 38 of the Bodleian's foliation), Tolkien writes in ink:

I will quote you — though this may seem an unpardonable digression in the manner of the poor <u>Beowulf</u> — poet — two modern poems on the dragon. The two together for all their defects (especially the first I shall quote) seem to me more important for <u>Beowulf</u>-criticism, for which they were not written, than very much that has been written with that purpose.
<u>Iúmonna Gold Galdre Bewunden</u>

[Below the title of the poem is written in pencil: "(omit last stanza) here we see the old enemy is within man as well as without"]

Then follows in ink:

"Lewis's Poem: — "

Followed by the text of "The Northern Dragon" from *Pilgrim's Regress*.

In the 'B' Text of *Beowulf and the Critics*, on the Bodleian's folio 147 (originally page 60), Tolkien wrote at the top of the leaf in pencil: "Eft ongan eldo gebunden gioguðe cwiðan. He wintrum fród worn gemunde" (afterwards it happened that the man bound with age lamented for his youth. Wise in winters, he remembered much); this is a condensation of lines 2111–2114 of *Beowulf*. This pencilled text is followed by the pencilled numeral (ii) centered on the page, and the Anglo-Saxon phrase "atol inwit gæst," also in pencil and centered. "The Northern Dragon" (untitled in the manuscript) follows immediately thereafter.

It seems to me clear that when Tolkien prepared the original lecture ('A') he intended to bring the text of *Iúmonna Gold* with him on separate sheets of paper and read them aloud. Similarly, on folio 42 in 'A' he writes "Read Cha. Foreword to Strong's translation p. xxvii "Yet Professor Chadwick ... to xxix .. painful on xxx end of Ector de Mari's [sic] speech"; see below, note 171), which suggests that he simply intended to bring Strong's translation of *Beowulf* with him to the lecture rather than copying out the long passage by hand.

The layout of the text on page 56 of 'B' (146 in the Bodleian's foliation) provides additional information: the main text written in ink on this leaf stops about one third of the way down the page, where Tolkien states that he is going to quote two modern poems on the dragon: "The two together, whatever their defects as poems, or dragon-poems, are in some respects, I think, more important for *Beowulf*-criticism (for which they were not written) than much that has been written with that purpose." The remainder of the text on the leaf is a scrawled pencil note for some text that, in a different form, is later integrated into the argument. It seems reasonable to infer that when Tolkien came to the portion of 'B' where he intended to insert the dragon poems, he had pages 57–59 already written on separate leaves; otherwise he would have simply continued the text on 56 (it is possible that the pencil text on 56 was in his way, but I do not think this is the case). At this point 'B' is still a fair copy of 'A' and there is no reason to think that Tolkien would have started the text on a leaf he had already written on; at the very least he would have turned the leaf over and written his fair copy on the verso of the scrawled notes, as he did elsewhere in the MS. But unless there is some additional information to be found in the foliation or the handwriting, I do not think it is possible to determine if pages 57–59 are the leaves Tolkien had in mind when he wrote only the title of the poem on folio 38. In any event, it it clear that Tolkien removed folios 57–59 (what would have been 147–149 if they had remained with the manuscript) when he was readying *Iúmonna Gold* for publication in *The Oxford Magazine*.

These pages were recently found by Christopher Tolkien, who kindly sent copies of them to me. The text of the poem (printed above) is quite similar to that of the 1937 version in *The Oxford Magazine*; the base text which Tolkien revised is closer to the 1937 version than it is to the 1923 version of the poem, although it is clearly intermediate between the two.

I have printed in the main text the version of *Iúmonna Gold Galdre Bewunden* which Christopher Tolkien sent to me, but since this version cannot be proven to be the version that J. R. R. Tolkien intended for the 'A' text, I have printed it the smaller font that I use to indicate editorial insertion or expansion. The version in the 'B' text I have printed as it appears on the leaves in the possession of Christopher Tolkien, although it is important to note that Tolkien's revisions of this version may not have been made when *Beowulf and the Critics* reached its final form, but instead may have been made for the 1937 publication of *Iúmonna Gold* in *The Oxford Magazine*. Nevertheless the version in the main text includes all of Tolkien's emendations; the base text can be reconstructed, if necessary, from the Textual Notes. Following J. R. R. Tolkien's instructions in the text, I have omitted the last stanza in the 'A' text but, since he did not put such instructions in the 'B' text, I have included it there. I print below the texts of the 1923 and 1937 versions of the poem for the sake of comparison.

When the moon was new and the sun young
of silver and gold the gods sung;
in the green grass they silver spilled;
and the white waters they with gold filled.
Ere the pit was dug or hell yawned,
ere dwarf was bred or dragon spawned,

there were elves of old, and strong spells
under green hills in hollow dells
they sang as they wrought many fair things,
the bright crowns of the Elf-kings.
But their doom fell, and their song waned,
By iron hewn and steel chained.
Greed that sang not, nor with mouth smiled,
in dark holes their wealth piled,
graven silver and carven gold:
over Elvenhome the shadow rolled.

There was an old dwarf in a dark cave,
to silver and gold his fingers clave;
with hammer and tongs and anvil-stone
he worked his hands to the hard bone,
and coins he made, and strings of rings,
and thought to buy the power of kings.
But his eyes grew dim and his ears dull,
and the skin yellow on his old skull;
through his bony claw with a pale sheen
the stony jewels slipped unseen.
No feet he heard, though the earth quaked,
when the young dragon his thirst slaked,
and the stream smoked at his dark door;
the flames hissed on the dank floor.
He died alone in the red fire,
and his bones were ash in the hot mire.

There was an old dragon under grey stone;
his red eyes blinked as he lay alone.
His joy was dead and his youth spent,
he was knobbed and wrinkled and his limbs bent
with the long years to his gold chained;
in his heart's furnace the fires waned.
To his belly's slime gems stuck thick,
silver and gold he would snuff and lick:
he knew the place of the least ring
beneath the shadow of his black wing.
Of thieves he thought on his hard bed,
and he dreamed that on their flesh he fed,
their bones crushed, and their blood drank:
he ears drooped and his breath sank.

Mail-rings rang. He heard them not.
A voice echoed in his deep grot:
a young warrior with a bright sword
called him forth to defend his hoard.
His teeth were knives, and of horn his hide,
but iron tore him, and his flame died.

There was an old king on a high throne:
his white beard lay on knees of bone;
his mouth savoured neither meat nor drink,
nor his ears song; he could only think
of his huge chest with carven lid
where pale gems and gold lay hid,
in secret treasury in the dark ground
whose strong doors were iron-bound.
The swords of his thanes were dull with rust,
his glory fallen, his rule unjust,
his halls hollow, and his bowers cold,
but king he was of elvish gold.
He heard not the horns in the mountain pass,
he smelt not the blood on the trodden grass,
but his halls were burned, his kingdom lost;
in a cold pit his bones were tossed.

J. R. R. Tolkien, "Iumonna Gold Galdre Bewunden," *The Oxford Magazine* 55.15 (1937): 473.

The 1923 version of the poem is also published in *The Annotated Hobbit*. I give this version below:

Iúmonna Gold Galdre Bewunden

There were elves olden and strong spells
Under green hills in hollow dells
They sang o'er the gold they wrought with mirth,
In the deeps of time in the young earth,
Ere Hell was digged, ere the dragon's brood
Or the dwarves were spawned in dungeons rude;
And men there were in few lands
That caught some cunning of their mouths and hands.
Yet their doom came and their songs failed,
And greed that made them not to its holes haled
Their gems and gold and their loveliness,
And the shadows fell on Elfinesse.

There was an old dwarf in a deep grot
That counted the gold things he had got,
That the dwarves had stolen from men and elves
And kept in the dark to their gloomy selves.
His eyes grew dim and his ears dull.
And the skin was yellow on his old skull;
There ran unseen through his bony claw
The faint glimmer of gems without flaw.
He heard not the feet that shook the earth,
Nor the rush of wings, not the brazen mirth
Of dragons young in their fiery lust:
His hope was in gold and in jewels his trust.
Yet a dragon found his dark cold hole,
And he lost the earth and the things he stole.

There was an old dragon under an old stone
Blinking with red eyes all alone.
The flames of his fiery heart burnt dim;
His was knobbed and wrinkled and bent of limb;
His joy was dead and his cruel youth,
but his lust still smouldered and he had no ruth.
To the slime of his belly the gems stuck thick
And his things of gold he would snuff and lick
As he lay thereon and dreams of the woe
And grinding anguish thieves should know
That ever set finger on one small ring;
And dreaming uneasy he stirred a wing.
He heard not the step or the harness clink
Till the fearless warrior at his cavern's brink
Called him to come out and fight for his gold,
Yet iron rent his heart with anguish cold.

There was an old king on a high throne;
His white beard was laid on his knees of bone,
And his mouth savoured not meat nor drink,
Nor his ears song, he could only think
Of his huge chest with carven lid
Where the gold and jewels unseen lay hid
In a secret treasury in the dark ground,
Whose mighty doors were iron-bound.
The swords of his warriors did dull and rust,
His glory was tarnished and his rule unjust,

His halls hollow and his bowers cold,
But he was the king of elfin gold.
He heard not the horns in the mountain pass,
He smelt not the blood on the trodden grass,
Yet his halls were burned and his kingdom lost,
In a grave unhonoured his bones were tossed.

There is an old hoard in a dark rock
Forgotten behind doors none can unlock.
The keys are lost and the path gone,
The mound unheeded that the grass grows on;
The sheep crop it and the larks rise
From its green mantle, and no man's eyes
Shall find its secret, till those return
Who wrought the treasure, till again burn
The lights of Faery, and the woods shake,
And the songs silent once more awake.

J. R. R. Tolkien, "Iúmonna Gold Galdre Bewunden," *Gryphon* n.s. 4.4 (1923): 130.

J.R.R. Tolkien, *The Annotated Hobbit*, ed. Douglas A. Anderson (Boston: Houghton Mifflin, 1988), 288–89.

161. **Lewis's poem:** —
"The Northern Dragon" from

C. S. Lewis, *The Pilgrim's Regress: An Allegorical Apology for Christianity, Reason and Romanticism* (London: Geoffrey Bles, 1933, rev. 1943; repr. 1956), 192–93.

Folio 40

162. **a baited badger.**
Badger-baiting was a blood sport in which dogs were set upon a badger (*Meles meles*). Because the badger was trapped in a pit from which it could not escape, the outcome of the contest was never in doubt: it was watched merely to see how many dogs the badger could fight against, and for how long. Tolkien is here suggesting that the traditional epic hero "caught in a net of fate" is not particularly moving as a poetic spectacle (just as badger-baiting was hardly a thing of poetic merit) because the outcome was certain, and bloody. A baited badger may be brave and fight hard, but that is all he can do. Poetry and tragedy, Tolkien seems to be arguing, require more.

163. **(has not Chambers himself made a** <u>motorbike</u> **the symbol of the lay, and a** <u>Rolls Royce</u> **of the epic)**

The men who wrote short lays wrote them for their own pleasure: they were not thinking of providing material convenient for the purpose of some epic poet who was to come after them. Therefore it should not be assumed, without evidence, that these lost lays of heathen times were of such a character that an epic could easily be made by fitting them together. Half a dozen motor-bikes cannot be combined to make a Rolls-Royce car.

Chambers, "Beowulf and the Heroic Age," xxv. For Chambers, see above, note 8.

164. Byrhtwold in the <u>Battle of Maldon</u>:
See above, note 149.

165. a received and honoured gnomē
A "gnome" here is a short, well-established expression of a general truth. Tolkien is suggesting that Byrhtwold would have inherited from his culture this set of words to express this sentiment.

Folio 41
166. man at war with the infest world
The word in the manuscript is clearly "infest." Tolkien's adjectival use of it is unusual, but can be justified etymologically from the Latin "infestus", "hostile", which is in fact the sense of the passage: man at war with the hostile world (the obsolete adjective is listed in the *Oxford English Dictionary*, 7. 926c.). Compare also the Latin *Vita Sancti Guthlaci* (*Life of Saint Guthlac*), which Tolkien cites in another context (see below, note 168):

> Contigit itaque in diebus Cœnredi Merciorum regis, cum Brittones, *infesti* hostes Saxonici generis . . .

> [Now it happened in the days of Cœnred King of the Mercians, while the Britons, the implacable enemies of the Saxon race . . .]

Bertram Colgrave, *Felix's Life of St. Guthlac* (London: Cambridge University Press, 1956; repr. 1985), 108–11, here 108–9.

167. It transcends astronomy.
Compare C. S. Lewis's *The Discarded Image* (Cambridge, Cambridge University Press, 1969), 92–102.

Folio 42
168. Cynewulf or the author of St. Guthlac
Cynewulf, who is generally thought to have lived in the early part of the ninth

century (although there is now significant dispute about this point), was from either Mercia or Northumberland. He "signed" his poems with runes worked into the text. A substantial number of poems were once attributed to Cynewulf based upon supposed similarities in style, but scholars are now certain only that he composed *Christ II* and *Juliana* in the *Exeter Book* and *Elene* and the *Fates of the Apostles* in the *Vercelli Book*. See *Cynewulf: Basic Readings*, ed. Robert E. Bjork (New York: Garland, 1996).

The author of *St. Guthlac* is unknown. There are various textual and source problems associated with the poem, which is found in the Exeter Book. A Latin *Life of Guthlac* by Felix of Crowland was written in the early eighth century: see above, note 166 (also available in part in Dorothy Whitelock, ed. *English Historical Documents*, 2nd ed. [New York: Oxford University Press, 1979], 1: 770–75). The Old English poem bears some relation to this text, but scholars cannot agree if the first half of the poem is at all based on the Latin text (the second half of the poem is).

Guthlac was a member of the royal Mercian house born in 673. He became a monk at Repton and then retreated into the wilderness of the Lincolnshire fens where he spent the remaining fifteen years of his life. According to the poem he was tormented by devils but held firm in his faith. He died in 714.

169. **It has been said that there is mirth and music and gentle talk in <u>Beowulf</u>, but the 'light is but a foil to the dark'.**
I cannot find an exact source for the quotation, but cf. Strong:

> The background of darkness and strife against which this brightness is set is intensified not only by the suggestion of fatalism, made both overtly and subtly throughout the poem, but by many of the poet's descriptions of nature.

Strong, *Beowulf Translated*, xliv. For Strong, see above, note 9.

170. **So deadly and so ineluctable is the theme that those who play only in the little circle of light with the toys of wit and refinement, looking not to the battlements, either hear not the theme at all, or recoiling shut their ears to it. Death comes to the feast, and they say He gibbers.**
I cannot find a direct source for the conjunction of "Death comes to the feast" and "He gibbers." Tolkien may be referring to the sixteenth-century poem "A Comparison of the Life of Man" by Richard Barnfield and then linking it to the use of "gibber" to describe ghosts in *Hamlet*, Act I, Scene 1, line 119. My interpretation of the juxtaposition of the passages (if Tolkien was intentionally linking *Hamlet* and Barnfield) is that when the witty and the refined who do not guard the battlements of civilization do finally see Death, they interpret him merely as a *sign* of death, not as the thing itself, and so do not recognize until

too late their doom. This explanation does scant justice to the phrase, which is one of the most powerful and poetic passages in both *Beowulf and the Critics* and "*Beowulf*: The Monsters and the Critics." The quotation may also recall Banquo's ghost at the feast in *Macbeth*, Act III, Scene 4. Also compare Stephen Phillips, *Ulysses* (1902), Act III, Scene 2: "... who gibbers at the feast of evil days." (cf. also Shippey, *Author of the Century*, 193.)

A Comparison of the Life of Man

Man's life is well compared to a feast,
Furnisht with choice of all varieties
To it come Tyme; and as a bidden guest
Hee sets him downe, in Pompe and Maiastie,
The three-fold Age of Man, the Waiters bee,
Then with an earthen voyder (made of clay)
Comes Death, and takes the table clear away.

Richard Barnfield, *Poems 1594–1598*, ed. Edward Arber (London: Unwin Brothers, 1882), 124.

In the passage from *Hamlet*, Horatio is speaking of the ghost that walks the battlements.

Hamlet, Act 1, Scene 1, lines 116–129.

HORATIO: A mote it is to trouble the mind's eye.
In the most high and palmy state of Rome,
A little ere the mightiest Julius fell,
The graves stood tenantless and the sheeted dead
Did squeak and gibber in the Roman streets;
As stars with trains of fire and dews of blood,
Disasters in the sun; and the moist start
Upon whose influence Neptune's empire stands
Was sick almost to doomsday with eclipse.
And even the life precurse of feared events,
As harbingers preceding still the fates
And prologue to the omen coming on,
Have heaven and earth together demonstrated
Unto our climatures and countrymen.

171. **Read Chambers' Foreword to Strong's translation p xxvii "Yet Professor Chadwick ... to xxix.. painful) — on xxx end of Ector de Maris' speech.**
Because there are deviations from Malory in Chambers's text, there are some difficulties in the reconstruction of this passage. I have corrected Chambers's "earthy" to Malory's "earthly," but for consistency (not always Malory's strong

suit) I have retained Chambers's "were" in the phrase "and thou were the meekest man . . ." in place of Malory's "was."

Chambers, *"Beowulf* and the Heroic Age," vii–xxxii.

Folio 43

172. **It has a kinship with St. Guthlac, Ælfric, even with medieval homilies on hell equally balanced with a lay like Voluspá, Hávamal or Sigurd's lay.**
For *Guthlac* see above, notes 166 and 168.
For Ælfric see above, note 63.

Völuspá ("The Prophesy of the Seeress") is the first poem in the *Elder Edda*, the oldest collection of Old Norse poetry. *Völuspá* provides the most developed verse account of the ancient mythology and cosmololgy of the ancient North.

Hávamál is the longest poem in the *Elder Edda* (it follows *Völuspá*). It is a collection of sententious sayings attributed to Odin.

Sigurd's Lay (*Sigurþurarkvia hin skamma* — "The Short Lay of Sigurth") tells part of the story of Brynhild and Sigurd and contains much material used in *Völsungr Saga*.

Tolkien is here arguing that *Beowulf* shares as much with the very obviously and overtly "Christian" poetry in Anglo-Saxon as it does with the most clearly "pagan" poems in Old Norse. He believes that it is not possible to put *Beowulf* into either camp, but neither can either influence be denied. Rather, *Beowulf*, being Anglo-Saxon, occurs at a unique moment when the old tales of the North had not been forgotten but had in fact been enriched (in the minds of Christian poets) with new meaning now that the Christian world-view had been adopted.

173. **book-Latin**
Latin learned from study, as opposed to spoken Latin. The Latin used for oral and informal written communication between, let us say, members of the Church from different countries was a simplified form of the language (which was not, by the Anglo-Saxon period, a cradle-tongue for anyone). Book-Latin was more formal and elaborate in construction.

174. **Angolcynn**
Literally "the kin of the Angles," the people of the Angles, one of the three tribes (the others are the Saxons and the Jutes) who, according to Bede, made up the migration of Germanic tribesmen from the continent to England.

175. **Aldhelm (whom Theodore considered best of the vernacular poets — though his vernacular verse is lost)**
I believe Tolkien made an error here that he later corrected in the B-Text of *Beowulf and the Critics* (see below, note 474). It was Alfred who considered Aldhelm the best of the vernacular poets (we know this by way of William of Mal-

mesbury). As far as I have been able to determine there are no comments on
Aldhelm's vernacular poetry attributed to Theodore.

The first great native-born English scholar, Aldhelm (c. 640–709), was abbot
of Malmesbury and later bishop of Sherborne. He wrote in a highly ornamented
and complex "hermeneutic style" and composed verse in Latin and, apparently,
Old English. His various compositions include *De Virginitate*, a set of "Enig-
mata," and two treatises on metrical composition. Although none of Aldhelm's
Old English verse has survived, William of Malmesbury notes that Aldhelm was
King Alfred's favorite Anglo-Saxon poet. Aldhelm is said to have used his ability
to compose and sing vernacular poetry to lead people to salvation: he would
wait on a bridge to intercept people returning from mass, and there he would
sing Old English verse into which he inserted words of scripture. See Andy
Orchard, *The Poetic Art of Aldhelm* (Cambridge: Cambridge University Press,
1994), 1, 5, 119–25; and Michael Lapidge, "Aldhelm's Latin Poetry and Old
English Verse," in idem, *Anglo-Latin Literature 600–899* (London: Hambledon,
1996), 247–69, 505–6.

> William of Malmesbury, *Gesta Pontificum*, ed. N. E. S. A. Hamilton (London:
> Rolls Series, 1870), 332–33.

176. Theodore
Theodore of Tarsus was a Greek missionary sent by Pope Vitalian to England.
He became Archbishop of Canterbury in 668. Theodore organized the adminis-
trative system of the English church. See Michael Lapidge, ed., *Archbishop Theo-
dore* (Cambridge: Cambridge University Press, 1995), esp. idem, "The Career of
Archbishop Theodore," 1–29.

177. ... Alfred the revivalist than the Latin learning which he strove to reestablish.
See above, note 66.

Folio 44

178. Virgil, Statius and Lucan are given among the books studied in the school of York, by Alcuin in his poem on the Church of York.
Alcuin (c. 735–804) was born in York and became a monk and eventual master
of the cloister school there. He became part of Charlemagne's court in 781, and
eventually became abbot at Tours. He wrote works on grammar, theology, and
the lives of saints, as well as many letters, one of which Tolkien quotes below
(see note 197). The poem on the school of York lists some of the authors whose
works the monastic library possessed:

> Quid quoque Sedulius, vel quid canit ipse Iuvencus,
> Alcimus et Clemens, Prosper, Paulinus, Arator,

Quid Fortunatus, vel quid Lactantius edunt,
Quae Maro Virgilius, Statius, Lucanus et auctor

[Whatever also Sedulius or Juvencus himself sings, Alcimus and Pruden-
tius, Prosper, Paulinus, Arator, whatever Fortunatus or Lactantius produced, or Virgil, Statius or the poet Lucan . . .]

Alcuin, "Carmen I," in *Monumenta Alcuiniana*, ed. P. Jaffé, Bibliotheca Rerum
Germanicarum 6 (Berlin: Apud Weidmannos, 1873), 128 (lines 1551–1554).

And see also W. P. Ker's comments:

The English epic is possibly due to Virgil and Statius; possibly to Juvencus
and other Christian poets, to the authors studied by Aldhelm and Bede. It
may be that the *Hildebrand* for the Western Germanic Group, and the *Atlamál* for the North, fixes the limit of epic size in the old Teutonic school;
that is was difficult or impossible to get beyond this without the encouragement of the Latin poets, showing how to amplify and embroider, to
compose orations for combatants, and to discriminate the particulars of
their wounds.

Ker, *Dark Ages*, 251.

Chambers: quotes Ker through ". . . studied by Aldhelm and Bede" on page
xxv, of the Foreword.

Chambers, "Beowulf and the Heroic Age," vii–xxxii.

179. Alcuin from circa 725
See above, note 178.

180. sea-burial, or the blazing pyre, and piled tumulus!
These three methods of burial are all described in *Beowulf*. The body of Scyld
Scefing is laid upon a ship with all his treasures and set out to sea (lines 32–52).
In lines 1114–1125, Hildeburh commits the bodies of her sons to the funeral
pyre. Beowulf's body is also burned, and his memorial is a mound and barrow
built on a headland (lines 3156–3168).

181. Avoidance of all glaring anachronism in this respect (such as is found heed-
lessly in Judith)
In *Judith* the poet does not even make an attempt to maintain a historical illusion. While the battle of the Bethulians and the Assyrians happens many years
before the birth of Christ, in lines 83–86a Judith calls upon the "Son of the All-
Ruler" and God the "powerful Trinity." Needless to say, invocations of the Son
and of the Trinity were not in the repertoire of Old Testament speakers (although traditional exegesis always attributed a kind of 'pre-knowledge' of the

Incarnation and the Trinity to the Old Testament patriarchs and matriarchs).

Ic ðe, frymða god   ond frofre gæst,
bearn alwaldan,   biddan wylle
miltse þinre   me þearfendre
ðrynesse ðrym.

[I wish to ask you, God of kindness, spirit of solace, Son of the All-Ruler,
for your mildness towards me in my need, powerful Trinity.]

Judith, lines 83–86
Dobbie, ed., *Beowulf and Judith*, 101.

Folio 45

182. **Woden and Þunor**
These are the Old English versions of the names of the Norse gods Odin and
Thor, respectively the Father of the Gods and the Thunder God.

183. **The last heathen kingdom Sussex had only been converted in 681–6.**
The South Saxons (Kingdom of Sussex) were heathen even though Ecgfrith,
their king, was Christian. Around the end of 680 or the beginning of 681 Wilfrid of Ripon, former head of the Northumbrian church, traveled to Sussex and
"within the next five years, [he] and a band of followers" had converted the
kingdom of the South Saxons. (For Wilfrid, see below, note 186).

Frank Merry Stenton, *Anglo-Saxon England*, 2nd ed. (Oxford: Clarendon Press,
1950), 138.

184. **Bede's story of Coifi and his sparrow**
The mis-spelling of the name "Coifi" (Tolkien spells it "Cefi" in the 'A' manuscript) and the conflation of Coifi with the unnamed advisor to Edwin who
actually tells the story of the sparrow, shows, I believe, that Tolkien was here cit-
ing Bede from memory.
    In Book II, Chapter XIII of his *Ecclesiastical History*, the Venerable Bede tells
the story of the conversion of Edwin, King of Northumbria. In the year 627 St.
Paulinus, Bishop of York and later Bishop of Rochester, receives some unlikely
help in converting Edwin when Coifi, the chief pagan priest, suddenly responds
to the words of the missionary:

Cui primus pontificum ipsius Coifi continuo respondit: 'Tu uide, rex,
quale sit hoc, quod nobis modo praedicatur; ego autem tibi uerissime,
quot certum didici, profiteor, quia nihil omnino uirtutis habet, nihil utili-
tatis religio illa, quam hucusque tenuimus. Nullus enim tuorum studiosius
quam ego culturae deorum nostrorum se subdidit; et nihilominus multi
sunt qui ampliora a te beneficia quam ego et maiores accipiunt dignitates,

magisque prosperantur in omnibus, quae agenda uel adquirenda dispo-
nunt. Si autem dii aliquid ualerent, me potius iuuare uellent, qui illis in-
pensius seruire curaui. Vnde restat ut, si ea quae nunc nobis noua prae-
dicantur, meliora esse et fortiora habita examinatione perspexeris, absque
ullo cunctamine suscipere illa festinemus.'

Cuius suasioni uerbisque prudentibus alius optimatum regis tribuens
assensum continuo subdidit, 'Talis' inquiens, 'mihi uidetur, rex, uita hominum praesens in terris, ad conparationem eius quod nobis incertum est
temporis, quale cum te residente ad caenam cum ducibus ac ministris tuis
tempore brumali, accenso quidem foco in medio et calido effecto cenaculo,
furentibus autem foris per omnia turbinibus hiemalium pluuiarum uel
niuium, adueniens unus passerum domum citissime peruolauerit; qui
cum per unum ostium ingrediens mox per aliud exierit, ipso quidem tempore quo intus est hiemis tempestate non tangitur, sed tamen paruissimo
spatio serenitatis ad momentum excurso, mox de hieme in hiemem re-
grediens tuis oculis elabitur. Ita haec uita hominum ad modicum apparet;
quid autem sequatur, quidue praecesserit, prorsus ignoramus. Vnde, si
haec noua doctrina certius aliquid attulit, merito esse sequenda uidetur.'
His similia et ceteri maiores natu ac regis consiliarii diuinitus admonitit
prosequebantur.

[Coifi, the chief of the priests, answered at once, 'Notice carefully, King,
this doctrine which is now being expounded to us. I frankly admit that, for
my part, I have found that the religion which we have hitherto held has no
virtue nor profit in it. None of your followers has devoted himself more
earnestly than I have to the worship of our gods, but nevertheless there
are many who receive greater benefits and honour from you than I do and
are more successful in all their undertakings. If the gods had any power
they would have helped me more readily, seeing that I have always served
them with greater zeal. So it follows that if, on examination, these new
doctrines which have now been explained to us are found to be better and
more effectual, let us accept them at once without any delay.'

Another of the king's chief men agreed with this advice and with
these wise words and then added, 'This is how the present life of man on
earth, King, appears to me in comparison with that which is unknown to
us. You are sitting feasting with your ealdormen and thegns in winter
time; the fire is burning on the hearth in the middle of the hall and all
inside is warm, while outside the wintry storms of rain and snow are rag-
ing; and a sparrow flies swiftly through the hall. It enters at one door and
quickly flies out through the other. For the few moments it is inside, the
storm and wintry tempest cannot touch it, but after the briefest moment
of calm, it flits from your sight, out of wintry storm and into it again. So
this life of man appears but for a moment; what follows or indeed what

went before, we know not at all. If this new doctrine brings us more certain information, it seems right that we should accept it.' Other elders and
counsellors of the king continued in the same manner, being divinely
prompted to do so.]

Bertram Colgrave and R. A. B. Mynors, eds., *Bede's Ecclesiastical History of the
English People* (Oxford: Clarendon Press, 1969; repr. 1991), 182–85.

**185. in Ireland of the seventh century profane classical literature with its inher-
ent mythology was widely cultivated even in monasteries.**
The idea that profane literature was read in Irish monasteries of the seventh
century was a truism in the 1930s, when Tolkien wrote *Beowulf and the Critics*,
but see now Michael Herren, "Classical and Secular Learning Among the Irish
Before the Carolingian Renaissance," in idem, *Latin Letters in Early Christian Ireland* (Aldershot: Variorum, 1996), 1–39.

Folio 46
**186. St. Paulinus of Nola (born at Bordeaux) — 5th century — cried that 'Hearts
vowed to Christ have no welcome for the goddesses of song; they are barred
to Apollo."**
Born Pontius Meropius Paulinus, St. Paulinus of Nola was a Roman apologist
for Christianity who wrote in the late fourth and early fifth century. The particular quote Tolkien cites is taken from a poem written to Ausonius, a close
friend who succeeded Paulinus to the suffect consulship in Aquitania in 378
(Paulinus's *Carmen* 10). It is one of two poems that are the only surviving verse
letters from Paulinus' side of a long correspondence with Ausonius, who was a
Christian, but a far less devoted adherent to the religion than was Paulinus.

The poem can be dated to some time between 389 and 395, when Paulinus
lived in Spain. Soon afterwards, Paulinus left Spain and founded a monastic
community at Nola in the Italian province of Campania, where he was gov-
ernor. Paulinus wrote Latin verse in a classical style that showed him to be a
"literary disciple of Virgil, Horace, and Ovid," but his matter was entirely Christian (P. G. Walsh, trans., *The Poems of St. Paulinus of Nola*, 4).

The specific quotation Tolkien uses, "Hearts vowed to Christ have no welcome for the goddesses of song; they are barred to Apollo" comes from the
opening of the letter. It seems that Ausonius must have wished Paulinus the
good fortune of being inspired by the Muses to write verses in reply to Ausonius' letter. Paulinus does not take the request as a formulaic wish for good luck
in composing, but instead rather severely asks Ausonius why "do you bid the
deposed Muses return to my charge?" followed by the quote Tolkien uses, and
continuing with the declamation that that he must no longer seek to summon
"deaf Apollo from his cave at Delphi, invoking the Muses as deities, and seeking
from groves or mountain sides that gift of utterance bestowed by divine gift."

Clearly Paulinus has no room for any pagan, heathen, or pre-Christian literature at all: God commands Christians to "not spend our days on the emptiness
of leisure and business, or on the fictions of literature" (Walsh, *Poems*, translating *Carm*. 10. 33–35). On *Carmen* 10 see Dennis E. Trout, *Paulinus of Nola:
Life, Letters, and Poems* (Berkeley: University of California Press, 1999), 78–86.

Tolkien quotes Paulinus as an example of "severe" Christianity, under whose
regime *Beowulf* would not have been created. In a letter to Sulpicius Severus
(*Ep*. 1), whom Tolkien quotes in the next line, though in a slightly different context, Paulinus writes that "Even though a man be a brother and friend and
closer to you than your right hand and dearer than life itself, if he is a stranger
and an enemy in Christ, let him be to thee as the heathen and the publican . . ."
(P. G. Walsh, trans., *Letters of St. Paulinus of Nola* [Westminster, MD: Newman
Press, 1966], 1: 32 [*Ep*. 1.5]). The Latin text is Paulinus of Nola, *Epistolae*, ed.
Wilhelm von Hartel, CSEL 29 (Vienna: Tempsky, 1894), 4.

Quid abdicatas in meam curam, pater,
      redire Musas praecipis?
negant Camenis nec patent Apollini
      dictata Christo pectora.
fuit ista quondam non ope, sed studio pari
      tecum mihi concordia
ciere surdum Delphica Phoebum specu,
      uocare Musas numina
fandique munus munere indultum dei
      petere e nemoribus aut iugis
nunc alia mentem uis agit, maior deus,
      aliosque mores postulat,
sibi reposcens ab homine munus suum,
      uiuamus ut uitae patri.

Paulinus of Nola, *Carmina*, ed., Wilhelm von Hartel, CSEL 30 (Prague: Tempsky, 1894), 25 (*Carm*. 10. 19–32).

Why, father, do you bid the deposed Muses return to my charge? Hearts
dedicated to Christ reject the Latin Muses and exclude Apollo. Of old you
and I shared common cause (our zeal was equal if our poetic resources
were not) in summoning deaf Apollo from his cave at Delphi, invoking the
Muses as deities, seeking from groves or mountain ridges that gift of utterance bestowed by divine gift. But now another power, a great God, in-
spires my mind and demands another way of life. He asks back from man
His own gift, so that we may live for the Father of life.

P. G. Walsh, trans., *The Poems of St. Paulinus of Nola* (New York: Newman Press,
1975), 58–59.

187. **Sulpicius Severus in the preface to his life of St. Martin asks "what good will it do posterity to study the philosophy of Socrates or to read the battles of Hector."**

Sulpicius Severus (c. 363–c. 420) was a Church historian and hagiographer. He was a lifelong friend of St. Paulinus of Nola and the author of the *Life of St. Martin of Tours*.

Ker quotes:

> Quid posteritas emolumenti tulit legendo Hectorem pugnantem aut Socratem philosophantem?

Which he translates as:

> "What profit is there in the record of pagan gods or pagan sages, the labors of Hercules or of Socrates?"

Ker, *Dark Ages*, 24 n. 1.

Tolkien's point is that Sulpicius Severus, who is writing of a "French" saint, is completely intolerant of any pre-Christian culture, knowledge or achievements, which is, however, not the case, see C. Stancliffe, *St. Martin and His Hagiographer* (Oxford: Clarendon Press, 1983), 17–19.

> Plerique mortales studio et gloriae saeculari inaniter dediti exinde perennem, ut putabant, memoriam nominis sui quaesierunt, si uitas clarorum uirorum stilo inlustrassent. quae res utique non perennem quidem, sed aliquantulum tamen conceptae spei fructum adferebat, quia et suam memoriam, licet incassum, propagabant, et propositis magnorum uirorum exemplis non parua aemulatio legentibus excitabatur. sed tamen nihil ad beatam illam aeternamque uitam haec eorum cura pertinuit. quid enim aut ipsis occasura cum saeculo scriptorum suorum gloria profuit? aut quid posteritas emolumenti tulit legendo Hectorem pugnantem aut Socraten philosophantem? cum eos non solum imitari stultitia sit, sed non acerrime etiam inpugnare dementia: quippe qui humanam uitam praesentibus tantum actibus aestimantes spes suas fabulis, animas sepulcris dederint: siquidem ad solam hominum memoriam se perpetuandos crediderunt, cum hominis officium sit, perennem potius uitam quam perennem memoriam quaerere, non scribendo aut pugnando uel philosophando, sed pie sancte religioseque uiuendo.

Sulpicius Severus, *Vita Sancti Martini*, ed., Karl Halm, CSEL 1 (Vindobona: Apud C. Geroldi Filium Bibliopolam Academiae, 1867), 1.1–4.

Most men, vainly pursuing the glory of the world, suppose that by writing the lives of great men they shall acquire a lasting reputation for themselves. Yet the profit which they expect to derive from such an undertaking turns out to be neither durable nor great; for although they may hand down their names to posterity, and may excite in their readers an emulation of the great men whose example they set forth; still they gain nothing by their writings in respect to the felicity of eternal life. For what profit shall they reap from the fame of their writings, which must perish when the world is destroyed? And what good has posterity derived from reading how Hector fought and Socrates philosophized? — When it is not only folly to imitate, but madness to do less than resist the influence of their example: seeing that they who estimate human life only by its present actions, build their hopes upon fables invented by poets and philosophers, and surrender their souls to the corruptions of the grave; for they seek to live only in the memory of mankind: whereas it is the duty of man to seek eternal life, rather than eternal fame: — and *that*, not by writing nor fighting nor philosophizing, but by living a pure and religious life.

The Life of St. Martin of Tours (Willits, CA: Eastern Orthodox Books, 1989). Also, Jacques Fontaine, ed. and trans., *Sulpice Sévère: Vie de Saint Martin*, Souras Chrétienne 133 (Paris: Cerf, 1967), 250–53. Also, an English translation by B. M. Peebles, *The Life of St. Martin of Tours* (New York: Paulist Press, 1949).

188. vita Sancti Wulframni

The *Life of St. Wulfram* of Sens. Wulfram was a Merovingian bishop and missionary. After he had set his see in Sens in order he traveled to Frisia to evangelize. He died in either 695 or 700.

Bruno Krusch and W. Levison, eds., *Vita Vulframni*, Monumenta Germaniae Historica, Scriptores Rerum Merovingicarum 5 (Hannover, 1910), 668.

189. The Odin and Þór of Snorri in the early 13th century are in any case nearly as remote from Woden or Þunor (or any ancient tradition concerning Danish heathendom the English may have possessed), as Jupiter and Apollo or mythology in Ovid is from Greek religion in the days of the long-haired Achaeans.

Snorri Sturlson (1179–1241) was an Icelandic chieftain as well as a poet and historian. He wrote the *Heimskringla*, the history of the kings of Norway, and the *Edda*, a combination of a poetic handbook and a selection of mythological prose. The mythological section of the *Edda*, the *Gylfaginning* ("The Deluding of Gylfi"), is the source for much of what we know of Northern mythology. But Snorri was a Christian, so he describes the Æsir, the Norse gods, as historical figures who convince the world that they are gods (rather than being actual gods).

Odin and Þór in Snorri's poetry are thus depicted more as mighty and legendary heroes than as gods to be worshipped and sacrificed to; pagans in pre-conversion England and in Iceland, however, actually worshipped and sacrificed to Woden and Þunor. Likewise the Jupiter and Apollo of the "mythological" gods of historical Rome are representative beings with stereotyped personalities: they do not require actual sacrifice and they do not seem to intervene in the world of men directly as does, say Poseidon in the *Iliad* and *Odyssey*, which take place in the world of the "long-haired Achaeans" (a Homeric formulaic epithet).

190. St. Wilfrid

Wilfrid was head of the Northumbrian church, but he was expelled by King Ecgfrith. In 677 Wilfrid left England to go to Rome to protest his loss of power, office, and property. He spent the winter of 677 in Frisia (the Netherlands) preaching and making converts, thus setting the stage for future English missionaries. He is also responsible for converting the last heathen kingdom in England, Sussex, which due to the work of Wilfrid and a band of his followers was Christian by 686 (see above, note 180).

Frank Merry Stenton, *Anglo-Saxon England*, 2nd ed. (Oxford: Clarendon Press, 1950), 135–36, 138.

191. St. Wulfram of Sens (died 695).

See above, note 188.

192. Wictberct in 689

According to the Venerable Bede, Wihtbert was a hermit who was both very ascetic and very learned. He tried to convert King Radbod of Frisia to Christianity but failed and returned to his self-imposed exile in Ireland.

Colgrave and Mynors, eds., *Bede's Ecclesiastical History of the English People*, 478–80.

193. Aldgisl

According to the Venerable Bede, Aldgisl was a Frisian king who hospitably received St. Wilfrid and allowed him to preach in Frisia. (For Wilfrid, see above, note 190.)

Colgrave and Mynors, eds., *Bede's Ecclesiastical History of the English People*, 522–23.

Folios 46–47

194. the famous story concerning the Frank St. Wulfram of Sens

For Wulfram, see above, note 188.

Radbod was a Frisian king. The missionary Wihtberht (see above, note 192):

"et Fresiam perueniens duobus annis continuis genti illi ac regi eius Rathbedo uerbum salutis praedicabat, neque aliquem tanti laboris fructum apud barbaros inuenit auditores"

[Traveled by ship to Frisia and "spent two whole years preaching the word of life to the nation and to its king Radbod, but he reaped no fruit for all his labour among the barbarians who heard him."]

Colgrave and Mynors give a further note, just after "Radbod":

This king of the Frisians was said to have been on the point of baptism at the hands of St. Wulframn, archbishop of Sens, when, after having been told that his ancestors were all in hell, he refused to be parted from them in heaven and rejected baptism (*Vita Vulframni*, MGH, SRM v. 668). He was constantly at war with the Franks under Pippin and Charles Martel and died in 719.

Colgrave and Mynors, eds., *Bede's Ecclesiastical History of the English People*, 479–81.

On Radbod and the missions to Frisia see Wolfert van Egmond, "Converting Monks: Missionary Activity in Early Medieval Frisia and Saxony," in *Christianizing Peoples and Converting Individuals*, ed. Guyda Armstong and Ian N. Wood, International Medieval Research 7 (Turnhout: Brepols, 2000), 37–45.

195. **The story relates that once he approached the baptismal font but stopped on the way to ask Wulfram whether, if he were baptized, he might hope to meet in heaven his Frisian ancestors. 'Do not deceive thyself' was Wulfram's reply, 'it is certain that they have received the just sentence of damnation.' Radbod therefore withdrew from the font, and said that he preferred to join his own people, wherever they might be, rather than sit down in the Kingdom of Heaven with a handful of beggars.**

Praefatus autem princeps Rathbodus, cum ad percipiendum baptisma inbueretur, percunctabatur a sancto episcopo Vulframno, iuramentis eum per nomen Domini astringens, ubi maior esset numerus regum et principum seu nobilium gentis Fresionum, in illa videlicet caelesti regione, quam, sit crederet et baptizaretur, percepturum sit promittebat, an in ea, quam dicebat tartaream dampnationem. Tunc beatus Vulframnus: 'Noli errare, inclite princeps, apud Deum certus est suorum numerus electorum. Nam praedecessores tui principes gentis Fresionum, qui sine baptismi sacramento recesserunt, certum est dampnationis suscepisse sententiam; qui vero abhinc crediderit et baptizatus fuerit, cum Christo gaudebit in aeternum.' Haec audiens dux incredulus — nam ad fontem processerat, — et, ut fertur, pedem a fonte retraxit, dicens, non se carere posse consortio praedecessorum suorum principum Fresionum et cum parvo pau-

perum numero residere in illo caelesti regno; qui potius non facile posse
novis dictis adsensum praebere, sed potius permansurum se in his, quae
multo tempore cum omni Fresionum gente servaverat.

Krusch and Levison, eds., *Vita Vulframni*, 668.

Folio 47

196. <u>Alcuin</u> (born about 735 and therefore almost certainly alive at time as the
poet of Beowulf)
See above, note 178.

197. In a letter to Speratus, bishop of Lindisfarne, of A.D. 797 we read: Verba
Dei legantur in sacerdotali convivio; ibi decet lectorem audiri, non citharistam, sermones patrum, non carmina gentilium. Quid Hinieldus cum Christo?
Angusta est domus; utrosque tenere non poterit — the King of Heaven must
not be mentioned with pagan kings who are lamenting in hell. (see Chambers
note <u>Widsith</u> p. 78). The reference to Ingeld is not, however, in the received
text of the letter (see Chambers note to <u>Widsith</u> p. 78) and may possibly therefore not derive actually from Alcuin, though the name <u>Hinieldus</u> seems to
show that it is of English origin.
Because Ingeld is mentioned in the letter and in *Beowulf* (see above, note 137),
this letter has been used in nearly every history of Old English literature to
show that stories with a Germanic hero were popular in the eighth century in
monastic contexts. But the evidence is somewhat more complicated. D. A. Bullough has shown that the letter is not directed at a monastic audience, but an
episcopal one: Speratus is probably Alcuin's nickname for the Mercian bishop
Unuuona of Leicester, and therefore the letter has nothing to do with the
monks of Lindisfarne.

Tolkien's comment about the Ingeld comment not being in the received text
of the letter brings in another set of complications. In the first edition of the
letter (from 1617) by A. Duchesne, the passage regarding Ingeld is missing. But
Duchesne's source was a manuscript (Vatican City, Biblioteca Apostolica Vati-
cana, MS. Reg. Lat. 272) that does contain the Ingeld passage.

Donald A. Bullough, "What has Ingeld to do with Lindisfarne?" *Anglo-Saxon
England* 22 (1993): 93–125, particularly 93–95 and note 6.

The complete text of Chambers' note is:

"The King of Heaven must not be mentioned with pagan kings who are
lamenting in Hell. The passage is quoted by Oskar Jänicke in his <u>Zeug-
nisse und Excurse zur deutschen Heldensage</u> (Z.f.d.A. xv, 314) on the
authority of a MS of which he does not give particulars. The reference to
Ingeld does not occur in the received text (<u>Letter to Speratus</u>, ed. Froben,

1, 1, 77). It will be found however in P. Jaffé's <u>Monumenta Alcuiniana</u> (<u>Bibliotheca Rer. Germ. VI</u>), Berlin, 1873, p. 357; <u>Epistolæ</u>, 81."

Chambers, *Widsith*, 78 n. 4.

The complete citation for the quotation from Jänke is:
Oskar Jänke, "Zeugnisse und Excurse zur deutschen Heldensage," *Zeitschrift für deutsches Altertum und deutsche Literatur* 15 (1871): 310–32.

The complete Latin quotation is:

> Verba Dei legantur in sacerdotali convivio; ibi decet lectorem audiri, non citharistam, sermones patrum, non carmina gentilium. Quid Hinieldus cum Christo? Angusta est domus; utrosque tenere non poterit. Non vult rex celestic cum paganis et perditis nominetenus regibus communionem habere; quia rex ille aeternus regnat in caelis, ille paganus perditus plangit in inferno. Voces legentium audire in domibus tuis, non ridentium turbam in plateis.

Alcuin, *Epistola* 81, in *Monumenta Alcuiniana*, ed., P. Jaffé, Bibliotheca Rerum Germanicarum 6 (Berlin: Apud Weidmannos, 1873), 357.

> [Let the words of God be read at the refectory of the priests; there let the lector be heard, and not the lyre-player, the sermons of the fathers, not the songs of the heathens. What has Ingeld to do with Christ? Narrow is the house; it cannot hold both of them. The Heavenly King does not desire to have communion with pagan and forgotten kings listed by name; the Eternal King reigns in heaven, while the forgotten king laments in hell. The voices of readers should be heard in your houses, not the laughing rabble in the courtyards.]

The reference of course is to the famous question "What has Athens to do with Jerusalem?" (Tertullian, *Adv. Haer.* 7) and its derivatives; it itself echoes 2 Corinthians 6: 14–16 (cf. Jerome, *Ep.* 22.29 [PL 22. 416 A]). Cf. W. F. Bolton, *Alcuin and Beowulf* (New Brunswick, NJ: Rutgers University Press, 1978), 102 with n. 7.

Folio 48

198. **were not ousted by Moses and the warriors of the Israelites, or by St. Matthew and St. Andrew, but transmuted and recoloured the conception of these figures of Christian tradition**
These are references to the Anglo-Saxon poems *Exodus* and *Andreas*. *Exodus* retells in Old English poetic form the Old Testament story of the Israelites' flight from Egypt under the leadership of Moses. *Andreas*, which is based on a lost Latin version of the Greek *Acts of St. Matthew and St. Andrew*, relates the tale of the rescue of St. Matthew from the cannibalistic Mermedonians by St. Andrew.

Tolkien's edition and translation of *Exodus* was edited by Joan Turville-Petre: J. R. R. Tolkien, *Exodus*, ed. Joan Turville-Petre (Oxford: Clarendon Press, 1981).

See also:

Exodus.
G. P. Krapp and E. van K. Dobbie, eds. *The Junius Manuscript*, The Anglo-Saxon Poetic Records 1 (New York: Columbia University Press, 1936), 91–107.

Andreas.
Krapp and Dobbie, eds., *The Vercelli Book*, 3–51.

Folio 49

199. Wells' Time Machine

The time traveler first sees a Morlock (the dark underground dweller) on page 100 and first learns the name of the creature on 109. An explanation of the relationship between Morlocks and Eloi (the beautiful above-ground creatures) is to be found between pages 100 and 109.

Harry M. Geduld, ed., *The Definitive Time Machine: A Critical Edition of H. G. Wells's Scientific Romance with Introduction and Notes* (Bloomington, IN: Indiana University Press, 1987), 100–9.

For an extremely interesting parallel between Tolkien's unpublished thoughts and those of a later critic see Geduld, *The Definitive Time Machine*, 211–13.

200. **For in Norse at any rate the gods are enmeshed within time, they are doomed to the agony of death — even if a rebirth glimmers faintly far ahead;**

In Norse mythology (as found in *Völuspa*, "The Prophesy of the Seeress" the first poem in the *Elder Edda*, the oldest collection of Old Norse poetry) after the doom of the Gods a new earth will be born that is green and fair and in which plants are grown without the sowing of seed. Baldr will return. All evil will be passed and gone. And a new hall, called Gimlé, bright and shining, will arise.

Völuspá, 59–65.
Sigurdur Nordal, ed., *Völuspá*, trans. Ommo Wilts (Darmstadt: Wissenschaftliche Buchgesellschaft, 1980), 127–28.

201. **Euhemerism**

Euhemerism is a theory of mythology that suggests that the gods are the deification of great, but mortal, historical persons. Tolkien thought that while such a theory preserves the names of the gods, it does so at the price of robbing them of any true power or mystery. A Thor who is only the euhemerization of some ancient chieftain is hardly the figure of power and terror that a thunder-god would be for those who believed in him. In fact the names of putative northern

gods appear high up in the lists of ancestors given in the Anglo-Saxon gene-
alogies and the *Life of King Alfred*. (Cf. above, note 189.)

Folio 50

202. **They are in their very beings but the shadows of great men and warriors
cast upon the walls of the world.**
A dual allusion, both to Plato's Cave and to Lucretius *De Rerum Natura* 1.73.

203. **(Hel: Gods can go there and not come out — Baldr).**
Baldr was the most beloved of the gods. He was troubled with evil dreams that
seemed to predict his death, so the gods convinced every living and non-living
thing in the world to swear not to injure him. They then took great sport in
throwing rocks and other missiles at Baldr and watching them fail to harm him.
But Loki discovered that the mistletoe had not been asked to swear the oath
because it appeared to be too young, soft and powerless. Loki fashioned a rod
out of the mistletoe and gave it to Hod, a blind god, to throw at Baldr. The
mistletoe killed Baldr, and he went down to Hel. The gods asked Hel to release
Baldr, and she agreed, but only if all things, living or dead, would weep for him.
Thokk the giantess (who was in fact Loki in disguise) refused to weep, and so
Baldr was forced to remain with Hel.

204. **Loki is among them it is true, an evil and a lying and a clever spirit — of
whom many monsters come.**
Loki is of the offspring of giants, but he is included among the gods. He causes
them much suffering, but also aids them through his cleverness. He is either the
blood-brother or the adopted son of Odin and the father of the Wolf of Fenrir,
the Midgard Serpent, and Hel.

205. **Gods of Asgard**
The Æsir, the greater gods in Norse mythology, including Odin, Thor, Freyja,
and others. They live in Asgard, the heavenly home of the gods.

206. **Wolf of Fenrir**
Also known as the Fenris Wolf, this enormous beast is the offspring of Loki and
the giantess Angrboda. The wolf remains chained until the doom of the gods,
but then it will escape and swallow Odin. Vidarr will in turn kill the wolf by rip-
ping its jaws apart.

207. **eoten and ylfe the álfar and jötnar of Norse mythology.**
"Eoten" is the Anglo-Saxon word for "giant" or "monster" (Tolkien adapts the
word in the "Ettenmoors" or "Troll-fells" mentioned in *The Lord of the Rings*).
"Ylfe" is the Old English word for "elf." Both words have clearly had an ex-

tensive, pre-Christian tradition. Uses of "ælf" (equivalent to "ylfe") in names like Ælfred ("elf-counsel") and Ælfgifu ("elf-gift") and the compound "ælf-sciene" (used to describe Judith) appear to suggest strong positive connotations surrounding elves. But charms against "wæteralfádl" ("water-elf disease") as well as the word's context in *Beowulf*, where in line 112 elves are included — "eotenas ond ylfe ond orcnéas" — among the monstrous descendants of Cain suggest another set of connotations.

The Norse mythological tradition is clearer because we have more mentions of álfar (elves) and jötnar (giants) and thus can develop a more detailed and nuanced understanding of their mythological interactions with humans than we can from the very few mentions of these creatures in Old English texts.

Beowulf, line 112
Klaeber, ed., *Beowulf and the Fight at Finnsburg*, 5.

Folio 51
208. **Dryhten, Líffreá,**
"Dryhten" means "lord," literally the leader of a "dryht," or "troop." "Líffreá" means literally "Lord of Life."

209. **þyrs This very word in Middle English survives only precariously as a synonym of the Devil.**
The word þyrs means "giant" or "demon." Beowulf calls Grendel a þyrs in line 426:

> ond nu wið Grendel sceal,
> wið þam aglæcan   ana gehegan
> ðing wið þyrse.

[And now against Grendel, alone against the terrible monster, I must carry out a meeting with the demon.]

Beowulf, lines 424b–426a
Klaeber, ed., *Beowulf and the Fight at Finnsburg*, 16.

In the poem *Maxims II* we read that:

> Þeof sceal gangan þystrum wederum.   Þyrs sceal on fenne gewunian
> ana innan lande.

[A thief must go forth into dark weather. The monster must dwell in the fen, alone in the land.]

Elsewhere in the same poem we read:

> Draca sceal on hlæwe,
> frod, frætwum wlanc.

[A dragon must be in a barrow, wise, proud with treasure.]

Maxims II, lines 42–43a and 26b–27a
Dobbie, ed., *The Anglo-Saxon Minor Poems*, 56.

These descriptions suggest that the Anglo-Saxons had traditions of appropriate places and attributes for their monsters.

Folio 52
210. **The devils that tempt and torment St. Guthlac have nothing to distinguish them from the mediæval assailants of saints.**
For St. Guthlac, see above, note 168.

The Welsh-speaking devils are not mentioned in the *Exeter Book* poem *Guthlac*. They do appear, however, in the *Vita Sancti Guthlaci* (*Life of Saint Guthlac*) by Felix, the source for parts of the Anglo-Saxon poem. In chapter 34 of the *Life* we read:

> Contigit itaque in diebus Coenredi Merciorum regis, cum Brittones, infesti hostes Saxonici generis, bellis, praedis, publicisque vastationibus Anglo- rum gentem deturbarent, quadam nocte, gallicinali tempore, quo more solito vir beatae memoriae Guthlac orationum vigiliis incumberet, extim- plo, cum velut imaginato sopore opprimeretur, visum est sibi tumultuantis turbae audisse clamores. Tunc dicto citius levi somno expergefactus, extra cellulam, qua sedebat, egressus est, et arrectis auribus adstans, verba lo- quentis vulgi Brittannicaque agmina tectis succedere agnoscit; nam ille aliorum temporum praeteritis voluminibus inter illos exulabat, quoadus- que eorum strimulentas loquelas intelligere valuit.

> [Now it happened in the days of Coenred King of the Mercians, while the Britons, the implacable enemies of the Saxon race, were troubling the English with their attacks, their pillaging and their devastations of the people, on a certain night about the time of cockcrow, when Guthlac of blessed memory was as usual engaged in vigils and prayers, that he was suddenly overcome by a dream-filled sleep, and it seemed to him that he heard the shouts of a tumultuous crowd. Then, quicker than words, he was aroused from his light sleep and went out of the cell in which he was sitting; standing, with ears alert, he recognized the words that the crowd were saying, and realized that British hosts were approaching his dwelling: for in years gone by he had been an exile among them, so that he was able to understand their sibilant speech.]

The "British hosts" turn out to be British-speaking (i.e., Welsh-speaking) devils whom Guthlac is able to disperse by reciting the first verse of the sixty-seventh psalm.

Colgrave, *Felix's Life of St. Guthlac*, 108–11.

211. **The Sigelhearwan in Ælfric are perfectly mediæval bogeys.**

Ælfric, in various texts, including his *Homilies*, *Lives of the Saints*, and the Old English *Heptateuch* (first seven books of the Bible), consistently uses the word "sigelhearwan" to gloss the Latin term Æthiopes ("Ethiopians"). In a long article printed in two parts in *Medium Ævum* in 1932 and 1934, Tolkien argued that the sigelhearwan were Northern mythological beings, perhaps related to the giants, who possessed red-hot eyes that emitted sparks and whose faces were black as soot (Tolkien, " 'Sigelwara Land': Part 2," 110). This native, Germanic image was taken up by Ælfric (who was consistently concerned about making his writings understandable to the widest possible audience) and used to explain the unfamiliar term "Æthiopes."

J. R. R. Tolkien " 'Sigelwara Land': Part 1," *Medium Ævum* 1 (1932): 183–96.
J. R. R. Tolkien " 'Sigelwara Land': Part 2," *Medium Ævum* 3 (1934): 95–111.

For Ælfric's texts see:

Ælfric, *Ælfric's Lives of Saints*, ed. Walter W. Skeat, Early English Text Society, Original Series 76, 82, 94, 114 (London: Oxford University Press, 1881–1900; repr. 1966).

Ælfric, *Ælfric's Catholic Homilies: The First Series*, ed. Peter Clemoes, Early English Text Society, Special Series 17 (London: Oxford University Press, 1997).

Ælfric, *Ælfric's Catholic Homilies: The Second Series*, ed. Malcolm Godden, Early English Text Society, Special Series 5 (London: Oxford University Press, 1979).

Ælfric, *The Old English Version of the Heptateuch, Aelfric's Treatise on the Old and New Testament, and his Preface to Genesis*, ed. S. J. Crawford, Early English Text Society, Original Series 160 (London: Oxford University Press, 1969).

212. **(vide Wanderer and Seafarer)**

These poems are among the most famous and most studied in the Old English corpus. Both are considered "elegies" and are found in the Exeter Book. Tolkien and E.V. Gordon were working on editions of the poems in 1933, but the editions were unfinished at the time of Gordon's death in 1938. Gordon's widow completed the edition of the *Seafarer* and published it in 1960 (my thanks to Douglas A. Anderson for assistance with this material; cf. Carpenter, *J. R. R. Tolkien: A Biography*, 140, 187).

The Wanderer and *The Seafarer*.
Krapp and Dobbie, eds., *The Exeter Book*, 134–37, 143–47.

213. **such as we find in fragmentary state in Old Norse (largely preserved only in ruinous condition in a time of faulty memories during the disappearance of paganism or even long after it when such things had become only conventional properties like Jove and Mars): a warrior's heaven and a shadowy hell.**

Most Old Norse mythology is preserved in a fragmentary state in a very few manuscripts that were saved as much by luck as by the efforts of a few diligent collectors. We thus know very little about actual Icelandic or Norwegian religious practice before the conversion to Christianity. The gods of Norse mythology were no longer being actively worshipped or believed in when many of the poems and tales we possess were written down, and so they became, like Jove and Mars in the eighteenth century, more conventional figures in literature than actual gods to be worshipped or sacrificed to.

The "warrior's heaven" is Valhalla, the hall of the slain, where Odin gathers the spirits of dead warriors in preparation for the final doom of the gods when gods and men will fight against monsters.

The "shadowy hell" is the place where the dead go who do not travel to Valhalla. It is ruled by Hel, one of the offspring of the evil "god" Loki, from whom we get the Old English name for Christian hell (and see above, note 203).

Folio 53

214. Eschatology

Eschatology is the branch of theology that deals with the fate of the soul after death. We do not know, because they left no written records about such matters, what English pagans believed happened to their souls after death.

215. Snorri — almost as far from real paganism as an 18th century Jove or Mars.

For Snorri, see above, note 189.

Tolkien's point is that just as no one in eighteenth-century England believed in the actual existence of Jove or Mars but rather used them in literature for their complex symbolic values, so too Snorri used Odin and Thor in his poems.

216. men against their common enemy in Chaos and Darkness.

Compare:

> The realm of Chaos and old Night is to rise against the gods and overcome them.

Ker, *Dark Ages*, 56.

Ker's phrase is an allusion to Milton, *Paradise Lost*, I. 543: "Frighted the Reign of Chaos and old Night," where "Reign" refers to the realm of hell.

John Milton, *Paradise Lost*, in Flanagan, ed. *The Riverside Milton*, 348–710, here 371.

217. the viking period

From approximately the eighth century (beginning around 737), when raiders from Denmark and Norway had developed their superior naval technology and began to attack the coasts of Europe, until the twelfth century.

218. lof
"Lof" means literally "praise." Tolkien's interpretation represents mainstream opinion of the meaning of this term. And see below, note 221.

Folio 54

219. So was it explicitly said of men of might in the last days of Norwegian heathendom that their fate was simply ek trúi á mátt ok megin.
In the *Færeyínga Saga*, Jarl Hakon asks Sigmundr Bestisson what he believes in.

"Sigmundr svarar: ek trúi á mátt ok megin."

C. C. Rafn and G. C. F. Mohnike, *Færeyínga Saga oder Geschichte der Bewohner der Färöer im isländischen Grundtext mit Färöischer, Dänischer und Deutscher Übersetzung* (Kopenhagen: Verlage der Schubothescher Buchhandlung, 1933), 101.

"I put my trust in my own might and main," said Sigmund to Earl Hacon.

F. York Powell, trans., *The Tale of Thrond of Gate commonly called Færeyinga Saga* (London: David Nutt, 1896), 33.

220. Certainly we see them often goðlausir
"Goðlausir" or "godlausir" means "godless," i.e., not worshipping any god, pagan or otherwise.

In the Icelandic *Landnámabók*, "The Book of Settlements," Hallr and his father Helgi are called godhlauss:

Hallr godhlauss het madr; hann var son Helga godlaus þeir fedgar villdu ekki blóta, ok trudhu aa matt sinn.

Finnur Jónsson, ed., *Landnámabók I–III: Hauksbók, Sturlbók, Melabók* (København: Thieles Bogtrykkeri, 1900), 134.

There was a man called Hall the Godless, son of Helgi the Godless. Father and son believed in their own strength and refused to hold sacrifices.

Hermann Pálsson and Paul Edwards, trans., *The Book of Settlements: Landnámabók* (Winnipeg: University of Manitoba Press, 1972), 22.

221. Earle long ago pointed out the prominence of lof in Beowulf.
The complete quotation from Earle is:

In the last clause of this inner Prologue occurs a word LOF praise to which I attach a peculiar value. This word occurs again in the closing line of the Poem, but in the interval it appears only once, and then in a position which, whether mechanically or mentally considered, is central. More than any other word that can be named, that word LOF is the Motto of this

Poem. What a prince must aim at is PRAISE, that is to say, the moral approbation of his peers.

Earle, *The Deeds of Beowulf*, xvi. For Earle, see above, note 42.

222. **. . . at the end of the first 'strophe' of the exordium occurs as a** <u>leitmotif</u>: <u>lofdædum sceal</u> **in** <u>mægþa gehwam man geþeon</u>. **The last word in the poem is** <u>lofgeornost,</u>
A "strophe" is a technical term that means a separate section of a poem that is not repeated elsewhere in the poem. An "exordium" is an introduction. A "leit-motif" is a repeated musical (and by extension, poetic) theme. Thus Tolkien is arguing that the first twenty-five lines of *Beowulf* serve as a section of a designed introduction (in *"Beowulf*: The Monsters and the Critics" he says that lines 1–52 are the exordium) to the rest of the poem and that at the end of the first section of that introduction, when the poet has described the great deeds of Scyld Scefing, he gives the theme that will be repeated throughout the poem:

> Swa sceal geong guma   gode gewyrcean,
> fromum feohgiftum on   fæder bearme,
> þæt hine on ylde   eft gewunigen
> wilgesiþas,   þonne wig cume,
> leode gelæsten;   lofdædum sceal
> in mæagþa gehwam   man geþeon.

> [So must a young warrior accomplish brave deeds, by means of splendid treasure-gifts, while he is under the protection of his father, so that later, when he is old enough, comrades will dwell with him when war comes, the people will stand behind him. By praiseworthy deeds a man shall prosper anywhere.]

Thus a recurring theme throughout the poem is the value of praiseworthy deeds, from the deeds a young man must do, to those accomplished at the end of the hero's life. The last word in the poem, which describes Beowulf, is "lof-geornost" ("most eager for praise"), supporting Tolkien's claim. (Note that Tolkien emends gehwære to gehwan in 25a.)

Beowulf, lines 20–25 and line 3182b
Klaeber, ed., *Beowulf and the Fight at Finnsburg*, 2, 120.

223. **to make an Anglo-Saxon pun this is** <u>last-worda betst</u>.
A reference to *The Seafarer*, line 73b:

>   Ic gelyfe no
> þæt him eorðwelan   ece stondað.
> Simle þreora sum   þinga gehwylce,

ær his tid aga,   to tweon weorþeð;
adl oþþe yldo   oþþe ecghete
fægum fromweardum   feorh oðþringeð.
Forþon þæt bið eorla gehwam   æftercweþendra
lof lifgendra   lastworda betst,
þæt he gewyrce,   ær he on weg scyle,
fremum on foldan   wið feonda niþ,
deorum dædum   deofle togeanes,
þæt hine ælda bearn   æfter hergen,
ond his lof siþþan   lifge mid englum
awa to ealdre,   ecan lifes blæd,
dream mid dugeþum.

[I do not believe that earthly riches will stand eternally. One of three things will always become uncertain before a person's time passes: sickness or age or the violence of swords will wrest away the spirit from the one fated to die, the doomed one. Because for every man the praise of the living, speaking afterwards, is the best of last words. So that he, before he must go on his way, must accomplish great deeds on earth against the hatred of enemies, with brave deeds against the devil, so that the sons of man may afterwards praise him, and his praise afterwards will live with the angels always for life, and the splendor of his eternal life and joy endure with the heavenly troop.]

The Seafarer, lines 66b–80a
Krapp and Dobbie, *The Exeter Book*, 145.

224. **1386ff Ure æghwylc sceal ende gebidan worolde lifes. Wyrce se ðe mote domes ær deaþe; þæt bið drihtguman unlifgendum æfter selest.**
Hrothgar seems to despair after he learns that Grendel's mother has killed Æschere, Hroðgar's most favored retainer. But Beowulf, vowing to destroy Grendel's mother as he has killed her son, addresses the aged king thus:

Ne sorga, snotor guma!   Selre bið æghwæm,
þæt he his freond wrece,   þonne he fela murne.
Ure æghwylc sceal   ende gebidan
worolde lifes;   wyrce se þe mote
domes ær deaþe;   þæt bið drihtguman
unlifgendum   æfter selest.

[Do not sorrow, wise man! Better it is that each man avenge his friend than mourn overmuch. Each one of us must live in expectation of the end of this worldly life. Let him who can earn good fame before death; that is the best thing, afterwards, for the unliving man.]

Beowulf, lines 1384–1389
Klaeber, ed., *Beowulf and the Fight at Finnsburg*, 52.

225. **The poet himself as commentator recurs again to this in 1534 swa sceal man don þonne he æt guðe gegan þenceð <u>longsumne</u> lof; na ymb his lif cearað.**
During Beowulf's fight with Grendel's mother, the great sword Hrunting shatters when Beowulf swings it against the monster. Refusing to despair, Beowulf tosses aside the hilt and trusts to his bare-handed strength until he is able to find the giant sword hanging in the cavern. The poet says:

> Swa sceal man don,
> þonne he æt guðe   gegan þenceð
> longsumne lof;   na ymb his life cearað

[So must a man do, when he hopes to win long-lasting glory at battle; he will not be too concerned about his own life.]

Beowulf, lines 1534b–1536
Klaeber, ed., *Beowulf and the Fight at Finnsburg*, 58.

226. **c.f. the end of <u>Widsith</u> referring to the minstrel's part in achieving for the noble and their deeds the prolonged life of fame — He says of his noble patron: <u>lof se gewyrceð, hafað under heofonum heahfæstne dom.</u>**
> Swa scriþende   gesceapum hweorfað
> gleomen gumena   geond grund fela,
> þearfe secgað,   þoncword sprecaþ,
> simle suð oþþe norð   sumne gemetað
> gydda gleawne,   geofum unhneawne,
> se þe fore duguþe wile   dom aræran,
> eorlscipe æfnan,   oþþæt eal scæceð,
> leoht ond lif somod;   lof se gewyreð,
> hafað under heofonum   heahfæstne dom.

[So the minstrels of the people, fated to wander, fare through many lands. They tell about their need, speak words of thanks. Always, south or north, they will meet someone wise about songs and generous with gifts who wishes to increase his fame before the troop, to sustain his earlship, until all passes away, light and life together. He earns praise who has under heaven enduring fame.]

Widsith, lines 135–143
Krapp and Dobbie, eds, *The Exeter Book*, 153.

Folio 55

227. <u>Seafarer</u> 66 <u>ic gelyfe no</u> carefully with Hroðgar's sermon or gidd — noting
especially the close resemblances between <u>Beowulf</u> 1735 ff and especially
1761–8 (which I believe original and not "revised") and <u>Seafarer</u> 66–71. After
teaching that man will die, the <u>Seafarer</u>-poet says: "Therefore this is for all
noble men the best "<u>last word</u>" (i.e. memorial in tale and song) and praise of
the living that commemorate him in words, that ere he is obliged to depart, he
merit and achieve on earth by heroic deeds against the maker of enemies
(<u>feonda</u>) opposing the Devil (<u>deofle</u>) so that the children of men may praise
him afterwards and his "lof thereafter may live with the angels for ever and
ever, the splendour of eternal life, rejoicing (<u>dream</u>) among the hosts (<u>du-
geþum</u>)."

For *Seafarer*, see above, note 212. For the passage in question see above, note 223.
Hrothgar's "sermon":

> "Wundor is to secganne,
> hu mihtig God   manna cynne
> þurh sidne sefan   snyttru bryttað,
> eard ond eorlscipe;   he ah ealra geweald.
> Hwilum he on lufan   læteð hworfan
> monnes modgeþonc   mæran cynnes,
> seleð him on eþle   eorþan wynne
> to healdanne   hleoburh wera,
> gedeð him swa gewealdene   worolde dælas,
> side rice,   þæt he his selfa ne mæg
> his unsnyttrum   ende geþencean.
> Wunaþ he on wiste;   no hine wiht dweleð
> adl ne yldo,   ne him inwitsorh
> on sefan sweorceð,   ne gesacu ohwær
> ecghete eoweð,   ac him eal worold
> wendeð on willan   (he þæt wyrse ne con),
> oðþæt him on innan   oferhygda dæl
> weaxeð ond wridað.   Þonne se weard swefeð,
> sawele hyrde;   bið se slæp to fæst,
> bisgum gebunden,   bona swiðe neah,
> se þe of flanbogan   fyrenum sceoteð.
> Þonne bið on hreþre   under helm drepen
> biteran stræle   (him bebeorgan ne con),
> wom wundorbebodum   wergan gastes;
> þinceð him to lytel   þæt he lange heold,
> gytsað gromhydig,   nallas on gylp seleð
> fædde beagas,   ond he þa forðgesceaft
> forgyteð ond forgymeð,   þæs þe him ær god sealde,

wuldres waldend,   weorðmynda dæl.
Hit on endestæf   eft gelimpeð
þæt se lichoma   læne gedreoseð,
fæge gefealleð;   fehð oþer to,
se þe unmurnlice   madmas dæleþ,
eorles ærgestreon,   egesan ne gymeð.
Bebeorh þe ðone bealonið,   Beowulf leofa,
secg betsta,   ond þe þæt selre geceos,
ece rædas."

["It is a wonder to tell, how mighty God in his generous-in-spirit wisdom distributed wisdom, land and earlship through mankind. He possesses power over all. Sometimes he in his love allows the mind of a man, from famous kin, to turn, gives to him joy in the homeland of the earth, a stronghold of men. He also makes dependent upon him portions of the world, a wide kingdom, so that the man himself in his unwisdom cannot anticipate its end. He remains in happiness. Nor in any way do sickness or old age mislead him, nor does sorrow darken his spirit, nor strife anywhere bring about hostility, but to him the whole world turns according to his will. He does not know a worse part of himself, until a portion of arrogance grows within him, while the guardian of the soul sleeps. Too deep is that sleep, bound up with cares. The slayer, who shoots from his bow with fiery darts, is near. It is then that, because he is unable to guard himself, he is struck beneath his helm with the bitter, sharp arrow by the twisted and strange commands of the spirit of evil. It seems to him that all he has long held is too little; he, angry-minded, covets. He gives out no ornamented rings, and he forgets and neglects the future because God, the Ruler of the world, has already given him a portion of honor. In the end it happens that the loaned and fated-to-die body declines and falls. Another succeeds him, one who willingly deals out portions of treasure, the ancient treasure of earls. He turns away from terror. Protect yourself, then, from pernicious enmity, my dear Beowulf, best of men, and choose for yourself the better part, everlasting wisdom."]

Beowulf, lines 1724–1760a
Klaeber, ed., *Beowulf and the Fight at Finnsburg*, 64–66.

228. **perhaps prolonged vaguely awa to ealdre in song.**
            Þu þe self hafast
dædum gefremed,   þæt þin [dom] lyfað
awa to aldre.

[You yourself have accomplished deeds such that your glory will live always for life.]

Beowulf, lines 953b–955a
Klaeber, ed., *Beowulf and the Fight at Finnsburg*, 36.

Folio 56

229. **186 ff. Wel bið þæm þe mot æfter deaðdæge Drihten secean, 7 to Fæder fæ-**
þmum freoðo wilnian.
[It shall be well for him who on his death day is able to seek the Lord, and to
seek safety in the embrace of the Father.]

Beowulf, lines 186–188
Klaeber, ed., *Beowulf and the Fight at Finnsburg*, 8.

230. **"helle gemundon" — they know about hell and this is a fact. Beowulf**
prophesies it for Unferð 588.

Swylce wæs þeaw hyra,
Hæþenra hyht;   helle gemundon
in modsefan

[Likewise the hope of the heathens had become their custom. They remembered hell in their hearts.]

Beowulf, lines 178b–180a
Klaeber, ed., *Beowulf and the Fight at Finnsburg*, 7.

þæs þu in helle scealt
werhðo dreogan,   þeah þin wit duge.

[For that you must endure punishment in hell even though your wit be
strong.]

Beowulf, lines 588b–599
Klaeber, ed., *Beowulf and the Fight at Finnsburg*, 23.

The *Beowulf* manuscript is defective at 588b; the word given above as "helle" has
disappeared due to damage to the manuscript. Both Thorkelin transcripts, A
and B, record "helle," and this reading was adopted by Klaeber and used by
Tolkien in his argument. It is possible, however, that the correct reading for
588b would be "healle" (hall), suggesting not that Unferth would suffer in the
afterlife, but that he endured his punishment (for slaying his kin) in the com-
munal hall. See, Fred C. Robinson, "Elements of the Marvellous in the Characterization of *Beowulf*: A Reconsideration of the Textual Evidence," in Robert
B. Burlin and Edward B. Irving, Jr., eds., *Old English Studies in Honour of John C.*
Pope (Toronto: University of Toronto Press), 119–37.

231. **The reward which he foretells to Beowulf (955) is that his dom shall live**
awa to ealdre, a fortune also in Norse bestowed on Sigurd (that his name æ
mun uppi).

> Þu þe self hafast
> dædum gefremed,   þæt þin [dom] lyfað
> awa to aldre.

[You yourself have accomplished deeds such that your glory will live always for life.]

Beowulf, lines 953b–955a

Klaeber, ed., *Beowulf and the Fight at Finnsburg*, 36.

I believe Tolkien is quoting the Old Norse from memory here. Of Sigurd it is said in *Völsunga Saga*:

"Ok hans nafn mun uppi, meþan veröldin stendr" (chapter 12)

and

"Heill, herra min! mikinn sigr hefir þú unnit, er þú hefir drepit Fafni, er engi varþ fyrr svá djarfr, at á hans getu þorþi sitja, ok þetta fremþarverk mun uppi, meþan veröldin stendr." (Chapter 19).

Wilhelm Ranisch, ed., *Die Völsungasaga* (Berlin: Mayer and Müller, 1891), 20, 31.

"And his [Sigurd's] name will endure while the world remains." (chapter 12).

"Hail, my lord. You have won a great victory, as you have killed Fafnir. None before were so bold as to dare to sit in his path. And this glorious feat will live on while the world remains" (chapter 19).

Jesse L. Byock, ed. and trans., *The Saga of the Volsungs: The Norse Epic of Sigurd the Dragon Slayer* (Berkeley, CA: University of California Press, 1990), 53, 65.

The phrase "æ mun uppi" is found in *Hálfs Saga ok Hálfsrekka*, stanza 31:

> Hrindum heilir
> hallar bjóri!
> nú taka súlur
> í sundr þoka;
> æ mun uppi,
> meðan öld lífr,
> Hálfsrekka för
> til hertoga.

A. Le Roy Andrews, *Hálfs Saga ok Hálfsrekka* (Halle: Verlag von Max Niemeyer, 1909), 108.

> Hack we down
> Hall's whole wall

Rip asunder
Stave and post.
E'er will be told,
While men still live,
This king visit
by Half's champions.

W. Bryant Bachman, Jr. and Gudmundur Erlingsson, eds., *The Sagas of King Half and King Hrolf* (New York: University Press of America, 1981), 21.

In "*Beowulf:* The Monsters and the Critics," Tolkien changes the quotation from "æ mun uppi" to the quotation from chapter 12 of the *Völsunga Saga*: "hans nafn mun uppi, meþan veröldin stendr."
Tolkien, "*Beowulf*: The Monsters and the Critics," 16.

232. **Thus the author tells us that Beowulf's soul gewat . . . secean soðfæstra dom**
Him of hræðre gewat
sawol secean   soðfastra dom.

[His soul departed from him to seek the judgment of those fast in truth.]

Beowulf, lines 2819b–2820
Klaeber, ed., *Beowulf and the Fight at Finnsburg*, 106.

233. **heofon in the singular or plural, and synonyms such as rodor, are of course frequent, but refer either to the particular landscape, or to the sky under which men dwell in general. These words are of course used with names of God — Lord of the Heavens and so on — but are parallels rather to God's general governance of nature (e.g. 1609 ff), and His realm which includes land and sea, even if heofon is his especial seat and the sun His candle.**
ðonne forstes bend   Fæder onlæteð,
onwindeð wælrapas,   se geweald hafað,
sæla ond mæla;   þæt is soð Metod.

[when the Father releases the bonds of frost, unwinds the bindings on the waters, he has the power over times and season. That is the true Measurer.]

Beowulf, lines 1609–1611
Klaeber, ed., *Beowulf and the Fight at Finnsburg*, 60.

234. **C.f. the celebrated reference to the death of Holofernes which so remarkably recalls certain features of Völuspá. Judith 115 wyrmum bewunden, 119 of ðam wyrmsele — Völuspá 38 sá er undinn salr orma hryggjum**
Læg se fula leap
gesne beæftan,   gæst ellor hwearf

under neowelne næs   on ðær genyðerad wæs,
susle gesæled   syððan æfre,
wyrmum bewunden,   witum gebunden,
hearde gehæfted   in hellebryne
æfter hinsiðe.   Ne ðearf he hopian no,
þystrum forðylmed,   þæt he ðonan mote
of ðam wyrmsele,   ac ðær wunian sceal
awa to aldre   butan ende forð
in ðam heolstran ham,   hyhtwynna leas.

[The body of the man lay behind, dead; the spirit turned away elsewhere, deep under ground, and he afterwards was ever given into torment, wound round with snakes, bound with tortures, imprisoned hard in hell-fires after journeying there. He had no need to hope, surrounded by darkness, that he might be able to go from that snake-hall, but must dwell there always for life, without any end, in that dark secret place, deprived of the joys of hope.]

Judith, lines 111b–121
Dobbie, ed., *Beowulf and Judith*, 102.

Völuspá, 38 lines 7–8
Nordal, ed., *Völuspá*, 122.

"Its [the hall's] walls are clad with coiling snakes"

Hollander, ed., *The Poetic Edda*, 8.

235. Holofernes

Holofernes is the evil chieftain of the Assyrians who, after drinking himself almost into unconsciousness, orders that the captured Bethulian maiden Judith be brought to his tent for his lustful purposes. Judith slays him after he passes out from inebriation, and she and her handmaiden carry his head back to the Bethulians and display it to inspire them to fight against the Assyrians.

236. Völuspá

See above, note 172.

Folio 57

237. Yet <u>Beowulf</u> himself though troubled by dark doubts at first (2729), and later declaring his conscience clear, thinks at the end only of his barrow and memorial among men, and of his childlessness, and of Wiglaf the sole survivor of his kin to whom he bequeaths his helm and gear. His funeral is quite unchristian, and his memorial is the virtue of his kingship and the hopeless sorrow of his people.

After the dragon has burned the gift-hall of the Geats, Beowulf wonders why he and his people have been afflicted by the beast:

> Þæt ðam godan wæs
> hreow on hreðre,   hygesorga mæst;
> wende se wisa,   þæt he Wealdende
> ofer ealde riht   ecean Dryhtne
> bitre gebulge;   breost innan weoll
> þeostrum geþoncum,   swa him geþywe ne wæs.

[To that brave man it was quickly the greatest of high sorrows. The wise one wondered if he had bitterly enraged the Ruler, the eternal Lord, due to an offense against ancient law. In his breast welled dark thoughts that were not customary for him.]

After Beowulf has received his death-wound from the dragon, he says to Wiglaf:

> "Nu ic suna minum   syllan wolde
> guðgewædu,   þær me gifeðe swa
> ænig yrfeweard   æfter wurde
> lice gelenge.   Ic ðas leode heold
> fiftig wintra;   næs se folccyning,
> ymbesittendra   ænig ðara,
> þe mec guðwinum   gretan dorste,
> egesan ðeon.   Ic on earde bad
> mælgesceafta,   heold min tela,
> ne sohte searoniðas,   ne me swor fela
> aða on unriht.   Ic ðæs ealles mæg
> feorhbennum seoc   gefean habban;
> forðam me witan ne ðearf   Waldend fira
> morðorbealo maga,   þonne mid sceaceð
> lif of lice."

["Now I would have wished to give my battle-dress to my son, if it had been granted that any inheritor, related by body, had come after me. I have led this people for fifty winters. No folk-king of the surrounding nations has dared to challenge me to battle or oppressed me with swords. I have abided the conditions of destiny, held my own well, and not sought out conniving enmity, nor have I sworn many false oaths. Though I am sickened with mortal wounds I may take comfort in this: that the Ruler of men cannot charge me with the murder of kin when my life leaves my body."]

Later, after Beowulf has seen the great treasure taken from the dragon's barrow, he says:

"Hataŏ heaŏomære   hlæw gewyrcean
beorhtne æfter bæle   æt brimes nosan;
se scel to gemyndum   minum leodum
heah hlifian   on Hronesnæsse,
þæt hit sæliŏend   syŏŏan hatan
Biowulfes biorh,   ŏa ŏe brentingas
ofer floda genipu   feorran drifaŏ."
Dyde him of healse   hring gyldenne
þioden þristhydig,   þegne gesealde,
geongum garwigan,   goldfahne helm,
beah ond byrnan,   het hyne brucan well —
"Þu eart endelaf   usses cynnes,
Wægmundinga;   ealle wyrd forsweop
mine magas   to metodsceafte,
eorlas on elne;   ic him æfter sceal."

["Command the battle-renowned ones to create a mound, bright after the fire, on a headland by the ocean. It must tower high on Hronesness as a memorial to my people so that seafarers afterwards will call it the barrow of Beowulf, when they guide their ships to fare over the dark flood." He then, the bold-minded king, took from his neck the golden ring, and gave to the thane, the young spear-warrior, the gold-decorated helm, the ring and the byrnie. He commanded him to use them well: "You are the last survivor of our kin, the Waegmundings. Fate swept away all my kin to their destiny, the earls in valor. I must follow them."]

Beowulf, lines 2327b–2332, 2729–2743a, and 2802–2816
Klaeber, ed., *Beowulf and the Fight at Finnsburg*, 88, 102–3, 105–6.

238. **Though there are special problems such as Hroŏgar's gidd (especially 1724–1760) and particularly lines 175–188,**
For Hrothgar's "sermon" or "gidd," see above, note 222.

Hwilum hie geheton   æt hærgtrafum
wigweorþunga,   wordum bædon,
þæt him gastbona   geoce gefremede
wiŏ þeodþreaum.   Swylce wæs þeaw hyra,
hæþenra hyht;   helle gemundon
in modsefan,   Metod hie ne cuþon,
dæda Demend,   ne wiston hie Drihten God,
ne hie huru heofena Helm   herian ne cuþon,
wuldres Waldend.   Wa biŏ þæm ŏe sceal
þurh sliŏne niŏ   sawle bescufan
in fyres fæþm,   frofre ne wenan,

wihte gewendan!   Wel bið þæm þe mot
æfter deaðdæge   Drihten secean
ond to Fæder fæþmum   freoðo wilnian!

[At times they offered — at the heathen temple — sacrifice to heathen
idols, bade with words that the spirit-slayer might give them help against
the nation's calamity. Likewise the hope of the heathens had become their
custom. They remembered hell in their hearts; they did not know God,
the Judge of deeds, nor did they wish to know to praise the Lord God, the
protector of the heavens, the Ruler of glory. Woe will it be to them who
must, due to terrible persecution, thrust their souls into the bosom of the
fire, not at all to hope for relief or for any change at all. Well will it be for
one who is permitted to seek the Lord and to seek after peace in the bosom of the Father.]

Beowulf, lines 175–188
Klaeber, ed., *Beowulf and the Fight at Finnsburg*, 7–8.

Folio 58

239. **The sort of thing that is achieved by the latter process is illustrated by the
drihten wereda for drihten Wedera in 2186. Though this is clearly ultimately
due to some gentleman more familiar with the biblical "Lord of Hosts" than
with Hreðel Lord of Wederas**
The manuscript at this point reads "drihten Wereda" "the Lord of Hosts," but
the context clearly indicates that the poet is referring to the "Lord of the Weders" ("Lord of the Geats"). Scholars are in agreement that the text here must be
emended to eliminate the apparent scribal error.

            Hean wæs lange,
swa hyne Geata bearn   goden ne tealdon,
ne hyne on medobence   micles wyrðne
drihten Wedera   gedon wolde.

Beowulf, lines 2183b–2186
Klaeber, ed., *Beowulf and the Fight at Finnsburg*, 82.

240. **He says that Dryhten will decide the issue of his combat with Grendel, and
follows immediately with gæð a wyrd swa hio scel (441 ff)**
            ðær gelyfan sceal
dryhtnes dome   se þe hine deað nimeð.
Wen ic þæt he wille,   gif he wealdan mot,
in þæm guðsele   Geotena leode
etan unforhte,   swa he oft dyde,
mægen Hreðmanna.   Na þu minne þearft

hafalan hydan,   ac he me habban wile
dreore fahne,   gif mec deað nimeð;
byreð blodig wæl,   byrgean þenceð,
eteð angenga   unmurnlice,
mearcað morhopu;   no ðu ymb mines ne þearft
lices feorme   leng sorgian.
Onsend Higelace,   gif mec hild nime,
beaduscruda betst,   þæt mine breost wereð,
hrægla selest;   þæt is Hrædlan laf,
Welandes geweorc.   Gæð a wyrd swa hio scel.

[He whom death carries off must acknowledge the judgment of the Lord. I believe that [Grendel] will, if he is permitted to win, fearlessly eat the people of the Geatas, the kin of Hreðel, in this battle-hall, as he often did. You will not have any need to bury my body, but he will have me stained with gore if death takes me. He will bear away the bloody slaughter, thinking to gulp it down. Without sadness the alone-goer will eat, staining his marshy lair. You will have no need to long sorrow over what to do with my body. Send to Hygelac, if battle takes me, the best of battle-corselets that I wear on my breast. It is the heirloom of Hrethel and the work of Weland. Fate always goes as it may.]

Beowulf, lines 440b–455
Klaeber, ed., *Beowulf and the Fight at Finnsburg*, 17–18.

241. (2) In 570 ff. in describing his escape from the sea he calls the sun leoht eastan ... beorht beacen Godes, but ascribes his conquest of the nicors to luck, saying
See above, note 119.

Folio 59

242. hwæþere me gesealde 574 (words which are precisely repeated of Sigemund later, to whom Beowulf is compared, 890). Grendel's success he ascribed simply to Danish feebleness 591.

Hwæþere me gesælde,   þæt ic mid sweorde ofsloh
niceras nigene.

[So to me it was given that I with my sword slew nine nicors.]

Beowulf, lines 574–575a
Klaeber, ed., *Beowulf and the Fight at Finnsburg*, 22.

Hwæþre him gesælde,   ðæt þæt swurd þurhwod
wrætlicne wyrm,   þæt hit on wealle ætstod,
dryhtlic iren;   draca morðre swealt.

[So it was given to him that that sword passed through the splendid drag-on, so that it stood in the wall, the lordly iron; the dragon died from the injury.]

Beowulf, lines 890–892

Klaeber, ed., *Beowulf and the Fight at Finnsburg*, 34.

For 591, see above, note 119.

243. **it is said by the poet that Beowulf on the eve of his combat (669) trusted in <u>Metodes hyldo</u>, but this was manifested in his possession of <u>modgan mægnes</u> — <u>georne truwode modgan mægnes, Metodes hyldo</u>. It would be quite wrong to put an "and" in here.**

Huru Geata leod   georne truwode
modgan mægnes,   Metodes hyldo.

[Indeed the leader of the Geatas eagerly trusted in his own mighty strength, the protection of the Measurer.]

Beowulf, lines 669–670

Klaeber, ed., *Beowulf and the Fight at Finnsburg*, 25–26.

Translators are wont to place an "and" between "mægnes" and "metodes hyldo." Bradley, for example, translates the passage as: "And certainly the Geatish leader readily trusted in his own intrepid strength and the protection of the ordaining Lord" (*Anglo-Saxon Poetry*, 429); Kennedy: "The Geatish hero put all his hope / In his fearless might and the mercy of God!" ("Beowulf," 44); Crossley-Holland: "Truly, the leader of the Geats fervently trusted / in his own great strength and in God's grace" (*The Anglo-Saxon World*, 90); Raffel: "And Beowulf was ready, firm with our Lord's / High favor and his own bold courage and strength" (*Beowulf*, 44). Even Edward B. Irving inserts an "and" in his an-alysis of the passage: ". . . Beowulf is not mentioned as placing trust in anything other than his own strength and God's favor" (*A Reading of Beowulf*, 134 n. 6).

Tolkien's point, borne out by the syntax of the passage, is that the "Metodes hyldo" (the favor of the Measurer) is set in apposition to "modgan mægnes" (mighty strength); that is, the mighty strength that God has given to Beowulf is (and has been already) the favor of God; Beowulf, in this passage, at least, is trusting in his already granted strength and not in some additional favor.

S. A. J. Bradley, trans., *Anglo-Saxon Poetry* (London: Dent, 1982).

Charles W. Kennedy, trans., "Beowulf" in *Medieval English Literature*, ed. J. B. Trapp (London: Oxford University Press, 1973).

Kevin Crossley-Holland, ed., *The Anglo-Saxon World* (New York: Oxford Univer-sity Press, 1982).

Burton Raffel, trans., *Beowulf* (New York: New American Library, 1963).

Edward B. Irving, Jr., *A Reading of Beowulf*, rev. ed. (Provo, UT: The Chaucer Studio, 1999).

244. **Beowulf says that <u>witig God</u> .. <u>halig Dryhten</u> (685ff) can decide the combat as He wishes.**

> ond siþðan witig God
> on swa hwæþere hond   halig Dryhten
> mærðo deme,   swa him gemet þince.

[and afterwards wise God, holy Lord, may decide the glory on whichever side as it seems right to him.]

Beowulf, lines 685b–687
Klaeber, ed., *Beowulf and the Fight at Finnsburg*, 26.

245. **967: Beowulf says that Metod did not will that he should kill Grendel outright.**

> Ic hine ne mihte,   þa Metod nolde,
> ganges getwæman,   no ic him þæs georne ætfealh,
> feorhgeniðlan.

[the measurer did not wish that I might stop him from going, I did not cling to him strongly enough, the spirit-foe.]

Beowulf, lines 967–969a
Klaeber, ed., *Beowulf and the Fight at Finnsburg*, 25–26.

246. **(6) 977: Beowulf says that Grendel shall abide <u>miclan domes</u> and what <u>scir metod</u> shall doom for him.**

> ðær abidan sceal
> maga mane fah   miclan domes,
> hu him scir Metod   scrifan wille.

[there he must abide, the young one stained with crime, whatever great judgment the glorious Measurer wishes to impose upon him.]

Beowulf, lines 977b–979
Klaeber, ed., *Beowulf and the Fight at Finnsburg*, 37.

247. **(7) 1272-3 The poet says that Beowulf gemunde <u>mægenes strenge</u>, <u>gimfæste gife</u>, <u>ðe him God sealde</u> ond him to <u>Anwaldan are gelyfde frofre ond fultum</u>.**

> Hwæþre he gemunde   mægenes strenge,
> gimfæste gife,   ðe him God sealde,
> ond him to Anwaldan   are gelyfde,
> frofre ond fultum.

[yet he remembered the strength of might, the wonderful gift, which God gave to him, and he entrusted himself to the One-Ruler, to his relief and support.]

Beowulf, lines 1270–1273
Klaeber, ed., *Beowulf and the Fight at Finnsburg*, 48.

248. **We note in his comforting of Hroðgar he says <u>domes ær deaþe</u> (fame before death) is the best thing for a dead man**
See above, note 224.

249. **and in his speech before he plunges into the accursed waters he makes <u>no reference to God</u>. His last 'will' is that Hroðgar should secure his <u>dom</u> by sending his "gifts" to Hygelac.**
See above, note 240.

250. **(8) Beowulf (1658–1665) acknowledges God's protection <u>nymðe mec God scylde</u>; and says that by his favour (<u>me geuðe ylda Waldend</u>) he saw the giant sword which enabled him to win the battle under the water. He adds <u>oftost wisode winigea leasum.</u>**

    ætrihte wæs
guð getwæfed, nymðe mec God scylde.
Ne meahte ic æt hilde mid Hruntinge
wiht gewyrcan, þeah þæt wæpen duge;
ac me geuðe ylda Waldend,
þæt ic on wage geseah wlitig hangian
ealdsweord eacen — oftost wisode
winigea leasum —, þæt ic ðy wæpne gebræd.
Ofsloh ða æt þære sæcce, þa me sæl ageald,
huses hyrdas.

[Immediately the battle would have been ended if God had not shielded me. Nor might I have been able to accomplish anything in the fight with Hrunting, though the weapon itself was strong; but to me was granted, by the Ruler of men — often He has guided the friendless — that I should see hanging on the wall a beautiful, mighty old sword. I drew that weapon. Then I slew at battle, when it was the time permitted to me, the keeper of that hall.]

Beowulf, lines 1657b–1666a
Klaeber, ed., *Beowulf and the Fight at Finnsburg*, 62.

Folio 60
251. **(9) In his recapitulation of events to Hygelac (2000–2151) he makes no**

reference to God at all. **Næs ic fæge þa gyt** (2141) is his explanation of his escape from the water.

Næs ic fæge þa gyt

[I was not yet then fated.]

Beowulf, line 2141
Klaeber, ed., *Beowulf and the Fight at Finnsburg*, 80.

252. (10) (2329 f) Beowulf in his old age — now **frod** cyning — is said by the poet to wonder if he had offended God (who was consequently punishing him with the dragon) : **wende se wisa þæt he Wealdende ofter ealde riht ecean Dryhtne bitre gebulge.**
See above, note 237.

253. (11) 2469. Beowulf says of the heartbroken death of Hreðel: **gumdream ofgeaf, Godes leoht geceas.**

He ða mid þære sorhge,   þe him to sar belamp,
gumdream ofgeaf,   Godes leoht geceas.

[He then, on account of that sorrow which had sorely afflicted him, gave up the joy of men and chose the light of God.]

Beowulf, lines 2468–2469
Klaeber, ed., *Beowulf and the Fight at Finnsburg*, 93.

254. (12) 2526f. Beowulf definitely equates **wyrd** and **metod**: ac unc sceal weorðan æt wealle, **swa unc wyrd geteoð Metod manna gehwæs.**

          Nelle ic beorges weard
oferfleon fotes trem   ac unc [furður] sceal
weorðan at wealle,   swa unc wyrd geteoð,
Metod manna gehwæs.

[I do not intend to fall back even a foot-length from the guardian of the barrow, but we two against the wall will fare as our fate, the Measurer of each man, determines.]

Tolkien does not here accept Klaeber's addition of "furður" in line 2525.

Beowulf, lines 2524b–2527a
Klaeber, ed., *Beowulf and the Fight at Finnsburg*, 95.

255. **Compare his words again 2814f eall wyrd forsweop mine magas to metodsceafte.**

Þu eart endelaf   usses cynnes,
Wægmundinga;   ealle wyrd forsweop

mine magas   to metodsceafte,
eorlas on elne;   ic him æfter sceal.

[You are the last survivor of our kin, the Waegmundings. Fate swept away
all my kin to their destiny, the earls in valor. I must follow them.]

Beowulf, lines 2813–2816
Klaeber, ed., *Beowulf and the Fight at Finnsburg*, 106.

256. **And contrast the words of the poet 1056 <u>nefne him witig God wyrd forstode,</u>
<u>7 þæs mannes mod,</u>**
                  ond þonne ænne heht
     golde forgyldan,   þone ðe Grendel ær
     mane acwealde, —   swa he hyra ma wolde,
     nefne him witig God   wyrd forstode
     ond ðæs mannes mod.

[and then he [Hygelac] commanded the gold be given for the one whom
Grendel had previously killed in crime — so he would have killed more
except that wise God and the courage of that man [Beowulf] staved off
fate.]

Beowulf, lines 1053b–1057a
Klaeber, ed., *Beowulf and the Fight at Finnsburg*, 40.

257. **Compare Old Norse mjötuðr, dispenser (of fate), ruler — also doom, fate,
death.**
According to the Cleasby-Vigfusson Old Icelandic-English Dictionary, mjötuðr
means "measurer, helper" or even, metaphorically "bane"; "the word itself is of
heathen origin."

Richard Cleasby and Guðbrand Vigfusson, *An Icelandic-English Dictionary*, 2nd
    ed., with supplement by William A. Craigie (Oxford: Clarendon Press, 1957).

258. **Old Saxon metod is singly "ambiguous" and like Old English Gabriel in the
<u>Heliand</u> says of John the Baptist that he will not touch wine — <u>so habed</u> im
<u>uurd giscapu metod gemarcod endi maht godes</u> (128);**
     So habed im   uurdgiscapu
     metod gimarcod   endi maht godes.

Eduard Sievers, ed. *Heliand* (Halle: Verlag der Buchhandlung des Waisen-
    hauses, 1878), 11–12.

"this is the way the works of fate made him, time formed him, and the
power of God as well."

G. Ronald Murphy, S.J., ed., *The Heliand: The Saxon Gospel* (New York: Oxford University Press, 1992), 7.

259. **again it is said of Anna the widow when her husband died that sie thiu mikila maht <u>metodes</u> tedelda, uured <u>uurdigiscapu</u> (511). In both "fate" is nearer than God. In Old Saxon metod(o)<u>giscapu</u> and <u>metodigisceaft</u> equals fate as Old English meotodsceaft.**

that sie thiu mikila maht   metodes tedelda
uured uurdigiscapu.

Sievers, ed. *Heliand*, 38–39.

"that the mighty power of the Measurer separated them, the cruel workings of fate."

Murphy, ed., *The Heliand: The Saxon Gospel*, 20.

Folio 61

260. **Beowulf in his penultimate speech (2729ff)**
See above, note 237.

261. **The list of crimes (avoided) is similar to those which in Völuspá doom men to wade in the heavy streams (þunga stramma) of Hell: there are <u>menn meinsvara, ok morðvarga, ok þanns annass glepr eyrarúnu. Namely perjurers, murderers, and adulterers.</u>**

For Völuspá, see above, note 172. Náströnduá is the "strand of the dead," the place where Hel's hall stands.

The relevant section of the poem is:

Sá hon þar vaða
þunga strauma
menn meinsvara
ok morðvarga
ok þanns annars glepr
eyrarúnu;
þar s'ygr Niðhöggr
nái framgengna,
slítr vargr vera.
Vituð ér enn — eða hvat?

Völuspá 39.
Nordal, ed., *Völuspá*, 122–23.

Waist-deep wade there   through waters swift
mainsworn men   and murderous,

eke those who betrayed   a trusted friend's wife;
there gnaws Níthhogg   naked corpses,
there the Wolf rends men —   wit ye more, or how?

Hollander, ed., *The Poetic Edda*, 7.

262. **In his last speech Beowulf says thanks to Frean Wuldorcyninge ... ecum Dryhtne for all that his eyes now see of treasure, and because in dying he has won treasure for his people. But his last thoughts are for his barrow, and his kindred — ealle wyrd forsweop mine magas to metodsceafte.**

"Ic ðara frætwa   Frean ealles ðanc,
Wuldurcyninge   wordum secge,
ecum Dryhtne,   þe ic her on starie,
þæs ðe ic moste   minum leodum
ær swyltdæge   swylc gestrynan.
Nu ic on maðma hord   mine bebohte
frode feorhlege,   fremmað gena
leoda þearfe;   ne mæg ic her leng wesan.
Hatað heaðomære   hlæw gewyrcean
beorhtne æfter bæle   æt brimes nosan;
se scel to gemyndum   minum leodum
heah hlifian   on Hronesnæsse,
þæt hit sæliðend   syððan hatan
Biowulfes biorh,   ða ðe brentingas
ofer floda genipu   feorran drifað."
Dyde him of healse   hring gyldenne
þioden þristhydig,   þegne gesealde,
geongum garwigan,   goldfahne helm,
beah ond byrnan,   he hyne brucan well —
"Þu eart endelaf   usses cynnes,
Wægmundinga;   ealle wyrd forsweop
mine magas   to metodsceafte,
eorlas on elne;   ic him æfter sceal."

["With these words I thank the Lord, the King of the world, the eternal God, for all of these treasures, which I look upon, because I have been permitted, before my death day, to acquire them for my people. Now I have given my allotted life for the treasure hoard, fulfilled the needs of the people. I may not remain here any longer. Command the battle-renowned ones to create a mound, bright after the fire, on a headland by the ocean. It must tower high on Hronesness as a memorial to my people so that sea-farers afterwards will call it the barrow of Beowulf, when they guide their ships to fare over the dark flood." He then, the bold-minded king, took from his neck the golden ring, and gave to the thane, the young spear-warrior, the gold-decorated helm, the ring and the byrnie. He commanded him to use them well: "You are the last survivor of our kin, the Waegmundings. Fate swept away all my kin to their destiny, the earls in valor. I must follow them."]

Beowulf, lines 2794–2816
Klaeber, ed., *Beowulf and the Fight at Finnsburg*, 105–6.

263. **so 441ff, 685ff, 967**
For 441ff see above, note 240; for 685ff, note 244; for 967, note 245.

264. **as where gæð a wyrd swa hio scel immediately follows his assertion (441) that Dryhten holds the balance in his combat;**
See above, note 235.

265. **(2526f — with which compare 2814f. where wyrd is more active and metodsceaft equals doom, death).**
For 2526f see above, note 254; for 2814f see note 250.

266. **the poets' comment on the man who escapes the dragon 2291f Swa mæg unfæge eaðe gedigan wean 7 wræcsið se ðe Waldendes hyldo gehealdeþ**

Swa mæg unfæge   eaðe gedigan
wean ond wræcsið   se ðe Waldendes
hyldo gehealdeð.

[So may an unfated one easily endure woe and the exile-path, he who holds the favor of the Ruler.]

Beowulf, lines 2291–2293a
Klaeber, ed., *Beowulf and the Fight at Finnsburg*, 86.

Folio 62

267. **Beowulf twice explicitly thanks God or acknowledges His help: (1) 1658–1661 he acknowledges God's protection and the favour of ylda Waldend — oftost wisode winigea leasum — in his combat under water.**
See above, note 255.

268. **in his last speech of all he thanks Frean Wuldorcyning ... ecum Dryhtne for all the treasure his eyes can see and for helping him to win it for his people. But his last thoughts are for his memorial on earth, and his family, and successor.**
See above, note 262.

269. He ascribes his conquest of the nicors (570ff) to luck — 'hwæþere me gesælde' (cf. Sigemund episode 890).
See above, note 119.

270. In his account to Hygelac his only explanation of preservation from the water-den is Næs ic fæge þa gyt 2141 : he never in this speech refers to God.
See above, note 251.

271. beorht beacen Godes (bright beacon of God) (571)
See above, note 119.

272. Godes leoht geceas (chose God's light) 2469
See above, note 253.

273. his declaration (977) that Grendel shall abide miclan domes and the decision of scir metod.
See above, note 246.

274. There remains 2729ff: where Beowulf examines his conscience and says that Waldend fira cannot accuse him of morðorbealo maga — his death is, however, actually comforted by the sight of the gold he has won. (With the crimes Beowulf says he has avoided compare the crimes that are punished in hell in Völuspá 36)
For 2729ff, see above, note 237. For *Völuspá*, see above, note 172. For the relevant section of *Völuspá* see above, note 261.

Folio 63

275. Thus 669 georne truwode modgan mægens Metodes hyldo [N.B. no "and" should be inserted; the favour of Metod is the possession of strength];
See above, note 243.

276. 1272-3 gemunde mægenes strenge gimfæste gife ðe him God sealde ond him to Anwaldan are gelyfde frofre ond fultum.
See above, note 247.

277. Finally the poet tells us that when the dragon's ruinous attack was reported wende se wisa þæt he Wealdende ofer ealde riht ecean Dryhtne bitre gebulge.
This quotation is from lines 2329–2331a. See above, note 237.

Klaeber in his note to 2330 writes: "Beowulf did not yet know the real cause of the dragon's ravages, see 2403 ff. The phrase ofer ealde riht, 'contrary to the old law' . . . is here given a Christian interpretation" (211).

Tolkien clearly disagrees with Klaeber's assertion. The "ealde riht" could just as easily refer to an "old custom" as it could to an "ancient law."

278. **Cædmonian tradition (among which ranks especially the <u>Genesis</u> of which we have a damaged and late copy)**
The "father of English poetry," Cædmon, the Venerable Bede tells us, was a simple herdsman. He was afraid to take his turn at the harp when it was passed to him at the feast, and to avoid this duty fled to the barn where he fell asleep. In a dream an angel came to him and commanded him to "sing the creation." Cædmon replied that he could not sing. "Nevertheless you must sing," the angel replied, and when Cædmon awoke he had been given the gift of producing poems, in English, about biblical matters. Because the subjects of the poems in the list Bede gives of Cædmon's poems match, at least generally, the subjects of quite a number of the surviving Old English poems, for many years the biblical paraphrase poems, those that tell a story from the Bible in Old English verse (including *Genesis* and *Exodus*), were called "Cædmonian." The only poem we can directly attribute to Cædmon is "Cædmon's Hymn," and even this is an Old English translation of Bede's Latin translation of the original poem.

By calling the version of *Genesis* in the Junius Manuscript "late", Tolkien is suggesting that the tradition of biblical paraphrase poems goes back in Old English literary tradition at least to the time of the historical Cædmon in the seventh century.

Genesis.
Krapp and Dobbie, eds. *The Junius Manuscript*, 3–87.

Folio 64
279. **folces hyrde, Hroðgar**
    Þa wæs on salum   sinces brytta
    gamolfeax ond guðrof;   geoce gelyfde
    brego Beorht-Dena;   gehyrde on Beowulfe
    folces hyrde   fæstrædne geþoht.

    [Then the giver of treasure was in the hall, white-haired and battle-brave, believed in the help, the lord of the Bright-Danes, the guardian of the folk, listened to Beowulf firmly resolved in thought.]

Beowulf, lines 607–610
Klaeber, ed., *Beowulf and the Fight at Finnsburg*, 23.

280. **<u>Heorot</u> (Hleiðr) as a place of originally heathen religious import which he derived from native tradition.**
Tolkien here follows Chambers in accepting the idea that some historical structure lies behind Heorot, probably a hall or town that was built in Leire near the north coast of the Danish island of Seeland. As Chambers notes: "Just as Arthur holds court at Camelot, or Charlemagne is at home *ad Ais, á sa capele*, so the Scandinavian traditions represent Rolf Kraki as keeping house at Leire

(*Lethra, Hleiðar garðr*)." Rolf Kraki is the great hero of the Danes, and his Leire
is the place "to which the North ever after looked for its pattern of chivalry . . .
where the grave mounds rise out of the waving corn-fields" (16–20). The presence of the grave mounds at Leire may also indicate a pre-historic association of
the place with actual heathen religious practices.

Chambers, *Beowulf: An Introduction to the Study of the Poem*, 16–20.

Folio 65

281. **The old fashioned criticism of "putting the best things on the fringes"**
See above, note 41.

Folio 67

282. **It "lacks steady advance" — so Klæber heads a critical section.**
"Lack of Steady Advance"

Klaeber, ed., *Beowulf and the Fight at Finnsburg*, lvii.

Folio 68

283. **The sluggish bear's son with his hug who wakes up and becomes famous is
a very old folk tale,**
See above, note 155.

284. **the legendary association of the Danish and Heorot with a marauding monster, and of the arrival from abroad of a "champion" of the "bear-anger" was
not invented by our poet.**
The text is difficult at this point. "Bear" is definitely the first word in the
pairing, but "anger" is unclear. I have chosen to print "bear-anger," working
under the assumption that Tolkien is making a not quite literal (though basically the same in meaning) translation of "berserks-gangr" (literally "berserks
fit-of-frenzy") and thus "bear-shirt's" (i.e., one who wears a shirt of bear skin,
the literal translation of "berserk") "fit-of-frenzy," hence "bear anger." In the 'B'
Text Tolkien changes the phrase to "of bear-origin."

Cleasby and Vigfusson, *An Icelandic-English Dictionary*.

Chambers argues that there are parallels between Beowulf the hero and Bothvar Bjarki in the *Saga of Rolf Kraki*. Bothvar Bjarki leaves his homeland (the
land of the Götar) and travels to the Danish court at Leire (which Chambers argues elsewhere is Heorot). Bjarki means "little bear", thus the connection between a champion from abroad of bear-origin and the legendary Danish court.

Chambers, *Beowulf: An Introduction to the Study of the Poem*, 54–61.

Folio 69

285. **There is a special connexion between Beowulf and Andreas**
There are quite a number of lines in *Andreas* which are identical to lines in *Beowulf*. *Beowulf* is generally presumed to be the older of the two poems and to have influenced the poet of *Andreas* (though we do not know if the *Andreas* poet had access to the actual *Beowulf* manuscript or was simply familiar with a tradition of *Beowulf* stories and literary formulae). For *Andreas*, see above, note 198.

286. **to the great missionary epoch of the 8th century.**
During the eighth century Anglo-Saxon missionaries set out to convert the pagan kingdoms of northern continental Europe. They were, in general, quite successful, and some religious traditions (such as penitential practice) traveled from Ireland to England in the early years of the conversion, and thence to the continent. These continental (but originally English) traditions were then reintroduced to England from the continent during the Benedictine Reform in the tenth century.

See:
Wilhelm Levison, *England and the Continent in the Eighth Century* (Oxford: Oxford University Press, 1946).
Allen J. Frantzen, *The Literature of Penance in Anglo-Saxon England* (New Brunswick, NJ: Rutgers University Press, 1983).

287. **the half surprised almost ironic question of Hygelac (ac ðu Hroðgare widcuðne wean wihte gebettest)**
          Ac þu Hroðgare
    widcuðne wean   wihte gebettest,
    mærum ðeodne?

[But did you, for Hrothgar, remedy at all his widely known affliction?]

Beowulf, lines 1990b–1992a
Klaeber, ed., *Beowulf and the Fight at Finnsburg*, 74.

288. **the emphasis on the friendly relations now established between nations once hostile**
This reading of Beowulf's report to Hygelac as a demonstration of the hero's political acumen (a reading that I have not encountered elsewhere in the intervening *Beowulf* criticism) anticipates by more than six decades the innovative anthropological and political criticism put forth by John Hill in *The Cultural World in Beowulf*.

John Hill, *The Cultural World in Beowulf* (Toronto: University of Toronto Press, 1995), 104–7 and *passim*.

'B' Text

Folio 92

289. **The Rev. Oswald Cockayne**
See above, note 1.

290. **the Rev. Joseph Bosworth, D.D., F.R.S., Rawlinsonian Professor of Anglo-Saxon:**
See above, note 2.

291. **'I have long entertained [the conviction] that Dr. Bosworth is not a man so diligent in his special walk as duly to read the books ... which have been printed in our old English, or so-called Anglosaxon tongue. He may do very well for a Professor.'**
See above, note 3.

292. **Bosworth's dictionary,**
See above, note 4.

Folio 93

293. **a 'litteratur'**
The German word for "literature," but also the accumulation of scholarly articles that address any given literary work. As Shippey notes, Tolkien plays with these two definitions of "literature" in "Beowulf: The Monsters and the Critics": "... 'literature' was 'books about books', the dead Latin 'letter' opposed to the ancient English spirit," (*Road to Middle-earth*, 5).

Tolkien, "*Beowulf*: The Monsters and the Critics," 5.

Folio 94

294. **'research'**
See above, note 10

295. **the best criticism (such as that of W. P. Ker or R. W. Chambers)**
For W. P. Ker, see above, note 6.
For R. W. Chambers, see above, note 8.

296. **Nordic Summa Theologica**
The *Summa Theologica*, the "Summation of Theology," is St. Thomas Aquinas's great work that unifies Christian and Hellenistic philosophy. A Nordic *Summa Theologica* would presumably be a work that provided a complete theological explanation of Old Norse cosmology and mythology in its own terms.

297. **Beowulf <u>and the Heroic Age in England</u>, sixteen pages and all too short, contributed by Chambers to Sir Archibald Strong's translation,**
See above, note 7.

Folio 95

298. **A man found a mass of old stone . . . they turned the stones upside down to look for hidden carvings and inscriptions;**
See above, note 11.

Folio 96

299. **<u>Beowulf</u> is steadily pronounced to be 'worth studying'. It is true that this is often qualified — 'it is the most worthy of study amongst Anglo-Saxon remains'**
Compare:

> "The story is commonplace and the plan feeble. But there are some qualities in it which make it (accidentally or not, it hardly matters) the best worth studying of all Anglo-Saxon poems."

W. P. Ker, *English Literature: Medieval* (London: Williams and Norgate, 1912), 30.

300. **a tone that suggests that Andaman Islanders might be substituted for Anglo-Saxons**
See above, note 13.

Folio 98

301. **the late Sir Archibald Strong, who had read <u>Beowulf</u> with attention;**
See above, note 9.

302. **<u>A Short History of English Literature</u>. O. U. P. (Milford) 1921.**
Strong, *A Short History of English Literature.*

303. **Indeed he cared for it sufficiently to translate it into verse. <u>Beowulf, translated into modern English Rhyming verse</u>. Constable 1925**
Strong, *Beowulf Translated.*

304. **he selected from all those available the one metré most foreign in mood and style to the original (the metré used by Morris in <u>Sigurd</u>) and not in itself a good metré.**
See above, note 17.

305. **of which <u>Beowulf</u>, probably justly (though it is one of the more important**

single pieces produced in all those 1200 years) gets less than two.
Strong, *A Short History of English Literature*, 2–3.

306. **pausing only to note that it opens thus:** <u>**Beowulf is the only poem of any**</u>
<u>**length — it runs to 3182 lines — which has come down to us, of the early he-**</u>
<u>**roic poetry of the Teutons.**</u> **And it ends:** <u>**Though biblical allusions abound,**</u>
<u>**and the heathen deities have, for the most part, vanished before the editing —**</u>
<u>**if we may call it editing — of the Christian reviser, the background is not**</u>
<u>**Christian but heathen.**</u> **Bear these in mind.**
The complete quotation is:

> *Beowulf* is the only poem of any length — it runs to three thousand one
> hundred and eighty-two lines — which has come down to us, of the early
> heroic poetry of the Teutons. There is no certainty about the date of its
> composition. It is extant in a manuscript of the tenth century, but this
> manuscript must be a copy of a much older original. The possibilities are
> that the poem, which contains several references to the narrative of the
> Old Testament, and speaks frequently of the God of the Christian religion,
> was put together in the late seventh century by a Christian poet who
> interested himself in the songs and lays of his heathen forefathers, and,
> making a selection of them, worked them into a consecutive story. Wheth-
> er he rewrote and refashioned the old lays, or merely edited them without
> making any great changes, it is impossible to say; in the present state of
> our knowledge it may be nearer the truth to speak of him as the shaper or
> editor rather than as the actual author. There is nothing distinctively Eng-
> lish in the poem. The scenes are laid in Denmark and South Sweden: the
> tribes who play a part in the action are Danes, Geats, Swedes, and Frisians.
> It is clear, therefore, that, if the poem was written in England — and of
> that there can be little doubt — the legends were carried, in likelihood in
> the form of short lays, by the English from their continental home, and re-
> mained current among them for many years after the settlement. Though
> biblical allusions abound, and the heathen deities have, for the most part,
> vanished before the editing — if we may call it editing — of the Christian
> reviser, the background is not Christian but heathen.

Strong, *A Short History of English Literature*, 2.

Folio 99

307. **"The main story deals with the adventures of Beowulf in his contest with**
ogres and dragons" ... **"does scant justice to the poem."**
See above, note 18.

308. <u>**A History of English Literature**</u> **(in 111 pages) in the 'Peoples Books,' a**
potting by Dr. Compton Rickett of his own larger work.

See above, note 19.

The "larger work" (it runs a full 702 pages) referred to by Tolkien is:

Arthur Compton-Rickett, *A History of English Literature* (London: T. C. and E. C. Jack, 1918).

Folio 100

309. **"In outline the story is <u>trivial</u> enough, a <u>typical folk-tale</u>; . . . <u>The Christian allusions show up rather incongruously against the pervading paganism.</u>**
The quotation is verbatim; the underlines and parenthetical comments are by Tolkien.

Strong, *A Short History of English Literature*, 2–3.

Folio 101

310. **Thus the old and rather dreary debate, which shows signs of breaking out like measles again, whether the <u>Géatas</u> of <u>Beowulf</u> are the Gautar of Sweden or Jutes has much technical evidence in favour of either side, but though to my mind the probability on linguistic and historical grounds lies with the <u>Gautar</u>, the real decision lies with the interpreter rather than the philologist or historian; for the Jutish case is really founded on the notion that <u>Beowulf</u> being in Old English must be a "national epic" and must relate the glories of Jutes not Swedes. But this is a primitive and quite erroneous conception and with its dismissal the Jutish-case with all its special pleading fails. It should never have been brought forward. If Beowulf is a national epic it is an epic of a peculiar kind which includes both Gautr and Jutes.**
What Tolkien calls the "Jutish hypothesis" is the identification of the Geatas in *Beowulf* with either the Gautr (Old Swedish Gøtar) "the inhabitants of Väster- and Östergötland, south of the great Swedish lakes" (Klæber, *Beowulf*, xlvi) or "the Jutes (Iuti, Iutae) of Bede (i.e. the tribe which colonized Kent, the Isle of Wight and Hampshire)" (Chambers, *Beowulf: An Introduction to the Study of the Poem*, 333). The linguistic evidence supports the Swedish identification. The case for Jutes is made by the idea of linguistic confusion that led to the Jutes being called "Geatas" at the time of the composition of *Beowulf*, and by the idea that in lines 2910–2921 we learn that with Beowulf's death, the Geatas have to fear both the Franks and Frisians. Since the Geatas fear the Franks, the argument goes, they must have been reachable by land (the Franks were a land power) and therefore not separated from them by the sea. Also, the Geatas and Swedes are said to fight "ofer sæ" ("on the sea") and if they both lived in Sweden, their battles would likely be on land. Finally, since *Beowulf* is seen as an epic about England (since it is written in Old English) it seems to make sense that the heroes of the poem would be one of the three tribes of the migration (the Jutes), not a people of southern Sweden. None of these arguments is particularly convincing, however, if one does not approach the poem with the

pre-formed hypothesis that *Beowulf* is a national epic of the English (see Chambers, *Beowulf: An Introduction to the Study of the Poem*, 333–45).

Folio 103

311. "**Beowulf is the only poem of any length ... which has come down to us, of the early heroic poetry of the Teutons.**"
See above, note 306.

Folio 104

312. **Beowulf is primarily an English poem of a special period,**
Tolkien believed *Beowulf* to have been written around 750, at the height of the so-called "golden age" of Anglo-Saxon monasticism before the Viking raids and social dislocations of the ninth century. (See above, note 31.)

Folio 105

313. **For essential criticism Shakespeare was a dramatist, an English dramatist of a special English period.**
Tolkien is here pointing out that critics, when it comes to Shakespeare, recognize him as a specific Elizabethan dramatist and do not (generally) assume that his works speak for all English literature for four or five centuries. And see above, note 29.

314. **The ancient legends mention the particular fame of the maker of verse such as Heorrenda no less than the maker of sword or jewel such as Wéland.**
See above, note 24.

315. **The fame and names of the individual Icelandic poets have been better preserved even than their works.**
See above, note 25.

Folio 106

316. **Great differences can be observed even among the Norse lays of the so-called Elder Edda**
See above, note 26.

317. **He seems to be lost in a crowd of 'ancestral voices prophesying war'.**
See above, note 27.

318. **His grandchildren were at grips with such Teutons par excellence, the viking invaders, and regarded them as the very devil.**
See above, note 28.

319. **More recent hypotheses concerning Frisian intermediaries seem hardly less fantastic, but do not radically affect what is here said.**
Elis Wadstein argued that the Geatas in *Beowulf* were in fact Jutes, the form of the name being due to Frisian intermediary forms through which the poem had passed.

> Elis Wadstein, *Norden och Västeuropa i gammal tid* Populärt vetenskapliga föreläsningar vid Göteborgs Högskola, Ny följd 21 (Stockholm: Albert Bonniers Forlag, 1925).
> Elis Wadstein, "The Beowulf Poem as an English National Epos," *Acta Philologica Scandinavica* 8 (1925): 273–91.

Folio 107

320. **from Aidan to Stígand anymore than Icelandic history from the <u>Landnám</u> to the cruel feuds of the great houses and the submission to the Norwegian crown in the 13th century; anymore one might add than Rome from Tarquin to Augustus or Augustus to Diocletian.**
For Aidan, Stigand, and Landnám, see above, note 30.

Tarquin (Lucius Tarquinius Priscus) is by tradition the seventh and final king of Rome, who ruled from 534 to 510 B.C. The rape of Lucretia by Tarquin's son Sextus and his general cruelty is supposed to have so infuriated the people of Rome that they expelled him and began the Roman Republic.

Augustus (Gaius Julius Caesar Octavianus) was the first Roman emperor, ruling from 63 to 14 B.C.

Diocletian (Gaius Aurelius Valerius Diocletianus) revived the Roman empire after the turmoil of the third century. He was proclaimed Emperor by the army in 284 but really achieved complete control over the formerly divided empire only in 296. In 303 he launched a severe persecution of Christians.

Tolkien's point here is that no one would say that Roman history is monolithic throughout several hundred years of change and development. There are distinctions to be drawn between types of literature and art from each century of Roman history. Likewise no one should believe that Icelandic or Anglo-Saxon history is monolithic and "one thing" across the changes of the centuries. See above, note 30.

Folio 109

321. **But <u>biblical allusions</u> do not 'abound' in <u>Beowulf</u> ; while on the other hand <u>heathen deities</u> have not 'for the most part vanished,' but vanished altogether.**
See above, note 32.

322. **save for the obscure name of <u>Ing</u>, occurring in Ingeld and in <u>Ingwine</u> (an 'epic' name of the Danes): the first was doubtless the historical name of a real person and no longer analyzed any more than <u>Edward</u> is today;**

For Ing, see above, note 34.

Likewise Edward, Anglo-Saxon "Ead-Weard" ("guardian of prosperity") is today thought of simply as a personal name; only philologists and Anglo-Saxonists translate the old knowledge it encodes.

Folio 110

323. in his own introduction to his translation he speaks not of the '<u>heathen</u> <u>background</u>' nor of the '<u>Christian editor</u>,' but of the <u>Christian colouring</u> which the <u>author</u> has given to <u>his</u> story.
Strong, *Beowulf Translated*, xxxv–xxxvi.

Folio 111

324. **In Chambers' Foreword to this same translation — this Foreword should be read by all, whatever else, save the poem itself, is unread — only the shadow of the historical document fallacy is left, and the solution of the Christian-heathen debate is trembling on the verge of explicit expression.**
See above, note 38.

325. **On page xxvi, when everything seems to be going right, we hear yet once again "that the main story of 'Beowulf' is a <u>wild folk-tale</u>."**
See above, note 39.

326. **Quite true, of course. It is true of <u>King Lear</u>, unless in that case one would prefer to substitute <u>silly</u> for <u>wild</u>.**
See above, note 40.

327. **But more — we are told that the same sort of stuff is found in Homer, yet there it is kept in its proper place.**
Compare:

> The fault of *Beowulf* is that there is nothing much in the story. The hero is occupied killing monsters, like Hercules or Theseus. But there are other things in the lives of Hercules and Theseus besides the killing of the Hydra or of Procrustes. Beowulf has nothing else to do when he has killed Grendel and Grendel's mother in Denmark

Ker, *Dark Ages*, 252–55. And see above, note 136.

328. **"<u>The folk-tale is a good servant</u>," . . . "<u>but a bad master: it has been allowed in 'Beowulf' to usurp the place of honour, and to drive into episodes and digressions the things which should be the main stuff of a well-conducted epic</u>."**
See above, note 41.

Folio 112

329. **One may assent to Earle's quotation from Dowden : 'The happiest moment in a critic's hours of study is, when seemingly by some divination, but really the result of patient observation and thought, he lights upon the central motive of a great work;'**
See above, note 43.

330. **Earle's particular divination, which ascribed the work to Hygeberht, Archbishop of Lichfield (787–803?) and made the whole poem into a kind of early political Utopia.**
See above, note 44.

Folio 113

331. **the mere manuscript date of <u>Beowulf</u> (c. 1000 A.D.)**
The *Beowulf* manuscript can be dated by the handwriting of the scribe to between 975 and 1025 A.D. There is much scholarly controversy as to whether or not that range of fifty years can be narrowed, but at this time there is no real consensus.

332. **the introduction to an anthology compiled by Mr. Shane Leslie speaks of <u>Beowulf</u> as 'small beer.'**
See above, note 47.

333. **Mr. Chesterton.**
See above, note 48.

334. **Vercelli <u>Vision of the Cross</u> (Dream of the Rood)**
See above, notes 49 and 50.

335. **plough-candidates in a provincial university**
See above, note 51.

Folio 115

336. **Bellocian prejudice**
A reference to Hilaire Pierre Belloc (1870–1953), the French-born British writer and poet. And see above, note 48. Tolkien, a Roman Catholic, wanted to distance himself from the popular "Chesterbellocian" image of Roman Catholicism.

337. **At any rate Jusserand's <u>Literary History of the English People</u>**
See above, note 109, 110.

338. **There is in any case no insularity quite so insular as that of the Île de France.**

A pun on the two meanings of "insular," one meaning "of or from an island," the other meaning "narrow-minded or illiberal." The Île de France is the historic section of France that includes Paris and the regions surrounding it, where Jusserand and other unsympathetic French literary scholars had presumably received their training.

Folio 116
339. **'woodnotes wild'**
See above, note 111.

340. **Jusserand says actually 'the charm of a wildflower'**
See above, note 112.

Folio 117
341. **'the charm of a wildflower' This, by the way, he says of Ælfric!**
See above, note 113.

342. **Ælfric**
See above, note 63.

343. **Old English translation of Boethius, treating the legend of Orpheus and Eurydice.**
See above, notes 116 and 117.

344. **'The dog of hell he should have three heads'** !
See above, note 115.

Folio 118
345. **the speech of Beowulf to Unferth (ll. 530–606), we are told, may be summed up thus: 'liar, drunkard, coward, murderer!'"**
See above, note 119.

346. **So may many brilliant speeches in the houses of Parliament today, and judging by report still more in the similar institutions in Paris.**
See above, note 120.

347. **the great court of Heorot, the ambiguous figure of Hroðulf, and the sinister figure of the evil counselor Unferth**
See above, note 121.

Folio 119
348. **litotes**
See above, note 124.

349. **beore druncen**, in line 531.
   See above, note 123.

350. **Guðrún in the 'Lay of Attila', where of the great Lady of the Burgundians, Queen of the Goths, it is said, as she greets her brothers riding to their doom in Attila's hall, bjóri vas hón litt drukkin.**
   See above, note 125.

351. **(cp. the similar symbolism at the beginning drukku dróttmegir vín í valhöllu).**
   See above, note 126.

352. **"To their excessive enthusiasm" we are told "succeed periods of complete depression, their orgies are followed by despair."**
   See above, note 122.

Folio 120

353. **'swaggering upspring' and heavy headed revel that the Prince of Denmark thought 'a custom more honoured in the breach than the observance' should be ascribed to the "Elizabethans."**
   Hamlet, Act 1, Scene 4, lines 8–16:

   > HAMLET: The King doth wake tonight and takes his rouse,
   > Keeps wassail, and the swaggering upspring reels;
   > And as he drains his drafts of Rhenish down,
   > The kettledrum and trumpet thus bray out
   > The triumph of his pledge.
   > HORATIO: Is it a custom?
   > HAMLET: Ay, marry, is 't,
   > But to my mind, though I am native here
   > And to the manner born, it is a custom
   > More honored in the breach than the observance.

354. **'orgies' are nowhere praised and very seldom recorded — unless it be of alien pirate chieftains, or of Assyrians and such highly cultured people of the ancient world.**
   See above, note 127.

355. **'They sacrifice their life in battle without a frown, and yet when the hour for fight comes they are harassed by the thought of death'.**
   See above, note 128.

356. **E.V. Gordon has dealt recently with this piece of traditional nonsense**

concerning the Germanic warrior in literature in his <u>Introduction to Old Norse</u>. In point of origin it is derived rather from classical accounts of ancient Celts and Gauls than from attention to Old English or Old Norse literature. See above, note 129.

Folio 120–121

357. "<u>The strange poem of 'Beowulf'</u>" he wanders on . . . "<u>Its heroes are at once pagans and Christian, they believe in Christ and Weland</u>."
See above, note 130.

Folio 121

358. "<u>They fight against the monsters of Scandinavian mythology, and see in them the descendants of Cain; historical facts such as the battle of the sixth century (mentioned by Gregory of Tours) are mixed up with fantastic deeds beneath the waves.</u>"
See above, notes 130, 131.

359. <u>they believe in Christ and Wéland</u>
See above, note 133.

360. **At this point the gentleman is seized from behind by Grendel and put in a bag, and for once one's sympathies are with the troll.**
See above, note 132.

361. **They believe in the Trinity and Merlin; while professing Catholics they imagine good violins were made by Stradivarius; though serious Calvinists they ascribe their furniture to Chippendale**
See above, note 133.

362. **Q.E.D. <u>Roma locuta, causa finita</u>!**
Quod erat demonstrandum ("which was to be demonstrated").
Roma locuta, causa finita ("Rome has spoken; the matter is settled").

"Roma locuta, causa finita" is the language of medieval papal bulls and other pronouncements. Tolkien is attacking Jusserand for making pronouncements rather than supporting his ideas with logic or evidence (Tolkien believes the ideas to be insupportable).

Folio 122

363. <u>word-hord</u>
See above, note 52.

364. <u>Ars longa</u> indeed — <u>the lyf so schort, the craft so long to lerne, so hard th'</u>

assay, so scharp the conquering, as Chaucer says.
See above, notes 54 and 55.

Folio 124

365. **variant jotted down from an old wife's lips, or unearthed in an old chap-book.**
The collection of many variations of a single folk-tale from numerous infor-
mants was one of the practices of the Grimms and other folklorists. The reference to an old chap-book could be a suggestion of some of the paper (as
opposed to parchment) variations of the Norse Sagas that were collected in Iceland. The variant versions were generally compared to each other and the critic
would then develop (as did the brothers Grimm) a version of the tale that
seemed to him to best represent the sense of the collected variations. Tolkien is
here suggesting that such an approach ignores the essential fact that, at least in
the case of *Beowulf*, an individual poet with enormous skill and craftsmanship
has shaped his folk-tale material into a poem.

366. **As different as the Lear of Shakespeare from the same tale recounted in the
chronicle of Layamon**
For *Lear* see above, note 40.

Layamon (properly spelled "Laȝamon" using the letter "yogh") was a priest
at Arley near Radstone. He was a poet and chronicler of English history, writing
in early Middle English. His *Brut* is a long (over 32,000 half-lines) poem that
traces the history of England from its supposed settling at the time of Brutus,
who settled England out of the wreck of Troy. *Brut* was written around 1205.

The basic outline of much of the Lear story is present in *Brut*, including the
contest among the three daughters to say how much each loves the father, Cordelia's failure to flatter, Lear's anger at and disinheritance of her, and his abuse
at the hands of the two favored daughters. But Cordelia does not die, the in-
trigues of Regan and Goneril are not really a factor, and the whole story is told
in chronicle form without Shakespeare's development of the characters, their
inner lives, and their motives.

Joseph Hall, ed., *Layamon's Brut: Selections, Edited with Introduction, Notes and Glossary* (Oxford: Clarendon Press, 1924), 2–17.

367. **Its meeting with William Morris was not under the happiest auspices; but
in any case Morris was not a learned or scholarly poet. He was too fond of employing a living crib or interpreter. In his dealings with Beowulf he was perhaps not so fortunate in his crib as in his (still somewhat casual) dealing with
Icelandic through Magnússon. But Morris had a wild and willful way even
with his cribs, and these cannot take the blame of his transgressions. The
'Morris and Wyatt' translation of Beowulf remains an oddity — quite outside
the main line of development.**

William Morris collaborated with the Icelandic scholar Eiríkur Magnússon (1833–1913) to translate a number of Norse Sagas. His translation of *Beowulf* was based on the work of Anglo-Saxon scholar A. J. Wyatt.

> The Story of Beowulf
> 1. And first of the Kindred of Hrothgar.
> What! we of the Spear-Danes of yore days, so was it
> That we learn'd of the fair fame of king of the folks
> And the Athelings a-faring in the framing of valour.
> Oft then Scyld the Sceaf-son from the hosts of the scathers,
> From kindreds a many the mead-settles tore;
> It was then the earl fear'd them, sith hence was he first
> Found bare and all lacking; so solace he bided,
> Wax'd under the welkin in worship to thrive,
> Until it was so that the round-about sitters
> All over the whale-road must hearken to his will
> And yield him the tribute. A good king was that.

> William Morris and A. J. Wyatt, eds. and trans., *Beowulf* in *Three Northern Love Stories, Beowulf*, The Collected Works of William Morris: With Introductions by his daughter May Morris 10 (London: Longmans Green and Company, 1911), 179.

Folio 125

368. (such as the **Epistola Alexandri** and the **Wonders of the East**) that occurred before it and after it.
See above, notes 56 and 57.

369. the scattering of manuscript remains in the sixteenth century
See above, note 58.

370. Lawrence Nowell
See above, note 59.

371. Humphrey Wanley
See above, note 60.

372. On page 218 of his **Catalogus** of manuscripts in volume II of Hickes **Thesaurus** (1705) he describes it thus: "In hoc libro qui **Poeseos** Anglosaxonicae **egregium est exemplum** descripta videntur bella quae Beowulfus quidam Danus ex regio Scyldingorum stirpe artes gessit contra Sueciae regulos."
See above, note 62.

373. **For long reasonably competent translation of Old English prose, such as that of Ælfric . . .**
See above, note 63.

374. **Cottonian Collection**
See above, note 61.

Folio 126
375. **Grim Johnson Thorkelin,**
See above, note 64.

376. **'editio princeps' in 1815.**
See above, note 65.

377. **had two transcripts made**
See above, note 67.

378. **by the gentle descendants of the barbarous Anglo-Saxons, when they bombarded the old city of Copenhagen.**
See above, note 68.

379. **Pastor <u>Grundtvig</u>**
See above, note 70.

380. **'Anglo-Saxon Verse' written in dedicatory commendation of his patron <u>Bülow</u>,**
Grundtvig, *Bjowulfs Drape*, xvii–xviii.

Folio 127
381. **N. F. S. Grundtvig, Præst.**
See above, note 70.

382. **first discerning <u>Sigemund Wælsing</u> for instance; and it was he who first identified <u>Hygelac</u> with <u>Chochtilaicus</u> in Gregory of Tours, a discovery of cardinal importance.**
See above, note 73.

383. **<u>Bjowulfs Drape. Et Gothisk Helte-Digt af Angel-Saxisk paa Dansk Riim ved Nic. Fred. Seve. Grundtvig, Præst. Kjöbenhavn, 1820</u>.**
See above, note 74.

384. **Professor B. Nerman in <u>Det Svenska Rikets Uppkomst</u>, Beowulf is still a**

prime document.
See above, note 79.

385. Thorkelin's title: <u>De Danorum Rebus Gestis Secul</u> III & IV <u>Poema Danicum</u>
<u>Dialecto Anglosaxonica</u>.
See above, notes 64 and 65.

Folio 128
386. Sharon Turner in 1807, in his <u>History of the Anglo-Saxons</u>.
See above, note 76.

387. the most interesting relic of Anglo-Saxon poetry which time has suffered us
to receive. The subject is the expedition of Beowulf to wreak the <u>fæhðe</u> or
deadly feud on Hrothgar for a homicide which he had committed. It abounds
with speeches, which Beowulf and Hrothgar and their partisans make to each
other, with much occasional description and sentiment.
See above, note 78.

388. As Earle says, proper names excepted, this has no more to do with <u>Beowulf</u>
than with the <u>Iliad</u> or the <u>Chanson de Roland</u>.
See above, note 81.

389. In his <u>History</u> of 1823 there is a considerable change, and <u>Beowulf</u> has become a 'poetical Romance' or a 'metrical Romance' which celebrates the heroic deeds of Beowulf who fell in <u>Jutland</u> in the year 340 A.D. This is a borrowing from the Danes — from Thorkelin, from the Danish historian Suhm,
who derived it from Saxo Grammaticus, by identifying Beowulf with the <u>Bous</u>
son of <u>Odin</u>, whom Saxo relates to have fallen in battle with <u>Hotherus</u> about
that date.
See above, notes 84 and 87.

390. These titles are challenges to Ritson and others, who denied the existence
of poetical Romance before the Norman Conquest.
See above, notes 85 and 86.

Folio 129
391. Geats and Jutes is that long controversy, which has complicated the detail
of <u>Beowulf</u> -criticism, concerning the identity of the <u>Géatas</u>.
See above, note 310.

392. The Jutish hypothesis has still vigorous supporters such as Professor Elis
Wadstein. Ultimately to my mind the Jutish theory, in any case the weaker,

breaks down since its foundation (the only thing that would give it any probability) is the view that <u>Beowulf</u> is a national epic glorifying the English or some part of their supposed ancestry.
See above, note 319.

393. It is to Conybeare perhaps in <u>Illustrations of Anglo-Saxon Poetry</u> (1826)
See above, notes 89 and 90.

394. Yet we may note that he rejects Thorkelin's <u>Bous</u> and <u>Jutland</u>, remains an agnostic about ultimate origins (<u>Illustrations</u>, page 33), and says of the writer (or perhaps the translator or modernizer of the 'Dano-Saxon' period to whom he is inclined to ascribe the poem as we have it) that "<u>it is evident that he was a Christian</u>."
See above, note 92.

Folio 130
395. the work of J. M. Kemble of (Trinity College, Cambridge).
See above, note 5.

396. Kemble's first limited edition — the effective beginning of Anglo-Saxon scholarship — came out in 1833: <u>The Anglo-Saxon Poems of Beowulf, the Traveller's Song, and the Battle of Finnesburh</u> edited together with <u>a glossary of the more difficult words and an Historical Preface</u>. London. Pickering. It was sold out in a few months (!) and soon replaced by the corrected second edition (1835).
See above, note 94.

397. it is Kemble's work of 1837 that marks the definite crossing to a new era. This was <u>A Translation of the Anglo-Saxon Poem of Beowulf with a copious Glossary, Preface and Philological Notes</u>. London. Pickering.
See above, note 96.

398. Grein's <u>Sprachschatz</u> and so of the modern 'Grein-Köhler',
See above, note 97.
    "Grein-Köhler" is the revised and updated edition of Grein's original work undertaken by J. J. Köhler in 1912.

Christian W. M. Grein, *Sprachschatz der angelsächsischen Dichter*, ed. J. J. Köhler (Heidelberg: Carl Winter's Universitätsbuchhandlung, 1912)

Folio 131
399. But already in the Preface we begin that swing from a blind belief in the historicity of the hero and all other characters in the poem, save perhaps Grendel

and the Dragon, to the "mythological" or "allegorical" explanation of everything which is now as wearisome as it was once irresistibly fascinating.

"The works which I made use of, and more especially Suhm's *History of
Denmark*, laborious as they are, are subject to one serious reproach: they
treat mythic and traditional matters as ascertained history."

Kemble, *A Translation of the Anglo-Saxon Poem of 'Beowulf'*, i–lv.

400. **founded upon the authority of Wolf and Lachmann, and their sentence
upon it was inevitable.**
See above, note 98.

401. **As Earle says: "That great works in early literature forsooth were not made
by art and device, but that they grew spontaneously and blindly, this was that
imagination in the air which attended the first entertainment of Beowulf in
the Fatherland."**
See above, note 99.

Folio 132

402. **Chambers notes (with something, it would seem, of unnecessary surprise)
that it is on such a piece as <u>Widsith</u> that the older scholars were at their best:**
See above, note 101.

403. **Kemble, Leo, Lappenberg, Ettmüller, and later Möller, Ten Brink, Müllenhof.**
See above, notes 93 and 102.

404. **in the appendix to the second edition (1932) of his <u>Introduction</u>, dealing
with recent work down to 1930, Chambers begins with Klaeber's edition of
<u>Beowulf</u> (1922, 1928²), and rightly calls it the most important since Kemble's
nearly a century ago, in 1833.**
See above, note 104.

405. **Klaeber's edition of <u>Beowulf</u> (1922, 1928²),**
See above, note 104.

Folios 132–133

406. **Decision, a view, a conviction are now imperatively desired as Chambers
rightly says: but oddly, since he is himself a master of indecision and takes
characteristically as the motto of his voluminous <u>Introduction</u> the words of
Uncle Remus, when faced with the problem of the comparison of the history
of the flood in his animal story and in Scripture: <u>Dey mout er ben two deloojes : en den agin dey moutent.</u>**

In "The Story of the Deluge, and How It Came About," Uncle Remus tells how at an animal assembly the crayfish were angered because the other animals would not listen to them. Finally, the crayfish and the spring lizard went underground and loosed the fountains of the earth. All the other animals were drowned. When the young boy to whom Uncle Remus is telling the story asks "What about the ark?" Uncle Remus replies:

> Don't you pester wid ole man Noah, honey. I bou' he tuck keer dat ark. Dat's w'at he wuz dar fer, en dat's w'at he done. Leas'ways, dat's w'at dey tells me. But don't you bodder longer dat ark, ceppin' your mammy fetches it up. Dey mought er bin two deloojes, en den agin dey moughtent. Ef dey wuz enny ark in dish yer w'at de Crawfishes brung on, I ain't heern tell un it, en w'en dey ain't no arks 'roun', I ain't got no time fer ter make um en put em in dar.

> [Don't you pester with old man Noah, honey. I bound to believe he took care of that ark. That's what he was there for, and that's what he did. At least that's what they tell me. But don't you bother any longer with that ark, unless your Mammy brings it up. There might have been two deluges, and then again there might not. If there was any ark in the deluge that the crawfishes brought on, I haven't heard tell of it, and when there aren't any arks around, I don't have time to make them up and put them in there.]

Harris' dialect spelling is inconsistent from one published version of the story to the other, explaining the discrepancy between Chamber's epigraph and the form quoted above.

Chambers, *Beowulf: An Introduction to the Study of the Poem*, title page.
Joel Chandler Harris, *The Complete Tales of Uncle Remus*, ed. Richard Chase (Boston: Houghton Mifflin, 1955), 14–17.

407. **amid the tulgy wood of conjecture and the burbling of the jabberwocks,**
Tolkien develops the metaphor further in "*Beowulf*: The Monsters and the Critics." The poetic context of the quote from *Alice's Adventures in Wonderland* is:

> He took his vorpal sword in hand
> Long time the manxome foe he sought
> So rested he by the Tumtum tree
> And stood awhile in thought.

> And as in uffish thought he stood
> The Jabberwock, with eyes of flame,
> Came Whiffling through the tulgey wood,
> And burbled as it came!

Lewis Carroll, *The Complete Illustrated Works of Lewis Carroll*, ed. Edward Guiliano (New York: Avenel Books, 1982), 95–97.

408. Earle wrote for his translation, <u>The Deeds of Beowulf</u>, in 1892.
See above, note 42.

409. apart from his own private theory at the end, the political allegory to which I have already alluded, which only added one more tum-tum tree to the forest.
For Earle's private theory, see above, note 44. For the Jabberwockian tum-tum tree, see above, note 407.

410. the sketch by <u>Brandl</u> in <u>Paul's Grundriss</u>.
Alois Brandl (1855–1940) was a German philologist who studied English dialect forms as well as the history of English literature.

Grundriss der germanischen Philologie (Foundations of Germanic Philology), edited by Hermann Paul, is an enormous compendium of scholarship that includes a long and thorough survey of the scholarship on Old English literature.

Alois Brandl, "Englische Literatur," in *Grundriss der germanischen Philologie*, ed. Hermann Paul (Strassburg: Karl J. Trübner, 1901–1909), 980–1024.

411. the metrical work of that renowned scholar Sievers, appearing first in the 'eighties' and issuing in his <u>Altgermanische Metrik</u> 1893.
Eduard Sievers (1850–1932) did more than any other scholar to establish the foundations of a metrical theory for Old English poetry. His most noted accomplishment, and what may be one of the greatest triumphs of the philological method, was his prediction, based on comparative philological studies, that a section of the Anglo-Saxon poem *Genesis* (this section is now generally called *Genesis B*) was a West Saxon translation of a continental Old Saxon original. When part of a fragment of a Saxon poem on Genesis was subsequently discovered, Sievers' prediction was borne out: lines in the fragment corresponded to lines in *Genesis B* as Sievers had predicted they would.

Eduard Sievers, *Altgermanische Metrik* (Halle: Max Niemeyer, 1893).

There is a partial English translation:
Eduard Sievers, "Old Germanic Metrics and Old English Metrics," in *Essential Articles for the Study of Old English Poetry*, ed. Jess B. Bessinger Jr. and Stanley J. Kahrl, trans. Gawaina D. Luster (Hamden, CT: Archon Books, 1968), 267–88.

412. W. P. Ker's <u>Epic and Romance</u> (1896); and one of the principal services of this work was, as has been said, to assist in shattering "the belief that (in the

words he was fond of quoting) 'all epic poetry is written by A, B, and an Interpolator.'"
Ker expresses these sentiments in *Epic and Romance* on pages 145–47, but I cannot find the exact quote in the published version and wonder if the exact remark was made orally rather than written down.

Ker, *Epic and Romance*, 145–47.

Folio 134
413. **Odium prosodicum excels odium theologicum**
Literally: "The hatred of prosodists exceeds the hatred of theologians." A reference to the exceptionally nasty and personal nature of some academic arguments even when (or perhaps especially when) the stakes involved in the argument are not particularly large.

414. **for those with small experience of poetry itself, and none of its composition.**
Another reference to Tolkien's dual roles as scholar and author, roles which perhaps afforded him a different set of insights into the nature of the construction of *Beowulf* that were perhaps not available to other critics.

Folio 135
415. **Olrik.**
Axel Olrik (1864–1917) was a Danish scholar whose work undermined the *Liedertheorie* which was used to interpret *Beowulf* as a conglomeration of shorter poems. He saw *Beowulf* as an important part of Danish historical tradition (see Shippey and Haarder, *Beowulf: The Critical Heritage*, 63–65).

Axel Olrik, *Danmarks Heltedigtning: I. Rolf Krake og den ældre Skjoldungrække* (Kobenhavn: G. E. C. Gad, 1903).
Axel Olrik, *The Heroic Legends of Denmark*, trans. Lee M. Hollander (New York: American-Scandinavian Foundation, 1919).
Shippey and Haarder, *Beowulf: The Critical Heritage*.

416. **The 'folk-lorists' are also busy, and especially in Panzer's Studien zum germanischen Sagengeschichte (1910) a vast knowledge of "folk-tale' is brought to bear on Beowulf,**
Friedrich Panzer, *Beowulf* in *Studien zur Germanischen Sagengeschichte* 1 (München: C. H. Beck'sche Verlagsbuchhandlung Oskar Beck, 1910).

417. **"Beowulf's adventures with Grendel and Grendel's mother belonged rather to folk-lore than to mythology."**
Tolkien here quotes Chambers, who is summarizing Panzer:

Chambers, *Beowulf: An Introduction to the Study of the Poem*, 392.
Panzer, *Beowulf*.

418. **this story was actively mythopoetic, or even apprehended as a myth of nature, sun, the seasons and the sea, when the poem was written, if indeed it ever had any such significance.**
See above, note 107.

419. **primitive mythopoeia**
"Mythopoeia" is the making or perpetuation of myths. The word (and the idea) were important to Tolkien and to C. S. Lewis, both of whom felt that England needed more northern myths to replace or augment the southern (Greek and Latin mythological stories) that had grown stale or never truly taken hold on English soil.

Carpenter, *The Inklings*, 43, 138–39.
Carpenter, *J. R. R. Tolkien: A Biography*, 146–48, 168–71, 190–92.
Shippey, *Author of the Century*, 150, 180–81, 231–36, 256, 314–15.

420. **At the same time modern archaeology began to be important for Beowulf study also — especially in the many essays of Knut Stjerna, and in further studies by Swedish historians and archaeologists (such as Professor Birger Nerman).**
Knut Stjerna (1874–1909) was an archeologist and historian of early Swedish history.

Knut Stjerna, *Essays on Questions connected with the Old English Poem of 'Beowulf'*, trans. John R. Clark-Hall (Coventry: Viking Club Society for Northern Research, 1912).

Birger Nerman (1888 1971) was a Swedish archeologist and historian whose work has been used to investigate the potential relationship of the Geatas in *Beowulf* to the tribe of the Gautar in Sweden.

Birger Nerman, *Det Svenska Rikets Uppkomst* (Stockholm: Litografiska Anstalt, 1925).

421. **The views as to the amalgamation of epics from earlier lays, which had seemed axiomative to Lachmann and his pupil Müllenhoff, and the mytho-allegorical and allegorical assumptions which Müllenhoff had inherited from Kemble, had ceased to be believed.**
Verbatim quotation from:
Chambers, *Beowulf: An Introduction to the Study of the Poem*, 45–47.

For Lachmann and Müllenhoff, see above note 98.

Kemble discussed myth and allegory in *Beowulf* in the following article as well as in his editions:

John Mitchell Kemble, *Über die Stammtafel der Westsachsen* (München, 1836). This thirty-five page booklet is preparatory to much of his "Postscript to the Preface" in his revised edition of the poem.

Folio 135–136

422. **Even, for instance, in the Lawrence-Klaeber-Chambers combine, which Chambers himself, in his <u>Introduction</u> (2nd ed. pp. 392 ff.) sets forth, perhaps a shade too solemnly, as an almost undivided trinity.**
See above, note 105.

Folio 136

423. **an almost undivided trinity.**
This phrase may be a reference to Trinity College, Oxford, whose title is "of the Holy and Undivided Trinity."

424. **in the age of Bede — in the 'Anglian,' not the 'Saxon' parts of England.**
The Venerable Bede writes that three tribes, the Angles, Saxons, and Jutes, migrated to England. They settled different parts of the country. The Angles occupied East Anglia and Middle Anglia, Mercia and Northumbria. The Saxons occupied Essex (East-Seaxna), Wessex (West-Seaxna) and Sussex (South-Seaxna).

425. **W. P. Ker the revered master of Chambers. He would deserve reverence, of course, even if he had not <u>ellor gehworfen on Frean wære</u>, on the high mountain in Switzerland.**
For Ker, see above, note 6. Ker was Chambers's teacher. The Old English can be translated as "was turned elsewhere, to the Lord" and is a reference to line 55b in Beowulf: "fæder ellor hwearf" ("his father turned elsewhere"), a reference to the death of Scyld Scefing. But Tolkien is here incorrect in detail: Ker died while climbing Mt. Macugnaga in Italy (not Switzerland) on July 17, 1923.

Folios 137–138

426. **I will quote you a well-known passage from his <u>Dark Ages</u> (pp. 252–3): 'A reasonable view of the merit of <u>Beowulf</u> is not impossible, . . . <u>Yet with this radical defect, a disproportion that puts the irrelevances in the centre and the serious things on the outer edges, the poem of Beowulf is unmistakably heroic and weighty. The thing itself is cheap; the moral and the spirit of it can only be matched among the noblest authors</u>."**
The underlines are Tolkien's. Otherwise the quotation is verbatim from:
Ker, *Dark Ages*, 252–53.

Folio 139

427. 'correct and sober taste'

A reasonable view of the merit of <u>Beowulf</u> is not impossible, though rash enthusiasm may have made too much of it, while a correct and sober taste may have too contemptuously refused to attend to Grendel or the firedrake.

Ker, *Dark Ages*, 252–53.

428. **a little suggestive of some contraption or Brock-effect, for the astonishment of the simple.**
See above, note 137.

429. **"<u>The thing itself is cheap; the moral and the spirit of it can only be matched among the noblest authors.</u>"**
See above, note 147.

430. **Chambers in <u>Widsith</u> (p. 79), where he is studying the story of Ingeld son of Froda and his feud with the great Scylding house of Denmark, which is in <u>Beowulf</u> introduced merely as an allusion. "Nothing" he says "could better show ... a wilderness of dragons."**
See above, notes 138 and 139.

431. **Jusserand, who speaks contemptuously of 'one of these ever-recurring treasures.'**
See above, note 140.

Folios 139–140

432. **<u>Book of St. Albans</u>. Let the poet retort upon his critics from the same Book a '<u>pride of lions</u>, <u>a kindle of young</u> cats, <u>a raffle of knaves</u>, and a <u>gaggle of geese.</u>' It would be more pointed and more just to the critics. As for the poem, one dragon does not make a summer nor a host.**
See above, note 141; and note the play on the commonplace "one swallow does not a summer make," a quotation traditionally attributed to Aristotle.

Folio 140

433. **If we omit from consideration the vast and vague figure of the Encircler of the World (<u>Miðgarðsormr</u>), the doom of the Gods, we have but the dragon of the Volsungs (Fáfnir), and Beowulf's bane.**
See above, note 142.

434. **Indeed the allusion to the more renowned and ancient worm killed by the <u>Wælsing,</u>**
See above, notes 143 and 144.

435. But Chambers later repeats this same criticism; and even in the Foreword to Strong's translation we meet it still, though it is now toned down, and is no longer in Ker's actual words. There still, as we have seen, we are told that the folk-tale "<u>has been allowed</u> in <u>Beowulf</u> <u>to usurp the place of honour, and to drive into episodes and digressions the things which should be the main stuff of a well-conducted epic.</u>"
See above, note 145.

Folio 141

436. Milton had conducted a children's Bed-time Hour and told the story of Jack-and-the Beanstalk in excellent blank verse.
See above, note 146.

437. that remains 'thin and cheap' when he has finished with it; or that he should in the selection of his material, in the choice of what to put forward, what to keep subordinate "upon the outer edges,"
See above, note 147.

Folio 142

438. The sophisticated mind, or 'correct and sober taste,' may refuse to admit
See above, note 427.

439. how they seize on Byrhtwold's words in <u>Maldon</u>!
See above, note 149.

Folio 143

440. The heroic stories are in themselves essentially more valuable!
See above, note 150.

441. There is no disputing about tastes, it is said, foolishly; for we must or should dispute about them.
See above, note 151.

Folio 144

442. In any case Chambers is not, I think very happy in his particular choice. He gives battle on dubious ground. In so far as we can now grasp its detail and atmosphere the tale of Ingeld the twice faithless, the easily persuaded (and perhaps not too intelligent) is chiefly interesting as an episode in a longer theme
See above, note 152.

443. as part of a tradition, that had acquired legendary and dramatically per-

sonalized form, concerning moving events in history, the arising of Denmark
and the wars in the isles of the North.
See above, note 153.

Folios 144–145

444. **the conception nonetheless approaches <u>draconitas</u> rather than <u>draco</u>**
See above, note 159.

Folio 145

445. **the prince of the heroes of the North, supremely memorable, whose fame
æ <u>man</u> <u>uppi</u>, was the Wælsing or Völsung — Sigemund (O.E.), Sigurðr, Siegfried. And his most memorable deed, from which in Norse he derived his title
<u>Fáfnisbani</u>, was the killing of a dragon, of <u>the</u> dragon, the prince of legendary
worms.**
See above, note 143.

446. **he was wreccena wide mærost ofer werþeode**
This description is given of Sigemund after he kills the dragon and seizes its
treasure. (Tolkien changes the first word of the passage from "se" to "he.")

> Se wæs wreccena   wide mærost
> ofer werþeode,   wigendra hleo,
> ellendædum   — he þæs ær onðah —,
> siððan Heremodes   hild sweðrode,
> eafoð ond ellen.

> [he was the most famous, throughout the nations of men, of warriors-in-
> exile, protector of warriors, on account of his deeds — by which he pre-
> viously achieved greatness — after Heremod's aggressiveness, strength
> and valor, subsided.]

Beowulf, lines 898–902a
Klaeber, ed., *Beowulf and the Fight at Finnsburg*, 34.

Folio 147

447. **Eft ongan eldo gebunden gioguðe cwíðan. He wintrum fród worn gemunde**
[Afterwards it happened that the man bound with age lamented for his youth.
He, wise in winters, remembered much.]

This is a modified version of lines 2111–2114 of *Beowulf*:

> hwilum eft ongan   eldo gebunden,
> gomel guðwiga   gioguðe cwiðan,
> hildestrengo;   hreðer inne weoll,
> þonne he wintrum frod   worn gemunde.

[At times afterwards the one bound with age, the old battle-warrior, mourned for his youth, his battle strength; sorrow welled inside, when he, wise in winters, remembered much.]

Beowulf, lines 2111–2114
Klaeber, ed., *Beowulf and the Fight at Finnsburg*, 79.

448. Atol inwit gæst

Æfter ðam wordum   wyrm yrre cwom,
atol inwit gæst   oðre siðe
fyrwylmum fah   fionda niosian,
laðra manna.

[After those words the dragon came in anger, the terrible unwanted guest, decorated with flames, to attack his enemies, the hated men.]

Beowulf, lines 2669–2672a
Klaeber, ed., *Beowulf and the Fight at Finnsburg*, 100.

Folios 147–148

449. Once the worm-laid egg broke in the wood, ... That I may sleep, go when I will to drink!

See above, note 161.

Folio 149

450. as moving as a baited badger.

See above, note 162.

451. Chambers himself has made a <u>motor-bicycle</u> the symbol of the lay, and a <u>Rolls-Royce</u>

See above, note 163.

Folio 150

452. Byrhtwold at the battle of Maldon:

See above, note 149.

453. honourable <u>gnomē</u>

See above, note 165.

454. man at war with the infest world

See above, note 166.

Folio 151

455. So deadly and ineluctable is the theme that those who in the little circle of

light play only with the toys of wit and refinement, looking not to the battlements, either hear it not at all, or recoiling, shut their ears to it. Death comes
to the feast, and they say He gibbers.

See above, note 170.

456. **Cynewulf or the author of <u>Guthlac</u> had a great command of dignified verse.**
See above, note 168.

457. **which we are told is "the real beauty of <u>Beowulf</u>."**
But the great beauty, the real value, of <u>Beowulf</u> is in its dignity of style. In
construction it is curiously weak, in a sense preposterous; for while the
main story is simplicity itself, the merely commonplace of heroic legend,
all about it in the historic allusions there are revelations of a whole world
of tragedy, plots different in import from that of <u>Beowulf</u>, more like the
tragic themes of Iceland. Yet with this radical defect, a disproportion that
puts the irrelevances in the centre and the serious things on the outer
edges, the poem of Beowulf is unmistakably heroic and weighty. The thing
itself is cheap; the moral and the spirit of it can only be matched among
the noblest authors.

Ker, *Dark Ages*, 253.

Folio 152

458. **It has been said that there is mirth and music and gentle talk in <u>Beowulf</u>,
but 'the light is but a foil to the dark.'**
See above, note 169.

459. **They (says Jusserand, meaning the Anglo-Saxons who he seems to think
wrote Beowulf in committee over a surfeit of beer) fight against the monsters
of Scandinavian mythology and see in them the descendants of Cain.**
See above, note 130.

460. **To quote Sir Arthur Quiller-Couch**
Chambers quotes Arthur Quiller-Couch from a lecture entitled "On the Lineage
of English Literature." Quiller-Couch is arguing against Stopford Brooke's idea
that *Beowulf* is the first English epic:

Now I am not only incompetent to discuss with you the more recondite
beauties of *Beowulf* . . . on the whole I rather incline to accept the cautious
surmise of Professor W. P. Ker that 'a reasonable view of the merit of
Beowulf is not impossible, though rash enthusiasm may have made too
much of it; while a correct and sober taste may have too contemptuously
refused to attend to Grendel and the Firedrake' and to leave it at that . . .

Quiller-Couch then compares Hrothgar's lament over the death of Æschere with a passage from the twenty-fourth book of the *Iliad* and writes:

> Can you — can any one — compare the two passages and miss to see that they belong to two different kingdoms of poetry? I lay no stress here on 'architectonics.' I waive that the *Iliad* is a well-knit epic and the story of *Beowulf* a shapeless monstrosity. I ask you but to note the difference of note, of accent, or mere music. And I have quoted to you but a passage of the habitual Homer. To assure ourselves that he can rise even from this habitual height to express the extreme of majesty and of human anguish in poetry which betrays no false note, no strain upon the store of emotion man may own with self-respect and exhibit without derogation of dignity, turn to the last book of the *Iliad*, and read of Priam raising to his lips the hand that has murdered his son. I say confidently that no one unable to distinguish this, as poetry, from the very best of *Beowulf* is fit to engage upon business as a literary critic.

> . . . I am confident . . . that, venerable as Anglo-Saxon is, and worthy to be studied as the mother of our vernacular speech (as for a dozen other reasons which my friend Professor Chadwick will give you), its value is historical rather than literary, since from it our Literature is not descended. Let me repeat in words that admit of no misunderstanding — *From Anglo-Saxon Prose, from Anglo-Saxon Poetry, our living Prose and Poetry has, save linguistically, no derivation.* (emphasis in original).

Arthur Quiller-Couch, "On the Lineage of English Literature," in *Cambridge Lectures* (London: J. M. Dent and Sons, 1943), 21–25.

Folios 153–154

461. **A champion of <u>Beowulf</u> might reply ... Seventh-Century England <u>did</u> produce men of that type ...**
This long quotation is taken verbatim from:
Chambers, "Beowulf and the Heroic Age," vii–xxxii.

462. **Monstrum horrendum ...**

Vix ea fatus erat summo cum monte videmus
ipsum inter pecudes vasta se mole moventem
pastorem Polyphemum et litora nota petentem,
monstrum horrendum, informe, ingens, cui lumen ademptum.
trunca manum pinus regit et vestigia firmat;
lanigerae comitantur oves; ea sola voluptas;
solamenque mali ...

Aeneid, Book 3, lines 655–661

Virgil, *The Aeneid*, ed. J. W. Mackail (Oxford: Clarendon Press, 1930), 124.

He had no sooner spoken
Than we all saw, high on the mountainside,
The shepherd Polyphemus' giant mass
In motion with his flocks, advancing shoreward.
Vast, mind-sickening, lumpish, heaven's light
Blacked out for him, he held a pine tree staff
To feel his way with, and the woolly sheep
Were all his company and the ease
Of comfort that he had.

Virgil, *The Aeneid*, trans. Robert Fitzgerald (New York: Random House, 1983), 3.

463. **Beowulf's loyalty, when he refuses to take the throne at the expense of his young cousin Heardred**
After Hygelac's death his son Heardred succeeds to the throne of the Geats. Hygd, Hygelac's queen and Heardred's mother, offers the kingship to Beowulf because she fears that Heardred is not yet old or strong enough to rule the Geats. But Beowulf refuses the throne and instead offers his support to Heardred until the latter is killed as a result of the feud with Ongentheow and Onela. Only then does Beowulf assume the throne.

Beowulf, lines 2369–2396
Klaeber, ed., *Beowulf and the Fight at Finnsburg*, 89–90.

Folio 155
464. **'For all this may I have joy, though sick with deadly wounds, that the Ruler of men may not charge me with the slaughter of kinsfolk.'**
This is Tolkien's translation and condensation of Beowulf, lines 2739b–2743a. See above, note 237.

465. **Professor Earle quoted the words of Sir Ector de Maris over Lancelot dead as being 'like an expansion of these closing lines of the <u>Beowulf</u>':**
And now I dare say, said Sir Ector, thou, Sir Launcelot, there thou liest, that thou were never matched of earthly knight's hand; and thou were the courteoust knight that ever bore shield; and thou were the truest friend to thy lover that ever bestrad horse; and thou were the truest lover of a sinful man that ever loved woman; and thou were the kindest man that ever struck with sword; and thou were the goodliest person that ever came among press of knights; and thou were the meekest man and gentlest that ever ate in hall among ladies; and thou were the sternest knight to thy mortal foe that ever put spear in the rest.

Tolkien's quotation is verbatim from the William Caxton edition of Malory (which was the only edition available before 1934).

Le Morte D'Arthur, Book 21, Chapter 13.

Thomas Malory, *Le Morte D'Arthur* (New York: The Modern Library, 1999), 936–37.

Earle, *The Deeds of Beowulf*, xvi.

Folio 156

466. . . . **Agamemnon and Achilles and all the Achaeans into the sea more decisively than the Greek hexameter routs the alliterative line (though this is highly probable).**

Tolkien is here obliquely arguing that even if the hexameter of Homeric poetry is demonstrably superior to the alliterative line (a critical commonplace that Tolkien did not directly contest but clearly did not accept), the military and heroic superiority of the Anglo-Saxons over the ancient Greeks might be worth considering.

Folio 156–157

467. **Ker has said: 'What is distinctively Northern in the myth of the Twilight of the Gods ... carried to its noblest terms ...'**

The complete quotation is:

> What is distinctively Northern in the myth of the Twilight of the Gods is the strength of its theory of life. It is this intensity of courage that distinguishes the Northern mythology (and Icelandic literature generally) from all others. The last word of the Northmen before their entry into the larger world of Southern culture, their last independent guess at the secret of the Universe, is given in the Twilight of the Gods. As far as it goes, and as a working theory, it is absolutely impregnable. It is the assertion of the individual freedom against all the terrors and temptations of the world. It is absolute resistance, perfect because without hope. The Northern gods have an exultant extravagance in their warfare which makes them more like Titans than Olympians; only they are on the right side, *though it is not the side that wins. The winning side is Chaos and Unreason; but the gods, who are defeated, think that defeat no refutation.* The latest mythology of the North is an allegory of the Teutonic self-will, carried to its noblest terms, deified by the men for whom all religion was coming to be meaningless except "trust in one's own might and main" — the creed of Kjartan Olafsson and Sigmund Brestisson before they accepted Christianity.

> [Ker inserts footnotes to *Laxdæla Saga* after "Kjartan Olafsson" and to *Færeyinga Saga* after "Sigmund Brestisson."]

Ker, *Dark Ages*, 57–58.

Folio 158

468. **Take Ælfric, for instance; he is classed by Ker as belonging "to the Latin world, the common educational tradition." Yet his homilies are written in Anglo-Saxon, in a prose "which is English in rhythm and founded on the model of Teutonic verse,"**

> The poetical prose of Ælfric, which is English in its rhythm and founded upon the model of Teutonic verse, is also greatly under the influence of the ornamented and rhythmical Latin prose: without that example it might not have occurred to an Englishman to beautify his sermons in that particular manner.

Ker, *Dark Ages*, 36.

> (cf. J. Hill, "Translating the Tradition: Manuscripts, Models, and Methodologies in the Composition of Ælfric's 'Catholic Homilies'," *Bulletin of the John Rylands University Library* 79 [1997]: 43–65.)

469. **It has a kinship with Cynewulf, <u>St. Guthlac</u>, Ælfric, even with mediæval homilies, no less than with the lays of the gods and heroes of the North preserved in Icelandic.**
See above, note 172.

470. **And even the bogies of Ælfric, the Sigelhearwan, with fiery eyes, that are regarded as devils, and yet equated with Ethiopians, have a purely native name and derive in one line from native northern 'folk-tale,' and are distant relatives of Grendel.**
See above, note 211.

471. **The earlier age was not less learned than the days of Eadgar and Æthelred II, but more learned and certainly not less two-sided.**
Eadgar (944–975) and Æthelred II (968–1016) ruled England during the revival of literature and culture in the tenth century that is known as the Benedictine Reform. During the Benedictine Reform the majority of the manuscripts containing Anglo-Saxon literature were, at the very least, copied (if not actually written). Tolkien is arguing that the previous flowering of Anglo-Saxon culture in the eighth century was even more "learned" and more open to understanding the non-Christian elements than were the Benedictine Reformers, who had to struggle to rebuild institutions damaged by the Viking invasions and political strife of the ninth and early tenth centuries.

472. **Not all the learning was in 'Book-Latin,' nor all the love of the learned for what was written in the new letters.**
See above, note 173.

473. within Christendom there was the <u>Angolcyn,</u> converted, yet nonetheless of the North, with its own language, its own laws, its own history, and its own poetry.
See above, note 174.

474. And these were not beneath the study of the early scholars, such as Aldhelm, whom Ælfred considered the best of the vernacular poets (though his vernacular verse is lost); and they were still loved no less by Ælfred the revivalist
See above, note 175.

Folio 159

475. Virgil, Statius, and Lucan are cited among the books studied in the school of York by Alcuin in his poem on the church of York
See above, note 178.

476. It has been held that the influence, if no more than the exciting of emulation, of the classical Latin epic, is perceptible in <u>Beowulf</u>, and a necessary part of the explanation of the development of the long poem in England in the eighth century.

There is too much education in *Beowulf*, and it may be that the larger kind of heroic poem was attained in England only through the example of Latin narrative. The English epic is possibly due to Virgil and Statius; possibly to Juvencus and other Christian poets, to the authors studied by Aldhelm and Bede. It may be that the *Hildebrand* for the Western Germanic group, that the *Atlamál* for the North, fixes the limit of epic size in the old Teutonic school; that it was difficult or impossible to get beyond this without the encouragement of Latin poets, showing how to amplify and embroider, to compose orations for combatants, and to discriminate the particulars of their wounds.

Ker, *Dark Ages*, 251–52.

477. He is not a half-Christian because he describes heroic sea-burial, or the blazing pyre!
See above, note 180.

Folio 160

478. This is specifically recorded even of <u>Hroðgar</u> and his Danes in the famous passage 175 ff.: <u>Hwílum hie gehéton æt hærgtrafum wígweorþunga</u> (of which more later).
See above, note 238.

479. such as are found heedlessly in <u>Judith,</u> for instance
See above, note 181.

480. references to Woden and Þunor
See above, note 182.

481. The last heathen kingdom, Sussex, had only been converted in 681–6
See above, note 183.

Folio 161
482. Bede's story of Coifi and the sparrow
See above, note 184.

483. In the Gnomic Verses of the Exeter Book we are told that <u>Wóden worht wéos, wuldor Alwalda, rume roderas: þæt is ríce God.</u>
[Woden wrought idols, the All-Ruler the world, the wide heavens; that is the kingdom of God.]

Maxims I, lines 132–133
Krapp and Dobbie, eds., *The Exeter Book*, 153–56.

Folio 162
484. The special conditions in Iceland, and the very special nature of the fragments of Norse mythology, must not be allowed to confuse the judgement of this matter.
Because the Icelandic materials make up almost all of what we possess of Norse mythology, it is easy, Tolkien argues, to view Norse paganism as easily accommodating, with gods who are more characters and types than deities. This false sense of the original pagan religion, however, is due more to the preservation of the mythological materials in the post-conversion work of Snorri Sturlson. Real Norse pagans were probably far more fierce in the practice of their religion and their intolerance for Christianity.

485. The Óðinn and Þórr of Snorri in the early 13th century, are nearly as remote from Wóden and Þunor or Ing as divine beings, and the persons of cult and temple-worship, as Jupiter and Apollo in Ovid are from Greek <u>religion</u> in the days of the long-haired Achaeans.
See above, note 189.

Folios 162–163
486. St. Paulinus of Nola (born at Bordeaux), in the fifth century, had cried that "Hearts vowed to Christ have no welcome for the goddesses of song; they are barred to Apollo."
See above, note 186.

Folio 163

487. Sulpicius Severus in the preface to his life of St. Martin asks: "What good will it do posterity to study the philosophy of Socrates or to read the battles of Hector?"

See above, note 187.

488. The missions to Frisia were English not Frankish — partly because of the interference of politics, and the intense hatred of Frisians, in their struggle for independence, of the Frankish realm. The missions were begun by Wilfrid in 679 and again by Wihtberht in 689, soon after Radbod's succession. Wulfram died in 695, and there is no evidence, outside the late Vita Sancti Wulframni, that he ever visited Frisia. Radbod died in 719.

See above, note 188.

489. ... Frank St. Wulfram of Sens. King Radbod of Frisia, the successor of Aldgísl who had harboured the English St. Wilfrid, was a fierce enemy of Christians and Franks, and the last defender both of Frisian heathendom and Frisian independence. The story tells that once he approached the baptismal font, but stopped on the way to ask Wulfram whether, if he were baptized, he might hope to meet in heaven his Frisian ancestors. 'Do not deceive thyself' was the reply; 'it is certain that they have received the just sentence of damnation.' Radbod therefore withdrew from the font, and said that he preferred to join his own people wherever they might be, rather than sit down in the Kingdom of Heaven with a handful of beggars. He remained heathen to his death in 719.

See above, notes 190, 192, 183, 194, 195.

Folio 164

490. ... Alcuin, we have recorded a saying that sounds similar. In a letter to Speratus, bishop of Lindisfarne, of A.D. 797 we read: Verba Dei legantur in sacerdotali convivio; ibi decet lectorem audiri, non citharistam, sermones patrum, non carmina gentilium. Quid Hinieldus cum Christo? Angusta est domus; utrosque tenere non poterit — the King of Heaven must not be mentioned with pagan kings who are lamenting in hell.

See above, note 197.

491. The reference to Ingeld is not, however, in the received text of the letter (see Chambers note to Widsith p. 78) and may possibly therefore not derive actually from Alcuin, though the name Hinieldus seems to show that it is of English origin.

See above, note 197.

492. such fairy-story matter as we find in Gylfaginning

The mythological section of Snorri Sturlson's *Edda*, the *Gylfaginning* ("The

Deluding of Gylfi") is the source for much of what we know of Northern mythology. But Snorri was a Christian, so he describes the Æsir, the Norse gods, as historical figures who convince the world that they are gods (rather than being actual gods). Thus, since Snorri does not even pretend to believe in its historicity or even mythological accuracy, *Gylfaginning* takes on more the feel of a fairy-tale than a true creation myth.

Snorri Sturlson, *Edda*, trans. Jónsson, 8–77.
Snorri Sturlson, *The Prose Edda*, trans. Young, 29–93.

Folio 165

493. **were they not wholly ousted by Moses or the Israelite warriors, or by St. Matthew and St. Andrew**
See above, note 198.

494. **A point especially to note in Chambers' words is this: "the Cyclops is himself god-begotten, and under divine protection, and the fact that Odysseus has maimed him is a wrong Poseidon is slow to forgive."**
Take for example the tale of Odysseus and the Cyclops — the No-Man trick. Odysseus is struggling with a monstrous and wicked foe, but he is not exactly thought of as struggling with the powers of darkness. Polyphemus, by devouring his guests, acts in a way which is hateful to Zeus and the other Gods: yet the Cyclops is himself god-begotten and under divine protection, and the fact that Odysseus has maimed him is a wrong which Poseidon is slow to forgive.

Chambers, "Beowulf and the Heroic Age," xxviii.

495. **may allow the ogre in certain cases to triumph. 'per sidera testor ... Of dampening his haunches.**
The Latin is from:
Virgil, *The Aeneid*, Book III, lines 600–665
Virgil, *The Aeneid*, ed. Mackail, 122–125.

The translation is taken from:
Virgil, *The Aeneid*, trans. Fitzgerald, 87–89.

496. **But of Grendel it is said Godes yrre bær.**
Ða com of more   under misthleoþum
Grendel gongan,   Godes yrre bær.

[Then came from the moor, under the misty cliffs, Grendel going: he bore God's ire.]

Tolkien's point is that we are told specifically in Beowulf that Grendel is the enemy of God. We do not hear the same judgment made of the Cyclops or other monsters in the Greek and Latin epics.

Beowulf, lines 710–711

Klaeber, ed., *Beowulf and the Fight at Finnsburg*, 27.

Folios 166–167

497. **In Norse at any rate the gods are enmeshed within time; they are doomed to the agony of death — though (probably by a late addition) a rebirth glimmers faintly far ahead for some of them.**

See above, note 200.

498. **Already before euhemerism saved them by embalming them, and they dwindled in learned antiquarian fantasy to the mighty ancestors of northern kings**

See above, note 201.

Folio 167

499. **When Baldr is slain and goes to Hel, he cannot escape thence any more than mortal man.**

See above, note 203.

500. **Loki is among the gods, it is true, an evil and a lying and clever spirit, of whom many monsters come.**

See above, note 204.

501. **But the gods of Ásgarðr do not recognize kinship with Fenris Wolf anymore than men with the Dragon.**

See above, notes 204, 205, and 206. Tolkien's point is that although the Fenris Wolf is the offspring of Loki, a putative god, the gods obviously do not consider it as being part of their kin, since they chain it in a remote place.

502. **giants of northern myth, the ever-watchful foes of Ásgarðr. The undoubted mention of Cain connects him with eotenas and ylfe, the jötnar and álfar of Norse mythology**

See above, note 207.

503. **Thus through the passages in Beowulf concerning the giants and their war with God (1689–93 and 113–114)**

Hroðgar maðelode —   hylt sceawode,
ealde lafe,   on ðæm wæs or writen
fyrngewinnes,   syðþan flod ofsloh,
gifen geotende   giganta cyn,

frecne geferdon;   þæt wæs fremde þeod
ecean Dryhtne;   him þæs endelean
þurh wæteres wylm   Waldend sealde.

[Hrothgar spoke, showed this hilt, the old heirloom, on which was in-
scribed with a point the story of ancient strife, after the flood, the flowing
of the ocean, overcame and killed the kin of the giants — they had acted
wrongly. That was a people foreign to the eternal Lord. To them this final
reward, through the welling of the waters, the Ruler gave.]

Beowulf, lines 1687–1693
Klaeber, ed., *Beowulf and the Fight at Finnsburg*, 63.

                    Fifelcynnes eard
wonsæli wer   weardode hwile,
siþðan him Scyppend   forscrifen hæfde
in Caines cynne —   þone cwealm gewræc
ece Dryhten,   þæs þe he Abel slog;
ne gefeah he þære fæhðe,   ac he hine feor forwræc,
Metod for þy mane   mancynne fram.
Þanon untydras   ealle onwocon,
eotenas ond ylfe   ond orcneas,
swylce gigantas,   þa wið Gode wunnon
lange þrage;   he him ðæs lean forgeald.

[The unhappy creature dwelled for a long while in the land of monster-
kin since the Creator had condemned him as part of the kin of Cain — the
eternal Lord punished that killing because he slew Abel. Nor was there rejoicing in that feud, but they were banished far from mankind by the Lord
on account of that crime. From them all awoke the evil brood, the ettens
and elves and evil spirits, likewise the giants, who fought against God for
a long time. For that he completely repaid them.]

Beowulf, lines 104b–114
Klaeber, ed., *Beowulf and the Fight at Finnsburg*, 5.

Folio 168
504. **the devils blended into the monsters and took visible shape in the hideous
bodies of the þyrsas and sigelhearwan of heathen imagination.**
        See above, notes 209 and 211.

Folio 169
505. **þyrs**
        See above, note 209.

506. **The 'mediaeval' is fully developed already in later Old English. There is nothing but the older language and the metre to distinguish Cynewulf's <u>Juliana</u> from the thirteenth century homily <u>Juliene</u> of MS. Bodley 34 (which is probably lineally connected with Cynewulf). The devils that tempt and physically torment <u>St. Guthlac</u> cannot be distinguished save perhaps by the odd fact that they speak Welsh) from the mediæval assailants of Saints.**

Juliana is one of the poems "signed" by Cynewulf with a runic signature in the text. The homily *Juliene* is found in the Oxford, Bodleian Library manuscript Bodley 34. It is written in Middle English and is one of the "Katherine Group" texts that Tolkien discusses in "*Ancrene Wisse* and *Hali Meiðhad*." Tolkien's claim that *Juliene* is directly discended from the Cynewulfian poem is controversial.

Juliana.

Krapp and Dobbie, eds. *The Exeter Book*, 113–33.

For the devils and St Guthlac, see above, notes 168, 210.

Folio 170

507. **Beowulf's <u>byrne</u> was made by Wéland, and the iron shield he bore against the dragon was made by his own smiths: it was not the breastplate of righteousness, nor the shield of faith for the quenching of all the fiery darts of the wicked.**

Beowulf says that his corselet, an heirloom of Hrethel, is "Welandes geweorc."

Beowulf, line 455

Klaeber, ed., *Beowulf and the Fight at Finnsburg*, 17–18.

The second part of the quotation is a reference to Ephesians 6:13–17 from the King James Bible (though as a Roman Catholic, Tolkien would also have dealt with the Donai-Rheims Version).

> Wherefore take unto you the whole armour of God, that ye may be able to withstand in the evil day, and having done all, to stand. Stand therefore, having your loins girt about with truth, and having on the breastplate of righteousness; And your feet shod with the preparation of the gospel of peace; Above all, taking the shield of faith, wherewith ye shall be able to quench all the fiery darts of the wicked. And take the helmet of salvation, and the sword of the Spirit, which is the word of God.

508. **Virgil: multa putans sortemque animo miseratus iniquam (pondering on so much, and stood in pity for the souls' inequitable fates)**

The context of the quotation is Æneas' seeing the dead in Hades, where they are unable to find rest. Tolkien finds Æneas' same sadness in the *Beowulf* poet, who looks back on the condemned (because they were not Christian) souls of his ancestors.

Virgil, *Aeneid*, Book 6, line 332
Virgil, *The Aeneid*, ed. Mackail, 226.
Virgil, *The Aeneid*, trans. Fitzgerald, 171.

509. **Eschatology**
See above, note 214.

510. **antiquarians such as Snorri Sturlson**
See above, note 189.

511. **nearly as far from real paganism as Jove and Mars in our eighteenth century.**
See above, note 215.

Folio 171
512. **So was it explicitly said of men of might in the last days of Icelandic heathendom that their creed was simply <u>ek trúi á mátt ok megin</u>.**
See above, note 219.

Folio 172
513. **Earle long ago pointed out the prominence of <u>lof</u> in Beowulf**
See above, note 221.

514. **At the beginning of the poem, at the end of the first "strophe" of the exordium there occurs as a <u>leitmotif: lofdædum sceal in mægþa gehwam man geþeon</u>. The last word of the poem is <u>lofgeornost,</u>**
See above, note 222.

515. **To make an Anglo-Saxon pun, this is <u>lást worda betst</u>**
See above, note 223.

516. **For Beowulf had lived according to his own philosophy, which he explicitly avowed (1386ff): <u>úre æghwylc sceal ende gebídan worolde lífes. Wyrce se ðe móte dómes ær déaþe: þæt bið dryhtguman æfter sélest.</u>**
See above, note 224.

517. **The poet himself as commentator recurs again to this in 1534: <u>swá sceal man don, þonne he æt guðe gegan þenceð longsumne lof: na ymb his líf cearað.</u>**
See above, note 225.

518. **<u>Lof</u> is ultimately (and etymologically) 'value' or 'valuation' — praise as we**

say (itself derived from <u>pretium</u>
"Pretium" is the Latin word for "price," "value," or "reward."

519. <u>Seafarer</u> from lines 66 to 80 with Hroðgar's <u>giedd</u> or sermon in <u>Beowulf</u>,
from 1735 onwards.
For *Seafarer*, see above, note 223; for Hrothgar's sermon, see above, 227.

520. **C.f. the end of <u>Widsith</u> which refers to the minstrel's part in achieving for
the noble and their deeds the prolonged life of fame. It is said of the noble
patron: <u>lof se gewyrceð, hafað under heofonum heahfæstne dom</u>**
See above, note 226.

Folio 173

521. **The Seafarer says: ic gelýfe nó ... feorh oðþringeð. [I believe not that the
joys of earth will abide everlasting. Ever and in all cases will one of three
things trouble his heart before the appointed day: sickness, or age, or the foeman's sword from the doomed men hastening hence will his life ravish.]**
The translation is Tolkien's of lines 66b–71 of the *Seafarer*. Tolkien emends the
manuscript readingof "tid aga" in line 69a to "tid-dæge."

For the passage in *Seafarer*, see above, note 223.

522. **Hroðgar says to Beowulf: eft sóna bið ... Swiftly will it come that thee, o
knight, shall death conquer.].**
The translation is Tolkien's, of lines 1762a–1768 of *Beowulf*.

Beowulf, lines 1762a–1768
Klaeber, ed., *Beowulf and the Fight at Finnsburg*, 66.

523. **Somewhat expanding the <u>þreora sum</u> are lines found elsewhere either in
great elaboration as in the <u>Fates of Men</u> or in briefer allusion to the well recognized theme as in <u>Wanderer</u> 80ff.**
The poem that Tolkien refers to as the *Fates of Men* is also known as the *Fortunes
of Men*. It lists a variety of outcomes for human lives.

The Fortunes of Men.
Krapp and Dobbie, *The Exeter Book*, 154–56.

Sume wig fornom,
ferede in forðwege,   sumne fugel oþbær
ofer heanne holm,   sumne se hara wulf
deaðe gedælde,   sumne dreorighleor
in eorðscræfe   eorl gehydde.

[One is taken by war, he goes forth on the journey. One the bird carries

off, over the high waves. One the hoary wolf rends to death. One, sad-
minded, is hidden, the eorl in the earth-scrape.]

The Wanderer, lines 80b–84
Krapp and Dobbie, *The Exeter Book*, 136.

Folio 174

524. **the sense of the ambiguous <u>feonda</u> is in the surviving poem made clear to
be <u>deofle togeanes</u>; secondly in enlarging the <u>lof</u> to include the angels and the
future life. <u>Lofsong</u>; <u>loftsong</u> are in Middle English specially used of the heavenly choirs.**
For the quotation, see above, notes 218, 221.
Tolkien is here arguing that the "feonda" ("enemies") in line 75b, which
conceivably refers to worldly enemies, is clarified by "deofle togeanes" ("against
the devil") in 76b. "Lof" ("praise") here includes not only the praise of noble
peers, but the reward of the angels in heaven. In fact Tolkien understates the
case for the religious connotations of "lofsong" ("praise song"). In the two hundred and forty-four appearances of "lofsong" and its various inflected forms in
the corpus of Anglo-Saxon prose and poetic texts the word is not used in anything resembling a secular, heroic, or elegiac context: "lofsong" is always religious in character, quite often used to gloss the Latin hymn "te deum laudamus"
("we praise you, God"). For further discussion see Drout, "Imitating Fathers,"
167–70.

Michael D. C. Drout, "Imitating Fathers: Tradition, Inheritance and the Reproduction of Culture in Anglo-Saxon England," Ph. D. diss., Loyola University
Chicago, 1997.

525. **these expressions are rather parallels to others describing His general governance of nature (e.g. 1609 ff.), and His realm which includes land, sea, and
sky, even if heofon is already regarded as his especial seat and the sun as His
candle. We may have simply lack of differentiation between symbol and state.
But in the pagan North the sky was not a symbol of the opposite of Hell —
which had originally been the place of <u>all</u> departed (so Baldr).**
See above, notes 223, 233, and 203.

Folio 175

526. **<u>Judith</u> to the death of Holofernes, which recalls remarkably certain features
of Hel in <u>Völuspá</u>. Cf. <u>Judith</u> 115 <u>wyrmum bewunden</u> and 119 <u>of ðam wyrm-
sele</u> with <u>Völuspá</u> 36 <u>sá er undinn salr orm a hryggjum</u> (which would translated into Old English be <u>se is wunden sele wyrma hrycgum</u>).**
See above, note 234.

527. his <u>dom</u> shall live <u>awa to ealdre,</u> a fortune also in heathen Norse bestowed
on Sigurðr (that his name <u>æ mun uppi</u>).
See above, note 231.

Folio 176

528. **What the precise theology concerning the subject of the just heathen was is
now perhaps not important**
The fate of the soul of the "just heathen" was a significant problem for Christianity in early England. The Church had to maintain the contradictory goals of
requiring baptism and true conversion for salvation while at the same time not
offending the sensibilities of new or potential converts who might wonder why
their good and kind and just ancestors would be consigned to hell by a just and
righteous God. Dante attempts to solve this very same problem by putting the
"virtuous pagans" in the first circle of hell — they are not tormented, but they
cannot enter into heaven since they were never baptized.

529. **<u>Wigláf</u>**
Wigláf is the only one of Beowulf's companions who does not desert him during
the fight with the dragon. Wigláf stabs the dragon in the belly, enabling Beowulf
to finish it off. Beowulf bequeaths to Wigláf his armor, but the kingship does not
appear to pass to the young warrior.

Folio 177

530. **The kind of thing that 'accident' achieves is illustrated by <u>drihten wereda</u>
'lord of hosts,' a familiar Christian expression, which is plainly an alteration,
probably casual, of <u>drihten Wedera</u> 'Lord of the Geats' in line 2186.**
See above, note 239.

531. **<u>Dominus Deus Sabaoth</u> than with <u>Hreðel</u> and <u>Weder-Geatish</u> house.**
"Dominus Deus Sabaoth" means "Lord God of Hosts." Tolkien is suggesting
that the scribe who copied the *Beowulf* manuscript, almost certainly a Christian
monk, would have been more familiar with the "Lord of Hosts" (a commonplace
of Christian prayer) than with the "Lord of the Weder-Geats," and would have
thus mis-copied "wereda" from the presumed "wedera" in his exemplar.

Folio 178

532. **Thus Cynewulf - Elena: huru wyrd gescreaf.**
　　　　　Huru, wyrd gescreaf
þæt he swa geleaffull   ond swa leof gode
in worldrice   weorðan sceolde,
Criste gecweme.

[Indeed, fate declared that he should become so full of belief and so loved
by God in the kingdom of the world, so pleasing to Christ.]

Elene, lines 1046b–1049a
Krapp and Dobbie, eds., *The Vercelli Book*, 95.

Folio 179

533. **(there is probably nearly one hundred years between Cædmon and <u>Beowulf</u>)**
For Cædmon, see above, note 278. According to the Venerable Bede, Cædmon
composed his first poem in 680. Tolkien believed *Beowulf* to have been composed around 750.

Colgrave and Mynors, eds., *Bede's Ecclesiastical History of the English People*, 414–
20.

534. **not only the old heroic language occasionally misused in application to
Christian legend (as in <u>Andreas</u> or <u>Elene</u>),**
See above, notes 198 and 285.

Folio 180

535. **We observe in <u>godes leoht geceas</u> an instance of this. All is not perfect in
<u>Beowulf</u>. In the very long speech of Beowulf from 2425–2525 the poet has
hardly attempted to keep up the pretense of <u>oratio recta</u> throughout. Just before the end he reminds us and himself that Beowulf is supposed to be speaking with a renewed <u>Beowulf maðelode</u> (2510). From 2446–2489 it is hardly a
monologue in character at all.**
For the first quotation see above, note 253.

Tolkien is here pointing out that the poet's statement that Hrethel at his
death "chose the light of God" is inappropriate, since Hrethel is supposed to be
a pagan character. In the "very long speech" of Beowulf (lines 2425–2525) the
hero ostensibly tells about his youth in the court of Hrethel, of the battles of
revenge with the Swedes and Franks, and how Beowulf carried out his duties as
a retainer of the Geatish court. Tolkien is correct in noting that the narration
could just as easily be by the poet directly as by the character Beowulf: we get
none of the interior thoughts of Beowulf or any explanation of his reactions to
the events he narrates.

536. **<u>Völuspá</u>, where the grim hall <u>Náströnduá</u> contains especially <u>menn meinsvara ok morðvarga</u> (perjurers and murderers).**
See above, notes 172 and 261.

537. **Thus 669: <u>georne truwode modgan mægnes, metodes hyldo.</u> No <u>and</u> is
possible metrically in the original, none should appear in translation.**
See above, note 243.

Folio 181

538. **Fóstbraeðra saga where it is said in describing a grim pagan character: ekki var hjarta hans sem fóarn í fugli, ekki var þat blóð ult, svá af þat skylfi at hræðslu, heldr var þat hert af enum hæsta höfuðsmið í öllum hvatleik (ch 2)**
Fóstbræðra Saga, chapter 2.
Konrad Gislason, ed., *Fóstbræðra Saga* (Kjöbenhavn: Berlingske bogtrykkeri, 1852), 8.

For his heart was not like the crop of a bird, nor was it so full of blood that it shook with fear. It had been hardened in the Almighty Maker's forge to dare anything

Viðar Hreinsson, ed., "The Saga of the Sworn Brothers," in *The Complete Sagas of Icelanders* (Reykjavík: Leif Eiríksson Publishing, 1997), 2: 333.

Ker also quotes this description of Thorgeir from *Fóstbræðra Saga*.
Ker, *Epic and Romance*, 275 n. 1.

539. **and again Almáttigr er sá sem svá snart hjarta ok óhrætt lét í brjóst orgeiri: ok ekki var hans hugþryði af mönnum ger né honum í brjóst borin, heldr af enum hæsta höfuðsmið (ib.)**
Fóstbræðra Saga, chapter 16.
Gislason, ed., *Fóstbræðra Saga*, 56.

It was the Almighty who touched Thorgeir's heart and put such fearlessness into his breast, and thus his courage was neither inborn nor of humankind but came from the creator on high.

Hreinsson, ed., "The Saga of the Sworn Brothers," 368.

540. **It has been said (Klaeber note to 2330) that ofer ealde riht, 'contrary to ancient law' is here given a Christian interpretation; but this would not seem to be so.**
See above, notes 237 and 277.

541. **the Cædmon tradition, and among this especially Genesis.**
See above, note 278.

Folio 182

542. **The Völuspá describes Chaos and creation of sun and moon,**
Ár var alda,
þats ekki var,
vara sandr né sær
né svalr unnir;
jörð fannsk æva

né upphiminn,
gap var Ginnunga,
en gras hvergi.

Áðr Burs synir
bjöðum of yppðu
þeir er Miðgarð
mæran skópu;
sól skein sunnan
á salr steina,
þá var grun gróin
groenum lauki.

Sól varp sunnan
sinni mána,
hendi inni hoegri
um himin-jöður;
sól þat né vissi,
hvat hann megins átti,
stjörnur þat né vissu,
hvar þær staði áttu.

Völuspá, 3–5.
Nordal, ed., *Völuspá*, 117–18.

In earliest times   did Ymir live:
was not the sea nor land   nor salty waves,
neither earth was there   nor upper heaven,
but a gaping nothing,   and green things nowhere.

Was the land then lifted   aloft by Bur's sons
who made Mithgarth,   the matchless earth;
shone from the south   the sun on dry land,
on the ground then grew   the greensward soft.

From south the sun,   by the side of the moon,
heaved his right hand   over heaven's rim;
the sun knew not   what seat he had,
the stars knew not   what stead they held,
the moon knew not   what might she had.

Hollander, ed., *The Poetic Edda*, 2–3.

543. **and extremely similar language appears in the Old High German fragment**
(Wessobrunner Gebet).

Wessobrunner Gebet (*Wessobrunn Prayer*) is an Old High German poem written in a Bavarian dialect. It was found in or near the monastery of Wessobrunn in a manuscript of the later eighth to early ninth century. There are nine lines of alliterative poetry followed by a prayer in prose. Scholars believe the poem shows evidence of some Anglo-Saxon influence (Bostock, *Handbook*, 114–20; rev. ed., 126–35). Tolkien is referring to the poetry.

Dat gafregin ih mit firahim   firiuuizzo meista,
Dat ero ni uuas   noh ufhimil,
noh paum <...>   noh pereg ni uuas,
ni <...> nohheinig   noh sunna ni scein,
noh mano ni liuhta,   noh der mareo seo.
Do dar niuuiht ni uuas   enteo ni uuento,
enti do uuas der eino   almahtico cot,
manno miltisto,   enti dar uuarum auh manake mit inan
cootlihhe geista.   Enti cot heilac <...>

Wilhelm Braune, ed., rev. Ernst A. Ebbinghaus, *Althochdeutsches Lesebuch*, 14th ed. (Tubingen: M. Niemeyer, 1969), 85–86.

I have heard tell among men of marvels the greatest,
that earth once was not, nor the heaven above,
nor tree ... nor hill was,
not .... none, nor sun nor stone,
nor did the moon shine, nor the great (or "the shining") sea.
Then there was nought, neither space nor time (?),
and there was the one almighty God,
the most merciful of men, and there were also with him many
good spirits. And God the Holy ...

John Knight Bostock, *A Handbook on Old High German Literature* (Oxford: Clarendon Press, 1955), 117, notes 1 and 2; rev. ed. (Oxford: Clarendon Press, 1976), 129; also 127, 130 on Anglo-Saxon influence.

Ker compares *Das Wessobrunner Gebet* (The Wessobrunn Prayer) to the opening lines of Völuspá.
Ker, *Dark Ages*, 240.

544. **The song of the minstrel in the first Æneid is also in part a song of origins.**
    Cithara crinitus Iopas
  personat aurata, docuit quem maximus Atlas.
  hic canit errantem lunam solisque labores,
  under hominum genus et pecudes, unde imber et ignes,
  Arcturum pluviasque Hyades geminosque Triones;
  quid tantum Oceano properent se tingere soles
  hiberni, vel quae tardis mora noctibus obstet.

Virgil, *The Aeneid*, Book 1, lines 740–746
Virgil, *The Aeneid*, ed. Mackail, 44–45.

> And Lord Iopas,
> With flowing hair, whom giant Atlas taught,
> Made the room to echo to his golden lyre.
> He sang the straying moon and toiling sun,
> The origin of mankind and the beasts,
> Of rain and fire; the rainy Hyadës,
> Arcturus, the Great Bear and Little Bear;
> The reason winter suns are in such haste
> To dip in Ocean, or what holds the nights
> Endless in winter.

Virgil, *The Aeneid*, trans. Fitzgerald, 30.

545. **Saturni gentem haud vinclo nec legibus aequam, sponte sua, verterisque dei se more tenentem (Virgil VII 202 ff)**

> neve ignorate Latinos
> Saturni gentem haud vinclo nec legibus aequam,
> sponte sua, veterisque dei se more tenentem.

Virgil, *The Aeneid*, Book 7, lines 201–203
Virgil, *The Aeneid*, ed. Mackail, 267.

> Know that our Latins
> Come of Saturn's race, that we are just —
> Not by constraint or laws, but by our choice
> And habit of our ancient god.

Virgil, *The Aeneid*, trans. Fitzgerald, 202.

546. **From 175 to <u>helle gemundon in modsefan</u> (which is strikingly true). 180 we can confidently accept as original. . . . 180–188 is unlike the rest of the poem in style and verse or rhythm, it becomes a more than probable certainty that we have here an instance of later interference with the poet's plan and purpose.**

Tolkien is arguing that it makes very little sense for the poet to have had the minstrel in Heorot sing a song praising God's creation of the world and then, only 90 lines later, say that the Danes did not know God. But if a later interpolator added lines 175–188 to more fully explain what the Danes had done in response to the scourge of Grendel, then the minor discrepancy can be explained. Tolkien works through this argument in greater detail in the appendix to "*Beowulf:* The Monsters and the Critics."

þær wæs hearpan sweg,
swutol sang scopes.   Sægde se þe cuþe
frumsceaft fira   feorran reccan,
cwæð þæt se Ælmihtiga   eorðan worhte,

[There was the song of the harp, the clear singing of the minstrel. He who knew how to tell about the creation of men from afar, said how the Almighty wrought the earth.]

Beowulf, lines 89b–92
Klaeber, ed., *Beowulf and the Fight at Finnsburg*, 7–8.

For lines 175–188, see above, note 238.

547. **Similarly it is the very marked character already by the poet given to Hroð-gar which has made possible the probable revision and expansion of the giedd without serious damage — though, well done as the passage is in itself, the poem would be better with the excision of 1724 wundor is to secgan to 1760 éce rædas, which are on independent grounds (that I do not here go into) under very strong suspicion as a later addition.**
For the passage, see above, note 224.

The lines Tolkien points out as being "under suspicion" are in fact awkward in syntax and do not seem to fit well into the rest of the passage.

Folio 184

548. **Æneid — especially felt as soon as Æneas reaches Italy, and the Saturni gentem .... Sponte sua veterisque dei se more tenentem. Ic þa leode wat ge wið feond ge wið freond fæste geworhte, æghwæs untæle ealde wisan.**
For the Virgilian text, see above, note 545.

Ic þa leode wat
ge wið feond ge wið freond   fæste geworhte,
æghwæs untæle   ealde wisan

[I know that nation, fast in purpose against enemy and with friend, in every respect blameless as known from of old.]

Beowulf, lines 1863b–1865
Klaeber, ed., *Beowulf and the Fight at Finnsburg*, 69–70.

549. **The criticism of Ker that the important matters are put on the 'outer edges' misses this essential point of artistry**
See above, note 41.

Folio 185

550. **The poem "lacks steady advance" — so Klaeber heads a critical section in his edition.**
See above, note 282.

Folio 186

551. **Let us think, say, of Malory, were all his sources lost beyond recall.**
See above, note 465.

Folio 187

552. **The sluggish bear's son, with his dreadful hug, who suddenly wakes up and surprises his family and becomes famous is a very old folk-tale.**
See above, note 155.

553. **As is true enough of Shakespeare's use of old material. <u>King Lear</u> is a specially clear example.**
See above, note 40.

Tolkien is arguing that from the relatively straightforward material of his source, Shakespeare created one of the great works of literature in English. The "plot" of the Lear story is somewhat similar to the finished play, though Shakespeare felt free to adapt and change it for his dramatic purpose. Similarly, the *Beowulf* poet inherited a plot of old material and, perhaps adhering more closely to the "plot" than Shakespeare did to his source, adapted the old and infused it with a thematic and poetic quality that the original material does not possess.

554. **Even the legendary association of the Danish court with a marauding monster, and with the arrival from abroad of a champion of bear-origin, was not invented by our poet.**
See above, note 284.

Folio 188

555. **bringing of the tale of Grendel to Gautland. As Beowulf stands in Hygelac's hall and tells his story,**
Gautland, probably in southern Sweden, is the home of the Geats. In lines 2000–2189 Beowulf reports to Hygelac all that has occurred at Heorot.

Beowulf, lines 2000–2189
Klaeber, ed., *Beowulf and the Fight at Finnsburg,* 75–82.

556. **the pregnant words <u>oþ þæt hine yldo benam mægenes wynnum, se þe oft manegum scód).</u>**

       þæt wæs an cyning
æghwæs orleahtre   oþ þæt hine yldo benam

mægenes wynnum,   se þe oft manegum scod.

[That was an incomparable king, without any flaws, until old age, which has destroyed many, took from him the joys of strength.]

Beowulf, lines 1885b–1887
Klaeber, ed., *Beowulf and the Fight at Finnsburg*, 70.

557. **There is a special connexion between <u>Beowulf</u> and <u>Andreas</u>, both in the language and phraseology and in the 'plots.'**
See above, note 285. And cf. Alan Thacker, "In Search of Saints: The English Church and the Cult of Roman Apostles and Martyrs in the Seventh and Eighth Centuries," in *Early Medieval Rome and the Christian West: Essays in Honour of Donald A. Bullough*, ed. Julia M. H. Smith (Leiden: Brill, 2000), 247–77, esp. 265–74.

Folio 189
558. **the great missionary epoch of the eighth century.**
See above, note 286.

559. **set out to win their spurs <u>déorum dædum déofle tógéanes</u>**
See above, note 223.

560. **They went to the courts of kings and wrestled with <u>Godes andsacan</u>, and some were destroyed like Beowulf's companion.**
"Godes andsacan" is "the enemy of God"; Grendel is called "Godes andsacan" in line 786b. In Christian theological terms (which is how Tolkien is interpreting the challenge of the heathen courts to the Anglo-Saxon missionaries), "the enemy of God" is the devil, who may take many forms but is always the same being. "Beowulf's companion" is the man whom Grendel eats (lines 739–745a) whom we later learn (2076) was named Hondscio.

Beowulf, lines 786b, 739–745a, and 2076.
Klaeber, ed., *Beowulf and the Fight at Finnsburg*, 28–30, 78.

Folio 190
561. **ironic question of Hygelac: <u>ac ðu Hróðgáre wídcúðne wéan wihte gebéttest?</u>**
See above, note 287.

562. **and the emphasis laid on the friendly relations now established between kindred nations that had been estranged**
See above, note 288.

Folio 192

563. **Though there is no hint (indeed there are many hints to the contrary) that it was a war to end war, a dragon fight to end dragons or the foes of men.**
The "war to end war" quotation is obviously a reference to World War I. Having (barely) survived that conflict and lost most of his good friends to war, and then having watched, as he wrote *Beowulf and the Critics*, the gathering shadows of Hitler's National Socialist Germany and Stalin's Soviet Russia creep across Europe, Tolkien's assertion that Beowulf's battle with the dragon is not worthless even though it cannot ultimately save his people is rather poignant (cf. Shippey, *Author of the Century*, 163–65).

564. **'In structure' it is said of <u>Beowulf</u> 'it is curiously weak, in a sense preposterous,' while allowing great merits of detail.**
See above, note 41.

565. **There may have previously existed stirring verse dealing in a straightforward manner and even in natural narrative sequence with the fall of Hygelac, with Beowulf's deeds, or again with the fluctuations of the feud between the houses of Hréðel the Geat and Ongenþeow the Swede, or with the tragedy of the Heathobards, or the treason that destroyed the glory of the Scyldings.**
Each of the stories mentioned above are "digressions" in *Beowulf*: the fall of Hygelac (lines 2354–2366), Beowulf's deeds in battle with other warriors in the Swedish wars (lines 2391–2396), the feud between the Geats and Swedes (lines 2379–2390 and 2922–2998), the story of the Heathobards and the story of Ingeld and the fall of the Scylding house in Denmark (lines 2009–2068). Tolkien's point is that critics should not take the *Beowulf* poet to task for not writing poems about these events, since in the poet's time there may well have been other verse in existence dealing with these plots and themes. It is only due to chance that we possess *Beowulf* alone and not any of the other poems that must have been written and told at the same time, and the poet can hardly be blamed for not including everything in his one poem.

566. **I have heard it said by more than one <u>úþwita</u> of yours that it is monsters in both halves that is so disgusting.**
The use of "úþwita" is another very clever jibe on Tolkien's part. For while the first definition of the word is "scholar," it can also be read as "Pharisee."

Folio 195

567. **There are creatures of similar orders, symbols (not allegories, my good sir) of a similar kind, and of like significance.**
Tolkien is here arguing that the monsters should not be simply read allegorically: that, for example, the slaying of the dragon by Beowulf is meant by

the poet to be seen as the destruction of wrath by mercy. Rather the monsters may represent aspects of evil, but they are fully developed "characters" in their own right and cannot be reduced merely to representing abstract qualities.

568. **then a poet might have arisen who told first of Ashdown, when Alfred, not yet king, left his brother and charged up the hill to the bitter fight about the thorn-tree, achieving great victory,**
The story of Ashdown is told in Asser's *Life of King Alfred*. In 871, when the Viking army was marauding in England, King Æthelred and his brother Alfred advanced their armies against the Vikings at Ashdown. The Vikings split their forces, and the English kings did also, one force being led by the king, one by his brother. Alfred "acting courageously, like a wild boar, supported by divine counsel and strengthened by divine help" engaged the enemy. The Vikings held the high ground, but Alfred led his forces in a charge and fought the Vikings near "a rather small and solitary thorn-tree" that was growing at the center of the battle. Soon, "the entire Viking army was put to flight, right on til night-fall and into the following day, until such time as they reached the stronghold from which they had come."

Simon Keynes and Michael Lapidge, *Alfred the Great* (New York: Penguin Books, 1983), 78–80.

Folio 196
569. **mere fortunes of the house of Wessex**
Alfred was the king of the West Seaxna Theod (the West-Saxon people). The house of Wessex can be traced back to Ecgbert (802–839) and from Alfred's son Edward the Elder forward to subsequent kings of Wessex and of England.

570. **A light starts — líxte se léoma ofer landa fela**
　　　　Guman onetton,
signon ætsomne,　　oþ þæt hy [s]æl timbred
geatolic ond goldfah　　ongyton mihton;
þæt wæs foremærost　　foldbuendum
receda under roderum,　　on þæm se rica bad;
lixte se leoma　　ofer landa fela.

[the men hastened, the warriors together, until they were able to see the high hall-timbers, adorned and gold-ornamented, the most famous among earth-dwellers of halls under the heavens, where the great warrior abided. Light from it shone out over many lands.]

Beowulf, lines 306b–311
Klaeber, ed., *Beowulf and the Fight at Finnsburg*, 12.

Folio 197

571. also a parody of man misformed by hate (<u>earmsceapen on weres wæstmum</u>)

     oðer earmsceapen
on weres wæstmum   wræclastas træd,
næfne he wæs mara   þonne ænig man oðer;
þone on geardagum   Grendel nemdon
foldbuende.

[another wretched creature in the shape of a man trod the exile track, except that he was greater than any other mortal; long ago the land-dwellers named him Grendel.]

Beowulf, lines 1351–1353

Klaeber, ed., *Beowulf and the Fight at Finnsburg,* 51.

TEXTUAL NOTES

I have taken advantage of recent technological developments in layout and presentation of texts in order to make these textual notes easier to use for both the scholar and the casual reader. Rather than obscuring the emendations and modifications in a sea of brackets, sigla, and abbreviations, I have tried to present the notes in a form that adheres as closely as possible to the form of the original text on the manuscript page. Thus text that is crossed out in the manuscript is crossed out in the notes, and text that is inserted from above the line is displayed above the line. I have adopted several conventions, however, to make the text a bit more readable.

To differentiate the layers of writing in the manuscript I have used italics to indicate all the text written in pencil, but where an original word has been crossed out in pencil and another word inserted in pencil I have simply italicized the word. Thus for the passage:

> certainly ~~*his*~~ *the* period ~~*represented the*~~ *was one of a certain* decline ~~*of*~~ *in* Anglo-Saxon study in England, *one* in which *it* was *?????* not ~~?????~~ so much dependent on foreign work as behind it and largely incompetent to appreciate it

the words "his," "represented the" and "of" are written in the original ink but are struck out with pencil. The words "was one of a certain," "in," and "one" are written in pencil interlinearly and inserted into the text as replacements for the crossed-out text. Readers may safely assume that any text that is both italicized and crossed out was originally written in ink and then struck out with pencil. On the rare occasions when Tolkien both wrote and crossed out a word in pencil I have made a note in the editorial commentary. Where Tolkien used carets or lines for insertions I have either reproduced them or described them in the commentary. Question marks indicate illegible text; they are otherwise formatted the same as the rest of the text, so that italicized question marks are illegible pencil text, crossed-out question marks indicate illegible struck out text, etc.

All editorial commentary (except for page numbers and indication of footnotes in the original) is written inside square brackets [ ]. On those occasions when Tolkien used square brackets in the text I have noted it in the commentary by writing [square brackets in original].

It is my hope that presenting the text in this manner will accomplish several goals: first, it preserves, as closely as a printed edition that is not a facsimile can, the actual layout and content of the manuscript. This preservation is important, since the manuscript is not written on acid-free paper and, despite the excellent preservation efforts of the Bodleian Library, is fading. While at the present time such information may not be immediately required by researchers studying Tolkien, it may come to pass that someone may want to perform a study that involves examining the process of composition. This text should allow that study to be performed even if the manuscript continues to fade. Second, I hope to allow students, novice scholars and interested readers who have not had time to master the arcana of sigla and abbreviations to see for themselves how the text has been developed by Tolkien. Every edition is by necessity an imperfect and highly subjective rendering of the manuscript page. I have not shied away from making editorial decisions, but I have tried to lose no information in the process. Even casual readers may wish to examine particular passages in order to follow Tolkien's line of reasoning and understand his writing process.

Cover Page
   ii (ult)
   [written in the top right corner.]

   folktale is a good servant but a bad
   master xxvi Ch. -- ??? place of ?????
   [written at the top of the page, 1/3 of the way across.]

   Beowulf ~~with~~ & the Critics
   [written at the center of the page in larger letters.]

   completely xxxviii : The Olympic gods belong to _kindred_ with monsters so why gmc gods
   being so identified with monsters -- ??? ??? ???? & this clicked with Christianity. to what
   idea of anti-monster = anti to powers of Darkness is a virtual equal
   [written at the bottom of the page.]

Folio 1
   "Shrine"
   [written in the margin next to the first line of text.]

   . . . of the Rev. Joseph Bosworth, D.D, F.R.S. Rawlinsonian Professor of Anglo-Saxon . . .

[There is no period after the second capital "D" in the original, and no comma after F. R. S.]

... which have been printed in our old English, or so-called AngloSaxon tongue.

... He may do very well for a Professor ..
[there are only two dots after "Professor.]

... certainly ~~his~~ the period ~~represented the~~ *was one of a certain* decline ~~of~~ *in* Anglo-Saxon study in England, *one* in which *it* was not so much dependent on foreign work as behind it and largely incompetent to appreciate it.

... when literature was not wide in range, or ~~di~~ in possession of a diversified store of themes and ideas ...

... such criticism as I notice is principally that which is still current, potent, and influential, *and even interesting;* and insofar as I allude to its history at all it is to point to what I think is the explanation of ~~the~~ *certain* critical commonplaces which I attack.

And ~~that which~~ all this is but a background against

Folio 1 verso

But oddly enough I have read Beowulf itself with close attention and even some understanding of its language. ~~The~~ This would not appear to have been the universal practice of critics. Yet this concentration on the poem itself has certain compensations denied to a wider ~~on~~ learning.
[written in black ink.]

Folio 2

Indeed ~~it is what was usually~~ antiquarian analysis of the content of <u>Beowulf</u>, and research into this, has ~~was~~ usually *been* considered identical with 'criticism',
[There is no obvious paragraph break between "showing structure and motive." and "So overshadowed, as I have said ..."]

So overshadowed, as I have said, has this critical function been by ~~the~~ the ~~???~~ other ...

Chambers, the greatest of living Anglosaxon scholars,

... nearly all censure, and a great deal of the praise, of <u>Beowulf</u> has been due
∧ ^{either} to believing it to be something that it is not (e.g. primitive, ~~Teutonic~~ or
rude, or Teutonic) ...

Footnote Text
[The note is inserted between " — a thing about" and "which it is possible".]

¹⁾ First edn ~~1884~~ 1833, 2nd edn. 1835; and esp. "A translation of the Anglo-
Saxon poem of Beowulf, with a copious Glossary, Preface and Philological
notes", 1837.

Folio 3
(e.g an ancient heroic lay of slaughter and divided allegiances).

... is due to a mental background due to 'research' — to too much 'research'
~~and a lack of balance in its prosecution~~ of the kind that is not ∧ ^{so} much criticism of the poem as mining in it."

... he has <u>not</u> sense of proportion, poor man

when they were told the gardener was an Anglosaxon

... but that yellow hair unfortunately ~~does not grow on a head~~ grows always on
a muddled head.

I will quote from some critics — only very few and ∧ ^{generally} the most recent...

In the meanwhile let us skip swiftly ~~of the~~ over the heads of the mass of the
critics. Their conflicting babel mounts

It sounds ~~as though~~ something like this:

Ten B
[written in the left margin next to "development of which".]

Folio 4
[between "antiquarianly" and "aping" the pen changes to a dark blue that
lightens towards the bottom of the page.]

amidst all this babel we catch one constant refrain

It is true that this is often qualified ~~by~~ thus:

... in tones that suggest that ~~the~~ Andaman-islanders could be substituted for Anglo-Saxons ...

the sort of thing that ~~a~~ scholars do not read

Students without formed ~~noti~~ ideas read them; and if one wonders whence the strange nonsense ^ comes which examinations produce, in spite of ex cathedra vociferations, the answer is from ~~these books~~ statements in these books ...

and makes the background of ~~ideas~~ current ideas.

Folio 5

Secondly it states ~~very~~ explicitly the reasons why, amid all the ~~m~~ dispraise, we have an agreement that <u>Beowulf</u> ought to be studied

of which <u>Beowulf</u> (one of the ~~single~~ greatest ^ single things in that tongue) gets less than 2.

It would take far too long, however, to criticize all the remarks even in this brief entry; and I pass ^ now over the first and longest paragraph

the first and longest paragraph (mostly tentative and not dogmatic and therefore innocuous, more or less, even in error), ~~citing only the beginning and the end: "Beowulf is the only poem of any length — it runs to three thousand one hundred and eighty-two lines — which has come down to us, of the early heroic poetry of the Teutons ...", and "Though biblical allusions abound, and the heathen deities have, for the most part, vanished before the editing — if we may call it editing — of the Christian reviser, the~~

Footnote Text

[Note 2 is inserted between "who had read" and "<u>Beowulf</u> with attention"; Note 3 is inserted between "said many things" and "nearer to the point".]

Footnote 2

... which is ^ the most foreign in mood and style to the original of almost all the ~~possible~~ available metres.

Folio 6

. . . crosses the sea to help Hrothgar, and in fight in his hall mortally wounds Grendel."

[the "a" before "fight in his hall" is missing in both the Tolkien manuscript and the source Tolkien quotes from, Archibald Strong's *A Short History of English Literature*, page 2. See above, Explanatory Notes, note 9, for additional information.]

". . . The poem ends with an account of his burial amid the mourning of his whole people. This short summary does scant justice to the poem."

[In Tolkien's source for the quotation, Archibald Strong's *A Short History of English Literature*, page 2, there is a paragraph break between the two sentences.]

A story ~~can~~ cannot be judged from its summarized plot,

. . . to try indeed to form any conception of it $\wedge$ ^{from stuff of this sort} . is to attempt an estimate of a great man from his skeleton.

But I have quoted ^{it} because it is accurate

. . . and because this mental subtraction of all that gives $\wedge$ ^{it} life from a story ["From a story" is circled and an arrow indicates that it is to be moved to the space between "subtraction" and "of".]

Footnote Text

[Note 4 is inserted at the bottom of the page after ". . . all that gives it life".]

Note 4

<u>A History of English Literature</u> (in 111 pages!) *by Dr. Compton Rickett, a potting of his longer work (which is as erroneous*

Folio 6 verso

~~The 'background' is certainly not heathen — but the critic has probably not made clear to himself what he means by 'background.'~~

Folio 7

must precede the forming ~~so that ju~~ ^{of} such judgements as the following.

I must omit ~~;~~ all except one sentence

This taken with what ^ *I have just cited* ~~precedes~~ . . .

[from "(i. <u>Beowulf</u> is the only poem of any length" to "the background is not Christian but heathen" is underlined faintly in pencil.]

Though ^ they are closely interconnected . . .

["The story is trivial a typical folk-tale" is underlined faintly in pencil.]
I reserve my fire. ~~The the~~ ^ ~~chief purpose in quoting from~~ ~~real reason for the quotation from Sir Archibald at this point was to fin his~~ frank statement of the
[the second struck-out "the" is written in the left margin.]

At this point I ~~principa~~ should like attention concentrated on ~~his~~ ^ Sir Archibald's frank statement of the reasons for studying <u>Beowulf</u>.

It had never occurred to me to approach this or any other poem in such a spirit — but ~~if such is the spirit then~~ ^ once one knows the spirit exists, one sees in this spirit is an admirable explanation of ^ the errors ~~??what~~ in <u>Beowulf</u>-criticism; it is their natural source.

Folio 8

. . . is the only one ~~in~~ which can ^ to-day attract a rational person of culture ~~today~~ or in search of it) — <u>which is false</u>, or else the two different ~~purposes to which~~ ^ attitudes which one can have towards a a document which is at once old (and preserved from an important but ill-represented period) as well as a work of art, ~~can be~~ have been confused.

The operations are distinct, and ~~it is~~ no excuse for confusing them

. . . the 'research' process may, and ~~often~~ *sometimes* does, assist and illuminate the other.

. . . the appreciation of that merit is the right and natural ~~prime~~ and indeed the prime function of ^ its study. ~~The Iliad and the Odyssey are great mines or quarries in fact~~

. . . the lordly ~~th~~ 'us' that means all reasonable living men.

Footnote Text

[The note marked with a penciled asterisk is inserted between "interest is for us not" and "purely literary." The note has a left margin extending 1/2 inch beyond the main text margin.]

much of the ~~history~~ literature and something of the history of that period

Folio 9

[there are no obvious paragraph breaks in the manuscript.]

It is *at the* ~~back of what~~ cause of what is false in the sentences I have already quoted. But for it the ~~sentence that~~ critic would never have written

"Beowulf is the only poem of any length . . ^{which} ~~that~~ has come down to us, of the early heroic poetry of the <u>Teutons</u>."
["Teutons" is underlined in pencil.]

. . . and does not in consequence see what <u>is</u> there. ~~There is indeed no "early heroic poetry of the Teutons" of any kind or any size, short or long, in existence~~
["is" is underlined in pencil. After "indeed," the ink changes from blue to black.]

Too many ^ ^{other} factors, some known, some unknown, intervene . . .

or German or Gothic as just "Teutonic" Or rather

. . . especially in dealing with ^ ^{individual} works of literature . . .

Folio 10

So Norse is Norse and English English. ~~Though~~ There is indeed

and for these lost things "Beowulf" is ~~not~~ ^{neither} a satisfactory substitute,

Were all mediæval English literature swept away, but for a few scraps ~~(perhaps)~~, and the allusions and stories in the plays of Shakespeare . . .

. . . investigating Shakespeare and comparing him with other ~~the mediæval~~ material of ^{similar period} ~~a plot, or allusions,~~ outside England, and so seeking to detect what in him was derived from the period behind ^ ^{him} in matter or in spirit.

This would be a legitimate procedure — ~~but it~~ to use Shakespeare ~~as~~ in the

~~process of some private~~ ^{course} research prompted by a special curiosity about the past.

Folio 11

'Beowulf' is then the only ~~heroic~~ poem of any length . . .

[there is no footnote marker for the note inserted in the text after the line that ends "Or, if you".]

"It is the longest and most elaborate ~~poem which has survived~~ surviving poem . . . it is the principal surviving example, ~~and probably a late~~ of the early ~~period~~ ^{heroic} poetry of this ~~northern tradition~~ vernacular tradition as it developed under peculiar circumstances in <u>England</u>; ~~of this development it is probably an example~~ and it comes probably from the end of that development."

For a moment we will turn to this ^ ^{last} point, usually unnoticed.

rights of authorship were less and different ~~in~~ we may assume in ancient days, we still cannot dismiss the author ~~inf~~ and thrust him back into the tribal genius.

The ancient legends ~~are~~ mention no less the particular fame of the maker of verse . . . There ~~are more~~ ^{fame &} names of ^ ^{individual} Icelandic poets have been better preserved ^ ^{even} than their works.

. . . but we have no right to assume that ~~it~~ ^{he} was ordinary ^ ^{& negligible} or that ~~this~~ his ^ ^{authorship} was of no concern to him;
["his" is inserted from the right margin; "authorship" is inserted from the left margin.]

~~Such~~ ^ ^{This "Teutonic"} criticism suggests, however, that '<u>Teutons</u>' had a ~~special kind of poetry, a~~ universal kind of poetry . . .

What of the maker of "Beowulf" in particular.

Folio 12

But he must be ~~considered~~ distinguished

If one really comes to think of it, he would have disliked ^ ^{many of} these Teutons heartily . . .

What ever their tongue they would ^have written them down rather in kin of Grendel than of Hrothgar (for even Grendel may ^probably well have spoken Danish).
["probably" is written in later pen.]

The life and spirit of the poem "Beowulf" is then — [This is my view and bias, and will of course be further elaborated] — not Teutonic ...

It has its roots in a past which was shared a by at least some of ^the historical speakers of Teutonic tongues ...

and code of (kinship and loyalty for example).

But it is a all these are transmuted: they belong to a special time, with and also a special temper, and also to a special man.

in a period whose original wealth is not now represented only by ...

But we must not forget him even if this means no more than hesitating to ^a caution in ascribing everything in "B" to Anglo-Saxons in general (let alone Teutons), and a remembrance that a factor exists, the personal ^one, for which we have not allowed (even if we cannot help it) this omission)

Folio 13
'Correctly' I say because A-S. history is not one thing ...

any more than Icelandic is all one & the same from the Landnám in the 9th century to the cruel wa feuds of the great houses and the submission to Norwegian crown in the 13th or Rome from Romulus to C????.
[lines are written in the top margin and inserted with an arrow after "Stigand." I cannot make out the name of the Roman emperor whose name begins with C. The word is short enough to be "Caligula," but "Constantine" not only makes more sense but more effectively fits the development of the passage in the B text.]

This is the reverse of the historical ^document bias of which I have spoken ...
["document" is written in the left margin and its insertion point marked with a caret.]

But the "Beowulf" critic, <u>as such</u>, must go first ~~for~~ ^{to} the ~~prime external~~ evidence ~~of the~~ ^ ^{for the period} outside his poem ~~for the period~~.

Đ There is not much danger of this . . . The poem fits well into the period (8th C.)

The murmurs of the primeval Teutonic forest, and the sounding of the Scandinavian seas, may still be heard ^ ^{there} and move the imagination ^ ^{of the} ^{listener}, but they are memories already in that day of a far past ~~, and~~ caught and coloured in the ^ ^{shells and} amber of tradition and refashioned by the jeweller of a later day

Footnote Text

[The note marked in the text with a pen and in the note body with a penciled asterisk is inserted between "it was composed" and "then this great poem . . .".]

The 8th. c. is now, probably universally agreed

Folio 14

— if we ^ ^{may} call it editing — of the Christian reviser, the background is not ~~heathen~~ Christian but heathen."

This and <u>not</u> their relative frequency is the important point, and will later ~~on~~ be considered.

. . . <u>wyrd</u> was not and is not a god, but the master of gods and men, ^{a theory that ~~melted~~} ^{~~insensibly int~~ was absorbed insensibly by an omnipotent god.} or rather was ~~simply an~~ ^ ^{indeed ~~esp~~ from} ^{the beginning} an apprehension of ~~h~~Him.

[from "or rather" to "of Him" is inserted from the left margin.]

. . . is that he consciously and explicitly regarded his story as taking place in heathen <u>times</u> and ~~there~~ also in <u>past times</u>, but either ~~knew~~ ^{could} not or would ^{not} _{name any of the ancient divinities}

Certainly but look at the contrast made, the ~~ha~~ creation

That is <u>worth</u> discussing; and ~~clearly with the~~ becomes, so expressed, a natural part . . .

Its discussion can be delayed ~~for the moment~~, therefore; and we need for the moment say no more ^ than what Sir A himself after profounder study speaks in his own introduction to his translation not of the "heathen background" but of the "Christian colouring" which the author has "given to ~~his story~~ "his story".

Folio 15

In Chambers <u>foreword</u> to this same translation (which should be read by all whatever else, save the poem itself, is unread) only the ~~hin~~ shadow of the old historical document bias is left, and the final solution of the Christian - heathen debate is trembling on the ~~brink~~ verge of expression . . .

. . . if "Beowulf" analysed is not quite so good as ^ *it is* in general impression . . .

~~The folk~~ One thing only remains unresolved — and here the shadow of the old bias is most dark ~~m~~.

On page xxvi, when everything seems going right, ~~were~~ hear once again that "the main story of <u>Beowulf</u> is a wild folk-tale". Quite true of course, as it is of <u>King Lear</u> ^ except that silly would in the latter case be a better adjective .

. . . <u>and to drive into episodes and digressions the things which should ~~have~~ be the main stuff of a well-conducted epic"</u> ~~and so we have come full circle we must who said Beowulf~~

. . . and ~~ho~~ who has legislated for what <u>should</u> be the main stuff of any poem. Only, I fear, the antiquarian historian, who prefers ^ semi historical legend to folk-tale . . .

And so we have come full circle, & the cloud hangs over us still!

Folio 16

I started with a ~~mere~~ chance-selected ~~and~~ but not unrepresentative criticism ^ *from a recent compendium* .

I have been led to digress from the ~~antiquated to the mo~~ the path I perhaps ought to have followed: I have hurried on too far & left out the beginning, and must loop backward.

. . . as well as the greater and more ~~sane~~ wise.

One may assent to Earle's quotation from [in left margin: "Deeds. p. xcix.]
Dowden

Hygeberht, [in left margin: "bp & tempor. abp" inserted with arrow at "Abp".]
Abp of Richfield $^{(787–803?)}$ and made the whole poem into a kind of early
political Utopia.

. . . at the expense of the fools who have ~~rushed in~~ trespassed in the confidence
of their ignorance on paths too difficult for their dainty feet) chiefly illustrate [in
left margin, inserted with arrow after "illustrate": what we have already seen are
the principal points of critical debate".] ~~So far then we already see what are to
be the main points~~.

. . . and finally we shall reach at the end as at the beginning the ~~it~~ old ogre in his
lair — the typical (or the 'wild') folk-tale ~~whi~~ usurping even in the courtly
Anglo-Saxon 8th c. the throne of the heroes.

Folio 17

a substitute for poetic merit is due to 2 distinct things.

. . . insensitiveness to poetry ~~except a few well known~~ (especially in unfamiliar
mould) to grasp — to hear or to feel — the poetic merit ~~merit~~ of <u>Beowulf</u>

[The passage beginning "Thus the introduction to Mr. Shane Leslie's . . ." is
here inserted with an arrow from the bottom of the page, where it follows the
line "And in any case I leave the poem itself to . . ."]

~~Thus Mr. Shane Leslie in an anthology~~ Thus the introduction to Mr. Shane
Leslie's anthology . . .
. . . the 'Dream of the Rood" in translation, but ~~what~~ in content $^{\text{is more}}$ ~~is unlike~~
wholly unlike that poem . . .

~~That~~ He might as well judge of ~~his beer in a New~~ English beer by ~~sample~~
visiting an American ~~?dive?~~ *speak-easy*
[I cannot make out the struck-out word before "speak-easy." It looks almost as
if it could be "dive," but that word does not really fit the sense of the passage.]

Old English verse — less perhaps in essence than because it is now strange and
unfamiliar in metre and manner, ~~a ???~~ and ~~in schol~~ and methods of diction —

does not unlock the treasures of its <u>word hord</u> readily, and least to the hasty and
the proud ^{conceited}.

This department, the ???? texture of Old Verse (of which "Beowulf" is a part but
∧ ^{yet} an individual, and much the best part ^{individual}), though it is part a section
department of 'general criticism,' I shall not here in detail explore.

Folio 17 verso

[written upside down in black pen at the bottom of the leaf and the entire
passage is struck out with pencil.]

The exaltation of historical interest at the or in substitute for the absence of r

Folio 18

[Above the top line is written: "so hard the assay so scharp the conquerynge",
which is inserted below with an arrow after "craft so long to lerne".]

hands of students trained in this scholarly ^{Oxford} school <u>with confidence.</u> Though
<u>Ars longa vita brevis</u> . . .

. . . even unto those whose knowledge and feeling for Old English is pre
eminent.

. . . and no ^{real} critic of its poetry has ever been not also to some extent an
amateur also ^{as well} of history and antiquity.

. . . receded from us that even the least se this historical interest — this ancestral
voice out of the distance — has an inscrutable appeal.

["inscrutable" is my best guess at a word in the manuscript that looks very much
like "incertable".]

Nonetheless it remains true that that we must attempt to get back to that time
this is only an accident, and not an essential.

It was firs It first awakened real hist interest . . .

. . . the poem is contained in a composite Mss. too together . . .

such as Laurence Nowell, made have made or thought of it

Folio 19

. . . a criticism that has constantly been repeated ~~in spite of~~ even amidst mispraise and has never been reversed), though it deals with "history," ~~Had this balance been kept things would not have been so bad. Actually Wanley's words~~ and with Danes and Swedes. Wanley's words in fact suggest that if he had ˄ had more time for scrutiny . . .

For in general the language of O.E. verse was ˄ as yet in his time almost entirely unknown.

For long reasonably competent translations of O. E. prose,

It is not surprising therefore that the ~~scene~~ story goes next to Denmark, to Grim ~~Jon~~ [inserted from just after Thorkelin: "Johnson"] Thorkelin — who eventually published the editio princeps in 1815.

. . . when he visited England & had his transcripts made.

Folio 20

although his 2 transcripts were saved.

. . . a gallant effort for an old man. ~~He is thus robbed of the distinction, such as it is, of next mentioning "Beowulf in print, after Wanley. Actually this was in~~

And from Thorkelin we pass to ˄ Pastor Gruntvig . . .

This is the first stage of Beowulf criticism ~~an~~ — and though criticism rapidly...

Footnote Text

[The long footnote, marked with an ink asterisk overwritten with a pencil asterisk, is inserted after "though criticism rapidly," and fills the rest of the leaf.]

I have not here time to say ~~more~~ much about him.

. . . of O.E. verse language brilliantly, & made such advances that his own . . .

though it will not now pass muster ˄ except where it is mere quotation . is nonetheless recognizably "like" in metre and idiom.

... to those unable ~~to~~ yet to swallow the notion that other languages than Latin Greek and Hebrew had any shape or rules.

and served to ~~create a rumour in~~ reawaken a belief

ignorance of the field and the achievements of A-S scholarship

Among examples of G's sagacity

It was G. who published the first translation of <u>Beowulf</u> into any modern language: <u>Bjowulfs Drape. Et Gothisk Helte-Digt af Angel-Saxisk paa Danske Riim ved. Nic. Fred. Sev Gruntvig, Præst. Kjöbenhavn, 1820</u>.

Folio 21

[From "sufficiently indicated by the title" to "Dialecto Anglosaxonica" is inserted from the top margin with an arrow after "Scandinavian history".]

This distinction, such as it is, goes to <u>Sharon Turner</u> in 1807 in his <u>History of</u> ^the <u>Anglo-Saxons</u>.

that any A-S might be too difficult for him

a disciple of the more ~~rath~~ humble and patient Thorkelin.

In his History of 1823 there is a considerable change, and the ^poem is a "poetical Romance" or "metrical Romance" *
[asterisk in pencil.]

Footnote Text

[The first footnote, marked with an asterisk, is inserted between "Scandinavian history" and "Thorkelin was not." The second footnote, also marked with an asterisk, is inserted at the bottom of the page after a penciled horizontal line.]

So it is to Prof. B. Nerman in <u>Det Svenska Rikets Uppkomst</u> "Beowulf is ^still a prime document.

Folio 22

[in the right margin is written in pencil: "Wardstein critical view gives coup de grace".]

With this ^ *the* identification or <u>confusion</u> of Geats and Jutes

... which we can safely neglect, as it ~~has little or no own interest from the present problem~~ concerns primarily the elucidation of the traditions enshrined in Beowulf for their own sake.
["for their own sake" is circled and marked for insertion with an arrow after "enshrined in Beowulf".]

'<u>Beowulf</u>' was derived from ~~contempora poems~~ a hand contemporary

It is ^ *to* Conybeare perhaps in "Illustrations of Anglo-Saxon Poetry" (1826) ...

and remains an agnostic about ultimate origins (<u>Illustr</u>. p 33);

Little later however with the work of J. M. Kemble (of Trin. Coll. Camb.) accurate scholarship began — also comparative philology ~~intruded on the scene~~ of a scientific kind was introduced, and ~~it~~ proved ~~the gre~~ here its worth: by it the meanings of innumerable words have been recaptured, and ~~to it is due~~ if we can now to a great extent appreciate the diction and verbal effects of O.E. verse it is due in the main to ~~this new a~~ philology.

Folio 23
This in ~~an~~ turn was due to Germany ...

... was sold out in a few months and soon replaced by the ~~more~~ corrected second edition (18~~3~~85)
[the "8" is struck out and corrected to "5" in later pencil.]

But though ~~only~~ the text represents a great advance on Thorkelin, and the discussion of archaic and difficult words was something quite new, it is ~~the~~ Kemble's work of 1837 that marks a definite ~~tra~~ crossing to a new era.

it was indeed the foundation of Grein's <u>Sprachschatz</u>, the possession of which ~~gives the~~ puts the merest beginner of today ~~in possession~~ in a position which 100 years ago could only be gained by years of work on largely unprinted ms.

But in this preface we begin ~~an~~ that swing from a blind belief in ^ *the* historicity of the hero and all other characters in the poem to the ~~wearisome~~ "mythological" explanation of everything which is now as wearisome as it was once ~~irresistibly~~

fascinating. ~~But still we~~ And already research begins to bury the poem

speculation as to what ~~wi~~is the nature

So deep has the dust grown since that it is difficult now to ~~dig~~ ^{see} the poem ~~from~~ ~~under~~ ^{beneath} it . . .

It is to Germany or scholars there trained and writing in German, as I have said that in the main

I say research advisedly, for it produced rather the materials of criticism (and as plentifully lumber that was of no use ~~of~~ ^{to heosu})

Folio 24

. . . either by studying his ancestors, or by ~~p~~ dissecting his person.
[the crossed out letter is simply a downstroke, but it is consistent with the other appearances of "p" in this section of the manuscript.]

. . . fortuitously ^{or} arbitrarily — became conjoined into an "epic."

The notions were grafted upon Beowulf-criticism in Germany, and ^ ^{came} from current classical scholarship . . . with ingrained ~~notions~~ ^ ^{beliefs} about the accidental growth of epics, founded upon the authority of Wolff and Lachmann [Tolkien spells Wolf's name with two fs in the manuscript.]

["Deeds xxix" is written in the left margin next to "As Earle says".]

All Earle's Introduction is valuable, except his own private gambol at the end. [this note is written in the margin next to the word "illuminating".]

It is small wonder that little illuminating ^ ^{general} criticism was produced in such an atmosphere . . .

~~Yet the con~~ Though the contributions of many illustrious German scholars cannot be despised — we ~~lean heav~~ depend heavily upon their patient and ingenious work . . . that it is on such a ~~p~~ piece as <u>Widsith</u> that older scholars are at their best.

such a poem — which has little poetry ~~and no~~ and only that

Small wonder then that in his appendix to the 2nd edn (193~~1~~2) of his <u>Intro-</u>
<u>duction</u> ~~Ch~~ on recent work down to 1930

Folio 25

And it contains in its introduction studies of structure tone ~~style~~ ideas ~~an~~ style
language in which ~~at last we hear like the~~ have ^ ^{some} synthesis as well as research, and ^ ^{some} sanity as well as learning.

Decision, a view, a conviction are as Cha. says essential and now imperative; yet
~~for~~ with few exceptions <u>Beowulf</u> ~~crit~~ study has wandered in a maze of theories
for 90 years and more. ~~Of~~ This wandering and development until we come to
~~Klaeber~~ Lawrence, Klaeber and <u>Chambers</u> I make no attempt to sketch. I will
quote you Chamber's own summary

. . . the principal points in his ~~synthetic~~ neglected synthetic and constructive side
— since 1890 ~~hardly in~~ (it was hardly in evidence before) and pass on . . .
[between "pass on" and "In brief this summary" the words: "*Cha. Introd. II. p.*
391–392" are centered on the line.]

. . . the dissector has vanished ~~his~~ with the ghost of his own interpolation and we
are face to face with a poem by an Englishman c. 725–750!

. . . and the ~~dogma~~ dead dogmas of buried scientists ~~in scie~~ often in mythopoeic
perversion are the science of popular belief ~~today~~ and the journalist today. So
we can still hear of Grendel as symbolic of the sea, ^ ^{and Beowulf of the sun} and of the
redacting Christian monks . . .

~~to~~ There is still some~~thing to be~~ fun to be got out of the major critics, the
monuments of learning,
~~We have said enough about the "historical document" bias.~~
~~A view of the Christian heathen debate will later be put forward~~ indeed the very
reverend masters . . .

Folio 26

/Of these Chambers is the most technical . . .

Of all the critics of "Beowulf" he is the most sympathetic and the most penetrating, and the least condescending. ~~It would not be fair to call him stay-at-~~
~~home.~~

His criticism offers little opportunity to the critic of criticism, since ^ *he has done*
more than any one ~~he has~~ other person to set criticism right . . .

. . . he never lacked depth and insight in spite of ^ *his* enormous literary and
linguistic range . . .

. . . than they were to some less-read ^ *old or* medieval authors and their audiences,
& that he did not always realize this. *]*
[The ampersand is written very large in the left margin.]

But first I will take ~~as~~ a representative

While men like Ker — and ^ *this* is perhaps a token of the peculiar ^ *intermediary*
cultural and mental (and linguistic) situation of the English-speaker in Europe
. . .
["this" is inserted in later pen.]

. . . in Latin or in Norse in French or in German ^ *in Italian or in Russian*, there is a
Gallic kind . . .

. . . second-hand opinions upon literary* works will take people. To the least
worthy, by some ~~strange~~ perverse instinct, it often . . .
[the asterisk refers to no footnote.]

Folio 27
. . . the perusing of which is more irksome & more dull . . .

. . . and secondarily because ~~though~~ it offers an example, though an exaggerated
one, of the weakness and insensitivity of the ~~Gaul~~ *Latin or Latinized* in dealing with
the un ~~Gallic~~ *Latin* elements in English . . .

. . . nor the insensitiveness ~~to~~ always (though it is sometimes) due to ill will. If
any reason for them ~~;t~~ is to be sought,

. . . which is as pleasant ~~to possess~~ as it is fatal to possess.

The ~~first~~ *former* is an axiom, the latter ~~as~~ charitable afterthought.

Folio 28

attempt ~~to~~, if the period is worth considering at all, ^^{to} study its language and idiom until one recaptures something of ^$^{the\ full}$ meaning and the connotation of what is said,

~~Or rather~~ Ignorance is bliss . . .

. . . a sentence from the ^$^{O.E.}$ translation of Boethius,

That means in mod. E. precisely:

A most unrustic attitude ~~(if imb~~$^{to.}$~~ibed from Boethius himself~~

Footnote Text

[The footnote is marked with an asterisk and inserted between "* — jots down" and "as a sample." It extends into the left margin. Short pen lines above and below also separate it from the main text.]

You may ~~be profoundly~~ have ~~no~~ $^{so\ little}$ liking for his matter, ~~and~~ that the virtues of ^^{his} manner are obscured.

Folio 29

~~But still~~ ^{and} it is still believed ^$^{by\ many}$ that O.E. (or M.E.) should yield its meaning readily . . .

. . . which notices ~~only~~, when the village maiden does not briefly appear, . . .

. . . speeches in the houses of Parliament to-day, and ~~more~~ possibly ^^{more} : in the house of deputies.

. . . the artistic purpose of that speech in ~~O.E.~~ $^{the\ poem}$.

. . . though the ^^{actual} words liar, drunkard, coward, or murderer are not anywhere used.

Folio 30

Footnote Text

[The note is inserted between "But we will pass now to major points — " and "observing, nonetheless, that throughout <u>Beowulf</u> . . ." It is written further into the left margin than the main text, from which it is separated by penciled lines above and below.]

. . . our modern used of <u>drunk(en)</u> = ~~incb~~ helplessly inebriated is a <u>litotes</u>, and that in O.E. ^ ^{druncen} it means still normally as here "having drunk."

Footnote Text

That a man has spoken ~~indiscreetly~~ ^{rashly} owing to wine or beer at a feast is a thing that can be observed even in Latin countries. In O.E. and O.N. poetry, however, words of this kind ~~mean~~ imply more — not bestial orgy, but the mirth, freedom, and sense of security where friends were gathered ~~ab~~ in hall about their patron.

Footnote Text

What would these drink-maniacs make of the tragic words ~~of~~ ^{concerning} Guðrún in <u>Atlakviða</u>, where ^ ^{of} the great Lady of the Burgundians, Queen of the Goths, ~~says of herself~~ it is said . . .

But ~~on these principles~~ our discerning ~~critics~~ would doubtless imagine that the poet

[While it is not so marked, the following sentences are repeated in clarified form on leaf 31 and were probably intended to be cut from leaf 30: "You could hardly guess we were speaking of a poem for ~~where narrative methods~~ which contrasts and changes of fortune are a necessary narrative method. Still less that Anglo-Saxons are nowhere referred to throughout the poem".]

Folio 31

to the "Anglo-Saxons." You could hardly guess that the critic is speaking of a poem, to which contrasts and changes of fortune are a necessary narrative method; still less that 'Anglo-Saxons" are nowhere in that poem referred to at all! ~~and pagan~~
[The above is written in smaller writing in the top margin and appears intended to replace the wording at the bottom of leaf 30.]

And actually, in A-S. as we have it not as it might have been . . .

"They sacrifice their life in battle without a frown" ~~he~~ ^ ^{the critic} proceeds.

Dear old nonsense, recently dealt with by Professor E.V. Gordon in his Introduction to O. Norse.

"the most important monument of A-Saxon literature"

which do not concern Beowulf (the hero) in particular, and of historical facts ..
[there is a small circle with a hyphen inside at the end of the ellipsis.]

Folio 32

though the difference is fundamental, & its perception essential to an understanding of England and Europe

???? They believe in the Trinity and Merlin, in God and Sir Orfeo; while
professing Catholics they imagine ~~all~~ good violins were made by Stradivarius;
while serious ~~agnostics~~ ^{Calvinists} they tell tales of ~~the Sea Serpent~~ ^{Robin Hood} — the
joke allows of ~~infinite~~ indefinite expansion, but its original perpetrator ~~meant~~
~~the right~~ never smiled

Even the famous Anglo-Saxons must look to the*ir* laurels as champions ~~in~~ of
muddle and incoherence.

Q. E. D. What brilliance! ~~But what shall we say of all the Western culture, composed of many elements, even of a blend of Palestine and Greece and Rome
(and other things)? What a medley. But the some have seen in the result a culture worthy of some honour.~~ ???? We have only to apply the method to all living
poems to see how thoroughly satisfying it is.

... the incoherence to perceived in Europe wherever you like to turn — compound of many elements, made of ~~mix~~ commixture of Palestine, Greece, Rome,
and other things.

It is one of the central points ∧^{for a critic} to seize upon, to ponder, and if he can
explain,

Folio 33

a name of great reverence, a critic who could read and move as in his home ∧ⁱⁿ
many tongues, ancient medieval and modern, as illuminating as a critic of ~~poet~~
prose and verse as he was biting as a critic of critics.

... he has among things of astonishing worth ~~he has~~ said several that are ^ill
^considered ~~wrong~~. And his influence has been ~~so~~ strong ...

I shall read you a passage from the <u>Dark Ages</u> pp. 252–3.
[the passage is not written out in the manuscript. I have inserted it.]

There is much that is ~~good~~ excellent here ...

... the poem <u>Beowulf</u> is unmistakably ~~weighty~~ heroic and weighty."

the <u>dignity, loftiness ; in converse, the well-wrought finish</u>

Folio 34

we have a situation, which the old ~~poets~~ heroic poets loved, and would not have
sold for a wilderness of dragons." Alas the poor rock-gardener — he gave them
flowers ~~only~~ and they wanted ~~above~~ only stones!

the sharper for coming from Chambers, the Beowulf-poets' best friend; ~~and~~ we
might have expected it of Jusserand, who speaks of "one of these ever-recurring
treasures."
[the apostrophe after "poets" is found in the original.]

This is à la <u>Book of St. Albans</u> — then why not say "a ~~superfluity of nuns,~~ a pride
of lions, *draught of butlers*, a kindle of young cats, and a raffle of knaves" as that
book does.
["draught of butlers" is inserted from the left margin.]

In all Northern literature there are but three ^that really count: ~~the great Serpent~~
~~of the~~ the Encircler of the World of Men (Miðgarðsormr),
["the" before "Encircler" is written in the right margin.]

The last two are both in <u>Beowulf</u> (one in the ^main story and the other spoken
of) ...

... a dragon of well-founded purpose, ~~and~~ even as he carefully compared
<u>Beowulf</u> ...

He knew the ~~me~~ uses of dragons as I hope some do still;

Folio 35

Yet it is all wasted on an unprofitable theme we are to understand as if ~~Wi Dr. Johnson~~ *Milton* had conducted a Children's Bed-time Hour and told the story of Jack and the Beanstalk in ~~rolling periods~~ *blank verse*

~~Yet~~ A ~~yet a~~ man may depict lower things than he knows . . .

~~an~~ It is, I should have said, antecedently improbable that such a person should have spent 2000 lines on ~~????????~~ matter that is not worth serious attention

~~At~~ theory that will at least allow that what he did was of design . . .

to be moved by it *myth*] 52 and misunderstand ~~the sensation~~ yourself — to deny the attraction or to ascribe it ~~to some~~ wholly to something also present, tone, style, or what not. The sophisticated *scholarly* intelligence may refuse to admit that it has been moved by ogres or dragons, since it believes ~~th~~ such things have ~~long be~~ in our day long been relegated to the nursery. O impoverished day!

Folio 36

fact that myth is ~~at its~~ best treated by an author who ~~himself~~ feels, rather than makes consciously explicit ~~to himself~~ what his tale portends; who even presents it as a fact in time, and bolsters it about with history (as our poet has done) *we desire our myths to be incarnate.*
["we desire our myths to be incarnate" is circled in the top margin and inserted here with a line.]

[the section beginning with "And behind this lies . . . and continuing to "Deliberately provocative this." is faintly struck out with a large X in pencil.]

And behind this lies the shadow of ^ *19th c* 'research,' . . .

you are puzzled or disappointed.
[Next to "disappointed" is written faintly in the margin *End of 52* ~~end of sec.~~]

The 'heroic,' as Chambers calls it, is the <u>more</u> valuable — an axiom, there is no argument about it.
[in the margin next to "axiom" is written ^ *53.*]

Research suggests that ~~both as an artistic form, and~~ in the development of O.E. poetry the 'heroic' lay precedes such stuff as <u>Beowulf;</u>

"No!' The hero worshippers cry in chorus.
[in the margin next to "axiom" is written *54*.]

~~In fact~~ *Yet* here ^*indeed* there has hardly been any dispute . . .

This story of the *Ingeld* twice faithless and easily led ^*(and the not too intelligent)* has to me
— and I suspect its undoubted popularity among the English was due to much
the same course — its chief interest not in ^*to ?????? work* . itself but as ^*but its being* part of
a great whole, part of a tradition concerning moving historical events, the arising of Denmark and the wars ~~of the~~ in the islands ~~while even granting~~

And in any case ~~while~~ ^*even* granting the superlative ~~method~~ ^*merit* of the "heroic" in
general, we have yet given no reason for refusing to consider ~~with~~ stuff of other
kind, for valuing Beowulf as it is.

[At the bottom of the page in larger characters is written *ETC.*]

Folio 36 verso
[on the verso of the leaf is written a short rider, labeled 36a, which is to be inserted between 36 and 37. It begins with "Are we to have no tragedy of fact . . ."
and ends with "Need we even debate which is more valuable?"]

. . . no tragedy of the mind but divided allegiances or conflicting duties.
[there is no question-mark in the text.]

Are we to refuse King Lear either because it is founded on a silly folk-tale (the
old naif details of which ~~hav~~ still peep through as they do in Beowulf) or because it is not ~~"Hamlet"~~ ^*"Macbeth"* ? Need we even debate which is more valuable?
Or ~~Rich~~ Henry Vth — historical or semi-historical as they are
["either" is written in the left margin.]

Folio 37
~~But the presupposition is not self-evident~~ There is ^*of course,* a value in heroic
tales of divided allegiance and ~~unrel~~ unacknowledged defeat.

~~Ernest Newman~~ The musical critic Ernest Newman . . .

. . . something inexplicable ^*by analysis* , inimitable, about old ~~(so-called)~~ traditional 'folk-airs' — remarking that any competent ^*mod.* musician ~~who~~ with any

melodic invention could turn them out by the score to ~~???~~ defeat ^{of} their most enthusiastic amateurs $\wedge^{the}$ powers of discrimination.

[an arrow indicates that "^{of} their most enthusiastic amateurs" is to be moved after "discrimination." The word in the manuscript certainly appears to be 'amateurs,' and there is a sense of the word which could apply, but for the sake of clarity I have emended to "admirers".]

for being a dragon, but rather for not being ~~dragon pure an~~ dragon enough,

Already $\wedge^{nonetheless}$ he approaches ~~rather~~ "draconitas" rather than'draco'

$^{In\ the\ poem}$ The balance is nice, but it is preserved.

The vast symbolism is near the surface of the exterior narrative ~~but not~~ but it does not *quite* burst through.

["quite" is written in the margin.]

Something larger than a standard hero, faced with a foe greater than any $\wedge^{human}$ enemy of house or realm is before us, and yet incarnate in time, walking as it were in $\wedge^{heroic}$ history, and treading the named lands of the ^{legendary} North.

that its poet coming in a time rich in legends and histories of heroic men, has used them afresh: he has not given us just one more, but given us ~~just~~ something ~~else ????? ??? quite different and mar-~~ different and also unique

Footnote Text

[the note is written in the left margin at "few good dragons" ; spelling of "all-though" as in the manuscript.]

Allthough ~~parts of the poem~~ there are some vivid touches (2293ff) in which the dragon is real enough with an animalic life and thought of his own.

Folio 38

The [stands alone at the top left corner of the leaf.]

"Yes, yes" $^{No,\ no}$ they say impatiently — $^{it\ won't\ do}$ he has given us a dragon."

Even today you ~~might~~ ^{may} find men ~~of intelligence~~ not ignorant of legend and of literature, who have ~~seen the hero and~~ heard about the hero, and indeed seen him, and who yet though they ~~who~~ would scarcely dream of writing an

heroic tale, ~~who are~~ ^{have been} caught by the fascination of the 'worm.'
["they" is written in the left margin. The section "not ignorant of legend . . . and who yet though" is inserted from the top margin with a line; there are in fact two arrows, one indicating the section is to be inserted after "worm", one indicating after "men." This second arrow is struck out.]

though this ~~perhaps~~ ^{may seem} an unpardonable

two modern poems on the dragon ~~The first is~~ The two together for all their defects (especially the first I shall quote) seem to ~~be~~ me more important for Beowulf-criticism, for which they were not written, than very much that has been written ~~for~~ with that purpose.

(omit last stanza). Here we see that the old enemy is within man as well as without

Folio 39
They whisper of me in a low voice, ~~to~~ laying plans,

Folio 40
The last are the indomitable will, undefeated in defeat
[the above line is written in the top margin.]

So much (at the moment) ~~of~~ ^ ^{for} the foe . . .

. . . but not very intelligible (not always very intelligent), as moving as a baited badger.

Or rather ^{*perhaps fairer*} I fancy Beowulf plays a larger part than is recognized in assisting in the understanding of him; and if these very critics had not had Beowulf to read they would have less loved the ~~heroic legends, and~~ the other heroes.

The heroic lay ~~will deal~~ ^{may have dealt} . in its own way, more vigorous and brief per-haps, if more harsh and noisy — (has not Chambers himself made a motorbike the symbol of the lay, and a Rolls Royce of the epic)

In it we ~~may perceive ???? shall see~~ ^{could have seen} the exaltation of the will undefeated

the poet of <u>Maldon</u>, but a solemn repetition of a received and honoured gnome; a terse exposition of a dominant idea.
["Maldon" is underlined in pencil. There is a faint pencil line drawn across the bottom of the page to separate the main text from the footnote.]

Folio 41

from a line here or a tone there, the background of ~~mind~~ imagination which gives to this indomitability,
["imagination" is inserted with a line from the top margin.]

we may see man at ~~word~~ war with the infest world
[The word in the manuscript is clearly "infest." Tolkien's adjectival use of it is unusual, but can be justified etymologically from the Latin "infestus", "hostile", which is in fact the sense of the passage.]

Nonetheless we at any rate against his ~~??~~ great scene

the shoreless ocean ~~and~~ unknown beneath the sky's inaccessible roof, wherein as in a little circle of light ~~made and~~ defended by mortal hands

That even this geography (~~as it~~ ^{once} held as material fact) might now by the supercilious be classed as 'mere folk-tale' ~~even thin and cheap~~, affects its value little or nothing.

Beowulf is not a hero of an heroic lay — ^ ^{not} quite. He has no enmeshed loyalties or hapless love. He is a <u>man</u>, & that for him and many is a sufficient tragedy.
[the large ampersand is written in the left margin.]

Folio 42

For all the machinery of "dignity" is present elsewhere. Cynewulf or the author of St. Guthlac had a great <u>feel</u> ~~of virtue~~ dignified verse and ~~could in~~ and you will find lofty converse weighty words, high-wrought finish, all in fact precisely which they say is the real beauty of Beowulf. Yet there is no one at all who doubts that Beowulf is more beautiful, that a line (even when it is the same line) as in the other OE poem. ~~the best~~ about where then lies the special virtue of B. if the common element is withdrawn. It is the theme.
[the above is written very faintly in the top and upper left margins. I have edited it for coherence and inserted it between "makes us feel so deeply" and "So deadly and so . . .".]

It is the theme in its deadly seriousness that begins^gets the dignity of tone.

So deadly and so ineluctable ^is the theme that those who play only in the little circle of light with the toys of wit and refinement, looking not to the battlements, either hear not the theme at all, or recoiling shut their ears to it. Death comes to the feast, and ~~one~~ they say He gibbers.

in its deadly seriousness that begets the dignity of tone *makes us feel so deeply*.

[in the left margin is written: Strong, in his Introd. to his transl.]

but not because the O.E. poet did not value the light, passionately.

If we like to forget the ~~author on an island~~ encircling foe

but ~~both~~ he loved the island all the more.

Though I have ~~for~~ long laboured the point myself, *I have only observed.* Chambers has grasped it ~~and~~ (in one aspect) and put ^it in words that I shall not attempt to better

Read Cha. Foreword to Strong's translation p xxvii
"Yet Professor Chadwick . . . to ~~xxviii~~ xxix . . painful) — on xxx end of Ector de Mari's speech . . .

[I have replaced the notation to read Chambers's Foreword to Strong's translation with the actual text of the passage.]

barbarians tells of many a deed as griesly as that to which Achilles feared that he might, despite himself, be driven
[The odd spelling of "grisly" is in Chambers's original text. I have emended it.]

Folio 43

["Which had provided . . . by this time" is written in the left margin. I have inserted it between "Christianity" and "infused into".]

In other words Christianity + ^*infused into* the Northern ~~tradition~~ would make what we call the <u>medieval</u>, and that process begins <u>at once</u> — some of ~~its~~ ^the most fundamental changes of that alchemy are almost immediate.

... the memories themselves ∧ ^are seen in different perspective.

[inserted from the left margin: It is better than either ~~it~~ as an O.E. one.]

[interlinearly] ^It has ~~more~~ a kinship with S. Guthlac, Ælfric, even with med. homs on hell ~~than with~~ equally balanced
with a lay like Völuspá, Hávamal or Sigurd's lay

.

But there is yet one point remarkable. It ~~was~~ ^came from a learned age, and yet
(though the accidents of survival tend constantly to make us forget this) ^from a
two-sided one.

~~The~~ Not all the learning ∧ ^was in book-Latin nor all the love of the learned ~~was~~ for ~~the~~
what ~~book-Latin~~ ^was written in the new letters.
["was written in the new letters" is interlinear and extends into the left margin.]

There was never any sign of a new pseudo-latin people being ~~forged~~ fabricated

And these were not ~~eit~~ beneath the study of the early scholars such as Aldhelm
(whom ~~Theodore~~ Alfred considered ~~mo~~ best of the vernacular poets — though
his vernacular verse is lost), and were loved no less by Alfred the revivalist than
the Latin ~~which he strove to~~ learning which he strove to ~~ret~~ reestablish.
[Theodore is written in the left margin with a large caret beneath the word.]

Folio 44
— a poem that supposes the ~~study of Virgil and Statius~~ ^knowl. of classical Latin epic
they say — but also a body of northern historical and legendary tradition for the
"educated" and christianized mind to ponder ~~on~~.

as a modern poet may ^still (or once used to) draw upon his history and his
classics ...

quite learned enough in this ^*vernacular* department

He casts his time back into the long ago — ^because the long ago has for him so at the date a
^poetic appeal, and also . justly because ^so set the struggle of man stands out all the more
naked — but ~~he~~ knew much about ~~that~~ ^old days: not least ...

This is specifically recognized even of Hrothgar ^and his Danes The discrepancy
~~looking~~ dealt with later in the famous passage from 175–178
["The discrepancy looking dealt with later" is written in the left margin.]

Avoidance of all glaring anachronism in this respect (such as is found heedlessly in ~~Judith~~) ~~to~~ in the absence of all specifically <u>Christian</u> references* is natural, deliberate, and essential. ~~Yet with a~~ One can ~~no~~ only stand amazed at the willful stupidity

Of course we at this distance of time
That the poem contains only a half-baked paganism–is not in this respect true but is dramatic true might be understood. But is a wholly other matter to which ???

Footnote Text

[the note marked with a dagger is written in the upper left margin. There is no mark in the main text or at the note.]

Virgil Statius Lucan are given among the books studied in the school of York, by Alcuin in his poem on the Church of York. Alcuin from c725 must have been nearly contemp with Beo. poet.

[the note marked with an asterisk is written below the main text at the bottom of the page. Asterisks are present in both the main text and the note.]

It should be noted that Abel 108 Cain 108 (1261) out of what wanting names ?? only occur where the poet is speaking. He is giving you his view of the origin and nature of such monsters; not a view contemporary with his hero.

Folio 45

[in the top margin is written in pencil] *Wulfram 44 mun 80Single p 85 89 pagan also*

~~Woden an~~ We should not hesitate to trot out references to <u>Woden</u> and <u>Þunor</u>

In protesting against a view that a man sufficiently cultured to write a long poem did not clearly know ~~what was what~~ the difference between Christian and pagan, we rather emphasize than obscure the potency still of paganism — as a belief.

Saxons (or the Frisians and the continental Saxons which were later~~)~~ and the Swedes later~~)~~ still) had been fanatically heathen — the sort of pale ~~din~~ lassitude ∧ without resistance which we get in Bede's story of Cefi and his sparrow is not a picture that can be applied universally to Germanic heathendom or to all parts of England.

We get no heathen gods, only the Lord, the Almighty, often Metod the Apportioner — in which ~~often times~~ the conception
[the name of the pagan priest is spelled "Cefi" in the A text. Tolkien corrects it
to Coifi in the B text.]

["*and which remains . . . our individual wills*" is inserted with an arrow from the left
margin, where it is written perpendicular to the main text.]

that $^{\text{in early}}$ Ireland ~~and England~~ $^{\text{of the seventh century}}$ ~~secular~~ ^{profane} classical literature with its inherent mythology ~~is more~~ $^{\text{was widely}}$ cultivated ~~at this period less~~
~~frowned on~~ $^{\text{even in monasteries}}$ ~~by the church than in heathen lands~~ — marked contrast to the Latin lands ~~at our end~~ while the pagan religion of the Empire was
still a serious thing [an arrow indicates that the text at the bottom of the leaf
"and indeed . . . active paganism" is to be inserted here.]

Folio 46
It ~~is a fruit of~~ ^{was} the English temper — ^{in} its strong Englishry connected with its
nobility and its dynasties and ~~cou~~ many small courts . . .

. . . we could hardly expect the gods to be given ~~even~~ ^{yet} the twilight reverence
of antiquarian record.
["Yet" is written in later pencil.]

~~Like~~ St. Paulinus of Nola (born at Bordeaux) — 5th c — ~~who~~ cried that 'Hearts
vowed to Christ
[here in the left margin is written: "quot. Crawford p. 80.]

~~St. Cassian~~ Sulpicius Severus in ~~his life~~ the preface to his life of St. Martin asks
"what good will it do posterity to study the philosophy of Socrates or to read the
battles of Hector."

Apocryphal — but nonetheless ~~memorable~~ $^{\text{to be noted}}$ for such an attitude was
possible — is the famous story concerning the Frank St. Wulfram $^{\wedge \text{ of Jens}}$ ~~much~~
~~later (early 8th C.)~~ $^{\text{(died 695)}}$. Radbod ~~son of~~ (successor of Aldgisl who had harboured ~~St. W~~ the English St. Wilfrid) . . .

Footnote Text
The Odin and Þór of Snorri in the early 13th century are in any case nearly as
remote from Woden or Þunor (or any ancient tradition concerning Danish

heathendom the English may have possessed, as Jupiter and Apollo or mythology in Ovid is from ~~the~~ ^{Greek} religion ~~of~~ in the days of the long-haired
Achaeans.
["nearly" is written in the left margin.]

Footnote Text

The footnotes are written at the bottom of the page. The second footnote,
marked in both the main text and the note by two asterisks, is separated from
the first footnote by a horizontal line that runs the width of the page]

Second Footnote

Wulfram died 695 & there is no evidence of (outside the late vita Sancti Wulframni) that he even visited Frisia.

Folio 47

[in the top left corner of the leaf is written: Crawford p. 44.]

"Do not deceive thyself" was Wulfram's reply,'it is certain that they have received the just sentence of damnation".

He remained heathen to his death in 719.
~~(Radbod only succeeded about 689 another and there is no evidence that
Wulfram ever visited Frisia).~~

It ~~is~~ ^{was} perhaps not altogether in the result regrettable that the Gallic or rather
new Frankish church fell into confusion demoralization and decay and that the
reenergizing of it and the reclamation by missionar~~ys~~ of Frisia and large areas
of Germany was due in principal measure to the English (of the age of Beowulf
the muddleheaded!), to whom may be ascribed indeed the foundation of the
medieval church *in Europe.*

Yet even ~~from~~ ^{of} the best known figure in that process Alcuin ... (born about
735 and therefore almost certainly alive at time as the poet of Beowulf)

In a letter to Speratus of Bp. of Lindisfarne

Angusta est domus; utroque ~~non~~ tenere non potent

This reference to Ingeld is not in the received text of the letter (see Cha. note
Widsith p. 78).

In any case it is rather evidence that in England even those trained and professed in religion as monks could ~~disagree~~ preserve ancient tradition.
["preserve ancient tradition" is inserted from the bottom margin with a line.]

Folio 48

. . . but it was not necessarily improper that the same minds should ~~per~~ contain
the old histories and the new faith. The house is wide and has many rooms. ~~The~~

. . . their going was ~~not disastrous~~ nonetheless not disastrous to the theme . . .

~~but ??? were each~~ and not only were not ousted by Moses

A point especially to not^e in Chambers'

are identified with the foes of God.

There is probably a truth in ~~such~~ a generalization ~~as the~~ which contrasts the
inhumanity^{ness} of the Greek deities with the humanity^{ness} of the Northern.

remember as we well may paint in what is left us of later mythologies that do not
exactly fit;

Folio 49

~~Though of divine shape~~ at the least ~~they are not or at least~~ not partners of lesser
men in war against them. Their race is rather like that far off vision of t men in
Wells' Time Machine divided into two ~~yet of one origin~~, the fair ~~of~~ who live in
the sun . . .

Maybe this makes them better gods, $^{maybe\ ??\ of\ one\ or\ the\ other}$ more fair

They are timeless and know not death — and such beliefs hold promise of a ^{higher}
wider and ^{or} profounder thought, so that Greece could make philosophy, but
the Germanic north claimed especially the 'hero' the artist in ~~act~~ conduct. $^{He\ is}$
conception when or how of that freedom by G ?????

. . . even if a rebirth glimmers faintly far ahead; their battle is with the monsters,
and with the dark. They fight ^{along} with men and ~~WOdin rallies men and gather~~
gather heroes from the same war. ^ *They are men writ large on a vaster scale of time* . Already before
euhemerism saved them by embalming them, and they dwindled ^ $^{in\ belief}$ to the

~~ancestors~~ mighty ancestors of the northern kings, ∧ *that had been* raised by ancestor worship to false lords

Folio 50

They ~~appear~~ are in their very beings but the shadows of great men and warriors cast upon the walls of the world. (*Hel: Gods can go there and not come out — Baldr*). Loki is among them
[the parenthetical expression is written in the left margin. I have inserted it where it seems to fit best.]

do not recognize *re???? their* kinship

But ~~this~~ this is ~~only~~ true of humanity in whom both Grendel and the dragon in their hatred, cruelty, malice and greed find part.

with God (1689–1693~~)~~ and 113–114) are certainly related

as is esp. <u>Genesis</u> ch. II, they cannot nonetheless be dissociated from the giants of northern mythology the ~~besiegers~~ ever encircling foes of <u>Asgard . . .</u>

[in the left margin next to "reference to Cain" is written: 112.]

just as the undoubted reference to Cain connects him with <u>eoten</u> and <u>ylfe</u> the <u>álfar</u> and <u>jötnar</u> of Norse mythology.

It is precisely therefore at this point that Christian~~ity~~ Scripture and pagan tradition fused . . .

begotten the gods fought on.
[inserted from bottom margin after "fought on"] *or wove from* ∧ *splendid forms* ~~their~~ ~~own~~ *fantastic banners of human courage*

[in the bottom left corner is written: ~~Vg. Cenlas~~.]

Folio 51

~~But the monsters were foes of God~~ Yet the war had changed. ~~Dryhten, the one Lord~~ For now there is

time thus takes on its ~~latest most~~ greatest aspect

the vision is ~~changing~~ *dissolving* and the visible world is changing into a*ⁿ* ~~mere~~ incarnation ~~or allegory of the~~ spiritual *and an allegory is near.*

~~it has not yet become "medieval" fully.~~ "Beowulf' is not a stupid medley of
Christian and pagan but a *re-* treatment of a theme which had already been
hammered out; tha~~nt~~

Yet it would not be so treated *?????*, but for the nearness of paganism.

As the poet looks back into the past, he sees that ~~it ends~~ all ∧ *that man* <u>*as man*</u> *can*
accomplish ends in night. ~~But the~~ He is still thinking primarily of man and men in
the world & their glory

Their art & science).

~~The~~ In spite of the terminology applied to <u>Grendel</u> he is not yet "medieval" —
we have not yet devils as hideous as this þyrs,⁺ this ogre and his dam, and as
fleshly, who are yet "evil spirits" whose proper purpose is to destroy the soul, to
tempt the spirit.

. . . whose proper purpose is destroy the soul, to tempt the spirit

Footnote Text
[The footnote is written within parentheses at the bottom of the leaf.]
This very word in M.E. survives only precariously

Folio 52
[There is some very faint pencil writing in the top margin. Most is illegible, but
what can be made out is] *Siglhearwan described . . . but they are not always visible . . .*
they are . . . . But . . . by a sheer . . . of a visible method . . . in

We are in fact just in time to get a poem from a man who knew enough of the
old *tales* ~~heroic tragedies to perceive~~ heroic tales as his contemps. did. vide W &
Seafarer. to perceive their common tragedy of inevitable ruin, and to feel it perhaps more poignantly because he was a little removed ~~in~~ from the direct pressure of its despair;
["as his contemps. did. vide W & Seafarer." is written in the left margin.]

a period which has in Christian*ity* *teaching* a ~~philosophy which the way~~ a justification of what had hitherto been ~~an ar~~ ^{dogma} not so much of faith as of instinct . . .

. . . though in what plane such value was realized the Germanic North never ~~in~~ ^{found} (and prob. unaided never would have found) a coherent or explicit theory. He was still dealing with this old universal theme.
[there are some faint penciled words that follow "theme," but they are illegible.]

~~Apart from~~ ^{The wise} – myths — the ~~poetic~~ counterparts of which in pagan England are lost.
[From "The myths" to the end of the leaf ("shadowy hell") is struck out with three diagonal pencil lines.]

Footnote Text

[the footnote is written so that it extends into the left margin. It is separated from the main text by faint pencil lines above and below.]

is fully developed in O.E. in this respect.

The Sigelhearwan in Ælfric ~~and~~ ^{are} perfectly medieval bogeys.

[MS Tolkien A 26 1 ends with this leaf.]

Folio 53

[MS Tolkien A 26 2 begins with this leaf.]

. . . however different the details, from ∧^{the} Scandinavian.

What little we know of the latter is, however, difficult enough to ~~assess for Scandinavia~~ estimate as a picture of Scandinavian imaginative beliefs . . .

. . . in tattered form from ~~a~~ times of confused and faulty memories

. . . antiquarians like Snorri — ∧^{almost} as far from real paganism as an 18th c. Jove or Mars.

We ~~see~~ ^{glimpse} there a heaven and a hell the one rather ~~me~~ the reward of courage the other the punishment of feebleness ^{;B}; but among much that is crude or ~~s~~ unshapen, ~~un~~ or confused the most dominant motive is that of courage, apprehended mystically as ~~loyalty~~ valuable in the war of Gods and men

But of definite mythological ~~of~~ treatments of this idea

It $\wedge$ ^{spirit} survives as a flavour a temper a mood.

the noble pagan's desire for $\wedge$ ^{the} merited praise of the noble, which is not confined to northern pagans.

For if this "limited immortality" $\wedge$ ^{or prolonged life} can exist as a strong motive together with detailed pagan beliefs and practices,

when the pagan gods decay ~~and for reasons with~~ whether unbelief comes

a pagan time was not far away from the poet, and $\wedge$ ^{its mood} was well grasped imaginatively by him

Footnote Text

[the footnote is written at the bottom of the page, separated from the main text by a horizontal line drawn completely across the leaf.]

a crueller colder and more barbarous one exalting slaughter and rapine, & encouraging at once unbelief and fantasy.

Folio 54

~~a twilight per~~ the end of English paganism was marked ^{much before the ??? culture of Chrs.} (at least among the noble and the courtly classes for whom and by whom such traditions were preserved) by a ~~similar~~ twilight period similar to that which we see historically in Scandinavia.

their fate was simply ek trúi á mátt ~~og~~ ok megin"

Certainly we see them often godlausir ~~either~~ or at best patronising towards to their eclectically formed deities — giving them a belief often of not much greater than that which modern men will accord to ~~amu~~ omens, or talismans in motorcars.

At the beginning of the poem ^{at} the end of the first 'strophe' of the exordium

The last word in ~~"Beowulf"~~ the poem is <u>lofgeornost</u>

Ure ~~sceal~~ æghwylc sceal ende gebidan worolde lifes.

["The poet himself . . . his lif cearað" is inserted between "<u>æfter selest</u>" and "<u>Lof</u> is ultimately . . ." with an arrow from the top margin.]

swa sceal man don þonne he æt guðe gegan þenceð <u>longsumne</u> lof; na ymb ~~lif cearað~~ his lif cearað.

the other into the ^conception of the judgement seat of God, the particular and the general judgements of the dead.

Footnote Text

[The footnote is inserted with asterisk and arrow from the left margin.]

prolonged life of fame — ~~lof se gewyrceð, the~~ He says of his noble patron: <u>lof se gewyrceð, hafað under heofonum heahfæstne dom.</u>

Folio 55

To appreciate this it is necessary to compare S. 66

noting especially the close resemblances between B. 1735 ff and esp 1761 – 8 (which I believe original and not "revised") and <u>Seafarer</u> 66 – 71.

"Therefore this is for all ~~men~~ noble men the best "<u>last word</u>" (i.e. memorial in tale & song) and praise of the living that ~~remember~~ him. ~~in words~~ commemorate him in words, that ~~he merit~~ ere he is obliged to depart, he merit and ~~carry o~~ achieve ^on earth by ~~(t????~~ heroic deeds ~~on~~ against the maker of enemies (<u>feonda</u>) ~~in~~ opposing the Devil (<u>deofle</u>) ^so that the children of men ~~should~~ may praise him afterwards and his "lof thereafter ~~should~~ may live with the angels for ever and ever, the splendour of eternal life, rejoicing (<u>dream</u>) among the hosts (<u>duguþum</u>)."

In any case it is a modification of heathen <u>lof</u> in 2 directions

by saying that this <u>lof</u> on earth should be for deeds of Christian value

<u>lof</u> remains pagan <u>lof</u> — the esteem of one's peers, ~~and the~~ perhaps prolonged

vaguely <u>awa to ealdre</u> in song. ~~there is nowhere in Beowulf any mention of heaven~~ There is in <u>Beowulf</u> <u>hell</u> ~~a native word which already had a significance long before~~

Folio 56

An exception might be made ~~fo~~ in case of 186 ff.
["in case of" is circled and inserted with an arrow from the top margin.]

They refer to <u>hell</u>** — *"helle gemunde"* — *they know about hell and this is a fact.*
Beowulf prophesies it for Unferð 588; but even the noble monotheist ~~as his~~
Hroðgar
[from "helle gemunde" to "a fact" is written in the left margin. There is no obvious insertion point.]

The reward which he foretells to Beowulf (955)
[955 is written in the left margin. There are no parentheses in the MS.]

a fortune also in Norse bestowed on Sigurd ~~as the~~

<u>gewat .. secean soðfæstra dom</u> ~~in which we~~ that is

<u>soðfæstra dom</u> by itself cd. have meant "the esteem of the just and good", the <u>dom</u> which B.

Footnote Text
[The footnotes are written at the bottom of the page, extending into the left margin. They are separated from the main text and from each other by horizontal lines.]

Footnote 1
<u>heofon</u> in the sing. or plural,

Footnote 2 Text
which is seen coloring references first in Chr. lit.

<u>of ðam wyrmsele</u> — V. 36 <u>sá er undinn salr orm a hryggjum</u>

Folio 57
as a young man had declared to be the prime ~~object~~ motive of good conduct

Yet Beowulf himself though troubled by dark doubts at first, and ~~at the end~~
^ later declaring his conscience clear, thinks at the end only of his barrow and
memorial among men, and ~~the extinction~~ of his ~~lineage the~~ childlessness, and
~~the~~ of Wiglaf the sole survivor of his kin . . .
["2729" is written in the left margin. "Beowulf" is underlined and the underline
crossed out.]

his memorial ~~is t~~ is the virtue of his kingship

Though there are special problems such as Hroðgar's ~~sermon~~ ^gidd ~~172~~ (esp
1724–1760) and particularly ll. 175–188

(in one poets' mind or of ~~a period~~ a whole period's thought!)

starting with the hypothesis that the poet ~~had reason, and~~ tried to do something
definite

~~In prefa~~ I should say that the strongest argument that ~~a~~ the actual situation of
the poem . . .

we find in the poem differentiation. ~~M~~

we can ~~for instance~~ distinguish plainly for instance

Folio 57 verso
[the following text is written upside down at the bottom of the leaf. The text is
struck out with a large pencil scrawl.]

^Rather The sole reference is in ll. 186 ff <u>wel bið þæm þe mot æfter deaðdæge</u>
<u>Drihten secean</u>, 7 to <u>Fæder fæþmum freoðo wilnian</u>; ~~&~~ if we accept this as genu-
ine (a point I will come to in a moment) it is expressly denied to the heathens
spoken of (Hroðgar and the Danes).

Folio 58
accidental tinkering by "monks" or others concerned only to ~~introduce~~ ^graft on
^at random familiar Christian matter.

Though this is clearly ~~eventually~~ ^ultimately due to some gentleman . . .

. . . extract from the poem all references to religion, ~~m~~ fate or mythology . . .

those things <u>which are said in speech or reported</u> ~~of~~ as actually said or thought by characters.

<u>Hroðgar</u> & <u>Beowulf</u> are quite distinct.

wise and pious a noble monotheist who refers all things to the favour of God ~~(halig God, wigtig Dryhten, Alwealda)~~ and never omits explicit thanks for mercies. [<u>Beowulf</u> refers to God only . . .

[The square bracket before "Beowulf" is very heavy and large, and there are penciled lines separating from "Beowulf refers" to "nicors to luck, saying" from the main text and the footnote.]

and follows immed. with gæð a wyrd swa hio scel

<u>leoht eastan</u> . . ~~Godes~~ <u>beorht beacen Godes,</u>

Footnote Text

[The footnote is separated from the main text by a horizontal pencil line. It extends into the left margin beyond the main text margin.]

<u>halig god</u> 381, <u>god</u> 478 ^ 930, 1397 ~~716~~ <u>Alwealda</u> 928 ^ 955, 1314, <u>wuldres hyrde</u> 931, ^ Dryhtnes miht 939 <u>Eald metod</u> 945, <u>mightig Drihten</u> 1398, <u>mihtig God</u> 1716, Metod 1778 <u>ecean Dryhtne</u> 1779, <u>wigtig Drihten</u> 1341. — I omit the <u>gidd</u> 1724–1760.

[In Klaeber, the line given as 939 above is 940.]

Folio 59

[a penciled vertical line is drawn through the entire left margin of the leaf.]

It wd. be quite wrong to put an "and" in here.

(4) B. says

(5) 967: B

(6) 977: B says

(7) 1272–3 The poet says that B. ~~trusted~~ gemunde . . .

Though we still ^ [see] the preeminen~~eet~~ ~~of~~ ^ [trust in personal] might — ~~the~~ even of God's gift ~~up ??? this is the most religious thing said of Beowulf as a younger man~~

Folio 60

[a penciled vertical line is drawn through the entire left margin of the leaf.]

(10) ^ [(2329 f)] Beowulf in his old age — now frod cyning — is said by the poet to wonder if he had offended God (who was conseq. punishing him with the dragon) : wende se wisa þæt he Wealdende ofer ealde riht ecean Dryhtne bitre gebulge. Perhaps the least Chrs. thing said of him

(11) 2469. B. says

But this is a mere phrase (from Chr. poetry?)

the expression is \ rather that of the poet as narrator.

Beowulf definitely equates wyrd and metod: ac unc sceal weorðan æt wealle, swa unc wyrd geteod metod manna gehwæs.

[Here JRRT does not accept Klaeber's insertion of furður.]

where God and wyrd become merely death or ill fate are opposed.

It is in Metod originally ~~orderer measurement and ordinance fate (O.N. mjötuðr fate dispenser (of fate) rule, but also — doom, fate, death: O.S. metod, endurer~~ measure or measurer — ordainer or ordinance — destiny* we see ~~that~~ [a] coalescence point of the pre Chr. with the Christian

Footnote Text

[the footnote is written at the bottom of the leaf with a left margin extending past the left margin of the main text.]

C.f. O.N. mjötuðr, dispenser (of fate), ruler — also doom, fate, death. OS. metod is singly "ambiguous" and like O. E. Gabriel in the Heliand says of John the

Baptist that he will not touch wine — <u>so habed</u> im <u>uurd gescapu metod ge-</u>
<u>marcod endi mahti godes</u> (128); again it is said of Anna the widow when her
husband died that sie thiu mikles maht <u>metodes</u> tedelda, uured <u>uurdigiscapu</u>
(511). In both "fate" is nearer than God. In O.S. metod (or <u>giscapu</u> and <u>metodi-</u>
<u>gesceaft</u> = fate as OE meotodsceaft.

Folio 61

[a penciled vertical line is drawn through the entire left margin down to the end
of the paragraph that ends with "metodsceafte.]]" The two square brackets at
the end of this paragraph are quite large and dark.]

(13)   Beowulf in his $\wedge$ ^penultimate^ speech
sc. ~~swearers of wrongful oaths or for~~ perjurers, murderers, and adulterers.

[Tolkien in the manuscript has used the abbreviation sc. (Latin "scilicet",
"namely")]

(14)   In his last speech B. says
and his kindred — ealle <u>wyrd</u> forsweop mine magas to <u>metodsceafte.</u>]]
[The two square brackets are large and heavy.]

so 441ff, ~~???ff~~ 685ff, 967. Thus we have in *Beowulf's* <u>his</u> language

as where <u>gæð a wyrd swa hio scel</u> immed. follows his assertion

that *Dryhten* holds the balance in his combat; or where <u>wyrd</u> and <u>metod</u> are definitely equated ~~(2526f)~~ — with which compare ~~equation~~ 2814f. where <u>wyrd</u> is
more active and <u>metodsceaft</u> = doom death).

It is B. who says <u>Wyrd</u>

(immed after calling the Sun ~~(beacen Godes)~~,

Swa mæg <u>unfæge</u> eaðe gedigan

Folio 62
B. ~~He~~ only ~~once~~ ^twice^ explicitly thanks God ^or ackn. His help^:

"(1) 1658–1661 . . . under water" is inserted from the top margin with an arrow
after "explicitly thanks God"

he thanks <u>Frean Wuldorcyning</u> .. <u>ecum Drhytne</u>
[only two dots in ellipsis.]

~~Other references are more formal~~ Other references are the merely formal

is under no possible ~~þ~~ suspicion of later addition or revision. More remarkable,
but ~~som~~ having some simil. to Beowulf's other references to God as Doomsman,
is his declaration ~~that~~ (977)

There remains ~~2429f and~~ 2729ff: ~~in the first t~~ where Beowulf examines his
conscience

his death is, however, ^ *actually* comforted by the sight of the gold he has won.
[With the crimes Beowulf says he has avoided cp. the crimes that are punished
in hell in Völuspá 36.]
[square brackets are used in the text.]

Footnote Text
[A horizontal line drawn across the bottom of the leaf separates the footnote
from the main text.]

It would be truer to regard ^ the language of Beowulf as Christian ~~poetry~~ diction
partly "paganized"

it seems to me ~~to~~ clear that the language of poetry — as known to the poet, as it
<u>was</u> before our <u>Beo.</u> poem ever took the shape we see — was already Chris-
tianized, and familiar with Christian ~~themes and~~ and Hebraic terms (O & N.T.).
We have ∴ in O.E. not only "heroic" language misused but also ~~or eas~~ Christian
language misused

Folio 63
Even where reference to B's <u>thought</u> is made

Finally ~~when~~ the poet tells us that when the dragon's ruinous attack was reported <u>wende se wisa þæt he Waldendes ofer ealde riht ecean Dryhtne bitre</u>
<u>gebulge</u> ~~further perhaps the most pagan of all thought of all unwitting "sin;"~~
~~trespass punished~~

We have thus actually in ~~poe~~ "Beowulf" an historical poem or an attempt at one
(though ^ lit. historical fidelity was not ever attempted).

looking back on the heroism ~~darkness~~ and gloom and seeing in it something

The man who wrote <u>Beowulf</u> so far from being a muddleheaded semi-pagan —
an historical~~ly~~ impossibility ^{probability} in any part or period of England to which
our poem can be ascribed . . .
["probability" is inserted above the "possibility" in "impossibility".]

Footnote Text

[the footnote is written at the bottom of the leaf with a left margin extending
past the left margin of the main text.]

F - Ch 2 (p 8 Reyky) again ch. 17 (R. p. 73) Almátigr

Folio 64

in delineation of the great king of <u>Heorot</u> we ~~have~~ see strongly the influence of
the O.T. — and in the <u>folces hyrde</u>, Hroðgar, have something of the devout ~~me~~
shepherd patriarchs ~~who trust~~ ^ ^{servants of the} one God.

the noble pre-Christian — ~~which~~ ^{who} can lapse nonetheless (as could the Israelites) in times of stress into "idolatry". ~~This is how~~ ^ ^{in ll 175ff} ~~he links on his
traditional home of the~~ <u>heathendom</u> ~~of the Danes, prob. also of special religious
assoc. of Hroðgar's capital, with the general atmosphere he is depicting. On the
other hand, the tradition of poetry (and traditional of co al code among the
aristocracy) would enable him~~It is of O.T. lapses and idolatries rather than of
events in England (such as northern reversions in the 7th century) that he is
thinking about 175ff,* ~~when~~ and which colour his manner of allusion to knowledge of the Danes as heathens and prob. of <u>Heorot</u> (Hleiðr) as a place of originally heathen religious import which he derived from native tradition.

in the code of conduct ~~and~~ of the nobles of England

Footnote Text

[The footnote is written at the bottom of the leaf, separated from the main text
with a horizontal line. The left margin of the note extends beyond the left
margin of the main text.]

From 175 ~~wið þeodþreaum~~ 179 <u>hæþenra hyht</u> we can confidently accept as
original.

wholly different grounds — style, rhythm tone. I find it v. difficult to believe
that 180–188 was by same hand

But it is really preposterous that an author who has carefully (& for good
reason) depicted <u>Heorot</u>

shd. say 180 <u>Metod hie ne cuþon</u> etc. of Danish counsellors.

Folio 65

The whole must have succeeded admirably in creating in the minds of the poet's
contemporaries ~~a feeling of~~ the illusion of surveying a past,

This last is an effect of and a justification ~~which the old fashioned criticism of
poetry ?good? "the best things on the fringes" of the use of~~ of the use of
episodes and allusions to old tales
[The "use of" that is not struck out is written in the left margin.]

The poet has made the appeal of antiquity so ~~exp~~ deeply appealing. ^{I think ??? deeply}
_{who ???}

[From "The old fashioned criticism . . . so deeply appealing" is written at the
bottom of the leaf and inserted with an arrow between "than the foreground"
and "To us perhaps".]

To us perhaps, in a way he could **t** hardly have hoped for this appeal, is
strengthened since the poet himself and his work has slipped back far into time

of ^{~~Now with a strange~~} ~~the ancient days bewailing~~ ^{we hear this only now} of sorrows that were
ancient already in ancient days.

Folio 66

The poem has ^ ^{then} both a theme (or interwoven themes) and a structure

The pagan theme ~~the~~ <u>man upon earth</u> and his war with the ~~chaotic~~ ^ ^{inhuman}
world, doomed to perpetual defeat in particular, and to <u>final defeat in general</u>
— in which his chief stay and reward is <u>dom</u> (self-approval and the approval of
all good men) — is presented not only by a contrast in ~~and~~ the foreground
between ~~youth and~~ successful youth and old age defeated, which is made sharp
and ~~deliber~~ definite, but also symbolized by the nature of his adversaries.

But this is ~~a certain extent~~ somewhat changed ~~by God~~ by Christian thought.
["Somewhat" is written in the right margin.]

The defeat in time, in spite of favours and answers to prayer, <u>death inevitable</u>,
is still emphasized ~~But God is a now with man, and the fight is good~~ remains in
fact the really ~~inevitably this has shifted~~ dominant idea.

~~It~~ The battle is not in vain ultimately and though all human glory þ success,
victory ~~pow~~, wealth, power, majesty wisdom ~~go~~ will ~~down~~ fall defeated physically by the inhuman ...

In the war with the world his battle is that of the Spirit . Grendel, too, as we have seen becomes
more "devilish" and less merely elemental — more like the inner enemy the evil
possibilities of debased human nature, ~~even~~ ^{just} as in defining him and his
broods as <u>Godes andsaca</u> he has become ~~þa~~ in fact offspring of Cain; that is ult.
of Adam

The Dragon ~~whom we see~~ remains more elemental, more pure malice whelming
good and evil alike, at once the destroyer of Beowulf individually, and ^{also} the
kin of the great serpent devourer of the world at last.

Folio 66 verso
connexion of this with the metre — art more that of painting or sculpture than
music

Folio 67
The structure of the poem ~~is~~ is plain enough — if we take only the main ~~and~~
points,

But it does not ~~serve~~ mean to advance steadily or unsteadily.

a description of two "moments" in a life. It is divided therefore into two
contrasting ~~halves~~ ^{portions},

A from 1–2199 including the Exordium of 52 lines. B 2200–3182. The proportion cannot be caviled at — it is for the purpose and the production of the
effect right.
[there is a crossed-out descending stroke between "it" and "is".]

~~Within~~ This simple structure is in each ~~half~~ ^{portion} much diversified and adorned.

But to my mind there is ^{actually} one point in each ~~half~~^{portion} ~~the against~~ which ~~ser~~ can be seriously raised.

In the first ~~half~~ portion I would instance the report of Beowulf to Hygelace
["portion" is written in the right margin.]

and is in any case imposed on the poet by his more or less static contrast-structure with its two ~~pictu~~ opposed picture, it is not wholly successful ~~in the~~
["in any case" is written in the right margin.]

Folio 67 verso
[the following text is written right-side-up, in pencil, at the bottom of the leaf:]
We may think rather of <u>*Malory*</u> *— were all or most of pre-Malory lost. Discrepancies* <u>*not*</u> *a proof of composite authorship in final story. It is extraordinarily difficult even in an invented tale* <u>*to avoid minor discrepancies*</u> *Not often noticed by author or audience. Critics have seldom written.*

[the following text is written upside-down, in ink, at the bottom of the leaf:]
In <u>structure</u> — to take only the most large and general points the strategy (omitting the consideration of the tactics of this and that method of narrative
∧ ~~and~~ mu or allusion) ~~in~~ is plain enough, and if once the notion that

Folio 68
reminiscence is too long in proportion and not ~~sufficiently~~ always sufficiently suitable in the ~~rest of~~ character and atmosphere . . .
["character" is written in the right margin.]

Yet without <u>all</u> that we have got the magnificent final movement, ~~the last~~ 3137 – end,

The recapitulation, granted, is necessary is done very well

and serves to demonstrate vividly the portrait of a young man, singled out ~~of~~
∧ ^{by destiny for} great things ~~by destiny, until t~~ as he steps suddenly out into his full powers.

The old tale was not first told by our ~~all~~ author. ~~nor even~~ tThe sluggish bear's son with his hug ^who wakes up and becomes famous is a ~very old~ folk tale~:~, ~But~ the legendary association of the Danish ~eo~ and Heorot with a marauding monster, and of the arrival from abroad of a "champion" of the "bear-argr" was not ~made~ ^invented by our poet.

[The period after "folk tale" is modified in pencil to change it into a comma. "Very old" is circled.]

The "plot" is not his, though ^he has poured feeling ~has flowed~ into it quite different from its simple crude essentials.

~Yet~ And that plot is not ~qu~ perfect

it would have been better if ~it~ we had no journeying. ~and~ If ~It~ the single nation and land of the <u>Geatas</u> had been concerned
["If" is written in the right margin.]

in one people and their hero, ~hu~ the human whole and their heroes.

Folio 69

the essentials of the previous part are taken up and compacted ~into~ so that all the tragedy of Beowulf' is contained

["in essentials in the section 1888–end." Is written after "the secondary contrast of <u>age</u> and <u>youth</u> in the persons of Hroðgar and Beowulf — " but inserted with an arrow after "all the tragedy of Beowulf' is contained".]

The one really silly thing to do with "Beowulf" ∴ is to read only 1–1888 and not the rest.

An interesting point ~in this connexion~ may be mentioned here.

since the passages of close similarity in the 2 poems are found ~rather~ in ~their near~ natural surroundings and applications in Beowulf ^rather than in the Christian'romance'.

the connexion ^is undoubted and serves to suggest that "Beowulf" itself ~is s~ has some relation to the great <u>missionary epoch</u> of the 8th century.

They ~were adv~ went to the courts of kings

Folio 70

Granted that "Beowulf" was written in the 8th c.

~~One~~ The "allegory" ~~as it is~~ ^{cd}. hardly have escaped contemporaries, although the poet has actually done nothing to ~~make it~~ ^ ~~*paint a moral in*~~ underline it ~~explicit~~.
["underline" is written in the right margin; "it" is in the left margin.]

for the half ~~iron~~ surprised almost ironic question

All this is ^ ^{nonetheless} purely subsidiary — and hardly affects the real feeling and movement of the poet's mind. ~~Having said so much we have said~~

Folio 71

one ought as a kind of appendix to General Criticism point out that ~~p~~ it should fall in his department to assess the art and technique in detail of the poet — was he good as an O. ~~P~~ E. poets go, was he good in a general literary view.

It is one of the misfortunes of E. which possesses at the beginnings of its career a language and a verse technique such as O. E.

For this language ~~is a tr~~ and verse is a true one — we have just enough preserved to reveal that. And (since this is but another way of saying the same thing) this requires considerable study for lit. appreciation. Old English

those tones and echoes that come from long lit. cultivation.

It is a worthy and enriching lit. experience.

one real reward of O.E. scholarship which a student of European Lit (a mere student of E. Lit is an inconceivable monster) cannot leave out of the picture — Beowulf.

[*Beowulf* and the Critics: B-Text]

Folio 92

. . . the Rev. Joseph Bosworth, D.D. , F.R.S. Rawlinsonian Professor of Anglo-Saxon
[No comma after F. R. S.]

He may do very well for a Professor . .'

[Only two dots in the ellipsis.]

Shrine
[written in the left margin next to "D.D., F.R.S."]

[A vertical pencil line is draft in the left margin from "D.D., F.R.S." to ""the study of Anglo-Saxon." Next to this line is a penciled "1".]

These words were inspired] by annoyance with Bosworth's dictionary,

the study of Anglo-Saxon had ~~considerably~~ ^{perhaps} declined in England, ^{and} where this study was ^{had for} not so much dependent

"token insider 2"
[written in the margin next to "on foreign (German) work".]

[From "by annoyance with Bosworth's dictionary" to "the serious problem of books <u>about</u> Anglo-Saxon." is underlined in pencil.]

the books that have been printed ^^{on} about, around . . .

some understanding of its language — ~~a thing which a practice~~ though this does not appear to have been the universal practice of the critics.

The dwarf ~~intensive student~~ ^{on the spot} sometimes sees deeper

[There is a faint vertical line in the left margin next to the final two lines of the leaf.]

Folio 93
period when literature was ~~of~~ less wide in range

repeated below
[written in the upper left corner of the page.]

[there is a faint vertical pencil line in the left margin alongside the first three lines of text.]

ideas which are still afloat although supposed to have been long exploded.

[written in the left margin alongside "that which is still current and influential, whether for bad or good".]

It began over 200 years ago,

[There is a faint vertical pencil line in the margin alongside the five lines of text beginning with "I pass, therefore . . .".]

whose ~~now~~ accumulated results we inherit

what was still 100 years ago large ∧^*ly* unintelligible ∧^*in detail* a poem

Folio 94

and last ^*later* actually in time (though not least in ~~p~~ importance)

Poetry has indeed ~~by~~ ∧^*been so* overshadowed by others,

<u>Beowulf</u> and the Heroic Age in England, 16 pages and all too short, ~~in~~ contributed by Chambers to Sir Archibald Strong's translation,

"Constable"
[written in pencil in the left margin.]

Folio 95

"A man found a mass of old stone : it was ~~as a matter of fact~~ part ^*an old ruined house* ^*under whose shadow he had built him* of the old wall of his small house and in a garden which had recently ~~built~~ been considerably altered and enlarged. Of this stone he ^*built* ^*a tower in a* made a rock-garden. But his friends coming at once perceived that the stones had formerly been part of a more ancient building; and they <u>turned</u> ^*pushed* ^*the tower over* the stones upside down to look for hidden carvings and inscriptions; some suspected a deposit of coal under the soil and began to dig for it. They all said "Thi~~se~~ garden ^*tower* is <u>most</u> interesting!" but they also said "What a jumble and confusion it is in!" And even the gardener's best friend, who might have been expected to understand, or at least to enquire, what he had been about, was heard to say : "He's such a tiresome fellow — imagine his using these beautiful old stones just to ^*build a nonsensical tower without even a bed-room* set off common-place flowers that are found in every back-garden : he has no sense of proportion, poor man!" ^*But the tower looked upon the sea* I might add that, of course, the less friendly when they ^*but from ~~that tower~~ the top of that tower ~~you~~ he could see the sea* were told that the gardener ^{man} was an Anglo-Saxon and often alluded to beer, understood at once. A love of freedom may go with beer and blue eyes, but that yellow hair unfortunately grows always on a muddle*d* head.

[the underlines are written in pencil. "In a" after "of his small house and" is written in the left margin.]

~~That allegory is perfectly just. Before we~~ ⁺ ~~come face to face with the more recent and more intelligent critics and attack the picture of Beowulf as it is becoming fixed and perpetuated~~

Folio 95 verso

[paradigms and exercises in Gothic.]

Folio 96

it is clever allegory of contemporary politics

Folio 97

which I have deliberately selected as a representation of a common view as expressed in English — the quintessence of research, that residuum that finally gets home to the public

[written in pencil in the top margin.]

qualified commendation. /Why is this so? The answer is important. /
[square brackets in the text in pencil.]

the sort of thing that scholars, young or old, ~~seldom~~ ^ ^{do not} read though they occasionally write them

and if one wonders ^ ^{whence} ~~where~~ the strange nonsense comes

it states explicitly the reason ^ ^{why}, amid all dispraise,

Folio 98

and ^ ^{was} nearer to the point than any critic other than Chambers.

Beowulf, probably justly (though it is one of the more important single pieces produced in all those 1200 years) gets less than 2.

We will now pass on and consider the summary and ^ ^{the} comment on it
[the passage from "Beowulf is the only poem" to "of the Teutons" is underlined,

as is the passage from "Though biblical allusions" to "Christian but heathen."

heroic poetry of the Teutons. ~~Bear that in mind. And the passage~~ And it ends:

Footnote Text

[The first footnote is inserted between "with attention; indeed" and "he cared sufficiently." Its margin extends into the left margin beyond the margin of the main text. It is separated from the main text by a line above it.]

[The second footnote is inserted after "and in the introduction" and before "to his translation. Its margin extends into the left margin beyond the margin of the main text. It is separated from the main text by horizontal lines above and below it.]

I remain of opin~~ar~~ion that

(the metré used by Morris in <u>Sigurd</u>) *and not in itself a good metré.*

Folio 99

We are told how the hall of Hrothgar, King of the Danes
~~321 26 48~~
[the numbers are written in the right margin.]

Footnote Text

[The footnote is inserted at the bottom of the leaf. Its margin extends into the left margin beyond the margin of the main text. A horizontal line separates the main text from the note.]

For example ~~in~~ ^{there is} a more meagre and baser variety of the genre to which Strong's book belongs: <u>A History of English Literature</u> (in 111 pages) in the 'Peoples Books,' a potting by ~~C~~Dr Compton Rickett of his ^ ^{own} larger work. ["Dr." over-writes "C".]

Folio 100

Though ^ ^{they are} closely inter-connected, there are some distinct points

[MS Tolkien A 26 2 ends with this leaf.]

Folio 101

[MS Tolkien A26 3 begins with this leaf.]

The works of Homer contain some of the greatest of ~~the~~ recorded poetry,

the main interest of these works is 'not purely literary', to whom they are
^ primarily 'important historical documents.'

Footnote Text
[The footnote is inserted between "perfectly" and "legitimate." A horizontal line
above it separates it from the main text.]

~~The critical~~ Criticism and interpretation

Sometimes it alone can ~~su~~ give the decision

to my mind ~~this is~~ the probability

must relate ~~d~~ the glories of Jutes ~~?????~~ not Swedes. But this is ^ a primitive and
quite erroneous conception and with its ~~contemptuous~~ dismissal

It should never have been brought forward. *If Beowulf is a national epic it is an epic
of a ?peculiar kind? which includes both Gautr and Jutes. near no ??? why ???*

Folio 102
Svenska riht
[written at the top of the leaf.]

greater than (in ~~nearly~~ most all respects) than that of <u>Beowulf,</u>
["most" added in later pencil.]

as mainly of historical interest in a literary survey
[underline is in pencil.]

in places poetry so powerful, that ~~its~~ any historical value it ~~might~~ may possess

~~But~~ While in truth its historical value is dubious

But the air has been clouded for Strong, ~~and~~ as for critics worse and better

he was really *in large measure* moved by the poetical treatment ~~of semi-historical legend.~~
["in" is written in the right margin; "large measure" is written in the left
margin.]

a quarry, is ~~indeed~~ ^{*largely*} a product of art — an art that has used ~~a sen~~ indeed a sense of history, ^^{but} for the purposes of poetry, with a poetical ~~object~~ not an historical object.

[two vertical pencil lines are written in the left margin from the beginning of the paragraph that begins "But the air" to the end of the leaf. Two asterisks are written at the top of the vertical lines.]

Folio 103

or fall into ~~th~~ fallacies after Sir Archibald Strong. Lest the glamour of Poesis over come them

twists the judgement [even of those who do not explicitly ~~declare it &~~ approve ^{of} it, as Strong does.]
[square brackets in the text in pencil.]

But for this ~~example~~ false historical bias the critic

The <u>historian</u> would like ^^{*to have*} some of this early poetry of the Teutons

and does not in consequen see what <u>is</u> there.

Alas there ^^{is} no "early heroic poetry of the Teutons"

or indeed ^^{any such} Teutons.

which roughly corresponds ~~in~~ to the known and definite community

race, or ethics, ~~still less~~ ^{or} of poetry.

Folio 104

Germanic (or Teutonic) spirit, and ^^{it} is appreciable

For those lost and unguessable ^^{'Teutonic'} things

thus in the course of research prompted by ~~a~~

Folio 105

But it would ^<u>not</u> be the chief function

But here ~~still~~ 'early' is ^ *still* misleading.

ancient Germanic or Northern ~~verse~~ heroic verse;

This last point is ~~usually neglected except for purposes of~~ important, . . . that is a defect ~~to~~ in criticism to be deplored rather than concealed.

the individual Icelandic poets have been ~~p~~ better preserved *even*

Folio 106
>   The "Teutonic" *kind of* ~~sort of~~ criticism suggests ~~however,~~ that 'Teutons' had a universal ~~sort~~ kind of poetry and no individual poets.
>   ["of" is written in the left margin.]

Footnote Text
>   [the note is written at the bottom of the leaf with a left margin that extends past the left margin of the main text. It is written below a horizontal line.]

More recent ~~views~~ ^ hypotheses concerning Frisian intermediaries

Folio 107
>   The life, the times and the spirit, then of ~~B~~ the poem <u>Beowulf</u>

by some at least of the speakers of ^ *other* "Teutonic" tongues in later days — it has much that is perceptibly ~~common~~ similar

chief negative — in not ascribing
[written in the left margin next to "<u>The individual man</u>".]

to the cruel feuds ~~and~~ of the great houses and the submission to ^ the Norwegian crown in the 13th c;

tha~~t~~n Rome from Tarquin to Augustus ^ *or Augustus to Diocletian* .
[the "n" in "than" over-writes a previous "t".]

Folio 108
>   the period in which ^ *it* was composed, then ~~would~~ it is not only ~~be~~ illuminated by history, but illuminates that history in return. It ~~will~~ becomes a considerable document

The poem fits so well into the period, the eighth century $^\wedge$ *after 700*

~~and~~ that it can hardly any longer be doubted

already in the poet's day $^\wedge$ *memories* of a far past,

refashioned by a jeweller of a later time

the great time of the Anglo-Saxon $^\wedge$ *Christian* spring.

~~æ~~ what are we to make of ~~the~~ such statements as the one I quoted above?

in <u>Beowulf</u> "<u>Though</u> biblical allusion,
[There is a tiny cross-out beneath "in"; "Though" is written in the right margin.]

and that such ~~token~~ signs of Christianity as are to be perceived are ~~due~~ not integral, but due to the ~~confusion of and~~ $^{~~mental state~~\ confused\ mind}$ of the original author ["mental state" is added and crossed out in pencil.]

Footnote Text
[the footnote is inserted between "that" and "it can." Its left margin extends past the left margin of the main text. It is separated from the main text by horizontal lines above and below it.]

Folio 109
It would be only fair here to remark that better criticism ~~of~~ is actually moving in the direction I intend. Namely (1) towards regarding the Christianity as produced by an editor (2) by later making that editor an effective ???? who was trying to Christianize pagan tradition, but as you will see, this seems to me, though ^{a} saner view ~~probably the reverse~~ probably ~~an~~ perversion of the truth

[the above is written in pencil in the top and left margin. The section in the top margin runs from the beginning to "this seems." The section in the left margin runs from "to me" to the end. I have edited the section as best I can and inserted it where it appears to fit best.]

perhaps $^\wedge$ *of* some later writer who recast the antique poem.

But <u>biblical allusions</u> do <u>not</u>'abound' in <u>Beowulf</u> ; ~~and~~ ^ ^{while on the other hand}
<u>heathen deities</u>

This ^{then is where} and <u>not</u> their relative frequency is the important point

Nor does a heathen deity ~~eve~~ appear

the total ~~sche~~ history past present

was absorbed insensibly by ~~the~~ an omnipotent God

their names were <u>*not*</u> forgotten

Folio 110

the creation ~~of~~ half-hearted it is true) of an editor or scriver who is ~~heathen and~~
not the poet and ~~no~~ it would appear not in sympathy with the poet.

but original and effective author ^ ^{or authors}

a fundamental question — ^{to} which I will return later.
[The interlinear "to" is added above the dash.]

Sir A. Strong, chosen to represent ~~an~~ a common and still current kind of criticism makes himself after profounder study
["himself" is circled, and an arrow indicates that it is to be moved to just before
"makes".]

But Strong was essentially ~~a~~ more intelligent and perceptive
[immediately before "But Strong" is a wider space with a penciled mark that
could be an "a".]

from ~~pseudohistorical~~ ^{hypothetical} Teutons to Englishmen, from ~~phantasy to the~~
bogus history to real poetry.

Folio 111

to this same translation — ~~which~~ this Foreword should be read by all,

however, still — ~~in this ????~~ we gather

But ~~at~~ nonetheless it is real history

the period to which 'Beowulf' ^{*as given*} belongs is delineated,

"The folk-tale is a good servant Chambers' says

(made though it is to save the face of Homer to throw stones at whom would be impious), for ~~it~~ he continues

Folio 112
Deeds, p. xcix
[written in the left margin, next to "quotation".]

but one need not (as ⟨ Earle himself admitted) ~~attend the~~ give

fools who have ~~trespassed on paths too~~ rushed in with clumsy

Folio 112 verso
under heading of'historical document' I shall say all I need to about history of B. study.

Folio 113
that like Grendel in Heorot, is said ~~to have~~ wið rihte, against all propriety

If we can lay them, then indeed criticism of Beowulf will be gefælsod.
[The MS is clearly "lay," and the second word appears to have a dot above it, suggesting "therein" spelled as "therin." Such a reading could make sense (i.e., laying within the hall through the night so that it might be cleansed), but a missing "s" in front of "lay" seems a simpler explanation.]

'Bwf . 16:
[written in the left margin in the break between the two paragraphs.]

Few ^ ^{European} vernaculars have anything so old to boast

Many ^{*who have criticized*} 'critics' ^B have ^{*not*} possessed ^{???} none of these

quite unqualified for their self-appointed pulpits
["their" was originally "the"; the "ir" was added later.]

for I do not possess the worthless book
["worthless book" is lightly circled in pencil".]

(it is in fact so bad that it ~~might be~~ would seem to be by Mr. Leslie himself)

construe a line of the poem he ~~has the effrontery to~~ ^{slightingly} to refer to ^{refers} to, but has depended

Folio 114

or near beer in a self????'s parlour.
[written in pencil in the top margin. An arrow indicates that it is to be inserted after "hooch," though such a placement does not make grammatical sense. I cannot make out the word before "parlour"; it could be "soft????" or "self???" but neither leads to a compound word that makes sense in the context.]

It is ~~stuff~~ casual 'criticism' of this Chestertonian kind, of course, that is ^ ^{really} the 'small beer' or ^ ^{the} sour wine

it may be ^ ^{as} unworthy of mention in serious lectures as Grendel has ^ ^{been} held to be in an epic poem,

~~Like~~ I will venture to its lair.
balanced linguistically and culturally between ~~the~~ what we may casually define

or lame in one leg. ~~There is something of fashion to accord these gentlemen more attention than they deserve~~ Of these ~~Jusserand~~ there are ~~som~~ several examples (more important in such affairs than Mr Chesterton).

whither the thirst for second-hand opinions upon literary works will take p~~l~~eople.

the perusing of which is ~~much~~ more irksome

Folio 115

At any rate Jusserand's <u>Literary History of the English People</u> is ~~still~~ on the shelves of the English library

it is like potting a ~~blind rabbit~~ one-eyed rabbit on the blind side

a critical method, ~~and~~ as popular still as it is worthless.

There is a deal of history behind this, ~~for which if the ??? be softer one~~ ^ ^{and} ~~can~~
the men of today cannot be held entirely ~~responsible~~ to blame ~~in their ?????~~. Yet
there is usually present also ~~an exaggerated~~ an easy sense

Folio 116

~~no insularity quite so insular as that of the Île de France.~~
[written at the top of the leaf.]

Old English, is <u>primitive</u>, and has the savage ~~and~~ ^{or} rustic vices of incoherence
and boorishness

Such notions go with and are ^{usually} founded upon mere linguistic ignorance.

implications of what is said ~~be~~ can be understood

And actually therefore this ~~refers~~ sort of criticism commends itself

Jusserand, for instance ~~— just after he~~

Folio 117

That is precisely in modern English: 'whose name was Cerberus, and who has
been reported to have three heads'.
[there is a faint circle around the period that follows "heads".]

The original Old English is a ~~fairly~~ competent,

The attitude is ^ ^{the} quite unrustic one of incredulity

Folio 118

we pass to <u>Beowulf</u> — prepared ~~only~~, as I have said, to notice,

... may be summed up thus: 'liar, drunkard, coward, murderer!"

even when it is describing a Dane?
[written in the left margin, next to "behaviour".]

in a poem written in Anglo-Saxon is ~~the equivalent of~~ just a picture

and the ~~au~~ actual words 'liar, <u>drunkard</u>, <u>coward</u> or <u>murderer</u> are, of course ~~nowhere found~~ not employed at all.
[the single quote before "liar" is struck out in the manuscript.]

and of bringing ~~in~~ part of his earlier history before us, at the same time relating it and interlinking it cunningly with $\wedge$ ^{the} large and ominous background

Folio 118 verso
Of the study much elementary work had to be done. The text had to be deciphered, the language learned, the purport of the major allusions discovered, and last in fact (but far from least in importance) the metre analyzed. History, mythology, folk-lore, archaeology, and Philology rather than poetry were the fairy-godmothers at the christenings. But the inevitable if unfortunate fact that <u>Beowulf</u> belonged to a past the tradition of which was almost completely lost (unlike the case of the classical tongues) so that a long apprenticeship of 'research' was necessary has had a considerable effect upon the tone of criticism.

[the above passage is struck out with two heavy diagonal lines. The ink is smeared, but there are no matching smears on 119 recto.]

Folio 119
It is hardly necessary to point out that the ~~genesis of the~~ whole prejudiced misconception

that it has ~~been~~ not been observed that our modern use

in Attila's hall, <u>bjóri vas hón litt drukkin——</u>.
[the dash is struck out in the manuscript.]

<u>Atlakviða</u>
[written in the left margin halfway down the page.]

we shall still observe that, throughout, <u>Beowulf</u> is taken

Folio 120
The poet speaks of Danes
[written in the top margin and inserted after "referred to at all".]

the Prince of Denmark thought ~~in~~ 'a custom

Assyrians and such ~~likely~~ highly cultured people of the ancient world.

Though we can hardly avoid ^ ^{also} the suspicion

and acknowledges gratefully the gentleman's condescension✱)
[a superscript asterisk is struck out after "condescension)".]

Footnote Text
[The footnote is written at the bottom of the page. Its left margin extends past
the left margin of the main text.]

concerning the Germanic warrior in literature in ~~the~~ his <u>Introd. to Old Norse</u>.

Folio 121
<u>and of historical facts . . .</u>°
[There is a small circle with a dot in the center at the end of the ellipsis.]

[There is a vertical line in the left margin for five lines, beginning with "<u>fight
against</u>" and ending with "behind by Grendel".]

*The French Romances are as full of ???? to the ???? Dumas ????? by his brother
???????*
[written in the left margin next to the paragraph that begins "Old Celtic Tales!"]

though serious Calvinists they ascribe their furniture to ~~Sheraton~~ Chippendale

Folio 122
and any satisfactory interpretation ^ ^{*of the poem*} has to explain

that has rendered it now ~~???~~ unfamiliar

I do not deal here with the ~~di~~ diction and texture of Old English verse

The writing ~~and~~ in detail, the tactics,

~~But~~ But ~~ma~~ though some may ~~of~~ have lacked, not a few critics of <u>Beowulf</u> have
possessed an eminent scholarship in Old English.

It is not solely due ^ ^{*then*} to inability to 'read' Old English with understanding;
~~It ???and~~ and we

Folio 122 verso

We have only to apply this principle to any long poem to see how thoroughly and satisfyingly destructive it is. But is is capable of even wider application. 'No need to expatiate on the incoherence' to be observed in Europe, wherever you turn even if it be to France), a commixture of Celt and Goth and Frank ~~with ans~~ Roman with notions got from all quarters, barbarians, Jews, Greeks.
[the passage above is struck out with diagonal pencil strokes.]

Folio 123

the causes of this attitude (in different degrees) ~~an~~ even among the better

equipped for the reading of a ~~p~~ poem as poetry. ~~This~~ ^It^ is due in some part

the importance or function ~~of~~ ^that^ the reference or allusion

Real critics of <u>Beowulf</u> as poetry have always also been ~~love~~ in varying degrees lovers of history and antiquity as well.

though this anticipates ~~what shou~~ a point

the surviving manuscript was ~~com~~ written out.

~~A~~ And so far have the days when

[there is a horizontal pencil line in the left margin alongside the first three lines of the paragraph that begins "Nonetheless a far more potent cause . . ."]

Folio 123 verso

~~Need to consider the reasons for this attitude even among those who could n~~

Folio 124

not a mere example of ~~mer~~ 'story-motives.'

^A glance at^ the rise and progress of <u>Beowulf</u> studies ^will^ help us to understand how we have got to our own present position, and may help ~~us~~ us to go on further.
[interlinear "will" is added in later pencil.]

a living crib ~~in the~~ or interpreter. In his dealings with <u>Beowulf</u> he was perhaps not so fortunate $\wedge$^{in his crib} as in his ($\wedge$^{still} somewhat casual) dealing with Icelandic through Magnússon.

But Morris had a wild and wilful way $\wedge$^{even} with his cribs, and these cannot take the blame of his ~~certain~~ transgressions.

~~Much~~ The 'Morris and Wyatt' translation

The sole MS. in which it is preserved is a composite one,

Folio 125
  no 34
  [written in the top margin.]

  See R. Flower ? Dr or B He ?? vol xxi
  [written in the top left margin.]

  after the scattering of MS. remains in the 16th century

  On page 218 of his <u>Catalogus</u> of MSS. in vol II of Hickes <u>Thesaurus</u> (1705)

  However, we see $\wedge$^{here} if not the 'historical document' bias

Footnote Text
  [The note is inserted between "page" and "218." Its left margin extends past the left margin of the main text.]

  at any rate in its contempt and ignorance of the national ~~tongue and~~ ^{linguistic and} ^{literary antiquities} ~~language and literature.~~

Folio 125 verso
  More potent still the belief that it is impossible for adult men and women to really take pleasure in the actual main story of <u>Beowulf</u> — the 'wild folk-tale' — so that ~~the~~ he is thrown back on the allusions, which are largely (but not entirely) more 'historical.' This article of belief seems to me radically false, although I have never see it anywhere questioned or attacked. It ~~is~~ has grown up because become established because owing to the way in which Beowulf study has progressed from 19th-century 'research' painfully to criticism
  [The above passage is struck out with one vertical and one diagonal line.]

Folio 126

I have not ~~now the~~ here ~~much~~ time to say much about him.

his own 'Anglo-Saxon Verse' ^ ^written^ in dedicatory commendation of his patron

[the lines from Grundtvig are written in pencil in the left margin.]

His emendations of Thorkelin's faulty text, were often found actually to be in the MS, which he had not seen

Folio 127

and served to awaken ~~at~~ the notion

as secure still in its ignorance of the field ~~of Anglo-Saxon and Northern~~ and the achievements of Northern scholarship

he who first made out ~~among~~ many of the proper names

<u>Beowulf</u> was valued simply ^*mainly*^ as a <u>document</u>

<u>De Danorum Rebus Gestis Secul.</u> III & IV <u>Poema Danicum Dialecto Anglo-saxonica</u>
[the "D" in "Danicum" is written over a previously existing "S".]

Footnote Text

[The footnote is written in the bottom margin. Its left margin extends past the left margin of the main text.]

Folio 128

any Anglo-Saxon might be too difficult for him (without further study) to appreciate the magnitude of his offence.

relic of Anglo-Saxon poetry ~~time~~ which time

to wreak the <u>fæhðe</u> or deadly feud on Hrothgar, for a homicide
[<u>fæhðe</u> is underlined in pencil.]

But we need not be too severe ~~upon~~ ^*to upon*^ Turner:

eight at dov?? In age of B even
[written in the lower left margin.]

Footnote Text
[The footnote is inserted between "heroic" and "deeds." Its left margin extends
past the left margin of the main text. It is separated from the main text by pencil
lines above and below.]

Folio 129
Suhm, ~~and~~ ^{who} derived ^^{it} from Saxo Grammaticus,

~~Here it is the history of Saxo fo enters the field~~ With this theory

which was soon to ~~contend history~~ compete with history

see above ^
[written in the left margin approximately one-third of the way down the page.
This annotation seems to indicate that JRRT thought the note and the text
repetitive, and perhaps indicates that the author skipped ahead to write the
note and then returned to the main text to include the similar material.]

the nature of <u>Beowulf</u> than the reverse, ~~while~~ and because the elucidation of the
problem concerns ~~rather~~ the study of the traditions

remains an agnostic about ultimate origins (<u>Illustr</u>. p. 33),

Footnote Text
[The note is inserted between "employment" and the paragraph that begins "It
is to Conybeare." Its left margin extends past the left margin of the main text.
The note is lightly struck out in pencil. There is no note marker in the main
text; I have inserted the dagger.]

The Jutish hypothesis has still vigorous supporters such as Professor Elias
Wardstein.

Folio 130
and seldom even ~~in~~ approximately accurate,

from Germany, where he had studied; ^^{and} ; in general after Kemble ~~that~~ to
Germany the ball passed

B as best seller
[written in the left margin next to "it was sold out in a few months(!)".]

But though the text ~~marks~~ ^{shows} a great advance

copious as it claimed to be, and $\wedge$ ^{*in*} its day invaluable.

in a position which 100 years ago could only be gained by years of work

Footnote Text
[the note is inserted between "together with" and "<u>a glossary of the more difficult words.</u>" Its left margin extends past the left margin of the main text.]

Folio 131
to the "mythological" "*allegorical*" explanation of everything *save perhaps Grendel
& the Dragon* which is now as wearisome as it was once irresistibly fascinating.
["allegorical" is added in the right margin. "save perhaps Grendel & the Dragon" is added from the top margin.]

for there was produced ~~rather~~ the materials for criticism

Of these the ~~least~~ *less* useful process is dissection.

Introd. to <u>Deeds</u>. xxix
[written in the left margin alongside the line that includes "As Earle says:".]

which attended the first entertainment of Beowulf in the Fatherland" It is small
wonder

Footnote Text
[the note is inserted between "welcomed" and "by scholars;" its left margin extends past the left margin of the main text, and it is separated from the main
text by horizontal pencil lines above and below it.]

Folio 132
Chambers notes ~~almost~~ (with something, it would seem, of unnecessary
surprise) that it is on such a piece as <u>Widsith</u> that the older ~~were~~ scholars

Preface to Widsith
[written in the left margin next to "that Chambers notes".]

[a vertical pencil line runs in the left margin from the beginning of the leaf to "nature-myth-monger is most innocuous".]

the changes in the world, and in lesser world

studies of structure, tone, ideas, style ^ and language,

is not a man ~~of p~~ of ^ great originality nor of great penetration and poetic insight,

Decision, a view, a conviction are ^ now imperatively desired as Chambers rightly says: but oddly, since he is ~~the~~ ^ himself a master of indecision and ~~with~~ takes characteristically
[the colon after "rightly says" seems to have been a period changed to a colon with the addition of a dot in pencil.]

[there is a vertical pencil line that runs in the left margin alongside the last two lines on the leaf.]

Folio 133
[There is a vertical pencil line in the left margin extending down three lines from "The wanderings of Israel".]

in a maze of theory for 90 years or more.

~~The synthetic and~~ Synthesis and general literary interpretation and judgement

Oct 23.
[written in the left margin next to the paragraph that begins "As a representative of the sort".]

... amid the tulgy wood of conjecture ...

There was *also* other work, of equal or greater importance on the continent,

appearing first in the ~~80s~~ ^ 'eighties' and issuing in his
[the first "i" in "issuing" is dotted in pencil.]

the study of poetry — has become a thing which ~~can with study be~~

Folio 134

not only $\wedge^{\text{can}}$ be employed as a weapon of textual criticism, ~~can~~ but can be appreciated as an instrument of art.

is apt to seize on less intelligent minds, ~~indeed~~ and has curiously a special attraction

the measure, the $\wedge^{\text{pattern}}$ selection from the rough material of language.

[there are two three-line-long vertical pencil lines drawn in the left margin alongside the end of the first paragraph on the leaf.]

Cha. <u>Introd.</u>₂ 391.
[written in the left margin next to "Turning once more ..." is written: ".]

the general literary study of early ~~literature~~ *poetry*

one of the principal kings of the period to mention is W. P. Ker's Epic and Romance (1896); & One of the principal services of this work
["kings" could be "things," though it certainly appears to be "kings" in the manuscript.]

The study of legends and their interconnexion, and of ~~th~~ the history enshrined in legends,

"the belief tha~~n~~*t* (in the words he was fond of quoting)
[the penciled "t" over-writes the ink "n" in "than".]

Folio 135

Cha. <u>Introd</u> ₂. 292
[written in the left margin next to "adventures with Grendel".]

that "Beowulf's adventures with Grendel ~~s~~ and Grendel's mother

~~But~~ The death-blow was dealt to the mythical-allegorical interpretation

it ever had ~~???? ???? ????? past~~ any such significance.

'mere folktale' exists rather in as an abstraction of the student of origins

[there is a vertical pencil line in the left margin, three lines long, beginning with the paragraph that begins "At the same time modern archaeology".]

Cha. loc. cit.
[written in the left margin next to "as to the amalgamation".]

[There is a vertical pencil line in the left margin seven lines long, running from "Englishman" to the end of the leaf.]

Slowly but ~~with~~ inevitably the obvious becomes discovered, that we have to deal with poem by an Englishman using ^ *afresh* ancient and traditional material ~~???????? — though for what purpose~~ and it becomes plain that at any rate in addition to ~~explaining that~~ enquiring whence ~~it~~ ^ *this matter* came from, we must now consider what *the* ~~*he*~~ *poet* did with it.

["the" between "what" and "he" is added in the right margin.]

e.g. the Exordium. Actual use is to give glory — and historical perspective. M. Arnold [written in the bottom left corner of the leaf. A vertical ink line is drawn between these words and the main text.]

Folio 136

though it may have suffered accidents ~~of damage~~ of tradition (even occasional alterations here and there) — as may a*n* Elizabethan play.

Its 'religion' ~~is that~~ belongs to that man and is not a product of mere editing.

though largely concerned with Scandinavian tradition and history, are <u>English</u> ^ <u>traditions,</u> or traditions , ~~and in~~ thoroughly <u>Anglicized</u>

He ~~deserves~~ would deserve reverence, of course, even if he had not <u>ellor gehworfen on Frean wære</u>, ~~in~~ on the high mountain in Switzerland.

[the main text only fills 75% of the page. A horizontal pencil line is drawn across the page immediately below the main text.]

Folio 137

~~We have only to apply the method to all long poems to see how thoroughly satisfying it is.'No need to expatiate on the incoherence' to be observed in~~

~~Europe, wherever you like turn (even if be to France) compounded as it is of~~
~~many elements, a commixture of Palestine, Greece, Rome, and much beside.~~
~~You imagined you perceived a culture, which has been held worthy of honour,~~
~~and you find a 'medley'. As for Cain — here is a chance for genuine critic. The~~
~~making of the monsters the children of Cain is used as a stone to throw at a fool.~~
~~The thrower was the fool. For here we have one of the central points for a critic~~
~~to seize upon, to comprehend not to sneer at why Cain and Abel alone of the~~
~~names of Scripture appear in Beowulf. To this point we shall now soon come.~~
~~But there is still some elementary work to be done first.~~
[the above section is crossed out both word-for-word and with a diagonal pencil
line. It fills the top one-third of the leaf. There is a horizontal ink line across the
page after the large crossed-out section.]

~~I will turn now (with relief) to W. P. Ker, a name of reverence~~ 47
[this line appears below the horizontal line. "47," which is written in the right
margin, is the correct page number.]

A ~~critic~~ ^scholar who could read and move ~~and~~ intelligently in many tongues

old and mediaeval authors and their audiences~~;~~.
[there is a struck-out semi-colon before the period.]

Inter se passu *
[written in the right lower half of the right margin in pencil between two horizontal lines.]

1904.
[written at the bottom right corner of the page.]

which ?verse? shall he care of critics
[written in the bottom margin. The illegible word could be "news" or "?re?".]

Folio 138
[there are two short vertical pencil lines alongside the sentence "Beowulf has
nothing else to do . . ."]

the descent under water to ~~com~~ encounter Grendel's mother

There is much that is excellent there. ~~though not a little that is perverse.~~ It becomes still more remarkable if one reflects that it was written at least 30 years ago or & has not ^{seriously} been surpassed.

to penetrate the heart of the matter, and is content

Folio 139

But the sentence chiefly to note is the concluding one of my quotation. [Requote.]
[square brackets are in the manuscript. I have replaced "[Requote]" with the quotation itself.]

has become a commonplace of ^ ^{the better} criticism, a paradox ~~above~~ the strangeness of which has been forgotten in the process of swallowing it

he gave them ~~flowers~~ ^{a tower} and they wanted only stones!

Chambers, the <u>Beowulf</u>-poet's ~~m~~ best friend

~~As for~~ As for the poem, one dragon does not

Folio 140

make a ^{summer nor a host}. And dragons

part both of the machinery <u>and</u> the ideas of a poem or tale
["and" is underlined in pencil.]

Indeed the allusion to the ~~e~~ more renowned

he had his reasons. ~~which were not those of inst???ance~~

though it is now ~~turned~~ toned down,

we are told that that the folk-tale "<u>has been allowed</u> . . .

Folio 141

the story of Jack-and-the Beanstalk ^{the Giant-Killer} . in ~~??~~ excellent blank verse

we should surely ^{probably} look twice and pause to consider what in the process of his poetic effort he had made of ^ ^{it}, what alchemy he worked upon his trivial tale~~,?~~ ~~his monsters thin and cheap?~~

A man may ~~things~~ depict things lower

Paradox in Grim
[written in the left margin alongside the paragraph that begins "A man may . .."]

matter that is really not worth serious attention ~~and that is thin and cheap~~ ^that
remains'thin and cheap' when he has finished with it; ~~and~~ ^or that he showed in the selection of
his material,

A theory that will at least allow ^*us to believe* that what he did was of design and
that for that design there is a defense that is still of some force, is plainly ~~int~~ in
itself a good deal more probable.
[the "th" in "there" is written over "is".]

~~These~~ value of myth or folk-tale

with little ~~imagin~~ potential ~~power~~ virtue, besides much that is far more powerful, and which cannot be sharply separated from'myth' being derived from it, or
capable ~~of~~ in poetic hands of turning into it

It is quite possible to be moved ~~in~~ by'myth'

Folio 142
to deny ~~even~~ it, or ascribe it

'Myth' also labours under this ~~disability~~ disadvantage

A myth must ^*is mythological when* — be incarnate ~~not only~~ in human form,

We must have tragedy, and tragic conflict, and that of an especial kind, a kind
& form that drama could treat with success. If other modes ~~and~~ of imagination,

Folio 143
and such 'research' does ^not lead you into the higher regions of literature.

so much that ^*the enquirer* you come eventually to value the "outer edges" chiefly

I should like to know why. ~~But even if were proved up to the hilt as a general
proposition, we could still make two points. First, that Chambers~~ ^*in any case*

~~fights on poor ground when electing to give battle on the particular behalf of Ingeld. The story of~~

Folio 144

qua 'plot'

There may be been a treatment that made it so

[written in the left margin. I have inserted it where it best seems to fit the text.]

the easily persuaded (and perhaps not too intelligent) ~~has~~ is chiefly interesting as an episode

Let us get rid, then, of the cant, as it has almost ~~arisen to~~ become,

Beowulf's dragon, if you wish ~~to~~ really ^ to criticize, is not to be criticized for being a dragon,

Although there are in the poem some vivid touches (2293 ff) ^2285 of the right kind, in which the dragon is real worm, with an animalic ^bestial life and thought of its own,

Footnote Text

[The Old English text is written in pencil in the left margin. There is no footnote marker, and I have inserted the material where it best seems to fit the text of the passage.]

Folio 145

Something more significant than a standard hero, ^ ~~is~~ a man faced with a foe greater than any human enemy

used them afresh in an original ~~and indeed unique~~ fashion

or "old heroic poets": ~~;~~ as far as we know

Wælsing or Völsungr — Sigemund (O.E.), Sigurðr, Siegfried.

already it had for the author these 2 salient features — the Dragon, the killing of which ~~which is~~ mentioned ^ as his greatest deed and the supreme glory of the dragon-slayer:

["killing of which" is written in the left margin and inserted with a line and caret.]

Whatever dire origins Hhe has in prehistoric facts or fears
[The capital "H" is overwritten with the lower-case "h".]

Folio 146

and who yet, ~~they~~ though ^*they* would scarcely think of writing an heroic tale, have
been caught by the fascination of the worm.
["they" is added in later pencil.]

I think the shadow of research lies upon the critics, even when they are dealing with a
question of taste. ~~Summarized quite.~~ For one thing … nakedness. But there are more
modes of imagination than one. There is beside the ~~myth~~ hero legend the ~~mythical~~ and there
are blends. Myth suffers the disadvantage that it is best treated when not personally ? ? ? ?
and cannot be dissected & proved on paper, it dies under vivisection. I doubt very much
whether the an
The shadow of research.
[the above text is written on the bottom half of the leaf and struck out with a
diagonal line.]

Folio 147

Eft ongan eldo gebunden gioguðe cwíðan He wintrum fród worn gemunde

(ii)

Atol inwit gæst

Often an owl flying ~~unde~~ over the country of stones

They make plots in the ~~cities~~ towns to steal my gold.

[At this point three leaves are missing from the manuscript, though not from
the Bodleian's foliation. See above, Explanatory Notes, note 160. These leaves
are numbers 57 through 59 in Tolkien's original foliation.]

[57]

(i)

Iúmonna Gold Galdre Bewunden.

When ^ ^the moon was new and the sun young
[the "W" in "When" is several point sizes larger than the rest of the letters in the
line.]

in the green grass <u>was</u> silver spilled,
["they" is written in the right margin.]

~~and~~ the white waters <u>were</u> with gold filled.
["they" is written in the right margin.]

Ere the pit was dug ~~and~~ ^{or} Hell yawned,
there were ~~old~~ elves $\wedge^{of\ old}$, and strong spells
~~they~~ under green hills in hollow dells
by iron hewn and $\wedge^{by}$ steel chained.
Greed that ~~wrought~~ ^{sang} not, nor with mouth smiled,
graven silver and carved^{n} gold:
~~oer~~ ^{over} ~~Elfinesse~~ the shadow rolled.
["Elvenhome" is written in left margin, first in pencil, then copied over in ink.
"Elfinesse" is underlined in pencil, struck out in pen.]
There was an old dwarf in a dark ~~grot~~ ^{cave} ,
[the "T" in "There" is several point sizes larger than the rest of the letters in the
line.]

~~fingering~~ ^{to} silver and gold ~~he had got~~; his fingers clave

No feet he heard, though the earth quaked,
[the "N" in "No" is several point sizes larger than the rest of the letters in the
line.]

*with*Single ~~through~~ the long years to his gold chained;
["with" is written in the left margin in pencil.]

beneath the shadow of his ~~????~~ ^{black} wing.
~~and their blood drank~~, their blood drank:
["their bones crushed and" is written in the left margin, first in pencil, then
pen.]

and his bones were ash in the hot mire.
[58]
There was an old king on a high throne:
[the "T" in "There" is several point sizes larger than the rest of the letters in the
line.]

The swords of his thanes were dull with rust,
[This line is indented five letters.]

~~yet~~ his halls were burned, his kingdom lost;
["but" is written in the left margin.]

in a cold pit his bones were tossed.
[59]
There is an old hoard in a dark rock

old /Single ~~its~~ <u>dark</u> secret shall the earth keep.
["old/" is written in the left margin.]

Folio 148
[this is the final leaf of MS Tolkien A 26–3.]

Folio 149
[this is the first leaf of MS Tolkien A 26–4.]

one of the ever-recurring treasures recur again.

They have, in fact, no excuse. *It is only a result in an*
not wholly intelligible (not $^{often\ ????}$ always very intelligent),

[there is a vertical pencil line in the left margin beginning the sentence that
begins "Or rather ..." and extending six lines down to the end of the
paragraph.]

unless of course they ~~in~~ ^^{are} merely counting the heads of slain in the spirit of
the game-hunter.

pages 63 —
taken out for B Dead
[written at the bottom of the leaf.]

Folio 149 verso
There are of course by some quite
[written upside down.]

Folio 150
[a horizontal pencil line is drawn across the page between "... which informs
the whole" and "Of course I do not mean ..."]

Of course I do not mean ~~necessarily~~ ~~*of course*~~ to say that the poet,
[the first "Of course" is written in the left margin. The second "of course" is both written and struck out in pencil.]

his poem would ~~almost~~ certainly have been the worse.

hung with tapestries woven of ancient tales ∧ ^of ruin^ (each in itself a little world)

Folio 151

That even this 'geography,' once held as a materia*l* fact . . .

In them you will find well-wrought~~y~~ finish
[the "y" at the end of "wrought" is circled and struck out in pencil.]

if the common element ^~~and~~^ which ~~is~~ of course to some extent belongs to the language itself, to a greater extent to a literary tradition, —

∧ ^*It must be*^ In the theme,

For in fact if there is a real discrepancy between theme and style, that style will not be felt as beautiful, but as false. That falsity is present ~~??????????????????????????????????~~ ~~????????~~ *???????? in all the long A-S poems save one — Beowulf.*

Folio 152

Strong: in introd. to his translation
[written in the left margin next to the beginning of the first paragraph.]

'the light is but a foil to the dark.' ~~This is true — or rather it~~ This should perhaps

But if we ∧ ^*now*^ like to forget the encircling foe and its ultimate victory *in* ^*on*^ ~~time~~
the temporal ^*plane for each individually and for mankind as a whole*^ , despising <u>Beowulf</u>
[the section "for each . . . as a whole," is inserted from the left margin with an arrow.]

They (says Jusserand, meaning the Anglo-Saxons who he seems to think wrote Beowulf in committee over a surfeit of beer) fight against the monsters of Scand. mythology & see in them ~~to~~ ^*the*^ *descendants of Cain. But here is the critical point of a criticism (as distinct from contempt) to seize.*

[inserted from the top margin with an arrow.]

It is *a* ^{at} this point that the question of Cain

It has long been used as a stick to beat an ass.
[inserted from the left margin with a caret.]

who has grasped (and recorded this in print) the point,
["the point" is circled in pencil and an arrow indicates that it is to be moved and
inserted between "grasped" and "(and recorded".]

They should lead ~~to~~ direct to a more penetrating apprehension of Beowulf
["should" is circled in pencil.]

*[Chambers Foreword: xxvii — xxx From quotation of Quiller-Couch to the end
of Sir Ector de Maris' speech.]*
[square brackets in the manuscript in pencil.]

Folio 153

[there is a very large penciled square bracket written in the left margin that
runs from the paragraph that begins "A champion of . . ." to the paragraph that
ends "to which Achilles feared he might, despite himself, be driven".]

the folk-tale being'a good ~~master but~~ servant but a bad master'

the twenty-fourth Iliad: perhaps the greatest thing even when read in in
translation:

Yet Professor Chadwick has shown us how ~~the~~ a study of Beowulf

For in both we have a picture of ~~a~~ society in its Heroic Age.

and with all the civilization of the Mediterranean which came ~~into~~ England with
~~the~~ Christianity.

the rough outline of ~~the~~ what later becomes the mediæval ideal of the knight *[*
or the modern ideal of the gentleman.]
[square brackets in the manuscript in pencil.]

And ~~yet~~ the history of Europe during the incursions of the Germanic barbarians
tells of many a deed as grisly as that to which Achilles feared he might, despite
himself, be driven.]
[square bracket in the manuscript in pencil.]

In the epoch of <u>Beowulf</u>, ^{he is} a Heroic Age more old and primitive than that of
Greece is brought into touch with Christendom, with the Sermon
[this last sentence is repeated, with a slight improvement in phrasing, on the
following leaf, so I have deleted it here.]

?? 67 take with for the ?ending?
[written in the lower right corner of the leaf.]

Folio 154
[there are two lines of penciled writing at the top of the page that have been
erased.]

In the epoch of Beowulf ^{as} (he says) a Heroic Age more wild & primitive than
that of Greece is brought into touch with Christendom, with the Sermon on the
Mount, with Catholic theology ; and ideas of Heaven and Hell
[the comma between "theology" and "and ideas of" is struck out.]

/Polyphemus, by devouring his guests, acts in a way which is hateful to Zeus and
the other gods/ *yet the]* is Cyclops is himself
[square brackets in the manuscript. The second "the" is written in the left
margin.]

who where always in ambush ~~to t~~ to waylay a righteous man.

[If Spenser had known <u>Beowulf</u>, he would have found a hero much nearer to
his Red Cross Knight than Achilles or Odysseus . . . ."]
[square brackets in the manuscript. The first square bracket is written in pen
and overwritten in pencil; the second square bracket is in pencil.]

though a part ~~not~~ often not put into practice.

Virgil. Bk iii 600–66r. monstrum horrendum, informe, ingens
[the quotation from Virgil is inserted interlinearly between "forgive" and "But
the gigantic foes." It is written in pencil.]

Part of which it may change worked because as we shall see the ???? North indisputably move to monsters foes at once of gods and men
[written in the left margin.]

[A horizontal pencil line separates the paragraph that begins ".... Here we find" from the rest of the leaf. It is joined in the left margin with a vertical line that ends at the bottom line of text; there is a short horizontal line attached to the bottom end of the vertical line extending for approximately one centimeter.]

Folio 155

[the entire page is crossed out with one long upper-right to lower-left diagonal pencil stroke.]

Beowulf rejoices that he has sought no cunning hatred, nor sworn unright-eously oaths
["oaths" is circled and an arrow indicates that it is to be moved to before "un-righteously".]

that thou were never matched of earthly knight's hands;

and thou were the truest friend ~~that~~ to thy lover

to thy mortal foe that ever put spear in the rest.
[the "y" in "thy" is large and over-writes "ou".]

the combination ~~of~~ in Beowulf of valour

Seventh-Century England ~~i~~ did produce men of that type ..."
[the quotation marks at the end of this passage are exceptionally large.]

Folio 156

the imaginative apprehension of ~~things~~ the world.

but one filled with thought ^passion^ and emotion
[both the interlinear insertion and the cross-out are in pencil.]

the theory, one might ~~almost~~ call it, of courage, that is the great contribution of early Northern literature.
["almost" is struck out in pencil.]

[there is a vertical pencil line in the left margin running from "if the Trojans.." down for four lines.]

they would have ~~handed~~ ^{driven} Agamemnon and Achilles and all the Achaeans into the sea ~~an~~ ^ ^{more} decisively than the Greek hexameter routs the alliterative line

But rather — since ^ ^{with} ~~in~~ due reserve we may here turn to the tradition of pagan imagination in ~~Norse~~ ^{Icelandic} — with the central position

D.A. 57
[written in the left margin alongside "Ker has said . . ."]

As far ~~it~~ as it goes, and as a working theory

Folio 157

The relative part of the ?????
[written in the left margin 1/3 of the way down the page.]

into the tenth century. *This temper must (whatever difference & distinct c??) have found utterance as a fundamentally similar pagan eschatology* ~~Beowulf in~~

monsters
[written in the left margin 2/3 of the way down the page and is struck out with two diagonal pencil lines.]

some of the most fundamental changes of that alchemy are almost immediate.
^ ^{indeed instantaneous} /In a Christian country
[square bracket in the manuscript in pencil.]

as it is in the case of an individual.] *The new is a spirit the old is the material.* You do not
[square bracket in the manuscript in pencil; the penciled writing is written interlinearly.]

Folio 158

[It ~~is~~ would thus be a lesser error to think of <u>Beowulf</u> as an early medieval poem
[square bracket in the manuscript. The struck-out square bracket is larger than the other textual elements in the line.]

[~~If we~~ Take Ælfric, for instance
[square bracket in the manuscript. The square bracket is larger than the other textual elements in the line. There is an erased word beginning with "N" between the bracket and "~~If we~~".]

D.A. 12.
D.A. 36.
[written in the margin next to the quotations from Ker.]

Yet ~~they~~ *his homilies* are written in Anglo-Saxon,

the Sigelhearwan, with fiery eyes, ~~and~~ that are regarded as devils

The earlier age was not ~~how~~ less learned

such as Aldhel*m*, whom Ælfred considered

and they were stilled loved no less by Ælfred

Folio 158 verso
Part reached last time
'Beowulf' comes from a learned and educated & even reflective age, which remained <u>*English,*</u> *and had beside the newer learning a learned native tradition. The 'historical' temper not wholly due to extraneous influence. It is part of the whole diff. between say E & Iceland. The Chronicle & the sagas. Beowulf and the shapen Eddaic lays.*
[the above passage is struck out with one diagonal, upper-right to lower-left pencil mark.]

Folio 159
he strove to re-establish.] *It is the blending of the Northern pagan and Christian* It is thus
[penciled square bracket in the manuscript.]

to a poet who sets out to write a poem *such as B* — <u>write</u> it on a scale and with a structure of epic proportions quite unlike any mere minstrel's lay — such as Beowulf
["such as B" is circled in pencil and inserted from the top margin; "write it" and "of epic proportions" are circled in pencil. I have excised the second "such as <u>Beowulf</u>" for reasons of style even though the phrase is not crossed out in the manuscript.]

[Virgil, Statius, and Lucan are cited among the books studied
[penciled square bracket in the manuscript.]

nearly contemporary, possibly ~~an~~ actual*ly* contemporary, with the author of
<u>Beowulf</u>] ~~But whatever~~ It has been held
[penciled square bracket in the manuscript.]

∧ ^{It has held that} the influence, if no more than the exciting of emulation,

in the eighth century, ~~as has been held, is not~~ However that may be

This is clear ~~from the connected and~~ both from

a modern poet might ~~and all could~~ draw upon history

He is not a half-Christian because he describes heroic sea-burial,
[there is faint and illegible interlinear writing over "describes heroic sea-
burial".]

Folio 160

[there is a pencil line in the left margin that begins at the top of the page and
extends six lines down to "Avoidance of all . . .".]

was that <u>the days were heathen</u>. /This is specifically recorded even of <u>Hroðgar</u>
and his Danes in the famous passage 175 ff ~~178~~:
[penciled square bracket is in the manuscript. Underline is in pencil.]

Avoidance of all obvious ~~and glaring~~ anachronisms

that this silence has been con- strued

a distant antiquarian interest in ~~them~~ ^{*their figures*}; once so dominant, and so strong.
/But that was not so
[penciled square bracket is in the manuscript.]

Footnote Text

[the note is inserted between "con-" and "strued," separated from the main text
by horizontal pencil lines. Its left margin extends past the left margin of the
main text. The note and the footnote reference marks in the main text and in
the note are in pencil.]

Note text: and giving you ~~a~~ his own view of the origin of the monsters
[the asterisk that indicates the footnote is written in pencil in both the text and the note.]

Folio 161

Christian and pagan, ~~an~~ we emphasize rather than minimize

~~Saxons, as the Saxons and~~ Saxons in England, as the Saxons on the continent

The ~~sort of~~ pale lassitude, as it were,

to all parts of England. *]*
[there is an illegible struck-out pencil insertion above "parts." The square bracket is in the manuscript in pencil.]

*[*or referred to generally by the poet himself, ⟨ speaking as a Christian, as the devil (gástbona).*]*
[the square brackets are in the manuscript in pencil.]

often <u>Metod</u> ~~me~~ (Order or Ordainer)

which remains ^{ed} and remained ^{s today} a natural mode of reference

This cannot be defended as ^{archeologically} strictly accurate ^{∧ for the times depicted} ~~and not an anachronism since~~ we know nothing of ancient English ~~???~~ accounts of their Gods,

can they have ~~had~~ formed anything but the merest glimmer of an Almighty God, ~~and that~~ at most.

wynsyn f
[written very faintly in the left margin.]

Folio 162

in marked contrast to the Latin lands, while *where* the pagan religion was still in being, or later ^{∧ (as in Gaul)} when a tradition of warfare had survived ~~??????~~ it.
["where" is inserted from the top margin.]

A foreign paganism has little danger. *We get more doomed gods & ??? but only a ??? reflections of ???*

and many small courts — , strengthened,

Abroad ~~þe~~ they are stronger and more frequent.

Crawford p. 80
[written in the left margin next to "St. Paulinus of Nola (born at Bordeaux), in
the fifth century".]

Footnote Text
[The left margin of the footnote extends beyond the left margin of the main
text. The note is separated from the main text by horizontal lines before and
after it. The asterisks in the note and the main text are in pencil. The note is
struck out with one diagonal upper-right to lower-left pencil stroke.]

that were probably ~~quite forgotten~~ *not perceived at all by the Icelanders who handed them on* were
nece<u>ssar</u>y to courtly and <u>cul</u>tured verse.
["not perceived at all the by Icelanders who handed them on" is inserted with
an arrow.]

rapid *(*but at the same time astonishingly effective and deep-going*)* conversion
taking place at a much more primitive, more religious and less literary, stage.
Hybet disappeared — wihta or walcyrie

Folio 163
[the entire page is struck out with a diagonal upper-right to lower-left pencil
stroke.]

Frisian independence.
[there is faint, illegible writing in pencil above these two words.]

One may be ~~refl~~ permitted to reflect that

the <u>aristocratic</u> nature of pagan tradition ~~and its concern for the royal~~
[the underline is in pencil.]

Footnote Text
[There is no footnote-call marker in the text. The note is inserted between
"nonetheless to be" and "noted." The left margin of the note extends beyond
the left margin of the main text. The note is struck out with four diagonal pencil
strokes.]

the intense hatred of Frisia^{ns} ~~for the~~, in their struggle for independence, of the Frankish realm

Radbod died in ~~(~~719

Folio 164
[from the top of the page to "pagan kings who are lamenting in hell" is struck out with one diagonal upper-right to lower-left penciled line. There is a horizontal penciled line after "lamenting in hell" that indicates that the cross-out ends there.]

But this is ^ *also* evidence that ~~eve~~ in England even

It might certainly be regarded $^{by~all~most}$ ~~as~~ then (as still) <u>indecens</u> that
[interlinear additions and cross-out are in later pen.]

This was evidently $^{a~prevalent~feeling}$ ~~the prevailing temper~~.
[interlinear insertion and the cross-outs are in later pen.]

"The house is wide and has many rooms. To such a time and temper <u>Beowulf</u> belongs.
[no closing quotation mark in the manuscript.]

Almost one might regard a poem generated by the very century, being as one object to show the virtues of that path which ???
[the lines are written between the paragraph that ends ". . . <u>Beowulf</u> belongs" and the one which begins "The old gods disappeared . . .".]

in jest
[written in the margin next with two short vertical lines next to the passage "Almost one . . . path which ???".]

Footnote Text
[the note is inserted between "verba dei legantur" and "in sacerdotali . . ." Its left margin extends past the left margin of the main text and is separated from the main text by horizontal lines, one above the note and one below, that run from the left margin approximately one-third of the way across the page. The asterisks are both ink overwritten in pencil.]

Folio 165

   B 740

ac he gefeng hraðe forman siðe / slæpendne rince, slat unwearnum / bat banlocan, blod edrum dranc, synsnædum swealh; sona hæfde unlyfigendes eal gefeormod / fet 7 folma.
[written in the top margin.]

& nonetheless their going was not disastrous to the theme.

and not only were they not $\wedge$ *wholly* ousted by Moses or the Israelites^e warriors,

[there is a large square bracket in the left margin that begins at "and not only were they . . ." and ends at "of these figures . . ."]

A point especially to note in Chambers' ??? words is this:

He may accord *to* victory to either side

the Juno inigua *of Vergil, which is at all times what ?? of a ??? one must see in the world of ?????*
[written in the left margin along with the long Latin quote from Virgil. The writing here is exceptionally faded, and all I can make out from the manuscript is the notation "Virgil 600–665." I have therefore inserted these lines from Virgil into the text even though it is clear, simply from length alone, that not all these lines are written by Tolkien in the margin.]

assist in the ~~making of this~~ formation of this attitude.

The late Norse mythological survivals are not English, and are only ^{at} *a* best a possible illustration

Folio 166

The Titania pubes the $\wedge$ *fulmine deiecti* that Æneas sees c???on $\wedge$ *and hell* ??? ?? *fundo volvuntur in uno*
[mostly illegible pencil writing in the top margin. The above is all I can make out. An arrow indicates that this writing is to be inserted after "Olympian".]

Gods defend ????
[written in the top of the left margin.]

~~They~~ ^{The gods} neither need ~~their~~ ^{men's} help, nor are concerned in their struggles.

Men may worship or propitiate one or the other ∧^{gods or monsters} but he is not an ally of either.
[interlinear insertion in later pen.]

not as part of a great strategy that includes ∧^{the whole of} mankind, if only as the infantry of battle.
[interlinear insertions are in later pen.]

The wages of heaven are deeds
[written in the left margin. I have inserted it where it seems to best fit.]

Such beliefs may hold promise of a ~~higher and~~ profounder thought

the darkness. They fight along

Folio 166 verso
the contrast between the legends of the punishment ^{torture} of Prometheus, and of Loki — ~~for~~ one for assisting man, the other for begetting monsters ~~treachery for treachery~~ for ???the powers of darkness; high the ??? is who another if at all differ

Folio 167
Poseidon & Cyclops

gigept

gigant
[and some illegible pencil marks are written in the left margin]

they are in their very being but the ∧^{enlarged} shadows of great men and warriors

Loki~~s~~ is among the gods,

do not recognize kinship with ~~the~~ Fenris wolf any more than men with Grendel ∧^{Dragon} ~~and the~~.

in a poem *dealing* ^{deliberately} *with the noble heathen* ^{before Christ} *and his war with the world*

????

[interlinear insertions and underlining is in pencil.]

[there are two short vertical pencil lines in the left margin alongside "Cain and Abel . . . with the world".]

The monsters had been the foes of the gods, *who were* the captains of men, and the monsters would win <u>in time</u>; and in ~~the~~ heroic siege and last defeat [underlining in pencil.]

For the monsters also ~~still~~ remained.

Folio 167 verso
  Gods 56. ???????
  [written upside down, in erased pencil, at the bottom of the leaf.]

  79
  [written right side up.]

Folio 168
  ece Dryhten
  [written in the left margin.]

and the monsters were <u>His</u> foe *as of the old feuds*.
[underline in later pencil; "as of the old feuds" is written in pencil in the top margin and inserted with a line.]

The tragedy of the great ^ *temporal* defeat is poignant, but no longer of supreme
final . importance.

or the devils ~~became~~ *blended into* the monsters
[the first word in the interlinear insertion is not legible, and while it does not appear to begin with "b", I have chosen "blended" because Tolkien used this word in similar context in the appendix to "Beowulf: The Monsters and the Critics".]

its author is still primarily *??? of interest* concerned

It is indeed no defeat: ~~but~~ the end of the world ^ *is* but part of the design of its ^ *own* Maker,

[the caret before "is" is in pencil; the other interlinear insertions are in later pen.]

treated in this poem but for the <u>nearness</u> of paganism
[underline is in pencil.]

The work of defeated valour $\wedge$ *in the world* is still felt deeply.
[interlinear insertion in later pen.]

the history of kings and warriors $\wedge$ *in the old tradition* he sees that

and he is still thinking primarily of m~~a~~en in the~~ir~~ world and their glory
[the "e" in "men" over-writes the previous "a".]

Folio 169
by the door. ~~It is~~ Later we have

a poem from an ^{pregnant} ~~interesting~~ moment

in traditional forms ~~as~~that descended often from actual pre-christian authors
[the "th" in "that" over-writes "as".]

from the direct pressure of its despair, ~~and~~ He could

Footnote Text
[the first note is inserted between "even of doing" and "bodily hurt." Its left margin extends past the left margin of the main text, and it is separated from the main text by horizontal pencil lines above and below it.]

[the second note is inserted between "itself *" and "We are dealing . . ." Its left margin extends past the left margin of the main text, and it is separated from the main text by horizontal pencil lines above and below it.]

First Note
survives in M. English only precariously

Second Note
The 'mediaeval' is fully developed already in $\wedge$ *later* Old English. There is nothing but $\wedge$ the older language & the metre to distinguish

(which is prob. lineally connected with Cynewulf)

Folio 169 verso

For if Virgil is as he has been called ?????? education may attest of the spirit if not ????
the ???? of Anglo-Saxon Beowulf

Folio 170

Eph. v, vi.

[written in the left margin alongside "it was not the breastplate of righteousness,
nor the shield of faith for the quenching of all the fiery darts of the wicked".]

Virgil: multa putans sortemque animo miseratus iniquam

[written interlinearly between "darts of the wicked" and "Of pagan English
eschatology".]

Paganism is not ~~uni~~ usually ~~a~~ unified and coherent;

the ~~mo~~ dominant motive is that of courage,

Footnote Text

[the note is written at the bottom of the page in smaller script separated from
the main text by a faint horizontal pencil line.]

~~It was~~ Between the old Gmc. North and Christianity intervened an age crueller,
colder & more barbarous, one exalting slaughter and rapine, & encouraging
both unbelief and fantasy

Folio 170 verso

~~could view it with a~~

[written upside down on the page and struck out in pencil.]

83

[written and circled in pencil with a long horizontal arrow pointing from the
number to the right margin.]

Folio 171

is the idea of <u>lof</u> ^ *or dóm* — the noble pagan's desire

Folio 172

the praise of the dead hero. To make an Anglo-Saxon pun, this is <u>lást worda</u>
<u>betst</u> For Beowulf had lived
["To make an Anglo-Saxon pun, this is lást worda betst" is inserted with a line
from the left margin.]

Footnote Text

The note is inserted between "since the two" and "words were not . . ." Its left
margin extends beyond the left margin of the main text and a box is drawn
around it in pencil. The asterisk in the main text is over-written in pencil.]

Folio 173

[The poetic quotations are written without caesura.]

[I believe not that ~~for a man~~ the joys of earth
[square bracket in ink in the manuscript; strike-out is in pencil.]

one of three things ~~are with~~ trouble

will his life ravish .]
[square bracket in ink in the manuscript.]

þæt þðec, dryhtguma, déað oferswýðeð

[Soone hereafter it will come to pass . . . eyes shall foul and darken. ~~Soon~~ Swiftly
will it come that thee, o knight, shall death conquer.] .
[square brackets in ink in the manuscript.]

Footnote Text

[The first note is written in the left margin next to the quotation from the Wanderer. The second note is written at the bottom of the page after a single horizontal pencil line that runs from margin to margin. Its margins are the same as
those of the main text.]

First Note
+ MS tidaga

Second Note
Somewhat expanding the <u>þreora sum</u> on ~~the~~ lines found elsewhere

or in briefer allusion to thie well recognized theme
["the" was originally written "thi," the "e" was then written on top of the "i".]

Folio 174

that commemorate him ~~after d~~ in words after his death

praise him afterwards, ^*and* ~~is~~ his'<u>lof</u>' may live

This is a passage which, for its syntax alone, would ^*certainly* appear ~~certainly~~ to have been revised.

the sense of ^*the ambiguous* <u>feonda</u> is in the surviving poem made clear to ^*be* <u>deofle togeanes</u>;

Lofsong; loftsong are in M.E. specially used of the heavenly choirs.
[written in the left margin and inserted after "future life" with an arrow.]

the esteem ^*praise* of one's peers,

as a place or state of reward, ~~as~~ of eternal bliss

Footnote Text

[The note is written at the bottom of the page. Its left margin extends past the left margin of the main text. It is separated from the main text by a horizontal pencil line that runs across the entire page and a vertical line that runs in the left margin from the beginning of the note to the last line written in ink: "especial seat and the sun as His candle." The asterisks in the main text and in the footnote are overwritten in pencil.]

<u>heofon</u> in the sg. and pl. and its synonyms such as <u>rodor</u> are, of course, frequent but refers either to the particular landscape

and so on — but ~~are rather~~ these expressions
[both crossed-out words are written in ink. "Are" is struck out in pencil; "rather" is struck out in ink.]

~~In a sense of course~~ we may have simply lack of differentiation ~~betwee sy~~ between ^*??*
symbol & state — but in the pagan North the sky was ^*???* *not a symbol of the opposite of Hell which had originally been the place of <u>all</u> departed (so Baldr)*

["simply" and "~~betwee sy~~ between $^{??}$ symbol & state" are written in pen, while the rest of the section is in pencil.]

Folio 175

If this and the passage in which it ~~is~~ occurs is genuine

Footnote Text

[the first note is inserted between "For the passage" and "is definitely . . ." Its left margin extends past the left margin of the main text. It is set off from the main text by two horizontal pencil lines that run margin to margin and a vertical pencil line that links the two horizontal lines in the left margin. The second note is inserted between "even the" and "noble monotheist . . ." Its left margin extends past the left margin of the main text. It is set off from the main text by two horizontal pencil lines that run margin to margin and a vertical pencil line that links the two horizontal lines in the left margin. All asterisks are in pencil.]

and expressly deny^{ies} any such knowledge to the Danes

that his name <u>æ mun uppi</u>

Note 1 Text

and style they ~~are q~~ introduce a 'voice' quite different

Note 2 Text

definite physical location, ~~and also a native idea~~ $\wedge$ *for an originally native pagan conception,* symbolism of which is seen colouring the references to ~~it~~ $\wedge$ ^{hell} in Christian literature

with <u>Vol</u>. 38 <u>sá er undinn salr orm~~um~~ a hryggjum</u> (which would translated into O.E. be <u>se is wunden sele wyrm~~um~~^{a} hrycgum</u>)

Folio 176

What ~~????~~ precise theology concerning the subject of the just heathen was ~~ever~~ now perhaps not important but we may take this as a comment. B was too distant to ?allow? little of punishment begin reckoned
[written in the top margin; there is no obvious insertion point.]

but was reckon^{ed} among the

[there is one illegible word in ink struck out at the top of the left margin.]

~~in~~ There is probably a Christian **t** transmutation of significance. ~~Though~~ sóð-fæstra dóm could by itself

the prime motive of noble conduct, ^{both} here combined

the recognized virtue of his king-ship

heathen thought in <u>Beowulf</u> is then usually ^{has often been} misconceived.

he muddled up ~~the very after all very different~~ Christianity and Germanic paganism, ~~he prob~~ the author

distinctions (more than one distinction), ~~distinctions not~~ and to represent moods

(such as ~~169–70~~ 168–9,

and ^ ^{esp.} lines 175–188)

Folio 177
poem ~~by~~, if we start rather

though the ~~pe~~ execution may not have been entirely successful

The strongest argument ~~to my mind~~ that the actual situation

distinguish plainly for instance
["plainly" is circled in pencil.]

confused in mind, or by ~~mere accident~~ haphazard

~~Though~~ This alteration is plainly due to some man

. . . with Hreðel and Weder-Geatish ~~his~~ house.

^ ^{But} No one has ventured to ascribe this confusion at any rate to the poet

But it can I think be observed

[I leave ^*it* to your study. The simplest method is to *]* ~~But~~ *if we* extract from the poem all references to religion, fate, or mythology, and observe *remember* the circumstances in which each appears,

[square brackets are in the text in pencil. "But it can I think be observed" interlinearly before the start of the paragraph and inserted with a line.]

Folio 178

[this leaf is misbound upside down.]

We have in Beowulf's language ??????? little differentiation

he thanks <u>Frean Wuldorcyninge</u> . . <u>ecum</u>
[only two dots in ellipsis.]

Footnote Text

[the first note is inserted between "Beowulf" and "refers sparingly to God." It is delimited by horizontal pencil lines above and below and a vertical line in the left margin that connects the two. The note's left margin extends beyond the left margin of the main text. The asterisks in the main text and the footnote are in pencil.]

[the second note is inserted between "<u>Wyrd oft</u>" and "<u>nereð unfægne eorl</u>", It is delimited by horizontal pencil lines above and below and a vertical line in the left margin that connects the two. The note's left margin extends beyond the left margin of the main text. The asterisks in the main text and the footnote are in pencil.]

while <u>metodsceaft</u> = doom, death.

Cf. O.N. <u>mjötuð</u>r which has the senses 'dispenser, ruler' — and also to the side of *the* inscrutable (and even hostile) *Fate*. ^*applied to worldly works*

<u>uurd (=wyrd) giscapu</u>

when her husband died ~~in~~

In ~~the~~ O.S. <u>metod(o)giscapu</u> and <u>metodigisceft</u> = Fate as O.E. <u>metodsceaft</u>.

Folio 178 verso

[from "of course the expressions" to "Swa huru wyrd gescreaf" is written on the verso of 178. There is no obvious insertion point, but the text seems to fit the section of the manuscript where I have inserted it".]

~~Of course at no time do such words~~ ^{things} ~~as 'fate' perish from thought~~ Of course ~~such~~ the expressions implying a belief in 'fate'

Certain words such as metod — ordinance ^{or ordainer} — naturally took over that part of the action of the God as the ~~governor~~ ruler of all

and is for all practical daily purposes dealt with as 'chance' as fate or ~~if you w~~ or else luck, ~~chance~~.

The ????? chr. poets continue to use wyrd which ~~remained~~ did not become a word ~~applicable~~ equateable with God or ???

Thus Cynewulf - Elen Swa huru wyrd gescref.

Folio 179

When he plunges into the mere he offers no prayer, and his only request is that Hygelac should be told ???? ??? bravery
[written in the top margin and inserted between "Sigemund 890)" and "In his account." I have replaced illegible words with text that seems to make sense of the passage, but the words I have chosen are not similar in shape to the illegible words in the manuscript.]

and for helping him to win ^^{it} for his people.

to luck — <u>hwæþre me gesea^xlde</u> (cf. The similar words use*d* of Sigemund 890)

to God throughout this report.
[the "t" in "this" is added to an existing "his" in later ink.]

for a heathen passable. ^^{~~in such a per~~} The second is

The whole story is a *~~pagan~~* ^{heathen} and hopeless one turning on blood-feud, and the ~~heathen~~ motive that when

The explanation is not to be sought in Christian reason,
[there is a large asterisk in the margin next to the above line.]

that <u>before</u> ~~Ch~~ <u>Beowulf</u> was written Christian poetry was already well-developed, and was ^well known to the author.
[there are three pencil underscores beneath "before".]

The diction of <u>Beowulf</u> is in fact ^??? ^'re- paganized,' with a special purpose ^by ^its author , rather than Christianized later without clear purpose by ~~later~~ revisers.

and familiar with ^????? Christian

Old Testament themes. ^*There is a gap important ??? between ?? & Beowulf* We

but in <u>Beowulf</u> ^*of a Christian time* Christian language occasionally ^*(actually very seldom)* ^*placed* ~~used~~ inadvertently in ^*the mouth* ~~unsuitable application~~. *There is prob. nearly 100 years between Cædmon & Beowulf*
[insertions and cross-outs are in pencil.]

??? ?? ??? devil knew of one God
[written in the left margin.]

He would either ?? ???
[written in the left margin.]

the pagan king or else sent him to hell
[written in the left margin.]

Folio 180
Bwf Godes leoht geceas is about the ??? cycle
[written in the top margin.]

^*of a heathen character* ~~to intentionally heathen themes:~~ We observe ~~that~~ in <u>godes leoht geceas</u> an instance of this.
["of a heathen character" is written immediately above the top line of text.]

throughout. ~~A~~ Just before the end

and finally his ^last examination of conscience ~~as~~ where he says that are closely paralleled in $\wedge$ *the heathen* <u>Völuspá</u>,

allowance for $^{??? \ ??? \ ???}$ <u>Godes leoht geceás</u> (which the poet, and even for some modification of character in age (when Beowulf becomes *a little* *much* more like Hroðgar

Norse saga. Everyone thus 665

Folio 181

can be offended inadvertently $^{In \ fact \ of \ a \ man \ who \ thought \ he \ ??? \ ??? \ God, \ and \ was \ eager \ for \ '????s', \ was}$ *far es????? of a ???? ????? ????? into ?????*

To sum up. *We* have in <u>Beowulf</u> $\wedge$ *then* an historical poem about the pagan past, or an attempt at one

(historically improbable $\wedge$ *for a man of this sort* in the period to which <u>Beowulf</u> belongs) $^{??????}$ brought <u>first</u> to his task

Footnote Text

[the first note is inserted between "Finally the poet tells us" and "that when . . ." Its left margin extends past the left margin of the main text and it is set off from the text with two horizontal pencil lines, one above and one below, that run from margin to margin.]

[the second note is written at the bottom of the page after "especially <u>Genesis</u>.* He". Its left margin extends past the left margin of the main text and it is separated from the main text by a horizontal pencil line that runs margin to margin and a vertical pencil line in the left margin that runs from the start of the note to the bottom of the page.]

Note 1

Compare, for instance, *the Christian commentary in* <u>Fóstbræðra saga</u>

Note 2

The <u>Genesis</u> which we have is a late and damaged poem copy of a poem . . . the same period as e as <u>Beowulf</u>. *The actual priority in composition of <u>Genesis A</u> compared with <u>Beowulf</u> is generally recognized.*

Folio 182

The song of the minstrel in the first <u>Æneid</u> is also in part a song of origins ?????? ch

[written in the top margin and inserted with a line into the text after "Wessobrunner Gebet)".]

The V̈olúspá describes ~~from~~ Chaos & the creation of sun and moon ~~of~~, and extremely similar language appears in the O.H.G fragment (Wessobrunner Gebet).
["& the" is written in the left margin.]

the poet brought a considerable learning $\wedge$ $^{in\,vernacular\,traditions}$ (for only by training

born naturally into eighth-century $^{seventh\,or}$ Englishmen

at birth by men of today $^{British\,School\,boys}$) ~~in vernacular English traditions~~.

Virgil Bk i 740
Cithara crinitus Iopas / personat aurata, docuit
quem maximums Atlas / hic canit errantem lunam
solisque labores,
unde hominem
genus et pecudes,
unde imber
et ignis
cf. Beo 91–98
[written in the left margin.]

Virgil
    Latium
Ne fugit hospitium
Neve ignorate Latinos
Saturni gentem
haud vinclo nec
legibus aequam
sponte sua, veterisque
dei se more tenentem
VII 202ff
[written in the in left margin, boxed in pencil, and struck out with a penciled "x". An arrow indicates that the passage is to be inserted after "Old Testament ~~and the patriarchs~~".]

the desire of the good $\wedge$ $^{of\,all\,ages}$ for truth

[interlinear insertion in later pen.]

turn largely to the Old Testament ~~and the patriarchs~~.

It is ^prob^ of Old Testament lapses
["prob" inserted in later pen.]

(of which he is not speaking), ~~such as Northumbrian apostasies in the seventh century,~~ that the poet ~~was~~ is thinking

Footnote Text
[the footnote is inserted between "in lines 175ff" and "and these colour his manner." It is written at the bottom of the page and wraps onto the next leaf after "then the poet must have." Its left margin extends past the left margin of the main text. The note is separated from the main text by a horizontal pencil line across the leaf. A vertical pencil line runs in the left margin from the beginning of the note to the end of the leaf.]

~~179~~ ^180^ we can confidently accept as original.

Folio 183
The hand would seem to be one or the other side of the century
[written in the top margin.]

B
[in the right margin at the beginning of the main text is a large penciled "B".]

?? The Tabernacle (muðour) Heaghægen ??
[written in the lower left margin, next to the main text.]

the heathen North *and the point of fusion between old* ^*lays*^ *& new.*
[from "and the point" to "& new" is inserted with a line from the right side of the bottom margin.]

Footnote Text
[the note continues from leaf 182, beginning at the top of the leaf. The note's left margin extends beyond the left margin of the main text. In the left margin a vertical line runs the length of the note, and written from bottom to top along the left side of this line is written "note continues from above".]

<u>Hroðgar</u> (who certainly ^*delivered from the gastbona* knew of God) and ~~has~~ a certain section of more pagan Danes. But it would remain a ~~very serious~~ blemish on the poem.

For it is undeniably ~~absurd~~ *as inept* for an author

how <u>se Ælmihtiga</u> wrought the world,
[underline is in pencil.]

poetic discrepancy in the ^*whole* poem.

but ^*&* note at the same time

poem ^*in style & verse or rhythm* . it becomes

it becomes a practical *more than probable* ~~certainty~~ that we have here

which has made possible the ^*probable* revision

Folio 184
[six lines in ink are written over erased pencil in the top margin. They are marked by a large square bracket to their left, and inserted into the text between "than the foreground" and "The criticism of Ker." The inserted text begins with "To the same . . ." and ends with "of a new thing".]

The 'discrepancies' are no greater than those to be found in Virgil's Æneid.
[written in pencil in the left margin and presumably is to be inserted just before "<u>Beowulf</u> is not an actual picture . . ."]

The whole must have succeeded admirably in creating ~~the~~ in the minds

episodes and allusions to old tales ~~*B is V*~~ — which are all
[interlinear insertion both added and struck out in pencil.]

a past that <u>itself had depth</u> and
[underline is in pencil.]

human sorrows. ~~to~~ This impression
[insertion and cross-out are both in pencil.]

~~To~~ the same sort of $^{sort\ of}$ change is probably due

similar effect of antiquity. $^{in\ the}$ ~~Virgil's~~ Æneid — especially felt

The criticism of Ker that the important matters are ~~be~~ put on the 'outer edges'
~~entirely~~ $^{???}$ misses this ~~essential~~ point of artistry, indeed it fails to see one of the
very reasons that $\wedge^{why}$ the old things
["of Ker" is circled in pencil.]

It is the poet $\wedge^{himself}$ who has made ~~the appeal of~~ antiquity so appealing.

[Yet there is no doubt of his allegiance. He is viewing ~~old~~ pagan heroism with
sympathy not ~~longing for its~~ regretting its supersession.]
[square brackets are in the text in pencil. The text between the square brackets
is lightly crossed out in pencil.]

His poem has more value in consequence ~~than that~~ and is a greater contribution
to ~~Christian~~ ^{mediæval} thought than ~~any modesty~~ the hard and intolerant $\wedge^{view}$ that
consigned all the ancestors to the devil.

The 'discrepancies' are no greater than those to be found in Virgil's Æneid.
[written in the left margin and struck out with a diagonal pencil stroke.]

So V had had believed even the ?? this ??? in back ??? as despair
[written in the left margin and struck out with a vertical pencil stroke.]

*We might wish for more of the old Italian stuff in Virgil & less of Greek or Trojan
infusion. But V was using not ?establishing? his old lore*
[written in the left margin and struck out with a diagonal pencil stroke.]

Folio 185
occasional tactics (in which $\wedge^{also}$ much is ^{still} deserving of high praise).
["still" is partially erased.]

a tale sequentially. [~~What tale? The life of Beowulf? Certainly we can piece most
of this out from the poem, but we if we take the narration of his life as plot of
Beowulf then we complaining shall be loud in our complaints.~~] The poem
[square brackets in the text. Brackets and cross-outs are in pencil. "Complaining" is struck out in ink.]

an elaboration of the ~~age-old~~ ^ *extremely ancient* and intensely moving contrast

This proportion cannot ^ *I think* be caviled at

This simple and <u>static</u> structure
[underline is in pencil.]

life is here ?????
[written in the lower left margin.]

Folio 186

and ~~in time~~ of his kingship

especially if it is captious or malicious ~~but also much praise if it is attentive~~ *but also much to praise if it is* ~~????~~ ~~attentive~~
[from "but also" to the end of the section is inserted from the top margin. The part of the selection not struck out is circled.]

[from "But to my mind" to "the general theme of Beowulf's fall" is struck out faintly. After this point a single heavy diagonal pencil line is drawn across the leaf from the right margin towards the lower left corner.]

has in place ~~*some*~~ *great* virtues,

too long in proportion *[*and ~~not clear the cha~~ ^ *the* nature and atmosphere of the things told is not always sufficiently suitable to the general theme of Beowulf's fall.*]*
[square brackets in the text.]

a piece of ~~*very*~~ great poetry ~~*one of the higher ??? of English poetry or lang*~~ where it stands
[interlinear insertion is both written and struck out in pencil.]

Footnote Text

[the note is written at the bottom of the page. Its left margin extends past the left margin of the main text and it is separated from the main text by a horizontal pencil line that runs from margin to margin.]

Note Text

even in a newly invented tale~~,~~ of any length,

Critics would seem seldom ^ *themselves* to have experienced

beyond recall. *I have now ?? ?? ?? ?? in which the heroine's very name changed from Edith to Ethel 170.*

Vergil ?? ??? in Bk vi Theseus is quite as an example of a ?? ?? ???
[written in the left margin next to the note.]

Folio 187

and becomes famous is very old folk-tale.

as the vehicle of the ~~ideas aroused in the poet in the making of his~~ the theme

Footnote Text

[the note is written at the bottom of the page. Its left margin extends past the left margin of the main text. It is separated from the main text by a horizontal pencil line that runs from margin to margin.]

and their hero, ~~this he~~ ^all mankind and its heroes

Folio 188

[from "I always feel" to "bogies that do not concern him" is circled and struck out with a diagonal pencil line.]

this defect is ~~to some extent~~ rectified by the bringing

and tells his story ~~before his own people~~, he sets his feet firm again

There is ~~in fact~~ ^thus a double division in the poem.

an important one, at 1887–8. ~~In a sense at 1888 we have "summary of previous chapters: now read on!"~~ The essentials

/The one really absurd thing to do with <u>Beowulf</u>, therefore, is to read only 1–1888 and not the rest [This procedure is in consequence directed or encouraged by several 'English syllabuses'!]
[square brackets in the text, the first bracket in pencil, the other two in ink. The entire passage is struck out with a diagonal pencil line.]

[For full understanding of this point we may also consider a further matter — interesting if subsidiary. There is a special connexion between <u>Beowulf</u> and <u>Andreas</u>, both in the language and phraseology and in the ~~tales~~ 'plots.' <u>Andreas</u> [square bracket in the text. the entire passage is struck out with a diagonal pencil line.]

B *But when criticism has carped its fill, without <u>all</u> that has gone before, the glimpses of the hero and the tragedies of the Geatish house, the magnificent final movement (3137– end) a piece of great poetry and great metrical art could not be so full of content* [written at the bottom of the leaf below a horizontal pencil line.]

[some pencil markings that are hard to make out suggest that perhaps the pen ciled passage at the bottom of the leaf is to be inserted after "manegum scód".]

Folio 189
since the similar passages ^*and expressions* in the poem are found

Folio 190
[from the top of the leaf to ". . . poet's mind lay far deeper." is struck out with a diagonal pencil line.]

and a??? plain reason for ~~its~~ close imitation of the poem

We get ^*thus* a sidelight, as it were, on the surprised

gebétest? , or the <u>joy in the traveller's return</u>, the <u>eagerness for a full account,</u> and
["eagerness for a full account" is underlined in pencil.]

[there is a vertical pencil line in the left margin beginning at "In any case" and extending ten lines down to ". . . than similar".]

In it there is no single ~~versa~~ rhythmic pattern

according to a tune. They depend

rather than similar. *They are more like masonry than music.* In this

as if it were ~~a~~ ^*in* modern accentual lines.

Beowulf is in fact the most successful OE poem because ~~it~~ ^*there the* *elements are all* ~~?or~~
~~nearly?~~ ^*most nearly* *in harmony, language, metre theme & structure*
[written in the bottom margin in pencil.]

Folio 190 verso
for missions

Folio 191
We have nonetheless, in <u>Beowulf</u> a method and structure that, within the limits
of the verse kind, approaches rather to sculpture or painting. It is a composition
not a ~~tune~~ tale.
[the commas are written in pencil.]

[there is a large penciled square bracket in the left margin touching at the top
the line that begins "This is clear . . ." and at the bottom "Grendel one can . . ."]

the practical certainty ^*of literary experience* that the hero will not in fact perish

the poem's plan. ~~Glory is over~~ Disaster is foretold.

Folio 191 verso
it as

Folio 192
is important chiefly to <u>Beowulf</u> himself.
["Beowulf" is underlined and the underline is struck out.]

Not many even ~~a~~ in dying can achieve

with him dies the hope of his people.
[there is a larger square bracket after "people".]

'In structure' ~~Ker said~~ ^~~it was said~~ of <u>Beowulf</u> it is curiously weak,
[the interlinear insertion is both written and struck out in pencil.]

In structure ^*it* actually it is ^*seems* curiously strong
[the first "it" is written directly overtop "actually".]

in spite of all that has ^*may* been said, is defensible, indeed ^*I think* admirable.

[interlinear insertions are in later pen.]

the feud between the houses of Hréðel ~~of~~ the Geat and Ongenþeow the Swede

Folio 193
a ^{*largely*} ~~in~~ connected and known whole,

chronicle fashion in *long* historical poems
["long" is inserted with a line from the top margin.]

but it used knowledge of these things ^ ~~in a~~ *for a different purpose*
["in a" is both written and struck out in pencil.]

[A horizontal line is drawn across the leaf just before from "The poet might reply . . ." From this point to the end of the leaf the text is struck out with a diagonal pencil line.]

the modern critics: "The history of the Danes
[quotation marks are large and in pencil.]

has often been treated ~~a~~ before, and well-handled — you have surely ~~must~~ heard the poems?

a tale that touched on these things, ~~but~~ and dealt with it in rather a new fashion,

At any rate, I made him walk in ~~history~~ poetic history. The things which now interest you most (poetry ~~do~~ in itself does not seem to be one of them), and ~~for~~ ^ *about* which you clamour

Folio 194
nor was I the ~~only~~ chief ^{*Anglo-Saxon*} poet ancient or modern.

[There were many good poems that were then well-known, though I never saw a copy of them or heard of them being written down.]
[square brackets are in the text, written in pencil.]

I do not think most of you have ~~caught~~ ^{seen} the point of it all,

But nothing ^ *at all* for mere reduction in numbers.

Folio 195

[from the beginning of the leaf to "death day" is struck out with two diagonal lines, one in ink, one in pencil. A vertical line in ink runs through this passage parallel to the right margin.]

symbols (not allegories) ∧ *my good sir* of a similar kind,

though the <u>nicors</u> that I alluded ∧ *to* show from the beginning
[underline is in pencil.]

and not during the ∧ *later* humdrum of recognized ability

upon his death-day"
[the first inverted comma of the quotation mark is in ink, the second is in pencil.]

~~I will for all represent my view in this way~~
[written on a separate line between "death-day" and "Let us ..." It is both written and struck out in pencil.]

*f*Let us to conclude consider this ~~on~~ once more on our own account.
[square bracket is in the text. It is written and struck out in pencil. The entire line is struck out faintly with pencil.]

in some desperate assault ∧ *had* achieved a victory

when Alfred, not yet king, left his brother and charged up the hill
[the commas are written in pencil.]

achieving ~~and~~ great victory, and ∧ *who* then past~~s~~ed to his last campaign and his dying battle, while he introduced allusively (or omitted) all the rest of ~~his~~ *Alfred's*
[the second "s" in "passed" over-writes a "t".]

Folio 196

an heroic ∧ *elegiacal* poem ~~in the ancient English manner and mood~~ — already perhaps
[the section that is struck out twice is struck out once in ink and once in pencil.]

It would be much better poetry than a verse *narrative* chronicle, however spirited,

or steadily advancing [~~of his birth, deeds, battles) then and death] in due order and proportion.~~
[both interlinear insertions and cross-outs in pencil. "then" is written in the left margin.]

greater significance than any _straight_ account of one man's deeds:
["straight" is written in the left margin.]

defeat and death. ^ _it would been just much your l??? poem or to his life ??? in_ But even

You would have to turn your Danes into ~~devils~~ _dragons_ for that.

Folio 197

[from "One may ask . . ." to "history turned myth" is struck out with one diagonal line.]

from the purely human point of view ~~could be more~~ ^ _could be however_ simple or
obvious

What symbol better ~~for these not~~ than the dragon

Even so ^ _in_ Grendel we see ~~also~~, as well as

made of the ^ _very_ _ stone of the world _being typical of the heights w_ , also _a parody of_ man
misformed ^ _to go_ ~~by sin~~ by hate.
[interlinear insertions and strike-outs are in later pen. "by sin" is written in the right margin; "by hate" is written in the left margin.]

the ancient human piety of _toward the past_ ~~the imagination (even Olaf Stapledon's 'Neptunians,' the survival of human evolution, ranged backward down the ages for the enrichment of their minds) :~~
[the interlinear insertion and all the strike-outs are in pencil.]

Folio 198

a day already changing and passing ~~then~~, which has now

weighted with ~~the~~ regret, and he expended ^ _his_ art in making ~~poignant~~ _keen_
that ~~lay upon~~ _touch upon_ the heart which sorrows have ^ _that are_ both poignant and
remote.

it has nonetheless its own individual character $^{\text{& peculiar solemnity}}$ which no comparisons can take away, ~~its own ancient cadences of verse, and its own thought~~.

[To recapture such echoes is the final ~~reward~~ ^{fruit} of scholarship in an old
tongue. ~~&~~ it is the most honourable object — rather than the ~~scient~~ analysis of
an historical document. fruit that is good for all to eat if they may, but which can
be gathered only in this way]for such reasons ultimately do we study 'Anglo-
Saxon.']
[square brackets are in the text. The above section is struck out with a diagonal
line; "the most honourable effort . . . an historical document" is inserted interlinearly." The cross-outs with the exception of "reward" and "scient" are in pencil. "Scient" is struck out both in ink and in pencil.]

while light lasts until the dragon comes
until the dragon comes while like lasts
until he
[written in the left margin.]

that could now be recognized, ~~its~~ $^{\wedge\ \text{much of its poetic}}$ value would remain

APPENDIX I

Transcription of Legible Portions of Folios 71–91:
Notes and Jottings

Folio 71 verso

comparative judgements are more difficult. Beowulf has this position for us. Accident—or was it really so? Partly the th???—which has reached and inspired better art.

But we really do not know. ~~of a~~ The great collections of O.E. do not repeat. [L. Riddle Soul & Body. Azarius R. B of B]. This alone suggests that we have a selection of chance out of a considerable wealth even written. Contrast O.N. —one C. Ryrus & a frequent yet we have repetition in which is fragment of 6 pieces, fragment & only 1 newly.

Nearly each new fragment of O.E. is fresh. B.th. Wald. Finn. These were diff trad. Contrast Beowulf with Genesis. Here is a total difference in power. But Beo represents ?? of the old heroic and the newer.

Chances of survival are better for much admired stuff. Prob B. was well thought of to survive and be copied so late (c 1000) — also it plainly has had a careful * & nearly continuous textual history.

Folio 72 recto

But we must be content to allow praise for the Beo poet even if some of it belongs to a time and a school rather than to an individual — even to a language.

Wherever he learned he learned well.

The noble but brief exordium. Places us just this side of the ancient myths and beginning: we are just in history. The ship burial.

We come then rapidly to "history"

There are practically no traces in B of the poet ever having felt the trammels of his verse at all—~~bu~~ it helps not hinders . He chooses his words as a free artist

~~The~~ He can <u>tell things</u> (which does not make his poem a narrative poem.)
Choice of detail grace & discuss

Ship burial. 32–52
?? ? ? 86–89 Grendel.
C??? <u>sunge</u> <u>702ff</u>
<u>Desc</u> of mere 1355–1376
v. 1400 not <u>diff.</u>
Dragon 2287

Folio 72 verso

It is metrical ??? art always at hand — but only ?? ?? likely the responsiveness of
large & ???? easy touches

as <u>Streamas</u> <u>wundon</u> 212 <u>ff</u>
Com passage 702.

The <u>D.E.</u> passage Grendel 739 <u>ff</u>

Or the constant changes of pas as <u>heald þu</u> nu, hruse 2247.

Or the many touches & devices of the last and resplendent 80 lines 3137 —

3142 hæleþ <u>hiofende</u> <u>hlaford</u> <u>leofne</u>
3150 <u>geo meowle</u>
3172 <u>wrecan</u> — <u>sprecan</u>

Note in the dialect shift &wig????<u>dum</u>
wide <u>gesene.</u>

Folio 73

[this is a half-sized leaf.]

charm of wild flower
The dog of hell he should have 3 heads.

Byrne well greatest of all

to ?? high

'useless ?oman' "Beowulf" says in what is not a touch of <u>regret</u> p. 521
　　out of respect towards the chief ?? ??? ???
Summed up — liar <u>drunkard</u> coward murderer
　　but it is all in expression. !!

Their excessive enthusiasm <u>precedes</u> <u>periods</u> of complete

——

make lines 870

——　　　　——

better effect
[written on the right side of the leaf at a 90-degree angle in pencil.]

Folio 74 recto

In standing on <u>Ein???</u> of <u>ehlt</u>

So we have ^ ^{before us} _a <u>half-baked</u>, ~~and~~ <u>Epos</u> that was <u>petrified</u> in the middle of
its development, without doubt it is the introduction of Christianity one of the
causes which destroyed the <u>????</u> lyric poets. The long <u>connexion</u> with mythical
tradition is interrupted new matter & ideas come gradually into the foreground
~~and~~ of consciousness.
The epic style contained <u>the germ of ruin in itself. The tendency to reflexion to</u>
<u>elegiac weakness.</u>

Folio 75 recto

'<u>Univosler</u>' of <u>Ettmuller</u>. Earl p <u>xxvi</u> <u>S?en</u> 1757-<u>1787</u>
<u>telescope.</u>
　　<u>Philological</u> (??? ???) really ?????? liking time the historical. for in a sense language
in such and such a state is the ??? by which with difficulty apprehended on ??? ?//????
language. Beowulf is the Beowulfian verse and vocabulary. If you would ask therefore for
proofs I would say old style <u>apprehended</u> <u>philologically</u>.

The 'historical' also a reaction against ??? But might had more truth in it — it
gets nearer to the dragon. Cosmic value.
[from "The 'historical' " to "Cosmic value" is written in blue pen.]

The dragon is not a mere idle silly tale — <u>modern</u> men of intelligence who <u>would not dream</u>
*<u>of writing an heroic tale</u> — can take interest in _dragon_ * Go with Lewis' poem.*
~~There~~ Ernest Newman once ~~said~~ remarked on the superstition that there was something

inexplicable, invaluable about ??? with folk lay.
Sounds of the same about "heroic tales"'s They can too

Folio 75 verso

wyrd 453,477,572,734,1205,2420,2526, 2574,2814
as 1056, 1233 = <u>eval</u> ???? <u>sp</u> 3020

~~dryhten~~ <u>metod</u>
?? <u>Ealdmetod</u>

Sy???ð?ny
S???? <u>wriht</u>

Eric <u>BrightEyes</u> (R. Haggard) is as good as most <u>sagas</u> and as heroic. ~~But~~ there
~~are very few good dragons~~ and many good <u>heroes</u> (and ??? similar) but there
are few good dragons (and each different). Beowulf's dragon is not <u>first-class</u> in
itself—for ~~he is draconitas already~~ he is already approaching <u>draconitas</u> <u>rather</u>
than a dragon: a personification of <u>malice</u>, greed, <u>destruction</u> (<u>the evil side of</u>
<u>heroic life</u>), and ~~But ??? is well even~~ of the ~~verse~~ <u>undiscriminating</u> <u>malice</u> <u>of</u> for-
tune which <u>distinguishes not</u> good or bad (<u>the evil side of all life</u>). But for Beowulf the poem that is as it should be.

Folio 76 recto

1876 — ~~So dear unto him was~~
To him the other was so dear, that he might not restrain ~~the~~ that <u>upwelling</u> of
his heart, but longing profound, ~~woven in his inmost soul with woven in his~~
~~heart~~ for that beloved one rooted in ~~fast in the chained chained in the his~~ heart-
string within his ???? now ~~ever~~ filled his blood with fire. Thence ~~did~~ Beowulf
went a warrior bold in golden ~~pride~~ <u>splendour</u>, treading the grassy sward, ~~or~~
~~exalting in his pride~~ his heart <u>uplifted</u> with rich gifts. The ~~se~~ <u>traverser</u> of the sea,
<u>awaited its lord and master</u>, ~~which~~ here ~~was riding~~ on its anchor riding; and ^ ^{as}
~~it~~ they went often was the ??? of Hrothgar praised: a king was he ~~?ruling?~~
~~without reproach~~ in all things without reproach, until age robbed him of the
~~glad poss~~ joys of valour , — ~~as it had often ?? it~~ often later it been the least of
many.
[the above text is struck out with one penciled diagonal line.]

2200
~~???~~ ^ ^{There was} a new 'canto' number ^ ^{at} <u>xxvii</u>. B. is often divided into two ???

there — but ? ? of the ??? of the canto numbers lest they at such odd places. This is a good ~~one~~ place. ???? we had the clearly almost one (<u>xxv</u>) in the middle of a sentence to ? new section beginning a ??/ ??/ <u>ob</u>! Quite impossible <u>generally</u> to believe these divisions go back <u>to the author. If so his practice was very much better than his consistency</u> — for look at xxxi — <u>which ends at xxxii a middle of</u> his ~~begin~~ approach to the dragon and the end strophe. Where about a ??? is the real ???? in ~~p~~ Beowulf, the real deliberate and important break. // At 2200 ~~at about~~ precisely *3/5*> ~~*2/3*~~ of the way to ?? we finish with the ???; glory, success, and turn to doom fall, and inevitable end. Triumph against the foes of man's precarious little <u>self-constructed</u> world with his world — ~~disaster~~ and the inevitable victory of the great <u>unformed</u> hostile and ?? ??/ inhuman another end of glory (except for the praise of his ??????? which we feel <u>is of ??????</u> <u>gradually fading as the ages lengthen. That the dragon dies too is important chiefly to B. within the limits of a human life</u> ^ ^{and its inevitable destru final} ___ ___ he neither lived nor died in vain ^ ^{the brave men who} But there is no hint that is was the end of ~~a~~ dragons or of ~~??~~ the foes of men — it is the end of Beowulf, and of his people. The real ???? at ????? 2200 ??? ??? ?? last the proportion is <u>exactly right.</u> ~~*2-2*~~> *3:2*> Is about the great <u>spirit</u> in a ??? life <u>repen</u>?? in us, achieved (21-end decline after . It is right at ?????? ?? ??? ?? ??? as each to give the

Folio 76 verso

[this page is mostly impossible to read except for scattered words. It seems to be an early draft of the end of the 'B' Text (Alfred and the Danes, Beowulf poet's direct address to the reader).]

Folio 77 recto

[It is also nearly impossible to form connected sentences from the faint writing on this leaf, but from what I can read it is clear that JRRT is working through many of the ideas in the sections about Cain and the Christianity of the poet.]

Folio 77 verso

<u>In fact the defect shown in these papers</u> ~~though not make, and~~ <u>one</u> ~~plainly be connected as direct with and ??? ??/ ?? with the and~~ <u>not dissociated from the looseness of the weaker lit end with ?? above.</u>

<u>In fact the defects in these papers, if more prominent, are</u> ~~of the same kind~~ ^ ^{not of a different order} <u>clearly selected in the looseness in the</u> ~~loose~~ _{weak}<u>work noted</u> <u>above</u> : ~~?? may and while content with a half and a superficial view, when where the acquisition of either~~ <u>ne</u> ~~seems the precise~~ ~~labour.~~

With these things philology would appear to have been confused.

[this side of the leaf is written upside down in black pen.]

Folio 78 recto
    B. 2200

Here is the real break not at 1887.

All the 50 years (<u>cf</u> l. 2209) interval of B's. reign is omitted, and his manner of gaining it by the death of <u>Hygelac</u>, & H's son <u>Heardred</u> only told at odd times in allusion. This does not prove that poem was not substantially all by one hand: — it can be parallelled even from modern work. It only proves author a faulty selector of incident, & a poor construction — according to modern views.
We may say that to tell of B's life we should like to know something of his early life, and of his <u>soul-searchings</u>: that ~~the~~ ^ ᵃ ᵐᵒʳᵉ central place should be occupied by the fight against the <u>Hetware</u> & <u>Hygelac's</u> death & B's ?eight?-hundred prowess; his loyal refusal of the throne in the <u>Geat's</u> dark hour, & loyal support of <u>Heardred</u>; his gathering of the remnants of the <u>Geats</u> after the Swedish invasion & the death of <u>Heardred</u>, and gradual <u>reestablishment</u> (just <u>non-historic</u>) of <u>Geat</u> power. The author replies that the fight with Grendel & the dragon are the most interesting & they are what my public wants—a scene at <u>Heorot</u> always goes down, and a dragon always increases sales. besides (he would <u>prob</u>. add) the other part of B's life are <u>well-known</u> & have been done. In answer to Chambers (that he would not sacrifice such as story as <u>Ingeld</u> for a wilderness of dragons)

[This leaf is made of very thin paper with blue lines. There are two hole punches in the left margin.]

Folio 78 verso
    He would no doubt say <u>personally I</u> find many agree with me that dragons <u>are highly</u> entertaining, and often not inferior to the ^ ⁇⁇ crooked ways of true love *or of <u>Ingeld</u>*. To me the spectacle of the aged king, almost deserted by his people in spite of a long and arduous rule for the good of his country fighting <u>single-handed</u> against the sudden destroyer and dying to save his ungrateful folk is a ~~tragic~~> situation of more gravity & dignity than the ~~mutable~~ conflict of unstable passions in the breast of the <u>fay</u> but not over intelligent <u>Ingeld</u>.
    You say there is no coherence or structure! There is ?mordant may? in the 2 pictures. (i) the young man in the <u>height</u> of his youth performing his first really

notable deed against a monster of evil—lauded with thanks by a foreign prince (ii) the same man at the other pole of his career performing his last great deed against a monster of evil & left to die by his own folk. The whole is done with ~~wel~~ very competent & occasionally very moving verse of the best models (though these scribes at <u>so much</u> line are a great curse to authors)—you posterity are hard to please.

B the <u>non-literary</u> problems—the amount of history enshrined in these legends, & Beowulf's place as a <u>prob-fictitious</u> <u>adornment</u> see Chambers & <u>Klaeber</u>.

[This leaf is made of very thin paper with blue lines. There are two hole punches in the left margin.]

[Folios 79r, 79v, 80r, 80v, 81r, 81v, 82r, 82v, 83r: contain a listing of uses of words for God in *Beowulf*, basically the same as those given in the 'A' and 'B' Texts.]

Folio 84 recto
  [in pencil]

  '<u>Lof</u> and its shift   [in pen] soþ<u>faestra</u> <u>dom</u>

                                                                        2820

                                                    of ??? are <u>aeghwylc</u>
  The theme

  Structure

  the repetition ??? gel <u>au</u>
          inherent weakness & not totally part
  in one land this is <u>divided</u>
  ???
  NB Beowulf & Andreas <u>missionary epoch</u>

  the discrepancies   <u>interpolator</u> (end of pagan passage . Hroðgar's
                                                    speech. no he him <u>???</u>)
                                                    but the main structure is clear.

[a penciled vertical line extends down the left side of the page from "the repetition" to "the main structure is clear".]

Folio 84 verso

The dragon is more <u>*unreasoningly*</u> *hostile* — *?????* *Also for the arm of* <u>*Grendel*</u> = *?style?* *who would also equal* <u>*deeds*</u> *of him* *???* *The Dragon is to be found and even for goodness.*

Folio 85

Vergil

This is real ??? about <u>Beowulf</u>

Vergil — read together. It <u>sundering</u> of <u>temper that makes things that are the</u> <u>??? ??? of ????</u> <u>as the accounts seem so similar. The great pagan who ???? ???? ??</u> <u>The great</u>   (??? if ??) <u>Christian</u> just over the threshold of <u>paganism</u>. multa putans sortemque animo miseratus iniquam VI 332

???

'Beowulf' almost a poem with a continuing ??? about '<u>pagans</u>. See Leslie p 71

~~Odo~~ Chartres passage is an apology.

Folio 86

210

On went the hours: on ocean afloat
under cliff was their craft. <u>Now</u> climb <u>blithely</u>
brave man aboard; breakers pounding
ground the shingle. Gleaming harness
they hove to ~~the~~ bosom of the bark, <u>armour</u>
with <u>cunning</u> forgéd then cast her forth
to voyage triumphant, valiant -hundred
fleet foam twisted. ~~as flies a bird~~ with flight of bird,
till at the same season of the second morning
her <u>bended</u> beak had <u>beaken</u> afar
and <u>labouring</u> at sea the lands ?by shore?
<u>shorewall</u> shining with sheer <u>headlands</u>
and vast capes the vessel of the sea
had ??? her errand. There up sprang ??
the <u>Weder-chieftans</u> and ??? shore
???? their ship, in all and ???
with gear <u>clanking</u>. <u>God</u> ??? praised
who planted ??? paths over ocean.

Folio 87 recto

{~~In any case if true the complain comsp The co~~} *In any case But at least a professor should have read the available <u>A-S</u> texts. He was not yet so <u>plagued</u> with foreign books about them. A modern professor even if he ~~does~~* ^*has* *read or even (* ^*& perhaps* ~~*occasionally*~~ *continues to read) A S books is faced by the serious problem of books about them. Even if he limits his attention to one "The Beowulf" ~~as~~ (as it was once called) though ~~????~~ solemn the sight is ??? which of <u>Beowulfiana</u>*

But the claim is just even if <u>if the</u> accusation was unfounded. The professor should re

2

["2" is written in the left margin.]

But the claim was just, even if ^possibility of his being in possession of even so ????<u>ly</u> insignificant chair. the accusation was unfounded. The professor should have read the available books in <u>Anglo-Saxon</u>. Not yet was he so plagued with foreign books about them ^*though ?? ?? ?? beginning* A ~~modern~~ professor now even <u>if</u> <u>he</u> has read <u>A-S</u> books is faced by ~~the~~ ^this serious problem of ~~these~~ ^*the* book about ^*his* books. Even if he concerns himself with one book only "The Beo-wulf" as it was once called — as one might refer either to the classics or the <u>measels</u>—he does not escape. The forest of <u>Beowulfiana</u> is already dense ~~and~~

although it is only just over 100 years since Scott confused Beowulf with Caed-mon the wood ^*is already* so <u>thick ~~that~~ with brambles that the trees are not easy to discern. If fear I</u> too am not

[a line runs from "and" to the bottom margin, where from "although it is" to "I too am not" is written. The folio is written on a sheet ruled with black lines. "Do not write in this margin" printed in the upper left corner.]

Folio 87 verso

The Rev. Oswald <u>Cockayne</u> wrote in 1864 of the Rev. Joseph <u>Bosworth</u> D D. <u>F.R.S.</u> , <u>Rawlinsonian</u> Professor of <u>Anglo-Saxon</u>: 'I have long entertained [the conviction] that Dr. <u>Bosworth</u>.
[Square brackets in the text; the above is written in pen, struck out with a curving pencil line.]

1855 Thorpe Beowulf. (1875)
   1876 Amend

<u>Hargh</u>. 1861 <u>A-S</u> <u>Sagas</u> <u>Helta</u> & Hr???

Chambers ???????? § 8 Questions of ??? History ?? ??? ??? B in that ??? of history, <u>archaeology</u>, ?? ??? mythology and folklore.
  When a ?? ?????

Beowulf only about 100 years old It is not much more than 100 years since Scott confused him with <u>Caedmon</u>.

??
The Beowulf <u>itself</u>, <u>Ch</u>. p. 524 <u>Earle</u> *

Folio 88 recto
  Vergil ???? ???? ???????

Folio 88 verso
  Close connection between <u>Anglian</u> and Scandinavian culture in ??? age. Prof. ??/ de in Norrige ??? ??? <u>pg</u>. 171-227-8. Hence similarity of aristocratic temper, <u>language</u> of poetry, & heroic temper. ?? ??? legends
  God <u>ana</u> <u>wat</u> <u>hwa</u> ???? ?? ???
  <u>*Byrhtwold*</u> *= Beowulf.*

* *huru <u>wyrd</u> <u>gescreaf</u> <u>ll</u> 1047*

Homer ends with noble funeral.

Folio 89 recto
  Chadwick (<u>Cha</u>) <u>Beo</u> to Homer. Time more like Vergil. Latin & Hroðgar. The simple heroic <u>looked back at</u> not lived (as in Homer)

Below Vergil lay the old lost aristocratic pagan. Below Beowulf lay the old lays. V ??? of these is a ??? p?? ??? ?? up and grey break a similar sense of depth in heroic time. The ??? <u>background</u> is clearly ancient in Æneas' day, and more rude & simple & carelessly discarded. The Germanic background in Beowulf is sudden & darker. Hroðgar ???? the good Christian King <u>in is</u> Æneas the civilized ruler.

[there is a blot of red wax at the top of the leaf, which is torn from an exam or exercise book.]

Folio 90 recto

<u>*Beowulf*</u>.

General Criticism.

[written in very large letters in pencil, centered on the page.]

Folio 91 recto

<u>'Beowulf'</u>

<u>gen</u> *Criticism*

[written in blue pencil, centered on the page.]

WORKS CITED

Ælfric. *Ælfric's Lives of Saints, being a Set of Sermons on Saints' Days formerly observed by the English Church, ed. from Manuscript Julius E. VII in the Cottonian Collection, with Various Readings from other Manuscripts*, ed. Walter W. Skeat. Early English Text Society, Original Series 76, 82, 94, 114. London: Oxford University Press, 1966.

———. *The Old English version of the Heptateuch, Aelfric's Treatise on the Old and New Testaments, and his Preface to Genesis; edited together with a Reprint of A Saxon Treatise concerning the Old and New Testaments, now first published in print with English of our times by William L'Isle of Wilburgham (1623) and the Vulgate Text of the Heptateuch*, ed. S. J. Crawford. Early English Text Society, Original Series 160. London: Oxford University Press, 1969.

———. *Ælfric's Catholic Homilies: The Second Series*, ed. Malcolm Godden. Early English Text Society, Special Series 5. London: Oxford University Press, 1979.

———. *Ælfric's Catholic Homilies: The First Series*, ed. Peter Clemoes. Early English Text Society, Special Series 17. London: Oxford University Press, 1997.

Alcuin. "Carmen I." In *Monumenta Alcuiniana*, ed. P. Jaffé, 128. Bibliotheca Rerum Germanicarum 6. Berlin: Apud Weidmannos, 1873.

———. "Epistola 81." In *Monumenta Alcuiniana*, ed. P. Jaffé, 357. Bibliotheca Rerum Germanicarum 6. Berlin: Apud Weidmannos, 1873.

Andrews, A. Le Roy. *Hálfs Saga ok Hálfsrekka*. Halle: Verlag von Max Niemeyer, 1909.

Arnold, Matthew. "On the Study of Celtic Literature." In *Lectures and Essays in Criticism*, ed. R. H. Super, 322. Ann Arbor: University of Michigan Press, 1962.

Bachman, W. Bryant, Jr. and Gudmundur Erlingsson, eds. *The Sagas of King Half and King Hrolf*. New York: University Press of America, 1981.

Barnfield, Richard. *Poems 1594–1598*, ed. Edward Arber. London: Unwin Brothers, 1882.

Benson, Larry D., et al., eds. *The Riverside Chaucer*. 3rd ed. Boston: Houghton Mifflin, 1987.

Berger, Harry, Jr., and H. Marshall Leicester, Jr. "Social Structure as Doom: The Limits of Heroism in *Beowulf*." In *Old English Studies in Honor of John C. Pope*, ed. Robert B. Burlin and Edward B. Irving, Jr., 37–81. Toronto: University of Toronto Press, 1974.

Bjork, Robert E., ed. *Cynewulf: Basic Readings*. New York: Garland, 1996.

———. "Grímur Jónsson Thorkelin's Preface to the First Edition of *Beowulf*, 1815." *Scandinavian Studies* 68 (1996): 291–323.

Bolton, W. F. *Alcuin and Beowulf*. New Brunswick, NJ: Rutgers University Press, 1978.

Bostock, John Knight. *A Handbook on Old High German Literature*. Oxford: Clarendon Press, 1955; rev. ed., Oxford: Clarendon Press, 1976.

Bosworth, Joseph. *An Anglo-Saxon Dictionary, based on the Manuscript Collections of the late Joseph Bosworth* ... Edited and enlarged by T. Northcote Toller. Oxford: Clarendon Press, 1898.

Bradley, S. A. J., trans. *Anglo-Saxon Poetry*. London: Dent, 1982.

Brandl, Alois. "Englische Literatur." In *Grundriss der germanischen Philologie*, ed. Hermann Paul, 980–1024. Strassburg: Karl J. Trübner, 1901–1909.

Braune, Wilhelm, ed. rev. Ernst A. Ebbinghaus. *Althochdeutsches Lesesbuch*. 14th ed. Tubingen: M. Niemeyer, 1969.

Bullough, Donald A. "What has Ingeld to do with Lindisfarne?" *Anglo-Saxon England* 22 (1993): 93–125.

Byock, Jesse L., ed. *The Saga of the Volsungs: The Norse Epic of Sigurd the Dragon Slayer*. Berkeley: University of California Press, 1990.

Cantor, Norman F. *Inventing the Middle Ages*. New York: William Morrow and Company, 1991.

Carpenter, Humphrey. *J. R. R. Tolkien: A Biography*. Boston: Houghton Mifflin, 1977.

———. *The Inklings: C. S. Lewis, J. R. R. Tolkien, Charles Williams, and their Friends*. Boston: Houghton Mifflin, 1979.

Carroll, Lewis. *The Complete Illustrated Works of Lewis Carroll*, ed. Edward Guiliano. New York: Avenel Books, 1982.

Chambers, Raymond W. *Widsith: A Study in Old English Heroic Legend*. Cambridge: Cambridge University Press, 1912.

———. "*Beowulf* and the Heroic Age." In *Beowulf Translated into Modern English Rhyming Verse*. ed. Archibald Strong, vii–xxxii. London: Constable, 1925.

———. *Beowulf: An Introduction to the Study of the Poem with a Discussion of the Stories of Offa and Finn*. 2nd ed. Cambridge: Cambridge University Press, 1932.

———. "William Paton Ker." In *Dictionary of National Biography 1922–1930*, 467–69. London: Oxford University Press, 1937.

———. *Man's Unconquerable Mind: Studies of English Writers from Bede to A. E. Housman and W. P. Ker*. London: Jonathan Cape, 1939

Cleasby, Richard, and Guðbrand Vigfusson. *An Icelandic-English Dictionary*. 2nd edition, with supplement by William A. Craigie. Oxford: Clarendon Press, 1957.

Clark, George. *Beowulf*. Boston: Twayne Publishers, 1990.

Cockayne, Thomas Oswald. *The Shrine: A Collection of Occasional Papers on Dry Subjects*. Vol. 1. London: Williams and Norgate, 1864.

Coleridge, Samuel Taylor. "Kubla Khan." In *The Poems of Samuel Taylor Coleridge*, ed. Ernest Hartley Coleridge, 297–98. London: Humphrey Milford for Oxford University Press, 1927.

Colgrave, Bertram. *Felix's Life of St. Guthlac*. London: Cambridge University Press, 1956.

———, and R. A. B. Mynors, eds. *Bede's Ecclesiastical History of the English People*. Oxford: Clarendon Press, 1969.

Compton-Rickett, Arthur. *A History of English Literature*. London: People's Books, 1912.

———. *A History of English Literature*. London: T. C. and E. C. Jack, 1918.

Conybeare, John Josias, ed. William Daniel Conybeare. *Illustrations of Anglo-Saxon Poetry*. London: Harding and Lepard, 1826.

Crossley-Holland, Kevin, ed. *The Anglo-Saxon World*. New York: Oxford University Press, 1982.

Davenport, Guy. "Hobbits in Kentucky." *New York Times*, 23 February 1979: A27.

Davidson, Hilda Ellis, ed. *Saxo Grammaticus' History of the Danes*, trans. Peter Fisher. Haverhill, Suffolk: D. S. Brewer, 1979.

Dobbie, Elliott van Kirk, ed. *Beowulf and Judith*. The Anglo-Saxon Poetic Records 4. New York: Columbia University Press, 1953.

———. *The Anglo-Saxon Minor Poems*. The Anglo-Saxon Poetic Records 6. New York: Columbia University Press, 1942.

Dowden, Edward. *Transcripts and Studies*. 2nd ed. London: Kegan Paul, Trench, Trübner & Co., 1896.

Doyle, Arthur Conan. *The Sign of Four*. London : Spencer Blackett, 1890.

Drout, Michael D. C. "Imitating Fathers: Tradition, Inheritance and the Reproduction of Culture in Anglo-Saxon England." Ph.D. diss., Loyola University of Chicago, 1997.

Earl, James W. *Thinking About Beowulf*. Stanford, CA: Stanford University Press, 1994.

Earle, John. *Anglo-Saxon Literature*. London: Society for Promoting Christian Knowledge, 1884.

———. *The Deeds of Beowulf: An English Epic of the Eighth Century Done into Modern Prose*. Oxford: Clarendon Press, 1892.

Ettmüller, Ludwig, ed. *Engla and Seaxna Scôpas and Bôceras. Anglosaxonum poëtae atque scriptores prosaici, quorum partim integra opera, partim loca selecta collegit, correxit et edidit*. Quedlinburg: Williams and Norgate, 1850.

Evans, B. I. *W. P. Ker as a Critic of Literature*. Glasgow: Jackson, 1955.

Farrer, Reginald John. *The English Rock-Garden*. London: T. C. & E. C. Jack, 1926.

Flanagan, Roy, ed. *The Riverside Milton*. Boston: Houghton Mifflin, 1998.

Fontaine, Jacques, ed. and trans., *Sulpice Sévère: Vie de Saint Martin*, Souras Chrétienne 133. Paris: Cerf, 1967.

Frantzen, Allen J. *The Literature of Penance in Anglo-Saxon England*. New Brunswick, NJ: Rutgers University Press, 1983.

————. *Desire for Origins: New Language, Old English and Teaching the Tradition.* New Brunswick, NJ: Rutgers University Press, 1990.

Fry, Donald K., ed. *The Beowulf Poet.* Englewood Cliffs, NY: Prentice Hall, 1968.

Fulk, R. D. "Preface." In *Interpretations of Beowulf,* ed. idem, ix–xix. Bloomington: Indiana University Press, 1991.

Geduld, Harry M., ed. *The Definitive Time Machine: A Critical Edition of H. G. Wells's Scientific Romance with Introduction and Notes.* Bloomington: Indiana University Press, 1987.

————. "*Beowulf* and *The Time Machine*: A Note on Analogues." In *The Definitive Time Machine,* 211–13.

Gislason, Konrad, ed. *Fóstbræðra Saga.* Copenhagen: Berlingske bogtryekkeri, 1852.

Gordon, E. V. *An Introduction to Old Norse.* Oxford: Clarendon Press, 1927.

Graff, Gerald. *Professing Literature: An Institutional History.* Chicago: University of Chicago Press, 1987.

Gregory of Tours. *Historia Francorum.* Monumenta Germaniae Historica, Scriptores Rerum Merovingicarum 1. Hanover: Impensis Bibliopolii Hahniani, 1884.

————. *The History of the Franks,* trans. O. M. Dalton. Vol. 2. Oxford: Clarendon Press, 1927.

Grein, Christian W. M. *Sprachschatz der angelsächsischen Dichter.* Cassel: G. H. Wigand, 1861–1864.

————. *Sprachschatz der angelsächsischen Dichter,* ed. J. J Köhler. Heidelberg: Carl Winter's Universitätsbuchhandlung, 1912.

Grundtvig, Nikolai Frederik Severin. *Bjowulfs Drape. Et Gothisk Helte-Digt fra forrige Aar-Tusinde af Angel-Saxisk paa Danske Riim.* Copenhagen: Trykt hos A. Seidelin, 1820.

Haggard, H. Rider. *Eric Brighteyes.* London: Longmans Green and Co., 1891.

Hall, Joseph, ed. *Layamon's Brut: Selections, Edited with Introduction, Notes and Glossary.* Oxford: Clarendon Press, 1924.

Hands, Rachel, ed. *English Hawking and Hunting in The Boke of St. Albans: A Facsimile Edition of sigs. a2–f8 of the Boke of St. Albans (1486).* London: Oxford University Press, 1975.

Harris, Joel Chandler. *The Complete Tales of Uncle Remus,* ed. Richard Chase. Boston: Houghton Mifflin, 1955.

Herren, Michael. "Classical and Secular Learning Among the Irish Before the Carolingian Renaissance." In idem, *Latin Letters in Early Christian Ireland,* 1–39. Aldershot: Variorum, 1996.

Hickes, George, ed. *De Antiquæ Litteraturæ Septentrionalis Utilitate, sive De Linguarum Veterum Septentrionalium Usu Dissertatio Epistolaris ad Bartholomæum Showere, Equitem Auratum, Non ita pridem Jurisconsultum apud Anglos, & Causarum Patronum Celeberrimum.* Oxford: E Theatro Sheldoniano, 1703.

Hill, John. *The Cultural World in Beowulf.* Toronto: University of Toronto Press, 1995.

Hill, Joyce. "Translating the Tradition: Manuscripts, Models, and Methodologies in the Composition of Ælfric's 'Catholic Homilies'." *Bulletin of the John Rylands University Library* 79 (1997): 43–65.

Hollander, Lee M., ed. *The Poetic Edda*. Austin: University of Texas Press, 1962.

Hreinsson, Viðar, ed. "The Saga of the Sworn Brothers." In *The Complete Sagas of Icelanders*, vol. 2. Reykjavík: Leif Eiríksson Publishing, 1997.

Irving, Edward B., Jr. *A Reading of Beowulf*, rev. ed. Provo, UT: The Chaucer Studio, 1999.

———. *Rereading Beowulf*, ed. Edward Peters. Philadelphia: University of Pennsylvania Press, 1989.

Jänke, Oskar. "Zeugnisse und Excurse zur deutschen Heldensage." *Zeitschrift für deutsches Altertum und deutsche Literatur* 15 (1871): 310–32.

Jónsson, Finnur, ed. *Landnámabók I–III: Hauksbók, Sturlbók, Melabók*. Copenhagen: Thieles Bogtrykkeri, 1900.

———. *Atlakviða*. Copenhagen, 1912.

Jusserand, J. J. *A Literary History of the English People from the Origins to the Renaissance*. Vol. 1. London: G. P. Putnam's Sons, 1895.

Kemble, John Mitchell. *The Anglo-Saxon Poems of Beowulf, The Travellers Song, and the Battle of Finnesburh*. London: William Pickering, 1833; 2nd ed. 1835.

———. *A Translation of the Anglo-Saxon Poem 'Beowulf' with a Copious Glossary, Preface, and Philological Notes*. London: William Pickering, 1837.

Kennedy, Charles W., trans. "Beowulf." In *Medieval English Literature*, ed. J. B. Trapp, 20–98. London: Oxford University Press, 1973.

Ker, W. P. *Epic and Romance: Essays on Medieval Literature*. London: Macmillan and Co., 1897; repr. New York: Dover, 1958.

———. *The Dark Ages*. London: Blackwood and Sons, 1904.

———. *English Literature: Medieval*. London: Williams and Norgate, 1912.

Keynes, Simon, and Michael Lapidge. *Alfred the Great*. New York: Penguin, 1983.

Kiernan, Kevin S. *Beowulf and the Beowulf Manuscript*. New Brunswick, NJ: Rutgers University Press, 1981.

Klaeber, Friedrich, ed. *Beowulf and the Fight at Finnsburg*. 3rd ed. Boston: D. C. Heath, 1950.

Krapp, G. P., and E. van K. Dobbie, eds. *The Junius Manuscript*. The Anglo-Saxon Poetic Records 1. New York: Columbia University Press, 1936.

———. *The Vercelli Book*. The Anglo-Saxon Poetic Records 2. New York: Columbia University Press.

———. *The Exeter Book*. The Anglo-Saxon Poetic Records 3. New York: Columbia University Press, 1936.

Krusch, Bruno and W. Levison, eds. *Vita Vulframni*. Monumenta Germania Historica, Scriptores Rerum Merovingicarum, 5. Hannover, 1910.

Lapidge, Michael, ed. *Archbishop Theodore*. Cambridge: Cambridge University Press, 1995.

———. "Aldhelm's Latin Poetry and Old English Verse." In idem, *Anglo-Latin Literature 600–899,* 247–69, 505–6. London: Hambledon, 1996.

———. "*Beowulf,* Aldhelm, the *Liber Monstrorum* and Wessex." In idem, *Anglo-Latin Literature: 600–899,* 270–311.

Lawrence, William Witherle. *Beowulf and Epic Tradition.* Cambridge, MA: Harvard University Press, 1928.

Lees, Clare A. "Men and *Beowulf.*" In *Medieval Masculinities: Regarding Men in the Middle Ages,* ed. eadem, 129–48. Medieval Cultures 7. Minneapolis: University of Minnesota Press, 1994.

Leslie, Shane, ed. *An Anthology of Catholic Poets.* London: Burns Oates, 1924; repr. 1952.

Lewis, C. S. "The Northern Dragon." In *The Pilgrim's Regress: An Allegorical Apology for Christianity, Reason and Romanticism,* 192–93. London: Geoffrey Bles, 1933; rev. 1943; repr. 1956.

Lewis. C. S. *The Discarded Image.* Cambridge: Cambridge University Press, 1969.

The Life of St. Martin of Tours. Willits, CA: Eastern Orthodox Books, 1989.

Liuzza, Roy M., ed. *Beowulf: A New Verse Translation.* Peterborough, Ont.: Broadview Press, 2000.

Malory, Thomas. *Le Morte D'Arthur.* New York: The Modern Library, 1999.

Morris, William, *The Story of Sigurd the Volsung and the Fall of the Nibelungs.* In *The Collected Works of William Morris: With Introductions by his Daughter May Morris,* 12. London: Longmans Green and Company, 1911.

———, and A. J. Wyatt, Eds. *Beowulf. Three Northern Loves Stories, Beowulf.* In *The Collected Works of William Morris: With Introductions by his Daughter May Morris,* 10. London: Longmans Green and Company, 1911.

Müllenhoff, Karl. "Der Mythus von Beóvulf." *Zeitschrift für deutsches Altertum und deutsche Literatur* 7 (1849): 419–41.

———. "Sceáf und seine Nachkommen." *Zeitschrift für deutsches Altertum und deutsche Literatur* 7 (1849): 410–19.

———. "Die innere Geschichte des Beovulfs." *Zeitschrift für deutsches Altertum und deutsche Literatur* 14 (1869): 193–244.

———. *Beovulf: Untersuchungen uber das angelsächsische Epos und die alteste Geschichte der germanischen Seevolker.* Berlin: Weidmann, 1889.

Murphy, G. Ronald, S.J., ed. *The Heliand: The Saxon Gospel.* New York: Oxford University Press, 1992.

Nerman, Birger. *Det Svenska Rikets Uppkomst.* Stockholm: Generalstabens Litografiska Anstalt, 1925.

Niles, John D. *Beowulf: The Poem and Its Tradition.* Cambridge, MA: Harvard University Press, 1983.

———. "Locating Beowulf in Literary History." *Exemplaria* 5 (1993): 79–109.

Nordal, Sigurdur, ed. *Völuspá,* trans. Ommo Wilts. Darmstadt: Wissenschaftliche Buchgesellschaft, 1980.

Olrik, Axel. *Danmarks Heltedigtning: I. Rolf Krake og den ældre Skjoldungrække.* Copenhagen: G. E. C. Gad, 1903.

———. *The Heroic Legends of Denmark*, trans. Lee M. Hollander. New York: American-Scandinavian Foundation, 1919.

Olrik, J., and H. Ræder, eds. *Saxonis Gesta Danorum.* Vol. 1. Hauniæ: Apud Librarios Levin et Munksgaard, 1931.

Orchard, Andy. *The Poetic Art of Aldhelm.* Cambridge: Cambridge University Press, 1994

———. *Pride and Prodigies: Studies in the Monsters of the Beowulf-Manuscript.* Cambridge: D. S. Brewer, 1995.

Overing, Gillian R. *Language, Sign, and Gender in Beowulf.* Carbondale, IL: Southern Illinois University Press, 1990.

Pálsson, Hermann, and Paul Edwards, trans. *The Book of Settlements: Landnámabók.* Winnipeg: University of Manitoba Press, 1972.

Panzer, Friedrich. *Beowulf.* Studien zur Germanischen Sagengeschichte 1. Munich: C. H. Beck'sche Verlagsbuchhandlung Oskar Beck, 1910.

Paulinus of Nola. *Sancti Pontii Meropii Pavlini Nolani Carmina*, ed. W. von Hartel. Corpus Scriptorum Ecclesiasticorum Latinorum 30. Prague: Tempsky, 1894.

Phillips, Stephen. *Ulysses.* New York: Macmillan, 1902.

Powell, F. York, trans. *The Tale of Thrond of Gate commonly called Færeyinga Saga.* Northern Library 2. London: David Nutt, 1896.

Quiller-Couch, Arthur. "On the Lineage of English Literature." In idem, *Cambridge Lectures*, 21–25. London: J. M. Dent and Sons, 1943.

Raffel, Burton, trans. *Beowulf.* New York: New American Library, 1963.

Rafn, C. C. and G. C. F. Mohnike. *Færeyínga Saga oder Geschichte der Bewohner der Färöer im isländischen Grundtext mit Färöischer, Dänischer und Deutscher Übersetzung.* Copenhagen: Verlage der Schubothescher Buchhandlung, 1933.

Ranisch, Wilhelm, ed. *Die Völsungasaga.* Berlin: Mayer and Müller, 1891.

Ritson, Joseph. *Ancient English Metrical Romances.* Vol. 1. London: W. Bulmer and Company, 1802.

Shakespeare, William. *The Merchant of Venice*, ed. David Bevington. In *The Complete Works of William Shakespeare*, vol. 2. New York: Bantam Books, 1988.

———. *Hamlet*, ed. David Bevington. In *The Complete Works of William Shakespeare*, vol. 3. New York: Bantam Books, 1988.

———. *King Lear*, ed. David Bevington. In *The Complete Works of William Shakespeare*, vol. 5. New York: Bantam Books, 1988.

———. *Macbeth*, ed. David Bevington. In *The Complete Works of William Shakespeare*, vol. 5. New York: Bantam Books, 1988.

Shippey, T. A. *The Road to Middle Earth.* London: Allen and Unwin, 1983.

———. *J. R. R. Tolkien: Author of the Century.* Boston: Houghton Mifflin, 2000.

———, and Andreas Haarder, eds. *Beowulf: The Critical Heritage.* London: Routledge, 1998.

Shirley-Price, Leo, ed. "Introduction." In *Ecclesiastical History of the English People*, 19–35. New York: Penguin Books, 1990.

Sievers, Eduard, ed. *Heliand*. Halle: Verlag der Buchhandlung des Waisenhauses, 1878.

———. *Altgermanische Metrik*. Halle: Max Niemeyer, 1893.

———. "Old Germanic Metrics and Old English Metrics." In *Essential Articles for the Study of Old English Poetry*, ed. Jess B. Bessinger, Jr. and Stanley J. Kahrl, trans. Gawaina D. Luster, 267–88. Hamden, CT: Archon Books, 1968.

Sowell, Thomas. *A Conflict of Visions*. New York: William Morrow, 1987.

Stancliffe, C. *St. Martin and His Hagiographer*. Oxford: Clarendon Press, 1983.

Stanley, Eric Gerald. *In the Foreground: Beowulf*. London: D. S. Brewer, 1994.

Steenstrup, Johannes C. H. R. *Historieskrivningen i Danmark i det 19de Aarhundrede (1801–1863)*. Copenhagen: B. Lunos Bogtrykkeri, 1889.

Stenton, Frank Merry. *Anglo-Saxon England*. 2nd ed. Oxford: Clarendon Press, 1950.

Stjerna, Knut. *Essays on Questions Connected with the Old English Poem of 'Beowulf'*, trans. John R. Clark-Hall. Coventry: Viking Club Society for Northern Research, 1912.

Strong, Archibald T. *A Short History of English Literature*. London: Humphrey Milford for Oxford University Press, 1921.

———. *Beowulf Translated into Modern English Rhyming Verse*. London: Constable, 1925.

Sturlson, Snorri. *Edda*, trans. Finnur Jónsson. Copenhagen: Gyldendalske Boghandel-Nordisk Forlag, 1931.

———. *The Prose Edda: Tales from Norse Mythology*, trans. Jean I. Young. Berkeley: University of California Press, 1954.

Suhm, Peter Friderich. *Historie af Danmark far de oeldeste Lider*. Vol. 1. Copenhagen: Ernst med Brøðrene Berlings Strifter, 1782.

———. *Geschichte der Dänen*, trans. Friedrich Gräter. Leipzig: Heinrich Gräff, 1803.

Sulpicius Severus. *Vita Sancti Martini*, dd. Karl Halm. Corpus Scriptorum Ecclesiasticorum Latinorum 1. Vindobona: Apud C. Geroldi Filium Bibliopolam Academiae, 1867.

Tacitus. *The Agricola and The Germania*, trans. H. Mattingly. New York: Penguin, 1971.

ten Brink, Bernhard. *History of English Literature*, trans. Horace M. Kennedy. Vol. 1. London: George Bell and Sons, 1895.

Thacker, Alan. "In Search of Saints: The English Church and the Cult of Roman Apostles and Martyrs in the Seventh and Eighth Centuries." In *Early Medieval Rome and the Christian West: Essays in Honour of Donald A. Bullough*, ed. Julia M. H. Smith, 247–77. Leiden: Brill, 2000.

Thorkelin, Grímur Jónsson. *De Danorum rebus gestis secul. III et IV. Poëma Danicum dialecto Anglo-Saxonica*. Copenhagen: Typis Th. E. Rangel, 1815.

Timpanaro, Sebastiano. *La genesi del metodo di Lachmann*. Padua: Liviana, 1985.

Tolkien, Christopher. "Foreword." In *The Hobbit: 50th Anniversary Edition*, i–xvi. Boston: Houghton Mifflin, 1987.

Tolkien, J. R. R. "Iúmonna Gold Galdre Bewunden." *Gryphon* n.s. 4 (1923): 130.

———. "Philology: General Works." *The Year's Work in English Studies* 4 (1923): 20–37.

———. "Philology: General Works." *The Year's Work in English Studies* 5 (1924): 26–65.

———. "The Devil's Coach Horses." *Review of English Studies* 1 (1925): 331–36.

———. *"Ancrene Wisse* and *Hali Meiðhad."* *Essays and Studies* 14 (1929): 104–26.

———. " 'Sigelwara Land': Part 1." *Medium Ævum* 1 (1932): 183–96.

———. " 'Sigelwara Land': Part 2." *Medium Ævum* 3 (1934): 95–111.

———. "Iumonna Gold Galdre Bewunden." *The Oxford Magazine* 55 (1937): 473.

———. *Farmer Giles of Ham*. London: Allen and Unwin, 1949; repr. 1975.

———. *The Silmarillion*, ed. Christopher Tolkien. Boston: Houghton Mifflin, 1977.

———. *Unfinished Tales*, ed. Christopher Tolkien. Boston: Houghton Mifflin, 1980.

———. *The Letters of J. R. R. Tolkien*, ed. Humphrey Carpenter and Christopher Tolkien. Boston: Houghton Mifflin, 1981.

———. *Exodus*, ed. Joan Turville-Petre. Oxford: Clarendon Press, 1981.

———. *Finn and Hengest: The Fragment and the Episode*, ed. Alan Bliss. Boston: Houghton Mifflin, 1982.

———. "*Beowulf*: The Monsters and the Critics." In *Beowulf: The Monsters and the Critics and Other Essays*, ed. Christopher Tolkien, 5–48. Boston: Houghton Mifflin, 1984. Originally in *Proceedings of the British Academy* 22 (1937): 245–95.

———. "On Translating *Beowulf*." In *Beowulf: The Monsters and the Critics and Other Essays*, ed. Christopher Tolkien, 49–71.

———. "On Fairy Stories." In *Beowulf: The Monsters and the Critics and Other Essays*, ed. Christopher Tolkien, 109–61.

———. "Valedictory Address." In *Beowulf: The Monsters and the Critics and Other Essays*, ed. Christopher Tolkien, 224–40.

———. *The Book of Lost Tales: Part II*, ed. Christopher Tolkien. Boston: Houghton Mifflin, 1984.

———. *The Hobbit: 50th Anniversary Edition*. Boston: Houghton Mifflin, 1987.

———. *Morgoth's Ring*, ed. Christopher Tolkien. London: Harper Collins, 1993.

———. *The Annotated Hobbit*, ed. Douglas A. Anderson. Boston: Houghton Mifflin, 1988.

———. *The Fellowship of the Ring*, rev. ed. Boston: Houghton Mifflin, 1999.

———. *The Two Towers*, rev. ed. Boston: Houghton Mifflin, 1999.

———. *The Return of the King*, rev. ed. Boston: Houghton Mifflin, 1999.

Trout, Dennis E. *Paulinus of Nola: Life, Letters, and Poems*. Berkeley: University of California Press, 1999.

Turner, Sharon. *History of the Anglo-Saxons*. London: T. Cadell and W. Davies, 1799–1805.

————. *The History of the Anglo-Saxons.* 2nd ed. London: Longman, Hurst, Rees and Orme, 1807.

————. *The History of the Anglo-Saxons: Comprising the History of England from the Earliest Period to the Norman Conquest.* 4th ed. London: Longman, Hurst, Rees, Orme and Brown, 1823.

van Egmond, Wolfert. "Converting Monks: Missionary Activity in Early Medieval Frisia and Saxony." In *Christianizing Peoples and Converting Individuals*, ed. Guyda Armstong and Ian N. Wood, 37–45. International Medieval Research 7. Turnhout: Brepols, 2000.

Virgil. *The Aeneid*, ed J. W. Mackail. Oxford: Clarendon Press, 1930.

————. *The Aeneid*, trans. Robert Fitzgerald. New York: Random House, 1983.

Wadstein, Elis. *Norden och Västeuropa i gammal tid.* Populärt vetenskapliga föreläsningar vid Göteborgs Högskola, Ny följd 21. Stockholm: Albert Bonniers Forlag, 1925.

————. "The Beowulf Poem as an English National Epos." *Acta Philologica Scandinavica* 8 (1925): 273–91.

Walsh, P. G., trans. *Letters of St. Paulinus of Nola.* Westminster, MD: Newman Press, 1966.

————, trans., *The Poems of St. Paulinus of Nola.* New York: Newman Press, 1975.

Wanley, Humphrey. *Librorum Veterum Septentrionalium, qui in Angliae Bibliothecis extant, nec non multorum Veterum Codicum Septentrionalium alibi extantium Catalogus Historico-Criticus cum totius Thesauri Linguarum Septentrionalium sex Indicibus*, Vol. 2. Oxford, 1705.

Whitelock, Dorothy, ed. *English Historical Documents.* 2nd ed. 2 vols. London: Oxford University Press, 1979.

William of Malmesbury. *Gesta Pontificum*, ed. N. E. S. A. Hamilton. London: Rolls Series, 1870.

Wilson, Edmund. "Oo, Those Awful Orcs!" *Nation* 182, 14 April 1956, 312–13. Repr. in idem, *The Bit Between My Teeth: A Literary Chronicle of 1950–1965*, 326–32. New York: Farrar, Straus and Giroux, 1965.

Wolf, Friedrich August. *Prolegomena ad Homerum, sive de operum Homericorum prisca et genuina forma variisque mutationibus et probabili ratione emendandi.* Halis Saxonum, Libraria Orphanotrophei, 1795; ed. Anthony Grafton. Princeton: Princeton University Press, 1985.

Wrenn, C. L. *A Study of Old English Literature.* London: George G. Harrap & Co., 1967.

INDEX

MRTS

MEDIEVAL AND RENAISSANCE TEXTS AND STUDIES
is the major publishing program of the
Arizona Center for Medieval and Renaissance Studies
at Arizona State University, Tempe, Arizona.

MRTS emphasizes books that are needed —
editions, translations, and major research tools —
but also welcomes monographs and
collections of essays on focused themes.

MRTS aims to publish the highest quality scholarship
in attractive and durable format at modest cost.

The most important essay in the history of *Beowulf* scholarship, J. R. R. Tolkien's "*Beowulf*: The Monsters and the Critics" has, rightly, been much studied and discussed. But scholars of both *Beowulf* and Tolkien have to this point been unaware that Tolkien's essay was a redaction of a much longer and more substantial work, *Beowulf and the Critics*, which Tolkien wrote in the 1930s and probably delivered as a series of Oxford lectures. This critical edition of *Beowulf and the Critics* presents both unpublished versions of Tolkien's lecture ('A' and 'B'), each substantially different from the other and from the final, published essay. The edition includes a description of the manuscript, complete textual and explanatory notes, and a detailed critical introduction that explains the place of Tolkien's Anglo-Saxon scholarship both in the history of *Beowulf* scholarship and in literary history.

Michael D. C. Drout is an assistant professor of English at Wheaton College.